The Annotated Constitution of Japan: A Handbook

The Annotated Constitution of Japan: A Handbook

Edited by Colin P.A. Jones

Routledge
Taylor & Francis Group
LONDON AND NEW YORK

First published in 2023 by Japan Documents and Amsterdam University Press Ltd.

Published 2025 by Routledge
4 Park Square, Milton Park, Abingdon, Oxon OX14 4RN
605 Third Avenue, New York, NY 10158

Routledge is an imprint of the Taylor & Francis Group, an informa business

ISBN: 9789048562015 (hbk)
ISBN: 9781041187202 (pbk)
ISBN: 9781003705161 (ebk)
NUR 823

Cover design: TransPac Communications, Greg Glover

For Product Safety Concerns and Information please contact our EU representative: GPSR@taylorandfrancis.com
Taylor & Francis Verlag GmbH, Kaufingerstraße 24, 80331 München, Germany

To the people of Japan, with gratitude and respect.

Table of Contents

Contributors

Giorgio Fabio Colombo is Professor of Law at the Nagoya University Graduate School of Law. He is also Visiting Professor of Japanese Law at "Ca' Foscari" University of Venice, Italy, Resident Research fellow of the Italian School of East Asian Studies (ISEAS), a member of the Editorial Board of the *Journal of Japanese Law/Zeitschrift für Japanisches Recht*, and a founding member of the Italian-Japanese Association for comparative law. Giorgio is also a lawyer admitted in Italy (Milan), and is listed as arbitrator with several arbitral institutions. His research focuses on ADR, arbitration, private comparative law, law and literature, legal cultures.

Tōru Enoki is a professor of Law at Senshu University, Tokyo. A graduate of the Faculty of Law, Kyushu University (LL.B.), he also obtained his PhD from the Faculty of Social and Cultural Studies, Kyushu University. He is interested in the constitutional issues of the Tennō (Emperor) system, same-sex marriage, freedom of expression, privatization and scope of application of constitutional provisions, and has published several scholarly articles in these areas. His single book is *Kenpō no gendaiteki igi—Amerika no suteito akushon hōri wo tegakari ni (Modern significance of constitutional law—Through consideration of the US State Action Doctrine)* (Hanashoin Press).

Koji Higashikawa is professor of law at Kanazawa University, Japan. He earned his PhD from the Kobe University Graduate School of Law in 2001 with a dissertation on the American election law system and minority voting rights, and has published numerous academic articles in the field of election law. As a free speech scholar, he has given presentations on the hate speech issue both in Japan and in the United States. One of his English publications is "Bold Solution from Easy Cases: The Development, Benefit, and Concern on Japanese Hate Speech Laws" (*Michigan State International Law Review*, 2021). He is a council and editorial board member at the Japanese American Society for Legal Studies, and a director at Japan Society of Comparative Law.

Mari Hirayama is a professor at the Faculty of Law of Hakuoh University in Tochigi, Japan. A graduate of Kwansei Gakuin Graduate School of Law (Master of Laws), she also completed the LL.M. program at the University of Minnesota Law School as a Fulbright scholar. She specializes in criminal procedure and criminal justice and has publications both in Japanese and English. Recent publications include: *Kensatu shinsa kai: Nihon no keijishiho wo kaeruka* (Prosecution review commissions—Will they change criminal justice in Japan?), co-authored with David T. Johnson and Hiroshi Fukurai (Iwanami Shinsho, 2022), "The First Ten Years of the Lay Judge System: Now, Do We Have "Hope" for Criminal Trials in Japan?" *Hastings Journal of Crime and Punishment* 1, No. 3 (2019); "Introduction of Videotaping of Interrogations and the Lessons of the Imaichi Case: A Case of Conventional Criminal Justice Policy-Making in Japan," co-authored with Setsuo Miyazawa, *Washington International Law Journal* 27, No. 1 (2017).

Colin P.A. Jones is a professor at Doshisha University Law School in Kyoto. A graduate of U.C. Berkeley, he did graduate work at Tohoku University (LL.M.) and Duke Law School (J.D., LL.M.). He is also a practicing lawyer admitted in New York and the Republic of Palau (inactive status) and sits on corporate boards. Colin has published widely in both Japanese and English, with a particular focus on Japanese law. His books include *The Japanese Legal System* and *The Japanese Legal System in a Nutshell* (both from West Academic and co-authored with Frank Ravitch) and *Obey, Not Know: Essays in Japanese Law and Society* (Kurodahan Press), which is based on his long-running column "Law of the Land" in *The Japan Times*. He also offers commentary on law in Japan on Twitter.

Mark Levin is a Professor of Law and the inaugural Director of the Pacific and Asian Legal Studies Program at the William S. Richardson School of Law, and is concurrently serving as the Director of the University of Hawai'i at Mānoa Center for Japanese Studies. Mark came to Hawai'i in January 1997 from the Law Department of Hokkaido University in Sapporo, Japan. His interest in Japan began after his 1983 graduation from Yale Law School, when he worked in international business and financial transactions at Masuda and Ejiri, one of the leading Tokyo international law offices at the time. From 1984 to 1986, Mark clerked for U.S. District Court Judge John C. Coughenour in Seattle, Washington, and then practiced in Seattle for five years as a corporate attorney, representing numerous Japanese clients. He earned an LL.M. from the University of Washington's Asian Law Program (Japanese Law Emphasis) in 1990.

Shigenori Matsui is a professor at the University of British Columbia, Peter A. Allard School of Law, in Vancouver, Canada. A graduate of Kyoto University Faculty of Law, he did graduate work at Kyoto University (LL.M., 1982) as well as Stanford Law School (J.SD., 1986), and obtained his LL.D. from Kyoto University in 2000. He is a well-known expert on freedom of expression, cyberspace law and comparative constitutional law. He has published over twenty books in Japanese as well as in English, including his *The Constitution of Japan: Contextual Analysis* (Bloomsbury, 2011), and *Law and Disaster: Earthquake, Tsunami and Nuclear Meltdown in Japan* (Routledge, 2019), in addition to numerous book chapters and journal articles.

Tetsuji Matsumoto is a professor at Doshisha University Law School in Kyoto. A graduate of the Faculty of Law, Kyoto University, he did graduate work at Kyoto University (LL.M.). He is a co-author of Japanese books including *Kenpō tekigōteki kaishaku no hikaku kenkyū* (Constitution-compatible interpretation on comparative perspective) (edited by Doi Masakazu, 2018, Yuhikaku, Tokyo); *Kenpō (I) sōron tōchi* (Constitutional law I: General theory & separation of powers); and *Kenpō (II) kihonteki jinken* (Constitutional law II: Fundamental human rights) (3rd ed., 2022, Yuhikaku). The International Academy of Comparative Law named him a National Reporter on *Human Rights: the justiciability of economic social and cultural rights* to the 2022 General Congress.

Sean McGinty is an Associate Professor at Nagoya University's Graduate School of Law where he is director of the School's Global 30 Program and teaches courses on Japanese and comparative law among other subjects. After graduating from the University of Victoria's Law School in Canada he briefly worked at a civil litigation law firm before coming to Japan to complete an LL.M. and LL.D. in international economic and business law at Kyushu University. Sean has published several articles and book chapters, some on Japanese corporate law and others on more niche topics such as the regulation of its shopping streets.

Andrea Ortolani is Associate Professor of Law at the University of Tsukuba, where he teaches Japanese law and other classes on comparative law topics. He holds a PhD from the University of Trento (2006) and a PhD from the University of Tokyo (2017). Andrea co-authored the first Italian hornbook on Japanese law and published articles, book chapters and other essays in English, Italian and Japanese on comparative law and Japanese law. He is one of the founders and current secretary of the Italian-Japanese Association for Comparative Law.

Kayoko Oshima is a professor of the Graduate School of Policy and Management at Doshisha University. She has been the Dean of Academic Affairs of the University since 2019. A graduate of the Graduate School of Law at Hokkaido University (Doctor of Law), she taught Japanese constitutional law and administrative law at Hokkaido Information University and Tezukayama University in Nara. She was a visiting scholar at UC Berkeley Law School (2006-2007), and at Columbia Law School (2013-2014), where she researched U.S. constitutional law and education law. She has published academic books and textbooks on Japanese and U.S. constitutional law and children's rights in schools (all are co-authored in Japanese).

Frank S. Ravitch is Professor of Law and Walter H. Stowers Chair in Law in Religion at the Michigan State University College of Law. He also directs the Kyoto Japan Program. Among the books he has written are: *Freedom's Edge: Religious Freedom, Sexual Freedom, and the Future of America* (Cambridge University Press, 2016); *Marketing Creation: The Law and Intelligent Design* (Cambridge University Press 2012), *Masters of Illusion: The Supreme Court and the Religion Clauses* (NYU Press 2007); *Law and Religion: Cases, Materials, and Readings* (West 4th Ed. 2021), *School Prayer and Discrimination: The Civil Rights of Religious Minorities and Dissenters* (Northeastern University Press 1999). He is co-author, with the late Boris Bittker and with Scott Idleman, of *Religion and the State in American Law* (Cambridge University Press 2015); and co-author with Colin Jones of *The Japanese Legal System* (West 2019) and *Japanese Law in a Nutshell* (West 2020). Professor Ravitch's articles, which have appeared in highly regarded journals, have primarily focused on law and religion in the U.S. and Japan. He speaks English, Japanese and Hebrew.

Yuichiro Tsuji is a professor at Meiji University Graduate School of Law in Tokyo. After earning an LL.M from Kyoto University Graduate School of Law in Japan, he completed his LL.M and JSD at UC Berkeley Law School. Tsuji has published widely in Japanese and in English, with a particular focus on Japanese law. He has published monographs on freedom of expression, *Jōhōka shakai no hyōgen no jiyu* (Nihon Hyronsha 2011) and the Chevron doctrine of the U.S. Supreme Court, *Sheburon hōri no kōsatsu* (Nihon Hyoronsha 2018). He is also the editor of *Amerika kikō hō to seisaku* (American climate change law, Keiso Shobo 2021) and *Hanrei amerika kankyō hō nyūmon* (American environmental law cases, Keiso Shobo 2022). He is a director of the Environmental Law Center at Meiji University.

Preface

Colin P.A. Jones

Statutory annotations are a standard reference work for law students, academics and legal practitioners in Japan. With respect to the Constitution of Japan a number of excellent works—some going by the name of *kommentāru* (the Japanese rendering of the German "kommentar")—are available and provide an article-by-article explanation of what the words of each provision of the charter mean. Depending on the version, there may also be capsule descriptions of important court cases in which a provision was interpreted, as well as summaries of what academia thinks about the subject. As a means of acquiring a basic grounding in what the constitution means, these books are a very useful starting point—if you can read Japanese.

There is, of course, a large body of scholarship in English on the Japanese constitution, including works by some of the authors who have contributed to this volume. However, a great deal of scholarship in English has tended to be focused on specific areas: criminal justice, freedom of speech, religion, and of course the famous "no war" provisions of Article 9. There are only a few books offering a comprehensive overview of the entirety of the constitution, and none offering a text-based, article-by-article explanation. This book is a collective effort by a team of scholars to remedy that deficiency; to make the Japanese constitution broadly accessible in its entirety to the many people who are interested in it or need to know about specific aspects of it for comparative purposes, but are unable to read about it in Japanese.

While this work will try to offer the basic "annotation" format familiar to Japanese readers, there are some necessary differences. First, being based on an assumption that many non-Japanese readers will know little or nothing about Japan or its legal system, an effort has been made to provide additional contextual information. Second, being also based on an assumption that readers will have little or no ability to read Japanese, this book will also point out some of the linguistic nuances in the Japanese version that are either missing or different in the English.

As an academic discipline, constitutional law in Japan can sometimes seem highly doctrinal, not to mention political, particularly with respect to controversial subjects such as the existence and use of the nation's Self-Defense Forces. The views of leading constitutional scholars are not merely academic: constitutional law is a subject in which a "correct" understanding must be demonstrated in order to graduate from law faculties and pass qualifying exams to become a public servant or enter various licensed legal professions. At the same time, however, with respect to parts of the constitution on which the Supreme Court of Japan has issued a clear interpretive ruling, academic commentary that diverges from or opposes that interpretation may be little more than a form of literary criticism in practice. With respect to interpretive issues on which the Supreme Court has not issued a ruling, the "government view" (*seifu kenkai*) is arguably the next most authoritative point of reference, since it informs how the government actually behaves as opposed to how it *should* behave, which is more commonly the purview of academics and activists. Accordingly, we have tried to limit our coverage of doctrinal squabbles and competing academic views.

Conventions, language and sources

Romanization

On the assumption that most readers will have little or no familiarity with the Japanese language, we have used the "Modified Hepburn" style of Romanizing Japanese terms, including the use of macrons to denote elongated vowel sounds. Japanese personal names are expressed in the English fashion—family name last, personal name first—a reversal of the way they are expressed in Japanese.

Paragraph numbers and headers

For articles of the constitution comprised of multiple paragraphs, it is common to refer to specific provisions by article, paragraph and clause number. However, such numbering was not a part of the English version as promulgated, and Japanese laws follow a different convention of only having numbers for the second and following paragraphs. As is common for commentaries in Japanese, we have added uniform paragraph and sub-clause numbering in all relevant provisions of the constitution, except the Preamble. Similarly, as is the common practice with many Japanese statutory compilations and annotations, we have added descriptive headers for each article of the constitution. However, this is an editorial choice for ease of reference only. Descriptive headers were not part of the constitution as promulgated and should thus not be considered for interpretive purposes.

Reference materials in appendices

Although also available on-line, we have included in Appendices to this book several other documents that we believe are useful to understanding the Japanese constitution: (1) The Constitution of the Empire of Japan (the so-called "Meiji Constitution") and (2) its English translation, (3) the Potsdam Declaration of 1945, (4) the Instrument of Surrender signed by Japan, (5) The "MacArthur Notes" which established the basic parameters for the initial draft, (6) the so-called "GHQ Draft" of the constitution, (7) the Japanese text of the present constitution and (8) the text of the Treaty of San Francisco, which brought about an end to the formal state of war between Japan and most of the Allied Powers when it took effect in 1952.[1]

Sources, citation formats, translations and abbreviations

In the interest of readability, we have tried to avoid the excessive and repetitive notations which bedevil authors and editors of US-style law review contributions and instead tried to use minimalist citation formats. Secondary sources are set forth in the bibliography and follow the AP Style Guidelines, with simple abbreviated citations in endnotes only when necessary for pinpoint cites or specific assertions. Miscellaneous sources (e.g., government reports or references to news or magazine articles) that are only referenced once are identified in notes only.

As is the case with Japanese annotations, throughout this book there are numerous references to academic interpretive theories. For the most part summaries of these can be found in one or more of the standard texts on Japanese constitutional law written by leading scholars. Some of these have been used by law students for decades and have gone through multiple editions. Moreover, these often root their own discussion of academic theory in references to contemporaneous or earlier "standard works." Working again on the assumption that most readers will be unable to read Japanese source materials, and in the interest of avoiding what would be a very large number of footnotes to this limited universe of standard texts in support of a statement about "academic theory," we have instead included in the bibliography a section listing the standard works, and tried to limit notes to instances where a specific scholar is being cited for a specific proposition. Asterisks next to a Japanese text in the bibliography are used as an attempt to offer one (but not the only) possible view of what might be considered "standard works."

We have also tried to be minimalistic in case citations. Although there are a number of official and privately-published case reporters which are commonly used in Japanese citation formats, we have generally avoided referencing them. Our assumption is that most readers will not have access to physical copies of Japanese case reporters and will not be able to read them even if they do. Moreover, most of the cases referenced in this volume are decisions of the Supreme Court of Japan, which are available (in Japanese) online at the courts.go.jp website, and can usually be located based on the date on which they were rendered. Most substantive Supreme Court judgments are also translated into English though there may be a time lag before they are available. Thus, on the assumption that most cases will be accessed online, pinpoint citations to case reporters and with page numbers are only used for (1) lower court rulings, or (2) Supreme Court rulings when it is necessary to distinguish between multiple rulings delivered on the same or similar issues on the same date (as occasionally happens).

The judiciary is discussed in more detail in Chapter VI, but a few preliminary notes are in order to assist in understanding citations to Supreme Court cases. First, Supreme Court judgments are not law, though lower courts are required to follow them in interpreting the law (the same is not true of lower appellate court rulings). Second, the Supreme Court is actually four courts: the three Petty Benches of five judges each which resolve most of the matters on the Court's docket, and all fifteen judges sitting *en banc* as the Grand Bench. Grand Bench rulings are comparatively rare, but are much more significant. Only the Grand Bench can find a statutory provision or other government act unconstitutional or contravene a prior Grand Bench ruling or interpretation.

The Supreme Court also renders two types of rulings. First, there are *judgments* (*hanketsu*). Judgments are rendered by a court in an adversarial trial with evidentiary proceedings, or a court sitting on appeals from such judgments. Second, there are *decisions* (*kettei*), which are rendered in "non-trial" proceedings, such as most of what happens in family courts, but also various types of procedural and special appeals (see discussion at Articles 32 and 82 regarding the significance of trial proceedings vs. non-trial proceedings).[2]

While some earlier western writing on Japanese law adopted the common law style of naming cases (*i.e.*, X v. Y), this is never done by Japanese writers. Instead, most cases are referred to by a descriptive title (*e.g.*, *The Lineal Ascendant Murder Case*) that quickly seems to become standardized. We have tried to replicate those titles wherever possible with some modifications where direct translations rendered them clunky or confusing.

Most important judgments of the Supreme Court of Japan have been translated into English and are available on its website at: https://www.courts.go.jp/english/index.html. English translations of many Japanese statutes are also available in translation at the government's Japanese Law in Translation website at: http://www.japaneselawtranslation.go.jp/. When quoting language from laws or cases we have used these "semi-official" translations whenever possible. Where translations from other sources have been used (including those by an author) a notation has been included.

We have generally used the English title for statutes used in government translations, subject to some modifications to render them less quirky, ponderous or repetitive.[3]

In the interests of brevity and minimizing repetitive references and citations the following tables set forth: (1) the titles and citations of Supreme Court cases referenced in more than one place in this book, and (2) commonly used acronyms, abbreviations, and English statutory names with citations. Citations for cases and statutes that are only cited in a single section (article or chapter summary) are included in the notes to that section.

Table 1 Cases Discussed in More Than One Section of This Book

Case Title	Citation	Discussed at:
After the Banquet Case	Tokyo District Court, judgment of 28 September 1964, 15 *Kaminshū* 2317	Articles 13 and 21
Confiscation of Third Party Property Case	Supreme Court, Grand Bench judgment of November 28, 1962	Articles 29 and 31
Courtroom Note-Taking Case	Supreme Court, Grand Bench judgment of March 8, 1989	Articles 17, 21 and 82
Ehime Tamagushi Case	Supreme Court, Grand Bench judgment of April 2, 1997	Articles 20, 81 and 89
Forest Act Case	Supreme Court, Grand Bench judgment of April 22, 1987	Articles 22, 29 and 81
Hakata Station TV Film Production Case	Supreme Court, Grand Bench judgment of November 26, 1969	Chapter III Introduction, Article 21
Hoppō Journal Case	Supreme Court, Grand Bench judgment of June 11, 1986	Articles 13 and 21
Hospital Director Suicide Case	Supreme Court, 3rd Petty Bench judgment of September 9, 1997	Articles 17 and 51
House of Representatives Malapportionment Case I	Supreme Court, Grand Bench judgment of April 14, 1976	Articles 14, 15, 47 and 81
House of Representatives Malapportionment Case II	Supreme Court, Grand Bench judgment of July 17, 1985	Articles 14, 15, 47 and 81
Ienaga Textbook Inspection Cases	Supreme Court, 3rd Petty Bench judgment of March 16, 1993; Supreme Court, 3rd Petty Bench judgment of August 29, 1997	Articles 21 and 26
Kathleen Morikawa Case	Supreme Court, 1st Petty Bench judgment of November 16, 1992	Chapter III Introduction, Article 22
Kimigayo Piano Accompaniment Case	Supreme Court, 3rd Petty Bench judgment of February 27, 2007	Articles 19 and 21
Lady Chatterley's Lover Case	Supreme Court, Grand Bench judgment of March 13, 1957	Articles 12 and 21

Case Title	Citation	Discussed at:
Lineal Ascendant Murder Case	Supreme Court, Grand Bench judgment of April 4, 1973	Articles 14 and 81
McLean Case	Supreme Court, Grand Bench judgment of October 4, 1978	Chapter III Introduction, Articles 14 and 22
Naganuma Nike Case	Supreme Court, 1st Petty Bench judgment of September 9, 1982	Articles 9 and 76
Nara Prefectural Reservoir Ordinance Case	Supreme Court, Grand Bench judgment of June 26, 1963	Articles 29 and 94
Nationality Act Case	Supreme Court, Grand Bench judgment of June 4, 2008	Articles 10, 14 and 81
National Police Reserve Case	Supreme Court, Grand Bench judgment of October 8, 1952	Article 9
Niigata Prefecture Public Safety Ordinance Case	Supreme Court, Grand Bench judgment of November 24, 1954	Articles 12 and 21
Osaka Airport Noise Pollution Case	Osaka High Court, judgment of November 27,1975, 797 *Hanrei Jihō* 36; appeal rejected	Articles 13 and 25
Osaka Anti-Prostitution City Ordinance Case	Supreme Court, Grand Bench judgment of May 30, 1962	Articles 31 and 94
Out-of-Wedlock Inheritance Rights Discrimination Case	Supreme Court, Grand Bench decision of September 4, 2013	Chapter III Introduction, Articles 14, 24 and 81
Overseas Voters Right to Review Supreme Court Judges Case II	Supreme Court, Grand Bench judgment of May 25, 2022	Articles 14, 15 and 81
Overseas Voting Rights Case	Supreme Court, Grand Bench judgment of September 14, 2005	Articles 15, 17, 44, 47 and 81
Pharmaceutical Affairs Act Case	Supreme Court, Grand Bench judgment of April 30, 1975	Articles 22, 29 and 81
Postal Act Case	Supreme Court, Grand Bench judgment of September 11, 2002	Articles 17 and 81
Postal Voting Case	Supreme Court, 1st Petty Bench judgment of November 21, 1985	Articles 15 and 17
Salaried Workers Tax Discrimination Case	Supreme Court. 3rd Petty Bench judgment of December 15, 1992	Articles 14, 22 and 30
Sarufutsu Case	Supreme Court, Grand Bench judgment of November 6, 1974	Articles 16, 21, 31, 41 and 73
Southern Kyūshū Tax Accountant Association Case	Supreme Court, 3rd Petty Bench judgment of March 19, 1996	Articles 19, 21 and 22
Sunagawa Case	Supreme Court, Grand Bench judgment of December 16, 1959	Articles 9, 76, 81 and 98
Sunagawa Sorachibuto Shrine Case	Supreme Court, Grand Bench judgment of January 20, 2010 (64 *Minshū* 1)	Articles 81 and 89
Tōdai Poporo Case	Supreme Court, Grand Bench judgment of May 22, 1973	Articles 23 and 26
Tokyo Prefecture Managerial Qualification Exam Case	Supreme Court, Grand Bench judgment of January 26, 2003	Articles 14 and 15

Case Title	Citation	Discussed at:
Tomabechi Case	Supreme Court, Grand Bench judgment of June 8, 1959	Articles 3, 7 and 76
Tsu City Groundbreaking Ceremony Case	Supreme Court, Grand Bench judgment of July 13, 1977	Articles 20 and 89
Women-only Remarriage Prohibition Period Case	Supreme Court, Grand Bench judgment of December 16, 2015, 69 *Minshū* 2427	Chapter III Introduction, Articles 14, 24 and 81
Yahata (Yawata) Steel Political Contribution Case	Supreme Court, Grand Bench judgment of June 24, 1970	Chapter III Introduction, Articles 15 and 19
Yodogō Hijacking News Redaction Case	Supreme Court, Grand Bench judgment of June 22, 1983	Articles 19 and 21

Table 2 Recurring Abbreviations, Acronyms and Names of Statutes

Term, Acronym or Abbreviation	Explanation/Citation
Act on General Rules for Application of Laws	Hō no Tekiyō ni Kansuru Tsūsokuhō, Law no. 78 of 2006
Act on Special Cases in Handling Gender Status for Persons with Gender Identity Disorder	Sei Dōitsu Sei Shōgaisha no Toriatsukai no Tokurei ni Kansuru Hōritsu, Law no. 111 of 2003
Amnesty Act	Onshahō, Law no. 20 of 1947
Attorney Act	Bengoshihō, Law no. 205 of 1949
Basic Act on Education	Kyōiku Kihonhō, Law no. 120 of 2006
Bank of Japan (BOJ) Act	Nihonginkōhō, Law no. 89 of 1997
Cabinet Act	Naikakuhō, Law no. 5 of 1947
CAT	United Nations Committee Against Torture
Child Rearing Allowance Act	Jidōfuyō Teatehō, Law no. 73 of 1971
Civil Code	Mimpō, Law no. 89 of 1896
Court Act	Saibanshohō, Law no. 59 of 1947
Criminal Compensation Act (CCA)	Keijihoshōhō, Law no. 1 of 1950
Disclosure of Information Held by Administrative Agencies Act	Gyōseikikan no Hoyūsuru Jōhō no Ōkai ni Kansuru Hōritsu, Law no. 42 of 1999
Diet	The national legislature (*Kokkai*) comprised of the House of Representatives and the House of Councillors
Diet Act	Kokkaihō, Law no 79 of 1947
Domestic Relations Case Procedure Act	Kajijiken Tedzuzukihō, Law no. 52 of 2011
Equal Opportunity in Employment Act (Act on Equal Opportunity and Treatment between Men and Women in Employment)	Koyō no Bunya ni Okeru Danjo no Kintō na Kikai Oyobi Taigū no Kakuhotō ni Kansuru Hōritsu, Law no. 113 of 1982
Family Register Act	Kosekihō, Law no. 224 of 1947
GHQ	"General Headquarters"; the term used to refer to the United States authorities overseeing the Occupation of Japan
GHQ Draft	The draft constitution prepared by GHQ and submitted to the Japanese government on February 13. See Appendix 6

Term, Acronym or Abbreviation	Explanation/Citation
Imperial House Law	Kōshitsu Tempan, Law no. 3 of 1947
Imperial Household Finance Act	Kōshitsu Zaiseihō, Law no. 4 of 1947
Judge Impeachment Act	Saibankan Dangaihō, Law no. 137 of 1947
Lay Judge (Saiban'in) Act (Act Relating to the Criminal Trials in which Lay Judges Participate)	Saiban'in no Sanka Suru Keiji Saiban ni Kansuru Hōritsu, Law no. 63 of 2004
Local Autonomy Act (LAA)	Chihō Jichihō, Law no. 67 of 1947
Local Public Service Act (LPSA)	Chihō Kōmuinhō, Law no. 261 of 1950
MacArthur Notes	The short February 3, 1946 memo by Douglas MacArthur to the GHQ drafting team setting forth his three "musts" for constitutional drafting. See Appendix 5
Meiji Constitution	The common term for Japan's first modern constitution, The Constitution of the Empire of Japan (*Dainihonteikoku kempō*), promulgated on February 11, 1889. See Appendices 1 and 2
MEXT	Ministry of Education, Culture, Sports, Science and Technology
MIC	Ministry of Internal Affairs and Communications
Minor Offenses Act	Keihanzaihō, Law no. 39 of 1948
MOD	Ministry of Defense
MOF	Ministry of Finance
MOJ	Ministry of Justice
Nationality Act	Kokusekihō, Law no. 147 of 1950
National Health Insurance Act	Kokumin Kenko Hokenhō, Law no. 192 of 1958
National Pension Act	Kokumin Nenkinhō, Law no. 141 of 1959
National Public Service Act (NPSA)	Kokka Kōmuinhō, Law no. 120 of 1947
Penal Code	Keihō, Law no. 45 of 1907
Protection of Specially Designated Secrets Act	Tokutei Himitsu no Hogo ni Kansuru Hōritsu, Law no. 108 of 2013
Public Offices Elections Act (POEA)	Kōshoku Senkyohō, Law no. 100 of 1950
Police Act	Keisatsuhō, Law no. 162 of 1954
Public Assistance Act	Seikatsu Hogohō, Law no. 144 of 1950
Public Finance Act	Zaiseihō, Law no. 34 of 1947
SCAP	Supreme Commander for the Allied Powers; the title of General Douglas MacArthur in his role as head of the Allied Occupation; often used more broadly to refer to the Occupation leadership or synonymously with "GHQ."
School Education Act	Gakkō Kyōikuhō, Law no. 26 of 1947
SDF	Self-Defense Forces (*jieitai*) – the name of Japan's national military
Self-Defense Force (SDF) Act	Jieitaihō, Law no. 165 of 1954
State Redress Act	Kokka Baishōhō, Law no. 125 of 1947
Subversive Activities Prevention Act	Hakai Katsudo Boshiho, Law no. 240 of 1952
Temporary Delegation of the Emperor's Acts in Matters of State Act	Kokujikōi no Rinji Daikōi ni Kansuru Hōritsu, Law no. 83 of 1964

Notes

[1] Next to dictionaries, one of the most common legal reference works sold in Japan may be a *Roppō*, a compilation of key statutes. These are key references for students and practitioners, and come in all shapes and sizes, some edited, others containing case annotations, and a brick-like two-volume works that includes all statutes currently in force. Interestingly, even the most basic minimalistic *Roppō* is likely to include the Meiji Constitution as well as the text of the Potsdam Declaration and the Treaty of San Francisco. Accordingly, they seem appropriate for inclusion in this volume also.

[2] One of the reasons for not using the "Bluebook" form of legal citation required by most American law journals, is that it's citation format does not indicate whether a case is a "decision" or a "judgment" or whether it was decided by a Petty Bench or the Grand Bench, both of which are basic, useful pieces of information.

[3] Among other things, the English translation of most statute names begin with "Act on" which, apart from being a formulation that causes momentary confusion to some English readers, would result in an unhelpful glossary and index.

Acknowledgements

This book was over ten years in the making. I originally—and naively—started it as a solo effort. It proved too much at the time and the publishers I talked to initially were strangely uninterested in what seemed to me a much-needed basic reference work on the Japanese constitution—an annotation in English. In addition, December 2012 saw the Liberal Democratic Party come back into power, giving birth to the second administration of Prime Minister Shinzō Abe, who had openly scorned his nation's constitution as "pathetic" (*mittomonai*). Moreover, the LDP had earlier the same year published its proposal for a sweeping set of amendments to the constitution I was proposing to annotate. All in all, it seemed best to turn to other things.

What has changed? First, Mark Gresham of MHM Limited kindly asked whether I would be interested in contributing something about Japanese law for his publishing company's *Japan Documents Handbooks* series. This seemed an ideal opportunity to revive my annotation project. Mark embraced the concept and that is why you have this book in your hands. For that I will always be grateful.

Second, the parameters Mark gave me for his series required the book to be an edited volume with multiple contributors. To be honest, I am not a huge fan of that format—at least in the field of law—since the results are often a disjointed collection of vaguely related, sometimes overlapping articles by contributors writing about whatever the subject of the book is. While they may contain numerous interesting insights, they often fail to present a coherent, comprehensive overview of the subject matter.

Japanese statutory and constitutional annotations, however, typically involve multiple authors contributing to individual sections or subsections with similar coverage but tighter parameters than typical edited volumes. Since they start from the text of the law under discussion, I find them particularly useful. With Mark's permission I agreed to do an edited volume along similar lines. This also solved a basic problem I had already encountered in my earlier effort—I no longer had to write everything by myself! I thus want to also express my deep gratitude to all the contributors whose time, expertise and mental energy made this work possible.

There remains a plausible chance that Japan's constitution may be amended within a few years of this book being published, given the LDP's repeated successes in Diet elections ever since Abe returned to power at the end of 2012. However, after over a decade of attempting to socialize various specific types of amendments (most relating to the Self-Defense Forces and emergency powers), it seems likely that if changes are made they would be much more limited in scope than the LDP's comprehensive 2012 proposal. It will in any case be useful to people seeking to understand whatever changes are made to know how the constitution was understood previous to them. And one of the nice things about the annotation format is that they are relatively easy to update.

In addition to the contributors who wrote chapter or article summaries, I would like to thank Larry Repeta for his helpful comments on the entire book, and Professor Craig Martin for his valuable insights on my efforts to summarize Chapter II, Article 9 and Article 14. I am also deeply grateful to Professor Yūichiro Tsuji for reading and offering helpful comments and corrections to all of the portions of the book written by me. Kieran Barnhardt provided invaluable service in organizing the bibliography and the footnotes and providing a second set of eyes. Thanks to Professor Shigenori Matsui for introducing him and for his own contribution and guidance.

This work would not have been possible without the support of Doshisha University and my colleagues on the faculty there, including two of the contributors to this work. And of course, my deepest thanks go out to my family, whose love, understanding and patience made this book and so many other positive things in my life possible.

Introduction
Historical Overview

Colin P.A. Jones

Japan's present constitution is, obviously, a product of its history. An important facet of that history is the constitution which came before, the Constitution of the Empire of Japan, more commonly called the "Meiji Constitution," after the Emperor Meiji who bestowed it on his subjects in 1889. A basic understanding of the historical background to both constitutions is thus important to understanding Japanese constitutional law today.

Since both charters are of comparatively modern provenance—at least when compared to the British or American constitutions—only a minimal inquiry into the history of Japan predating the Meiji Restoration of 1868 is necessary. There are numerous fine studies of the history of Japan after the Restoration by historians, so coverage of that period will also be brief. There are also several excellent accounts in English of the unusual circumstances of the constitution's birth during the postwar Occupation[1] and at the time of writing all of the key documents could be accessed through the National Diet Library's "Birth of the Constitution of Japan" on-line exhibit.[2] Thus, though a fascinating and dramatic story, only a brief outline of that part of the constitution's history will be provided in this work.

Prologue to Meiji: Ancient times through Tokugawa

Japan's legal system is comparatively modern. With the exception of emperors as a feature of government, virtually no Japanese laws or government institutions in existence today predates the Meiji Restoration of 1868, and most of those still in place can only be traced as far back as the birth of the Meiji Constitution or later.

The emperor system is a useful way of tracing the historical prelude to the Meiji Constitution. The first emperor, the probably mythical Emperor Jimmu, is said to have established the nation and acceded to the throne in 660 BC. According to the two earliest surviving historical narratives, the *Kojiki* (712) and *Nihonshoki* (721), Jimmu was a direct descendant of the deities that created the Japanese islands.

The supposedly unbroken lineage of emperors that followed Jimmu thus establishes a putative link between the imperial system and the divine origins of the Japanese nation. While this lineage no longer has formal political significance, it is relevant to the important role the emperor continues to play in the Shintō religion, including through forms of ancestor worship. When Emperor Naruhito, the 126th in the lineage ascended to the throne in 2019, in addition to various secular ceremonies, there was also a *daijōsai,* a Shintō ritual in which he entered specially-prepared chambers alone and made symbolic offerings of food, drink and clothing to *Amaterasu Ōmikami*, the sun goddess and one of the founding deities claimed by the emperors as an ancestor.

Due to its proximity to the Asian mainland, and the Korean peninsula in particular, from early times Japan had intercourse with and was influenced by imperial China. Buddhism was introduced in Japan in the 6th century CE from Korea, after its spread to China along the Silk Road. Other Chinese influences that appeared at the same time include the ideographic writing system and Confucian ideas about law and governance.

In the year 604, what is sometimes called Japan's first constitution—the Seventeen Article Constitution—was issued by the legendary Prince Regent Shōtoku Taishi. Its text is reproduced in full in the *Nihonshoki* and Article 1 famously begins with the exhortation: "Harmony is to be valued, and an avoidance of wanton opposition to be honored." Article 2 contains a call to revere Buddhist teachings, and Article 3 clearly establishes the emperor at the top of the hierarchy with the mandate "[w]hen you receive the Imperial commands, fail not scrupulously to obey them." However, this is counterbalanced by the opening sentence of the last article: "Decisions on important matters should not be made by one person alone." Collectively the charter contains a mixture of Confucian precepts of governance mixed with Buddhism and local modifications.

This "constitution" did not provide much in the way of detailed rules. These came in the form of law codes known as the *ritsuryō*, which were a more detailed set of rules relating to punishment for offenses (the *ritsu*) and administrative rules relating to the imperial court (the *ryō*). Although there are references to earlier bodies of *ritsuryō* law codes, the most well-known are the Taihō Code and the Yōryō Code of 757. These were modeled after the codes of Tang Dynasty China, subject to local modifications, including the lessening of the severity of some of the Chinese punishments (for example there was never a version of China's "death of a thousand cuts" punishment in Japan's *ritsuryō*). The Japanese also retained a hereditary bureaucracy rather than adopting the exam-based meritocracy of China. Because of the divine origins of the imperial lineage, the Japanese system also could not accommodate the notion of an emperor "losing the mandate of heaven" as happened periodically in China.

The Confucian underpinnings of the *ritsuryō* were reflected in Japanese law until the adoption of western models in the Meiji period. These included a preference for harmony that equated it with morality and good government, and a corresponding disfavoring of open disputes such as litigation, potentially a sign of bad government. This order included rules whereby the same behavior could be a serious crime or a minor offense depending on the respective family or status of the actors. In this system it was highly culpable for a son to beat his father, whereas the reverse would not be problematic. Shadows of this system remained into the 20th century with a provision of the Penal Code which established heavier punishments for the murder of parents or other lineal ascendants than for other types of murders and was found unconstitutional in 1973 (see discussion at Article 14).

The age in which the *ritsuryō* were promulgated saw the flourishing of culture under imperial rule, first in the capital of Nara during the Nara period (710–794), then in Kyoto during the Heian period (794–1184). The splendor and sensitivity of this period is epitomized by *The Tale of Genji,* commonly described as the world's first novel.

Over time the military class came to dominate politics, and generals—the shogun(s) appointed by the emperors for temporary military campaigns—came to usurp power permanently. The growth of largely autonomous private estates or *shōen*—including those controlled by Buddhist and Shintō religious establishments—denuded imperial power and tax revenues. The culmination of this saw the establishment of the shogunate or military government in 1192 CE, in the town of Kamakura, near present-day Tokyo.

The shogun continued to rely on the emperors for legitimacy through appointments, but supplanted them in increasing areas of life including law-making. Although the *ritsuryō* technically remained in force until the Meiji period, they were rendered increasingly irrelevant in the world outside of the imperial court. In 1232 the shogunate promulgated its own code of law, the *goseibaishikimoku*, which was devoted primarily to governing the military class, but included detailed rules about land rights under the system of feudal tenure, as well as punishments for various offenses. Buddhist and Shinto institutions competed with their own rules to govern their domains and adherents.

The feudal system established by the Kamakura shogun(s) collapsed with the Ōnin War of 1467, ushering in a "warring states" period that lasted for 150 years. This period culminated in the Battle of Sekigahara in 1600, which saw the feudal lord Ieyasu Tokugawa defeat his rivals and unify the nation again as the first of the Tokugawa shoguns. The Tokugawa shogunate established themselves in the town of Edo (now Tokyo).

The "Edo period" lasted until the Meiji Restoration and was characterized by several policies that were rigidly enforced by the samurai leadership. First was *sakoku,* or national seclusion, which forbade almost all interactions with the rest of the world. Second, and related to the first, was the proscription of Christianity, which had been introduced to Japan in the 16th century by Spanish and Portuguese missionaries. Third was the completion of an ongoing process of turning samurai into a legally distinct ruling class with hereditary stipends and a monopoly on the possession of weapons. Some Edo period rules devoted to ensuring the distinction between the samurai minority and the rest of the population were maintained through dress and behavior. Fourth, a feudal system was maintained with the Tokugawas having the most extensive domains while other lords were accorded hereditary domains (*han*), the size and location of which depended in part on whether their ancestors had been on the winning or losing side at Sekigahara. The domain lords had a degree of autonomy to set and enforce rules within their own domains, but were subject to various requirements that subjugated them to the shogunate, including a requirement that they leave family members as hostages in Edo, and periodically travel to and from the capital. The emperors remained a source of legitimacy, but the shoguns were powerful enough to significantly regulate and restrict their activities.

Most of the Edo period was marked by peace, prosperity, economic growth and a flourishing of commerce, art, literature and other cultural activities. This was disturbed in 1853 when the American Commodore Matthew Perry arrived with his fleet of "black ships" and a letter from President Fillmore demanding that Japan open itself to commerce with the world. The fact that this letter was addressed to the emperor rather than the shogun demonstrated how little the outside world knew about the political realities of the nation.

The American fleet also demonstrated that, among other things, in its isolation Japan had missed out on centuries of development in military technology. The shogunate was aware of the embarrassing defeat suffered recently by neighboring China at the hands of European

Powers in the Opium Wars and the humiliating treaties imposed as a result. Japan now faced a similar, potentially existential threat that shook its political establishment to the core.

Perry returned the following year and forced the shogunate to enter into the Treaty of Kanagawa which, among other things, required to Japan to open certain ports for commerce and allow the United States to establish an embassy in one of them. Two and a half centuries of isolation were over. This treaty was followed by a more expansive Treaty of Amity and Commerce signed in 1858, and similar treaties imposed by other western nations who rushed to take advantage of the opening created by the United States.

These treaties contained provisions similar to those which had been on imposed on Imperial China after the Opium Wars. First, Japan was forced to accord the citizens of treaty partners extraterritorial status: they were not subject to Japanese laws or the jurisdiction of Japanese courts in either civil or criminal spheres. Trials involving foreigners took place in consular courts staffed by diplomatic personnel, who naturally tended to favor their western compatriots. Second, Japan lost the ability to set its own tariffs, which were similarly put under foreign control. Third, foreigners gained an entitlement to reside in treaty ports (which were increased in number). Fourth, residence rights for foreigners included the right to practice their religion, meaning Christianity again gained a foothold. Finally, the most favored nation status contained in each treaty meant that if Japan subsequently signed a more favorable treaty with another nation, all previous signatories would enjoy the same benefits. Overall, these so-called unequal treaties represented a significant infringement on Japanese sovereignty.[3]

The arrival of the "black ships" had plunged the nation into political foment. Various factions expressed different views on how to respond, with many calling for the expulsion of the foreigners and continuation of national isolation. The Tokugawa shogunate sought to achieve national unity by taking the unprecedented step of presenting the 1858 treaty with the United States to the Emperor Kōmei for approval. This was a mistake, for he declined to do so.[4] The shogunate proceeded to sign this and other treaties anyway, thereby giving cause to the anti-foreign, anti-shogunate camp.

The remainder of the Edo period was a period of great upheaval. The shogunate struggled to retain political power while responding to external threats. The leaders of the domains historically disadvantaged by the Tokugawa feudal system saw an opportunity to enhance their standing, including through the adoption of western military techniques. Kyoto became a hotbed of intrigue as various factions sought to obtain imperial favor and use the emperor's prestige for their own ends. In 1863 the emperor was sufficiently empowered to issue an order to "expel the barbarians." The shogunate demurred, but some individual domains took it upon themselves to commence hostilities with foreign powers, with disastrous results for the Japanese side.

Military conflict also developed between upstart domains and the shogunate forces, in which the latter were defeated. The position of the shogun became untenable and in November 1867, Yoshinobu Tokugawa formally resigned as the last of the Tokugawa shoguns. The Emperor Kōmei had died earlier in the year, so the reins of government were formally returned to his son, the Emperor Meiji, who was 16 at the time. This "restoration" was formalized through an imperial edict issued on January 3, 1868 and the establishment of a new government.

A state of civil war (known as the "Boshin War") continued into the following year. Other incidents of political violence and open conflict arose in the years to come, including another civil war in 1877. However, the new system of government under the Meiji emperor survived and ultimately prospered.

The emergence of the "Meiji System"

The Meiji government was led by a fractious cabal of mostly samurai leaders from the former outsider domains far from Edo. Although "expelling foreign barbarians" had been a rallying cry for the anti-Tokugawa forces, it was quickly abandoned as unrealistic. Instead of renewing isolation, the new government focused on creating a nation that would be politically unified and economically and militarily powerful enough to be accepted as a modern nation by western powers. This involved a concentrated program of learning about the military, government, economy, and legal systems of these countries.

In the legal sphere, tremendous change was wrought. Feudal domains were replaced with prefectures. A more modern system of land tenure was introduced. The neo-Confucian class system that had dominated for centuries was eliminated, as was samurai as a legal status itself. This was replaced with a new system of hereditary aristocracy with the emperor at its apex. Conscription was implemented, as western armies had demonstrated the superiority of formations of quickly-trained conscripts with rifles over warriors who trained for years to master sword and bow. Domain (han)-based penal laws were replaced with national ones. The development of laws and legal institutions based on western models and to which foreigners would be willing to submit was critical to success in renegotiating the unequal treaties.

Politically the new leaders looked to the young Emperor Meiji as a source of legitimacy but also as a means of unifying the country. This entailed focusing on the divine roots of the imperial lineage, and the development of Shintō as a national religion (something that was actively countermanded through the current constitution). The end of exclusion meant a flood of western knowledge entering the country, including new ideas about government. Theories of democracy and representative government found fertile ground, particularly in the numerous sectors of society disaffected by recent changes.

In 1868 the Emperor Meiji marked his enthronement with the Charter Oath comprised of five articles promising, among other things, that "[d]eliberative assemblies shall be widely established and all matters decided by open discussion." Demands for a representative assembly were a feature of politics from early in the Meiji period. This was accompanied by both external "private" proposals for constitutions, together with discussion among the various factions of government. In 1876 the Emperor Meiji instructed his advisors to prepare constitutional proposals, and at an 1881 imperial conference a formal commitment was made to establish a national legislature by 1890. After this decision was made, key leaders such as Hirobumi Itō traveled to Europe for research.

While Britain's parliamentary system had many admirable qualities, to Japanese leaders it was problematic as a model due to the power of political parties. They did not believe the Japanese people ready for that level of democracy and worried about exposing emperors directly to grubby partisan politics. While France was a highly regarded source of models in law and influenced the development of Japan's Civil Code, its republicanism was problematic when it came to constitutions. Prussia and Austro-Hungary became the principal source of constitutional models, and the German scholars Lorenz von Stein, Rudolf von Gneist and

Karl Friedrich Hermann Roesler were particularly influential in shaping the charter that was eventually drafted.

The Meiji Constitution was promulgated on February 11, 1889, and took effect on November 29 of the following year, the date on which the new Imperial Diet commenced its first session. This represented a significant step in the development of Japan as a modern state, though the country was still in turmoil: the Minister of Education was assassinated on his way to the promulgation ceremony. While what can be described as the "Meiji System" of law and government under the Meiji Constitution was largely stabilized by the turn of the century, outbreaks of political violence, including political assassinations and coup attempts, would continue up until World War II.

The Meiji Constitution

"The Constitution of the Empire of Japan" (the formal title of the Meiji Constitution) was promulgated as a gift from Emperor Meiji. It was introduced with a *tsugebumi*, or Imperial Oath and a rescript of promulgation. The constitution itself consisted of a preamble in the form of another edict (*jōyu*) and 76 articles in seven chapters (see Appendices 1 and 2 for the Japanese text and English translation). The preamble reiterated the divine origins of the imperial lineage and the natural rights of sovereignty inherited with it. Article 3 reiterated this with the statement "The Emperor is sacred and inviolable."[5]

The promulgation ceremony for the Meiji Constitution was carried out in a manner intended to create the impression that the charter emanated from the emperor himself. This meant it was unassailable. The emperor himself also effectively existed outside the bounds of of the constitution, and other things characterized as emanating from his mouth or his pen could be of a quasi-constitutional character.

In fact, the Meiji System could be said to involve two constitutions: the Meiji Constitution, and what is now called the Imperial House Law, which was promulgated at the same time. Prior to its amendment after World War II (and subordination to the Diet, as discussed at Article 2), the Imperial House Law was essentially a constitution for the imperial family, not a law that could be amended by the Imperial Diet.

The relationship between the emperor and the army and navy was also established largely outside of the framework of the Meiji Constitution. Article 11 established the emperor as Supreme Commander of both, and Article 12 gave him, not the Imperial Diet, the power to control their organizations. The only constitutional control which the Imperial Diet could exercise over the military was the budgetary power, though even that did not extend to controlling the finances of the imperial household. Efforts to control the military through lower-level cabinet processes were also of limited effect.

Moreover, the Imperial Rescript to Soldiers and Sailors had already been issued in 1882. This was a code of ethics for military personnel that established a direct link between them and the emperor without any involvement of other branches of government. Given the disastrous defeat in World War II that ultimately resulted from Japanese military aggression, some might consider the Meiji Constitution defective for failing to provide suitable mechanisms for keeping the military under control. However, it should be remembered that Japan had direct historical experience with a clearly defined locus of military authority (i.e., the shoguns) usurping political power from the emperor.

The Meiji Constitution arguably suffered from several key flaws. First, in European constitutional monarchies at the time, the monarchs "reigned but did not rule." In such systems it was possible to maintain the fiction that the sovereign was infallible, because any mistakes or problems were the fault of the government. The Meiji leadership, however, had little inherent legitimacy beyond the emperor. So just as the Meiji Constitution itself was presented as having emanated directly from the emperor himself, the government it established required the emperor to be both infallible and seen as ruling directly, even though actual rule was carried out entirely by others.

This impossible premise meant that the constitution could only be applied by interpreting it broadly, since in reality the emperor was not actually performing all the roles it accorded to him. At the same time, constitutional interpretation was fraught with risk of lèse-majesté.[6] Paradoxically, therefore, efforts to "protect" the constitution through more conservative, strict interpretation rendered it dysfunctional.[7]

One facet of this dysfunction was manifested in the fact that any senior member of the government or the military appointed directly by the emperor—which included individual ministers of state and also senior military officers—could claim they answered to no other authority. Thus, although during the war it was common to portray Japan as a totalitarian fascist system like Nazi Germany, the governance system was highly fractious until the end. Wartime Prime Minister Hideki Tōjō sought to remedy this by "multi-hatting," also holding at various times the role of army minister, education minister, munitions minister, and chief of the general staff. For this he was criticized from some quarters as guilty of a "Tokugawa-like" usurpation of power.

The culmination of this dysfunction was the end of World War II, which was accomplished after the nation suffered two atomic bombings. By tradition usually silent, Emperor Hirohito spoke up and demanded that his ministers, generals and admirals seek peace. The terms of the Potsdam Declaration—the July 26, 1945 announcement by the Allied Powers of the terms for ending hostility (see Appendix 3 for text)—were accepted on August 14, 1945 and this was announced by Hirohito in a radio broadcast to the nation the next day.

The Occupation and a new constitution

Within two weeks of this broadcast, the advance guard of the Allied Occupation force arrived in Japan. Shortly thereafter, on August 30, General Douglas MacArthur arrived to assume the role of Supreme Commander for the Allied Powers (SCAP). A formal surrender ceremony took place on September 2, 1945, at which an Instrument of Surrender was signed (see Appendix 4).[8]

A key term announced in the Potsdam Declaration was the destruction of Japan's war-making potential. This was thus an important goal from the earliest stage of the Occupation, though one that changed with the international situation in the years that followed, rendering the reconciliation between geopolitical reality and the high ideals expressed in the new constitution complicated (see discussion at Article 9).

Although MacArthur may not have arrived with a specific agenda to amend the Meiji Constitution, the Allies did see Japan as having an oppressive totalitarian system of government. The Potsdam Declaration mandated "The Japanese Government shall remove all obstacles to the revival and strengthening of democratic tendencies among the Japanese people. Freedom of speech, of religion, and of thought, as well as respect for the fundamental human rights shall be established." MacArthur thus did arrive with an immediate goal of "democratizing" Japan.

On October 4, MacArthur's general headquarters (commonly referred to as "GHQ") issued a directive restoring civil liberties and abolishing a wide range of restrictive laws and regulations. On the same day, MacArthur made his first of several suggestions to senior Japanese leaders that constitutional revision might be appropriate.

On October 25, a newly established Cabinet under Prime Minister Kijūrō Shidehara created a committee to investigate the "Constitutional Problem" to consider possible amendments. It was headed by Jōji Matsumoto, a former law professor and government official. By the end of 1945, Matsumoto's committee had prepared drafts, though they were not made public. Through a mysterious set of circumstances, one of the Matsumoto committee's drafts made it into the hands of reporters, and it was published in the *Mainichi Shinbun* on February 1, 1946.

This created a problem for MacArthur: the contents of the proposed amendments were not the type of significant changes he considered necessary. By this time he had a deadline of sorts, in the form of the newly-established Far Eastern Commission (FEC) comprised of representatives of Allied Powers which was supposed to perform oversight of his administration of the Occupation MacArthur thus wanted to establish constitutional change as a *fait accompli* of Japanese origin before the FEC could interfere too much. One reason for this was to protect Emperor Hirohito, who some allied leaders and citizens felt should be tried as a war criminal and executed. MacArthur, however, had concluded that the Occupation could be managed much more smoothly by keeping the emperor in place. To accomplish this required having a constitutional proposal ready as quickly as possible.

On February 3 MacArthur issued a memo ordering a team of GHQ lawyers and other personnel to prepare a draft constitution. This memo (sometimes referred to as the "MacArthur Notes," see Appendix 5 for the full text) outlined three key principles he considered essential for the new constitution: (1) the emperor to be the head of state and determined by dynastic succession; (2) Japan would renounce war and be prohibited from having any military forces; and (3) the elimination of the feudal system and the hereditary nobility. The GHQ team worked in great secrecy over an intense period of a little over a week to produce their draft, based on what limited reference materials they had at their disposal or which they could borrow from Japanese libraries without attracting attention. They also had the benefit of various private amendment proposals already in circulation, including one prepared by the Constitutional Research Association (a group of scholars and intellectuals) which had already been translated into English and analyzed by GHQ.

On February 8, the Japanese government submitted to GHQ its proposed constitution based on the efforts of the Matsumoto Committee. On February 13, GHQ informed the Japanese that the Matsumoto draft was unacceptable, and instead shocked them with GHQ's own English language draft. This is commonly known as the "MacArthur Draft" or the "GHQ Draft."

Several weeks of intense negotiations between the Japanese government and GHQ followed, with the former pushing back and the Americans insisting on their language, or at least its substance. MacArthur threatened to publish the American draft and to submit it to the Japanese people for consideration, which would have doomed the Shidehara Cabinet. This process culminated in an intense drafting session spanning March 4 and March 5 at which parallel English and Japanese versions of a draft were hammered out by negotiators from the two sides. Further changes were made at this time.

On March 6, the Japanese government announced the new constitution in draft form, and on April 17 the full text of the proposed constitution was published. No mention was made of the American involvement in its creation. To help obfuscate the fact that parts of it were fairly obvious translations or reflected American ideals, it was published in vernacular Japanese, rather than the archaic language that had previously been used to draft laws and regulations. This began a process of Japanese laws in more accessible language that continued long into the postwar period.[9]

In reading the constitution in English it is thus important to remember that it was prepared under tremendous time pressure by two groups of people with sometimes conflicting interests or understandings, working across two very different languages. Thus, the relationship between the Japanese version (which controls, of course) and the English is not just merely that of a source text and its translation. Rather they were two versions developed in parallel and as a result there are some discrepancies between the English and the Japanese that go beyond mere mistranslation. These will be pointed out where appropriate throughout this book.

Procedurally, the new constitution was enacted as an amendment to the Meiji Constitution, proposed by the emperor pursuant to Article 73 of that law. Substantively, it represented a complete rewriting of the national charter, with the shadow of the prior constitution remaining only in the order of the chapters.

The draft was submitted to the Imperial Diet on June 20, 1946 pursuant to an imperial edict. The House of Representatives had been reconstituted by an election held on April 10. By this time, GHQ had already eliminated proscriptions on left-wing political parties, purged many politicians associated with militarism, and forced a change of electoral laws expanding the franchise to all men and women older than 20. The legislature that deliberated on the constitution was thus different than before, and included women, socialists and even communists.

The deliberations in the two houses are a useful record of how the draft constitution was viewed, the types of questions asked and the official view of the government in its response. Various additional changes were made to the draft during this process, as noted where appropriate elsewhere in this book. Both chambers voted overwhelmingly in favor of the draft, even though for the House of Peers this meant voting itself out of existence. The new constitution was promulgated on November 3, 1946, the Emperor Meiji's birthday (now celebrated as Culture Day), and took effect on May 3, 1947 (also a national holiday: Constitution Day).

Under the Occupation the constitution became a part of a new system of government that saw wholesale reform of laws and legal institutions, not to mention society at large. The constitution eliminated the hereditary nobility created in the Meiji period. A Diet Act, Cabinet Act and Court Act were all passed in 1947 to reconstitute the three branches of government in accordance with the new charter. A new code of criminal procedure was enacted to reflect the new constitutional procedural norms, and the family law and inheritance provisions of the Civil Code were recrafted to reflect the new constitutional requirements of equality regardless of birth order or gender. Numerous other laws were also passed during this period. However, notwithstanding the new constitution, laws and institutions, a great deal of continuity remained in terms of the people who worked within the legal system, including judges, lawyers and prosecutors.

After the constitution took effect, GHQ continued to exercise its influence behind the scenes until the end of the Occupation. This included the implementation of policies that were clearly contrary to the constitution, including the confiscation and redistribution of land, suppression of labor unions and censorship of publications.

The Occupation continued until April 28, 1952 when the Treaty of San Francisco between Japan and most of the Allied Powers came into effect and Japan regained sovereignty over most of its territories. Exceptions were the Amami Islands (returned later in 1952 and 1953), the Ogasawara Islands (1968) and Okinawa (1972).[10] Japan also lost its colonies in Micronesia, Taiwan and Korea, though the latter two were already embroiled in conflicts of their own. Contemporaneously with the peace treaty, Japan entered into a defense alliance with the United States which allowed the latter country to maintain a military presence in Japan which has remained until today.

Considering the constitution's provenance, it would have been reasonable for Japan's leaders to consider amendment once sovereignty was restored. Under a now-defunct law, a Constitutional Investigation Committee was established under the Cabinet in 1956.[11] It deliberated for nine years and produced a weighty report but did not result in any constitutional amendments.

Pursuant to a 2000 amendment to the Diet Act, constitutional investigation committees were established in both houses of the Diet. As discussed at Article 96, as of the date of writing, the constitution has never been formally amended. While this is a source of great frustration to conservatives, perhaps enough Japanese people have been satisfied with their constitution as it is.

Notes

1 See, for example, Moore, R., & Robinson, D. (2004); Inoue, K. (1991); and Koseki, S. (R. Moore, trans.) (1997) Hellegers, D.M. (2001).

2 *Birth of the constitution of Japan*. National Diet Library. (n.d.). Retrieved May 24, 2022, from https://www.ndl.go.jp/constitution/e/.

3 The Japanese did learn from the Chinese experience in one respect: the treaties signed by the Japanese, though unequal, banned the import of opium.

4 It is worth noting that the full official title of the shogun actually meant "Commander-in-Chief of the Expeditionary Force Against the Barbarians." So, expelling foreign barbarians was arguably a key performance indicator.

5 Note that the application of terms such as "sacred" and "divine" to Japan's emperors was likely to have been regarded with great effrontery by those from monotheistic Judeo-Christian western nations. Shintō allows for the discovery of a divine essence in even rocks or trees, so in the context of emperors it may not be nearly as significant. Thus, that portion of the January 1, 1946 radio address in which Emperor Hirohito declared himself to be a mere human was regarded as highly significant by western observers, but apparently not by Hirohito himself. Nor were any of his Japanese listeners likely surprised by the revelation. As one Japanese writer has observed: "*No Japanese, even the most ignorant and superstitious, has ever believed the Emperor to be a god in the Western sense of possessing powers of control over natural phenomena or that he necessarily possessed even superior human quantities*" and "*The Japanese had known right along that the Emperor was a mortal man. So what, thought they, was the point in formally announcing the obvious?*" Kawai, K. (1960), 74, 84.

6 This was illustrated by the 1935 expulsion from the House of Peers of the constitutional scholar Tatsukichi Minobe for espousing the theory that the emperor was an "organ of the state," even though he had first done so in a 1912 publication and this theory had been widely accepted for many years before it became problematic for political reasons. His case is also discussed at Article 23.

[7] The views of the defects of the Meiji Constitution are informed by the work of Kawaguchi, A. (2017). An English summary of his work is available in "Different Constitutions, Similar Defect?" in Jones, C.P.A. (2019).

[8] Interestingly, while the Potsdam Declaration is still sometimes referenced in connection with the interpretation of the constitution, the Instrument of Surrender appears to have faded into insignificance.

[9] Another difference between the Meiji Constitution and the current constitution is linguistic. The former is rendered in *kana majiri bun,* which relies more heavily on kanji ideographs, uses a different phonetic alphabet to express verb conjugations and grammatical particles, eschews punctuation and uses the grammar of classical Japanese. The linguistic modernization of Meiji-era statutes took some time; the Civil Code was not entirely rendered into modern Japanese until 2004.

[10] Japan still has a territorial dispute over four islands which were occupied by Soviet forces shortly before the end of the war and remain under Russian dominion.

[11] Kempō chōsakaihō [Constitutional Investigation Committee Act], Law no. 140 of 1956.

The Constitution of Japan

Promulgated on November 3, 1946
Came into effect on May 3, 1947

The Preamble

Colin P.A. Jones

We, the Japanese people, acting through our duly elected representatives in the National Diet, determined that we shall secure for ourselves and our posterity the fruits of peaceful cooperation with all nations and the blessings of liberty throughout this land, and resolved that never again shall we be visited with the horrors of war through the action of government, do proclaim that sovereign power resides with the people and do firmly establish this Constitution. Government is a sacred trust of the people, the authority for which is derived from the people, the powers of which are exercised by the representatives of the people, and the benefits of which are enjoyed by the people. This is a universal principle of mankind upon which this Constitution is founded. We reject and revoke all constitutions, laws, ordinances, and rescripts in conflict herewith.

We, the Japanese people, desire peace for all time and are deeply conscious of the high ideals controlling human relationship, and we have determined to preserve our security and existence, trusting in the justice and faith of the peace-loving peoples of the world. We desire to occupy an honored place in an international society striving for the preservation of peace, and the banishment of tyranny and slavery, oppression and intolerance for all time from the earth. We recognize that all peoples of the world have the right to live in peace, free from fear and want.

We believe that no nation is responsible to itself alone, but that laws of political morality are universal; and that obedience to such laws is incumbent upon all nations who would sustain their own sovereignty and justify their sovereign relationship with other nations.

We, the Japanese people, pledge our national honor to accomplish these high ideals and purposes with all our resources.

The jōyu

Before talking about the Preamble, mention needs to be made of the *jōyu*, the brief statement by the emperor announcing that "according to the will of the Japanese people" an amendment to the constitution had been passed through consultations with the Privy Council and the decision of the Imperial Diet in accordance with Article 73 of the Meiji Constitution, and that it was now sanctioned and promulgated. The *jōyu* is followed by the imperial seal and countersigned by his ministers of state.

The Meiji Constitution had also had a *jōyu* which comprised part of that charter (the text preceding Article 1 which starts with the declaration "Having, by virtue of our glories..."). The *jōyu* which announced it is *not* considered part of the present constitution, and is of interest mainly because it establishes the continuity between the old constitution and the new, while illustrating the transition from a process notionally controlled by the emperor, to a substantive new law beginning with the stirring words "We the Japanese people."

The Preamble

Like most of the text of the Preamble, the words "We the Japanese people" were written by Lt. Colonel Milo Rowell, an American army lawyer.[1] Apart from the obvious influence of the US constitution, it is believed to have drawn on other well-known textual models, including Lincoln's Gettysburg Address and the Atlantic Charter of 1941. GHQ entertained few changes to their draft of the Preamble, as is evidenced by the high degree of concordance between the language above and that of the GHQ Draft.

Read as something written by an American immediately after defeating Japan in a brutal war, the Preamble can easily be understood as an aspirational statement projected onto the Japanese people by well-intentioned victors. Their view was that the Japanese people had been led into a disastrous war by bad leadership and should resolve to never allow such a thing to happen again through democratic control of their leadership and acceptance and fostering of international norms of peaceful co-existence and cooperation. This reading also makes it accord readily with Article 9, with which the Preamble is often associated in constitutional discourse.

However, the Japanese quickly made the Preamble their own text. Scholars described it as articulating three basic principles underlying the entire constitution, a view that was persuasive enough that children once had to memorize them in elementary school. The three principles are generally described as being: (1) popular sovereignty, (2) respect for human rights, and (3) pacifism.

There are some problems with these three principles, not the least of which is that they have changed over time and not all are immediately apparent from the text of the Preamble. For example, the text does not even mention human rights, whereas other parts of the constitution (Articles 11 and 97) contain much more clear statements of principle on that subject. Similarly, a clear statement of the locus of sovereignty is contained in Article 1, and the parameters of Japan's constitutional pacifism are articulated at Article 9. Why is it necessary to read more into the Preamble than is already there?

Most scholars agree that as part of the constitution the Preamble has effect as law. However most also agree it is not specific enough to be grounds for a stand-alone claim for judicial relief and that a lawsuit based only on an asserted violation of the Preamble alone would thus not go anywhere. There is some consensus to the effect that the text of the Preamble may support a ruling of unconstitutionality rooted in other parts of the charter.

Some scholars and a few lower court decisions have looked to the Preamble in combination with Article 9 as the source of a constitutional guarantee of a "right to a peaceful existence" (*heiwateki seizonken*).[2] However, the Supreme Court has only declared such a right to be "not clearly defined."[3]

There is academic debate over whether the "This is the universal principle…" and "We reject" language in the first paragraph of the Preamble prevent amendments of the constitution and if so, to what extent. It seems unlikely this debate will forestall any actual amendments if they are ever successful.

Chapter I
The Emperor
Articles 1–8

Introduction

Colin P.A. Jones

Overview

Just as with the Meiji Constitution, the first substantive provisions of the Constitution of Japan address the status of the emperor. A comparison of Chapter I of both charters reveals how much the role of the emperor has changed. Whereas under the Meiji Constitution he was vested with the vast powers of sovereignty, some of which were delegated to other parts of government (the judiciary, the Imperial Diet), under the current constitution he exercises a more limited range of powers and then only symbolically, always bounded by the "advice and approval" of the Cabinet.

Today the provisions of Chapter I are something of a constitutional backwater. Few court cases have arisen under any of its provisions and its eight articles generate almost no jurisprudence and little controversy, one exception to the latter being the question of succession, as discussed at Article 2.

The seemingly innocuous nature of Chapter I belies the controversy its generated at the time of the constitution's birth. Meiji constitutionalism had been dominated by the notion of *kokutai* (literally, the "body of the nation"), which under the Meiji Constitution became the expression of an entire system of Japanese society, religion and government with the emperor at the center. To question the role of the emperor, or even characterize it in a heterodox way could be a form of *lesè majesté*, or at least career suicide, as some constitutional scholars discovered the hard way. One of the reasons why communism was regarded as anathema in prewar Japan was because of its call for the abolition of the imperial system. To question the *kokutai* was a form of thought crime that led to the arrest of intellectuals and their "conversion" to the correct way of thinking. Seeking assurances from the allies about the preservation of *kokutai*—the emperor—as a possible condition for accepting the Potsdam Declaration arguably led to the dropping of the atomic bombs. Even in the face of total defeat, therefore, the dramatic changes demanded by the Americans in the role and characterization of the emperor were problematic for Japanese political leaders.

The eight articles comprising the GHQ draft of Chapter I thus generated some of the most heated arguments between the American and Japanese sides in their initial drafting session. Chapter I is where the Japanese side resisted the American proposal with particular vigor and the Americans pushed back just as forcefully. With most of the bargaining power being on the American side, however, their views on Chapter I generally prevailed (as is apparent from a comparison of the GHQ draft with the constitution).

Contextual guideposts

Some context will be helpful for the discussion that follows. The first is etymological: the Japanese word for the nation's emperor—*Tennō*—has nothing to do with the word for "empire" (*teikoku*). The use of the English term "emperor" predates but became normalized during the Meiji period, which is also when the nation began building an empire. However, the term *Tennō* has a much older provenance and its usage was intended to establish Japan's emperor as equivalent to the Chinese emperors, a show of resistance to a much older, larger and more powerful empire which had long regarded itself as the center of the worldand its neighbors as tributary states whose rulers were inferior in stature.

The second is a matter of political history. Anglo-American constitutional history developed around the struggle between monarchs with real political, military, economic and even religious authority and their "subjects," who were generally trying to resist, negate or even acquire some of that authority. Neither of Japan's constitutions have been the product of this type of history, since Japan's emperors went for centuries without exercising significant power outside the spheres of culture and religion. This means that the notion of the emperors (as opposed to the state, their advisors, shoguns or other "bad actors") as a source of oppression or tyranny never have really developed as a central feature of Japanese constitutionalism.

Third, the emperor and his immediate relatives—collectively the "imperial house"—are separate from the *kokumin*, the "people" from whom the constitution notionally originated and whose rights and freedoms it guarantees. Members of the imperial house do not have surnames, and are registered in a registry separate from the family registries in which the births, marriages, deaths and other changes in status of Japanese people are recorded. Marriage into or out of the imperial family involves moving from one register to the other.

Being a member of the imperial house means being subject to various restrictions and discriminatory rules that would be problematic if applied to ordinary citizens. Article 8 imposes restrictions on the property rights of members of the imperial house. Members of the imperial family are not free to marry without going through a consultative process involving the Imperial Household Council. They are prohibited from entering into adoptive relationships (a common practice in Japanese families), and women born into the family are subject to further restrictions, including the inability to succeed to the throne either directly or through their children.[4]

Under the Meiji system, a legal framework existed that provided rules of governance for the imperial family, which was much larger than it is now.[5] The old Imperial House Law functioned as a separate constitution for members of the imperial house, and, together with imperial edicts, provided a much more extensive set of rules than under the current version of that law.[6] These include rules relating to the emperor's religious status, which were excised under the new constitutional system.[7]

For example, under the Meiji system, in addition to the old Law,[8] the "Imperial House Trial Order" established rules for criminal and civil trials for members of the imperial family, other than the emperor, who was, constitutionally, "sacred and inviolable" (Article 3).[9] No similar rules or laws exist under the current constitution. The Supreme Court has held that "[i]n light of the Emperor's status as the symbol of Japan and the symbol of the Japanese people, it is appropriate to understand the jurisdiction of civil courts as not reaching him."[10] The question of criminal jurisdiction and the amenability of other members of other members of the imperial family to civil or criminal suit has never been tested, but provisions of the Imperial House Law and Temporary Delegation of the Emperor's Acts in Matters of State Act granting them temporary immunity from "legal action" when acting as proxies, but without completely impairing the right to take legal action against them suggests they are not immune from suit or prosecution except when standing in for the emperor.

Fourth, just as the emperor plays a low-key role in government, his presence is manifested in various other ways. Modern historical periods are still referred to using regnal titles that coincide with the reign of an emperor (e.g., the Meiji period, for the Meiji Emperor), who is more commonly referred to in Japanese by that title than by name (e.g., "the Emperor Meiji" rather than Mutsuhito, "the Shōwa emperor," rather than Hirohito, etc.). Official documents are still dated using regnal years. For example, this book was published in 2023, which is the 5th year of the Reiwa Period, the regnal title used to describe the reign of Emperor Naruhito, the 126th emperor in the lineage.

Many national holidays also have some imperial provenance. This includes not just the current emperor's birthday, but also "Culture Day" (November 3, the Meiji Emperor's birthday), "Green Day" (April 29, the Shōwa Emperor's birthday) and National Foundation Day (February 11) celebrates the accession of Japan's first emperor, Jimmu, to the throne.

The national anthem is also a paean to the emperors. Singing it has sometimes been controversial, particularly to those who object to elevating the emperor or having an imperial family at all. Such objections may have been stronger in the past, during the reign of Emperor Hirohito, due to views in some quarters that he was responsible for the suffering of World War II. The question of whether public school teachers can be forced to sing or perform the national anthem at school events has been the subject of several court cases, as discussed at Article 19.

Article 1: Popular Sovereignty and the Symbolic Emperor

Colin P.A. Jones

> **Article 1.**
> The Emperor shall be the symbol of the State and of the unity of the people, deriving his position from the will of the people with whom resides sovereign power.

Under Article 4 of the Meiji Constitution, sovereignty was clearly vested in the emperor. By declaring sovereign power to reside in the Japanese people and notionally subjecting the status of the emperor to their will, Article 1 represents a dramatic restructuring of the political foundations of government and was highly contentious at the time it was negotiated.

From the time it was deliberated by the Imperial Diet, constitutional scholars have had issues with the conceptual problem of using the amendment process set forth in the Meiji

Constitution—a gift to the people from a sovereign emperor—to relocate sovereignty to the people. One theory that was developed to overcome this problem was that of the "August Revolution." Under that theory, the acceptance of the Potsdam Declaration on August 14 was a form of "revolution" which resulted in a transfer of sovereignty to the Japanese people before it was formalized in the constitution. The principal benefit of this entirely academic theory seems to be in its facilitation of minimizing the American role in reshaping Japan's political foundations.

The use of the term "symbol" to describe the emperor's new role is thought to have been inspired by the 1931 Statute of Westminster, which established self-government for Canada and other parts of the British Empire and described the British crown as "the symbol of free association of the British Commonwealth of Nations."[11] What is meant by the Japanese term in the Japanese context is a matter of some debate, though again mostly academic.

Whether or not the Japanese would have used the term "symbolic" to describe it, the idea of a symbolic emperor is arguably not an American innovation. As noted by historian Kenneth J. Ruoff, some Japanese regarded a symbolic emperor as nothing more than a return to the traditional role of the imperial institution before it was hijacked by militarists.[12] Under this view, the emperor's status under the new constitution was not revolutionary at all: as described in 1973 by Yasuhiro Nakasone (who went on to become one of postwar Japan's most influential prime ministers): "I think that the essential character (*honshitsuteki seikaku*) of the Japanese emperor from time past until today was like the symbol emperor. The reason the emperor was supported for 2,000 years was that he in reality did not have political power and did not enter into the fray of political disputes."[13] This view needs to be taken with a grain of salt, given postwar efforts to reinvent Emperor Hirohito as a pacifist bearing no responsibility for the horrors of World War II. [14] If a symbolic emperor did indeed represent a return to tradition, it is difficult to explain the resistance of some Japanese leaders to the change.

Perhaps the most significant thing about Article 1 (or any other provision in Chapter I), is what it does *not* say: that the emperor is head of state. This was clearly stated in Article 4 of the Meiji Constitution, and was mandated as part of one of the three "musts" set forth in the MacArthur Notes.[15] However, it was never included in the text of the constitution. Who is the head of state is the sort of thing which generally cannot be assumed or interpreted into a written constitution, and since the emperor is no longer the locus of even nominal executive or foreign policy powers (which now reside in the Cabinet), some scholars are of the view that the emperor cannot be the head of state.

The Japanese government view has been highly nuanced. On the one hand, whether the emperor is head of state or not depends on the definition of the term, which is not provided in the constitution (or anywhere else). At the same time, however, given the emperor's albeit ceremonial role in foreign affairs (Article 7(ix)), it is possible to consider the emperor as head of state, at least for diplomatic purposes.[16] Since that is how he is in fact treated by both the Japanese government and foreign counterparties, other views are largely academic.

Article 2: Succession

Colin P.A. Jones

Article 2.
The Imperial Throne shall be dynastic and succeeded to in accordance with the Imperial House Law passed by the Diet.

> *"His succession shall be dynastic."*

This core mandate from the MacArthur Notes was duly reflected in Article 2, though without any gender-specific pronouns in the Japanese. The Meiji Constitution clearly limited succession to male descendants (Article 2). The constitution is silent as to gender, but the Imperial House Law (Article 2) currently limits succession to males born into the imperial family and their male descendants.[17]

As for who "his" referred to at the time the constitution was drafted, it did not necessarily mean Hirohito, whose abdication had been deliberated. Before it was pruned by MacArthur, the imperial family as defined by the old Imperial House Law was much larger, so there were other candidates. Outside the "official" imperial family, there was an even larger universe of people who could legitimately claim descent from imperial stock, at least one of whom presented himself to GHQ as an alternative.[18] In the end, however, Hirohito was retained.

Coming after the reallocation of sovereignty from emperor to people in Article 1, Article 2 contains a further subtle subversion of the emperor's status that is not apparent from the English. Under the Meiji system, the Imperial House Law was not a law that could be amended by the Imperial Diet (or a law at all). Converting what had previously been effectively a separate constitution for the imperial family into a law passed by the Diet was one more way in which the new constitution subordinated the emperor to the people and their democratically-elected representatives.[19]

The Imperial House Law only provides for a single means of succession: the death of a sitting emperor results in the next in line to the throne immediately assuming the title (Article 4). This means that being emperor is a lifetime job; the law contains no provisions for abdication.[20] This is by no means a matter of ancient tradition: in the past abdications by emperors had not been uncommon—58 had done so in the pre-modern age, the last in 1817. The emperor-for-life system was a product of the Meiji period and reflected concerns about the use of abdication (including compelled abdications) as a political tool.

In a 2016 broadcast to the nation, Emperor Akihito expressed a desire to abdicate. He was 82 at the time and had already experienced several episodes of poor health. After much debate, a special law was passed in 2017 allowing Akihito (only) to abdicate and creating for him and his wife a special new status of "emperor and empress emeritus." This law leaves in place for the current and future emperors the "succession only at death" provisions of the Imperial House Law.[21]

That future emperors were not also given the option to abdicate is understandable. The question of imperial succession leaves the imperial family in an existential crisis, which would be further exacerbated if its few remaining (male) members are able to quit either before or after assuming the throne.[22]

At the time of writing, the imperial family currently consisted of just 17 members spanning four generations. The youngest generation had just three members, only one of whom is male. Naruhito, the current emperor, has only one child, a daughter who is thus ineligible for the throne. Under the Imperial House Law rules of succession, the next in line after Naruhito would be his younger brother Crown Prince Akishino. After that would be Prince Akishino's son and the youngest member of the imperial family, Prince Hisahito, who was 16 at the time of writing.

Under the Imperial House Law, princesses who marry commoners lose their imperial status (Article 12). Since there are not any eligible male imperial family members of suitably diluted consanguinity, it can be assumed that if any of the the five unmarried princesses currently in the two youngest generations of the imperial family subsequently marry they will exit the imperial house. Thus, within a generation or two the imperial family may be reduced to a single nuclear family comprised of Prince Hisahito and his future wife, who will be under tremendous pressure to give birth to a male child. There are additional ramifications relating to the availability of proxies and regents, as discussed at Articles 4 and 5.

To western (and many Japanese) readers there would likely seem to be several obvious solutions: allow women to retain their status after marriage, allow their sons to inherit the throne, or even allow women to become emperor. Japan has had eight female emperors, though most were in the distant past, but they seem to offer historical precedents. Traditionalists will point out that while Japan has had female emperors in the past, they have always served effectively as placeholders until a suitable member from a male lineage was available to take over.[23] To allow even a male child of a female member of the imperial family to assume the throne would thus run contrary to centuries of tradition.

A committee of experts had been considering the possibility of relaxing some of the restrictions on female members at the behest of Prime Minister Jun'ichiro Koizumi in 2004 and 2005, at a time when it looked like there were no male heirs to take over the throne. Prince Hisahito's birth in 2006 made the problem less urgent and deliberations have not resumed in earnest since. Yet the long-term problem remains.

Article 3: Advice and Approval of Cabinet for Emperor's Acts in Matters of State

Colin P.A. Jones

> **Article 3.**
> The advice and approval of the Cabinet shall be required for all acts of the Emperor in matters of state, and the Cabinet shall be responsible therefor.

In the GHQ Draft, Article 3 was combined with the substance of Article 4. They were separated into separate articles but remained substantially the same otherwise. The meaning of "acts in matters of state" is discussed at Article 4.

The Meiji Constitution did not mention the Cabinet, containing only sparse references to ministers of state, the principal one being Article 55 which merely said: "[t]he respective Ministers of State shall give their advice to the emperor, and be responsible for it." This hewed to the fiction that the emperor ruled directly, and that individual ministers were responsible only for advice. This made cabinets weak since individuals could resign if they disagreed with government policy. The Army and Navy—each represented in the Cabinet by a general or admiral on active service—could cause governments to fail by pulling their respective cabinet minister and refusing to appoint a replacement.

Article 3 is both a rejection of the Meiji system of cabinets (further strengthened by provisions of Chapter V) and a further reinforcement of the strictly symbolic nature of the emperor. This is reflected not only in the addition of the "approval" requirement, but in linguistic changes not apparent in the English version.[24]

Article 3 makes it clear the Cabinet is in control, since the emperor cannot act without the consent of that body, whereas the formulation of the Meiji Constitution implied that final decision-making authority rested with the emperor. Under the present constitution, the emperor is, in the words of constitutional scholar Toshiyoshi Miyazawa, a "robot," to whom the constitution accords various duties but no free will in their exercise.

The manner by which the Cabinet proffers its advice and approval is left to practice. The 1947 removal of the Minister of Agriculture Rikizō Hirano by Prime Minister Tetsu Katayama has been criticized as violating the constitution because the emperor attested it (as required by Article 7) without a cabinet meeting taking place first (the "advice"). This was justified by the now common practice of cabinet decisions being made through signed circular resolutions in lieu of meetings.

Similarly, in the *Tomabechi Case*, the constitutionality of the 1952 dissolution of the House of Representatives was challenged on the grounds that proper cabinet procedures had not been followed in giving the necessary advice and approval. A trial court declared the dissolution void, but this was overturned on appeal and the Supreme Court declined to express a view on the grounds that it was a political question.[25]

Regarding the theoretical relationship between the emperor's role in state functions and the advice and approval requirement there are two main schools of thought. The first sees the advice and approval requirement as rendering the emperor's otherwise potentially substantive role in state affairs strictly formalistic. The second holds that the postwar constitution only accords the emperor formalistic, non-substantive functions in the first place, and that even these can only be performed with the advice and approval of the Cabinet. Neither interpretation seems wholly satisfactory. The prior viewpoint essentially assumes that the emperor still has some sort of inherent authority that is restrained by the constitution, a notion that is inconsistent with the principle of popular sovereignty. The latter viewpoint requires acceptance of the notion that the constitution mandates the emperor's performance of acts that are essentially pointless.[26]

This debate relates to another interesting but unimportant question: whether the emperor is a "constitutional monarch." On the one hand the emperor lacks some of the indicia of a constitutional monarch (including notional sovereignty). At the same time, however, it would be odd to describe a country with a hereditary emperor as a "republic." The government view has been that Japan's system of government can be described as a "constitutional monarchy."[27]

Article 4: The Limits of the Emperor's Powers; Proxies

Colin P.A. Jones

Article 4.

(1) The Emperor shall perform only such acts in matters of state as are provided for in this Constitution and he shall not have powers related to government.

(2) The Emperor may delegate the performance of his acts in matters of state as may be provided by law.

Acts in matters of state and other public acts

Article 4 purports to limit the role of the emperor to the performance of "acts in matters of state," a term of art that refers to the various roles accorded to him in Articles 6 and 7. As noted in Article 3, the emperor's performance of all such acts is bounded by the advice and approval of the Cabinet, and is thus wholly symbolic. "He shall not have powers related to government" represents another clear refutation of the Meiji Constitution, Article 4 of which declared the powers of sovereignty to be combined in and exercised by the emperor.

Notwithstanding the "only" language in paragraph (1), in practice the emperor performs numerous functions *not* clearly identified in any constitutional provision. These include attending state dinners, corresponding with, hosting and visiting heads of state from other countries, delivering speeches at the convocation of Diet sessions, conducting well-wishing visits to communities hit by disasters, and making appearances in myriad other public events. These are generally referred to as "public activities" (*kōteki kōi*) and there are various theories as to how they can be reconciled with paragraph (1) of Article 4.

The government view is that the emperor's activities can be categorized as: (1) matters in acts of state set forth in the constitution, (2) public activities that are derived from the emperor's role as a symbol and a public figure, and (3) other activities, which are mostly of a private character. The third category encompasses functions of the imperial household (including religious rites), as well as some activities that have a public face, such as attending cultural events. The government view is also that while the "advice and approval" of the Cabinet is not required for activities other than matters in acts of state, the Cabinet is still responsible for those activities of the emperor having a public character and for "assisting" (*hosa*) the emperor accordingly.[28] This is reasonably consistent with the paragraph (1) constraint on the emperor having "no powers related to government," but there are plenty of potential gray zones.[29]

A list of Emperor Akihito's activities in 2015 gives an indicator of the demands of the role. It includes over 1,000 matters in acts of state (mostly signing and affixing the imperial seal to official documents) and 529 public activities, 68 instances of "other" activities having a public character, and 19 religious ceremonies.[30]

Delegation

The details of the temporary delegation of the emperor's constitutional functions are set forth in the Temporary Delegation of the Emperor's Acts in Matters of State. The Act provides that in instances where the emperor is temporarily sick or incapacitated but not to the extent that the appointment of a regent is necessary, the emperor may, upon the advice and approval of the Cabinet, appoint (and subsequently terminate the appointment of) a member of the imperial family proxy to perform matters in act of state. Although not mentioned in the law, in practice proxies have also been appointed when the emperor has been abroad, presumably because government functions would be impaired if no proxies were available during his absence.

Those eligible for appointment and the order of precedence are the same as those eligible to act as regent (see Article 5), as set forth in the Imperial House Law. A 2017 legislative report identifies 28 instances of a proxy being appointed since the law was passed, mostly due to foreign travel by the emperor. The longer appointments, however, typically involved periods of sickness by the emperor, the longest being a 456-day period of delegation during the time leading up to the death of Emperor Hirohito. In all cases but one the designated proxy was the crown prince.

Article 5: Regency

Colin P.A. Jones

Article 5.
When, in accordance with the Imperial House Law, a Regency is established, the Regent shall perform his acts in matters of state in the Emperor's name. In this case, paragraph one of the preceding article will be applicable.

Regencies have not been uncommon in Japanese history. Just as in monarchies elsewhere in the world, they have occasionally been problematic from a governance perspective, representing an opportunity for the authority of a sovereign who is still a child or has been incapacitated to be usurped by someone whose constitutional status is unclear.

There have been no instances of a regency under the current constitution, though it was discussed as a possible alternative to Akihito's abdication. The most recent example of a regency was when, as Crown Prince, Hirohito performed the role during the prolonged incapacity of the Taishō emperor from 1921 until his death in 1926.[31]

The details of the establishment of a regency are left to the Imperial House Law. Under Article 16 of that law, a regency may be established if the emperor is still a minor or if the Imperial House Committee decides to do so in a situation where the emperor is unable to perform acts in matters of state due to physical infirmity or serious accident. The Imperial House Law designates those other members of the imperial house eligible to act as regent and the order of precedence, though this can be changed by a decision of the Imperial House Committee.

The crown prince is the first eligible to be regent, followed by other princes. Interestingly, unlike the emperor itself, women members of the imperial family can act as regent if no male family members are available.[32] Regardless of whether women born into the imperial family are ever allowed to become emperor, allowing them to retain their status after marrying would thus help alleviate a looming shortage of members to act as proxy or regent.

Article 6: Emperor's Appointment of Prime Minister and Chief Judge

Colin P.A. Jones

Article 6.

(1) The Emperor shall appoint the Prime Minister as designated by the Diet.

(2) The Emperor shall appoint the Chief Judge of the Supreme Court as designated by the Cabinet.

The prime minister is chosen by the Diet according to Article 6 and is typically the head of the political party which achieves a majority in the House of Representatives. The prime minister and chief judge of the Supreme Court are the only appointments actually made by the emperor. Unlike other high officials whose appointments and dismissal he attests under Article 7, the emperor is not involved in the dismissal or resignation of the prime minister or chief judge.

The special treatment accorded the prime minister and chief judge in Article 6 give rise to some theoretical questions. The first is whether these appointments need the advice and approval of the Cabinet under Article 3. The general consensus among scholars appears to be that the appointments are "matters of state" for which such advice and approval is required (in the case of the appointment of the prime minister, the advice and approval is apparently provided by a caretaker cabinet consisting only of the prime minister who has just announced his resignation).[33]

A second question is whether the emperor is *bound* by the Diet's designation. Here it is necessary to appreciate that in Japanese, paragraph (1) of Article 6 contains an ambiguity not adequately reflected in the English version, which might more accurately be rendered as: "[t]he Emperor shall appoint the prime minister *based on* the designation of the Diet."[34] This wording could be interpreted as permitting the emperor to appoint someone other than the Diet's designee or perhaps even for the Diet to designate two or more candidates for the emperor to choose from. Since it is generally accepted that the advice and approval of the Cabinet is required for appointments under Article 6, however, the real question is whether the Cabinet could recommend that the emperor appoint a prime minister different from the person designated by the Diet. Although so far this has only been a hypothetical issue, it does relate to the more basic (and unresolved) question of whether the emperor could have any inherent substantive powers that are not restrained by the advice and approval requirement, or whether instead the constitution only accords him roles that are non-substantive *ab initio.*

Under the GHQ Draft the chief judge of the Supreme Court was to be appointed by the Cabinet in the same fashion as the other judges on that court. The elevation of the chief judge to the same level as the prime minister through direct appointment by the emperor was an amendment made by the House of Councillors to bolster the status of the judiciary. [35]

Article 7: Emperor's Act in Matters of State

Colin P.A. Jones

Article 7.
The Emperor, with the advice and approval of the Cabinet, shall perform the following acts in matters of state on behalf of the people:
(i) Promulgation of amendments of the constitution, laws, cabinet orders and treaties.
(ii) Convocation of the Diet.
(iii) Dissolution of the House of Representatives.
(iv) Proclamation of general election of members of the Diet.
(v) Attestation of the appointment and dismissal of Ministers of State and other officials as provided for by law, and of full powers and credentials of Ambassadors and Ministers.
(vi) Attestation of general and special amnesty, commutation of punishment, reprieve, and restoration of rights.
(vii) Awarding of honors.
(viii) Attestation of instruments of ratification and other diplomatic documents as provided for by law.
(ix) Receiving foreign ambassadors and ministers.
(x) Performance of ceremonial functions.

Article 7 sets forth the list of other acts in matters of state performed by the emperor in the constitution. Given the "only" (*nomi*) formulation of Article 4, Articles 6 and 7 are considered a complete compendium of acts in matters of state performed by the emperor under the constitution.

Many of the items listed in Article 7 mirror the sovereign prerogatives of the emperor under the Meiji Constitution. However, Article 7 renders them symbolic through a repetition of the "advice and approval of the Cabinet" limitation and the added language about their performance being "on behalf of the people."

Promulgation of laws and regulations

The promulgation (*kōfu*) of laws, cabinet orders, treaties and constitutional amendments by the emperor pursuant to clause (i) is an integral part of the legislative and regulatory process. Promulgation is the process by which legislation that has been passed by the Diet is formally announced to the people. Under the Meiji Constitution a law did not take effect unless the emperor assented to it. The current constitution is different. Although it has never happened, academic theory posits that if the emperor refused to promulgate a law that did not meet his approval the promulgation could be carried out by the Cabinet or by the president of the House of Representatives.[36]

Promulgation of laws and regulations typically takes place in advance of the date on which they come into force, but this is not required. In early rulings the Supreme Court upheld promulgations having immediate effect, including by radio.[37]

Convocation of the Diet, dissolution of the House of Representatives and proclamation of elections

The convocation of legislative assemblies and proclamation of elections is probably a typical example of the type of ceremonial role performed by constitutional monarchs or other apolitical heads of state. The same can be said of the dissolution of those legislative chambers which are subject to dissolution. However, the emperor's role in dissolving the House of Representatives bears some additional scrutiny.

As is made clear in Chapter IV, the House of Councillors is not subject to dissolution. Articles 45 and 54 anticipate the House of Representatives may be dissolved before the end of its members' four-year term, but do not identify by whom or on what grounds. Article 69 references dissolution as an alternative to the resignation of the Cabinet after passage of a non-confidence motion, but is again silent as to who initiates the dissolution. The constitution is otherwise silent on the subject of dissolution in cases other than a no-confidence motion being passed (which rarely happens).[38]

In practice, decisions about dissolutions are made by the prime minister and through the Cabinet, and the official documentation used to formalize the process cites Article 7 as the constitutional basis. This is now well-established practice and most scholars accept Article 7 as being the grounds for dissolution. Earlier in the constitution's history there were more rigorous debates on the subject. In the *Tomabechi* case, which involved a challenge to the 1952 dissolution of the House of Representatives brought by a Diet member by the name of Gizō Tomabechi, who lost his seat as a result, the Supreme Court declined to rule on the issue on the grounds that it was a political question.[39]

Attestation of appointments, dismissals, "full powers and credentials" and diplomatic instruments; Receiving foreign diplomats

The constitution requires ministers of state to be appointed by the prime minister (Article 68) and Supreme Court judges other than the chief judge together with judges of inferior courts to be appointed by the Cabinet (Articles 79 and 80). The number of ministers of state, vice-ministers and judges are set by statute. Numerous other statutes establishing government bodies such as the National Personnel Authority, the Fair Trade Commission and the Imperial Household Agency also provide for the appointment of commissioners or chief executives.

Some of these statutes mandate that specific appointments (and dismissals of persons so appointed) be attested by the emperor, a process that involves a ceremony and the delivery of letters of appointment bearing the signature and seal of the emperor. Officials whose appointments are subject to this requirement are referred to as *ninshōkan*, or "attested officials."[40]

The attestation of the credentials of the ambassadors dispatched by Japan is one area where the emperor plays a symbolic role in foreign affairs. The use of "full powers" in the English may cause confusion, since it suggests the emperor is attesting the actual vesting of power. However, the Japanese version—*zenken ininjō*—clearly refers to a document granting its holder with plenipotentiary powers to represent the nation in dealings with foreign interests. *Shinninjō*, the Japanese term for "credential," is also clearly a reference to a credentialing document, rather than status. Finally, while the English version refers to "ministers" in Japanese it is clear that this is not a "minister of state" but a diplomat—a chargé d'affaires—who is not an ambassador.

Scholars note that there is an imbalance between the role the emperor plays in credentialing Japanese diplomats, which merely involves attesting appointments made by the Cabinet, and "receiving foreign ambassadors and ministers" under clause (ix), which is a power exercised directly by the emperor, albeit under the advice and approval of the Cabinet. In practice it may not matter much in diplomatic protocols, at least; the emperor is treated as head of state for most if not all purposes.[41] Also note the broader discussion of the public service at Article 15.

The attestation of the instruments for ratifying treaties and other diplomatic instruments executed by Japan is another formality. The substantive power to enter into such documents is vested in the Cabinet, subject to ratification by the Diet (see Articles 61 and 73).

Attestation of amnesties and other official acts of forgiveness

Relief from criminal punishment and other sanctions are decided by the Cabinet under Article 73. The details are provided for in the Amnesty Act of 1947, with a separate act (the "Exemption of Disciplinary Action and Other Matters in Relation to Public Officers Act" of 1952) providing for the rehabilitation of public servants subject to disciplinary actions in connection with amnesties. Individual pardons are not very common, but widespread amnesties have been a feature of the celebration of auspicious events—including the enthronement of a new emperor and imperial weddings. "Restoration of rights" refers to the removal of impediments to obtaining licenses or serving in specific roles in regulated sectors which may arise from a criminal record. The loss of the right to vote and stand for office are also provided for as additional punishments under Japan's public election law, meaning that some amnesties have been criticized for rehabilitating questionable political figures.

Honors

Japan's system of imperial honors is interesting for a number of reasons. Developing a system of medals and other honors was a high priority for the early Meiji leaders in part due to the need to exchange them with the royalty and dignitaries of other nations, as was the custom at the time. It also served as a means of encouraging and rewarding public service both in government and the military. In the prewar period, military honors came with a lifetime pension, and other honors were linked to the titled aristocracy. This is not a feature of the current system, in part because Article 14 prohibits any privilege or hereditary rights attaching to any honor.

Under the post war system, honors are a low-key feature of Japanese public life, yet one which may be overlooked by most westerners as a potential motivating factor for Japanese in both government and the private sector. The majority of honors are awarded to those who have worked in government either as bureaucrats or elected officials, and the level achieved in those spheres is a factor in the honors received after retirement, typically at or after the age of 70.

Most honors are in the form of medals of varying degrees within two categories, one for former public servants and the other for those who have made contributions in other spheres (including some non-Japanese recipients). There is also an Order of Culture for those who have made significant cultural or literary contributions. Decisions about honors are made by a bureau within the Cabinet Office and usually awarded during the two "honors seasons" in the fall and spring. The involvement of the emperor depends on the level of honors, with those at the highest level (usually reserved for former prime ministers of suitable repute) being presented directly by the emperor.

An even more subdued form of honor is the granting to leading citizens of a posthumous ranking based on notional proximity to the emperor and having roots in a system originally designed by the legendary prince, Shōtoku Taishi. Such rankings are announced in the official gazette.

The system of honors is also interesting because they represent the only instance of a constitutional provision being implemented by a cabinet order only, without Diet legislation. This is discussed at Article 73.

Ceremonial functions

The GHQ Draft framed the final item in the list of roles of the emperor as "performance of *other* ceremonial functions," suggesting it was both intended as a catchall and that everything listed in Article 7 was also "ceremonial." The final draft resulted in the present formulation which establishes "performance of ceremonies" as a separate role.

The provision is understood as referring to public ceremonies. There is uncertainty about where the line is drawn between ceremonies under clause (x) of Article 7 and the "public acts" of the emperor that are not clearly mentioned (see discussion at Article 4).

Clause (x) does not extend to the Shintō ceremonies which the emperor performs in connection with his role in that religion and which are considered to fall within the rubric of the private affairs of the imperial household. To the extent that public ceremonies include any religious element, as was the case in funerary rites for Hirohito after his death, and some of the rituals involved in the accession of a new emperor, there have been complaints about the violation of the Article 89 prohibition on the use of public funds for religious purposes, though none that stopped the government from doing so. [42]

Article 8: Receipt of Property by the Imperial House

Colin P.A. Jones

> **Article 8.**
> No property can be given to, or received by, the Imperial House, nor can any gifts be made therefrom, without the authorization of the Diet.

Article 8 is another seemingly innocuous provision that had great significance at the time it was drafted. Under the Meiji Constitution, the imperial house had become a vast financial conglomerate managed by the Imperial House Ministry. The emperor's finances were not subject to control by the Imperial Diet, as discussed in the Introduction to Chapter VII.

The imperial house was effectively one of the *zaibatsu* or financial conglomerates that GHQ felt it necessary to dismantle because of their perceived baneful influence on democratic institutions.[43] This is accomplished in part by Article 88, which effectively nationalized whatever property was left to the emperor. Article 8 prevented the emperor from reacquiring property that was divested during the Occupation, and prevents the imperial house from achieving any sort of extra-constitutional influence through the use of wealth.

The details of imperial finances are provided for in the Imperial Household Finance Act. It provides blanket authorizations for routine commercial transactions, diplomatic niceties and gifts made for public purposes. Separate Diet authorizations have been passed in connection with significant events resulting in the receipt of gifts, by members of the imperial family, such as the weddings of Akihito and Naruhito when they were crown prince, in 1959 and 1993, respectively.

Notes

1 There is no language corresponding to "we the" in the Japanese version, in any case.

2 Sapporo District Court, September 7, 1973 (712 *Hanji* 24); Nagoya High Court, April 17, 2008 (2056 *Hanji* 74); Okayama District Court, February 24, 2009 (2046 *Hanji* 124).

3 Supreme Court, 3rd Petty Bench Judgment of June 20, 1989.

4 Imperial House Law, Articles 28–37 (Imperial House Council), Articles 6, 9, 10, 11, 12 and 13 (restrictions). At the time of writing a translation of the Imperial House Law was not available at the government's Law in Translation website, but was available at the Imperial Household Agency website, at: *The Imperial House Law*. The Imperial House Law—The Imperial Household Agency. (n.d.). Retrieved June 10, 2022, from https://www.kunaicho.go.jp/e-kunaicho/hourei-01.html The Imperial House Council is an interesting body in that it is made up of representatives of all branches of the government including the chief judge and one other judge of the Supreme Court (Imperial House Law, Article 28).

5 One of the many Occupation-era reforms included drastically reducing the number of people enjoying "imperial" status. This pruning of the imperial tree may have been too zealous, since at the time of writing the youngest generation of the imperial house as currently constituted contains just one male, the imperial family could potentially be reduced to a single nuclear family within two generations. Some conservative politicians have suggested resuscitating some of former branches to imperial status by allowing male descendants of it to be adopted into the imperial family (the Imperial House Law currently prohibits adoptions by members of the imperial family). However, it is hard to imagine how many eligible men would actually want to submit themselves to the scrutiny and restrictions of freedom that would come with being a member of the imperial house.

6 Kōshitsu Tenpan [Imperial House Law (old)], 1889, chapter 2. Repealed in 1947.

7 Ibid., Chapter 2.

8 Ibid., Chapter 10.

9 Kōshitsu saibanrei [Imperial family trial order], Imperial House Order No. 16 of 1926 (repealed 1947).

10 Supreme Court, 2nd Petty Bench judgment of November 20, 1989.

11 Statute of Westminster, 1931 Chapter 4, 22 and 23 Geo 5. American use as a model: Moore, R., & Robinson, D. (2004), 297, 378. (n. 12).

12 Ruoff, K. (2001), 44–54, 84–86, 138–42, 255–56.

13 Quote from Ruoff, K. (2001).

14 Ruoff, K. (2001), 126–57.

15 Note that as with many other modern Japanese legal terms, *genshu* ("head of state") was essentially newly invented in order to translate foreign terms (in this case, the German *Staatsoberhaupt*) for which there was no ready cognate in the Japanese lexicon at the time. As noted by Ruoff, "[t]*he term genshu itself was not used in Japanese political or legal discourse before the Meiji era*." Ibid., 26.

16 Statement by head of first department of Cabinet Legislation Bureau to House of Councillors Cabinet Committee, October 11, 1988.

[17] This is one of the many examples of members of the imperial family being subject to discriminatory treatment that is prohibited by other provisions of the constitution (e.g., Articles 14 and 24).
[18] Dower, J. (2000), 306. The most famous of these was a shopkeeper named Hiromichi Kumasawa who in 1951 brought suit challenging the legitimacy of Hirohito's place on the throne on the grounds that he was a descendant of a 14th-century usurper, while Kumazawa was in fact a rightful descendant of the true imperial line. His suit was denied.
[19] Although bearing the same name, the current Imperial House Law was passed in 1947. Although it is clearly a law, the Japanese titles of both the old and new versions do not include the word "*hō*" or "*hōritsu*" (law), which are included in the titles of other statutes. Instead, the term is *Kōshitsu Tempan*, the *tempan* being more likely rendered a "canon" or "code of conduct."
[20] This is obviously inconsistent with the constitution's prohibition against involuntary servitude and guarantee of freedom to choose one's occupation at Articles 18 and 22, respectively.
[21] Insofar as the constitution seems to clearly require that succession be governed by the Imperial House Law, accomplishing the transition from Akihito to Naruhito through special legislation would seem problematic but has garnered little attention. Tennō no tai'i tō ni kansuru kōshitsu tempan tokureihō [Act for Special Case Under the Imperial House Law in Connection with the Abdication (Etc.) of the Emperor], Law no. 63 of 2017.
[22] Under the Imperial House Law even "voluntary" departures from imperial status require the approval of the Imperial House Council (Article 11).
[23] Prior to the modern period, emperors had multiple wives, making it easy for competing lineages of sons to arise; in this environment a female member of one lineage assuming the throne temporarily until a male child from that lineage became a viable successor would likely have been a preferable option to surrendering succession to a competing lineage.
[24] While "advice" is the term used in the English renderings of both constitutions, the Japanese terms are different. The Meiji Constitution uses "*hohitsu,*" a compound of now rarely-used kanji characters that some Japanese people might struggle to read or write, and referring specifically to the counsel given by a subordinate to someone of superior status. During the drafting negotiations the Japanese side sought to use this term but were rebuffed by the Americans, who insisted on "*jogen,*" a more familiar and status-neutral term also meaning "advice."
[25] Coming six years, two elections, and seven cabinets after the Tokyo High Court held that both advice and approval were required but finding that both had actually been procured, the Supreme Court's ruling in the *Tomabechi Case* could probably not have done much beyond ratify that decision. It still stands as a statement of the Court's intent not to involve itself in the details of how the Cabinet proffers advice and approval to the emperor.
[26] *See, e.g.*, Urabe, N., in Ashibe, N., et al. (Eds.) (2000), 194–99, for a discussion of the various views on this issue.
[27] Statement by Director General of Cabinet Legislation Bureau at House of Councillors Cabinet Committee meeting, June 28, 1973.
[28] See, statement by head of 1st department, Cabinet Legislation Bureau at House of Councillors Cabinet Committee, April 19, 1990, and discussion contained in pp. 31–40 of Chapter 1 of House of Councillors Legislation Bureau Report dated June 2017, available at: *Dai Isshō (Tennō) ni kansuru shiryō—shugiin.* (n.d.). Retrieved June 10, 2022, from https://www.shugiin.go.jp/internet/itdb_kenpou.nsf/html/kenpou/shukenshi095.pdf/$File/shukenshi095.pdf.
[29] One of the most controversial examples of the emperor performing a public act with potentially significant political ramifications can be seen in Emperor Akihito's apology for Japan's colonial policies in Korea, delivered in 1990 at a state banquet in that nation. *See* discussion at Ruoff, K. (2001), 151–53. More recently, Akihito's announcement of his desire to abdicate represented both an implicit request for a change in law and a particular characterization of the emperor as a *tsutome* (role) which could be cast off. The former appears to have been initially regarded as unwelcome by the Abe Cabinet, and the latter was objectionable to conservative commentators who regarded the emperor as a status which could not be terminated except by death. Interestingly, in the debate over abdication some commentators even expressed the view that the most important role performed by the emperor was praying for the nation.
[30] Shūgiin kenpō shinsa kai jimukyoku, Shuken Shiryō 95, "Daiisshō—Tennō" ni kansuru shiryō [House of Representatives Constitutional Review Committee Secretariat, Document No. 95, Documents relating to

"Chapter I—The Emperor"] (June 2017), available at: https://www.shugiin.go.jp/internet/itdb_kenpou.nsf/html/kenpou/shiryo.htm.

31 As noted by Professor Kawaguchi, the relative peace associated with the final years of the Taishō Period could be attributed in part to a regency being in effect. This meant nobody in the military could plausibly claim to engage in military adventures on behalf of the Taishō emperor (who was known to be incapacitated) and although the Regent, Crown Prince Hirohito, was an officer in both the Army and the Navy, but the rank he held was junior to the admirals and generals, so they could not pretend to be following his orders on that basis either. Kawaguchi A. (2017).

32 At the time of writing, Emperor Naruhito's younger brother Prince Akishino was crown prince, and next in line for the regency was Prince Hitachi, former Emperor Akihito's younger brother. Other than them, all other members available to acts as regent (or proxy under Article 4) were women.

33 Satō, K. (2020), 515–16. Iwama, A., *Kempō Rokujō—Tennō no Nimmeiken* [Article 6 of the Constitution: Appointments by the Emperor]. In Ashibe, N., et al. (Eds.) (2000), 251–52.

34 The GHQ Draft contained no such ambiguity, stating that "*The Emperor appoints as Prime Minister the person designated by the Diet.*"

35 The equality of the two roles is also reflected in both receiving the same official salary.

36 Yamamoto, H., *Dai Nanajō (Tennō no Kokuji Kōi (2))* [Article 7: Constitutional Functions of the Emperor (2)]. In Serizawa, H., et. al. (Eds.). (2011), 40. Article 66 of the Diet Act requires that laws be promulgated within 30 days of their presentment to the emperor. Promulgation takes place by publication in the *kampō*, the official gazette. Interestingly, there is no legal basis for promulgation taking place in this manner. Under the Meiji Constitution, this was mandated by the *kōshikirei*, a 1907 Imperial Edict governing the format and substance of official documents under the emperor's name. However, this was repealed in 1947 under the Occupation and never replaced. The *kōshikirei* continues to be followed in practice as a matter of custom.

37 Supreme Court (1st Petty Bench), 1 March 1951, 5 *Keishū* 478; Supreme Court (Grand Bench), 28 December 1957, 11 *Keishū* 3461; Supreme Court (Grand Bench) 15 October 1958 (*Keishū* 12, 3313).

38 The most recent example was the no-confidence resolution passed against the Cabinet of Prime Minister Kiichi Miyazawa in 1993.

39 Supreme Court, Grand Bench judgment of June 8, 1960.

40 Being an "attested official" does not have any legal significance beyond the process of appointment, though there are academic debates over whether the appointment is valid (and thus whether the appointee may exercise the powers of office) prior to attestation. Leaving this aside, attestation involves cache that may be underappreciated by western observers: it has bearing on the level of honor one is eligible for after leaving government service, and when a *ninshōkan* is involved in a scandal, it is not uncommon for the media to remind readers of this status, as if it were a compounding factor. In a sense, the concept of an attested official can be seen as a remnant of the Meiji Constitution when all officials were either directly or indirectly appointed by the emperor and, if directly appointed, could claim to be subject to no other authority. Currently the universe of *ninshōkan* consists of: the ministers of state comprising the Cabinet (other than the prime minister), the three deputy secretaries of the Cabinet Secretariat, the three commissioners of the National Personnel Authority, the 24 vice-ministers of the eleven ministries and the Reconstruction Agency, the Head of the Imperial Household Agency, the Grand Chamberlain to the emperor, the Chamberlain to the emperor emeritus, the chairman of the Fair Trade Commission, the ten most senior ranking prosecutors, the fourteen judges of the Supreme Court (other than the chief judge), the chief judges of the eight high courts, the chairman of the Nuclear Regulatory Authority, the three commissioners of the Board of Audit, and special ambassadors and envoys.

41 As noted by one scholar:

> *The Government insists upon a very careful wording of diplomatic instruments. For example, the emperor only "attests" to any ambassador's letters of accreditation, which are issued by the Cabinet of ministers. Yet such letters are all the same so skillfully drafted as to lead the foreign head of state who receives them to think that they were issued by the emperor himself.*

Higuchi, Y. The Constitution and the Emperor System: Is Revisionism Alive? In Luney, P.R., & Takahashi, K. (Eds.) (1993), at 63.

42 See *Tsu City Groundbreaking Ceremony Case* and related cases discussed at Articles 20 and 89.

43 This was back when excessive concentrations of wealth were considered inimical to democracy by at least some American leaders.

Chapter II
Renunciation of War
Article 9

Introduction

Colin P.A. Jones

Article 9 in a global context

The single article comprising Chapter II—Article 9—is by far the most famous feature of the Constitution of Japan, and the provision that likely has the most emotional dimension for the Japanese people. Many seem to take pride in their constitution's rejection of war and the pacifistic ideals it embodies. Others may have no objections to peace, but consider the restraints as a millstone around the neck that prevents the nation from protecting itself in a dangerous world.

Within Japan and elsewhere in the world there also appears to be a widespread perception of Article 9 as a uniquely Japanese contribution to constitutionalism. In 2014, Article 9 was even nominated for a Nobel Peace Prize. The large military described as a "Self-Defense Force" and existing under a constitution that disclaims "land, sea and air forces," could also be seen as a uniquely Japanese institution.

The reality is more complicated. The degree to which any particular aspect of Article 9 is actually unique is debatable, particularly given the Japanese government's longstanding interpretation of it as permitting the maintenance and use of military forces for self-defense. The French constitution of 1791 established its military to "to defend the State against enemies from abroad," and postwar constitutions of nations as diverse as (for example) Germany, Italy, the Philippines, Costa Rica and South Korea contain provisions comparable to at least parts of Article 9.[1] Some small countries simply do not have armed forces without addressing the subject in their constitutions. Nor do the contents of Article 9 in a constitution promulgated in 1946 make Japan an "early adopter" of some of the principles it articulates. The horrors of World War II and the numerous smaller regional conflicts that preceded it make it easy to forget that the leading nations of the world—including Japan—had already ratified an instrument formally entitled "The General Treaty for Renunciation of War as an Instrument of National Policy," more commonly known as the Kellogg-Briand Pact of 1928.[2] Japan almost immediately violated this treaty with the invasion of Manchuria in 1931, conflict with China starting from 1937, and the surprise attack on the United States and other Allied Powers in 1941. Thus, to the Americans who wrote the initial draft of what became Article

9, it was less likely intended as something new, but as a reiteration of promises Japan had already made to the world and broken.[3]

Abandonment of the use of force and disarmament were also ideals articulated by the US and British governments in the Atlantic Charter of 1941, and disarming Japan was one of the conditions of surrender conveyed in the Potsdam Declaration four years later. Announcing a new international order based on peaceful resolution of conflicts and international cooperation, the United Nations Charter was opened for signature before Japan had even surrendered.[4]

The drafting process

Renunciation of war and disarmament comprised one of the three basic principles of constitutional drafting articulated in the MacArthur Notes. That formulation went so far as to reject war as a sovereign right of Japan "even for preserving its own security." With some modifications, including the removal of this specific language, his principles were reflected in Article VIII of the GHQ Draft.[5] Paragraph 2 of Article VIII of the GHQ draft also expanded on the MacArthur Notes by adding to the proscription on land, sea or air forces an additional prohibition on "other war potential." These prohibitions were completely unqualified.

It was at the deliberations at the Imperial Diet that the infamous "Ashida Amendment"—the addition of the clause "in order to accomplish the aim of the preceding paragraph" to the second paragraph of what would become Article 9—was made.[6] While the historical record suggests the intent behind the change may have been more about aesthetics than substance,[7] these words subsequently facilitated arguments that Article 9 permitted the preservation and use of "war potential" for the limited purpose of self-defense. Although the country was not yet a UN member, some Japanese leaders were already thinking in terms of how Japan could plausibly become a member in a body whose charter specifically called for a collective approach to threats to peace, and recognized the rights to individual and collective self-defense of member states.[8]

The historical record is full of statements by various Japanese leaders offering interpretations of Article 9, both during the drafting process and in the years immediately following. A survey of these interpretive statements is beyond the scope of this book, but it should be remembered all were made during a military occupation and by Japanese leaders eager to see sovereignty restored as soon as possible. Any views on Article 9 expressed by government officials would likely have been made with a high degree of sensitivity as to how they would likely be received by GHQ. Even the American view of Article 9 was something of a moving target as the Cold War progressed and turned hot with the outbreak of the Korean War in Japan's former colony.

The US-Japan security alliance and the birth of the SDF

The Allied Occupation of Japan formally ended in 1952 when the Treaty of San Francisco went into effect, but the US military never left. Instead, it remained, pursuant to a security treaty between Japan and the United States executed the same day in 1951 as the Treaty of San Francisco. The security treaty committed the United States to use its military to defend

Japan, and even to suppress foreign-instigated internal unrest, if requested by the Japanese government.[9] However, the treaty expressed American willingness to defend Japan as being conditioned on the expectation that:

> *Japan will itself increasingly assume responsibility for its own defense against direct and indirect aggression, always avoiding any armament which could be an offensive threat or serve other than to promote peace and security in accordance with the purposes and principles of the United Nations Charter.*[10]

The 1951 security treaty was a temporary expedient with a ten-year term. In 1960 it was replaced by the Treaty of Mutual Cooperation and Security between Japan and the United States, which remains in force to this day. Under this treaty the US continued to enjoy basing rights, but Japan now assumed a positive obligation to "act to meet the common danger in accordance with its constitutional provisions and processes" in the event of an attack on the US forces in Japan.[11] Japan also committed to "maintain and develop, subject to [its] constitutional provisions, [its] capacities to resist armed attack."[12] The 1960 treaty no longer allowed for the use of US forces to combat domestic uprisings in Japan. By the time it was signed Japan was already developing its own capabilities for doing so.

The first major step in Japan's rearmament was the establishment in 1950—by order of GHQ—of Japan's National Police Reserve. This was in part a response to the sudden need to relocate US ground forces to the Korean peninsula due to the outbreak of the conflict there, leaving Japan largely undefended. While this police reserve was initially focused on combatting internal unrest and thus lightly armed, by the following year it was negotiating with the US to procure tanks.[13]

Japan's nascent military also experienced its first constitutional challenge in the form of a lawsuit brought by a socialist Diet member demanding judicial confirmation that all acts in connection with the creation and maintenance of the National Police Reserve were void. In the *National Police Reserve Case*, this challenge was rejected by the Supreme Court in 1952 as being too abstract to satisfy case or controversy requirements (see discussion at Chapter VI).

Before this judgment was rendered, the National Police Reserve was already being transformed into the Security Agency which in 1954 became the Self-Defense Forces (SDF), the collective reference to Japan's current tripartite military comprised of land, sea and air arms. The naming can be said to reflect both the constitutional conundrum and the solution—Japan's military exists for the limited purpose of self-defense and as such is *not* an army, navy, air force or other war potential.

Upon the birth of the SDF the Cabinet announced a basic interpretation of Article 9: that it does not negate Japan's inherent right as a sovereign nation to defend itself, and that Japan is permitted to have military capabilities so long as they do not exceed the scope of what is necessary for self-defense.[14] This interpretation has been surprisingly robust and, with some modifications, has prevailed until the present date.

Article 9 in postwar history

The limiting of the SDF to "self-defense" created many new conundrums. What type of forces and equipment were within the bounds of mere self-defense, and what might constitute prohibited "offensive" capability has always been a highly subjective question. Moreover, the boundaries of self-defense have changed over time in response to economic, technological and geo-political situations.

During the Cold War, when the most likely threat was a Soviet invasion in conjunction with a broader conflict with the US and its allies elsewhere, Japan could focus primarily on having a force structure that could, with US assistance, fend off attacks on Japanese territory. In this environment, policies such as acquiring fighter aircraft with in-flight refueling capability were controversial: why would such a capability be necessary unless to attack foreign territories?

The end of the Cold War brought new challenges. China developed into a military superpower and claims several remote Japanese islands as its own territory. North Korea—whose bellicose leaders have in the past threatened to turn Tokyo into a "sea of fire"—has developed nuclear weapons and missiles that can easily carry conventional and nuclear warheads to Japan. Whether Japan should develop first-strike capabilities to preempt attacks such of these is also a constitutional question that must be analyzed in the framework of what constitutes self-defense.

The evolution of this ever-changing concept can be seen in the 2013 launch of the *Izumo*, the Maritime SDF's largest military vessel to date. Categorized as a "helicopter-carrying destroyer," most casual observers would likely call it an aircraft carrier. As of the time of writing that was what it was scheduled to become, with budget allocations for the purchase of US F-35 fighters, and the refitting of the *Izumo* to accommodate them.[15] That Japan now has weapon systems typically associated with the projection of military power far from the national territory is a useful indicator of how much the concept of "self-defense"—as both a justification for military capabilities and their use—has changed.

While some of this change is driven by domestic political forces wishing to cast off the burdens of Article 9, external events have also been a factor, particularly US pressure to shoulder a greater part of the burden of defending both Japan and the broader US-led world order. In this context Japan went from a localized Cold War defense posture, to being expected to assume greater responsibility for the security of the sea lanes it depends on for trade and energy. When Iraq invaded Kuwait in 1990, Japan was criticized for just "writing checks" without taking any of the risks borne by the broad international coalition that defeated Iraq the following year. This led to the SDF's first mission abroad, the dispatch to the Persian Gulf in 1991 of a Maritime SDF contingent to clean up naval mines.

The following year saw the first dispatch of SDF personnel on a United Nations peacekeeping mission in a non-combat role. Shortly after 9/11 Japan dispatched Maritime Self-Defense Force vessels to support the US-led campaigns in Iraq and Afghanistan as part of the Global War on Terror. In 2004 Ground Self-Defense Force units were dispatched on a "humanitarian" mission to Iraq. Although equipped with heavy weapons for the first time, the GSDF forces were subject to such restrictive rules of engagement that contingents from other participant militaries were needed to defend their bases. In 2009, MSDF vessels and aircraft were dispatched to participate in anti-piracy activities off the coast of Somalia, and Japan acquired its first overseas base in Djibouti, to support these operations.

In 2015, in connection with a broad set of amendments to Japan's defense-related laws, the SDF Act was amended significantly to, among other things, allow the SDF to provide logistical and material assistance to the militaries of Australia, India, Canada, France and the UK.[16] At the time of writing, the SDF, Japan's military forces, were actively engaged in joint exercises not just with their US alliance partner, but other regional powers such as Australia and India.[17] Each of these developments has been not only politically significant, but has involved enabling legislation (as discussed in the following section) and often virulent disputes as to if and how they can be accommodated within the constraints imposed by Article 9.

Article 9: Renunciation of War and War Potential

Colin P.A. Jones

Article 9.

(1) Aspiring sincerely to an international peace based on justice and order, the Japanese people forever renounce war as a sovereign right of the nation and the threat or use of force as means of settling international disputes.

(2) In order to accomplish the aim of the preceding paragraph, land, sea, and air forces, as well as other war potential, will never be maintained. The right of belligerency of the state will not be recognized.

Language and overview

In addition to creating a range of linguistic issues around terminology for SDF equipment and personnel, the Japanese version of Article 9 has certain aspects that are not apparent in the English.[18] First, the "sovereign right" (*kokken*) in paragraph (1) is the same term as is rendered "state power" in the English version of Article 41. Second, there is no clear corollary to the English "never" in the Japanese version of paragraph (2).

Third, "the right of belligerency" in paragraph (2) in Japanese is *kōsenken*—which could be more literally translated "the right to conduct war."[19] This means that it is a concept more closely related to the "war" (*sensō*) renounced in paragraph (1).

More substantively, the "right of belligerency" is a right that, at the time Article 9 was written, was in the process of dramatic change. The idea of nations having a "right" to engage in war and that doing so triggers various rights and duties vis à vis other countries when they exercise that right harks back to 19th century European thinking about international law. To the extent this view of international law was what was learned by the first generations of postwar constitutional scholars writing on Article 9, it may have been a factor in the various theories about what the clause means. However, insofar as the framework of the international law of conflict was already being restructured under the UN system at the time the constitution was being drafted, "right of belligerency" may describe a right that had been drastically changed. Paragraph (2) does not "renounce" the right, but refuses to recognize it in the first place.[20]

This also demonstrates a subtle but important feature of Article 9 that makes it special; it addresses a sphere where domestic law interfaces with international public law. Thus, it is possible to conceptualize Article 9 as addressing both *jus ad bellum* (the conditions under which nations are permitted by international law to conduct hostilities) and *jus in bello* (the rules which must be followed by nations engaged in hostilities, now commonly called

"International Humanitarian Law"), with paragraph (1) addressing the former, and paragraph (2) the latter. Moreover, although the two regimes of international law are generally considered separate, it is possible to conceptualize Article 9 as containing a unique waiver of *jus in bello* belligerency and other rights in paragraph (2) to backstop the waiver of *jus ad bellum* rights accomplished through paragraph (1).[21]

Judicial interpretations of Article 9

Article 9 received its first—and only—significant judicial interpretation by the Supreme Court in the *Sunagawa Case*, which was decided in 1959.[22] The *Sunagawa Case* arose from a large-scale protest over government efforts to expropriate farmland in order to expand the runway at a US air base in Tokyo. In the course of this protest, several demonstrators entered the base and were arrested for trespassing under special criminal provisions established in connection with implementing the US-Japan security treaty as well as the Minor Offenses Act. The defense argument was that the US military constituted "war potential" prohibited by Article 9(2), and that the special criminal statute used to prosecute the defendants thus violated Article 31.

This argument had a receptive audience at the initial trial; the Tokyo District Court agreed with the constitutional arguments and acquitted the defendants, resulting in a highly unusual prosecutorial appeal directly to the Supreme Court.[23] The court overturned the acquittals, finding that it was a high-order political question with implications to Japan's continuing existence as a sovereign nation and that such matters were not amenable to judicial resolution unless "obviously unconstitutional and void."

With this articulation of the Japanese version of the "political question" doctrine, the Supreme Court essentially effectively recused itself from the business of interpreting Article 9 absent obvious constitutional violations, and has maintained this policy ever since. Its approach to Article 9 can also be reflected in some of the techniques Japanese courts have used to avoid issuing rulings on constitutionality in other contexts as well.

At the same time, however, the view that the Court abdicated its role overshadows other aspects of its ruling in the *Sunagawa Case*. Among other things, the court held that since Article 9 does not address foreign military forces, and US forces in Japan were not under Japanese control, they did *not* constitute war potential, that nothing in Article 9 denied "the right of self-defense inherent in our nation as a sovereign power," and that the constitution did not prohibit Japan from seeking a security guarantee from another country, even outside the scope of the UN framework. None of these views is inconsistent with Japan's security policy in practice.

A few lower court decisions have addressed the SDF and Article 9-related disputes, and even generated excited headlines in doing so, but none have resulted in meaningful interpretive changes. For example, the *Naganuma Nike Case* involved challenges by local residents to the issuance of a permit to use part of a forest designated for conservation for the construction of an SDF missile base. The Sapporo District Court accepted the residents' claim on the grounds that the SDF was war potential prohibited by the constitution.[24] On appeal the Supreme Court avoided the constitutional issue by finding the residents lacked standing to challenge the permit issuance.[25] This case is also famous in the context of judicial independence (see Article 76).

Another case, the *Hyakuri Base Case* arose from an effort to block the construction of an SDF base through the purchase by an opposition group of land in the planned location. One party who had contracted to sell his land to the group grew dissatisfied because of their failure to tender full payment, cancelled the contract and sold his land to the government instead. This was challenged in court on the grounds that *inter alia*, the entry into a contract to purchase land was both an "other act of government" under Article 98 of the constitution and thus also a *void* act of government due to the Article 9 violations allegedly arising from the establishment and existence of the SDF and the Defense Agency. A second argument was that the contract was void on public policy grounds under Article 90 of the Civil Code due to its unconstitutional subject matter. The Supreme Court rejected these arguments on the grounds that Article 9 did not apply to private law acts such as contracts even when the state was a party.[26]

In 2008 the Nagoya High Court issued a ruling declaring the dispatch of the SDF to Iraq unconstitutional.[27] Although it generated a lot of headlines, it was a classic example of a *dasoku hanketsu* (literally "snake leg judgment"). Such judgments involve dramatic dicta that is not reflected in the court's disposition. [28] The case involved a claim for nominal damages and an injunction from a citizens group claiming to have been harmed by the unconstitutional dispatch. The court agreed the dispatch violated Article 9, and recognized the Preamble as articulating a right to live in peace, but found that since the plaintiffs had not suffered any actual damages their claims must be rejected. The plaintiffs got the headlines they presumably wanted, the government could not appeal—because it had won—but the judgment didn't require it to change its behavior either: a win-win for everyone!

Other interpretations of Article 9

In the absence of post-*Sunagawa Case* judicial guidance, interpretation of what the various provisions of Article 9 mean have fallen to academics and other government branches. An overview of the scholarly interpretations of Article 9 could easily fill a large book while potentially misleading readers about constitutional reality. For example, some constitutional texts make a point of identifying interpretive theories to the effect that Article 9 has resulted in Japan abandoning the right to even self-defense, relying instead on "the justice and faith of the peace-loving peoples of the world" (Preamble) and being prohibited from having even latent war potential (such as nuclear power). Yet these viewpoints are not just academic but incompatible with reality. Accordingly, other than pointing out the existence of a rich body of academic literature on the meaning of Article 9, the discussion in this book will not delve into them deeply.

As with other constitutional issues and questions that have proven difficult to resolve through judicial review, the next most authoritative interpretation is that given by the government—cabinet members or high-level government officials. These interpretations may be generated through responses to questions asked at legislative committee meetings, press conferences or interpellations from (opposition) Diet members (see Article 63). This last category of questions is perhaps the most formal, and involves a well-established documentary process (reflected in part in Articles 74 and 75 of the Diet Act), and the responses are prepared and vetted by the Cabinet Legislation Bureau (CLB) and other relevant government institutions before being formally approved by the Cabinet.

Thus, to the extent Article 9 creates constraints on the Japanese government's scope and use of its military power, these constraints are most likely to manifest themselves in the contours of answers to questions that are often very specific in nature. To a distant observer it may seem that the government is able to "arbitrarily" announce a constitutional interpretation that is convenient at the time, but the interpretation is "binding" in the sense that future changes or diversions from that interpretation will be challenged and require explanation. For example, the government's longstanding view was that three conditions had to be met for the constitutional use of force in self-defense: (1) the minimum use of force necessary, used to (2) eliminate an immediate threat to Japan, that (3) cannot be removed through other appropriate means. As discussed below, the process of interpretively changing these "three conditions for self-defense" was by no means easy or uncontroversial.[29]

These question-answer based interpretations are diverse and widely dispersed as a source of information.[30] For example, on November 9, 1990, Sumiko Shimizu, a socialist Diet member, submitted a series of questions about the Japanese government's contribution of funds to assist in the liberation of Kuwait, including whether funding the use of force by the United States outside the scope of the mutual defense treaty did not constitute "collective self-defense" prohibited by Article 9 (under the interpretation at the time). On November 27 the government issued its response which included its interpretation that merely providing money did not constitute overt acts comprising collective self-defense activities.[31]

Participation in collective self-defense activities—using military force to assist allies and other friendly nations from attacks not made directly against Japan—has been a particularly controversial issue for decades. To the frustration of multiple prime ministers (some of whom preferred to expend political capital on economic development rather than resolving constitutional questions), the Cabinet Legislation Bureau, which, in addition to vetting cabinet legislative proposals, provides legal advice to the Cabinet, for decades held to the view that, even though collective self-defense was an inherent right of sovereign nations and anticipated by Article 51 of the UN Charter, Article 9 prohibited Japan from exercising this right.[32]

In 2013, Prime Minister Shinzō Abe appointed a CLB outsider as Director General of the CLB, for the purpose of engineering a change of its interpretation. The CLB dutifully did so (in a meeting at which no minutes were kept), and the new interpretation was articulated in a 2014 cabinet resolution.[33] This resolution announced a much more expansive interpretation of Article 9, including addressing what had been gray areas such as what was a permissible response to attacks from non-state actors such as terrorists and pirates and threats to the safety of Japanese citizens abroad, as well as use of weapons by SDF personnel abroad.[34] It also greatly expanded and redefined the scope of SDF activities abroad, including in collective security activities protecting countries with which Japan shares common interests, to the extent Japan's own security is implicated.

This reinterpretation also involved the articulation of three *new*, greatly relaxed conditions for the constitutionally permissible use of force in self-defense: (1) the minimum amount of force suitable to (2) respond to an attack on Japan or an attack on a country having a close relationship with Japan and which clearly threatens to fundamentally impact the lives, liberty or right to the pursuit of happiness of the Japanese people, (3) when there are no other appropriate means for removing the threat and ensuring the survival of Japan or the protection of the Japanese people cannot be accomplished through other appropriate means.[35] Note the reference to "life, liberty and the pursuit of happiness" is a reference to

Article 13, which has long been considered an additional basis for the right of self-defense (i.e., not protecting the nation would result in a failure to protect those rights).[36]

The manner in which the prime minister engineered this reinterpretation (which, at the time of writing was bearing "fruit" in tangible forms such as aircraft carriers and in expanded military cooperation with the United States and other countries) has been the source of significant criticism, including from numerous constitutional scholars as well as former Supreme Court judges and CLB leaders.[37]

At the same time, however, it needs to be born in mind that with the Supreme Court having in the *Sunagawa Case* effectively abdicated its role as final arbiter of what Article 9 means, the task of interpretation necessarily falls to some other branch of government. One might argue that constitutional changes should be made through the amendment process, not interpretation, yet the same argument can also be made about Supreme Court decisions interpreting the constitution, including instances where the court overturns or amends prior precedents. Similarly, complaints about Prime Minister Abe's unprecedented "interference" in well-established CLB practices in choosing a director general, ignore the reality of its status an institution subordinated to the Cabinet.[38]

Morevoer, key aspects of the new interpretation were reflected in the 2015 defense legislation package mentioned in the Introduction to this chapter. Among other things the resulting amendments to the relevant laws specifically authorized the use of force for collective self-defense activities and clarified the ability of SDF personnel to use lethal force in various situations.[39] Thus, two of three branches of Japan's government can be said to have ratified this new constitutional interpretation.

Article 9 and Japanese legal and political culture

Given the existence of the SDF and its increasingly visible role as a "normal" military, it is tempting to conclude that Article 9 is largely meaningless, or at best a political manifesto.[40] This would be too harsh; the constitutional norms expressed in Article 9, together with the historical experience of war and occupation that gave birth to it, can be said to have had broad ramifications on postwar policy, culture and law. Culturally, pacifism is a widely accepted value in postwar Japan. The impact of Article 9 and its underlying pacifism manifests itself within Japan's domestic legal system in numerous ways. For example, the extremely stringent restrictions on the possession of guns, swords, and even carrying knives can be attributed partially to occupation-era efforts to disarm the Japanese people in furtherance of the Potsdam Declaration. Article 9 can also be directly linked to longstanding government policies such as the famous "three non-nuclear principles"[41] and the less well-known "three principles of weapons exports," which effectively kept Japan's manufacturing industries out of the international arms trade for decades before being recast (but not eliminated) in 2014.[42]

Moreover, unlike the president under the US constitution or even the emperor under the Meiji Constitution, nobody in the Japanese government can claim to exercise constitutionally vague, undefined or "inherent" powers as supreme commander of the military, immune from legislative interference.[43] A logical corollary of the SDF's existence being constitutionally limited to the needs of "self-defense," is that what the SDF may and may not do in furtherance of self-defense is necessarily defined by statute. This means that efforts to expand the remit of the SDF—the various international missions it has taken on as discussed in the Chapter summary—have each required legislation.[44] To the extent that some of this legislation has been controversial and sometimes involved acrimonious deliberations in the Diet, it means that the permissible use of Japan's military has been a frequent subject of public debate. This is probably not a bad thing, and the Japanese government demonstrably expends significant energy and political capital in reconciling what it seeks to do with the SDF with the current understanding of the constraints imposed by Article 9.

Another manifestation of this can be seen in the statutory foundations for the use of weapons by individual SDF personnel and units. For the most part there is a statutory foundation for any particular instance where a weapon might be used. Many (but not all) are contained in the SDF Act itself,[45] and may be characterized in different ways, such as the use of weapons when performing a police-like role, for the purpose of preserving defensive capabilities (e.g., guarding weapons and ammunition), or for self-defense. Some are oddly specific: for example, Article 93-3 of the SDF Act specifically authorizes the use of weapons to destroy ballistic missiles.

Self-defense is perhaps the most basic grounds for SDF personnel to use their weapons, and is sometimes described in natural law terms. Yet one subtle aspect of Article 9 is that SDF personnel cannot simply be assumed to enjoy the status of military personnel engaged in hostilities under international law. The use of weapons in personal or unit-level self-defense potentially constitutes an element of the state's use of force in self-defense, but the government has put significant effort into distinguishing between the two and sought a statutory basis for the use of weapons whenever possible. Most of the SDF Act provisions permitting the use of weapons tie it to Articles 35 and 36 of the Penal Code, which provide excuses for criminal liability in the case of self-defense and "averting present danger." Given the applicability of Penal Code provisions criminalizing murder and numerous other offenses when committed abroad by Japanese citizens, how these exculpatory provisions apply to SDF personnel dispatched abroad can be a complicated determination.[46]

Given the statutory basis for the use of weapons by SDF personnel, the absence of a legal authorization can also be problematic. For example, when SDF personnel first started participating in UN Peacekeeping missions under the so-called "PKO Law," the statute permitted SDF personnel to use small arms to protect themselves and other members of their unit, but not to protect any other parties involved in the operation, including peacekeeping forces from other countries and UN personnel.[47] Similarly, despite a decades-long alliance relationship, there was uncertainty as to whether SDF personnel could use weapons to defend American forces (or the forces of other countries) in various situations that were not clarified until the amendments passed in 2015.[48]

Together with other provisions of the constitution, Article 9 has also had an impact on the legal status of the SDF in other respects. Pacifist sentiments and lingering suspicions that any law dealing with the SDF or national security was part of an effort to subvert Article 9 or shift the country back to militarism made it difficult—or at least controversial—to pass many laws of a character that are "normal" for other countries with militaries. For example, despite Japan having assumed treaty obligations to do so appropriately decades previously, the possibility that the SDF might have to be responsible for taking care of foreign prisoners of war was not addressed legislatively until 2004.[49] Similarly, it was not until that year that a general legislative framework was created for the use of ports, airports, roads and other public infrastructure to respond to attacks.[50] Until 2013 Japan also lacked a national secrets act—a precondition to any meaningful military cooperation with friendly nations outside the scope of the US-Japan security alliance.[51]

In the sphere of governance, Article 9 together with related constitutional provisions has presented challenges in establishing laws and institutions necessary for the effective development and use of military forces, even for the limited purpose of self-defense. For example, the "Defense Committee" established in 1954 to provide top-level leadership was structured in part to prevent ex-military leaders from re-establishing a controlling faction, and was focused primarily on defense planning and procurement.[52] It was not converted into a more broadly focused and constituted Security Council until 1986, and only become the present National Security Council in 2013.[53] Similarly, despite having the most personnel of any national government institution, the SDF was not directly represented at the cabinet level until the establishment of the Ministry of Defense (of which the SDF is a part) in 2007.[54]

The SDF is an all-volunteer force and conscription is considered constitutionally impossible.[55] Nor is it possible to have a separate system of criminal justice with especially harsh punishments for SDF personnel, since Article 76 prohibits such special tribunals.[56]

Finally, Article 9 has provided a powerful bulwark—or obstacle, depending on your point of view—to constitutional reform of any type. To grossly oversimplify a complex and changing historical situation, for decades Japan's opposition parties were able to garner votes—enough at least to prevent the LDP from obtaining supermajority control of one or both houses—in part based on the simple platform of protecting Article 9. However, with changing geopolitical conditions and the SDF having become a long-established and even respected institution, many Japanese people seem amenable to the prospect of amending the constitution at least to the extent necessary to acknowledge the military's existence. Whether that will open the door to other amendments will remain to be seen.

Notes

1 Title IV(1) of the French constitution of 1791. The German federal constitution of 1949 (Article 87A(1)) states that its armed forces shall be "for defense." Under Article 11 of the Italian constitution that nation "… rejects war as an instrument of aggression against the freedom of other peoples and as a means for the settlement of international disputes." The Philippine constitution of 1987 also "renounces war as an instrument of national policy" (Article 2). South Korea's constitution renounces "all aggressive wars" (Article 5(1)). Article 12 of the Political Constitution of the Republic of Costa Rica abolishes the army and only permits other military forces to be organized either under a continental agreement or for national defense.

2 In Article I of the treaty, the signatory nations undertook to "condemn recourse to war for the solution of international controversies, and renounce it, as an instrument of national policy in their relations with one another." In Article II they further "agree that the settlement or solution of all disputes or conflicts of whatever nature or of whatever origin they may be, which may arise among them, shall never be sought except by pacific means."

3 As noted by Craig Martin, it is unlikely that the GHQ drafting team had a copy of the UN charter or were fully aware of the finer nuances of the new *jus ad bellum* regime of international law being introduced through it. Martin, C. (2008), 293–94. He also notes that the GHQ drafters have acknowledged being "guided by the language" of the Kellogg-Briand pact, and being aware of the preparations being made for the Tokyo War Crimes Tribunals to be convened "just a few blocks away." Ibid., 295.

4 Indeed, when the United Nations charter was executed in June of 1945, the signatory nations were effectively proclaiming themselves "united" against the one remaining axis nation which had yet to be defeated—Japan. A remnant of this can be seen in several provisions of the Charter (specifically, Articles 53, 77 and 107) referencing "enemies" of the signatories.

[5] The Memo's statement about Japan relying upon "the higher ideals which are now stirring the world for its defense and its protection" were reflected in the Preamble rather than Article 9.
[6] The amendment was named after Hitoshi Ashida, the chair of the Imperial Diet subcommittee from which it originated.
[7] See, e.g., Moore, R., & Robinson, D. (2004), 247–50.
[8] UN Charter, Articles 1 and 51.
[9] The Security Treaty between Japan and the United States of America of 1951, Article I.
[10] Ibid., Preamble, para. 3.
[11] Article V.
[12] Article III.
[13] There was also a degree of quiet Japanese participation in the Korean War, including through the dispatch of minesweepers and other vessels. Morris-Suzuki, T. (2012).
[14] See, e.g., *Jieiken no umu (Shūdan teki jieiken o fukumu) to jieitai no ichizuke* [On the existence of the right to self-defense (Including the right to collective self-defense) and the tatus of the SDF]. (n.d.). Retrieved June 10, 2022, from https://www.kenpoushinsa.sangiin.go.jp/kenpou/houkokusyo/houkoku/03_12_01.html (explanatory note from home page of the Commission on the Constitution of the House of Councillors).
[15] Toropin, K. (2021, October 27). *With a Wink and a Nod, Japan Has an Aircraft Carrier Again*. Military.com. Retrieved June 10, 2022, from https://www.military.com/daily-news/2021/10/27/wink-and-nod-japan-has-aircraft-carrier-again.html.
[16] SDF Act, Article 100–7, *et. seq*. These provisions reflect Acquisition and Cross-Servicing Agreements (ACSA) between Japan and the respective nations.
[17] Muneo, N. (2014); *U.S., Japan, Australia, India Begin Joint Naval Drill amid China rise*. Kyodo News+. (2021, October 13). Retrieved June 10, 2022, from https://english.kyodonews.net/news/2021/10/4a33ffe422fe-us-japan-australia-india-begin-joint-naval-drill-amid-china-rise.html.
[18] The Japanese version of Article 9 has generated a number of linguistic issues. One of the reasons for the "SDF" naming is because paragraph (2) of Article 9 clearly prohibits "*gun*"—the generic term for "armed forces" whether on land (*rikugun*, army), in the sea (*kaigun*, navy) or in the air (*kūgun*, air force). Yet "*gun*" is a common component of numerous military terms (*gunkan*—the generic term for military vessels and *gunjin*—the generic term for military personnel), necessitating the creation of a whole new vocabulary of terminology used in connection with the SDF (and creating a parallel conundrum around the term "civilian" as used in Article 66). Similarly, the "*sen*" (war) in "*senryoku*" (war potential) is also a component of various common military terms such as "tank" (*sensha*) and "fighter" (*sentōki*). In the past similarly evasive terms such as "special vehicle" were used for such hardware, but one subtle sign of changing attitudes towards the military is in the gradual acceptance and official use of the more traditional term for some equipment, such as tanks.
[19] The "*ken*" in *kōsenken*" is "right," The "*sen*" is the same as described in the preceding note. One accepted translation of "*kōsen*" by itself is "war."
[20] The Japanese language does not have elements corresponding to definite and indefinite articles and is often unclear as to plurality of nouns. Thus, the latter sentence of paragraph (2) could also plausibly be translated as "The right of belligerency of states will not be recognized."
[21] This is an attempt to briefly summarize the very comprehensive treatment by Martin, C. (2008).
[22] Supreme Court, Grand Bench judgment of December 16, 1959. Note the case is sometimes also referred to as the Sunakawa Case.
[23] Tokyo District Court judgment of March 30 1959, 1 *Kakyū saibansho hanreishū* 776. The direct appeal was not the only thing unusual about the case. US diplomatic cables declassified in 2008 revealed that the US ambassador to Tokyo (MacArthur's son, Douglas MacArthur II) was meeting with Chief Judge Kōtarō Tanaka while the case was being deliberated by his court.
[24] Sapporo District Court judgment of August 5, 1976, 27 *Keishū* 1385.
[25] Supreme Court, 1st Petty Bench judgment of September 9, 1982.
[26] Supreme Court, 3rd Petty Bench judgment of June 20, 1989.
[27] Nagoya High Court judgment of April 17, 2008, 2056 *Hanji* 74.
[28] The "snake legs" is a reference to something unnecessary or surplus. On the odd dynamics of snake legs judgments by Japanese courts, see Jones, C.P.A. (2005).

[29] The three principles are articulated in a 1985 government response to a question from House of Representative member Kiyoshi Mori. Question: Shugiin.go.jp. (n.d.). Retrieved June 10, 2022, from https://www.shugiin.go.jp/Internet/itdb_shitsumona.nsf/html/shitsumon/a102047.htm. Answer: Shugiin.go.jp. (n.d.). Retrieved June 10, 2022, from https://www.shugiin.go.jp/Internet/itdb_shitsumona.nsf/html/shitsumon/b102047.htm.
[30] Some commercially-published compilations exist. *See, e.g.*, Urata, I. (Ed.) (2017).
[31] The questions and answers are available on the House of Councillors website: *Nihon seifu no Chūtō shiensaku ni kansuru shitsumon ni taisuru tōbensho: Tōben honbun: Sangiin* [Written response to questions concerning Japan's support operations in the Middle East]. House of Councillors. (n.d.). Retrieved June 10, 2022, from https://www.sangiin.go.jp/japanese/joho1/kousei/syuisyo/119/touh/t119005.htm and *Nihon seifu no Chūtō shiensaku ni kansuru shitsumon shuisho: Shitsumon honbun: Sangiin* [Questions concerning Japan's support operations in the Middle East]. House of Councillors. (n.d.). Retrieved June 10, 2022, from https://www.sangiin.go.jp/japanese/joho1/kousei/syuisyo/119/syuh/s119005.htm.
[32] The testimony of CLB Director General Ichirō Yoshioka at the September 14, 1974 meeting of the House of Councillors Audit Committee, is commonly referenced as the source of this view, but Yoshioka repeatedly refers to it as already being a longstanding view of the CLB. *69th Session of the National Diet. House of Councillors. Audit Committee. Closing of Fifth Session. September 14, Shōwa 47.* Minutes of National Diet Search System. (n.d.). Retrieved June 10, 2022, from https://kokkai.ndl.go.jp/#/detailPDF?minId=106914103X00519720914&page=1&spkNum=0¤t=-1
See also, Samuels, R.J. (2004).
[33] *Kuni no zonritsu o mattōshi, kokumin o mamoru tame no kireme no nai anzen hoshōhōsei no seibi ni tsuite* [Regarding the establishment of a security legislation framework that comprehensively protects the people and ensures the survival of the nation]. (n.d.). Retrieved June 10, 2022, from https://www.cas.go.jp/jp/gaiyou/jimu/pdf/anpohosei.pdf.
[34] This final point involved the use of the interesting euphemism "*kaketsuke keibi*" or "guarding a place after rushing to it."
[35] See Cabinet Secretariat. (n.d.). *Shin san'yōken no jūzen no kempōkaishaku to no ronriteki seigōsei ni tsuite* [On logically reconciling the new three conditions and previous constitutional interpretations]. Cabinet Legislation Bureau Memorandum of June 9, 2015. Retrieved June 10, 2022, from https://www.kantei.go.jp/jp/headline/pdf/20151111/sinsanyouken.pdf.
[36] Another comparatively recent addition to the corpus of defense legislation frames its purpose in part to protect the lives, persons and property (but not liberty or the right to pursuit of happiness!) of the Japanese people from armed aggression. Buryoku Kōgeki Jitaitō ni Okeru Kokumin no Hogo no Tameno Sochi Ni Kansuru Hōritsu [Act Relating to Measures Taken for the Protection of the Japanese People in the Event of Armed Attacks, etc.], Law no. 112 of 2004, Article 1.
[37] See, e.g., Martin, C. (2017).
[38] Under Article 2 of the law constituting the CLB, its head is appointed by the Cabinet. *Naikaku Hōseikyoku Secchihō* [Act Establishing the Cabinet Legislation Bureau], Law no. 252 of 1952. One interesting aspect of the change of the Director General was that the previous head—who had previously stated publicly that Article 9 prevented Japan from engaging in collective self-defense—was appointed to the Supreme Court, presumably in part because his views on the subject of what Article 9 means would not cause any trouble there.
[39] For a summary of the 2015 legislation, see Nasu, 2016.
[40] Writing in 2019 in his preface to the 7th edition of the late Nobuyoshi Ashibe's classic treatise on the constitution, Professor Kazuyuki Takahashi describes the need for constitutional scholars to move away from questioning the constitutionality of a military force that has existed for decades (the "Achilles heel" of constitutionalism, as he describes it), and instead seek reconciliation with government interpretations of Article 9. He prefaces this by noting that in 1995 even Professor Ashibe had considered whether it would be necessary to develop a theory of Article 9 as being a "political manifesto." Ashibe, N., (2019), v–vi.
[41] Statement by Prime Minister Eisaku Satō at the Budget Committee in the House of Representatives (December 11, 1967): "My responsibility is to achieve and maintain safety in Japan under the Three Non-Nuclear Principles of not possessing, not producing and not permitting the introduction of nuclear weapons, in line with Japan's Peace Constitution." (*Three Non-Nuclear Principles.* MOFA. (n.d.). Retrieved June 10, 2022, from https://www.mofa.go.jp/policy/un/disarmament/nnp/.) "Introducing" is a poor translation of "*mochikomi*" which means "allowing into Japanese territory." This last principle has involved a longstanding theater of the

Japanese government not asking whether US forces in Japan have nuclear weapons at any given time, and the US government not telling, or even secretly agreeing to ignore them when necessary.

[42] These were first clearly articulated in a speech by Prime Minister Satō on April 21, 1967 as being a prohibition on Japan exporting weapons to: communist countries, countries where a UN resolution prohibiting the export of weapons was in force, and countries presently engaged in conflict. In 1976 Prime Minister Takeo Miki added an additional "principle" of "refraining" from exporting weapons to any other countries, which was essentially an outright prohibition on all exports. While these principles were not formally reflected in any law, the Foreign Exchange and Control Act imposed restrictions on weapons exports in any case. See, Tomita, K. (2011). Under the Abe administration, in 2014 these three principles were replaced by the more pleasingly euphemistic "three principles of transferring defense equipment" which are more complex but consist of: (1) a prohibition on transfers of weapons in violation of international agreements to which Japan is a party, UN resolutions or to countries presently in conflict, (2) a requirement that such transfers as do take place contribute to peace and Japan's security, and (3) ensuring suitable control over the use and further transfers. *The Three principles on transfer of Defense Equipment and Technology*. Ministry of Foreign Affairs of Japan. (n.d.). Retrieved June 10, 2022, from https://www.mofa.go.jp/press/release/press22e_000010.html.

[43] This may depend, however, on the theoretical view taken as to what constitutes the executive/administrative power under Chapter V (see discussion at Article 65). In the real world, under Article 7 of the SDF Act, the prime minister "representing the Cabinet" exercises overall command of the SDF. Under Article 8, the Minister of Defense exercises command to the extent provided for in the Act, but this is exercised through the appropriate service branch head.

[44] For example, SDF participation in UN peacekeeping operations required the passage in 1992 of the Act on Cooperation with United Nations Peacekeeping Operations and Other Operations, the use of Maritime SDF forces to combat international piracy saw the passage of the Act for the Punishment of and Response to Pirate Activities of 2009. Corresponding amendments to the SDF Act have also been required for these and other changes in the scope of its role and missions.

[45] SDF Act, Articles 84-3(1)(ii), 92-4, 92-5, 93-3, 95, 95-2 and 95-3.

[46] Penal Code, Article 3.

[47] This was addressed by a 2001 amendment. Kokusai Rengō Heiwa Iji Katsudōtō ni Taisuru Kyōryoku ni Kansuru Hōritsu [Act Relating to Cooperation in UN Peace-Keeping Operations, etc.], Law no. 79 of 1991 (see Articles 25 and 26 regarding permissible use of weapons).

[48] SDF Act, Article 95-2.

[49] Buryoku Kōgeki Jitai Oyobi Zonritsu Kiki Jitai ni Okeru Horyotō no Toriatsukai ni Kansuru Hōritsu [Law Relating to the Treatment of Prisoners (etc.) in the Event of Attack or Existential Crises], Law no. 117 of 2004. By contrast, within a year of regaining sovereignty in 1952, Japan had ratified all four Geneva Conventions of 1949 comprising the core of postwar international humanitarian law, including the one relating to prisoners of war (The Convention (I) for the Amelioration of the Condition of the Wounded and Sick in Armed Forces in the Field. Geneva, the Convention (II) for the Amelioration of the Condition of Wounded, Sick and Shipwrecked Members of Armed Forces at Sea, Convention (III) relative to the Treatment of Prisoners of War, and Convention (IV) relative to the Protection of Civilian Persons in Time of War). Note the Japanese term for prisoner of war (*horyō*) contains no war-related morphemes, so is not as problematic in the Article 9 context as it might seem in English.

[50] Buryoku Kōgeki Jitaitō ni Okeru Tokutei Kōkyōshisetutō no Riyō ni Kansuru Hōritsu [Act Relating to the Use of Designated Public Facilities (etc.) in the Event of Situations of Armed Attacks (etc.)].

[51] The Protection of Specially Designated Secrets Act was passed in 2013. A 1985 bill to prevent and criminal spying failed to pass. Prior to this SDF personnel were subject to the general prohibition on disclosing confidential information contained in the National Public Service Act (Article 100), with additional penalties imposed by the SDF Act. The punishments for violations of the latter are surprisingly light: a maximum of one year's imprisonment (SDF Act, Article 118(i)). A more obscure law passed in conjunction with the US-Japan security alliance imposes more stringent confidentiality obligations in connection with information relating to military equipment made available to Japan by the US. Nichibei Sōgo Bōei Enjo Kyōtei ni Tomonau Himitsu Hogohō [Act for the Protection of Secrets in Connection with the Japan-US Mutual Defense Agreement], Law no. 166 of 1954.

[52] Yasuaki, C. (2012).

[53] Kokka Anzen Hoshō Kaigi Secchihō [National Security Council Establishment Act], Law no. 71 of 1986.

[54] Prior to this upgrades its functions resided principally in two agencies: the "Defense Agency" under the Cabinet Office, and the Defense Facilities Administration Agency.
[55] In response to a government plan to convert Japanese merchant mariners into Maritime SDF reservists, there was an outcry that it was a form of conscription, to which the government responded nothing would be compulsory. "Jijitsujō no chōyō"—Kaiinkumiain ga hanpatsu" [Maritimer union outcry over "De-facto conscription"]. *Mainichi Shinbun.* (2016, January 30). Retrieved June 10, 2022, from https://mainichi.jp/articles/20160130/k00/00m/040/091000c.
[56] See discussion at Article 76 regarding the constitutional constraints on tribunals outside the scope of Chapter VI. Although the SDF Act imposes some criminal penalties on personnel for non-compliance, the most severe penalty is 7 years imprisonment, which can be imposed for certain dereliction of duty and desertion-like defenses. SDF Act, Article 122.

Chapter III
Rights and Duties of the People
Articles 10–40

Introduction

Sean McGinty

Overview

Article 10 of the Potsdam Declaration made the establishment of the respect for fundamental human rights a condition of Japan's surrender. Chapter III of the Constitution of Japan, which covers the rights and duties of the people, was in large part how this principle was put into effect. One major factor which contributed to making the protection of human rights such a focus was undoubtedly the very weak protection they had enjoyed in Japan under the Meiji system, a situation about which we may begin this chapter with a few words.

One well known anecdote related to Japan's selective adoption of a legal system based on western models in the Meiji era is that the language lacked a word that "right" could be translated into and one thus had to be invented from scratch (*kenri*).[1] The profundity of this story is somewhat blunted by the fact that the Japanese language produces huge numbers of new words each year without it really impacting the ability of people to use the thing being described, and also by the fact that Japan in the preceding Tokugawa era had long experience with concepts analogous to property and contractual rights in the field of private law. It does however usefully serve as a simplified metaphor for the discomfort that members of the Meiji ruling class felt towards the idea of creating a set of legal rights that the people could use specifically against the new state which they were in the process of building.[2]

This unease is reflected in the content of the Meiji Constitution's second chapter which, like Chapter III of the current one, covers rights and duties. The rights enshrined in the Meiji Constitution differed from those in the current constitution in three major ways. The first is that most current rights simply were not in it. Economic and social rights were completely absent while rights related to the criminal process, intellectual freedom and procedural rights against the state for the most part existed only in very rudimentary form. The second is that the small number of rights that were included were always qualified as being subject to the provision of law. While this did not necessarily deprive them of all meaning as they could still serve as a check on arbitrary abuse, it did mean that they could be limited or stripped away through regular legislation as the government saw fit (as it, not coincidentally, often did). Finally, the Meiji Constitution did not provide for a system of judicial constitutional review, which meant that in the prewar period Japanese could not challenge legislation or government actions which violated what rights they may have had before the courts.

As a result, Japanese citizens could at best be described as having had a very weak system of constitutional rights before 1947. This shortcoming is often cited as a significant contributing factor to the rise of a militant nationalist government in the 1930s which, not being confronted with an effective system for protecting rights, had little problem in ignoring them. Introducing both a more robust set of rights and a system for protecting them in the new constitution thus came to be a key reform for SCAP in the war's early aftermath.[3]

The new constitution sought to alleviate these problems with the Meiji Constitution. First, it dealt with the general problem of a lack of rights by, at the risk of oversimplification, making Chapter III a lot longer than its predecessor. Whereas Chapter II of the Meiji Constitution only contained fifteen articles, some of them stipulating duties rather than rights, Chapter III of the present constitution comprises thirty-one articles, only three of which mention duties. Second, it dropped the "subject to the provision of law" proviso for the rights enumerated, making them less susceptible to being over-ridden by legislation, though it also introduced general public welfare provisions which ensured that rights were not unqualified (and, as it would turn out, could be limited through legislation without too much difficulty). Finally, the inclusion of judicial review under Article 81 provided a means of using the courts to challenge legislation and government actions which violated constitutional rights.

An additional important distinction to be noted between the current and former constitution lies in the nature of the rights themselves. Whereas the preamble of the Meiji Constitution framed its contents, including the rights contained therein, as a gift from a benevolent emperor, rights under the new constitution are based on universalist and natural law ideals, influenced by a mix of both the 18th-century American constitution's Bill of Rights and mid-20th century concepts. This is reflected in Article 11's statement that the rights are "eternal and inviolate," a concept repeated later in Article 97's reminder that the rights have "survived the many exacting tests for durability and are conferred upon this and future generations in trust, to be held for all time inviolate."

As with the rest of the constitution, Chapter III was drafted mainly by American lawyers, though it departs from the American Bill of Rights in some areas and includes many concepts such as social and economic rights which are not contained therein, reflecting the vastly different context of its creation. A more apt comparison in terms of substance would perhaps be to the Universal Declaration of Human Rights, which was being drafted roughly contemporaneously and exhibits a significant degree of overlap with the Japanese constitution in terms of the rights being guaranteed. This is a reflection of both the universalist view of human rights, and the development of ideas about the relationship between the individual and the modern state, which clearly influenced the drafters of both. To a certain extent some elements of the content of Chapter III can also be described as a compromise between competing interests within Japan which had some input into its creation as its drafters also had access to various proposals from Japanese sources.[4] On the one hand conservatives associated with the government initially supported a draft that would have left most of the Meiji Constitution's provisions unchanged, a position that was immediately rejected by SCAP. In contrast more radical reformers proposed more extensive sets of rights than those that ended up in the constitution as promulgated, which makes no explicit mention of areas like minority rights or, with the exception of equality of marriage in Article 24, gender rights.

Classification of rights

We may also say something here about the typology and organization of rights contained in the current constitution, which is important for understanding differences in how they may be litigated (if at all) before the courts. We can begin by noting some categories of provisions in the Chapter which are not generally recognized as conferring rights on individuals which can be judicially enforced. One such category are the so-called programmatic provisions (*puroguramu kitei*) which are interpreted as merely requiring the state to enact a program to achieve a given end rather than granting an enforceable right. A notable example of this is Article 25's duty to promote the extension of social welfare and security and public health, which is viewed as requiring the government to create programs to achieve those objectives, but not as providing grounds for a suit against the government for failing to achieve them. A second type are institutional guarantee provisions (*seidoteki hoshō*) which do not directly affect individual rights but rather are focused on institutions. Article 23's guarantee of academic freedom, for example, while it does protect some individual rights (such as the right of law professors to write commentaries on the meaning of Article 23) is also recognized as protecting the independence of universities from state interference, a right on which the courts will not allow individuals to bring constitutional challenges since it does not apply to them as individuals. Additionally, there are some provisions which stipulate general principles, such as Article 11's guarantee of fundamental human rights, which courts have not generally recognized as judicially actionable.

In line with the Chapter's title, some provisions also impose duties rather than rights though these comprise a small minority of the provisions in the Chapter. These are Article 26, which requires parents to ensure the education of their children, Article 27's obligation to work, and Article 30's duty to pay taxes.

In contrast to these, Chapter III contains a significant number of rights which clearly do provide individual rights which have been used to challenge legislation or government actions. In no particular order, the first of these are rights related to spiritual or intellectual freedoms. The Meiji Constitution did contain very limited provisions on freedom of speech and religion, the former subject to the limits of the law and the latter given to subjects only to the extent that it was not "antagonistic to their duties as subjects." The new constitution significantly expanded these by introducing unqualified freedoms of thought and conscience (Article 19), religion (Article 20), assembly and speech (Article 21), and academic freedom (Article 23).

A third category of rights are those often referred to as economic and social rights. With the exception of the freedom to change one's abode (subject to the provisions of law) and the right to property, the Meiji Constitution was silent on these. Those found in the current constitution include the right to a wholesome standard of living (see discussion of the "programmatic declaration theory" at Article 25), to education (Article 26), to work (Article 27), to bargain collectively (Article 28), and to hold property (Article 29). Some elements of these are, as noted earlier, treated as programmatic provisions (Article 25) or contain duties (the second paragraph of Article 26).

A fourth category are what might be called procedural rights. These are provisions which create rights to bring actions against the state. While the Meiji Constitution allowed subjects to present petitions, provided the proper forms of respect were observed, it otherwise did not envisage enabling people to bring claims against the government. The new constitution in contrast enumerates several ways of doing so. These include the right to petition (Article 16), the right to seek redress for damages against the state (Article 17), the right to access the courts (Article 32) and the right for those acquitted after being arrested or detained to demand compensation (Article 40).

An additional category to note are the rights contained in Articles 31 to 40 which provide a wide range of protections from state actions primarily in the context of the criminal justice system. These include the warrant requirement for arrest (Article 33) and search or seizure (Article 35), the right to be informed of charges (Article 34), the right to a speedy and public trial before an impartial tribunal (Article 37), and the right not to be compelled to testify against yourself (Article 38).

Who can enforce these rights?

As noted above, programmatic provisions, institutional guarantee provisions and provisions which define duties generally do not confer rights on individuals, but most other provisions in Chapter III do. Two broad questions arise in respect of who can bring a claim with respect to these: what persons enjoy the protection of constitutional rights generally, and who has standing to bring a specific case.

The question of who enjoys the protection of constitutional rights has mainly been raised in respect of whether they extend to foreign nationals or legal persons. With respect to the former, the GHQ Draft contained a provision which explicitly stated that all aliens were entitled to equal protection under the law, but this was removed by the Diet during its passing and the constitution is thus silent on the status of foreign nationals, though the wording of individual provisions is open to differing interpretations. Many individual provisions of Chapter III, such as the right to equality before the law under Article 14, are addressed to "the people," using the Japanese term *kokumin* which suggests they apply to Japanese nationals. In contrast others, such as the right to petition under Article 16 use the phrase "every person" (*nampito*) which suggests a broader application. This distinction in phrasing is of somewhat limited use as a guide, however, since other provisions containing rights such as the right to freedom of thought and conscience under Article 19 use neither and simply say that the freedom is guaranteed. Reflecting this difficulty, the Supreme Court has taken a case-by-case approach to determining which rights extend to foreign nationals and which are reserved exclusively for Japanese nationals.

The *McLean Case* involved an American working in Japan as an English teacher whose application to renew his work visa was denied on the grounds that he participated in anti-war demonstrations while in Japan. When he challenged the denial on the grounds that he was effectively being punished for the exercise of constitutionally-protected rights (the right to freedom of conscience under Article 19, to freedom of speech and association under Article 21 and to choose one's residence under Article 22), the Grand Bench found that in principle the protection of fundamental rights do extend to foreign nationals.[5] The following language from the judgment is commonly used to summarize the meaning of the case as to the rights of foreign nationals:

It should be understood that the guarantee of fundamental rights included in Chapter Three of the constitution extends also to foreign nationals staying in Japan except for those rights, which by their nature, are understood to address Japanese nationals only. This applies to political activities, except for those activities which are considered to be inappropriate by taking into account the status of the person as a foreign national, such as activities which have influence on the political decision-making and its implementation in Japan.

In another case commonly referred to as the *Fingerprint Refusal Case*, the Court has also found that Article 13 protected individuals from being fingerprinted without just cause, and that it also extended to non-Japanese.[6] In both this and the *McLean Case*, however, the Court also found that legislation restricting the foreign national's exercise of such rights due to their being foreign nationals was reasonable and necessary and thus not unconstitutional. Thus, while foreign nationals may in principle be recognized as enjoying these rights, in practice this has not actually led to them having success in trying to enforce them. The Court has also held that there are some rights which foreign nationals do not possess, notably the right to vote under Article 15 which it found to exclusively apply to Japanese nationals and upheld legislation preventing foreign nationals from voting (see additional discussion at Article 14).

With respect to legal or juridical persons, the Court has also taken a case-by-case approach to recognizing the applicability of constitutional rights. In the *Yahata Steel Political Contribution Case*, the Grand Bench held, without referencing a specific provision, that the rights in Chapter III as a whole should be interpreted as applying to Japanese-owned legal persons wherever it was possible to do so. In that decision, which as a shareholder lawsuit against corporate directors provided an odd venue for a discussion of constitutional rights, the Court found that political donations by a corporation did not violate the corporate charter or the rights of shareholders who might have objected to them and were permissible. This followed an earlier case—the *Hakata Station TV Film Production Case* discussed at Article 21—in which it had held that the Article 21 right to freedom of expression extends to TV broadcasting corporations.[7]

The question of who has standing in a specific case can also have important implications for the litigation of constitutional rights. The courts will only hear a constitutional claim in the context of an actual legal dispute: there is no way for the courts to rule on constitutional questions via a reference or advisory process. This means that constitutional claims often first appear in a district court either *ex ante* as a result of an administrative suit which seeks the revocation of the application of an allegedly unconstitutional rule, or *ex post* as a result of someone having already broken a rule and raising its unconstitutionality as a defense.[8] With respect to administrative cases the Supreme Court has adopted a fairly narrow interpretation of who has standing, requiring the violation of a specific individual right of a plaintiff. This has created a barrier to bringing claims against administrative agencies whose actions impact the interests of the public as a whole, but not directly on individuals.[9] An additional problem in administrative litigation cases is posed by a doctrine that courts have developed, in respect to both civil and administrative litigation claims, which requires the existence of an interest at stake in a dispute for the courts to hear the case. Where such interest is lost, such as in cases where the plaintiff has died before trial, the courts will dismiss the claim without considering its merits.

The role of the courts

The introduction of judicial constitutional review in Article 81 allowed the courts for the first time to play a significant role in interpreting and applying constitutional rights as cases challenging legislation or government acts came before them. From a comparative perspective, however, observers have long noted the almost acrobatic ability of the Supreme Court to reason its way to the conclusion that any given piece of legislation or government action does not violate constitutional rights or avoid addressing such questions altogether.[10] While the success rates of plaintiffs are not uniform across all types of claims, with courts showing somewhat more willingness to rule against government actions (as opposed to legislation) which violate the constitution, in general it can accurately be said that parties face long odds in bringing constitutional challenges before the courts.

This deference shown by the Supreme Court in exercising its judicial review function has evolved somewhat over time. In early cases Article 12's admonition that rights be utilized for the public welfare and Article 13's public welfare clause were used to fashion a general public welfare exception to all constitutional rights which allowed legislation to be upheld even where it conflicted with them so long as it was deemed necessary for the public welfare.[11] In more recent years the Court has adopted a more nuanced approach, weighing the reasonableness and necessity of the impugned provision in achieving the purpose of the legislation against the seriousness of the breach of the right in question to determine whether it should be allowed, though in most cases this has led to the same outcome. In other cases, the Court has either avoided addressing the constitutional issue altogether or upheld a provision on the grounds that it was possible to interpret it in a way that complied with the constitutional right at issue.

While this change has not radically altered the pattern of mostly deferential outcomes of cases, the Court has recently shown a slight willingness to more actively advance rights in some areas. An example of this concerns the rights of children born out of wedlock, who have long been discriminated against in various pieces of legislation. In the 2013 *Out-of-Wedlock Inheritance Rights Discrimination Case* the Supreme Court struck down a rule in the Civil Code in respect of inheritance on the grounds that its discriminatory treatment of children born out of wedlock violated Article 14's guarantee of equality before the law (see discussion at Article 14). This was particularly noteworthy since in 1995 the Court had upheld the constitutionality of the same provision in an almost identical case. In the 2013 case the Court noted changes in society's views on family as a justification for its own change in position. That case also notably demonstrates the potential significance of dissenting opinions, as the majority in the 2013 decision largely adopted the reasoning of the dissent in the 1995 case. Another area where the Court has been more proactive has been in reviewing election laws for their conformity with the constitution. Since the 1970s the Court has on several occasions been willing to find that disparities in the apportionment of representatives across regions, which has tended to lead to the overrepresentation of rural areas in the Diet relative to their population size, have been unconstitutional (see discussion of *House of Representatives Malapportionment Cases* at Articles 15 and 44). These judicial pushbacks remain isolated examples, however, and the Court's output of deferential rulings remains the norm.

Process and remedies

One problem related to the litigation of constitutional rights is that even in cases where the Court might be willing to find legislation unconstitutional this may not result in a meaningful remedy. Since the courts require the existence of a dispute to hear a case it is not possible to request injunctive relief against statutes which have not yet come into force.[12] Additionally, when the underlying factual basis for the unconstitutionality no longer exists, the courts will decline to provide any substantive form of relief. This is particularly evident in the above noted string of Supreme Court decisions over the years which have found the apportionments of seats in national elections to violate the right to vote contained in Article 15. Despite these findings the Court has never actually voided the results of those unconstitutional elections, on the grounds that the state of unconstitutionality no longer existed at the time it rendered its decision. The Court's willingness to narrowly define the rule at issue may also result in pyrrhic victories for plaintiffs. This was illustrated in the recent *Women-only Remarriage Prohibition Period Case*, discussed at Article 24, which saw the Court finding a discriminatory prohibition replaced by the same prohibition applying for a shorter period of time, based on the "correct math" involved in eliminating conflicting presumptions of paternity.

An additional point to note is that as a result of the various difficulties faced by plaintiffs in bringing constitutional challenges, actions based on the State Redress Act have come to play a fairly significant role in litigating constitutional rights. These are tort claims against the government—which the people have a constitutional right to bring under Article 17—that can be used to raise challenges against both government actions and legislation. With respect to the former, where an issue of standing or some other hurdle otherwise precludes challenging an administrative action, the plaintiff can still bring a case arguing for damages. Thus, for example, teachers arguing that rules which required them to sing the national anthem in school ceremonies violated their freedom of conscience under Article 19 framed their claim as an action for damages resulting from their punishment for refusing to comply with it.[13] Likewise, legislative action, or inaction, can also form the basis for a claim for damages where this results in the violation of a constitutional right. Even when successful such claims often only result in nominal damages,[14] with the real aim being to attain a declaration that the rule or act in question violated the constitutional right. With respect to legislation such a decision does not automatically result in the voiding of the rule, but is communicated to the Diet which is expected to take legislative action to remedy it.[15]

Article 10: Nationality

Sean McGinty

> **Article 10.**
> The conditions necessary for being a Japanese national shall be determined by law.

As it was under the Meiji Constitution, the first provision in the modern constitution's chapter on the rights and duties of the people deals with Japanese nationality. A notable textual difference between the two is that Article 18 of the Meiji Constitution refers to Japanese "subjects" (*shinmin*) while Article 10 of the current constitution refers to Japanese "nationals" (*kokumin*). This change was introduced in the GHQ Draft. The change, and the position of the provision at the beginning of the Chapter on rights and duties, are significant since in the Japanese text many of the rights and duties are expressed as being those of nationals (*kokumin*). In most English translations, however, these rights are expressed as belonging to the more ambiguous "the people."

"Determined by law"

The provision states that the conditions necessary for being a Japanese national are to be determined by law. Note that the Japanese term used for "conditions" is *yōken*, which might more appropriately be translated "requirements."

Article 10 has been implemented by the Diet's enactment of the Nationality Act which replaced the previous Meiji-era legislation. The Act defines both the conditions for acquiring Japanese nationality and for losing it. With respect to the former, the Act creates a *jus sanguinis* system by which the principal means of acquiring Japanese nationality is through birth to a Japanese parent. Prior to 1984 the Act had created a *jus paternis* system which only allowed the children of Japanese fathers to acquire Japanese nationality by birth, though this was amended by the Diet to grant nationality regardless of the gender of the Japanese parent following lower court rulings which found it unconstitutional but before the Supreme Court had the chance to consider whether this conflicted with the right to equality before the law under Article 14.

The Supreme Court has taken the position that owing to the complex factors that must be weighed in creating rules which determine who gains (or loses) membership among a nation-state's citizenship, Article 10 should be interpreted as giving the legislature a high level of discretion in determining the content of said rules.[16] A number of cases have however tested the boundaries of this discretion.

In the immediate postwar period the territorial dissolution of Japan's prewar empire created some difficulties with respect to loss of nationality in particular. During the prewar period residents of Korea (and also Taiwan) were considered Japanese nationals under international law, but under Japanese law they were registered in a separate family register system from those in the rest of Japan. When Japan renounced sovereignty over Korea and recognized its independence the question arose as to how this change of territory affected the nationality of those who resided therein, a subject which the Nationality Act (and the Treaty of San Francisco) did not directly address. This was tested in a 1961 case before the Grand Bench in which the appellant, who was born Japanese, had married a Korean man in the prewar period and been removed from her original family register and placed in his. Following the war people registered under the Korean family register system were stripped of their Japanese nationality, including the appellant who brought a case challenging this and seeking the recognition of her Japanese nationality.[17] The Court interpreted Article 10 as simply requiring that any changes in nationality connected with a change in territorial jurisdiction be established in law. The Court held that the scope of those who lost Japanese nationality as a result of the peace treaty was all those whom Japanese law had classified as Korean, via the Korean family register system. This system continued during the Occupation period as GHQ classified Koreans as foreign nationals, and the Japanese government began requiring them to register as such. Since this distinction was legally established, and the appellant was solely registered under the Korean family register, it dismissed her claim.

More recently, however, the Supreme Court has shown a willingness to limit the boundaries of the legislature's discretion in defining nationality, particularly when it infringes on other rights in the constitution and even to apply a higher standard of review. In the *Nationality Act Case*, the Supreme Court found one aspect of the Nationality Act's rule on the acquisition of nationality by birth to infringe Article 14 of the constitution. The appellant was the child born out of wedlock to a Japanese father and Filipino mother and had not been acknowledged by the father at or before the time of birth. The Act precluded the appellant from attaining nationality through the simple process of notification of the birth to the Minister, since the Act required a legal relationship with the Japanese parent at the time of birth (through acknowledgment before birth, which was lacking) and the only alternative route required legitimation (which was also lacking since the appellants' parents had never married). The Act created a distinction between the eligibility of children born out of wedlock to a Japanese father based solely on whether he acknowledges paternity before or after birth.

The Court found that the initial rationale for the requirement of either acknowledgment before birth or subsequent legitimation to obtain nationality were as a means of measuring the closeness of the ties between the child and Japan. While it held that such an objective was a reasonable exercise of legislative discretion, it also found that in light of social changes requiring legitimation could no longer be said to be reasonably relevant to that purpose. Thus, the statutory provision was held to violate Article 14 and the majority found that the proper remedy was to construe the relevant provisions as not requiring legitimation as a precondition to acquiring nationality.

More recently, however, the Court rejected Article 14 challenges to provisions of the Nationality Act and Family Register Act which resulted in the loss of citizenship for children born to Japanese parents abroad who failed to register a notice of intent to preserve Japanese citizenship within three months of birth.[18]

Article 11: The Enjoyment of Basic Human Rights

Sean McGinty

> **Article 11.**
> The people shall not be prevented from enjoying any of the fundamental human rights. These fundamental human rights guaranteed to the people by this Constitution shall be conferred upon the people of this and future generations as eternal and inviolate rights.

Article 11 introduces the notion of fundamental human rights (*kihonteki jinken*) and marks a significant break from the Meiji Constitution which had no equivalent provision. The individual rights enumerated in the Meiji Constitution were generally prescribed as being "within the limits of the law," meaning that they could be limited through ordinary legislation. One of the main aims of the American drafters of the new constitution was to elevate the rights contained therein so as to prevent their abrogation in that manner.

The Supreme Court has generally refrained from recognizing Article 11 as providing an independent basis for challenging legislation. This was tested early in the 1951 *Escaping Convicts Case* in which the appellants challenged the constitutionality of the provisions of the Penal Code that made escape by persons detained by judicial order a criminal offence on the grounds that this violated the natural right of human beings to seek their own freedom and thus Article 11's guarantee of fundamental human rights.[19] The Court, noting that Articles 31 and 34 of the constitution were premised on the notion that the detention of people was allowable provided certain conditions were met, dismissed the claim and found that Article 11 did not apply, without engaging in any discussion of its scope or meaning. Similarly in the *Siberian Prisoners Case* the 1st Petty Bench dismissed a state compensation claim brought by former Japanese prisoners of war held captive by the Soviet Union in Siberia for several years after the end of World War II.[20] They based their claim on, *inter alia*, breaches of their rights under Article 11 resulting from Japan starting, carrying out, and then losing the war (which resulted in their imprisonment). Again, in this case the Court refrained from addressing the Article 11 argument head on. Scholarly opinion has interpreted this as indicating it cannot be used as a cause of action. Another question to note in passing, though the courts have never had to deal with it, is whether the wording of Article 11 precludes the amendment of the other provisions containing rights, given that they are "eternal and inviolate."

Article 12: Responsibility for Rights and Freedoms

Sean McGinty

Article 12.
The freedoms and rights guaranteed to the people by this Constitution shall be maintained by the constant endeavor of the people, who shall refrain from any abuse of these freedoms and rights and shall always be responsible for utilizing them for the public welfare.

Article 12 has played an important role in judicial review by the courts for the compliance of laws and government actions with other rights in the constitution. It requires that the people refrain from "abuse" (*ran'yō*) of their rights, and that they always be used for the "public welfare" (*kōkyō no fukushi*). Both of these concepts also appear in Article 1 of the Civil Code and are familiar principles of Japanese private law, with the courts having developed doctrines which limited the use of private rights when they infringed on the rights of others. The Meiji Constitution contained no similar provision. The GHQ Draft contained a different phrasing, stating that the rights involved "an obligation on the part of the people to prevent their abuse and to employ them always for the common good."[21]

Public welfare

The phrase "public welfare" also appears in Article 13 and as a limit to specific rights enumerated in Articles 22 and 29. Its appearance in Article 12 in particular, which applies it to all constitutional rights in general, has been used by the Supreme Court as a standard which for the most part has been used to uphold legislation that otherwise conflicts with constitutional rights.

This was established in several cases in the 1950s and 1960s, when there were a number of challenges to local ordinances that required permits be obtained for public demonstrations.[22] The criminal convictions of leaders of political demonstrations who had not obtained permits were challenged on the basis that they violated Article 21's guarantee of freedom of speech and assembly. As discussed at Article 21, a 1960 Grand Bench ruling saw these restrictions upheld on public welfare grounds—they were reasonable and necessary to prevent demonstrations from becoming riots. Numerous other cases saw the Court reaching a similar conclusion (see related discussion at Article 21).

Another prominent case where Article 12 was used was the 1957 *Lady Chatterley's Lover Case* also discussed at Article 21 in which, upholding an obscenity conviction against the novel's translator, the majority opinion for the Grand Bench held that despite the fact that Article 21 contained no mention of public welfare, its mention in Article 12 (and 13) applied to all rights in the constitution.

In more recent years the Court has made less explicit reliance on public welfare in Article 12 as a limitation on other constitutional rights and mention of it has become rarer in Supreme Court decisions.

Article 13: Respect for Individuals and the Right to the Pursuit of Happiness

Tōru Enoki and *Mark Levin*

Article 13.
All of the people shall be respected as individuals. Their right to life, liberty, and the pursuit of happiness shall, to the extent that it does not interfere with the public welfare, be the supreme consideration in legislation and in other governmental affairs.

Historical background

The Meiji Constitution had no provision comparable to Article 13. The Meiji Constitution adopted German *Rechtsstaat* principles from the Prussian constitution of 1850, which allowed for a highly qualified notion of individual rights. Moreover, rights and freedoms did not inherently belong to individuals, but were granted to Japanese citizens by the State as subjects of the emperor who was sovereign. The emperor, as sovereign, sat above this structure with unlimited authority to rule the Japanese nation.

Thus, presented together with language clearly inspired by the US Declaration of Independence, Article 13's notion of respect for individuals is an obviously imported aspect of the nation's fundamental law. Article 13 (Article XII in the GHQ Draft) was initially conceived to accomplish the abolition of Japan's feudal system, one of MacArthur's three essential requirements for constitutional reform (also see discussion at Article 14). Although the explicit first sentence ("The feudal system of Japan shall cease") was removed by the Japanese side, the remaining text in the GHQ Draft was otherwise mainly unchanged in Japan's later negotiations and parliamentary proceedings. During these the notion of respect for individuals was never seriously challenged. Rather, the debate was about whether proposed Article 13 alone was sufficient to protect social welfare rights, thus obviating the need for the more concrete and specific language that ultimately appeared as Articles 25 through 28.

"Respected as individuals"

The first sentence of Article 13 establishes individualism as a fundamental principle of the constitution (one that is reiterated in Article 24). Reflecting this constitutional norm, respect for persons as individuals is reflected in the general order of private law through Article 2 of the Civil Code stipulates that "[t]his Code must be construed in accordance with honoring the dignity of individuals and the essential equality of both sexes."[23]

The right to the "pursuit of happiness"

The three concepts of "life," "liberty," and "the right to the pursuit of happiness" are distinguished, but since there is no practical use in making a distinction between them, they are understood as a unified concept and in many cases referred to collectively as the "right to pursue happiness." The constitution has detailed human rights provisions, but it can be said that they are also a list of important rights and freedoms that have historically been often violated by state power. Moreover, the enumerated constitutional rights do not cover all the human rights that may be necessary today. Therefore, even if rights and freedoms are not stipulated in the constitution, legal interests that are considered worthy of protection due to social changes are understood to be human rights guaranteed under the constitution as "new human rights." These are based on the right to the pursuit of happiness in Article 13. Moreover, it is a common theory and feature of judicial precedent that the right to the pursuit of happiness can be *a source of* concrete rights that can be remedied judicially, as discussed in more detail below.[24]

The scope of the right to the pursuit of happiness

With regard to what kind of "new human rights" can be derived from the right to the pursuit of happiness, there is a conflict in constitutional theories between (1) the personal autonomy theory (*jinkakuteki jiritsu setsu*) and (2) the general freedom theory (*ippanteki jiyūsetsu*). This conflict extends not merely to the scope of the right to the pursuit of happiness, but also the question of how to view it under the constitution.

The "personal autonomy theory" limits the coverage of the guarantee of the right to the pursuit of happiness to those interests indispensable for personal life. This theory holds that only those rights closely related to individual autonomy are recognized as human rights under the constitution. It also warns that if the coverage of constitutional human rights is expanded without limitation, it will lead to the inflation of human rights; even rights that do not deserve to be described as human rights, such as the freedom to walk or take a nap, would be guaranteed under the constitution. Finally, the theory also argues that excessive expansion of the scope of constitutional human rights guarantees will result in an overall weakening of the effectiveness of constitutional rights in general guarantees, since constitutional rights are supposed to be used at a critical moment.[25]

On the other hand, the "general freedom theory" states that the coverage of the right to the pursuit of happiness is a broad guarantee of general freedom of action. In light of the original purpose of civil liberties, which is to secure a free sphere for the individual against state power, free actions of the individual should be broadly guaranteed. The theory holds that limiting the scope of constitutional human rights guarantees will substantially weaken the effectiveness of the constitutional human rights guarantees.[26] This is because the state should not restrict the freedom to climb mountains, swim in the sea, or drive a car without a justifiable reason, even if such acts do not involve personal autonomy. Therefore, the broader the scope of protection the better. In a refinement of this theory, some scholars argue that the degree of constitutional protection should be relatively weakened for activities that do not implicate personal values, and that a more lenient standard of review should be used in cases involving restrictions on such activities.[27]

The conflict between these two theories continues, with the personal autonomy theory gaining majority acceptance among scholars. Regardless of which theory is applied, however, the relationship between Article 13 and other individual constitutional rights provisions is considered to be that of a general overarching provision and more specific provisions. Therefore, Article 13 is considered to be applicable only when it is not appropriate to apply other more specific constitutional rights provisions.[28]

Specific constitutional rights derived from the right to the pursuit of happiness

Various academic theories advocate the recognition of a number of "new human rights" derived from the right to the pursuit of happiness under Article 13, and many have been tested in court. These include the right to privacy, the right to the environment, the right to sunshine, the right to tranquility, the right to a view, the right to beach access, the right to be free from tobacco smoke exposure, the right to health, the right to information, the right to access, the right to peaceful existence (in conjunction with the Preamble), and the right to self-determination (including as may be associated with indigeneity).[29] In order for these "new human rights" to be recognized, the courts need to provide remedies for their violation based on the right to the pursuit of happiness. Given that the creation of new rights in line with the progress of society is the role of the Diet as a legislative body, the creation of "new human rights" by the courts may be inconsistent with that role. This is because when the courts create new rights, they are legislating passively, which is considered to be in conflict with the exclusive legislative power of the Diet (see discussion at Article 41). In point of fact, the only right deriving from Article 13 that has been explicitly recognized in Japanese Supreme Court jurisprudence is the right of publicity as a right of privacy.[30]

The right to privacy

While the right to privacy developed through doctrines ultimately expressed in the famous 1965 US Supreme Court decision of *Griswold vs. Connecticut* (which arose in the context of the freedom to obtain contraceptives), in Japan it came into focus with the 1964 judgment in the *After the Banquet Case*, in which a violation of privacy was asserted by a person depicted in Yukio Mishima's novel *Utage no Ato*.[31] In this case, the Tokyo District Court stated that "the so-called right to privacy is understood as a legal guarantee or right not to have one's private life disclosed to the public." However, the Tokyo court was upholding a private law right, not a constitutional one.

The right to privacy under private law, came to be widely recognized as a constitutional right through two Supreme Court decisions. First, the *Kyoto Prefectural Federation of Student Unions Case* involved a privacy-based challenge to the police taking pictures of persons participating in demonstrations. In response, the Supreme Court declared that:

> *As part of such citizens' freedom in private life, any person has the right not to have his face or appearance photographed without consent or good reason. Apart from whether or not such right can be referred to as right of portrait* [publicity], *it must be said at least that if a police officer, without good reason, has photographed the face or appearance of a citizen, such an act should be regarded as being in violation of the purport of Article 13 of the constitution and therefore it is unallowable.*[32]

While thus acknowledging the existence of a constitutionally protected right of privacy, the Court went on to find it was limited by the public welfare and had not been infringed in the case at bar.

Second, the *Criminal Record Inquiry Case* was a tort case against the state brought by a person aggrieved by a town mayor's improper disclosure of their criminal record. In upholding the claim for damages, the Supreme Court held that:

> *A criminal record and criminal history (hereinafter referred to as "criminal record, etc.") are matters directly related to a person's honor and credibility, and a person with a criminal record, etc. has an interest worthy of legal protection in not having it disclosed to the public.*[33]

Although the Supreme Court does not use the word "privacy," it is understood to have substantially recognized the right to privacy in relation to public authorities. In the *Kyoto Prefectural Federation of Student Unions Case*, the Supreme Court did not say that protection from taking photographs of an individual's appearance, etc. without his or her consent and without proper reason is *guaranteed* by Article 13 of the constitution, but instead acknowledged that it could be contrary to the purport (*shushi*) of Article 13. This a formulation considered to be a lower degree of protection than a clearly stated "guarantee." In the *Criminal Record Inquiry Case*, although the Court used the expression "interest worthy of legal protection" to describe privacy of criminal records, it did not explicitly describe it as a *constitutional* interest; it was merely referring to interests capable of protection through the State Redress Act (see Article 17).[34]

The right to informational privacy

As for the meaning of the right to privacy, it was originally taken in the negative sense of the right to exclude others from intruding into one's private sphere, as per the holding in the *After the Banquet Case*. More recently, however, there is also an emphasis on a positive right to control personal information about oneself, which includes an aspect of claiming protection of privacy against public authorities.

In this way, the right to privacy has gone from being understood as a "liberty aspect" (freedom from intrusions on privacy) to a liberty aspect combined with a "claim aspect" (the right to claim the protection of privacy against public authorities). This is also related to the fact that the protection of personal information has become an important issue. In today's society where a great deal of personal information is centrally managed by government agencies, it has become necessary for individuals to have some control over their own information and the ability to request that their information be reviewed, corrected, or erased. In order to realize this goal, the Act on the Protection of Personal Information Held by Administrative Organs was passed in 2003, at the same time as a general Personal Information Protection Act, which protects data privacy in commercial and other private law relationships.[35] These can be seen as legislative implementations of the privacy right aspects of Article 13.

It is important to note that a privacy case requires an element of state action to implicate constitutional rights. Japanese law also recognizes rights to privacy in the context of relations between individuals, but such cases are addressed in the realm of civil law and private tort damages rather than constitutional matters. However, given the overlapping considerations, scholars often look to the larger body of jurisprudence from private law to gain insights as to the how courts are likely to think about privacy in both the constitutional and private law settings.

This approach applies to the treatment of the right to information privacy in the Supreme Court's decision in the *Basic Resident Register Network Case*, which involved various challenges to the creation and maintenance by the government of a computerized resident register containing personal information about individual citizens. In it, the Supreme Court noted that "as one of individuals' [sic] liberties in private life, every individual has the liberty of protecting his/her own personal information from being disclosed to a third party or made public without good reason." Nonetheless, the Court held that the "act of an administrative organ to collect, manage or use identification information of inhabitants ... even in the absence of the consent of the individuals to such act, does not infringe their liberty of protecting their own personal information from being disclosed to a third party or made public without good reason, which is guaranteed under Article 13..."[36]

In the *Waseda University Jiang Zemin Lecture Case*,[37] the Court offered further guidance on its views of privacy in a civil action for damages without state action, but with implications helpful in ascertaining its views in comparable cases with state action. The case involved a speech at Waseda University (a private university) by the President of China. For security reasons, the university, disclosed to police the names, addresses, and telephone numbers of students who had applied to attend the lecture without obtaining their consent. The Supreme Court upheld an award of damages against the university, holding that that even though the personal information disclosed by it was not particularly sensitive, based on the reasonable expectation of the people to whom it pertained, it "should be legally protected as information concerning the appellants' privacy."

Personal rights

The term "personal rights" is used in a variety of ways and can also include the right to privacy and the right to self-determination. Personal rights (other than the rights to privacy and self-determination, which are discussed above and below) are defined as being interests related to honor, life, and health.

In the *Hoppō Journal Case* (also discussed at Article 21) the Supreme Court acknowledged that reputation is a personal right protected by Article 13 of the constitution. Personal rights have also been asserted in the context of the protection of daily life and health. In the *Osaka Airport Noise Pollution Case*, the Osaka High Court referenced Article 13 in granting a civil injunction based on personal rights against aircraft noise.[38]

Right of self-determination

Another right that can arguably be derived from the right to the pursuit of happiness is the "right of self-determination" (*jiko ketteiken*). This refers to the right to make decisions about one's private affairs without interference from public authorities. Since the constitution is based on the concept of "respect for the individual," each person must be guaranteed the right to decide how to live their own lives. It goes without saying that the state should not be allowed to force people to live in a certain way. For example, whether to get married, who to marry, who to live with, whether to have children, where to live, what kind of occupation to have—being able to decide these things is important when a person thinks about what kind of life they want to lead.

The Supreme Court has not clearly acknowledged the right to self-determination. However, academic theories consider it to be the fundamental essence of the right to pursuit of happiness under Article 13, although some consider it as a part of the right to privacy while others claimed it should be thought of as a distinct inherent right.

The scope of the theoretical guarantee of a right to self-determination differs depending on one's understanding of the scope of the guarantee of the right to the pursuit of happiness. Under the "personal autonomy theory" described above, it is understood that the constitution guarantees the right of self-determination in matters essential to the personal survival of the individual. The details vary from one commentator to another, but such matters can generally be categorized (1) the right of self-determination regarding reproduction (freedom to bear or not to bear children, contraception, abortion, etc.); (2) the right of self-determination regarding lifestyle (hairstyle, clothing, etc.); and (3) the right of self-determination regarding the disposition of life and body (refusal of treatment, euthanasia/death with dignity, etc.)[39]

On the other hand, under the "general freedom theory," all matters of self-determination are protected by the guarantee of the right to self-determination. Even from the standpoint of the theory of general liberty, there is a view that distinguishes between the core and the periphery of personal survival, with the reasonableness of regulations being examined moderately in the latter case. According to this view, it can be evaluated that the element of personal interest is added to the judicial standard review.[40]

Although the Supreme Court has not made any clear pronouncements on the right of self-determination, issues where it is implicated arise frequently in Japanese society. For example, Japanese junior high schools and high schools often require their students to wear school uniforms and prohibit various hairstyles/hair color. While challenges have been brought asserting that the freedom of students to choose their own hairstyle is within the scope of the right of an Article 13 right of self-determination, courts have rejected such arguments and upheld school regulations governing hair styles and the exercise of discretion by school principals in making decisions on such matters.[41] By contrast, academic constitutional theories consider the right to choose one's own hairstyle to be guaranteed by the right to self-determination under Article 13, as either a part of the right to the pursuit of happiness or under a theory of personal autonomy or general freedom.

Questions have also arisen in the medical context over whether patients have a legally protected right of self-determination over their treatment. In a case of a member of the Jehovah's Witnesses who had clearly expressed objections to blood transfusions but was given one during surgery, the Supreme Court avoided the constitutional argument but ruled the doctor liable for damages in tort as compensation for mental anguish resulting from the infringement of the right of patients to make decision about their medical treatment.[42]

Issues related to marriage and gender have also come to receive attention in the context of Article 13. For example, although freedom of marriage is guaranteed in Article 24 it has not been extended to include legal recognition of same-sex marriage, as has been the case in many western countries as well as Taiwan. Article 13 arguments have been used (unsuccessfully, so far) in court cases challenging the constitutionality of provisions in the Civil Code that do not allow same-sex marriage on the grounds that not doing this violates the constitutional protection of the freedom to marry the partner of one's choice (see Article 24).

With respect to gender, in 2003 the Diet passed the Act on Special Cases in Handling Gender Status for Persons with Gender Identity Disorder. Under it a person may change their gender for legal purposes subject to satisfaction of certain requirements, including the removal of any external genitalia of the former gender and absence or removal of any reproductive glands.[43] Although one could argue that this legal requirement unduly curtails a constitutional right to self-determination regarding gender, in 2019 the Supreme Court found no violation of Article 13 (or Article 14).[44]

Article 14: Equal Protection of the Law

Colin P.A. Jones

Article 14.

(1) All of the people are equal under the law and there shall be no discrimination in political, economic or social relations because of race, creed, sex, social status or family origin.

(2) Peers and peerage shall not be recognized.

(3) No privilege shall accompany any award of honor, decoration or any distinction, nor shall any such award be valid beyond the lifetime of the individual who now holds or hereafter may receive it.

Background

As with many western countries, Japan has struggled to accommodate the relatively recent normalization of broad legal egalitarianism. The Meiji period began with a transition from a rigid caste-like system with a hereditary imperial lineage, samurai as a hereditary ruling class and women at all levels of society accorded inferior status. The development of the Meiji constitutional system saw the formalization of a new, legally defined system of inequality: an imperial family with their own separate constitution (see Article 2), a hereditary aristocracy with special rights and privileges, voting rights conditioned on gender and (until 1925) wealth, and family laws favoring first born and legitimate males over everyone else in both inheritance rights and control over other family members. One area in which the Meiji leaders struggled with the adoption of foreign legal models—particularly from France, which in the latter half of the 19th century was considered to have the most sophisticated Civil Code, but had also seen its aristocrats guillotined under the banner of "equality" the previous century—was in family and inheritance. While largely forgotten as an issue in western countries today, equality of inheritance once had profound implications for agrarian societies, since the cumulative impact of the equal subdivision of farmland over generations threatened to render it all unproductive. In the Japanese historical context, this represented a threat to the source of the samurai's feudal stipends, and the subdivision of farmland (through inheritance or otherwise) was banned by the Tokugawa Shogunate as early as 1673.

The Meiji legal system dealt with this issue in part through formalized inequality; the imposition of a system of family law that required each household to register as a formal family unit with a designated head, typically the eldest legitimate male. Head of household was a heritable legal status that came with any hereditary titles (in the case of aristocrats) and control over and authority to dispose of family property, the ability veto entry to the family through marriages, adoptions or recognition of children born out wedlock involving other members of the household. Unsurprisingly, the Meiji Constitution contained no mention of equality or provisions condemning discrimination.

The elimination of hereditary privilege

Paragraphs 2 and 3 of Article 14 can be dealt with in short order. Though largely of historical interest today, both reflect fundamental principles of constitutional reform set forth in the MacArthur Notes: the elimination of the feudal aristocracy and hereditary privilege outside the greatly reduced imperial family.

The rejection of "peers and peerage" in paragraph (2) may seem redundant in English, but in Japanese involve distinct terms with very different origins but which are still largely interchangeable in the constitutional context of today.[45] As discussed at Chapter IV, the new constitution also resulted in the elimination of the House of Peers and its replacement with the elected House of Councillors.

Paragraph (3) not only backstops the prohibition on any form of hereditary privilege, but also prohibits the use the various honors bestowed by the emperor as a financial reward. This reflects the fact that prewar militarism was facilitated in part by a system of imperial honors for valor and victory that came with lifetime pensions.[46] That the honors now granted by the emperor pursuant to Article 7 are merely symbolic and decorative can be said to be a constitutional requirement.[47]

Equality under the law and the prohibition on discrimination

Unlike the Meiji Constitution, equality is mentioned in the constitution thrice; as a general principle in Article 14(1), in connection with spousal equality in Article 24(1), and the principle of gender equality in Article 24(2).[48] The present constitution also contains two proscriptions on discrimination: the general one in Article 14(1), and the one addressing voting rights in Article 44. Article 14(1), however, is the more important provision in connection with equal protection and discrimination, and as discussed below, has been at least one of the grounds for a majority of the small number of instances in which the Supreme Court has found a statutory provision unconstitutional.

Most laws routinely treat people differently for perfectly acceptable grounds: children are not allowed to drive cars, and only licensed doctors are permitted to perform appendectomies. Absent a mechanistic interpretation requiring absolute equality in all respects, the challenge for any equal protection regime is in identifying between permissible distinctions and unlawful discrimination. In an appeal involving alleged age discrimination in public employment, the Supreme Court offered the following interpretation of paragraph (1) of Article 14 as:

> *not guaranteeing the Japanese people absolute equality; rather, it should rather be understood as prohibiting discrimination without any rational basis for such discrimination. The provision thus does not reject differing treatment that is found to be rational based on the nature of the matter."*[49]

Article 14(1) appears to provide guidance in its enumeration of "race, creed, sex, social status or family origin" as prohibited bases for discrimination. Although some scholars have argued that the enumerated categories should be subject to a heightened degree of scrutiny, in the same 1964 ruling as the excerpt above, the Supreme Court indicated it considered them merely illustrative.[50] Nonetheless, a brief explanation of each category will help understand how equal protection is understood in the Japanese context.

Race

The vast majority of popular discourse in Japan about discrimination and inequality that in other countries would be framed in terms of race or ethnicity, tends to be framed in terms of a "Japanese-non-Japanese" dichotomy in which the "Japanese" side of the equation is implicitly portrayed as racially homogeneous. The reality is, of course, more complex. Japan has minority communities, including the Ainu people native to Hokkaidō, who have been subject to various forms of historical discrimination. Moreover, in the Japanese context even the conception of "race" makes discussion problematic. For example, due to its colonial legacy, Japan also has a small but significant community of people of Korean and Taiwanese heritage who have also suffered from prejudice and unequal treatment, in part because they were stripped of Japanese nationality at the end of the Occupation. Some might argue this is due in part to their citizenship rather than race, but that merely illustrates the complexity of the problem. Indeed, the common tendency to equate Japanese ethnicity (whatever that means) with Japanese citizenship is arguably part of the problem; some people of foreign origin who naturalize as Japanese citizens report finding themselves treated differently than other "Japanese people" because of their appearance. Japan is party to the International Convention on the Elimination of All Forms of Racial Discrimination. However, litigation involving race-based discrimination cannot be said to have played a significant role in the development of Article 14 jurisprudence.

Creed

Though sometimes used in a religious context, creed (*shinjō*) is understood to be a broader reference to ideology or philosophical outlook.[51] There is no significant jurisprudence on discrimination based on this category.

Sex

Listing sex in Article 14(1) may seem duplicative given the separate guarantee of gender equality in Article 24. However, the latter Article addresses sex (gender) in the context of family law. Article 14(1) thus represents a more expansive category and has been used by the Supreme Court and lower courts to invalidate gender-based discrimination in the context of employment and property rights.[52] Article 14(1) is also usually cited together with Article 24 in cases involving gender-based discrimination in family law (see discussion at Article 24). Gender discrimination has also been a factor in the transmission of Japanese nationality, as discussed in Article 10.

Social status

There are various theories as to what this category means, particularly as something distinct from some of the others enumerated in paragraph (1). The Supreme Court has unhelpfully defined it as "a status a person continuously maintains in society," though in the context of rejecting old age as an example of social status for purposes of the provision.[53] There has been little other helpful jurisprudence on this category.

Family origin

The Japanese term "*monchi*" is both more obscure than "family origin" as used in English and more expansive. It would include the prewar aristocracy,[54] and some of the other remnants of the Edo-period class structure that continued to have influence into the Meiji period. The most well-known instance of historical discrimination under this category involves the so-called *burakumin*, the descendants of pre-Meiji outcast communities that traditionally lived in separate hamlets (*buraku*) and engaged in occupations such as those involving the handling of dead bodies and butchering animals, which traditionally were considered religiously "unclean" activities.[55]

Nationality/alienage/national origin excluded

The enumerated categories of prohibited discrimination do *not* include nationality, alienage or national origin. This is mentioned as a reminder that, as discussed in the Chapter Introduction, in the Japanese version the entire constitution frames its guarantee of "human rights" as applying only to the Japanese people (*kokumin*). That this omission is not accidental is also clear from the drafting history: the GHQ Draft not only included "national origin" as an enumerated category of prohibited discrimination in the provision that became Article

14, but also a separate provision stating "Aliens shall be entitled to the equal protection of law." Both of these were excised through amendments requested by the Japanese drafters.[56]

This lack of clarity has resulted in a number of cases in which the Supreme Court has had to examine the applicability of constitutional guarantees of supposedly "fundamental human rights" to human beings who are not Japanese citizens. In the course of deciding these cases the Court has successfully developed a body of broad, benign-sounding statements about the general applicability of constitutional protections to non-Japanese without ever deciding in their favor.[57] In addition to approving the loss of visa status for participating in political demonstrations in the *McLean Case* (discussed in the Introduction to this Chapter), the Court has upheld discrimination against foreign nationals in the field of public employment (as discussed at Article 15), ability to re-enter the country (as discussed at Article 22) and eligibility for national pension benefits and other welfare programs, and entitlement to compensation for wartime harm and military service pensions.[58] As noted at Article 15, there have also been cases rejecting voting rights for non-citizens. Finally, the limiting of the family register system to Japanese citizens results in basic family law operating differently for Japanese and non-Japanese persons.[59]

Thus, despite the fine-sounding statements of general principle on the subject, there is quite literally no instance of a non-Japanese party prevailing in a case challenging legal discrimination against non-citizens. The possible exception might be the *Nationality Act Case* discussed at Article 10. Even that judgment, however, contains the somewhat discomforting statement that:

> *Japanese nationality is also an important legal status that means a lot to* people in order to enjoy the guarantee of fundamental human rights, [and] *obtain public positions or receive public benefits in Japan, and in this respect,* it constitutes the critical basis for enjoying fundamental rights." *(emphasis added).*

Equality in the courts

Article 14(1) is one of the more heavily litigated provisions of the constitution and as already noted accounts for the majority of cases where a statute has been found to violate the constitution. Although some of these are discussed elsewhere in this book, for reference the cases are as follows:

- *Lineal Ascendant Murder Case (1973).* Discussed later in this section.
- *House of Representatives Malapportionment Case I (1976).* See discussion at Article 15.
- *House of Representatives Malapportionment Case II (1985).* See discussion at Article 15.
- *The Nationality Act Case (2008).* See discussion at Article 10.
- *The Out-of-Wedlock Inheritance Rights Discrimination Case (2013).* Discussed later in this section.
- *The Women-only Remarriage Prohibition Period Case (2015).* See discussion at Article 24.

The Lineal Ascendant Murder Case

The *Lineal Ascendant Murder Case* is significant as the first instance of Japan's Supreme Court exercising its power to strike down statutory provisions on constitutional grounds. However, the details of the case and the rationale for the Court's judgment may puzzle some readers, particularly those accustomed to the more broad-based "heroic" jurisprudence of the US Supreme Court in *Brown v. Board of Education* and other famous Civil Rights-era cases.

Article 200 of Japan's Penal Code established the murder of a parent or other lineal ascendant as a discrete offense that was punished more severely than murder of anyone else.[60] The case involved a woman who had been sexually abused by her father for over a decade, starting from the age of fourteen. She was effectively forced to live as his wife and bore his children, but stayed in order to protect a younger sister. A co-worker proposed marriage to her and when she told her father he locked her up and raped her again. This drove her to kill him. She was, in short, a highly sympathetic defendant.[61]

The problem was that even applying all possible mitigating factors available under the Penal Code, she would still have to spend several years in prison. Moreover, the Court had upheld the constitutionality of the enhanced punishments for the murder of lineal ascendants in two separate 1950 Grand Bench judgments, and dozens of subsequent Petty Bench rulings.[62]

In 1973 the Grand Bench was able to strike down Article 200 not because it considered punishing some murders more harshly than others based on the existence of a particular family relationship between the killer and the victim, but because a bare majority of the Court's judges agreed that the limited range of severe punishments the provision imposed on killers of lineal ascendants went "far beyond the legislative purpose, and makes an unreasonable discrimination in comparison with the provided punishments...for an ordinary homicide."[63] Thus, rather than anything remotely close to the categories of prohibited discrimination enumerated in Article 14(1), the *Lineal Ascendant Murder Case* sees the Court finding unconstitutional discrimination in the range of possible sentences for murderers based on the status of their victims.[64]

It is possible to frame the Court as struggling with remnants of "traditional" family values and the Tokugawa-era Chinese-influenced system of criminal law in which the severity of punishments varied greatly depending on the family or social relationship between offender and victim. The majority mentioned this "ideological background" but only to the extent necessary to note Article 200 was rooted in a family system that had been "abolished" by the constitution.

Beyond demonstrating that the Court could actually use the powers given to it by the constitution, the case did not have a huge impact. The following year it rejected constitutional challenges to a similar provision of the Penal Code imposing heavier punishments on manslaughter (injury resulting in death) of lineal ascendants.[65] Both provisions remained in the Penal Code until it was overhauled in 1995.[66]

The Out-of-Wedlock Inheritance Rights Discrimination Case

Article 900 of Japan's Civil Code sets forth the statutory share of inheritance to which spouses, children and other relatives of a decedent are entitled, absent a testamentary disposition. Until the case was decided, clause (iv) of Article 900 contained a proviso to the effect that, as between children of the decedent born in and out of wedlock, the latter were entitled to only half the statutory share of children born during the marriage.

When challenged, the Supreme Court unanimously found the proviso to be void on the grounds it violated Article 14(1).[67] In addition to being a rare instance of the Court using its power to find a statute unconstitutional, the case is significant for several reasons.

First, like the *Lineal Ascendant Murder Case,* it is an even rarer instance of the Court reversing prior constitutional precedents. The Grand Bench had found the Article 900 provisions constitutional in 1995, as had no less than five Petty Bench decisions in subsequent challenges, the most recent in 2009.[68] Second, in reversing this prior decision, the Court in the 2013 inheritance case nonetheless upheld what by now could be called the "rational basis" test for the review of discriminatory provisions in statutes it first articulated in 1964, i.e., that Article 14(1): "should be interpreted as prohibiting any discriminatory treatment by law *unless such treatment is based on reasonable grounds in relation to the nature of the matter* (emphasis added)."[69]

Third, this meant that in order to find the Civil Code provision unreasonable after having previously found it reasonable, the Court referenced a number of factors including social change including attitudes towards marriage,[70] trends in other countries and Japan's ratification of the International Covenant on Civil and Political Rights and the Convention on the Rights of the Child,[71] and what might be called a form of legislative history.[72] While the validity of each of these grounds is debatable, together they present an interesting study in how the Court goes about justifying a reversal under a "rational basis" standard.

Finally, the Court limited the effect of its decision to only those cases involving estates that had not yet been settled. Given that the Court rendered judgment in 2013 on a case triggered by a death occurring in 2001, but for such a limitation it could have potentially resulted in the reopening of thousands of inheritance cases and a tidal wave of new disputes. This was the first instance of the Court structuring an unconstitutionality ruling in this fashion.

Other categories of discrimination

While the courts have heard numerous Article 14 challenges, other than the cases noted above, none have been successful. Nonetheless there are a few areas of recurring litigation worthy of brief mention. First, the Court has rejected challenges of what might be called "discrimination by geography" based on different prefectures having different ordinances, some with criminal penalties and prohibitions. The Court has rejected such challenges because such differences are an obvious consequence of the rights of local self-government provided in the constitution (see Chapter VIII).[73] The *Salaried Workers Tax Discrimination Case* saw the Court reject an Article 14 challenge to tax rules giving the self-employed greater scope for deducting business expenses than salaried workers. In addition, although Article 14(1) addresses discrimination by the state, courts have used Article 90 of the Civil Code to find discrimination by private parties void on public policy grounds.[74]

At the time of writing the Supreme Court has yet to issue any definitive rulings on Article 14 in connection with sexual orientation. The constitutionality of not allowing same-sex marriage has been reviewed by lower courts as discussed at Article 24. A damage claim against Tokyo prefecture for improper discrimination in not permitting a gay rights group to make reservations to utilize a prefectural facility was upheld by the Tokyo High Court but not appealed further.[75]

Equality outside the courts

It should be remembered that constitutional provisions like Article 14 are not just the province of the courts; they also serve as mandates to the legislative and executive branches. Various important statutes exist that are either intended specifically to remedy discrimination or ensure equal treatment in various spheres of social and economic activity.[76]

Article 15: The Right of the People to Choose Public Officials

Sean McGinty

Article 15.

(1) The people have the inalienable right to choose their public officials and to dismiss them.
(2) All public officials are servants of the whole community and not of any group thereof.
(3) Universal adult suffrage is guaranteed with regard to the election of public officials.
(4) In all elections, secrecy of the ballot shall not be violated. A voter shall not be answerable, publicly or privately, for the choice he has made.

Structure and language

Article 15 enshrines the right to vote and is thus one of the core provisions that implements the democratic principles of the constitution. It marks a significant shift from the Meiji Constitution which, while it did provide for an elected House of Representatives, did not specifically include a right to vote, with the general right to appoint and dismiss public officials instead being given to the emperor. The GHQ Draft (Article XIV) was structured differently from the final version, with the first paragraph originally also stating "The people are the ultimate arbiters of their government and of the Imperial Throne." This phrase was later dropped and the third paragraph guaranteeing universal adult suffrage was added in an amendment in the House of Peers.

The four paragraphs which constitute the article are drafted in a somewhat awkward order. The first and third paragraphs are often read together as forming the overall right to vote which is universal among adults (third paragraph) and applies to both choosing and dismissing public officials (first paragraph). The paragraph between those two on the other hand does not relate to voting per se but rather states that public officials are the servants of the "whole community." This has been significant in defining the role of public servants in relation to the public they serve and the rules which govern their actions particularly with respect to political activities. The fourth and final paragraph in turn provides that elections are to be held by secret ballot and protects voters from being answerable for their voting choices.

Some awareness is needed about the use of the term "officials" as used in Article 15 and elsewhere in the English version. In Articles 15, 16, 17, 36 and 99 the Japanese term is *kōmuin* ("public servant"), which is widely used in other statutes and public discourse. In Articles 7 and 73 the Japanese is *kanri*, an archaic term that is now rarely used, but which under the Meiji constitutional system referred to military and civilian officials whose appointment was a prerogative of the emperor.[77] In 93(2) an even more obscure term (*riin*) is used where the English is "local official."

Moreover, even within Article 15 the term "public officials" (*kōmuin*) appears three times. but despite using the same term in both the Japanese and English versions it is defined in two quite different ways. With respect to its use in the first and third paragraphs, which relate directly to the right to vote, it has been interpreted as only applying to those public officials for which either the constitution or other legislation provides elections be held (notably Diet members under Article 43). Its use in the second paragraph on the other hand, as discussed later, applies to government employees more generally. The first paragraph also uses the word "choose" (*sentei*) rather than "vote for" (*tōhyō*), a distinction that does not raise an issue. The right to dismiss public officials has, with the exception of the review of Supreme Court judges provided under Article 79 of the constitution, not generally been implemented and has been described as irrelevant. In the *Overseas Voter Right to Review Supreme Court Judges Case* the Grand Bench held that the right to review Supreme Court judges was of the same nature as the right to vote and that the same constitutional rights attached to voting also applied to the review of judges (see discussion at Article 79).

The right to vote

The main piece of legislation which implements the right to vote is the Public Offices Election Act (POEA), which lays down a set of extraordinarily detailed and arcane rules governing how campaigns and elections function, and refers to the constitution in its first article.

The question of who is excluded from the right to vote under the first and third paragraphs of Article 15 has been tested in several Supreme Court decisions. In a 1955 case the Grand Bench found that a provision of the Public Offices Elections Act which deprived persons convicted of certain election-related offences from voting or running in elections was constitutional.[78] In a subsequent case the 2nd Petty Bench, making reference to the language in the constitution's Preamble and its holding in the *McClean Case*, has also specified that the right to vote is one of those reserved for Japanese nationals (*Nihon kokumin*) and thus does not extend to foreign nationals, upholding the provisions of the Local Autonomy Act which limited voting rights to Japanese citizens.[79] The 3rd Petty Bench carried this further in a subsequent case which tested the fact that Article 93 of the constitution requires local officials to be elected by "residents" (*jūmin*) finding that this should be interpreted as referring to Japanese nationals resident in the area of the local election.[80] The Court did, however, find that the constitution did not preclude measures which would allow foreign residents to vote in local elections, a conclusion that would seem to conflict with its finding that voting rights are exclusively held by Japanese nationals. In a 2005 case the Grand Bench found that the provisions of the POEA which precluded Japanese nationals living abroad from voting in the October 20, 1996 national elections due to their lack of a registered address within a voting district was in violation of the right to vote in Article 15.[81] In the *Yahata Steel Political*

Contribution Case discussed in the Introduction to this Chapter, the Court has held that political contributions by corporations do not infringe the right of natural persons to vote.

Another question which has arisen is the obligation on the state to make voting accessible. The Court has considered the matter in the context of a tort claim against the state in the *Postal Voting Case*, discussed at Article 17. Voting accessibility was further tested in a 2006 case in which the plaintiff had difficulty leaving home to vote at a polling station due to mental illness.[82] Though the Court dismissed the claim it did acknowledge that restrictions on exercising the right to vote were in principle not permitted and the state was under an obligation to take measures to enable citizens to exercise this right.

The Malapportionment Cases

Another important question the Supreme Court has had to deal with on numerous occasions over the decades is the disparity in the weight of votes across voting districts (sometimes referred to collectively as the *Malapportionment Cases).* Throughout most of the postwar era there has been a large gap in the proportion of voters to representatives between rural and urban areas which has greatly favored the former and, by extension, the ruling Liberal Democratic Party which has long relied on the rural vote. This is in large part due to the gradual migration of the population from the countryside to the city in the decades since the apportionment of seats was first set in 1950 which readjustments at regular five-year intervals have failed to keep pace with.

In the 1972 House of Representatives election the discrepancy was as high as 5:1 between some districts, meaning that some Diet seats represented five times as many voters as others.

In the *House of Representatives Malapportionment Case I*, the Grand Bench held that the right to vote, read in conjunction with Article 14's guarantee of equality before the law, required equality of the value of each citizen's vote as well. The Court, recognizing the practical difficulties it would present, held that this did not require precise mathematical equality between every vote cast. The Diet was thus recognized as having some discretion in setting rules on apportionment, taking into account factors such as size, population density, transportation considerations and the composition of residents. The Court did however find that the POEA allocation of House of Representatives seats resulted in a discrepancy in vote weight under the system used was severe enough and had continued un-remedied long enough that it violated the constitution. The Court thus ruled the apportionment unconstitutional though it did not void the results of the election as a remedy on the ground that invalidating the election would leave the nation without a Diet to pass the laws necessary to remedy the problem.

In the *House of Representatives Malapportionment Case II,* the Grand Bench again found an apportionment scheme (this time one resulting in a discrepancy of as high as 4.4:1) was unconstitutional on the same grounds, again with the results of the elections being allowed to stand.

In 1994, in part to ameliorate this problem, Japan's electoral system was substantially changed introducing a dual system in which the majority of seats in each were elected by a single seat constituency system (in the House of Representatives) or multi member district system (in the House of Councillors) while the remainder in both were elected through a proportional representation system based on the votes each party received. Elections for both are held simultaneously with voters casting separate votes in each, one for a candidate in their single seat constituency or multi member district and one for a party in the proportional representation system. The same reform aimed at keeping the maximum discrepancy in vote weight below a 2:1 ratio.

This reform did not completely resolve the problem, and cases challenging elections based on voting weight discrepancies have remained regular features of the Supreme Court docket. The August 30, 2009 elections which featured a maximum disparity of roughly 2.3:1 were challenged with a particular focus on a rule that automatically granted every prefecture a single seat in the House of Representatives apportionment of the single seat constituency system and only apportioned the remainder according to population, a practice which inflated the seat totals for low population prefectures. The Grand Bench found that this rule had "become contrary to the constitutional requirement of equality in the value of votes," but that since it could not be said that the problem had not been addressed "within a reasonable period of time as required by the constitution," there was no constitutional violation.[83] Similar results effectively "contrary to the constitution but not unconstitutional" have resulted in other challenges, including cases challenging House of Representatives elections in 2012, 2016 and 2017.[84] This middle ground enables the Court to signal the Diet the need to fine tune the electoral scheme.

The dual voting system introduced in the 1994 reform also raised several other questions with respect to its conformity with the voting right in Article 15 separate from the apportionment issue. Three of these, which related mainly to the fact that some candidates could simultaneously run as candidates in the single seat constituency race and also be named on their party's list for the proportional representation election, were raised as objections before the Grand Bench in a challenge against the 1996 Diet elections.[85] The first was that the system allowed a candidate who lost their election as a stand-alone candidate to nonetheless end up in the Diet through their being named on their party's list in the proportional representation portion. The second issue was that at the time voting took place the ranking of the party lists in the proportional representation election could not be known since it depended on the outcome of the single seat constituency elections being held at the same time. Third, not all candidates could run in both election systems since the proportional representation one was only open to political parties that met certain qualifying criteria. Thus an independent candidate could only run in the single constituency system, while a candidate affiliated with a qualifying party would be given a second opportunity to win a seat in the event that they lost as a single constituency candidate and were on their party's list for the proportional representation system. While noting that the right to stand as a candidate was an important ancillary of the right to vote which would be violated if it were limited without reasonable grounds, the Court held that owing to the significance of political parties in the national political system, the dual system fell within the discretion that the Diet was afforded to determine the particular mechanics of elections and dismissed these objections.

With respect to voting rights, Article 15 also accounts for two of the Supreme Court's rare unconstitutionality rulings; the *Overseas Voting Rights Case* (see discussion at Article 17) and the *Overseas Voter Right to Review Supreme Court Judges Case*. Voting rights in Diet elections are also discussed further at Article 44, and Supreme Court judicial retention elections at Article 79.

"Servants of the whole community and not of any group thereof"

While as noted earlier "public officials" in the first and third paragraph of Article 15 is interpreted narrowly, the same term in the second paragraph applies more broadly to civil servants in general. Their special status as "servants of the whole community" under that paragraph has been used to justify the imposition of limits particularly on their political activities which has sometimes created tension with other rights guaranteed by the constitution. The Supreme Court has upheld these restrictions with the result that one of the main effects of the second paragraph of Article 15 has been to severely curtail the ability of civil servants to participate in political activities.

Rules contained in the National Public Service Act, and in regulations thereunder which establish standards for members of the national public service, have been the source of most of the litigation before the Supreme Court which has tested the meaning of the second paragraph of Article 15. In a 1973 judgment the Court held that the Act's ban on strikes and work to rule campaigns by civil servants did not violate their right to collectively bargain guaranteed by Article 28 of the constitution mainly based on their special position as defined by the second paragraph of Article 15.[86] The majority of the Grand Bench found that restrictions on fundamental rights of civil servants are justified when there are reasonable grounds to impose them. Since strikes and similar acts could lead to the interruption of public services, leading to a negative impact on the common interest of the community, allowing such actions would be inconsistent with their special status and thus the restrictions on them were upheld. A concurring opinion which disagreed with the majority's conclusion on the point noted this interpretation of the second paragraph of Article 15 seemed to impose an absolute duty of obedience on public servants, which in light of the "and not of any group thereof" proviso at the end of the paragraph seemed to go far beyond what the intention of the paragraph actually was (to prevent bias for a specific group in the provision of public services).

Somewhat oddly, the special status of civil servants under paragraph (2) of Article 15 has also created a conflict with the voting rights contained in paragraphs one and three of the same Article. In order to maintain the political neutrality of the civil service in keeping with the second paragraph of Article 15 the National Public Service Act imposes a very broad prohibition on civil servants engaging in political activities of any sort other than exercising their right to vote. In a 2012 case, the Supreme Court confirmed the conviction of a bureaucrat at the Ministry of Health, Labour and Welfare for violating this rule by distributing copies of the Japan Communist Party's newsletter in mailboxes at a public housing facility during his personal time.[87] In his appeal he argued that the excessively broad nature of the ban had the effect of undermining the right of civil servants to choose their public officials by limiting their participation in the democratic process to the mere act of voting itself.

The 2nd Petty Bench held that while the objective of ensuring the neutral administration of the national government was a reasonable one, the necessity and reasonableness of the prohibition in achieving this end had to be weighed against the importance of the right being restricted. By interpreting the prohibition as only applying to acts that posed a substantial risk of undermining the political neutrality of public officials in the performance of their duties, the Court held that it was not excessive and was constitutional. After weighing several factors—the appellant's position, whether the act occurred during work hours, whether public facilities were used, whether he took advantage of his position as a public official when doing them, whether the act could be construed as being official—it found that it fell within the acts prohibited and thus upheld his conviction.

Citizenship requirements for public servants

In the *Tokyo Prefecture Managerial Qualification Exam Case*, the Supreme Court upheld the use of rules excluding non-Japanese citizens from public service positions involving the exercise of state power.[88] The case involved a prefectural employee of Korean heritage (see discussion at Article 14) who worked for the Tokyo prefectural government and applied to take the test for advancement into managerial roles. The request was refused on the grounds that she was not a Japanese citizen. The Court upheld the restriction, finding it reasonable and consistent with the overarching principle of popular sovereignty of the Japanese people.[89]

Secrecy of voting

Paragraph (4) of Article 15 protects the secrecy of voting. This is implemented through the POEA, which *inter alia* requires voters to fill in the name of their choice by hand.[90] There is mixed jurisprudence on the subject of the degree to which ballot and their provenance can be investigated for purposes of investigating electoral crimes.[91]

Article 16: The Right to Petition

Sean McGinty

> **Article 16.**
> Every person shall have the right of peaceful petition for the redress of damage, for the removal of public officials, for the enactment, repeal or amendment of laws, ordinances or regulations and for other matters; nor shall any person be in any way discriminated against for sponsoring such a petition.

While the Meiji Constitution stated that subjects of the emperor could present petitions provided the proper form was respected, it did not provide a right to do so. The right to peaceful petition was newly introduced in the GHQ Draft whose version became the final Article 16.

The right is implemented through the Petition Act, which establishes a process by which petitions are to be brought to the government agency having jurisdiction over the subject matter of the petition and requires that they be dealt with in good faith by the receiving body.[92] The Act also provides that petitions may be addressed to the emperor via the Cabinet. Additionally, Chapter Nine of the Diet Act establishes a process by which petitions may be brought to either house of the Diet and Articles 124 and 125 of the Local Autonomy Act establish a similar process for local governments. Though in the *Sarufutsu Case* the Supreme Court referred to the right to petition as being among one of the fundamental human rights found in the constitution that are important to political activities, it has never interpreted its meaning.

Article 17: The Right to Seek Redress Against the State

Sean McGinty

> **Article 17.**
> Every person may sue for redress as provided by law from the State or a public entity, in case he has suffered damage through illegal act of any public official.

Article 17 provides that every person may sue the State or a public entity for damages owing to illegal acts by any public official. This was a significant departure as the Meiji Constitution contained no equivalent provision and prewar legislation explicitly excluded the state and public officials from civil liability for official acts. The provision did not appear in the GHQ Draft either but was rather introduced through an amendment in the House of Representatives.

The term "illegal act" (*fuhō kōi*) is the same term used in Chapter V of the Civil Code to describe torts and is understood in basically the same way—the provision covers claims for compensation for damages caused by actions of the state or public officials in the exercise of their official duties. The main piece of legislation implementing this provision is the State Redress Act. Article 1 of the Act provides for the liability of the State or a public entity for damages unlawfully caused either negligently or intentionally by a public official in the exercise of their duties. Article 2 further makes the State liable for damages resulting from defects in the placement or administration of roads, rivers or other public structures. In addition to being used for run-of-the-mill compensation claims for damages due to the negligence of public officials, the Act has also come to play a role in the litigation of constitutional rights in cases framed as damages claims for government actions (or failures to act, including legislatively) that have violated the rights of the plaintiff.

"Every person"

The article applies to "every person" which suggests that it is one of the rights which applies not just to Japanese nationals but also to foreign nationals as well. Article 6 of the State Redress Act complicates this, however, as it states that when the victim is a foreign national the Act only applies when there is comity (which is to say when the law of the victim's home state provides the same rule). The Supreme Court has never ruled on whether this seeming inconsistency violates Article 17, though lower courts have not found it to do so.[93] A particular complication arises from the fact that a large number of Korean nationals reside in Japan, mostly descendant from residents who lost Japanese citizenship after the war (as discussed at Article 10). While South Korea does provide a similar guarantee in its law, North Korea does not. Lower courts have gotten around this since both Koreas recognize each other's citizens as their own and thus have recognized everyone with a Korean nationality as being able to sue under the State Redress Act.

"Public officials"

Both Article 17 and the State Redress Act make it clear that an action seeking damages lies against the state or public entity itself and not with the public official in their personal capacity.[94] Where the acts complained of were not conducted as part of their official duties, the injured party may seek damages from a public official directly using the regular rules of tort under the Civil Code.

Article 17 uses the term "public official" (*kōmuin*) which, as with its use in Article 15, raises the question of who qualifies as such. Particularly with Article 17 an issue has been whether or not this extends to lawmakers (a category of "public official") as well as unelected civil servants. The liability of the Diet in carrying out its legislative duties was tested in a 1985 case before the 1st Petty Bench commonly known as the *Postal Voting Case*, in which the appellant sought damages from the state owing to the Diet's revocation, and failure to later re-instate, a voting system that allowed those with physical disabilities to vote from home. Separate from the issue of whether the constitution required such a system was the question of whether the State would be liable to compensate an individual for damages (in this case for mental anguish resulting from his inability to vote) for its failure to enact legislation that was necessary to ensure constitutional rights (in this case the right to vote under Article 15 and the equality right under Article 14). The Court held that as a general principle, legislative acts of the Diet (or failures to act) are not subject to liability under the State Redress Act, but it noted that this did not apply in exceptional cases where laws that clearly violated the fundamental principles of the constitution were passed.

While it dismissed the appeal on the grounds that the constitution did not require the Diet to implement such a voting system, the exception it created established a precedent for a form of constitutional litigation: the use of the State Redress Act to seek compensation for "failure to legislate." One example of this was the 2005 *Overseas Voting Rights Case*—one of the rare instances of the Court finding legislation unconstitutional—in which the appellants successfully challenged the constitutionality of electoral rules which had the effect of excluding Japanese nationals residing abroad from voting in Diet elections. The Grand Bench found this exclusion to violate Article 15(1) and (3), Article 43(1), and the proviso of Article 44 and awarded a nominal 5,000 Yen in compensation under the State Redress Act for the Diet's failure. The judgment also confirmed that the plaintiffs had the right to participate as voters registered abroad in the next Diet elections.

In addition to legislation itself, liability for statements by Diet members during deliberations has also been litigated. In the *Hospital Director Suicide Case* the 3rd Petty Bench dealt with a case in which damages from the State were sought for negative statements a lawmaker had made in the Diet about the director of a hospital, who later committed suicide. While Article 51 of the constitution provides immunity from liability to lawmakers for statements made in the Diet, the Court noted this immunity did not extend to the State itself. Though it dismissed the claim on the facts, the Court found that the State would be liable for damages for statements by a Diet member alleging facts for an illegal or inappropriate purpose unrelated to their duties or where they knowingly made false statements.

Judges may also be "public officials" for purposes of Article 17. In the *Courtroom Note-Taking Case*, discussed at Article 21, the Grand Bench dismissed the appellant's claim for state redress, but indicated a claim might be possible if a judge was markedly unreasonable in the exercise of authority.

The Postal Act Case

Article 17 also accounts for one of the Supreme Court's unconstitutionality rulings; the 2002 *Postal Act Case*, which tested the extent to which the state could legislatively limit its liability for negligence. At the time, the postal service was run by the government and the Postal Act granted the service almost total immunity from claims under the State Redress Act in connection with its handling of the mail, and tightly limited who could raise claims in the few exceptions that applied.[95] This was challenged in a case involving a court order sent via special delivery (as required by the Code of Civil Procedure) to a financial institution to attach the proceeds of a debtor's bank account. However, the post office failed to deliver it properly and the resulting delay gave the debtor time to withdraw the funds, resulting in a significant loss to the appellant, who challenged the Postal Act immunity from tort liability as violating Article 17.

In its ruling, the Court noted that while Article 17 should be interpreted as giving the legislature discretion in determining the conditions for claiming redress from the State and what acts would be compensable, this discretion was not unfettered. Rather it had to be weighed in consideration of factors including the nature and extent of the interest being infringed, the scope of the exemption from liability, the legitimacy of the purposes of the exemption and its necessity in achieving those purposes. The Court found that while the purpose of the Postal Act immunity provision was legitimate in that it facilitated the operation of a low-cost postal service, excluding the post office from liability even for gross negligence or intentional acts and for mishandling particularly important mail sent by special delivery, was excessive and went beyond what was necessary to achieve that purpose and thus violated Article 17. It remanded the case for further fact finding. Its willingness to rule against the government in this case may in part be explained by the importance of the post office not just to business but also to the judicial system itself, since it is used by the court system to serve process and other court documents on litigants by special delivery, and thus at least that part of it needs to be reliable for the courts to function.

Article 18: Involuntary Servitude Prohibited

Sean McGinty

> **Article 18.**
> No person shall be held in bondage of any kind. Involuntary servitude, except as punishment for crime, is prohibited.

Article 18 is a slightly revised version of Article XVII of the GHQ Draft, the first sentence of which also mentioned enslavement and serfdom specifically. The Meiji Constitution did not prohibit bondage or involuntary servitude and in fact contained a provision that all subjects were amenable to service in the army or navy. While owing to the existence of Article 9 the question has never been tested in court, Article 18 would likely preclude military conscription in Japan.

The Japanese term used to express "bondage" in the first sentence is *doreiteki kōsoku*, which might be more accurately rendered "the bondage of slavery."

The qualifier in the second sentence "except as punishment for crime" is an important one since one of the main forms of punishment under the Japanese Penal Code has long been "imprisonment with labor."[96] Early cases before the Supreme Court found that ordinances prohibiting public officials from going on strike do not infringe the prohibition on involuntary servitude.[97] More recently it considered whether the lay judge (*saiban'in*) system introduced in 2009 under which trials for certain serious crimes are tried by a panel partially composed of lay persons drawn from voter rolls constituted a form of involuntary servitude.[98] While noting that being appointed as a lay judge imposed a certain burden, the Court characterized it as being more like the conferral of the authority to participate in the exercise of judicial power rather than a form of servitude and dismissed the claim, though it did not provide a clear definition of what *would* constitute involuntary servitude.

Article 19: Freedom of Thought and Conscience

Sean McGinty

Article 19.
Freedom of thought and conscience shall not be violated.

Article 19 guarantees freedom of thought and conscience. The Meiji Constitution contained no equivalent provision, with the concept being introduced in the GHQ Draft. Freedom of thought had been severely curtailed by prewar legislation, and further limited during the wartime period. Article 19 was intended as a rejection of such restrictions.[99]

Throughout the constitution's existence the Supreme Court has proven itself adept at finding an eclectic group of laws, ordinances and other government actions to not be in violation of Article 19. These have included a law requiring people to join the public health insurance scheme,[100] an ordinance restricting the ability of acupuncturists to make certain claims in their advertisements,[101] the use of public funds to pay for a ceremony honoring a local politician for his appointment to the Cabinet,[102] court orders requiring the losing defendant in a defamation case to publish apologies,[103] and a junior high school principal writing unflattering comments about a student's participation in political protests in a recommendation letter for high school applications.[104]

Whose right and against whom?

In the 1973 *Mitsubishi Resin Case*, the Grand Bench ruled that Article 19, and indeed constitutional rights generally, do not apply against the actions of private parties.[105] The appellant in that case had been dismissed from his job with a private corporation after it discovered that he had been involved with left wing groups during his days as a student. The appellant challenged his dismissal on the basis that it violated his rights under Article 19 (as well as Article 14). The Court dismissed the claim, holding that these rights only applied to government actions.

In the 1996 *Southern Kyūshū Tax Accountant Association Case*, however, the 3rd Petty Bench held that a resolution of a regional professional association approving the collection from members of a special fee to be used for making donations to a political party was invalid as it violated the Article 19 rights of its members.[106] Distinguishing the situation from corporate political contributions in the *Yahata Steel Political Contribution Case* (see Chapter Introduction), the Court noted that the association in the latter case was not a purely private body but one in which tax accountants were required by law to be members of in order to practice a licensed profession and thus it was beyond its purpose to make political contributions, even if they were for the purpose of influencing tax law and policy.

Reading, books and freedom of thought and conscience

The Supreme Court expanded on the meaning of freedom of thought and conscience in a line of cases that involved restrictions on prisoners' access to reading materials. In the *Yodogō Hijacking News Redaction Case* the appellants, detained members of militant left-wing groups, claimed that redaction of articles about a hijacking by another left-wing militant group from the papers they were allowed to read in jail violated their rights under Article 19 (Articles 13 and 21).[107] At issue was whether the freedom to access information and ideas, such as by reading newspapers or books, was an essential part of freedom of thought and conscience itself. The Court held that it was, noting that the freedom to absorb knowledge and opinions was key to developing a person's conscience and thought in the first place and necessary to realize the basic principles of a democratic society. While it did find that this "freedom to read" existed, it also noted that it was not an absolute right and could be subject to reasonable restrictions necessary for the public interest, in this case the maintenance of order in detention facilities. The provision in the Prisons Act under the authority of which the restrictions on reading were based would comply with the constitution if interpreted as only allowing them to the extent they were necessary to fulfill that interest, which the Court found to be the case. In a similar case in 1993 involving a prisoner being refused permission to read a book critical of prisons, the 2nd Petty Bench referenced the reasoning of the *Yodogō Hijacking News Redaction Case* to reach the same conclusion.[108]

In addition to the right to read, the Supreme Court has also curiously extended its interpretation of Article 19 to a right of authors themselves to have their books available to be read. In a 2005 case a librarian in Funabashi city had removed from the public library and discarded several books by a publisher of history textbooks on the grounds that she disagreed with their content. The association of authors brought a claim under the State Redress Act, arguing that this action violated their rights under Articles 13, 19 and 21 of the constitution.[109] The 1st Petty Bench agreed, finding that in light of authors' freedom of thought and conscience under Article 19 they had a legally protected interest in having their books available in public libraries which would be infringed if their works were removed in an unfair manner.

The national anthem and flag cases

Japan used a song called *Kimigayo* as a national anthem and its familiar flag (called the *hinomaru*) as a national flag since before World War II. However, it was not until 1999 that the government passed legislation which officially designated them as Japan's national anthem and flag, respectively. Owing to their association with Japan's wartime past (and, in the case of *Kimigayo*, the emperor system), this was not without controversy and was a subject of some disagreement across Japanese society. Following the enactment of the law the school boards in several prefectures introduced rules that formalized the use of both in public schools, including at graduation ceremonies. These were met with significant expressions of dissent by some teachers who objected to their use. Tokyo Prefecture's rules, in particular, not only required teachers to actively participate in the singing of *Kimigayo* during ceremonies, but also required schools to monitor compliance by teachers and report and punish those who failed to do so. Punishments meted out to teachers who failed to comply were the subject of a significant amount of litigation which raised the question of whether requiring someone to sing a song which they fundamentally objected to breached their right to freedom of thought and conscience under Article 19, several of which made their way to the Supreme Court.

In the first of these, the *Kimigayo Piano Accompaniment Case*, the plaintiff was a music teacher at an elementary school who had been reprimanded for refusing to play *Kimigayo* on the piano during the school's entrance ceremony. She did so partially on the grounds of her objection to its association with Japan's wartime aggression and partly on the grounds that she felt playing it without explaining the historical context to children violated their rights to an education (as an interesting alternative she also objected to the fact that musically the song was not intended to be performed on a piano). Over a strong dissent, the majority opinion characterized these as the appellant's views on history or the world and held that her refusal to play could not be inseparably connected with those views nor could the order be construed as denying them. Since playing the song was a common part of school ceremonies, it held the order to play could not be seen as forcing someone to have a particular thought or preventing them from holding one, but rather it was merely forcing them to perform obligatory duties and thus did not violate their rights under Article 19. This seemingly circular logic—if you are ordered to do something which goes against your conscience it cannot go against your conscience because you were ordered to do it—which was in part justified by the special status of public officials under the second paragraph of Article 15—was questioned in a dissenting opinion.

In 2011 a further trio of cases involving public school teachers who had refused to stand and sing *Kimigayo* during school ceremonies and been reprimanded in some way as a result, worked their way to the Supreme Court. Two of the cases were decided by the 3rd Petty Bench[110] while the other the 1st Petty Bench.[111] The majority opinion in each largely followed the same reasoning as the *Kimigayo Piano Accompaniment Case* while further developing the jurisprudence. The judgments went further however and acknowledged that forcing someone to stand and sing a song which they fundamentally disagreed with might indirectly impinge their freedom of thought and conscience by forcing them to externally manifest a thought which they disagreed with. Weighing this against the public interest, however, the Court found it to be no match for the need for school ceremonies to function smoothly and for teachers to be mindful of their special status as public officials under

Article 15 and thus the requirement was to be reasonably justified and thus not a violation of the teachers' Article 19 rights. Justice Mutsuo Tahara, who had sided with the majority in the piano teacher case, dissented in two of these cases, noting that the majorities failed to draw a distinction between standing and singing, the latter of which was arguably irrelevant to the smooth functioning of the ceremony and very directly created a conflict between the person's thoughts and conscience on the one hand and their actions on the other.

Article 20: Freedom of Religion; Separation of Religion and State

Frank S. Ravitch

Article 20.

(1) Freedom of religion is guaranteed to all. No religious organization shall receive any privileges from the State, nor exercise any political authority.

(2) No person shall be compelled to take part in any religious act, celebration, rite or practice.

(3) The State and its organs shall refrain from religious education or any other religious activity.

On its face Article 20 seems to provide strong protection for the free exercise of religion and a strong barrier against government support for religion. The reality is a bit more complex.[112]

Historical overview

Under Article 28 of the Meiji Constitution religious freedom for the Japanese people existed in theory, but as a practical matter it could be seriously limited when the government viewed a religious belief or practice to be outside the "limits not prejudicial to peace and order, and not antagonistic to their duties as subjects." Thus, citizens could be forced to take part in religious ceremonies supporting State Shintō (even if they were Christians, for example) and they could be punished due to their religious objections to State Shintō, militarism or other government policies.[113]

State Shintō was a government-created version of Shintoism that was blended with nationalism and fealty to the emperor. It placed the emperor and imperial ancestors at the center of belief, in stark contrast to traditional Shintō, which tends to focus more on local *kami* and family ancestors.[114] When GHQ was involved in drafting and negotiating the new Japanese constitution a significant focus was limiting the support for, and impact of, State Shintō as well as supporting religious freedom. Article 20 was created to protect religious freedom, but also to keep the government from promoting or supporting religion. Article 89 also furthers the latter goal.

Freedom of religion

As Article 20 states clearly in the first sentence, "freedom of religion is guaranteed to all." What freedom of religion means in practice, however, often comes down to whether those who practice a particular religion can gain an exemption from state action that places a significant burden on a religious practice and whether government can interfere with religion in other ways. Article 20 has served religious practitioners well in the context of religious exemptions, but the story is a bit more mixed in other contexts.

Perhaps the most famous case decided, at least in part, under Article 20 is the *Jehovah's Witness Kendō Refusal Case*.[115] In that case, which has become famous not just in Japan, but among constitutional law and law and religion scholars around the world, a municipal technical college in Kobe was the defendant in a suit brought by a student whose Jehovah's Witness faith prevented him from engaging in *kendō* (a martial art), one of the college's physical education requirements. This resulted in the student being unable to graduate and ultimately being expelled for failing to satisfy the requirement.

On appeal in an administrative suit challenging this disposition, the Supreme Court reasoned that for everyone to have the rights as expressed in the education laws and under the constitution (see Article 26), religious accommodations are appropriate because a seemingly neutral law can interfere with freedom of religion for some people. Thus, held the Court, the college should have provided an accommodation. The Court also rejected the college's argument that providing an accommodation would violate Article 20(3), explaining that accommodating someone's religion must be done without scrutinizing or favoring their faith and that when the government gives a religious accommodation it does not create a hierarchy of religions.

The Court held that religious accommodations must be given but need to be balanced against the interests of others and society. To deny an accommodation the government must have a very good reason to infringe on the interests of the religious individual. The Court explained that accommodations are a way to prevent a negative impact on the religious person resulting from the law, but that to the extent an accommodation allows a religious person to avoid a requirement or a hardship the government may require an equally demanding alternative.

There is some debate among Japanese scholars over whether the case was primarily decided under the constitution or under the education laws. The Court's judgment does reference Article 20 but has more extensive references to the School Education Act and its implementing regulations. The side supporting the argument that the constitution played at least an important role in the decision seems to have the stronger argument, and that position has garnered a great deal of support among Japanese constitutional law scholars. Regardless, after the case was decided many government entities began implementing systems to grant religious exemptions.

Another case that illustrates the complex relationship between religion and the constitution is the *SDF Officer Enshrinement Case*.[116] In that case the widow of a Christian SDF officer who had died in an accident while on duty brought suit objecting to his enshrinement in the local Gokoku Shrine (a Shintō shrine dedicated to the spirits of military and public safety personnel who die in the line of duty). The suit was brought against the SDF and the non-governmental veteran's association for their role in the enshrinement and sought damages for infringement of "religious rights of personality" and asserted violations of Article 20(3) of the constitution. The Court found that although the SDF had indirectly participated by cooperating with the veteran's association in performing clerical work, the actual enshrinement was carried out by the association. It also rejected the "religious rights of personality" argument, noting the freedom of religion guaranteed by the constitution also included the freedom of others to engage in religious behavior that the plaintiff might find objectionable in the context of her own beliefs.[117]

Thus, while the right to religious exemptions from generally applicable laws/rules seem well protected under Article 20, there are other ways in which the government can impact what a citizen might view as his or her religious freedom. The *SDF Officer Enshrinement Case* essentially found inadequate state action for a constitutional claim. Yet, the person was being enshrined because he died in the line of government service and the widow of the person being enshrined had religious objections to the enshrinement, and perhaps he himself would have too.

Separation of government and religion

The separation of government and religion is an important element of Article 20, and is addressed in Article 20 sections (1) and (3). As mentioned above, one of the main foci for the new Japanese constitution was the elimination of State Shintō and thus the history of State Shintō and its abandonment in the new constitution can have an impact on decisions under Article 20. The same is true for Article 89, which prohibits government financial support or the use of any government property to support religion or any religious organization. In fact, many of the cases discussed here also involve claims under Article 89, and some of the reasoning under both articles is interchangeable.

The *Tsu City Groundbreaking Ceremony Case* is another famous case under Article 20 (and 89). Shintō rites were performed at a city-sponsored groundbreaking for the construction of a municipal gym. The ceremony and offerings were paid for by the city. A case was brought by a local citizen under Article 20(3) and Article 89 alleging that the ceremony was an unconstitutional establishment of religion. In addressing the issue, the Court held that some traditional Shinto practices can be interpreted as cultural practices and therefore government recognition of Shinto was not problematic under Article 20(3) or 89 as state support of a religion.

In reaching its conclusion the Court held that the State must be religiously neutral, but all state connection with religion is not prohibited by the constitution. Rather, state connection with religion that, when considering Japanese social and cultural conditions and the purpose and effect of the state action, exceeds a reasonable standard consonant with the objective of religious freedom, is unconstitutional. A violation of Article 20(3) occurs when government conduct has a purpose with religious significance or the effect of the government conduct is to subsidize, promote, suppress, or interfere with religion.

Here, the rites were obviously connected to religion, but they were not unconstitutional when considering the totality of the circumstances, because the ceremony had the secular purpose of "marking the start of construction by a rite performed in accordance with general social custom to pray for a stable foundation for the building and accident-free construction work." According to the Court, the effects of the ceremony did not subsidize or promote

Shintō or suppress or interfere with other religions. Therefore, government support for, and involvement in, the ceremony was not a religious activity for purposes of Article 20 or Article 89. The reasoning from the *Tsu City Groundbreaking Ceremony Case* was followed in several other cases.

In 1997, the Supreme Court issued an opinion that continued to follow, and augmented, the legal framework set forth in the *Tsu City Groundbreaking Ceremony Case*, but which drastically departed from that case's application of the legal framework. The *Ehime Tamagushi Case* involved officials of the government of Ehime Prefecture, acting upon the instructions of its governor to use public funds for offerings to the Yasukuni Shrine and the Gokoku Shrine at ceremonies held by those shrines.[118]

The *Ehime Tamagushi Case* Court applied the legal test from the *Tsu City Groundbreaking Ceremony Case*, but explicitly condemned Meiji era practices that tangled religion and government, holding that, "the constitution should be interpreted as striving for a secular and religiously neutral state by regarding the total separation of state and religion as its ideal." The Court held this approach helps protect the freedom of religion.

The Court again recognized, however, that total separation between religion and the state is impossible, because anytime government regulates social norms it can affect religion indirectly. The test it established to determine whether religious neutrality is violated was the purpose and effects test used in the *Tsu City Groundbreaking Ceremony Case*, but with an endorsement gloss.[119] Specifically, under the new test a court must consider whether the government action under review favors religion in the eyes of the public. The Court applied this analysis to the case under Article 20(1), Article 20(3) and Article 89 and found that paying for and giving the offerings violated both the purpose and effect elements of the test and would be viewed as favoring religion in the eyes of the public.

The Court held that the offering of *tamagushi* (and *kumotsuryō*, another kind of offering made to the shrines) at public expense and in the name of the local government, directly supports the religious activity of the shrine.[120] Having found the offerings unconstitutional, the Court ordered the governor to repay the government for all the expenditures made in support of the offerings because he had ordered them. The enforcement of the holding through a judgment like this is quite significant. As demonstrated elsewhere in this book, Japanese courts sometimes find constitutional violations but do not enforce any sort of strict order against the government or government officials.

Prior to the *Ehime Tamagushi Case* the Court decided a case that involved government officials attending events at a war memorial in Minō City where in alternating years a Shintō priest or Buddhist monks were involved in the ceremony.[121] The government also financially supported the relocation of the monument because it needed the land the monument was originally on to expand an elementary school. The Court addressed both issues and held that the monument was not a religious monument, that the war dead family association which sponsored the event (and was formed by the families and friends of those who died during wars going back to the Edo Era) was not a religious organization, and that the attendance of the mayor and other public officials at the event did not violate Article 20 or Article 89 of the constitution.

Central to the holding was the notion that religious neutrality allows some connection between government and religion so long as that connection is limited and appropriate in light of social, cultural, and other conditions in Japan. In this case the fact that the war memorial was not a religious monument, the religious aspects of the ceremony were minimal (at least according to the Court), and that the association was not a religious organization, all pointed toward the presence of the government officials not violating Articles 20 (or 89) because their participation to support the bereaved families was appropriate in light of Japanese social, cultural and other conditions. Furthermore, the Court held that the government subsidizing the movement of the memorial was not unconstitutional because the monument was not religious, it was only being moved because the government needed the land for expansion of an elementary school, and the government was doing so to support the war dead family association which was not a religious organization because its primary purpose was not to carry out religious activities. This case echoes the Tsu City case and preceded the *Ehime Tamagushi Case*, but once the Court found that the war memorial, association, and ceremony were not primarily religious the outcome was unsurprising.

The approach from the *Ehime Tamagushi Case* has been followed in several subsequent cases, including two additional cases involving rulings of unconstitutionality of application, both of which are discussed at Article 89.

As discussed at Article 21, the government is involved in regulating religious corporations, which has potential implications on the constitutional guarantee of freedom of association.

Article 21: Freedom of Expression

Shigenori Matsui

Article 21.

(1) Freedom of assembly and association as well as speech, press and all other forms of expression are guaranteed.

(2) No censorship shall be maintained, nor shall the secrecy of any means of communication be violated.

Significance of protection

Article 21 protects freedom of assembly, association, and expression together with secrecy of communications. All elements are concerned with communication and information which can collectively be classified as freedom of expression. Freedom of expression is vital for personal development and for participation in liberal democracies. It is necessary to reach the truth in the marketplace of ideas and is one of the most cherished freedoms in the world. It is a cornerstone of liberal democracies but continues to be a vulnerable right which government often attempts to curtail out of fear of public criticisms against the government.

This is a lesson the Japanese people learned under the Meiji Constitution which was premised upon the sovereign power of the emperor.[122] Although it protected freedom of speech, it only did so within the limits of law. In other words, when freedom of speech was restricted by the legislations or imperial orders, there was no infringement of freedom of speech. Accordingly, the Criminal Code imposed punishment for insults against the emperor and various legislations were enacted to restrict freedom of speech, such as the Newspaper Act, Publication Act and Public Peace Preservation Act. The people's freedom of speech was severely restricted by these legislations.[123] It was therefore not surprising that the Allied powers quickly invalidated them right after the start of the Occupation. They strongly believed that absence of freedom of expression had led to the rise of extreme militarism in Japan and that the intensified protection of freedom of expression was vital for the nation's future as a liberal and democratic country. This strong commitment to freedom of expression and civil liberties ultimately led to the enactment of the Constitution of Japan and its protection of freedom of expression in Article 21.

The Supreme Court affirmed this commitment in the *Hoppō Journal Case*, which involved a party seeking an injunction against a newspaper to prevent publication of defamatory materials about a possible candidate for public office. Although the Court upheld the injunction on the grounds it was not constitutionally prohibited censorship, it also articulated a broad view of the Article 21 protection of freedom of expression:

> *In a democratic nation where sovereign power resides with the people the following is the foundation of its existence. That is, the people as constituents of that nation may express any doctrine, advocate any doctrine and the like as well as receive such information from each other, and by taking whatever he believes rightful from among them of his own free will, majority opinion is formed, and government administration is determined through such process. Therefore, the freedom of expression, especially the freedom of expression relating to public matters, must be respected as a particularly important constitutional right in a democratic nation. It is considered that this thought lies at the root of the paragraph 1, Article 21 of the Constitution.*[124]

As we will see, freedom of expression is thus believed to occupy the preferred position in the hierarchy of the fundamental human rights protected by the Constitution of Japan.

Scope of protection

The Supreme Court has never officially defined the scope of freedom of expression. Technically, it is a freedom of "speech, press and other forms of expression." Since the Court has never clearly distinguished speech, press and other forms of expression, it is meaningless to decide strictly what constitutes "speech," "the press" or "other forms of expression." Although television broadcasting and cyberspace were not developed at the time of the constitution's promulgation, the Court has acknowledged that television broadcasting enjoys the constitutional protection as a form of freedom of expression (despite the fact that there are significant differences between television broadcasting and print media, such as newspapers, books and magazines)[125] and that even cyberspace is entitled to receive constitutional protection (despite the fact that there are so many ambiguities in the legal status of the cyberspace).[126] The scope of the guarantee in Article 21(1), therefore, is quite broad and can include all forms of expression.

Moreover, the Supreme Court has also acknowledged that the right to receive information should be constitutionally protected and the right to gather information, which is vital for freedom of expression, needs to be respected.[127] However, the Court has also been somewhat reluctant to acknowledge that the right to gather information should be included in freedom of expression.[128] It has even denied that the right of access to government information is included in the constitutionally protected freedom of expression.[129]

Furthermore, the Supreme Court has not been clear when freedom of expression is implicated in some cases. For instance, in the *Kimigayo Piano Accompaniment Case* discussed at Article 19, the Court denied that freedom of thought was infringed when a public-school music teacher was ordered to play piano at a ceremony by the school principal for *Kimigayo*, the national anthem, but she refused to do so because of her political beliefs. Playing the piano is a form of expression, therefore forcing an individual to express despite his or her objection should have been regarded as an infringement of freedom of expression, since no one should be forced to express in a way he or she refuses. Yet, it seems the Court did not view this case as implicating an infringement of freedom of expression.

The Court has also denied the applicability of Article 21 to acts of private persons or corporations. As a result, when a private corporation disciplines its employees for their criticisms against it, the courts tend to find no constitutional freedom of expression issue.[130]

Framework of analysis by the Supreme Court of Japan

The Supreme Court has not clearly articulated its framework of analysis on constitutional issues involving freedom of expression. Despite its acknowledgement of the necessity of special protections for freedom of expression, the Court has been eager to sustain all kinds of restrictions against freedom of expression. Unlike the US Supreme Court, it has never clearly distinguished between content-based restrictions and content-neutral restrictions and has never employed strict scrutiny even in content-based restriction cases. Unlike the Supreme Court of Canada or Federal Constitution Court of Germany (FCCG), Japan's Supreme Court has not embraced a proportionality test as a constitutional framework. Instead, the Court has always applied a case-by-case *ad hoc* analysis. But the end result is always the same: it has always been very deferential to the legislature and has sustained the constitutionality of all restrictions on freedom of expression.[131]

In the *Lady Chatterley's Lover Case*—in which the Court upheld the conviction of the Japanese translator of D.H. Lawrence's famous novel for distribution of obscene materials—the Court made it clear that freedom of expression was subject to restriction for the public welfare as articulated in Articles 12 and 13 of the constitution.[132] No one believes that freedom of expression can be literally unlimited. However, the Court easily found the protection of sexual morality—the goal behind the ban on publication of obscene materials—to be consistent with public welfare, and easily concluded that the total ban on publication of obscenity imposed by the Penal Code was justifiable.[133] The Court never carefully inquired why sexual morality could be seen as a legitimate and important interest to justify the restriction on freedom of expression or why an absolute ban is truly necessary. This willingness to accept the government's restrictions on freedom of expression is a good indication of the Supreme Court's general stance in sustaining all sorts of restriction on constitutionally protected rights. And despite a gradual change in its judicial philosophy, the Court still sticks to this reluctance to seriously question the legitimacy and importance of government objectives or the necessity of a total ban on certain types of expression.[134]

Sometimes the Supreme Court has indicated a willingness to balance freedom of expression and competing government interests to see whether the restriction is reasonable and necessary. Yet, the result is no different: placing more emphasis on pressing government interest while minimizing the seriousness of infringement, the Court sustains a total ban on the targeted speech. For example, in the *Sarufutsu Case* the Court held that the rights of the public workers are subject to reasonable and necessary restrictions, and used a balancing of interests analysis to see whether a total ban on political activities of public workers could be justified.[135] It ended up holding that the governmental interest to secure political neutrality of public workers as well as the appearance of political neutrality is important enough that it outweighs any impact on their freedom of expression and therefore sustained a total ban on such activities by public workers.[136]

Censorship

In the United States, censorship used to be the primary target of freedom of expression, since censorship was the primary method used to control print media in Great Britain prior to US independence. In the US, therefore, it was generally understood that the absence of censorship was a hallmark of freedom of expression. The US Supreme Court has repeatedly confirmed this extreme hostility to censorship and has developed its freedom of expression jurisprudence through never accepting any censorship or prior restraint except in extremely exceptional cases.

The Constitution of Japan has clearly inherited this hostility towards censorship in Article 21, since it explicitly declared in paragraph (2) that "no censorship shall be maintained." This is a clear lesson from the experience under the Meiji Constitution, when publishers produced newspapers or books, they were required by law to submit these papers to the government for review and the government was authorized to issue a publication ban if it found the contents illegal or questionable. During the war, military officers were stationed in newspaper editorial rooms and there was total censorship: no article could be included in the paper if unapproved by the government. There was virtually no freedom of speech since everyone was mandated to actively support the government's war effort.[137]

The Supreme Court of Japan also adopted hostility towards censorship in the *Customs Inspection Case*, a challenge to the constitutionality of the Customs Act, which banned the import of obscene materials from abroad and authorized customs officers to inspect the materials imported to prevent any import of obscene materials, effectively forcing the importers to abandon them.[138] The Court held the constitution's ban on censorship to be absolute, leaving no room for justification. This is a clear indication that the Supreme Court accepted the lessons of the past. Nevertheless, the Court narrowly construed "censorship" to mean a system of subjecting the content of the publication to comprehensive and general review by administrative agencies before publication for the purpose of prohibiting its publication if found to be inappropriate. Since the customs inspection is conducted on materials already published abroad and the purpose of the inspection is for the enforcement of the Customs Act, it was found not to be a form of prohibited "censorship."

Prior restraint challenged

Currently there is no such comprehensive advance administrative censorship of publications in Japan. It is no wonder, therefore, that the Supreme Court has never struck down any prior restraints as constitutionally prohibited censorship.

In one of the *Ienaga Textbook Cases* (also discussed at Article 26), for example, the Supreme Court sustained the school textbook inspection system.[139] In Japan, even though they are produced by private publishers, all school textbooks to be used by public schools need a government approval for their content to be bought by the government and distributed to students free of charge. The government has subjected draft textbooks to stringent standards and content requirements, often requiring the publishers to revise the contents and sometimes rejecting textbooks entirely. When challenged on constitutional grounds, the Court followed its narrow definition of prohibited censorship and concluded that the inspection requirement was not censorship since it never precluded the publication as a regular book.

In the *Hoppō Journal Case*, the constitutionality of a judicial injunction against the publication of defamatory content about a possible candidate for public office was challenged.[140] Since it was a judicial injunction, the Court easily concluded that it was not "censorship." The Court nevertheless held that judicial injunctions being a prior restraint on freedom of expression, needed to be limited to truly exceptional circumstances where there was clearly no room to justify the defamatory content. In this case, however, the Court was convinced that the injunction was justified. Subsequent to this holding, the Court also upheld an injunction to prevent invasion of privacy in the *"Fish Swimming in Stones" Case*.[141] In this case, a famous author published a novel about the struggles of a woman with serious facial disfiguration, a story modeled after one of her close friends, who brought suit and won an award of damages and an injunction against further publication. On appeal, the Supreme Court upheld the injunction using the same balancing test as in the *Hoppō Journal Case* and concluded that there was no room for claiming protection as freedom of expression, but also showed no serious concern with freedom of expression since it was a fictional story modeled on a private person and thus was not concerned with matters of public interest.

Overall, compared to the US Supreme Court, the Supreme Court of Japan appears more willing to tolerate prior restraints.

Content-based restrictions

Content-based restrictions on expression are especially risky because they tend to proscribe or prevent expression of messages the government feels are problematic or bothersome. They can be used to suppress the political opposition and may thwart the very foundations of freedom of expression in a liberal democracy. That is the reason why the US Supreme Court applies strict scrutiny to content-based restrictions, demanding that the restriction needs to be justified by some compelling government interests and that the means used needs to be narrowly tailored. In Japan such restrictions have come up in a variety of contexts, but Japan's Supreme Court has not applied the same rigorous scrutiny.

National security

Restrictions on expression for the sake of national security are a prime example of content-based restriction. There are various restrictions on freedom of expression intended to preserve national security in the Japanese Penal Code as well as in individual statutes. For example, under the National Public Service Act, all public employees are subject to criminal penalties for leaking or disclosing confidential government information.[142]

In the *Nishiyama Case*, a newspaper reporter was prosecuted and convicted for solicitation of the leak of a confidential government document from his girlfriend, a Ministry of Foreign Affairs employee.[143] On appeal, the Supreme Court upheld the application of the solicitation ban against breaches of the confidentiality obligations established by the National Public Service Act for public servants to the newspaper reporter and, finding his conduct to be highly immoral (since he used his girlfriend to accomplish his objective of obtaining a secret document and dumped her after doing so), sustained his conviction. Although he argued that the leaked document revealed potentially wrongful conduct by the government, the Court held there was no constitutional violation and therefore the secrecy of the document deserved to be protected. It thus rejected the journalist's argument that greater public interest in revealing such secrets should outweigh the interest in protecting confidentiality. This holding confirmed that the constitutionality of the prohibition on leaks of government secrets and established that even mass media reporters could be convicted for soliciting them.

In addition to the general ban in the National Public Service Act against leaking government secrets, there are also special protections for military secrets in the Self-Defense Forces Act and a special protection for "specified military secrets" on weapons, and other materials provided by the US government based on the Mutual Security Assistance Agreement.[144] More recently in 2013, the government enacted the Protection of Specially Designated Secrets Act (over strong public protests), in order to grant further protection to "specifically designated secrets" relating to national defense, foreign affairs, specified harmful conduct, and terrorism. It imposes severe punishments for intentional as well as negligent leaks and, in certain circumstances, the acquisition of such secrets as well.

Japanese law contains no direct punishment for publication of national security information by the mass media, but because of all these restrictions, the media is seriously restricted in getting access to national security information even if they believe government wrongdoing is afoot. As a result, freedom of expression in Japan is significantly restricted with respect to the investigation and reporting of national security information.

Public safety

The Penal Code prohibits certain conduct that disturbs public order and safety. This includes riots, public disturbance using assault or intimidation by many people, refusal to disperse, arson, setting off explosives and so forth.[145] The century-old Explosives Control Declaration of 1884, prohibits the use of explosives disturbing of the public peace or to harm the life and body of the public.[146] Under the Penal Code, abetting or incitement of these crimes may be subject to criminal punishment.[147] Similarly, the Subversive Activities Prevention Act of 1952, in addition to providing for government control over groups that are involved in violent subversive conduct, imposes additional punishments on sedition, solicitation of riots, arson or other crimes for ideological or political reasons, printing, distributing or publicly displaying documents or pictures advocating riots.[148] These provisions inevitably restrict freedom of expression.

The Supreme Court indicated its willingness to sustain such restrictions in the *Food Supply Management Act Case of 1949*.[149] The Food Supply Management Act was a wartime law that required farmers to sell their produce to the government at stipulated prices so the government could distribute it to the public because of the extreme food shortage during World War II; the Emergency Food Supply Management Order was enacted in 1946 to implement food supply management after the war. Among other things these laws penalized advocating not selling food to the government. In response to an appeal of a conviction, the Supreme Court held that, while freedom of expression needed to be respected, solicitation of violations of the Act, which was enacted to secure vital foods for the public, went beyond legitimate criticism of the governmental policy and harmed the public welfare. It thus concluded that the solicitation ban was justified. The holding never discussed what the defendant actually said or what impact the defendant's expression had. Nevertheless, the Court easily sustained the conviction. Despite the wide-spread academic criticisms against its insensitivity to the necessity of protecting freedom of expression, the Court has clung to this stance ever since.[150]

In the *Okinawa Return Protest Case*, the leaders of a radical student group that opposed the return of Okinawa with US military bases still in place urged their members to attack and eliminate the police and caused a public disturbance resulting in a railroad station being set on fire and the death of a police officer.[151] The leaders were prosecuted and convicted under the Subversive Activities Prevention Act (discussed above), which defines "solicitation" as "conduct that causes the decision to commit the designated crimes or further stimulates the promotion of the decision already made to commit such crimes by documents, pictures or conducts with the purpose of causing the person to commit such crimes with the political aims"[152]—in other words, expressive conduct. On appeal the Supreme Court admitted that these provisions limit freedom of expression but, citing previous precedents, held that freedom of expression can be restricted in order to preserve public welfare and that the agitation in question involved very dangerous conduct which could cause very serious crimes such as arson or public disturbance and was thus against the public welfare. On that basis the Court concluded that such expressions deserved no protection. In light of the circumstances (including the death of a police officer), the radical defendants' punishment might seem justified, but once again the Supreme Court showed no interest in what the defendants actually said or whether there was a real or imminent danger of illegal action being triggered by their statements. It appears the Court will uphold any ban and punishment for advocacy or solicitation adopted by the Diet.

Political expression

Although the Supreme Court has emphasized the importance of protecting freedom of expression relating to matters of public concern, there are many restrictions on political expression in Japan. As shown in the *Sarufutsu Case*, public servants are banned from partaking in any political activities and the Court has sustained the constitutionality of these restrictions. As a result, public workers are only allowed to cast a vote in elections and may not engage in any political activities.

Moreover, the Public Offices Election Act imposes very tight regulations on election campaigning, which can only be conducted during the very brief period set forth in law and any campaigning prior to that period is banned. Even during the campaign period, many typical campaigning methods, including distribution of documents and door-to-door canvassing are also prohibited.[153] The Supreme Court has sustained all these restrictions as necessary and reasonable to secure the fairness of elections.[154] The Court evidently believes that election campaigning is a special category of political expression that needs to be strictly regulated to secure electoral fairness and equality of candidates. Although election campaigning is one of the most basic forms of political participation, it is far from free in Japan.[155]

Defamation

Defamation is subject to civil liability as a tort (Japanese law does not distinguish between libel and slander).[156] It is also subject to punishment as criminal defamation under Article 230 of the Penal Code. Defamation is a strict liability tort: the plaintiff can be awarded damages without proof of any injury caused by the statement and without proof of any intent or negligence on the part of the defendant. It has been held that civil liability could be attached to defamatory statements regardless of whether the published statement was true or false. In other words, truth is not a defense. The same is true with respect to criminal defamation: any publication of defamatory materials could lead to criminal punishment without room for a defense of truth.

It was once believed that civil and criminal defamation liability never raised any constitutional issues. However, with the adoption of the present constitution and its guarantee of freedom of expression, the Penal Code was revised to establish a limited defense of truth for defamatory statements if the statement was true, concerned with the matter of public interest and published solely to promote the public purpose.[157]

The Supreme Court initially believed this defense was a result of keeping the balance between freedom of expression and the need for protection of one's reputation and that it had been added to preserve the constitutionality of the criminal defamation provision. It thus rejected arguments that further protection was needed for defendants who could not prove their statement was true but honestly believed it to be true based on sufficient grounds.[158] Eventually, the Court reversed itself and accepted the possibility of such a defense in criminal defamation.[159] The Court also came to accept the same defense in civil defamation cases, even though there is no statutory language similar to the Penal Code granting immunity from tort liability.[160]

The judicial protection of defamatory statements has therefore significantly expanded. Nevertheless, the plaintiff still does not have to prove that they suffered any damage or harm, that the statement was false, or that the defendant was intentional or negligent. It is still the responsibility of the defendant to prove the elements of the defense. This is a far cry from the US Supreme Court's constitutional defamation jurisprudence granting constitutional protection for defamation for statement about public officials in the absence of proof that the statement was false and that the defendant had actual malice.[161]

The development of cyberspace has also presented opportunities for the Supreme Court to reconsider the liability of authors for online comments. Since most are made by bloggers or general Internet users, it is impossible to expect the same degree of due diligence as professional reporters and the rebuttal is much easier online. Nevertheless, the Court has recognized that the same limited defense in cyber defamation prosecutions should be applicable to offline defamation, rejecting the defense counsel's call to establish a different standard of care for cyberspace defamation.[162] This approach will seriously chill freedom of expression in cyberspace if it is left unremedied.

Invasion of privacy and insult

Invasion of privacy can also be tortious under the Civil Code. The *After the Banquet Case* (see discussion at Article 13) established that a victim could sue for damages for invasion of privacy.

The Supreme Court confirmed this in the *"Reversal" Case* which involved a non-fiction writer who published a book about a jury trial in US-occupied Okinawa, in which the author served as a juror. His book identified one of the persons convicted using his real name, thereby revealing he had a criminal record.[163] That person filed a suit claiming invasion of privacy and was awarded damages. On appeal the Supreme Court held that the plaintiff had a legal interest in keeping his real name and criminal record unpublished and that publication of it could be a tort. This determination was made upon balancing competing interests, including the importance of the case, the status and power of the named person, the nature of the book, and the necessity of using real names in it. The Court emphasized that in the case at bar many years had passed from the plaintiff's conviction: he had since married and was living a normal life and there was no justification to publish his real name. The Court also sustained an injunction against the invasion of privacy and insult in the *"Fish Swimming in Stones" Case* mentioned earlier.

There is no outright ban in the Penal Code on invasions of privacy by publication. However, the Revenge Porn Prohibition Act of 2014 introduced a criminal ban against disclosing private, intimate sexual images without consent.[164]

There is also a criminal ban on insult in the Penal Code.[165] Yet, since it used to be interpreted as a provision to protect social reputation, not involving statements of fact in contrast to statement of facts implicated by defamation, its reach was not clear, and its actual enforcement was quite rare. In recent days, however, egregious "trashing" directed against specific persons, especially celebrities, has become a huge social issue since in some cases it has resulted in suicide. The police seem willing to use this provision of the Penal Code as a means of combatting such behavior. Yet, many people remain disappointed by the absence of more effective means of addressing public "trashing." In response to such sentiments, in 2022 the Diet amended the Penal Code to increase the penalty for the crime of "insult."

Obscenity and sexual expression

Article 175 of the Penal Code prohibits "dissemination or public display of obscene documents, pictures, electronic records or other material as well as dissemination of obscene electronic record or other records by telecommunication" and authorizes criminal punishment. The Supreme Court, in upholding the constitutionality of its older version in the *Lady Chatterley's Lover Case*, held that the criteria for obscenity was whether the material "excites or stimulates sexual desires wantonly, harms the normal sexual sense of embarrassment of the average person and is against good sexual morality." It also held that artistic or literary value has nothing to do with whether something was or was not obscene; even materials with high artistic value could be criminally obscene. Finding the purpose of the obscenity ban in protecting sexual morality, it concluded that Article 175 was justified as a measure to secure public welfare. Believing that *Lady Chatterley's Lover* contained obscene material, the Court thus upheld the conviction of the novel's translator.

Constitutional academics as well as artists are generally critical of this holding. Many insist that expressive material having a high artistic or literary value should not be banned as obscene. Nevertheless, the Court has never allowed the publication or distribution of artistic or literally valued works if deemed obscene. In the *"l'Histoire de Juliette ou les Prospérités du vice" Case*, an 18th-century novel by the Marquis de Sade was translated into Japanese and published in 1959.[166] It was a story of a pious woman raised in a monastery who came to doubt God and sexual morality and subsequently committed various violent immoral acts. The translator and publisher were prosecuted and convicted under Article 175. On appeal the Supreme Court followed the *Lady Chatterley's Lover Case* holding and sustained the conviction, although it hinted that in exceptional cases, high artistic value or ideology might negate criminal obscenity.

The Court's current stance is only slightly changed since these rulings; in the *"Yojō-han Fusuma no Shitabari" Case*, it held that, in order to decide whether the material is obscene or not, it is necessary to consider the degree of patently and detailed description of sex in the material and its method, the relative weight of such description to the book as a whole, relevancy of such description to expressed thought, structure and development of the book, the degree of reduction of sexual stimulation by the artistic and ideological value and the motivation to appeal to the prurient interest as a whole.[167] In the end, after balancing all these factors, it turns on whether the material "excites or stimulates the sexual desire wantonly and harms the normal sexual sense of embarrassment of the average person and is against good sexual morality" in light of healthy social common sense of that age. The ultimate standard has not changed but with this the Court at least indicated its willingness to consider the totality of circumstances.

Enforcement practice has also changed slightly. In the past, Japanese police used to take the mechanical stance of not allowing any direct descriptions or depictions of sexual intercourse or genitalia or even showing pubic hair. At the same time, so long as these parts were obscured, police were generally reluctant to enforce the obscenity ban. However, by the 1990s the law enforcement agencies had become able to tolerate some pubic hairs in pictures. In the *Mapplethorpe Case*, which involved a decision by the Customs Agency to prohibit the import of a picture book by the famous photographer Robert Michael Mapplethorpe, the Court denied that the book was obscene, even though it contained some pictures showing male genitals.[168] The Court pointed out that the book had a high artistic value and given the nature and type of pictures, it was difficult to say that it was appealing to the prurient interest of readers. Although it made its decision based on the interpretation of the Customs Act rather than the constitution, this was the first time the Court tolerated pictures of male genitals as not obscene. Nevertheless, since the Court's decisions in this area depend on the totality of circumstances, it is hard to objectively say what is obscene in practice.

There were some doubts whether online pornography was prohibited by Article 175 of the Penal Code because the older version of the article prohibited sale, distribution and public display of obscene "materials," whereas online pornography is merely digital information and there is no sale or distribution of any physical "materials." Nevertheless, the Court held that digital information can be obscene if the data could create an obscene image on a computer screen and that the computer hardware which contains digital information consisting of pornography can be obscene "materials" and that transmitting the digital information can be a form of "public display," and thus subject to the Article 175 ban.[169] This was an unnatural interpretation of the statute but in 2011 Article 175 was amended to make it clearly applicable to "electronic record" and the prohibition is on dissemination and not only sale or distribution.

Police and courts remain committed to enforcing the obscenity ban. Recently, the Supreme Court re-confirmed its constitutionality in upholding the conviction of an artist who distributed a digital blueprint that could be used to create a replica of her vagina using a 3D printer.[170] The Court also held that it did not matter that she had an artistic motivation: to combat the notion of the vagina as obscene and to make it an everyday image in life, as well as to raise funds for that purpose.

The creation, import, display, publication, dissemination and possession of child pornography is banned by the Act on Child Prostitution and Child Pornography and Protection of Children.[171] It defines a "child" as anyone under the year of eighteen but not knowing the child's age is not a defense unless the offender can prove they were not negligent.[172] The scope of expression banned by the Act is significantly expanded from the definition of obscenity under the Penal Code, and simple possession or access is also prohibited. Nevertheless, unless the picture or image depicts an actual child, the sexually explicit pictures or images do not fall into the definition of child pornography; virtual child porn or child pornography using adult models does not constitute "child pornography" under the Act.[173] Many have thus criticized the insufficiency of Japanese anti-child pornography legislation.

Hate speech

Unlike many developed countries, Japan has no criminal ban on hate speech. Despite persistent hate graffiti against vulnerable *burakumin* who have been subjected to various kinds of discrimination (see discussion at Article 14) and the rapid increase of hate speech against resident Koreans, the national government has been reluctant to introduce a criminal ban. Faced with intensified criticisms from abroad, the Diet finally decided to enact a countermeasures against hate speech towards non-Japanese residents.[174] However, it only applies to hateful speech and behavior directed primarily at "persons from other countries or territories outside of Japan or their descendants, lawfully residing in Japan" which was apparently intended to serve the purpose of protecting resident Koreans, but does not address other forms of hate speech against racial, ethnic or religious minorities. No other country in the world has enacted such a narrow anti-hate speech law. Moreover, it contains no criminal penalties or administrative or civil remedies. It simply authorizes the government to take some countermeasures such as educational measures. It is simply a declaration of government anti-hate speech policy. Still, the statute prompted some municipalities to refuse to permit hate demonstrations on public streets and offers a potential justification for courts to issue injunctions against such demonstrations.

Although a growing voice can be heard calling for a criminal ban on hate speech, a criminal ban faces a serious challenge since the definition of hate speech is very vague, the reasons for punishment are difficult to specify and the scope of prohibition may be too broad.[175]

Content-neutral restrictions on expression

Advertising and bill-posting

There are various types of content-neutral restrictions on expression. Since such restrictions are not based upon the content of expressive statements, they do not create serious risks that the government can use them to suppress opposition or annoying criticism. As a result, they generally only need to be necessary and reasonable to achieve an important government objective in order to be found constitutional.

An example of a content-neutral restriction is the prohibition of posting advertising on public property under the Outdoor Advertisement Regulation Act[176] and local ordinances passed under the Act to protect the environment and public safety. The Supreme Court sustained such a ban as necessary and reasonable to maintain a pleasant civic environment.[177] Although some scholars question whether the total ban can be justified, the Court accepted it without serious inquiry. Some also question the discriminatory enforcement of the ban against political posters (posting of posters on funeral services or missing cats never was subject to police enforcement), but the Court simply dismissed such arguments, insisting that the possibility of discriminatory enforcement cannot be a reason to question the constitutionality of such a restriction. Billboard signs and billboard advertisements are subject to the same regulations and the Supreme Court has similarly sustained the constitutionality of such restrictions.[178]

Posting bills or signs on private property (such as utility poles owned by utility companies) is also prohibited by the Minor Offenses Act.[179] The Court has upheld this ban as reasonable and necessary to protect private property.[180]

The use of loudspeakers during parades or demonstrations is subject to local government anti-loudspeaker ordinances, which generally place limits on maximum permissible volume.[181] The Court has not addressed the constitutionality of such regulations, but in light of the other cases involving content-neutral restrictions, it is likely it would sustain them as necessary and reasonable.

Restrictions on public gatherings, parades and demonstrations

Content-neutral restrictions on freedom of expression raise especially difficult issues when they affect public gatherings, parades, demonstrations or protests in public places. People should be able to assemble in public parks or on public streets and be free to engage in demonstration or protests, as a form of a moving "assembly" or as "other forms of expression," but such rights are subject to restrictions to preserve public welfare. First, all assemblies, parades and demonstrations need to be peaceful. There are also various restrictions for the purpose of maintaining public safety and traffic safety and protection of public property and management. Again, the issue is whether such restriction can be viewed as necessary and reasonable.

Restrictions on the right to hold an assembly in a public park were sustained in the *Gathering in the Exterior Garden of the Imperial Palace Case*.[182] In this case, a labor union applied for a permit to hold a May Day rally in the exterior garden (a public park) of the emperor's palace in Tokyo, but was refused over concerns about the possibility of property damage to the garden. The Supreme Court dismissed the union's constitutional challenge as moot since the date of the planned gathering had already passed by the time the case was before the

Court. Nevertheless, it went on to rule on the merits *in dicta*, upholding the constitutionality of the permit refusal. The Court accorded very broad discretion to the government as the manager of the park and held that the refusal due to concern for property damage was a reasonable exercise of management power. This decision seems to indicate the Court's implied belief that public parks should be used for leisure rather than mass rallies.

Many local governments have public safety ordinances which require a permit or advance notification for demonstrations on public streets. In an early encounter with this issue, the *Niigata Prefecture Public Safety Ordinance Case*, the Supreme Court held that general advance permission requirements for public demonstrations would not be constitutionally acceptable, but demonstrations could be subject to necessary and reasonable restrictions (including requiring a permit as to specific places or methods) and even disallowed when there was a clear and present danger to public safety.[183] In a total reversal of this precedent, however, the Court subsequently held in the *Tokyo Public Safety Ordinance Case*, that, since public demonstrations could easily turn into riots, a general requirement to obtain a permit in advance was acceptable and denial of permits was justified if there is any risk of danger to public safety.[184] This was tantamount to saying that the local government could refuse a permit for any public demonstration since potentially any public demonstrations could become a riot. In other words, there is no constitutional right to public demonstrations.

Thereafter, the Supreme Court confirmed the constitutionality of similar public safety ordinances in all cases.[185] The Court has also upheld the use of traffic safety regulations to further restrict demonstrations.[186] Thanks to this jurisprudence, during the 1970s through the 1990s, it became very difficult to organize and participate in even lawful public demonstrations

To some extent, this was inevitable since most public demonstrations during these periods were quite often confrontational and ended in violence. Because of these tight restrictions, violent demonstrations decreased and the number of participants seriously dropped. In some cases, public demonstrations see demonstrators sandwiched between police who outnumber them, just for the purpose of walking through public streets. With a gradual increase of "family friendly" demonstrations in the 1990s, however, police have come to allow more peaceful demonstrations with family and labor participation.

Recently, public demonstrations by right-wing hate groups against resident Koreans have attracted widespread attention. With the passage of the anti-hate speech statute and ordinances described earlier, some municipalities have refused to grant permits for these demonstrations. However, it is unclear whether doing so is justified, since such demonstrations are objectionable because of the messages participants disseminate, any restrictions on holding them would be content-based rather than not content-neutral.

The public also has the right to hold meetings in public facilities such as civic halls and auditoriums. These facilities were created and made available for the public to use for various purposes, most importantly for exercising freedom of expression. The Local Autonomy Act mandates that municipalities operating such public facilities may not arbitrarily refuse to permit use, or discriminate against some prospective users.[187] Nonetheless, the Supreme Court upheld a municipality's refusal to allow use of a community hall to a radical group with a history of involvement in illegal activities, due to the public safety concern.[188]

Yet, when one union wanted to use one of the municipal facilities for the funeral service for its leader, the municipal government refused a permit due to fear that the opposing rival groups might come to disrupt the public peace. The Supreme Court disallowed this refusal because there was no concrete danger that the use might bring any harm to the public safety and because any disturbance could be controlled by the police.[189] In other words, such a refusal would be equivalent to allowing a "heckler's veto," which would limit the use of public facilities to only uncontroversial events.

The rights to receive and gather information, and to access government information

The right to receive information

In the *Yodogō Hijacking News Redaction Case* the Supreme Court acknowledged that, based on Articles 13, 19 and 21, the constitution protects the right to receive information. The context was a challenge to the authority of prison wardens under the Prison Act to prevent criminal suspects in detention pending trial from seeing specific newspaper articles on the grounds it might cause disturbances inside the detention facility (see discussion at Article 19).[190] Although the Court acknowledged detainees still have constitutional rights after detention and therefore should generally be entitled to continue enjoying the right to receive information, it nonetheless sustained the prison warden's restrictions on the basis of maintaining order within the facility.[191]

The *Customs Inspection Case* discussed above also addressed the right to receive information, though in the context of upholding prohibitions on importing illegal pornography. Although the simple possession of obscene materials for personal use is not banned by the Penal Code and there was a question whether the total ban on import is necessary, the Supreme Court believed that the total ban is justified since it is difficult to find out the purpose of imports and it was therefore necessary to ban all imports regardless of the purpose for the prevention of dissemination of obscene materials.[192]

The right to gather information

In the *Hakata Station TV Film Production Case*, the Supreme Court also acknowledged that the right to gather information needs to be respected, although it is not included within freedom of expression. The constitutional protection of the right to gather information is thus weaker than it is for freedom of expression.

One important case that presented the restrictions on the right to gather information was the *Courtroom Note-Taking Case.* All courts in Japan used to ban note-taking in the courtrooms during trials, except by journalists accredited to the Court. This was challenged by an American researcher. Although the Court declined to award damages to the researcher, it held that "in light of the spirit of Article 21" the act of note-taking by courtroom spectators should be "respected" by the courts and only restricted in exceptional cases (such as multiple spectators note-taking in unison to intimidate witnesses). Although procedurally a loss for the researcher, the case resulted in significant change to courtroom practices: spectators have been generally free to take notes since the Court's judgment. (See also discussion at Article 82).[193]

The right to gather information is also directly implicated when a journalist is ordered to reveal the identity of confidential sources. Whereas attorney-client privilege as well as doctor-patient privilege is explicitly stipulated in the Code of Criminal Procedure, there is no such express privilege for journalist-source relationships and the courts have been reluctant to create another privilege for journalists.

There have been other situations that raise similar concerns over the chilling effect on the right to gather information when the materials collected for expression are searched and seized by the government. For example, in the *Hakata Station TV Film Production Case*, TV news broadcasters were ordered by a court to produce film footage gathered in the course of news reporting due to its potential relevance to a trial, which they challenged as an infringement of the Article 21 right to gather information. This was not a situation involving a confidential source, but the media feared the use of their footage gathered for reporting for criminal justice purposes might hinder future news gathering: people might be reluctant to be interviewed or videotaped. The Court used a balancing test, weighing the needs of the criminal justice system against the harm suffered by the media, to ultimately uphold the lower court's production order. The Court considered the footage important as the only available evidence, while finding the threat of harm to future news gathering less significant given that it had already been aired. The Court has used the same balancing test when ruling against objections from TV stations over the search and seizure by law enforcement of master tapes used for news broadcasts when needed as evidence in criminal cases.[194]

The Court has shown more willingness to protect journalists and mass media in civil cases. In the *Shimada Case*, a reporter was summoned to the Court to testify as a witness in a civil proceeding but refused to reveal a source.[195] On appeal, the Court relied upon the same balancing test as in criminal cases to determine whether the reporter could be excused from testifying. However, in contrast to the outcome in criminal cases, the Court held that reporters should generally be accorded a privilege against being compelled to testify as to the nature of confidential sources, unless the case has public interest implications, the reporter's news gathering method was unlawful, the source consented to disclosure, or unless there were other special circumstances that weighed in favor of compelling the disclosure of the news source.

As of this writing, there were still no shield laws in Japan specifically protecting media outlets and journalists from compulsory production or seizure of information in criminal proceedings; everything is left to balancing of interests by the courts. But courts are much more likely to accept the disclosure of a news source or production order or seizure of information collected for a news report in Japan in comparison to the US.

Right of access to government information

The Supreme Court has been extremely reluctant to recognize a constitutional right to access to government information as an element of freedom of expression.[196] Instead, the right of the public to seek access to government information is provided by the Disclosure of Information Held by Administrative Organizations Act, which was passed in 1999 and grants citizens the right of access to government information, subject to certain exceptions. This Act has significantly expanded the right of access to government information, but the exceptions are very broad, especially with respect to national security exceptions.[197] Nor does it permit *in camera* inspections by courts in disputed cases, mandate the creation or storage of government documents or establish punishments for government actors who willfully ignore disclosure requests or destroy documents to avoid disclosure.

Furthermore, there is no general "open meeting" law requiring executive and administrative meetings to be open to the public, nor does the above statute apply to the legislative or judicial branches. Therefore, protection of the right to access government information provided by the 1999 statute is hardly sufficient. Many civil right advocates are calling for stronger freedom of information laws.

Broadcast regulation

Broadcast media is also implicated by Article 21. The Radio Act imposes a licensing requirement for basic broadcasting and the Broadcasting Act establishes the general requirements for all broadcasts. First, it declares broadcast programming free from interference or regulation by anyone, except in accordance with legal authority.[198] It also mandates the basic principles to be followed by broadcasters in their domestic broadcast programming: not to violate the public order or harm good morals, to be politically fair, not to distort the truth, and to present a variety of viewpoints on controversial subjects.[199] This is a Japanese version of the "fairness doctrine" once imposed by the Federal Communications Commission on US broadcasters (and subsequently abolished), except that it is statutory and applies to all broadcast programming, not just editorial content. Moreover, Japan's version extends to all domestic broadcasting programs, including cable services and even some Internet broadcasters. In addition, these requirements of the Broadcast Act are enforced directly by the Ministry of Internal Affairs and Communications (MIC), rather than an independent administrative agency (such as the FCC in the United States).

There are no criminal or administrative sanctions for violations of the mandated principles of the Broadcasting Act. As a result, there is a serious question as to whether the government can legally enforce them. Yet, the MIC has consistently argued that the government can enforce these mandates and uses its authority to impose sanctions under other provisions of the Broadcasting Act, and under the Radio Act and related laws and regulations. The MIC also often uses informal administrative warnings to broadcasters when it believes they have violated the "spirit" of the mandates, without clear guidance on legal standards or legal procedures to be followed. Since most broadcasters are subject to licensing requirements or certification and registration requirements for program distribution administered by the MIC, they have a powerful incentive to comply regardless of the absence of clear rules.

There are no similar overarching content-related principles in any statute governing print media and, given the applicability of constitutional guarantee of freedom of expression to broadcasting, one can wonder why such a comprehensive content requirement for broadcasting exists. While the government as well as most academics believe that the regulation of broadcasting is justifiable, serious questions remain as to the scope and rationale, since the legal definition of "broadcasting" in Japan is not limited to the use of air waves, but applies also to cable and other forms of content delivery. The traditional justification for broadcasting regulation—the need for government intervention to ensure proper allocation of available radio spectrum—is not applicable in such cases. The prevailing view is that broadcasting has a special social impact and is used for the function of conveying important information to the public. Yet the same could be said of print media or cyberspace, so it is seriously doubtful whether there is really a significant difference between them and broadcasting. Furthermore, it is doubtful whether the government must regulate broadcasting—but not print media—in order to preserve the important function of providing essential information to the public. In other words, the constitutionality of the current system of broadcast regulation is highly questionable.

This has a significant implication for mass media in Japan; the lack of strict anti-concentration policies has allowed for close ties of cross-shareholding and control to develop between broadcasters and newspapers. By controlling broadcasting, therefore, the government is also effectively able to control newspapers as well. As a result, tight administrative control over broadcasting has a tremendous impact on freedom of expression in Japan in general.

"New" media and cyberspace

As already noted, the Broadcasting Act treats newer forms of media, such as cable television, as a form of broadcasting, even though they do not use broadcast spectrum. This is also a far cry from the US where cable services are not directly subject to content-based regulations by the FCC.

In addition, despite serious doubt as to whether any government regulations of content in cyberspace (beyond the same content regulations as apply to print media) can be justified, the government established content regulations for certain Internet broadcasting based on telecommunication services (which are also regulated by the MIC). Now some forms of online "broadcasting" are firmly incorporated into the regulatory framework established by the Broadcasting Act. However, most Internet content platforms (such as YouTube), deliver specific content to specific users in response to user requests and probably do not constitute broadcasting under the Broadcasting Act. Yet, ambiguities of the definition and the absence of a more precise explanation leave many cyberspace observers perplexed.

The freedom of association

What is freedom of association?

The Article 21 guarantee of freedom of association protects the rights to create and join associations. The "association" referred to in Article 21 means all kinds of groups or organizations.[200] The right also includes the right to leave associations freely, and to not be forced to join them in the first place.[201]

Article 21 provides the general right to freedom of association, including the right of political association as well as other associations for civic and social causes, which are protected through the Article 21 general guarantee of freedom of expression. The freedom of association simply emphasizes the constitutional protections granted to individuals with respect to the association, and the right of associations themselves.

Freedom of association is also implicated by religion, which enjoys additional protections under Article 20. Also, unlike some countries in the world where a general right to freedom of association is relied upon as the source of constitutional protections for unions, this is unnecessary in Japan thanks to the specific constitutional guarantee of unions in Article 28.

Forming or joining an association

In part because of the constitutional guarantee, there are no legal formalities involved in creating or joining an association. Organizations that wish to enjoy the benefits of specific corporate forms must follow the rules involved in their establishment and membership, of course. There is, however, a special regulation for religious corporations in part due to the tax benefits they enjoy.[202]

There is no comprehensive statute or other regulation governing the formation and operation of political parties in Japan. There are regulations governing their participation in elections and their eligibility to receive financial subsidies, and the use and reporting of political funds.[203] These rules limit eligibility to public funding to parties that meet the necessary requirements, and allocate funds based on the number of Diet seats the party has. Some have questioned the constitutionality of this system, since it uses taxpayer funds to support political parties that many taxpayers have not voted for.

Electoral laws also favor qualifying political parties, including the advantage to some political party or political organization through proportional representation, giving only party-affiliated candidates two opportunities to win a seat in a single election (see discussion at Article 47).[204] There have been some calls for the enactment of a general "Political Party Act," but so far the effort has been unsuccessful.

There are few legal restrictions on freedom to form or join associations. Some licensed professionals are required by law to join professional associations that are granted autonomy and a degree of self-regulatory powers. Examples include: attorneys, tax attorneys, judicial scriveners, administrative scriveners, certified accountants and others. In the *Southern Kyūshū Tax Accountant Association Case* the Supreme Court upheld such mandatory association requirements if there is a suitable public interest justification, but also acknowledged that the requirement imposes limits on such association's activities, such as political donations (see also discussion at Article 19).

Government control over association activities

Some associations may also be subject to government control. For instance, the Subversive Activities Prevention Act allows the National Public Safety Commission to impose restrictions against organizations with a history of engaging in violent subversive conduct (including restriction on publishing), and ultimately to order their dissolution in the event of non-compliance.[205] Former officers and members of organizations dissolved in this way are also prohibited from engaging in any conduct in furtherance of the organization.[206]

Sometimes the freedom of association becomes a central focus, such as when a corporation is ordered to be dissolved by the courts at government application. The Supreme Court addressed this issue when an application was filed to dissolve the religious corporation of Ōmu Shinrikyō, the religious cult responsible for the deadly 1995 sarin gas attack in the Tokyo subway which caused 14 deaths and thousands of injuries.[207] In response to challenges asserting that the dissolution violated Article 20, the Court held that, even after a religious corporation is dissolved, its organization could be preserved and believers would not be prevented from believing or participating in religious activities. Accordingly, the judicial dissolution was not an unconstitutional infringement of religious freedom.[208]

Secrecy of communications

Article 21 also protects the secrecy of communications. The Meiji Constitution (Article 26) declared the secrecy of "letters" (*shinsho*) inviolate, but allowed the law to establish exceptions and there was no general guarantee of secrecy of communications. In contrast, the Constitution of Japan explicitly guarantees secrecy of communications. It is a matter of privacy. However, Article 21's protection of communications secrecy together with freedom of expression indicates the realization that secrecy of communications is also vital to securing freedom of expression. Whistleblowers and critics often need the protection of anonymity.

The protection of the secrecy of communications includes not only the contents being communicated, but also extends to metadata such as the name and other details about the author or recipient, and the frequency and time of communication. Because of the guarantee, the government, postal workers, and even private providers of communications services are prohibited from probing, examining or disclosing the contents of confidential communication.

Secrecy of communications is protected by a variety of statutes. The Penal Code prohibits opening of letters and mail without a legitimate reason as well as unjustified violations of confidentiality obligations.[209] The Postal Act and Telecommunication Service Acts also prohibit persons involved in handling mail or telecommunications from censoring or revealing secrets of communication and third parties from seeking to intercept or misuse such secrets.[210] The Illegal Access Prohibition Act protects the secrecy of communications through computer systems by prohibiting illegal access to such systems or the wrongful use or dissemination of information stored or extracted from them.[211]

The constitutional protection of secrecy of communications prevents the government from obtaining private communications, but the protection is not absolute. As discussed at Article 35, the government must obtain a judicial warrant based on probable cause to search and seize private documents. A similar requirement applies to wire-tapping and other forms of government interception of private communications, which also require a warrant.[212] Access to private communications can only be obtained by the government based upon such a warrant.

Secrecy of communications became an issue when Internet service providers were asked to reveal the identities of persons using those services to make illegal statements or disclosures of information. When a posting on a website or social media violates the Penal Code, the police can obtain a search warrant and obtain the information necessary to identify the offender from service providers. But if the matter is not criminal, such as when one party needs to identify an anonymous Internet user for purposes of serving them with a complaint in a civil lawsuit, for example, the obligation of telecommunication service providers to protect the secrecy of communications (including the anonymity of the communicator) became a significant hurdle. The problem was resolved through a specific statute (known as the "Provider Liability Act"), enacted to make it possible to demand a service provider to reveal information about user identity in certain circumstances, based on a reasonable belief that the disclosure of information online infringes the rights and legal interests of others.[213]

Article 22: The Freedoms to Choose One's Occupation, Emigrate and Divest Citizenship

Tetsuji Matsumoto

Article 22.
(1) Every person shall have freedom to choose and change his residence and to choose his occupation to the extent that it does not interfere with the public welfare.
(2) Freedom of all persons to move to a foreign country and to divest themselves of their nationality shall be inviolate.

Background

Article 22 of the Meiji Constitution provided that "Japanese subjects have the liberty of abode and of changing the same within the limits of law." This was not an insignificant right, since one of the features of the Tokugawa system of government was restrictions on internal travel and a lack of freedom to relocate to different communities. Hirobumi Itō's commentaries on this provision interpreted it as including a guarantee of the freedom to engage in business, but leading scholars at the time did not accept this interpretation.[214] In the GHQ Draft (Article XXI), freedom of "movement and choice of abode" were guaranteed together with freedom of association, subject to not conflicting with the general welfare. A separate clause also guaranteed the right to emigrate and to divest oneself of citizenship. The choice of occupation was guaranteed together with academic freedom under Article XXII. The Japanese drafters subsequently reorganized them into their current configuration.

Economic liberties and the constitution

The constitution has two provisions that explicitly guarantee economic liberties: Article 22 and its freedom of occupational choice, and the Article 29 guarantee of property rights. Both provisions reflect learning from *Lochner*-era constitutionalism of the United States, where excessive protection of "freedom of contract" frustrated the implementation of socio-economic regulatory legislation that is now taken for granted and widely accepted as constitutional.[215]

In this sense, Japan's constitution is a child of the New Deal. It is the first constitution in human history to guarantee welfare rights for individuals (see Article 25). It also contains provisions making it clear that economic liberties are widely restricted by socio-economic legislation (e.g., Article 27). It has a public welfare clause that generally restricts the scope of fundamental human rights (Article 13) and this qualifier is repeated in Article 22 as well as Article 29. Collectively these provisions establish that economic freedoms are subject to restrictions intended not only to prevent harm to others, but also to promote the welfare of socially disadvantaged people.

The freedom to choose one's occupation guaranteed by Article 22 is certainly an economic one. But it is important to understand it also has mental and personal aspects. To English speakers the use of the word "mental" (*seishinteki*) might seem unnatural in a constitutional context but, in Japanese, the freedoms guaranteed by Articles 19, 20, 21 and 23 are frequently referred to by academics as "mental" freedoms. This usage probably derives from the German "*geistige Freiheit*."

This is important to understand, since the personal or mental aspects of the Article 22 freedom are not as easily deemed susceptible to restrictions which may be legitimately imposed upon its economic aspect. However, before discussing this part of Article 22 in more detail, we will first review the other freedoms it guarantees.

The freedom to choose and change one's residence

This freedom is widely understood to include the right to travel. Both this freedom and freedom to choose one's occupation are significant as further steps in breaking down past feudalistic institutions that tied most people to locations and occupations, and thereby making it possible for people to freely engage in economic activities. That said, the freedom to choose and change one's residence should not be thought of as being of an economic nature. Even if restrictions on occupational freedom are permitted through socio-economic legislation, the same rationale cannot be used to restrict freedom to choose and change one's residence. Restrictions on these rights are limited to grounds such as preventing the transmission of infectious disease, administrating bankruptcy and regulating criminal procedure.

An example of such a restriction can be seen in the government's approach to Hansen's Disease (leprosy). Several decades after the disease became treatable, those suffering from it and their family members were legally required to live in isolated communities. In subsequent litigation, a trial court found this to constitute legislative nonfeasance and a violation of Articles 13 and 22.[216]

In Japan it is necessary to register as a resident of a municipality. After the sarin gas attack on Tokyo subway system by the Ōmu Shinrikyō cult in 1995, some municipalities refused to allow former cult members to register as residents. This was struck down by the Supreme Court as illegal, though not on constitutional grounds.[217]

The freedom to move to a foreign country

The Supreme Court and a majority of scholars understand "move" in this clause includes to include travel abroad. This view is nonetheless objectionable to some leading scholars, since in Japanese the "move" is *ijū*, which clearly means emigration rather than temporary visits.[218]

A freedom to travel abroad should naturally entail the freedom to re-enter Japan. However, while the Supreme Court has affirmed that non-Japanese have the right to leave Japan, in the *Kathleen Morikawa Case* it declined to recognize foreign residents as having a "right of sojourn"—the right to leave Japan and be readmitted (as was discovered by many during the global Covid-19 pandemic, when even holders of Japanese residential visas were restricted from entering or reentering Japan).[219] In the *McLean Case* the Court had already declared Article 22(1) to not guarantee foreign nationals a right to enter or continue to reside in Japan.

This freedom has been implicated occasionally in connection with passports. Under the Passport Act, the Minister of Foreign Affairs may deny issuance of a passport to a person reasonably believed likely to commit acts directly and significantly detrimental to the interests or public security of Japan.[220] During the Occupation this power was upheld (without detailed constitutional analysis) in the denial of a passport to a Japanese politician seeking to attend an international meeting at Moscow.[221]

More recently, the Japanese government used another provision of the passport law to force the return of a passport from a journalist covering the Syrian conflict so it could reissue one with restrictions on permissible destinations in order to prevent him traveling to conflict zones and potentially being kidnapped.[222] This restriction was upheld by lower courts and the Supreme Court summarily rejected substantive appeals.[223]

Freedom to divest oneself of Japanese citizenship

The essentially unconditional guarantee of the freedom to cease being Japanese is sometimes seen as a symbol of individualism underlying the Japanese constitution. However, the freedom does not extend to the freedom to be stateless, since the Nationality Act only allows divestiture of citizenship by those already having citizenship of another nation.[224] Nor does the freedom extend to granting citizens complete autonomy to choose if and when they cease to be Japanese. Japanese law prohibits dual nationality; under the Nationality Act those who become citizens of other nations by choice lose their Japanese citizenship, and those who are dual nationals by birth must renounce one citizenship upon adulthood, and there is a mechanism (albeit rarely, if ever, used) for forcibly stripping Japanese nationality from those who fail to renounce foreign citizenship (also see discussion at Article 10).[225]

Freedom to choose one's occupation

We can now return to the provision of Article 22 which has received the most attention from courts and scholars; the freedom to choose one's occupation. As described by the Supreme Court in the *Pharmaceutical Affairs Act Case*, an occupation is:

> *a continuous activity in which an individual engages in order to maintain his own livelihood. Furthermore, in a society in which there is a division of labor, an occupation is by nature an activity apportioned by social function through which one contributes to the continuity and development of society, and as the locus where each person fulfills his personally endowed individuality, it also has an inseparable relationship to the personal worth of the individual.*[226]

This understanding of what "occupation" in Article 22 means is widely accepted by academics. As well, as noted above, it is thus important to understand the freedom as having both economic and mental/personal aspects.

In the *Pharmaceutical Affairs Act Case*, the Court also held that the freedom encompasses not only choices regarding commencing, continuing and abandoning an occupation, but also to the nature and content of occupational activities. Thus, the freedom is not just one of choice of occupation, but of occupational activity.

The freedom to choose one's occupation, of course, includes the right to engage in business. But the occupation is not limited to business if it means independent activities for the sake of profit.

Occupational freedom and the public safety/social welfare regulatory dichotomy

The Article 22 guarantee of freedom of occupation is implicated in a wide range of business regulation which for the most part consist of constraints on freedom. It is thus useful to distinguish between two types of regulation: those aimed at preventing harm to others (public safety regulation), and those intended to promote the welfare of the people, especially the socially disadvantaged (social welfare regulation). As discussed below, courts have generally applied a somewhat stricter level of strict scrutiny to the former, while being quite lenient in their review of the latter.

A great deal of Japanese business regulation is related to preventing excessive competition and impact the freedom to choose one's occupation. The leading case on this type of "social welfare regulation" is the *Public Marketplace Act Case* of 1972.[227] The case involved criminal charges brought against a property owner for operating a public marketplace without the permit required under the Public Marketplace Act. Under the Act a permit would not be issued if there were any existing public marketplaces nearby, as was the case.

The Supreme Court upheld the restriction on the grounds that the purpose of the Public Marketplace Act was to protect individual shops within marketplaces from the threat of financial instability that would result from excessive competition among public marketplaces. The Court held that this was a reasonable regulatory purpose, and that it would not find this type of socio-economic regulation unconstitutional unless the regulatory measures taken were manifestly and substantially unreasonable. In all subsequent cases in which the *Public Marketplace Act Case* has been cited by the Court as a precedent, it has upheld the constitutionality of the law or regulation being challenged.[228] In other words, regulations intended to protect businesses from excessive competition are an acceptable form of "social welfare regulation" for the benefit of those engaging in such businesses.

By contrast, the different approach taken by the Court in reviewing challenges to "public safety regulations" can be seen in the *Pharmaceutical Affairs Act Case*, which was decided just a few years later, and is the second instance of the Court finding a statutory provision unconstitutional.[229] As with the *Public Marketplace Act* case, it involved proximity restrictions on the licensing of pharmacies. However, in this case the government's position was that the law was not about protecting pharmacies from the financial impact of excessive competition, but using a licensing system (with proximity-based requirements) to protect consumers from injury from poorly administered low-quality drugs that could result from such excessive competition.

In this case the Court first noted that "in general licensing systems go beyond simple regulation of the content and form of occupational activities and impose restrictions upon the freedom to choose an occupation itself in the narrow sense" and "[t]hus, because they are powerful limitations upon freedom of occupation, in principle in order to be able to affirm their constitutionality, they are required to be necessary and reasonable measures for an important public interest." Furthermore, the Court added that:

> [a]*lso in cases where they are not measures for a positive purpose with respect to social or economic policy, but rather negative, police measures for the purpose of preventing harm to the public brought about by free occupational activities, it is necessary to find that the above purpose could not be fully achieved through regulation of simply the form and content of the occupational activities, which is, in comparison with a licensing system, a looser restriction upon freedom of occupation. These requirements are demanded not only with respect to the licensing system itself, but also with respect to its content. And even in a case in which the adoption of a licensing system is itself approved, a separate determination must again be made concerning the suitability of the individual conditions for a license in the light of these requirements.*[230]

A leading scholar has described this as the Court adopting a "strict rationality" standard of review for public safety regulations.[231] More likely it is a kind of "intermediate scrutiny." Whatever the standard is called, the Court used it to find the Pharmaceutical Affairs Act's proximity restrictions unconstitutional, finding the mere assertion of a likely causal relation between competition and the harm being prevented inadequate grounds for the restriction, and finding it unreasonable to assume the danger asserted could not be "prevented by strict enforcement of supervision and regulation of [the pharmaceutical] dispensing businesses."[232]

Another important precedent is the *Public Bathhouse Act Case*, in which the Court upheld the constitutionality of the proximity restriction on public bathhouse partly relying on the fact that it served the objective of keeping the bathhouse sanitary.[233] Since this case predates the *Pharmaceutical Affairs Act Case*, one might think the latter case superseded it. However, the Court reaffirmed its ruling in the *Public Bathhouse Act Case* in two subsequent Petty Bench cases, both of which involved challenges to bathhouse proximity restrictions. One of these relied on the *Public Marketplace Act Case* and applied its very lenient standard of review.[234] The other made no such reference, but easily found the regulation to be necessary and reasonable for the purpose of making public bathhouses available to people without bathing facilities in their own house.[235]

With respect to the freedom to choose one's occupation, the Court has generally maintained the dichotomy between its standards of review for public safety regulations and social welfare regulation. However, some regulations do not readily fit into either category. For example, in the past the Liquor Tax Act required a license to sell alcoholic beverages. The liquor tax is a special type of consumption tax collected from consumers by liquor stores who pay it up through a hierarchy of wholesalers, breweries and distillers who finally pay tax to the National Tax Agency.[236] In a challenge to the licensing requirement on Article 22 grounds, the government argument was that the license was necessary to secure the payment of the tax. In the *Liquor Sales License Case*, the Court found the requirement constitutional, citing the *Pharmaceutical Affairs Act Case* but qualifying the standard of review with a reference to its holding in the *Salaried Workers Tax Discrimination Case* (see discussion at Article 30). Applying this methodology, the Court held that licensing requirements imposed in order to secure payment of a tax would not be found unconstitutional unless they were manifestly unreasonable.

Thus, while the *Pharmaceutical Affairs Act Case* is significant as a rare instance of the Supreme Court finding a statutory provision unconstitutional, it has had limited applicability in subsequent jurisprudence. The strict scrutiny applied in the case has been limited to cases involving the right to choose a particular occupation in the case of licensing schemes requiring prior administrative approval.

For example, in a case involving a challenge requiring the licensing requirement for judicial scriveners (a category of licensed legal profession), the Court upheld the licensing and qualification requirements required for entering the profession.[237] In doing so the Court relied on the *Pharmaceutical Affairs Act Case* but did not apply the higher level of scrutiny, instead offering a brief statement that the restrictions were necessary and reasonable. This is a reflection of the Court's differing approach for analyzing and reviewing professional qualification requirements and business licensing requirements; the former are generally upheld on a "rational basis" standard, while the latter are at least theoretically subject to potentially stricter scrutiny as in the *Pharmaceutical Affairs Act Case*, though in practice this has not been the case.

More recently the Court revisited the constitutionality of restrictions on pharmacies in the Internet age. In the *Online Pharmacy Case*, the Court upheld the constitutionality on the requirement that pharmacists have face-to-face interactions with customers seeking to buy certain pharmaceutical products and medical devices, even though they burdened the ability of on-line pharmacies to conduct business.[238] The Court found the prohibition to be a reasonable restriction on online pharmacies, insofar as it applied only to "pharmaceuticals requiring guidance," a category of over-the-counter drugs which had been approved for sale within the past five years. Though this was also a case involving "public safety regulation" and the Court referenced the *Pharmaceutical Affairs Act Case*, it again declined to apply the higher level of scrutiny articulated in that case, instead opting to accept the implicit judgment of the Diet that the legislation was "reasonable and necessary."[239]

In closing, it is appropriate to make a short comment on how the Court decides what level of scrutiny to apply with regulations affecting the freedom to choose one's occupation. Obviously, the manner and impact of the regulation in question is extremely relevant, and there is thus a significant substantive aspect which should be considered in determining the level of scrutiny to apply. At the same time, however, there is also an institutional aspect to the question that should not be forgotten. That is, whether the judiciary has the institutional capabilities necessary to make decisions about the relevant facts, particularly when compared with administrative or legislative branches of government. The underlying purpose of the regulations under consideration is particularly relevant in this regard.

Now, as in other countries all over the world, the constitutionality of laws and orders restricting people's freedoms to prevent the spread of Covid-19 have presented significant questions for the courts to address. While these restrictions are clearly imposed for the sake of public health and safety, it would seem appropriate for courts to apply a stricter standard of review on that basis, particularly given that there may not be enough public health information available to make an appropriate decision. Insofar as these restrictions impact economic freedoms, however, it seems that the Supreme Court will likely defer to the political and administrative judgments of the other branches, as long as they do their best to make their decisions based on what is scientifically necessary and reasonable. The same will likely prove true of restrictions impacting other constitutional freedoms as well.

Article 23: Academic Freedom

Yūichiro Tsuji

Article 23.
Academic freedom is guaranteed.

Historical background

Article 23 has a historical background which requires some explanation. It follows the German constitution,[240] under which special protection was given to universities as places where professors enjoyed the privilege and freedom to engage in research and other academic endeavors. This is notwithstanding the fact that the Japanese constitution was initially drafted by American-trained GHQ lawyers whose own constitution had no comparable guarantee.[241] The reason that the Japanese constitution followed the German type, and not that of the US constitution lies in its unique history.

It is not clear whether the academic freedom that appears in the GHQ proposal was stipulated by GHQ with reference to other constitutions or private constitutional proposals.[242] There are no Japanese government documents that reveal the intentions of GHQ in drafting Article 23, but there are hints in GHQ documents drafted before the GHQ Draft.

While the Matsumoto Committee was still preparing its draft amendments, US military lawyers Milo E. Rowell and Alfred Hussey Jr. had prepared a report entitled Report of Preliminary Studies and Recommendations of Japanese Constitution, dated December 6, 1945.[243] This report referenced the constitutions of various countries and constitutional proposals prepared by scholars not affiliated with the Japanese government. The Report recommended Japan adopt a constitution containing a bill of rights which guaranteed, among other things: "Freedom of educational institutions above the middle school level from governmental restrictions on curricula and instruction and non-interference in academic matters by the Ministry of Education or other administrative branch of government."[244]

The minutes of a February 8, 1946, meeting with the Committee on Civil Rights provide as follows: "[F]reedom of academic teaching, study, and lawful research, and restricted the authority for dismissal of teachers to professional organizations or societies.[245]

Records note that [t]he Steering Committee objected to the guarantee of research since the Allies intended to severely restrict some kinds of research and entirely forbid others. Then, the Committee on Civil Rights submitted the following report (February 1946) by GHQ, Memorandum for the Chief, Government Section containing the following directive: "Freedom of academic teaching, study and choice of occupation are guaranteed to all adults."[246]

This history is rooted in several well-known cases of government attacks on academic theories about law. In 1933 the Ministry of the Interior and the Ministry of Education led an attack on Kyoto University Professor Yukitoki Takigawa for his criticism of the unequal treatment of men and women under the law of adultery, which at the time was a crime if engaged in by married women, but not by married men. This view was problematic because the emperor had consorts in addition to his official wife, and Takigawa's book was banned, partly because of his criticism of the sacred and inviolable emperor.[247]

Perhaps the most famous instance of the suppression of an academic is that of constitutional scholar and Tokyo Imperial University Professor Tatsukichi Minobe. His scholarship included an effort to reconcile Taishō era theories of democracy with the Meiji Constitution (under which the emperor was sacred, the supreme leader and locus of sovereignty).[248] Minobe argued that the government or state was a legal entity, that the emperor was the supreme organ (agent) of the government or state, and that the emperor was essentially supported by his ministries.[249]

This was the so-called "Emperor as Organ of State" theory. Minobe first published it in 1912 and it became widely accepted among constitutional scholars. Starting in the mid-1930s Minobe and his views came under attack from militarists as contradicting the *kokutai*, under which the emperor was the state itself pursuant to Articles 1 and 4 of the Meiji Constitution. Minobe's book was banned, he was investigated under suspicion of *lèse majesté*, forced to resign his seat in the House of Peers, and injured in an assassination attempt by a right-wing zealot.[250]

Thus, Japanese constitutional scholarship has direct historical experience with the infringement of academic freedom. These incidents demonstrated that academics and researchers are vulnerable to governmental interference and pressure. This is why the constitution came to contain a specific guarantee of academic freedom in the form of Article 23.

The guarantee and its interpretation

The basic proposition of Article 23 is that the pursuit of knowledge by scholars and researchers should be free of government interference. It is based on an underlying presumption that academic research by professors and universities is devoted to seeking the truth.[251] Under the School Education Act, "The purpose of universities, as centers of science, shall be to impart knowledge widely, teach and study arts and sciences deeply, and develop intellectual, moral, and applied abilities."[252]

The Article 23 guarantee consists of three strands: (1) freedom to research and to publish the results of research, (2) the autonomy of universities, and (3) the freedom of education. The freedom to research and publish overlaps with the freedom of thought and conscience (see Article 19) and freedom of expression (Article 21). Academic and scientific research involves the critical investigation of existing knowledge and theories in order to develop new or different perspectives. Article 23 provides special protection for this process.

With respect to specific articles of the constitution, the term "public welfare" appears only in Articles 12, 13, 22, and 29. However, scholars believe that almost all human rights are subject to limitation by public welfare on the basis that it is not permissible to infringe on the rights of others. However, a person's innermost feelings are not subject to the restrictions of public welfare because they do not infringe on the rights of others unless they are acted upon. Thus, scholarly hypotheses still in the conceptual stage are protected under Article 19, and are thus not subject to the restriction of public welfare. When scholars publish their research or conduct experiments, however, they may be restricted by public welfare if their research or experiments infringe on the rights of others or pose a concrete danger, just like the freedom of expression under Article 21.

Particularly in the field of the natural sciences, research has become a highly-specialized and infrastructure-intensive endeavor. It is not practical for individuals to conduct such research without the support of a university or research institute. Each research field has its own discipline, methodology, and procedure for conducting research, and achievements are evaluated by a community of those engaged in similar or related research. Moreover, professors in universities need to maintain financial stability to fund their research. For this reason, Article 23 is understood to provide special protection for the autonomy of universities where researchers are affiliated. This autonomy extends to personnel decisions, maintenance of order, control of facilities and the treatment of students. More recently some constitutional scholars have argued that Article 23 should also extend to autonomy in budgeting and the method of evaluating educational achievement.[253]

Freedom of education refers to the lectures and curricular content delivered by professors and universities. As in Germany, this freedom is guaranteed primarily to institutions of higher education (see discussion at Article 26 regarding primary and secondary education).

The question of whether the guarantees of Article 23 extend to the activities of university students is, in fact, still an issue today when student activities are suppressed by universities. One view is that students do not enjoy academic freedom, because they are just users of the services and facilities of their university. Others argue, however, that students do enjoy it because they get involved in research with professors.

In the *Tōdai Poporo Case*, the Supreme Court explained that the academic freedom under Article 23 of the constitution shall be enjoyed by students in the same manner as by ordinary citizens. However, as students of a university, they enjoy greater academic freedom and have access to facilities under the self-governing control of the university authorities, which is founded in the nature of the university and one aspect of the special academic freedom and autonomy possessed by professors and other university researchers.

The *Tōdai Poporo Case* involved a theater-troupe (named *Poporo*) sanctioned by Tokyo University (commonly abbreviated as "*Tōdai*"). In 1952 the troupe performed a play depicting the *Matsukawa Case*, a highly controversial prosecution of national railway union members in connection with a 1949 fatal train accident. This took place during a tense cold-war environment in which universities were a hotbed of socialist thought which, combined with widespread labor unrest, was a source of great concern and attempted suppression by government authorities.

Students recognized four plain-clothes policemen in the audience. Three were captured and forced to write apology letters. The students were subsequently prosecuted for crimes of violence against the officers but acquitted on the grounds that they had been properly defending the autonomy of their university as guaranteed by Article 23 from police interference. On appeal from the prosecution, the Supreme Court vacated the acquittals and remanded for further proceedings (which duly resulted in convictions). In doing so the Court described Article 23 as broadly protecting the freedom of research and publication of research enjoyed in particular by professors and university students, but also by the Japanese people in general. The Court also acknowledged the importance of university autonomy. However, it rejected the notion that an activity was "academic" and thus entitled to the protection merely because it took place on campus and was sanctioned by the university; the troupe was putting on a clearly political play freely open to any member of the public who purchased a ticket. As such it was merely a political and social activity not entitled to Article 23.

Dual use and the Science Council of Japan

A more recent area of controversy under Article 23 arises in connection with so-called "dual use technologies"—technologies developed through university research which have both civilian and military applications. Japan's National Security Strategy of 2017 encourages research into dual use technologies.[254] In 2015 the Acquisition, Technology, and Logistic Agency of Ministry of Defense established a large budget for research into technologies for national security use.

Given that modern research in natural science fields requires financial support from the government and private sources, and that the source of funding can impact the objectivity of the research itself, research funding has great potential to infringe the autonomy of universities. In 2017, an announcement by the Science Council of Japan declared that military-funded research conflicts with the freedom of academic research.

Human cloning and Article 23

Another area of controversy arises in connection with human cloning. As with the exercise of other constitutional rights and freedoms, academic research is restricted by the public welfare, which prohibits the infringement of other rights.

The Act on Regulation of Human Cloning Techniques generally prohibits the transplant of human embryos or germ cells, and requires researchers in the field to follow guidelines established by the Ministry of Education, Culture, Sports, Science and Technology (MEXT).[255] The law allows the MEXT to issue orders to modify or refrain from research that does not follow these guidelines. Some scholars have argued that these guidelines should be put in statutory form to clarify and establish a firmer foundation for public-welfare based restrictions on academic freedom. When the judiciary reviews a law such as one that concerns cloning research, judges tend to respect the expertise of researchers. Yet there is no reason why courts should avoid judicial review on issues related to human dignity such as cloning research simply on the grounds of their lack of research expertise.

University regulation and funding

Despite the implicit Article 23 guarantee of university autonomy, universities are highly regulated by the MEXT. This control is particularly pronounced in the case of national universities. Their conversion into special corporations in 2013 was accompanied by legislative changes granting greater power to university presidents, and establishing management councils with memberships including university outsiders. Presidents at many universities are now chosen by these councils rather than through the long-standing tradition of election by faculty and staff. Previously autonomous faculties within universities (both national and private) were demoted to "advisory" bodies to university presidents who could ignore their decisions. The MEXT assigns medium-term (six year) objectives to each national university, which submits plans for achieving them and receives funding based on the MEXT's evaluation. Shrinking research budgets mean professors at national university corporations are increasingly required to seek external funds to maintain the minimum level of their research.

The long-term goal of these changes appears to be to make universities more "corporate" and subject to top-down control by a single person beholden to university regulators—the president. Whether these changes are consistent with the constitutional guarantee of academic freedom remains to be seen. Currently, both public and private universities receive substantial funding assistance from the government. This financial support is being reduced every year. When Article 23 was crafted, academic freedom was defined in opposition to the government's interference on the freedom of teaching in universities. Today, the threat to academic freedom appears to be likely to develop through reduction in funding and the resulting diminishment of the potential for research and new learning at universities in general.

Article 24: Marriage and Gender Equality in Family Life

Yūichiro Tsuji

Article 24

(1) Marriage shall be based only on the mutual consent of both sexes and it shall be maintained through mutual cooperation with the equal rights of husband and wife as a basis.

(2) With regard to choice of spouse, property rights, inheritance, choice of domicile, divorce and other matters pertaining to marriage and the family, laws shall be enacted from the standpoint of individual dignity and the essential equality of the sexes.

Historical background

The system of family law that developed after the Meiji Restoration and became embedded in the Civil Code and the family registration system was based on extended family units with a formal "head of household" (*koshu*). *Koshu* was a heritable legal status that usually vested in the eldest legitimate male. The status could not be freely abandoned, except through formal retirement at the age of sixty. By identifying a person clearly responsible for the family unit, this system also enabled the government to use the *koshu* as a means of implementing policies such as conscription and taxation. In exchange, the household heads were given broad authority over what happened within the family, including the power to veto marriages and adoptive relationships involving its members. Under this system marriages were essentially agreements between families agreed by the respective heads.

The Occupation authorities considered these family structures one of the factors that had enabled militarism to arise and to result in poor treatment of women who were accorded inferior status. Family law reform was thus one of the agendas of GHQ. This is reflected in Article XXIII of the GHQ Draft, which among other things declared that marriage should be "founded upon mutual consent instead of parental coercion, and maintained through cooperation instead of male domination."

In the drafting process that followed, the references to parental coercion and male domination were removed and other amendments made. Famously, Beate Sirota Gordon—"the only woman in the room"—is credited with both drafting the original language and preserving the gender equality language that survived in Article 14.[256] Similarly, the "based on the mutual consent of both sexes" language in Article 24(1) is an express rejection of the power of the male head of household to veto a marriage under the old Civil Code.

Occupation-era amendments to the Civil Code, family registration system and other related laws reflected the Article 24 mandates.[257] Article 2 of the Civil Code stipulates the dignity of individuals and the essential equality of both sexes as basic interpretive principles applicable throughout.

"Rational" discrimination permitted

That said, however, even after substantial amendment during the Occupation, the Civil Code (and the Family Register Act) contained a number of provisions that either expressly or implicitly embedded various forms of discrimination based on gender and birth status. Some have been removed either legislatively or as the result of litigation, but others remain.[258] And as discussed at Article 10, discriminatory rules based on gender and parents' marital status have been a factor in eligibility for nationality.

For example, Article 819 of the Civil Code vests sole custody over children born out of wedlock in mothers by default. Article 772 presumes the husband is the father of children conceived during marriage or born during the 300-day period after marital dissolution.[259] Under Article 774 the presumption of parent-child relationship under Article 772 can be overturned, but only on motion by the husband, not the wife or child. A constitutional challenge to this discriminatory treatment was rejected by the Supreme Court in 2020.[260] Finally, the Japanese system of family law is based on marriages, births, divorces, adoptions and other changes in family status being recorded in the family register pursuant to the Family Register Act.[261] However, insofar as the entire family registry system is limited to Japanese citizens, it necessarily results in differing treatment for non-Japanese residents and family members.[262] It also imposes significant impediments on the estimated ten thousand *mukosekisha*—Japanese people who do not have family registries because their births were not registered and thus lack the ability to provide a common form of proof of identity (family register extracts).[263]

Discrimination and Article 24 in the courts

Discrimination based on legitimacy has also been perpetuated by both the Civil Code and the Supreme Court, though the 2013 *Out-of-Wedlock Inheritance Rights Discrimination Case* discussed at Article 14 saw the Court take action against such discrimination in the context of inheritance rights.[264] Several other contemporaneous decisions reveal the continuing tension between more traditional family structures both assumed and reinforced by the Civil Code and the constitutional mandate of equal treatment.

The Spousal Surname Cases

Article 750 of the Civil Code requires spouses to share the same legal surname. This necessitates that one party to the marriage change their legal name. Although the requirement is framed in gender neutral terms, in 98 percent of cases the wife takes the husband's name. For working women who have developed a professional reputation under their maiden name this requirement can be a significant burden (and is arguably unnecessary in any case). In a 2015 Grand Bench judgment, the Supreme Court rejected challenges to the requirement rooted in Articles 13, 14 and 24 in part on the grounds that the marriage system including surname requirements was "a matter that needs to be discussed and determined by the Diet."[265] This reasoning was slightly ironic given that the claim was framed as a tort suit against the state for legislative nonfeasance (see Introduction to this Chapter). This procedural aspect of the case that made it possible for some justices to issue concurring opinions declaring the surname requirement to be unconstitutional, but nonetheless rejecting the appeals on the ground appellants the Diet had not yet had adequate time to remedy the problem legislatively.[266]

The Grand Bench revisited the question in 2021, this time in a challenge to provisions of the Family Register Act, which resulted in rejections of marriage registration filings that did not denote the same surname for both spouses.[267] Referencing its 2015 decision, the Court upheld the requirement again, though with some grumbling about constitutionality in concurring and dissenting opinions.

At the time of writing at least two other challenges to the surname requirement were being litigated but had not been addressed by the Supreme Court. One involved a Japanese couple who were married in New York and claimed that their New York law marriage should be recognized in Japan despite retaining separate surnames.[268] In an unreported March 25, 2021 judgment the Tokyo District Court rejected claims of unconstitutional discrimination based on the fact that the same surname requirement does not apply to marriages between Japanese and non-Japanese.[269]

The Women-Only Remarriage Prohibition Period Case

Article 733 of the Civil Code prohibited women from remarrying for six months following the dissolution of a prior marriage. Men were subject to no such restriction. In a 2015 judgment the Grand Bench found the restriction unconstitutional but only as to the extent that the prohibition exceeded 100 days. The logic of this seemingly strange result relates to other provisions of the Civil Code designed to prevent conflicting claims of paternity over children born during or shortly after marriage. Under Article 772(2) of the Code, children born 200 days or more after marriage or within 300 days of the dissolution of a marriage are presumed to have been conceived during marriage. Thus, assuming an average gestation time of 300 days, conflicting presumptions of paternity could be avoided merely by preventing a woman from remarrying for 100 days after divorce. Any restriction extending beyond that period was thus unnecessary given the legislative purpose, and thus unconstitutional. Following this decision, the Diet modified Article 733 to shorten the period from 6 months to 100 days.[270]

The *Women-only Remarriage Prohibition Case* can be said to demonstrate that despite the gender equality espoused by the constitution, substantive Japanese family law is still subordinated to outdated presumptions of paternity that date back to the 19th century. This was also demonstrated by the *Transgender Paternity Case*, which was not a constitutional case but saw the Supreme Court uphold the right of a transgender man (who had been born as a woman but legally changed gender) to be named as the father of a child born to his wife using donor sperm.[271] While it may seem a very progressive decision, it can also be understood as merely the consistent application of 19th-century presumptions of paternity that applied in other contexts.

Same-sex marriage

Japan has not recognized same-sex marriage and there are no Supreme Court rulings on the subject.[272] The 2003 law enabling persons to change their legal gender specifically prohibits married persons from doing so, in part to prevent same-sex marriages from arising.[273] At the time of writing, several cases challenging the constitutionality of not allowing same-sex marriage were being heard in the lower courts.

"Mutual consent of both sexes only*"*

An important nuance missing from the English version of the first paragraph of Article 24 is that the Japanese version reads as mandating marriage to be based only on the mutual consent of both sexes. In the historical context described above this is best understood as a rejection of the power of the head of household over marital decisions.[274] Textually, however, it can also be read as a rejection of any conditions on marriage beyond the parties' consent.

The "consent as sole condition to marriage" reading has been used (unsuccessfully) in arguments against the spousal surname requirement described above as well as in favor of same-sex marriage. However, it is widely accepted that the state can impose additional requirements on marriage including that they be registered in order to have legal effect (Civil Code Article 739), and not be bigamous (Article 732), or entered into by minors below statutory age (Article 731) or between persons within prohibited degrees of affinity (Articles 734–736).[275]

Nor does "consent" apply to remaining married; a "right to divorce" has never been identified in the Japanese constitution. Until 1987 Japan's Supreme Court had rendered it virtually impossible for the "spouse at fault" to obtain a judicial (i.e., non-consensual) divorce.[276]

Marriage and employment

It was once not uncommon for companies to require female employees to retire upon marriage. This was rejected by lower courts as unconscionable, and prohibited legislatively in 1972.[277]

Article 24 as a grant of legislative discretion

In closing the discussion of Article 24 it is worth revisiting a subject touched upon in the chapter introduction; the role of constitutional rights provisions as legislative mandates as opposed to judicially-enforced norms. The discussion above may lead some readers to feel that Japan still has family laws that are inherently discriminatory based on gender, legitimacy or nationality despite the seemingly clear wording of Article 24(2). However, the courts understand the provisions to be primarily a description of the scope of legislative discretion granted to the Diet in the sphere of family law. [278]

Article 25: Right to a Minimum Standard of Cultured Living

Mark Levin and *Tōru Enoki*

Article 25.

(1) All people shall have the right to maintain the minimum standards of wholesome and cultured living.

(2) In all spheres of life, the State shall use its endeavors for the promotion and extension of social welfare and security, and of public health.

The welfare right as a social right

Social rights are human rights that have come to be guaranteed in order to protect the socially and economically vulnerable from the adverse effects of unemployment, poverty and deteriorating working conditions that have accompanied the advancement of capitalism. Drawn from the German public law notion of *soziales Grundrecht*, social rights are based on the idea of a welfare state that broadly recognizes the involvement of the government and are the right to request positive action and consideration by the government so that the socially and economically disadvantaged can live a life that meets certain basic standards. Therefore, social rights have a different character from civil liberties, which means the elimination of interference by the government. They are the rights related to the quality of socio-economic life.

The Meiji Constitution had no stipulations pertaining to these rights. A fairly extensive approach to social welfare was included in Article XXIV of the GHQ Draft. This was then more narrowly presented in the Cabinet's submission of the draft constitution to the 90th Imperial Diet in 1946, suggesting early on that the Japanese government was not as comfortable including such broad rights for social welfare. During the deliberations in the House of Representatives, the Socialist Party further proposed that the welfare right be presented as an individual right, leading to the first paragraph being included in what became Article 25. Thus, the constitution stipulates these social rights explicitly, with Article 25 positioned as the most general provision for this purpose and Articles 26, 27, and 28 adding further particularity as to the right to receive an education, the right to work, and the rights of workers.

Welfare rights and related laws

Article 25 consists of paragraph (1), a provision declaring the right of every citizen to live a life that meets certain basic standards, and paragraph (2), which imposes on the government the obligation to make efforts to actualize the welfare right. In light of paragraph (2)'s clear exhortation for the state's affirmative action, the principal legal structures that effectuate Article 25 are legislative enactments.

These may be distinguished as laws pertaining to social welfare and security (i.e., insurance) and those pertaining to public health. In the first regard, this includes the Public Assistance Act, the Child Welfare Act, the Social Elderly Welfare Act and the Disabled Welfare Act.[279] Laws that concern social security insurance include the National Health Insurance Act, the National Pension Act, the Employment Insurance Act and the Long-Term Care Insurance Act.[280] In the area of laws for public health, there are the Community Health Act, the Food Sanitation Act, the Basic Environment Act, the Air Pollution Control Act[281] and others.

Article 1 of the Public Assistance Act expresses a legislative intent directly related to carrying out Article 25's obligations: "The purpose of this Act is for the State to guarantee a minimum standard of living as well as to promote self-support for all citizens who are living in poverty by providing the necessary public assistance according to the level of poverty, based on the principles prescribed in Article 25 of the Constitution of Japan." Meanwhile, Article 3 of the Act explicitly draws upon the constitutional phrasing: "The minimum standard of living guaranteed by this Act shall be where a person is able to maintain a wholesome and cultured standard of living." Similarly, the Public Assistance Act stipulates the institutions of public assistance in order to enable those in need of public assistance to lead a "the minimum standards of wholesome and cultured living,"

Thus, unlike many or most areas of rights-based attention in constitutional law, the guarantee of the welfare right provided for in Article 25 requires not *inaction* but *action* by the government, which can be realized through laws embodying the purpose of Article 25 and administrative regulations executing the mandates of those laws. The constitutional text is only broadly stated, leaving unclear to whom and what benefits the government will provide. Clarity is added through academic theory and jurisprudence.

Theories as to the legal nature of the welfare rights

Four leading theories on the legal nature of the welfare rights guaranteed by Article 25 have been presented in Japanese academic circles. These are all well-considered by scholars and further provide a framing for the jurisprudence as to the status quo as well as to possibilities for alternative approaches. Each have been named in leading scholarship, with literal translations to English provided here.

The Programmatic Declaration theory

The "programmatic declaration theory" represents the narrowest and most conservative interpretation, but is also the closest to the extant jurisprudence of Japan's Supreme Court. It holds that Article 25 of the constitution merely sets forth policy goals, i.e., ostensibly moral obligations of the government, but that it does not allow for specific justiciable rights claims by individual citizens. In short then, there is no enforceable *legal* right to be found. Proponents of this theory argue that the concept of "the minimum standards of wholesome and cultured living," with multiple possible means of achieving it is too ambiguous to be a judicially-actionable right, with further interference from interpretive complications when budgetary constraints are factored in. They believe that the embodiment of the welfare right should be left to the professional and technical discretion of the legislative and executive branches and would allow for no judicial inquiry whatsoever.[282] This is the theory reflected in much of the Supreme Court's Article 25 jurisprudence, as discussed below. Other articles of the constitution are also sometimes discussed in terms of being "programmatic provisions," like Article 25 under this theory.

The Abstract Rights theory

A more centrist view is found in the "abstract rights theory," whereby Article 25 is understood to generally (i.e., abstractly) impose an obligation on the government to implement measures that embody the welfare right through legislation and the budget. Thus, as with the programmatic declaration theory, failures of the legislature to implement Article 25 are not judicially actionable. However, once legislation such as the Public Assistance Act is established, then Article 25 can function as an interpretive standard to be accessed in judicial decision-making and for the imposition of justiciable remedies by the courts with regards to entitlements, due process and the sufficiency of the benefits provided.[283]

The Concrete Rights theory

Progressing further liberally, the "concrete rights theory" asserts that Article 25 imposes judicially cognizable duties on the Diet and the executive to realize the welfare right. Under this theory plaintiffs should be allowed to file suit seeking a declaration of unconstitutionality in the circumstances of the law and regulations, but with remedies limited to obtaining such recognition. Even if the Court ascertains a gap in the provisions of the law and regulations with regards to the state's Article 25 duties, there is no basis to obtain a judgment ordering performance.[284]

The Right to Claim Benefits theory

Finally, the "right to claim benefits theory" recognizes an affirmative right of citizens to sue and claim benefits that directly arise from Article 25(1). This theory calls upon the courts to objectively determine the content of "the minimum standards of wholesome and cultured living," which other theories regard as too ambiguous for such resolutions. Moreover, proponents of the right to claim benefits theory argue that welfare rights allow courts to impose budget-sensitive determinations, meaning that remedies may be recognized even when they will impose fiscal and other obligations on the state.[285]

The abstract rights theory has the most support in academic circles. However, this is partly because, as noted above, a host of laws in Japan now already effectuate welfare rights relating to Article 25. In practice the abstract rights theory and right to claim benefits theory have essentially merged into the prevailing academic understanding of Article 25.

Cases relating to welfare rights

In an ideal setting, if laws and the administrative regulations based on them to actualize Article 25's guarantee of welfare rights are appropriate, legal disputes as to their propriety and sufficiency might not arise. In reality, however, several court cases unpacking the question as to what is meant by "the minimum standards of wholesome and cultured living" present the Japanese judiciary needing to develop interpretive jurisprudence. Moreover, other matters invariably arise relating to eligibility and due process even when benefits may be sufficient.

Particularly at the Supreme Court level, Article 25 jurisprudence has been conservative, essentially implementing the programmatic declaration theory. In practice, its decisions allow discretionary authority regarding implementation to remain with the legislative and executive branches. That said, judicial decisions arising under Article 25 at the district and high court levels have been more diverse in their approaches, offering perspectives more closely approximating the more liberal theoretical approaches argued for by legal scholars. Accordingly, while the status quo for rights claims under Article 25 is limited, the possibility of an alternative future remains.

Despite scholarly criticism suggesting that the decision has become anachronistic in today's wealthier Japan, the Supreme Court's decision in the *Food Supply Management Act Case* of 1948 is generally recognized as the leading case in this regard.[286] The case involved an appeal from a defendant convicted of buying black-market rice, based on a wartime statute requiring farmers to sell their crops to the government and which was left in place to address postwar food shortages. The defendant argued that since the purchase and transportation of food was necessary for survival, the provision of the Food Control Act that made it illegal to buy food violated the Article 25(1) guarantee of the right to a wholesome living.

In response, the Supreme Court first held that Article 25(1) of the constitution only declares the general responsibility of the government to administer the national government so that all citizens may live wholesome and cultured living, and does not directly guarantee specific and practical rights to individual citizens. In addition, it further found that the Food Control Act itself had the purpose of benefitting the welfare of the people in general by stabilizing their living conditions as much as possible. Thus, it conformed to the purpose of Article 25(2). While the Food Control Act has since been repealed, the first portion of the judgment remains the Court's approach to interpreting Article 25.

This approach was sustained but further refined by the Supreme Court in the 1967 *Asahi Case*.[287] The case involved a challenge by a welfare recipient that the standard of financial support set by the government under the Public Assistance Act was insufficient to maintain a "the minimum standards of wholesome and cultured living." He prevailed at the district court level in a ruling implicitly built upon a cognizable capacity of individuals to sue for benefits arising from concrete rights under Article 25(1), such as would be consistent with the right to claim benefits theory introduced above, and even allowing for judicial determination of the nation's fiscal capacity to provide the benefits claimed as rights under Article 25.

The district court's ruling however, did not survive at either the high court or Supreme Court levels, and, notwithstanding Japan's greater relative national wealth in contrast to the early postwar years, the conservative views articulated by the programmatic declaration theory prevailed instead. Thus, over the objection of four separate dissenting opinions, the majority of the Supreme Court upheld the levels of financial support set by the government and affirmed the jurisprudential approach articulated in the *Food Supply Management Act Case* of 1948 of declining to recognize Article 25 as a source of concrete rights. However, the ruling did open a narrow crack in the door for judicial review of welfare benefit determinations in subsequent cases, but only in the event of extreme abuses of discretion by relevant authorities. Absent such an exception, the implementation of the constitutional "standard of living" as enacted in the law would be subject to nearly unfettered administrative discretionary authority:

> [i]*t is reasonable to understand that the authority to determine what constitutes the healthy, cultural and minimum standard of living is first vested in the discretionary power of the* [government], *and that* [its] *decision does not directly produce an issue of illegality, although such decision might produce an issue of propriety which might lead to a political debate about governmental responsibility. Only in cases where such decision is made in excess of, and by abuse of, the power bestowed by the law, against the objects of the Constitution and the Livelihood Protection Law, by ignoring the real condition of life and establishing extremely low standard of schedule, would such decision be subject to judicial review as an illegal action.*[288]

Subsequent lower court decisions continued to sometimes present alternate views of the Article 25 guarantee. However, the majority approach from the *Asahi Case* was reaffirmed in the 1982 *Horiki Case*, this time by a unanimous Grand Bench ruling, bringing the jurisprudence to the well-settled interpretation that remains intact today.[289] The case involved a challenge to a provision of the Child Rearing Allowance Act, prohibiting the payment of a child rearing allowance under the Act concurrently with a disability pension.[290] In response to the violations of Articles 13, 14 and 25 of the constitution alleged by Ms. Horiki, the plaintiff-appellant, a visually-impaired single mother dependent on government financial support, the Supreme Court reiterated that:

> [t]*he "minimum standards of wholesome and cultured living" provided in this article is an extremely abstract or relative concept. The concrete contents of this concept should be determined on a case-by-case basis, by taking into account the level of cultural progress, economic and social circumstances, and the ordinary status of people's living. Furthermore, in order to materialize the expectation of this provision into specific laws, the state's fiscal conditions cannot be ignored, and consideration should also be given to complex and diverse issues from a highly technical perspective and policy decisions should be made based on such consideration. Therefore, what legislative measures should be specifically taken under the purport of Article 25 of the Constitution is left to the broad discretion allowed to the legislative authority, and such choice or decision is not suitable for being subject to review or determination by court, unless it is extremely unreasonable and obviously goes beyond the bounds of the discretion or constitutes an abuse of the discretion.*[291]

In addition to avoiding the question of legislative inaction, the Court also avoided offering any specifics regarding claims under Article 25 or the basic merits of a scheme prohibiting an otherwise eligible person from receiving overlapping benefits, or the adequacy of the amounts received

Thus, the current framework of the Supreme Court's jurisprudence is that "the minimum standards of wholesome and cultured living" provision under Article 25(1) of the constitution does not generate a concrete right, but rather that its meaning and application is left to the nearly unfettered discretion of the legislature and the executive, subject to judicial review only "in cases of gross unreasonableness and clear abuse of discretion," circumstances that are extraordinarily unlikely to be found. While this does not *completely* exclude the possibility of judicial review, as proponents of the programmatic declaration theory would argue should be the case, for most practical purposes it limits the scope of judicial review to nearly the same degree. As scholars who support the other theories note, the constitution clearly declares the establishment of this conceptualization under a rights framework and there are laws that embody it. An overwhelming majority of scholars are critical of the extremely narrow scope of judicial review put forward in the *Horiki Case* and earlier decisions, because what constitutes a minimum standard of living can be determined objectively to some extent in a particular society at a particular time, and that setting a standard lower than that objective minimum standard may be unconstitutional or illegal.[292]

Other Article 25 interpretations under scholarly theory and lower court decisions

The cases discussed above represents the extent of the Supreme Court's jurisprudence on Article 25, or rather paragraph (1) of the provision. However, the Osaka High Court's judgment in the *Horiki Case* is considered significant in the way it addresses the relationship between paragraph (2) and paragraph (1) of Article 25, presenting a plainly bifurcated approach to the two paragraphs with paragraph (2) merely mandating general attention to societal circumstances causing disadvantage and paragraph (1) serving as the only concrete obligation to remedy individual circumstances where the system nevertheless leaves persons living below the minimum standards that the constitution entitles them to enjoy.

> *Paragraph 2* [of Article 25] *declares the obligation of the Government to make efforts to prevent poverty in advance, and paragraph 1 … declares that the Government has the obligation to take supplementary and individual measures for the relief of those who have failed in spite of the measures for the prevention of poverty set forth in paragraph 2.*[293]

Though the issue was left unaddressed in the Supreme Court's later ruling, according to this aspect of the high court decision, the government "has the obligation to take measures directly aimed at ensuring *the absolute standard* of guarantee of the minimum standards of wholesome and cultured living' set forth in paragraph 1," while with regard to the measures taken by the state under paragraph (2), it is not necessary for any particular measure to meet the minimum standard.

In other words, the Osaka High Court's approach resembled the Supreme Court's majority view in *Asahi* and later in *Horiki* in according extremely broad discretion to the government as to paragraph (2)'s purposes even in the case of inaction with regards to applicable legislative measures. It differed in finding that once legislation is put in place, courts should carry out a more careful review of consonance with paragraph (1) of legislative measures to prevent poverty, using a stricter "absolute standard" for evaluation in doing so. However, it qualified this by limiting the scope of measures subject to this higher standard of review to the Public Assistance Act (which was not at issue in the case), finding that disability pensions and child support allowances fell under the scope of paragraph (2).

This aspect of the high court decision has been criticized by scholars from the standpoint that other laws besides the Public Assistance Act should also be seen as implementing the guarantee "the minimum standards of wholesome and cultured living."[294] In any case, the Osaka High Court judgment illustrates an interpretive divide that is the subject of ongoing debate, but which has not yet been addressed by the Supreme Court.

The decision-making process regarding entitlements

Social security measures provided for by the government are subject to change. Unless recipients are grandfathered in with their existing benefits, changes which reduce benefits will disadvantage recipients who have come to rely on receiving benefits at a certain level. Thus, unfettered legislative discretion in making such changes can deliver a major blow to recipients, whose legal objections may be couched in the framework of constitutional entitlements.

The 2012 *Abolition of the Elderly Supplement Case* drew attention to this problem.[295] This case was brought by a public assistance recipient challenging a change in regulations under the Public Assistance Act which, *inter alia*, eliminated a supplemental welfare payment for the elderly, resulting in a reduction in benefits.

The Supreme Court rejected the plaintiff's claims, ruling that references to a "minimum standard of living" in the Public Assistance Act was an "abstract and relative content" requiring "highly specialized technical consideration and policy judgment" regarding implementation. As such the government's decision to revise such standards would only violate the "minimum standard of living" espoused by the Act if "deemed a deviation from or abuse of the scope of discretionary authority." Finding no such deviation, the Court found the reduction in benefits to be legal under the statutory framework and accordingly constitutional with respect to the ideals of Article 25 reflected in the statute.

Article 25 in the context of environmental rights

Environmental rights were first proposed by lawyers belonging to the Osaka Bar Association in 1970.[296] Those rights were asserted as a response to the destruction and pollution of the environment which accompanied Japan's rapid economic growth, and the resulting harm to human health. The idea of a constitutional guarantee of environmental rights was then endorsed by many constitutional scholars as well.

Environmental rights were asserted in litigation in the *Osaka Airport Noise Pollution Case* of 1975. Residents living near Osaka's Itami Airport filed an action against the governmental agency operating the airport seeking compensation for damages from noise pollution and an injunction against nighttime arrivals and departures. They prevailed at the Osaka High Court but then the Supreme Court, after deliberating on the matter for six years, rejected the request for an injunction and upheld only the claim for damages, without acknowledging any form of environmental rights.[297]

Environmental rights are not explicitly provided for in the constitution, but prevailing academic theories affirm the existence of an implicit constitutional right of some kind.[298] One of the most popular theories is that a right to a clean environment is founded in both Article 25's guarantee of the welfare right, and Article 13's guarantees of the right to life, liberty and the pursuit of happiness.[299]

Theoretical discussions reveal two aspects to such a right. The first is the right to demand positive measures from the government so that the people can enjoy a clean and healthy environment, whether through preservation or improvement.[300] For example, it is clearly within governmental authority to limit the time that airplanes can take off and land as a measure against noise, or to order factories to eliminate the odors caused by factory waste-water. However, while such a role of the government can be grounded in Article 25 of the constitution, which stipulates the welfare right, the ability of citizens to demand such right is limited by the jurisprudence described above that finds no justiciability in such claims. The courts have been generally unwilling to assert their own judgments over the environmental standards that are implicated by such rights or how they should be maintained and preserved in legislative and regulatory embodiments.

At the same time, if the people have a right to a clean environment, the government should not be a detrimental force by causing environmental harms. In other words, environmental rights may imply a right to be free from the degradation of a habitable environment by public authorities. The destruction of the natural and living environment by the construction of large roads and dams might be an example. The idea of eliminating such infringements and protecting the living environment of the residents comes from the environmental right as a civil liberty. Since it is a civil liberty, scholars have also recognized a constitutional basis pursuant Article 13 which is the general provision of human rights and the liberty aspect of Article 25.

Even if a broad constitutional notion of rights is to be recognized, many questions remain. For example, what would be the "environment" guaranteed by the constitutional right? Some would limit the understanding to the natural environment, such as air, water, and sunlight as benefits to be protected for human existence. Others would more broadly view the environment to also include historical and cultural features such as archaeological sites and temples, and the social environment, such as roads, parks and schools. Based on the history of the advocacy of environmental rights and the concern that a broader concept of environmental rights might potentially dilute protections that decision makers would allow for such rights, the academic world most commonly limits its constitutional framing in this regard to the natural habitat.[301]

In any case, the Supreme Court has not recognized environmental rights as a constitutional right so far. Some scholars call for caution as well, concerned that the content and scope of environmental rights and the scope of right holders are too vague, and private law remedies should be sufficient.[302] Moreover, many believe that even if we consider the concept of a constitutional environmental right to be valid, the abstract nature of this right makes it essential to have legislation that clarifies its purpose in the same manner as discussed above with regards to the welfare right.

Life itself in jeopardy: The limits of Article 25's potential as a programmatic ideal and the implications of concrete rights

The Supreme Court's approach in the *Horiki Case*, establishing a nearly impossibly high hurdle to judicial relief—"gross unreasonableness and clear abuse of discretion"—may not only be impacting "wholesome living" as to welfare and poverty reduction, but it may be a matter of life and death for the Japanese people. Some scholars believe that an Article 25 that allowed for concrete justiciable claims would have allowed judicial inquiry into whether the government policies in response to the global pandemic adequately protected human lives. This seems to be entirely consistent with Article 25's stated aims. It is unfortunate that the *Horiki Case* jurisprudence slammed the door shut so forcefully on its potential.

Similarly, government inaction in other spheres impacting the quality of life, whether in the field of public health, or the existential challenges we can anticipate in the 21st century from climate change, would also appear to be appropriately addressed within a human *rights* framework under Article 25 and informed by developments in the environmental jurisprudence of other countries which can be used for new legal actions in Japanese courts.

Article 26: The Right and Duty of Education

Kayoko Ōshima

Article 26.

(1) All people shall have the right to receive an equal education correspondent to their ability, as provided by law.

(2) All people shall be obligated to have all boys and girls under their protection receive ordinary education as provided for by law. Such compulsory education shall be free.

The constitutional guarantee

Japan's modern education system began with the promulgation of the Gakusei (Education System Order) in 1872. This was the order that established the first modern school system aimed at educating all the people. The obligation to attend elementary school for four years was established in 1886. Compulsory schooling was made free of charge in 1900 and elementary school was extended to six years in 1907.

The Meiji Constitution had no provision for compulsory education, but the Imperial Rescript on Education had been promulgated in 1890, and articulated the general principles of national education based on Confucian morality. The background for the promulgation of the Imperial Rescript on Education is said to have been the growing nationwide liberal civil rights movement and a sense of crisis over western individualistic ideology. Education was considered one of the fundamental duties of the emperor's subjects, including children who were obligated to receive education. Parents were also obligated to send their children to school. At this time, it was believed that basic regulations on education should be implemented not by laws passed by the Imperial Diet, but by imperial ordinances based on Article 9 of the Meiji Constitution (this is called the "Imperial Ordinance Principle"). This is one of the reasons why the Imperial Rescript on Education remained the basic "law" of education until it was repealed during the Occupation.

By contrast, Article 26(1) of the present constitution both guarantees the right to receive education and makes it the subject of laws passed by the Diet. Paragraph (2) provides for compulsory education at state expense. The duty to educate children is one of the three duties articulated by the constitution. The view that education contributed to the indoctrination of the Japanese people and the growth of authoritarianism under the Meiji Constitution and concern that it could re-emerge is reflected in both the constitution and subsequent controversies over educational policies.

The character of the right

The early prevailing theory emphasized the significance of the right to receive education as a "social right" and advocated that it is the right to demand economic support from the State in order to achieve equal educational opportunities.[303] However, in the early 1970s, a leading educational scholar criticized this understanding. He argued instead that Article 26 provides the right of the people to receive education in order to build a better life, but especially for children, it guarantees their right to learn.[304] Current constitutional theories understand that Article 26 guarantees the "right of the children to learn" in order to receive education and grow and develop as human beings. The Supreme Court has also confirmed that children have a constitutional "right to learn" in the *Asahikawa Achievement Test Case* of 1976.[305] Today, the right to receive education is understood to be a complex right that has both social right and liberty right aspects.

Who should decide the content of education?

Starting in the early 1970s, the question of who should decide the content of children's education was debated judicially in the *Ienaga Textbook Inspection Cases*, which were three lawsuits brought by the historian Saburō Ienaga against the state. Each challenged the refusal of the Ministry of Education to authorize Japanese history books he wrote for use in high schools.[306] At issue was whether the state can intervene in the content of education, whether textbook authors have the right to freedom of education, and whether the system of government authorization of textbooks constitutes censorship (also see discussion at Article 21).

The question of content causes clashes between two theories. On one hand, the theory of "the people's right to education" held that the entire nation—but mainly parents—should be responsible for the education of their children, and that the state should not be involved in the content of education, its role being limited to providing financial and other support.[307] On the other hand, a competing theory of "the right of the State to education" argued that the education of children is a matter of public concern and that the State should also determine the content of education by law.[308]

These two theories were sharply opposed to each other. However, in the *Asahikawa Achievement Test Case*, the Supreme Court held that "both theories were extreme and one-sided, and neither could be adopted in full." It then stated that the education of children should be exclusively for the benefit of the children, and while approving the freedom of parents, teachers and private schools to educate children based on their responsibility to realize the children's right to learn, the State has the authority to determine the content of the children's education to the extent "necessary and appropriate." The Court went on to say, "State intervention in the content of education must be restrained as much as possible," and "in particular, it was prohibited to prevent children from developing as free and independent human beings by forcibly teaching content that instills false knowledge or one-sided thinking."

In the first *Ienaga Textbook Inspection Case*, the Supreme Court held that the purpose of the textbook authorization system is to realize the requirements that the educational content of general education should be at a certain level nationwide and that the educational content should be in accordance with the students' stage of physical and mental development. The textbook authorization standards at issue could not be said to be beyond the "necessary and reasonable" extent for such purpose, and did not contain any content that would prevent children from growing as free and independent individuals. Thus, the Supreme Court concluded that the State's intervention in the content of education through the textbook authorization did not violate Article 26.[309]

Freedom of education for whom?

As stated above, in the *Asahikawa Achievement Test Case*, the Supreme Court held that parents, teachers, and private schools have freedom of education. Each of these freedoms is explained below.

Parents

The Supreme Court said that "the freedom of parents to educate their children is found mainly in the freedom to educate them outside of school, such as at home, and in the freedom to choose schools." Article 10 of the Basic Act of Education also establishes parents as having primary responsibility over their children's education. The prevailing theory argues that the freedom to choose private schools is derived from the freedom to choose schools. The freedom to choose between regular schools and special needs schools also can be said to derive from the freedom to choose schools.

Teachers

The Supreme Court held that even in general education (a term used for compulsory education up to junior high school and high school, which is not compulsory), teachers should be given a certain degree of freedom in terms of specific teaching contents and teaching methods. Some scholars argue that the freedom of education of teachers in general education is also guaranteed under Article 23.

In the *Tōdai Poporo Case*, the Supreme Court stated that the academic freedom guaranteed by Article 23 includes the freedom to conduct academic research and the freedom to publish the results of that research, and that Article 23 intends to guarantee those freedoms especially at universities. At the same time, it held that the freedom of education, while closely related to academic freedom, is not necessarily included in this freedom. However, the Court did acknowledge that, with respect to universities, the freedom of professors and other researchers to teach the results of their research is recognized under the intent of Article 23 of the constitution and the purposes of universities provided in the School Education Act.[310]

On the other hand, with respect to general education, in the *Asahikawa Achievement Test Case*, the Supreme Court denied teachers full freedom of teaching under Article 23, on the grounds that students have little or no ability to choose their school or teachers or to criticize the content of classes and teachers have a strong influence on students; and the law requires uniform educational standards throughout the country from the viewpoint of equal opportunity in education.[311]

Private schools

Private schools have freedom of education to a certain extent. For example, they are allowed to provide education based on a particular religion. However, as long as private schools are also "schools" recognized by the School Education Act, they must comply with a variety of educational laws and regulations.[312]

Free compulsory education system

Article 26(2) imposes on parents the duty to ensure their children receive a certain minimum level of education. The term "all people" as used in this section, means a parent or guardian who exercises parental authority over a child.[313] The constitutional duty is mirrored in Article 17 of the School Education Act which obligates parents and other guardians to send children to school. Such parental obligations may conflict with the parent's freedom of education.[314] The system of compulsory education is one in which the State undertakes on behalf of parents some of the education necessary for the human development of their children. As a result, the freedom of parents to educate their children must be used in a manner that advances the children's right to learn. Accordingly, the educational freedom of parents has its own limits.

As for the meaning of the mandate that education be "free," there are two main theories about what this means: one is that it means there should be no tuition, and the other is that it means all expenses related to school educational activities should be borne by the state. The Supreme Court has held that "free" means "tuition-free" and that it is also desirable to consider and make efforts to reduce other costs (such as textbooks, etc.) as much as possible, but that the latter is a matter of legislative policy.[315] In 1963 the government enacted legislation to provide free textbooks for use in compulsory education.[316] Although "compulsory education" extends to six years of elementary school and three years of junior high school, in order to achieve equal opportunities for students to study at high schools, there is a more recent program under which the State pays all or a portion of high school tuition as well for students whose parent or guardian falls below a certain income threshold.[317]

Article 27: The Right and Duty to Work

Colin P.A. Jones

Article 27.

(1) All people shall have the right and the obligation to work.
(2) Standards for wages, hours, rest and other working conditions shall be fixed by law.
(3) Children shall not be exploited.

"Lifetime employment" is a common misnomer used to describe the culture of work in Japan. It refers to a system under which high school or college graduates enter a company (or public service job) and remain with that employer for most of their productive lives until retiring at the mandatory retirement age established by the employer (or statute, in the case of public employment).[318] This involves a bargain whereby workers make an implicit long-term commitment to a company or institution in exchange for a level of job security that employees in many other countries would find enviable.

In reality, only a minority of Japan's working population enjoys this form of employment, which is itself constantly evolving. However, even those in more precarious modes of employment benefit from a complex variety of laws and regulations aimed at tilting the playing field in favor of workers. The difficulty of terminating employees, or even declining to renew fixed-term employment contracts is a well-known feature of Japan's business environment.

One reason for this can be attributed to the constitution, Article 27 of which guarantees the right to work. This is not understood to be a concrete right capable of assertion in court through litigation demanding (for example) that the government give the plaintiff a job. Rather the prevailing view is that it is a "social right" that can only be implemented through legislation. In that respect it might be possible to make a claim for legislative nonfeasance (see discussion in Introduction to this Chapter), but the ample supply of laws and regulations fostering and protecting employment would likely make it a losing proposition.[319]

In essence, the state seeks to fulfill its obligations under the first and second paragraphs of Article 27 and by extension, Article 25, through a complex set of employment regulations that effectively render employers a part of the social welfare state. This has involved legislative interventions into the ostensibly private law domain of employment contracts. The Labor Standards Act establishes a regime of detailed standards and restrictions on contractual practices that must be followed by private employers. The Labor Contract Act imposes additional requirements on labor contracts, including allowing fixed-term employment contractual arrangements that exceed five years to be converted to permanent employment by employees.[320] The Law for the Stabilization of Employment of Elderly Persons requires employers that have a mandatory retirement age to nonetheless make employment opportunities available to workers until the age of 65.[321] A special act restricts the ability of companies to use corporate spin-offs to divest undesired workers.[322] Companies with a workforce above a certain threshold are required to hire a certain number of persons with disabilities or pay into a fund used to provide subsidies.[323] Examples of additional statutory regimes include laws mandating minimum wage, workplace safety, worker's compensation insurance, unemployment insurance, regulating headhunting and establishing a network of government job banks, mandating equal opportunities in employment, protecting short-term and fixed term contract workers and establishing a byzantine framework for the use of "dispatched workers."[324]

The judiciary has also played a significant and surprisingly activist role in securing employment, though primarily in the sphere of private law. This has involved interpreting general principles and rules of contract in the Civil Code to level the playing field for employees. In the *Nippon Salt Case* of 1975 the Supreme Court used the Civil Code notion of "abuse of rights" to invalidate an employer's purported termination of an employment contract.[325] Two years later in the *Kōchi Broadcasting Case*, the Court similarly invalidated the termination by a broadcaster of an employee who overslept, resulting in the radio broadcasting silence instead of the news—twice in a two-week period.[326] The Supreme Court has also invalidated employer efforts to avoid renewing fixed term contracts with workers, analogizing them to improper terminations and applying the abuse of rights doctrine to reassignment of employees to unwelcome posts.[327] The judicial standards enunciated in cases such as these were ultimately codified such as in Article 16 of the Labor Contract Act, which states that "If a dismissal lacks objectively reasonable grounds and is not considered to be appropriate in general societal terms, it is treated as an abuse of rights and is invalid."[328]

Thus, although there are few significant court cases addressing Article 27 specifically,[329] the courts can nonetheless be said to have played a significant role in protecting the right to work. As for the *duty* to work enunciated in Article 27, this is best understood as being hortatory. Those who do not need to work are not required to do so, and both Articles 18 and 22 provide guarantees oppositional to compelled labor.

The prohibition on exploitation of children contained in paragraph (3) reflects conditions at the time of the constitution's drafting. The Meiji Constitution contained no comparable language (to paragraph (3) or any other part of Article 27), and children were subject to working conditions that would now be considered shocking. Nor was this limited to Japan; it should be remembered that for the Americans who drafted the language that ultimately came to be reflected in Article 27, both the mass unemployment of the Great Depression and the failure of the Child Labor Amendment to the US Constitution would have been events from recent memory.

Article 28: The Right of Workers to Organize

Colin P.A. Jones

Article 28.
The right of workers to organize and to bargain and act collectively is guaranteed.

Historical background

The Meiji system of government was markedly unfriendly to organized labor. The Security Police Act of 1900 criminalized strikes, and suppression of unions and related socialist and communist activities were a feature of Japanese politics until the end of World War II.[330] Needless to say the Meiji Constitution was silent on the subject of labor rights.

Article 28 (unchanged from Article XXVI of the GHQ Draft) can thus be said to reflect a certain American idealism about organized labor and political freedoms. By some estimates, however, over 40 percent of workers were unionized by 1946, before the new constitution had even taken effect.

With the advent of the Cold War globally and mass labor unrest in Japan, some in the Allied Occupation leadership may have come to regret this grant of liberality. In February of 1947 SCAP was banning general strikes and the following year, at MacArthur's instigation the Cabinet issued an order abolishing the right of public sector employees to strike, a prohibition that was subsequently codified into law.[331]

The influence and evolution of organized labor represents a significant aspect of the social, political and economic history of postwar Japan. The use of strikes as a political tool of the left and the response of governments and employers played out in a cold-war context in which socialism and communism were characterized as potential existential enemies of the West, yet at the same time had potentially broad appeal that was easily disseminated thanks to the political liberality western governments purported to be protecting.[332] Japan's economic miracle, policies aimed at redistributing at least some of the wealth it generated and the emergence and spread of "in-house unions" that are naturally less adverse to management, have made large scale industrial unrest a thing of the past—for now, at least. Thanks in part to the constitutional guarantee, however, unions remain a central feature of the employment landscape, though in a particularly Japanese form.

The three rights

Article 28 is understood to protect three distinct and fundamental rights of labor: the right to organize (*danketsuken*), the right to bargain collectively (*dantaikōshōken*) and the right to engage in collective action (*dantai kōdōken*). There are, of course, various theories as to the nature of these rights and which of them is most foundational.[333] The concrete implementation of the Article 28 rights has been legislative, particularly through the Labor Union Act, which contains prohibitions on employers taking various adverse actions towards union members and activities.[334]

The right to organize—the right to form and join unions—gives rise to a question of whether the constitutional protection extends to *not* joining unions. This is an important question in the context of "union shops" where employment with a company is contingent on joining and remaining in the company (or other specified) union, an arrangement which among other things simplifies the process of negotiating terms of employment for employers. Mandatory union membership potentially conflicts with the freedom of association guaranteed by Article 21 of the constitution, but most theories seem unsupportive of interpretations of Article 28 that establish a right *not* to organize. The Supreme Court has found overly restrictive union shop requirements in collective bargaining agreements to be void for public policy grounds under Article 90 of the Civil Code.[335]

The Court has also acknowledged that the right to organize involves giving unions and their leaders a certain amount of rights of control over union members, but only to the extent they are free to leave the union.[336] It has also made it clear that the right of unions to exercise control over their members does not extend to political matters.[337] Finally, by declining further appeals the Court also implicitly upheld a lower court ruling rejecting challenges to the Mayor of Osaka's refusal to make space in municipal offices available to public sector unions.[338]

The right to collective bargaining would be empty if management could refuse to participate. The Labor Union Act limits management's freedom to do so by prohibiting employers from refusing to bargain without due cause.[339] The Act also establishes a network of Labor Relations Commissions which provide a mechanism for investigating and resolving disputes between unions and management.[340]

The right to "act collectively" is a euphemism that encompasses strikes, work-to-rule, slowdown and other activities aimed at coercing management. Since they would otherwise be potentially actionable in tort or contract, the Labor Union Act disables employers from suing unions or their members for damages resulting from the exercise of their rights to engage in such activities.[341]

Strikes and other collective action can sometimes be used for political or economic reasons that are not directly related to the employment conditions at a particular company. The Supreme Court has declined to find strikes for political purposes to be legitimate, and has also been unsympathetic to collective action that infringes on the property or other rights of employers, such as taking over factories and workplaces.[342]

Limitations on the three rights

Just as with other constitutional rights, the three labor rights are not unlimited. The Labor Relations Adjustment Act imposes various constraints on strikes in certain situations and industries, and other statutes of questionable constitutionality also prohibit or restrict strikes by particular categories of ostensibly private sector workers.[343]

However, the most famous and controversial departure from Article 28's seemingly unequivocal guarantee of workers' rights involves public servants. National and local public servants are prohibited from striking and similar activities.[344] They are able to organize not into "unions" but "worker organizations" under the applicable public law and National Personnel Authority regulations.[345] However, police, prison, coast guard, and fire workers are prohibited from establishing or joining any organization for the purpose of collective bargaining.[346] These prohibitions are backed by criminal penalties which extend to even simply planning strikes or encouraging other public servants to engage in them.[347] A trade-off to the loss of these rights is that the National Personnel Authority effectively "negotiates" on behalf of public servants through its recommendations to the Diet regarding annual pay increases.

The Supreme Court started out as wholly supportive of the restrictions on the Article 28 rights of public servants, which it upheld in a 1953 ruling.[348] The following decade it softened its tone. In a 1966 ruling, the Court indicated that only the minimum reasonable necessary restrictions and the punishments should be imposed, and that some sort of alternate mechanism was necessary to compensate for the loss of rights.[349] This was followed by two other Grand Bench judgments which seemed to come close to finding some of the restrictions unconstitutional without actually doing so.[350] In 1973, however, the Court changed course again and issued a judgment supportive of broad restrictions backed by criminal sanctions, justified in part by the fact that public employees were paid by the state pursuant to laws passed based on National Personnel Authority recommendations, rather than private employers making decisions on how to allocate profits.[351] Moreover, while in the 1966 case the Court had rejected the idea of Article 15 of the constitution justifying the wholesale restriction of public workers' labor rights, in the 1973 judgment, the majority view held that pursuant to Article 15 "their employer is in substance the whole people and they owe their obligation of offering their labor force to the whole people." The Court's position was largely unchanged at the time of writing.

Internationally, Japan is a party to both the Freedom of Association and Protection of the Right to Organise Convention of 1948 and the Right to Organise and Collective Bargaining Convention of 1949. In connection with these the Committee on Freedom of Association of the International Labor Organization has repeatedly called on the government of Japan to ensure basic labor rights for public employees as ensured in those instruments.[352]

The exercise of labor rights and other laws

There is some tension between the Article 28 rights and the Penal Code, since many activities conducted in the course of strikes and related activity can be characterized as offenses such as extortion or obstruction of a business. Under Article 35 of the Penal Code acts "performed in accordance with laws and regulations" are not punishable. The Labor Union Act specifically references this provision to confirm collective bargaining and related activities enjoy the Penal Code justification, but only to the extent violence is not involved.[353] Nonetheless, police and prosecutors have sometimes been aggressive in the use of the criminal process against unions.[354]

Article 29: Property Rights

Tetsuji Matsumoto

Article 29.

(1) The right to own or to hold property is inviolable.

(2) Property rights shall be defined by law, in conformity with the public welfare.

(3) Private property may be taken for public use upon just compensation therefor.

Historical background

Article 27 of Meiji Constitution held "[t]he right of property of every Japanese subject shall remain inviolate" and required that "[m]easures necessary to be taken for the public benefit shall be any provided for by law."

The first two paragraphs of Article 29 are largely as set forth in the GHQ Draft (Article XXVII). Article XXVIII of the draft contained a much more expansive statement regarding the ultimately public character of property rights and the locus of the "ultimate fee" to the land and all national resources. Article XXIX further declared "[o]wnership of property imposes obligations. Its use shall be in the public good. Private property may be taken by the State for public use upon just compensation therefor." At first these provisions were misunderstood by one of the Japanese ministers involved as a revolutionary declaration of nationalization of the land, though it was mostly intended to establish the basic principles underlying eminent domain. In any case, most of the substance of the two articles was excised by the Japanese side and what little remained was moved to paragraph (3) of the current text; GHQ did not object.

While it may be hard to believe today whether it would be possible to introduce socialism or communism without amending the constitution was once a question of serious debate, at least during the early stage of the Cold War era. In other words, whether Article 29 would permit the abolishment of the system of private property was once a source of constitutional controversy in connection with the "institutional guarantee" theory discussed later in this section. With the end of the Cold War and the collapse of socialist regimes, this debate is now only a matter of historical interest.

Language and concepts of property

The use of the term "fee" by the American drafters in the GHQ Draft would likely have confused the Japanese side, given that Japan's system of property law was not based on the Norman-Anglo-Saxon feudalism of the common law, but on continental European (particularly Prussian and French) models. The Japanese word used for "the right of property" in Article 27 of the Meiji Constitution was "*shoyūken,*" which was a translation from German word "*Eigentum*"—property. *Shoyūken* is commonly translated into English as "ownership," but is more technically one of the categories of "real rights" (*bukken*) recognized by the Meiji-era Civil Code.[355]

By contrast, both "the right to own or to hold property" and "property rights" are rendered in the Japanese version of the current constitution as "*zaisanken*," which, is more comprehensive than "*shoyūken*," encompassing contractual rights and other claims that under the Civil Code would fall under the ambit of *saiken* (claims). Thus, almost all Japanese textbooks and commentaries on Article 29 start with an explanation to the effect that "'property rights' [*zaisanken*] means all rights having value, including not only the right to own property and other real rights, but also claims, intellectual property rights and other proprietary rights created by statute, such as mining rights and fishing rights."

The scope of the guarantee of property rights

Article 29 has a distinct structure not seen in any other article of Chapter III. First, the significance of paragraphs (1) and (2) needs to be carefully evaluated. By reading too much into paragraph (2), it is possible to interpret it as permitting any law which effectively violates property rights by the way it defines them. But that would result in the "inviolable" formulation of paragraph (1) having no inherent constitutional significance, and vest in the legislature an effectively unlimited power over property, subject only to "conformity with the public welfare." Thus, the reasonable interpretation is that paragraph (1) establishes something inviolable or, as discussed before and acknowledged by the Supreme Court, that there are limits on the legislative power to define property rights under paragraph (2).

The seminal case for understanding how the Supreme Court has addressed this question is the *Forest Act Case* of 1987.[356] The case arose between two brothers who each inherited from their father a half co-ownership in a forest. Article 256, paragraph 1 of the Civil Code provides that "[e]ach co-owner may demand the partition of property in co-ownership at any time." But Article 186 of the Forest Act provided that "a co-owner of a forest may not demand the partition of the forest in co-ownership; provided, however, that this does not preclude a co-owner from demanding partition by the majority in proportion to the values of the interests of co-owners."[357] The latter act thus prohibited demands for partition from a co-owner of less than a majority portion of a forest, even though it was possible under the Civil Code. Neither brother had a majority.

When the Forest Act restriction on partitioning was challenged, the Supreme Court held "the right to demand the partition of property in co-ownership has been developed as one that enables each co-owner to make the shift to sole ownership, which is the principle[d] form of ownership in modern civil society." On that basis it held that "denying co-owners' right to demand the partition of property in co-ownership"—particularly given that there was nothing about forest land that naturally made it impossible to partition—constituted "a restriction on property rights under the Constitution." The Court then held "legislation establishing such restriction should be considered to be required to conform to the public welfare as referred to in Article 29, paragraph 2 of the Constitution" and in failing to do so, Article 186 of the Forest Act was unconstitutional. Thus, the Court found constitutional boundaries on the ability of the legislature to define property rights under paragraph (2), and did so by looking to the public welfare. We will see this level of scrutiny applied in other contexts, such as the *Securities and Exchange Case* discussed below.

The "institutional guarantee" of Article 29

The *Forest Act Case* added a new facet to the Article 29 guarantee; that it "not only guarantees the private property system but also guarantees the individual property rights of the people that form the basis for social and economic activities as fundamental human rights." This formulation is thought to establish an "institutional guarantee" (*seido teki hoshō*) of the system of private property. Under this view, the core of the system (institution) is constitutionally protected from invasion by law.[358]

However, if there are constitutional limits on the power of the legislature to define property rights under paragraph (2), as was established in the *Forest Act Case*, it may be unnecessary to recognize a separate institutional guarantee of the private property system.

Nonetheless, the broad guarantee of "individual property rights" in the *Forest Act Case* has required further clarification. The implication of the Court's ruling is that not only are there constitutional limits on the property-defining power vested in the legislature by paragraph (2), but also on the power of the legislature to alter existing laws defining the property rights. In other words, it may amount to a protection of vested rights and/or the status quo. Thus, although the Diet is not absolutely prohibited from changing the content of property rights, once people have property rights under law, it is restricted in its ability to do so.[359]

A decade before the *Forest Act Case*, the Supreme Court had already ruled that "the constitutionality of the alteration [of property rights] must be determined with comprehensive examination of the nature of the property rights, the extent to which the law alters the content of the property rights, and the nature of the governmental interest promoted by the law."[360] This was a case involving laws addressing the aftermath of Occupation-era agrarian reform, which saw the widespread redistribution of land from large landlords to tenant farmers.[361] The laws in question enabled former owners to buy back farmland that had been expropriated but was no longer suitable for farming. The buy-back right was politically controversial because the statutory pricing mechanism resulted in a significant windfall for some former owners.[362] A subsequent law greatly increased the price former owners would have to pay.[363] A former owner challenged the change, arguing that changing a right to purchase at a particular price violated Article 29. The Supreme Court rejected the constitutional claim by a former owner who had been seeking to exercise his repurchase right at the time the law changed. In doing so, the Court arguably applied a stricter standard than in the *Forest Act Case*. Although it has been considered an unimportant case, it received notice when it was relied upon by the Court in dealing with *ex post facto* tax laws (see Article 84).

Evolving standards of judicial review

In the *Forest Act Case*, the Court found the purpose of the Forest Act provision under review was "to ensure stable forest management by preventing segmentation of forests and eventually promote the conservation and culture of forests and the enhancement of productivity of forests, thereby contributing to the development of the national economy." That being the case, it could not be said that the legislative purpose of the provision "does not conform to the public welfare." However, the Court found that the restrictions on co-ownership of forest lacked "reasonable relevance" to the legislative purpose. On that basis, it held it "impossible to affirm either reasonableness or necessity" of the Forest Act provision given its legislative purpose. The Diet had thus exceeded "the scope of its reasonable discretion" and the provision was invalid because it violated Article 29(2).

Coming after the *Pharmaceutical Affairs Act Case* (see Article 22), as the second ruling of unconstitutionality in the sphere of economic liberties, the *Forest Act Case* was originally thought by one of the leading scholars to be a similar application of the "public safety regulation" standard of review from the earlier case.[364] However, it is now widely accepted that the *Forest Act Case* was actually about social welfare regulation (see discussion at Article 22) "to ensure stable management." That said, however, the standard of review applied in the *Forest Act Case* was not as lenient as that enunciated for "social welfare regulation" cases in the Public Marketplace Case discussed at Article 22.

Article 22 jurisprudence was further developed through a case known as the *Securities and Exchange Act Case*.[365] Under the "short swing profit rule" of the Securities and Exchange Act (now the Financial Instruments and Exchange Act), a publicly-traded company can demand from board members or large shareholders any profits from purchases and sales conducted within less than six months of each other.[366] In a case where a company sought to recoup such profits against a large shareholder, the shareholder argued that the statutory provision violated Article 29. On appeal, the Court upheld the provision on the ground that it

> *establishes restrictions for the purpose of maintaining fairness and justice in the securities market and to ensure the credibility of the market in the eyes of investors in general. The purpose of the restriction is justifiable, and it is not evident that the means of restriction are either unnecessary or unreasonable, this* [provision] *provides for restrictions which are compatible with public welfare and therefore is not against Article 29 of the constitution.*[367]

Notably, the Court did not mention legislative discretion as it had in the *Forest Act Case*. In subsequent Article 29 rulings, the Court has repeatedly affirmed judgments upholding the constitutionality of other laws by referencing not the *Forest Act Case*, but the *Securities and Exchange Act Case*.[368] The significance of this choice of precedents is not yet apparent.

In the *Confiscation of Third Party Property Case*, the Court has also found the confiscation without notice of third party property as a criminal punishment to violate the constitution (see discussion at Article 31).

Regulation of property rights by prefectural or municipal ordinances

Since Article 29(2) permits property rights to be defined, and thus regulated by "law"—something only the Diet can pass—an interpretive question is whether property rights can be regulated by ordinances of local public entities (i.e., prefectural or municipal governments). In the *Nara Prefectural Reservoir Ordinance Case*, the Court answered this question affirmatively but ambiguously.[369] The case involved a challenge by a farmer fined under a prefectural ordinance that prohibited planting crops on reservoir dikes, something the farmer, his father and grandfather had done long before the ordinance. He appealed the fine on the grounds that the implementation of the ordinance violated Article 29.

The Court's reasoning was ambiguous because on the one hand it relied on the same types of reasoning it used to uphold laws of the Diet—citing the reasonableness and public welfare interest reflected in the ordinance.[370] On the other, it found that potentially destructive activities such as planting crops on a dike were not "property rights" protected by the Civil Code or the constitution, though this distinction between the content and use of property rights arguably begs the question. Despite this ambiguity, this case is now generally understood as supporting the proposition that property rights can be regulated by local government ordinances, and academics generally agree that it should be left up to local public entities to regulate property rights within the scope of laws granting them authority to do so (See discussion at Article 94, and related discussions at Articles 30, 31 and 84).

Takings of private property for public use

Paragraph (3) of Article 29 regulates "takings" which have been a common exception to the sanctity of property rights at least since France's Declaration of the Rights of Man and of the Citizen of 1789 (Article XVII). In this sense the guarantee of property rights is not the guarantee of the rights of property themselves but only of their monetary value. The Supreme Court has read the "for public use" requirement of Paragraph (3) quite broadly. Takings of private property (land, typically) for the construction of public facilities such as roads and railways has always been deemed a public use.

In the *Agrarian Reform Cases* the Court also upheld the Occupation-era land reforms described above, even though they involved forcing property owners to sell land at disadvantageous prices.[371] The Court held that taking property from one private person and giving it to another private person could be deemed as a "public use," so long as it is consistent with the public welfare. In other words, even expropriations of private property for the sake of private use (by different persons) could nonetheless be for public use. Agrarian reform was effectuated during the Allied Occupation and under the extra-constitutional control of SCAP. Nonetheless, these rulings are still considered valid.[372]

With both the judiciary and the majority of academics having accepted that the constitution is broadly permissive of takings for public use, and that this may include regulatory takings as well as takings for private uses that conform to the public welfare, the remaining issue is compensation. When is it necessary, and how much?

There is a common understanding among Japanese legal scholars, derived from German jurisprudence, that compensation for takings or restrictions of property rights is necessary when there is "*besonderes Opfer*," that is, a special sacrifice on the part of the rights holder. It is also widely agreed that two perspectives are important in making this determination. One is concerned with whether a restriction that may constitute a taking applies generally or to a specific person or persons. The other is concerned with the severity of the restriction on those who it affects.

In addition to this theoretical framing, in the *Nara Prefectural Reservoir Ordinance Case*, the Court held that compensation was not required in the case of restrictions imposed in the interest of public safety. However, this aspect of the ruling has been seriously questioned by critics who point to the *River Area Restriction Case*.[373] The case involved an entrepreneur who leased land by a river and hired workers to make gravel. Using a Meiji-era legal rule, the prefectural governor subsequently designated the area a "restricted river area," which prohibited the entrepreneur from continuing without a permit. He did so nonetheless and was fined. He challenged the fine on the grounds that the regulation imposed criminal punishment on him while depriving him of property rights without compensation in violation of Article 29(3).

The Court rejected the argument that the absence of provisions for compensation in the rule was an obstacle to imposing the punishment, since the purpose of doing so was to discourage certain activities for the public good. At the same time, however, the Court noted the absence of provisions clearly providing for compensation did not bar the appellant from bringing a claim, and compensation might be required by Article 29(3). Thus, it is conceivable that courts could still find it necessary to compensate for restrictions on property rights resulting from public safety regulations, at least to the extent of the cost of resources invested before the regulations were imposed.

The possibility of public safety regulations that infringe property rights triggering compensation requirements has become an issue of particular interest due to government "requested" closures of businesses to stop the spread of Covid-19. Although some opposition politicians have argued "no closure without compensation," according to the Supreme Court's reasoning in the *Nara Prefectural Reservoir Ordinance Case*, compensation would not be required by the constitution with respect to pandemic restrictions necessary to protect the lives and health of the people.[374]

What is "just" compensation?

Both academics and court precedents are collectively ambiguous as to what constitutes "just" compensation. In one of the *Agrarian Reform Cases*, the Court held it to mean "a reasonable amount calculated rationally based on the price that is assumed to be valid under the economic conditions of that time, and it is not required to be always completely consistent with said price."[375] The Court thus adopted "appropriate compensation" rather than "complete compensation" as an interpretation of "just compensation" requirement of Article 29 and upheld the constitutionality of the amount of compensation, even though it was ridiculed as "three salmon for a quarter acre rice field" by the land owners forced to accept it.

In sharp contrast, in the *Expropriation of Land Act Case I*,[376] the Court showed a different understanding of what compensation was required in takings cases. This case was not a constitutional challenge, but involved the interpretation of the compensation provisions of the Expropriation of Land Act.[377] The Court found the language of the Act required "complete compensation" which, in monetary terms, meant "compensation by which the owner can purchase similar neighboring substitute land, etc."

Scholars have interpreted this as the Court adopting a "complete compensation" for Article 29(3) purposes and quietly rejecting the "extra-constitutional" *Agrarian Reform Case* standard. Yet the Supreme Court has been more ambivalent in the *Expropriation of Land Act Case II*,[378] involving a challenge to Article 71 of the Expropriation of Land Act. Article 71 set compensation rates based on fair value as calculated based on market value of neighboring land at the time public notice of the project necessitating the expropriation is given, multiplied by a cost-of-living adjustment for the period until the compensation decision is made.[379] This complicated way of calculation (introduced through a 1967 amendment) was an effort to address both constant increases in land prices during postwar Japan's era of rapid economic growth, and the fact that the mere announcement of a project could have an impact on land values before the compensation decisions were made. These factors would have made it very difficult to apply the "complete compensation" standard of *Expropriation of Land Act Case I*.

The 2nd Petty Bench found the compensation methodology to be consistent with the Court's ruling in the *Agrarian Reform Cases*, but did so characterizing the statute as giving those whose land was expropriated as receiving compensation at "the same property value before and after the expropriation"—a formulation seemingly similar to "complete compensation." It is a questionable one at that, given the statute functioned to prevent landowners from being fully compensated for increases in land values attributable to the public project. One factor in the ruling may have been that the Court (the 2nd Petty Bench) was seeking to avoid the constraints on Petty Benches from issuing rulings inconsistent with earlier Grand Bench judgments on the constitutionality of a law (see Article 79).

Compensation for vaccine harm and Article 29(3)

Interestingly, the "special sacrifice" aspect of Article 29 has been used to justify compensation in lawsuits resulting from death and injuries caused by side effects of vaccinations. By analogizing vaccinations for the sake of public health to takings for the public welfare which result in a "special sacrifice" by those having a negative reaction, lower courts have found a basis in Article 29(3) for granting compensation.[380] However, this rationale shocked many people, since it implied the life or health of others could be unilaterally purchased with money, just as in the case of property rights. Appellate courts rejected these analogies and instead awarded damages in tort based on medical malpractice—the failure of the doctors to examine patients adequately before administering vaccinations in individual cases.[381]

War and compensation

The Supreme Court has denied all requests by war victims who have sought compensation under Article 29, paragraph (3).[382] The Court held that Japanese people had to equally endure damages caused by war. But there have been heated controversies whether some of them were "special sacrifices," comparing pension paid for former military personnel and injuries suffered by victims of carpet bombing to Japanese cities in the last months of the war.

Article 30: Taxation

Yūichirō Tsuji

Article 30.
The people shall be liable to taxation as provided by law.

Article 30 is one of the three constitutional provisions that imposes duties on the people rather than simply guaranteeing rights. These were proposed by the Japanese government during the drafting process with GHQ.[383]

As discussed at Article 84, the constitution requires that new taxes be imposed and existing taxes be changed by statute. The term "statute" (*hōritsu*) is considered to include ordinances established by local assemblies.[384] Either way, taxes must be set through legal rules passed by a lawfully-constituted body comprised of elected members. This basic principle prevents the tyrannical use of taxation powers by the executive branch.

Governments need money to plan and perform their functions. That is why taxes can be directly collected from the general public without their consent (other than through the electoral process). As did Article 21 of the Meiji Constitution before it, Article 30 of the present constitution describes the payment of taxes as a duty. However, it also presents taxes in the context of fundamental human rights, which links it to two additional constitutional provisions relevant to taxation. First, Article 29 states that property cannot be taken without fair compensation, meaning that the government needs to justify its financial demands on the people. Furthermore, Articles 83–85 require legislation in order for the government to impose taxes and use the funds so collected. This ensures that the fiscal powers of the government are controlled by laws that are passed by democratically elected representatives, in a manner consistent with the human rights provisions of the constitution.

The government should impose taxes equally. However, income taxes vary, with higher taxes imposed on wage earners than they are for those operating businesses. Such inequality was upheld in the *Salaried Workers Tax Discrimination Case*, in which the Supreme Court rejected an Article 14 challenge (by a university professor) asserting the unfairness of allowing business operators to deduct numerous expenses, but disallowing similar deductions to wage earners, resulting in the latter being taxed more heavily.[385] The Court found the differing treatment accorded by the tax laws to have a rational basis.

In 2020, the Supreme Court ruled on the Hometown Tax (*furusato nōzei*) system, which was developed as a way to encourage taxpayers (who tend to be concentrated in Japan's larger cities), to "donate" a portion of their taxes to a municipality other than the one where they live—their hometown, for example. As an incentive, municipalities seeking such donations could offer rewards such as gift boxes of local produce or delicacies. The result was intense competition among municipalities seeking tax revenues by offering increasingly extravagant rewards. The Ministry of Internal Affairs and Communications (MIC)—which has jurisdiction over local government affairs and taxation—established arcane rules governing the nature and value of rewards that municipalities could offer. Izumisano City had a particularly aggressive and successful program, but fell befoul of the MIC, which excluded it from participating in the system.

The city challenged the decision, first in the Committee for Settling National-Local Disputes, and then in an appeal to the Supreme Court. The Court ruled in the municipality's favor, noting that the MIC's notices and guidelines regarding the program and which Izumisano City had failed to follow were merely that—notices and guidelines. They were subsequently reflected in a law passed in 2019, but the MIC effectively applied them retroactively to punish the city for acting "rebellious." The Supreme Court found it unacceptable for the MIC to treat the city of Izumisano adversely on the basis of its failure to follow its recommendations which had no statutory basis.

Editorial Note on Certain Terminology

Colin P.A. Jones

The latter half of Chapter III is devoted primarily to constitutional rights and protections in the context of the criminal justice system. While efforts have been made throughout this book to identify areas where differences between the English and Japanese versions of the constitution may cause confusion, one area where such issues exist across multiple provisions is the use of terminology relating to arrest and detention.

The English term "apprehend" is used in Articles 33 and 50. The Japanese however, is *taiho* which is a legal term used in statutes and translated elsewhere (including the Japanese government's translation of the Code of Criminal Procedure), as "arrest." The same term was also used in the corresponding provisions of the Meiji Constitution (Articles 23 and 53) and translated as "arrest" in the English. That the English "apprehend" actually means "arrest" in Japanese is important in understanding why Article 33 has generally been found inapplicable to apprehensions outside the scope of the Code of Criminal Procedure.

By contrast, the paired terms "arrested or detained" or "arrest or detention" as used in Articles 34, 38 and 40 are *yokuryū* and *kōkin*, which could both be translated "detain," though the former would typically be used for a short-term detention, the latter a longer term (though to add to the confusion, *yokuryū* is also used to mean "internment" a much more long-term affair). However, neither *yokuryū* or *kōkin* are widely used in laws other than the Constitution; in fact, there is an impressive variety of different highly specific Japanese legal terms used to describe various forms of incarceration depending on the circumstances.

Thus, while the use of "apprehend" in Articles 33 and 50 may give the impression it has a particularly broad sweep, it is arguably the most technically specific in Japanese.

The opposite holds true for "arrest" and "detain" as used in Articles 34, 38 and 40, which seem more specific in English but are actually more vague in Japanese.

Note also that the term "judicial officer" (*shihō kanken*) used in Articles 33 and 35 is a term different than "judge" (*saibankan*) as used in Chapter VI. *Shihō kanken* is a more generic term with a broader scope that potentially encompasses prosecutors and law enforcement officers. However, it is not widely used in laws other than the constitution, and there are no serious arguments that warrants can be issued by anyone other than judges.

Article 31: Procedural Guarantee

Mari Hirayama

Article 31.
No person shall be deprived of life or liberty, nor shall any other criminal penalty be imposed, except according to procedure established by law.

Background

Although the state has a monopoly on rendering punishments for crimes, it is necessary to prevent the abuse of that authority. Article 23 of the Meiji Constitution stipulated that arrest, confinement, hearing and punishment could only be carried out against Japanese subjects in accordance with law, establishing the principle of "no punishment without law." However, this also meant that so long as there was a law permitting it, people could be deprived of their freedom. There were thus numerous cases of arbitrary deprivations of liberty by government officials under color of law.

Article 31 was modelled after the due process clauses of the Fifth and Fourteenth Amendments to the US constitution. The "procedure established by law" referenced in Article 31 is intended to protect the lives and liberty of the people through "due process of law," though that phrase is not used anywhere in the constitution.

One key difference between Article 31 of the Japanese constitution and the Fifth and Fourteenth Amendments to the US constitution is that the guarantee in the Japanese provision does not include the word "property." One of the reasons for this is that the GHQ drafting team included a number of "New Dealers" who had been disillusioned from watching the US Supreme Court use protection of property rights as a basis for striking down legislation seeking to regulate business. Accordingly, as a reflection of their ideals, property was left out of Article XXXII of the GHQ Draft, the substance of which became Article 31.[386] However, Article 31 does contain a catch-all reference to "other criminal penalties," and in the *Confiscation of Third Party Property Case* (discussed later in this section), the Supreme Court confirmed that the due process requirements of Article 31 also applied to infringements of property rights.

The scope of the Procedural Guarantee

Nulla poena sine lege (no punishment without law) is a fundamental doctrine of criminal law that is based on the demand of liberal democracy, where the substance of crimes and punishments must be only decided by a parliament elected by the people, in order to prevent the abuse of punishment by the state.

As to criminal procedure the "established by law" component of Article 31 is largely embodied in Articles 33 and 35 (which require judicial warrants for arrests and searches), Article 34 (which requires notice of reasons for detention) and Article 37 (which guarantees the rights to a fair trial). There is thus some question as to whether Article 31 adds anything that is not already addressed in more detail elsewhere in the constitution.

Academic views differ as to whether Article 31 is merely a procedural guarantee or whether it also applies more broadly to the propriety of the laws establishing crimes and punishment—a form of "substantive due process."[387] The predominant academic theory is that "procedure established by law" in Article 31 also includes the process by which crimes and punishments are defined in law.[388] Under this theory Article 31 should be interpreted as mandating not only procedural due process but also "no punishment without law" and thus a form of substantive due process. This means that not only must there be a legal foundation defining crimes and their punishment, but the balance between the two must be appropriate.

Even in a merely "procedural" context, due process also requires persons affected to be given advance notice of the nature of the proceedings and the opportunity to explain and defend themselves; the "notice and hearing" requirement. The Supreme Court confirmed this in a 1962 case in which it ruled that it violated both Articles 29 and 31 for the government to confiscate third party property together with the property (a boat) used by appellants convicted of smuggling offenses, without giving the third parties notice and the opportunity to defend their rights.[389] Three years later the Court applied a similar rationale to invalidate the confiscation from a third party of an amount paid to them as a bribe.[390]

"Established by law"

The language of Article 31 would seem to limit the definition of crimes and their punishment to laws passed by the Diet. Article 73(vi) of the constitution states that cabinet orders may not be used to impose penalties unless authorized by law. Thus, a legislative delegation is required in order for punishments to be imposed by secondary legislation. Moreover, it must not be a comprehensive "carte blanche" delegation, since cabinet orders and other secondary legislation are not drafted by democratic institutions, the delegation by law must be specific.

The most famous case in this regard is the *Sarufutsu Case*, which involved a challenge to the National Public Service Act prohibition on public servants engaging in political activities and the delegation to National Personnel Authority to define political activities subject to criminal punishment. The Court rejected constitutional challenges to the delegation based on Article 31 and other grounds, but four judges dissented, asserting, *inter alia*, that the wholesale delegation of power to define criminal behavior to the Authority violated Article 31.

Another question under this aspect of Article 31 is whether ordinances passed by municipal and prefectural governments and which impose criminal punishments satisfy the "by law" requirement. Since such ordinances are passed by elected assemblies, they arguably have a more democratic foundation than cabinet orders or other regulations. In the *Osaka Anti-Prostitution City Ordinance Case* the Supreme Court held that establishing criminal penalties through ordinances does not violate Article 31 if the enabling by the law is reasonably specific and limited. This requirement is satisfied by Article 14(3) of the Local Autonomy Act, which empowers municipal and prefectural governments to pass ordinances with punishments no heavier than two years of imprisonment with labor or fines of up to JPY 1 million (see also discussion at Article 94).

The death penalty

Article 31's reference to "life" can be interpreted as the constitution permitting the death penalty, so long as it follows procedures established by law. The Supreme Court first upheld the constitutionality of the death penalty on this basis in 1948, and it remains a feature of the criminal justice system today.[391] Death penalty opponents, however, argue that Article 31 merely requires due process be followed in imposing punishment and does not mandate or permit a particular form of punishment (see also discussion at Article 36 regarding torture and cruel punishments).

Applicability outside of the criminal sphere

Although clearly directed at criminal punishments, a final question relates to the applicability of Article 31's procedural requirement to administrative proceedings. Administrative agencies have broad powers that can impact the rights and freedom of the people. To the extent these powers can be used to impose sanctions that restrict such rights and freedoms, both the substance of regulations and the process by which they are enforced must be appropriate. In the *Narita New Act Case*, a law was passed permitting the Minister of Transportation to issue administrative orders prohibiting specific people from using structures near the international airport at Narita. Such orders could be issued without any prior notice or hearing for the benefit of the persons subject to them.[392] When challenged on Article 31 grounds, the Supreme Court acknowledged it would be "inappropriate to consider that all administrative procedures are automatically excluded from the scope of the guarantee under said Article just because they are not criminal procedures."[393] However, it also held that applicability would be case-by-case consideration and rejected the appeal in this particular case.

More recently, March 2021 amendments to the Act on Special Measures Concerning Novel Coronaviruses empowered prefectural governors to impose administrative fines on businesses that do not comply with requests and orders to temporarily shut down or reduce business hours in order to prevent the spread of infection. The law also gives governors the discretion to decide which businesses and industries should be subject to such orders and requests.[394] This has been controversial, and though it is too early to tell at the time of writing, it may prove to be an area where the relationship between Article 31 and administrative proceedings is tested in the courts.

Article 32: The Right to a Trial

Mari Hirayama

> **Article 32.**
> No person shall be denied the right of access to the courts.

Language and historical background

Article 32 is one of the provisions where the English version diverges most from the Japanese, which might be more properly translated: "No person shall be deprived of their right to receive a trial by a court." It is thus quite close to the guarantee contained in Article 24 of the Meiji Constitution, which is rendered more accurately in English as: "[n]o Japanese subject shall be deprived of his right of being tried by the judges determined by law."

The difference between a trial in a court and a trial by judges may seem insignificant,[395] but the Meiji Constitution's guarantee only applied to civil and criminal cases. Remedies in administrative cases were highly limited and available only through a special court in Tokyo which was not staffed by judges and from which appeals were not possible. Since Article 37 of the present constitution contains a separate guarantee of criminal trials and Article 31 contains a criminal due process guarantee, Article 32 is understood to be concerned primarily with due process in civil (including administrative litigation) cases.[396] It nonetheless has a significance in the criminal context as well.

The right to a trial

The right of access to the courts is regarded as the right to demand something from the state—a trial. The right to a trial protects the rights and freedoms of all people and guarantees procedures to eliminate unlawful infringements. Moreover, the right is guaranteed to all persons equally without discrimination; the guarantee in the Meiji Constitution, by contrast, was limited to "Japanese subjects."

The Japanese term for trial (*saiban*) has a specific meaning which has significance to the interpretation of Articles 32 and 82. In a 1960 case the Supreme Court, referencing both provisions, noted that the constitutional requirement that trials be adversarial proceedings conducted in open court was critical to the protection of human rights.[397]

However, not all proceedings conducted by courts are considered "trials," a distinction that is also important to the question of whether they need to be open to the public as required by Article 82. Examples of those that are not considered trials include juvenile criminal adjudications and various categories of "non-contentious" civil proceedings, including most family court proceedings. Similarly, when a family court renders a decree affecting the rights and duties of the parties in divorce cases, such as those relating to the division of marital property and allocation of parental authority under the Domestic Relations Case Procedure Act, the proceedings are not conducted in open court pursuant to adversarial rules of litigation. Does this violate Article 32? No: in 1965 the Supreme Court upheld the family court procedural regime then in effect, including mandatory conciliation, non-adversarial proceedings and closed courtrooms as necessary to resolving such disputes, and thus permissible under both Articles 32 and 82 of the constitution. It did so in part on the grounds that the procedures allowed for parties dissatisfied with a family court decree to seek subsequent resolution of matters relating to rights and duties through formal trial litigation.[398]

The Article 32 prohibition on deprivation of a right to a trial means that in civil and administrative litigation cases a person whose rights and interests have been somehow wrongfully infringed is guaranteed the right to seek redress for the damage from the Court. Courts are not permitted to refuse a trial as long as the suit filed is lawful and involves a legally-protected interest. It also means that in criminal cases only courts may conduct criminal trials and impose punishment (as is also required by Articles 31 and 37).

Article 32 does not, however, establish an absolute right to a trial on demand; "case or controversy" requirements must be satisfied (see discussion at Article 76) and courts may reject suits on grounds such as mootness or lack of standing.[399] The Supreme Court has also declined to find the right to a trial deprived by amendments to the Code of Civil Procedure narrowing the grounds for appeals,[400] or initial proceedings that are not "trials," but where recourse to a full trial is available.[401]

Trial by courts and lay participation

As used in Article 32, the terms "court" refers to courts constituting the judicial branch as set forth in Chapter VI. A question is whether the guarantee is compatible with lay participation in deciding trials.

From 1928 through 1943 Japan had a jury system that decided serious criminal cases. Its use was suspended due to the war, but the relevant statute was never repealed and the jury system could theoretically still be reinstated. [402] The jury system was compatible with the Meiji Constitution's guarantee of a trial by a judge and Article 32 is also not considered to preclude use of juries for trials by court, though it remains a theoretical consideration.

Less theoretical questions arise with the lay judge (*saiban'in*) system, which has been used since 2009 and follows continental European models of citizen participation, using a mixed panel of three professional judges and six citizens to engage in fact finding and sentencing decisions in crimes involving serious offenses. In response to challenges to this system alleging, *inter alia*, violations of Article 32, the Supreme Court held that:

> *the Constitution generally permits citizens' participation in judicial proceedings, and if any system is adopted for this purpose, the Constitution leaves it to the legislative branch to decide the details for the system, including whether the system should be formed as a jury system or any other criminal trial system involving the participation of citizens...*[403]

Cases involving non-Japanese in immigration and refugee proceedings have also been a source of issues. In recent years, Japan has often been subject to criticism in the international community for its reluctance in the refugee recognition process. In 1977 the Supreme Court rejected claims that deportation of a non-Japanese resident whose residency had expired deprived them of their right to appeal in the judicial resolution of their case, since they had the ability to pursue their appeal through counsel.[404] More recently, however, the Tokyo High Court awarded damages to two asylum seekers from Sri Lanka who had been deported the day after being notified their applications had been rejected. The Court found that the plaintiffs had been deprived of the opportunity to seek judicial review of the administrative decision, in violation of Article 32.[405]

Article 33: Requirements for Arrest

Mari Hirayama

> **Article 33.**
> No person shall be apprehended except upon warrant issued by a competent judicial officer which specifies the offense with which the person is charged, unless he is apprehended, the offense being committed.

Under the Code of Criminal Procedure (CCP) arrest (*taiho*) is one category of compulsory dispositions (*kyōsei shobun*); actions by law enforcement officials conducted against the will of their target but permitted by law. Arrest involves apprehending a suspect for short period of time. Despite the fact that Article 33 only appears to allow for two, the CCP provides for three categories of arrest; (1) general arrest pursuant to an arrest warrant; (2) arrest for an offense in progress; and (3) emergency arrest (see the Editorial Note at page 143 regarding the terminology used for arrest and apprehension in the English and Japanese versions).

As a general rule, arrests should only be conducted pursuant to a warrant (*reijō*) issued by a judge. This reflects a basic constitutional principle of Japanese criminal procedure derived from Articles 33 and 35 called the "warrant principle" (*reijō shugi*), which holds that compulsory dispositions in criminal proceedings should be conducted pursuant to a judicial warrant. Arrest warrants must specify the offense which the person arrested is suspected of committing.General (unspecific) warrants are prohibited.

Article 33 also acknowledges an exception to the warrant rule: when "the offense [is] being committed." Under Article 212(1) of the CCP: "A person who is in the very act of committing or has just committed an offense is a flagrant offender." When a suspect is caught in the act—meaning the crime was committed in the presence of the person making the arrest[406]—both the crime and suspect are obvious, making a warrant unnecessary. Also, under these circumstances, it is not feasible to request a warrant.

Article 212(2) expands the scope of "in process" warrantless arrests significantly, by deeming as flagrant offender persons committing an offense a short time before the arresting officer arrives at the scene, including: (1) a person engaged in fresh pursuit; (2) a person carrying evidence of a crime (i.e., stolen goods or a weapon); (3) a person with visible traces of the offense on his/her body; and (4) a person who attempts to run away when challenged.

The Supreme Court has found warrantless arrests constitutional in a case where the arrest was conducted over an hour after the crime and 4 km away from the scene of the crime.[407] The criteria for determining what constitutes an offense in process for purposes of applying the exception to the warrant requirement include how much time has passed since the offense was committed and how far from the location of the crime the offenders are found. But they are not the only the criteria. Other specific circumstances of individual cases may also be considered.

Article 210(1) of the CCP provides for the third category of arrest: when a law enforcement officer has sufficient grounds to suspect a serious crime has been committed and a warrant cannot be obtained first due to the urgency of the situation. This is "emergency arrest." Although it involves a warrant (which must be obtained *after* the arrest), it likely seems inconsistent with the clear wording of Article 33. Nonetheless, the Supreme Court found emergency arrest to be constitutional because "emergency arrests can be exercised in inevitable and emergent situations and only in a certain category of serious crime. Also, the warrant must be requested right after the arrest," though this is a rationale that merely articulates the statutory requirements rather than any meaningful constitutional interpretation.[408]

Another question arises from the practice of *bekken taiho* ("arrest for a different matter"), which involves either arresting a suspect for one offense for the purpose of investigating him for a different offense, or the use of a successive series of arrests to obtain a new detention warrant and prolong the pre-charge detention period in order to continue investigating a suspect. While lower courts have found this practice to be unlawful or even unconstitutional in some situations, the Supreme Court has always upheld specific instances of its use.[409]

The Court has also upheld the warrantless apprehension and detention of deportable aliens.[410] In doing so the Court avoided the question of whether such actions were "arrests," by analogizing them to arrests for crimes in progress.[411]

Apprehension and detentions by public authorities occur in a variety of other contexts outside the scope of formal criminal procedures, including committal of persons suffering from mental disease, police taking people into protective custody, and the imposition of punishments by judges for disruptive behavior in courtrooms. Although scholars have differing views on each category of apprehension, the courts have never found them constitutionally problematic, at least from an Article 33 perspective (since they are not considered "arrests").

Finally, in practice many arrests result from suspects voluntarily accompanying a police officer to a police station where they confess (again voluntarily) and are then arrested pursuant to a warrant procured based on the confession. Whether the accompaniment and confession are actually "voluntary" is questionable in some cases.

Article 34: Requirement of Cause for Arrest and Detention; Right to Counsel

Mari Hirayama

Article 34.
No person shall be arrested or detained without being at once informed of the charges against him or without the immediate privilege of counsel; nor shall he be detained without adequate cause; and upon demand of any person such cause must be immediately shown in open court in his presence and the presence of his counsel.

Deprivations of liberty and the criminal process under Article 34

Under the Meiji Constitution (Article 23), arrests and detentions had to be "according to law." However, this made it possible to impose prolonged warrantless detentions so long as there was a statutory foundation for doing so. By contrast, Article 34 establishes several basic constitutional guarantees in the criminal justice process, including the right to be informed of charges and a right of counsel additional to that set forth in Article 37.

Readers should refer to the discussion of terminology like "arrest" and "detain" in the Editorial Note at page page 143. As noted there, "arrest" as used in Article 34 in Japanese refers to a form of detention (*yokuryū*), though a potentially brief one. In any case, Article 34 requires a person subjected to a deprivation of liberty to be informed "at once" of "the charges against [them]," though in Japanese the term is *riyū*, which just means "reason." *Riyū* appears two more times in Article 34, where it is rendered "cause" in English. The article thus also requires that detentions be for adequate[412] cause, and that is understood to mean the facts of the specific allegation of facts and crime they constitute forming the basis of the arrest.

For purposes of an arrest—whether by warrant or otherwise (see discussion at Article 33)—the "informed of the charges" requirement is deemed satisfied by the statement of the crime alleged in the arrest warrant or as read out at the time of arrest.

Within 72 hours of an arrest prosecutors must seek a judicial warrant for further detention.[413] The grounds for detention are set forth in Article 60 of the CCP, i.e., the suspect: (1) has no fixed residence; (2) may conceal or destroy evidence; or (3) is a flight risk. The latter two grounds are highly subjective, include a presumption of guilt, and are all too easily accepted by judges in authorizing detention, a source of much criticism.[414]

Detention warrants are often issued *before* a decision to prosecute has been made. This is important in understanding how the criminal process works in a way that on the surface may seem incompatible with Article 34. After an arrest—at which time the suspect is informed of the reason—the first time a suspect is likely to appear before a judge is when the judge considers the prosecutor's application for a detention warrant at a time when a decision to prosecute has not yet been made.[415] This is not conducted in open court, does not implicate the right of counsel, and is *not* the explanation required in Article 34. The subject of the proceeding is the prosecutor's reason for seeking detention, *not* the crime for which the suspect has been arrested.

The requirements of the latter part of Article 34 are met through a process formalized in Article 84 of the CCP. This enables a detained suspect or defendant (or any other interested party)[416] to demand an explanation of the cause for his deprivation of freedom before they have been adjudicated guilty of any crime (or even put on trial). The prosecutors, defense counsel and/or suspect/defendant can make a statement to the Court, but this must not exceed 10 minutes per person.[417]

Until the 1980s there were a number of cases of demands being made in politically sensitive cases. More recently, however, the procedure has fallen into disuse, possibly because it is found to be a pointless exercise whereby judges simply reiterate the grounds for authorizing detention in the first place.[418] As a result, fewer than 1 percent of detained suspects/defendants now avail themselves of the procedure—despite its constitutional foundation.

The language providing for an opportunity to be informed of the charges in open court has its origins in Article XXXI of the GHQ Draft, and clearly anticipates some sort of *habeas corpus* relief. Japan does in fact have a *Habeas Corpus Act*, that was enacted at least in part to implement Article 34.[419] However, it never came to be widely used in the criminal justice sphere, in part due to Supreme Court procedural rules limiting its use to only "significantly unlawful" deprivations of liberty for which no other remedy is available.[420]

The Article 34 right of counsel

Article 37 guarantees the right of assistance of counsel to defendants who have been formally charged and are put on trial. Article 34 establishes an additional right to counsel for those earlier in the process: arrest and pre-charge detention.

This aspect of Article 34 is implemented through the CCP (Article 30(1)) which states that an accused or a suspect "may appoint defense counsel *at any time*" (emphasis added). This means that even suspects or defendants who are not in custody have a right to appoint defense counsel. The CCP (Articles 203(1) and 204(1)) also require police officers or prosecutors to inform suspects at the time of arrest of the charges and that he or she may appoint defense counsel.

The Supreme Court has held that the Article 34 right to counsel must be exercised by the accused himself; courts and prosecutors are not required to provide information about how to appoint counsel, nor is the state constitutionally required to bear the expense. The Article 34 requirement is satisfied so long as the Court and the prosecutors afford the opportunity to exercise the right.[421]

Thus, in practice, although the right to counsel under both Articles 34 and 37 implies the ability of a suspect or defendant to *communicate* freely with their counsel while detained, in practice significant restrictions are imposed on attorney-client contact, particularly during pre-charge investigations. CCP Article 39(1) states that a suspect or defendant may "without any official being present, have an interview with, or send to or receive documents or articles from defense counsel or prospective defense counsel..."[422] Yet paragraphs 2 and 3 of CCP Article 39 impose significant restrictions on the exercise of these rights, including in the case of suspects under pre-charge investigation, the ability of investigators to designate the time and place of attorney-client meetings.[423]

Article 35: Protections from Searches and Seizures

Mari Hirayama

Article 35.

(1) The right of all persons to be secure in their homes, papers and effects against entries, searches and seizures shall not be impaired except upon warrant issued for adequate cause and particularly describing the place to be searched and things to be seized, or except as provided by Article 33.

(2) Each search or seizure shall be made upon separate warrant issued by a competent judicial officer.

Criminal procedure frequently involves situations where police investigators search premises and seize evidence.[424] The places and property subject to these actions are highly relevant to the privacy of the people involved. Privacy and property rights are important, but so is securing evidence for trial. Article 35 thus seeks to establish a balance between competing rights and interests in a way which allows investigators to do their jobs without abusing their powers in a way that harms privacy or property rights.

This is accomplished through the parameters set forth in the first paragraph and the warrant requirement in the second (see discussion at the Editorial Note on page 143 regarding the meaning of "judicial officer"). In Anglo-American jurisprudence there is a very old and deeply rooted maxim: "a man's house is his castle." A similar belief also holds true in Japan; even under the Meiji Constitution the home was protected from unauthorized entry or searches (Article 25). The Japanese term in Article 35 is *jūkyo*, which would typically be translated "residence." Leading constitutional scholars have referred to this "home" in such terms as "the center of one's private life" [425] or "the place where one has a reasonable expectation in his or her personal life is protected."[426] The former view may be too narrow, as it seems limited to one's residence, while the latter may include a workplace or hotel room. The basic premise of Article 35 is consistent with the warrant principle-based nature of Japanese criminal procedure (see Article 33), and establishes the principle that searches and seizure should be conducted pursuant to a warrant issued by a judge, who is charged with determining whether there are suitable grounds for authorizing the search and seizure in connection with the crime alleged.[427]

Search and seizure warrants must describe the place(s) to be searched and thing(s) to be seized with particularity; in other words, general warrants are prohibited. As to the degree of particularly required in the warrant, the Supreme Court has held that:

> *Article 35 of the Constitution only requires that the place(s) to be searched and item(s) to be seized be specified; it should not be understood as requiring the warrant to specify that it has been issued based on probable cause. That being the case, the Constitution also does not require the offense at issue in the case under investigation or the applicable statutory reference to be set forth in the search and seizure warrant. Other than the place(s) to be search and the item(s) to be seized everything is left to the Code of Criminal Procedure.*[428]

In the same decision, the Supreme Court also declared that, to the extent a warrant enumerated various concrete things, it did not create a problematic lack of specificity if it also included a catch-all "all other items related to this case."

Paragraph (1) of Article 35 identifies the exceptions to the warrant requirement. This is accomplished through reference to Article 33, which addresses arrests, though there are different possible interpretations of what this means. One is that warrantless searches and seizures are permitted in connection with any arrest that is permitted under Article 33. An obvious interpretation would thus be that warrantless searches and seizures are permissible in conjunction with a lawful arrest of any type, and this is the interpretation reflected in the CCP (Article 220). This represents one of the very few exceptions to the *reijōshugi* principle, judicial warrants being required for forcible actions by the state in the course of the criminal justice process. It also makes the potential scope of searches and seizures broad.

Another possible interpretation of the reference to Article 33 would be that it is intended to allow warrantless searches and seizures in conjunction with warrantless arrests. Under that view, "the scope of the place of the arrest" would arguably limit searches and seizures to the suspect's person and immediate possessions.

The Supreme Court, however, has focused on the "[n]o person shall be apprehended ... unless he is apprehended, the offense being committed" construction of Article 33 to interpret Article 35 as allowing warrantless searches and seizures in any circumstance where an arrest for a crime in progress could have been made, *even if no arrest is actually made*.[429] While the Supreme Court has required that if there is a search and seizure in connection with an arrest, the former must relate to the crime for which the arrest is made, though it has acknowledged a degree of flexibility so long as there is a reasonable connection between the time and place of arrest and of search and seizure.[430] In doing so, the Court even went so far as to uphold a warrantless search and seizure conducted in connection with an emergency arrest (see discussion at Article 33), before the arrest took place.[431]

Although the Court has allowed for warrantless searches in connection with emergency arrest, there is no "emergency search and seizure" regime comparable to that for arrests. Therefore, conducing search and seizure first and obtaining a warrant later is not permissible.

Technological developments have given rise to new issues. In 2017, the Supreme Court issued a judgment in a case in which the police had attached a GPS tracker to the defendant's car and used it to track his movements for more than six months prior to his arrest. The Court found this to be an invasion of a private sphere, and that the use of GPS technology in this way was a form of "compulsory investigation" and thus required a warrant under Article 35.[432] Despite this ruling, the Court also ruled that there was enough evidence against the defendant without the GPS data to uphold his conviction. While the Court has acknowledged that evidence gathered in violation of the requirements of Article 35 could be subject to exclusion, it has rarely done so to the extent of invalidating a conviction.[433]

Although Article 35 is concerned primarily with criminal investigations, it is also potentially implicated by administrative investigations of a non-criminal nature. After all, when investigations are conducted by tax authorities, for example, it is possible that it could escalate into a criminal case. The Supreme Court has acknowledged the possibility of the Article 35 warrant requirement applying to administrative investigations, but has so far declined to reject any instances where a warrant was lacking and enunciated the need for a balancing test between the purpose of the investigation and the degree of coerciveness in the investigation.[434] Finally, justified in part by the administrative role of police officers in "preventing and suppressing crime," the Court has also upheld warrantless forcible searches of persons and their possessions in connection with stop-and-question activities under the Police Duties Execution Act.[435]

Article 36: Torture Prohibited

Mari Hirayama

Article 36.
The infliction of torture by any public officer and cruel punishments are absolutely forbidden.

Crime and punishments

Once a criminal defendant is convicted at trial, sentence is passed and executed. Japan's Penal Code provides for seven distinct categories of punishment: death (*shikei*), imprisonment with work (*chōeki*), imprisonment without work (*kinko*), fine (*bakkin*), misdemeanor detention without work (*kōryū*) and petty fine (*karyō*).[436] Confiscation (bosshū) is an ancillary punishment that may also be imposed in some instances.[437]

Fines and imprisonment with work are the most commonly imposed forms of punishment. Imprisonment can be for a defined term of no less than one month or no more than 20 years. The closest Japan has to "life imprisonment" is imprisonment without a defined term (*muki*). As discussed at Article 18, the constitution prohibits involuntary servitude, except as a punishment for crime.

Article 36 contains an absolute prohibition on "cruel" punishments. Which punishments are cruel and which are not? In 1948, the Supreme Court defined as cruel, those "punishments which are regarded as cruel on humanitarian grounds and which entail unnecessary mental and physical anguish."[438] Most people may agree that capital punishment—the death penalty—is the most extreme form of punishment and at least some may consider it cruel. In 1948, however, the Supreme Court of Japan upheld the constitutionality of death penalty. Dismissing the appeal from the defendant sentenced to death for committing a double murder, the Court famously declared "Life is precious. A single person's life weighs more than the entire earth. The death penalty is truly the harshest of all punishments, the ultimate punishment of last resort."[439] The Court then proceeded to point out that Articles 13 and 31 of the constitution anticipate capital punishment to the extent not inconsistent with the public welfare and imposed pursuant to a procedure established by law. Thus, "by itself, as a form of punishment, the death penalty does not generally and immediately constitute cruel punishment." The Court thus focused on the method of execution, not the taking of life itself in evaluating "cruelty." A concurring opinion by four of the Court's judges noted that the death penalty might be regarded as a cruel form of punishment at some point in the future when the people have developed a higher and more peaceful culture in which it is no longer needed to deter crime and advance the public welfare.

Over seven decades later, Japan still has the death penalty and it has not subsequently been deemed constitutionally "cruel." With respect to the method of execution (which in Japan has been hanging, since the Meiji period), in 1955 the Supreme Court ruled that there was no reason to find it a particularly cruel form of execution.[440]

The commencement in May of 2009 of the lay judge (*saiban'in*) system, whereby randomly-selected citizens sit with professional judges to try serious cases has brought new attention to the death penalty. This is in part because the lay judge system is only used to try offenses punishable by death or indefinite imprisonment, or where an intentional offense results in a death.[441] In a 2011 arson-murder trial before a lay judge panel which featured a former prosecutor testifying about their experience witnessing a hanging, questions were raised about the cruelty of this form of punishment. Referring to the 1948 Supreme Court judgment, the Osaka District Court held the death penalty constitutional but noted it was debatable whether hanging was the best way of implementing it.[442]

Torture by public officers

Under the Meiji Constitution, the police were able to use unlawful arrests and torture to obtain confessions from suspects. Article 36 represents a rejection of this practice, in expressing an absolute ban on torture by any public officer (which includes police and prosecutors).[443] This is further bolstered through the Article 38(2) exclusion from evidence of confessions procured through torture.

Despite this constitutional prohibition, Japan lacks any laws clearly defining "torture." As a constitutional term in the context of both Articles 36 and 38, torture is generally understood to mean the use by law enforcement officials of physical and psychological stress or pain against criminal suspects in the course of procuring a confession or other criminal investigations.[444] Some question whether the term needs to be limited to this context.

While not defined as torture, the Penal Code does establish an offense called "Assault and Cruelty by Special Public Officials," which potentially applies to abusive police and prosecutors.[445] The Code of Criminal Procedure also provides for a special procedure for bringing charges against public officials who abuse their authority (though they are rarely successful).[446]

In 1999 Japan acceded to the Convention against Torture and Other Cruel, Inhuman or Degrading Treatment or Punishment, which requires periodic review by the UN Committee Against Torture (CAT). In its 2007 and 2013 reviews the CAT expressed several concerns and made recommendations, including that Japan establish a legal definition of torture.[447] The CAT also expressed concern over the conditions of prisoners detained on death row, which includes prolonged solitary confinement while under uncertainty about the date when the sentence will be carried out. Under current practice, inmates are reportedly not informed of the date of their execution until the morning of the execution date.[448]

Article 37: Rights of the Criminal Defendant

Mari Hirayama

Article 37.

(1) In all criminal cases the accused shall enjoy the right to a speedy and public trial by an impartial tribunal.

(2) He shall be permitted full opportunity to examine all witnesses, and he shall have the right of compulsory process for obtaining witnesses on his behalf at public expense.

(3) At all times the accused shall have the assistance of competent counsel who shall, if the accused is unable to secure the same by his own efforts, be assigned to his use by the State.

Suspect, accused and defendant

Article 37 articulates several significant rights guaranteed to defendants at the criminal trial stage. In order to understand them, however, it will be helpful to clarify some areas of potential linguistic and procedural confusion.

In Anglo-American Law individuals who become targets of criminal investigations are called "suspects." If arrested, then that person may be called "the accused," a title that may be used even after being charged or indicted. Once on trial, they may be called "the accused" or "the defendant." However, most prosecutions end in plea bargains so actual courtroom trials are the exception rather than the rule. Accordingly, the English term "accused" covers a broad category of people at several stages in the criminal justice process.

Japanese criminal procedure is quite different. Those who become the target of a criminal investigation are called "*higisha*" (suspect). They are still called *higisha* after arrest and charging. After they are indicted and brought to trial by prosecutors (who effectively have the exclusive power of initiating prosecutions, there being no grand jury system in Japan),[449] they are then called "*hikokunin*," which is typically translated as "defendant."[450] Since there is no general plea bargain system in Japan, even those who freely admit their guilt go through a trial and will thus be called "defendant" until they are conclusively acquitted or convicted.[451]

While the English version of Article 37 uses the term "accused" and would thus appear to potentially apply to persons starting from the arrest stage of the process, the Japanese version uses *hikokunin*, and thus would be more precisely translated as "defendant." Under the Japanese text, therefore, it is clear that the protections of Article 37 only apply to accused once they have been charged. For this reason, to avoid further confusion the discussion that follows will use "defendant" rather than "accused."

Fair tribunal, speedy trial

Article 32 already guarantees the right of access to the courts. Article 37 adds a right of criminal defendants to a speedy and public trial by an impartial tribunal.[452] According to a very early Supreme Court decision, "trial before an impartial tribunal" means "a trial by a court which in its organization and other aspects is free from partiality and unfairness, and it is not indicative of a trial that in individual cases is concretely fair and valid in substantive detail."[453] In other words, the guarantee is *not* that each individual case will be "fair." The organizational fairness of courts is implemented in detail through the CCP, which seeks to ensure judges and other court personnel involved in individual cases are free from partiality.[454]

As the legal aphorism goes "Justice delayed is justice denied." Speedy trials are important because as time goes by, evidence can be lost, and the memories of witnesses can fade. This interferes with one of the important goals of the criminal trial process: finding the truth. Moreover, failing to identify and punish a wrongdoer in a proper and timely fashion is also contrary to the public interest. Finally, and most importantly, prolonged status as a criminal defendant involves numerous burdens and restraints on freedom, which should be minimized as much as possible. In a 1948 case, the Supreme Court declined to find a violation of Article 37(1) in a case in which the trial was demonstrably not "speedy" due in part to Occupation-era disruption and a shortage of court personnel.[455] Given that "speediness" is subjective and will vary greatly from case to case, and the absence of any provisions in the

Code of Criminal Procedure implementing it, the "speedy trial" guarantee in Article 37(1) has generally been considered a "program provision" (see discussion in the Introduction to this Chapter and at Article 25).

However, in 1972 in its ruling on the *Takada Case*, the Supreme Court dismissed an indictment for which no trial had been held for 15 years, declaring that:

> [T]*he provision of Article 37(1) not only requires that legislative and judicial administration measures should be taken as needed to generally guarantee speedy trial, but also recognizes that in individual criminal cases, if an extraordinary situation against the guarantee provision has actually been caused in which the defendant's right to speedy trial seems to have been violated due to a significant delay in the proceedings, an emergency relief means may be taken to discontinue the proceedings involving the defendant, even where there are no specific provisions on how to cope with such a situation.*[456]

The *Takada Case* was a significant decision, but since it was issued the Supreme Court has been quite reluctant to acknowledge other incidents of an "extraordinary situation against the guarantee provision" resulting in unconstitutional delays in trials. In fact, only three years later the Court found the rationale of the *Takada Case* to be inapplicable in a case that had dragged on for over 15 years, in part due to appeals by the defendant.[457]

In any case, as part of Japan's millennial judicial system reform, the Act on the Expediting of Trials was passed in 2003 with the stated purpose of concluding proceedings in the first instance (in both civil and criminal cases) "in as short a time as possible within a period of two years."[458] The introduction of the lay judge system also saw the introduction of a system of pretrial proceedings and concentrated trial proceedings held over consecutive days.[459]

Public trial

Article 82 mandates that trials shall be conducted and judgment declared publicly. This applies both to civil and criminal trials. Criminal trials, however, involve the possible deprivation of the personal liberty, property and even life of a defendant, so the need for criminal trials to be public is particularly important; hence the additional guarantee in Article 37. Here, "public" trial means that the general public can observe a trial. However, under the Rules of Criminal Procedure established by the Supreme Court (Article 215) observers are prohibited from taking photographs, and no broadcasting of court proceedings is permitted without the permission of the Court (and in the past spectators were prohibited from taking notes, as discussed at Articles 21 and 82). In practice, at trials which gather public attention, the media only broadcast images from the courtroom before the defendant and lay judges enter, for a short period of time.

Witnesses

The right to examine all witnesses is critical to criminal defendants. If a defendant is not permitted the opportunity to examine all witnesses, statements of such witnesses are not admissible at trial under the hearsay exclusion rule in Article 320 of the Code of Criminal Procedure. There are, however, some exceptions to its rules on excluding hearsay evidence (Article 321 *et seq.*), one of which permits use as evidence of an affidavit given before a public prosecutor (*kensatsukan menzen chōsho*) in a wide variety of circumstances even if they are unavailable to testify at trial. This is a questionable practice because prosecutors represent one of the parties in adversarial proceedings, so there is no reason documents prepared by them should be accorded special treatment that conflicts with the defendant's right to examine *all* witnesses. However, the Supreme Court has upheld this practice.[460]

Advocacy for the rights of crime victims resulted in amendments to the CCP being passed in 2000 to enhance the protection of witnesses in criminal trials. This includes practices such as allowing "those who are appropriate in easing the witness's anxiety or tension" to accompany them while testifying, making it possible for witnesses to testify without the witness and defendant to see each other, and allowing for witness testimony through video-link.[461] The Supreme Court has held that methods that enable witnesses to testify out of view of the defendant did not infringe Article 37(2), since "the defendant cannot see the witness but can hear the witness giving a statement and can also question the witness."[462]

Similarly, with increasing prosecutions of child abuse cases, how to use children's statements obtained through forensic interviews in court has become a controversial issue. In order to avoid the secondary victimization of children through the trial process, recording of children's statements at forensic interviews for use as evidence is one possible solution. These statements by children are, however, not amenable to examination through cross examination, so their use at criminal trials raises some difficult questions.

As for a defendant's right to compulsory process for obtaining witnesses, it does not equate to all witnesses requested by the defendant being summoned. The Supreme Court has held that it is sufficient "if the witnesses who are necessary and appropriate for that trial are summoned."[463] "At public expense" means the State will provide for every expense related to the witnesses, such as travel expenses and per diems. The Court also held, however, that Article 37(2) does not prevent the defendant from being ordered to pay these costs if convicted.[464]

Counsel

First, it should be noted that the Japanese version of Article 37(3) clarifies that the meaning of "competent," is only to be qualified (*shikaku wo yūsuru*).[465] Second, the English says "at all times," which adds to the impression that the protections of Article 37 apply across a broader range of the criminal justice process.[466] However in Japanese the language is (*ikanaru baai ni mo*), which would be more accurately translated "in all situations."

Third, while the English is an unqualified "shall have the assistance of competent counsel," the Japanese merely acknowledges a right to request the assistance of counsel (*irai suru koto ga dekiru*). Moreover, this right does not include the right to decline the assistance of counsel. There is no constitutionally-protected right of self-representation, and professional counsel is now effectively mandatory in all serious cases.

Similarly, the "inability to secure" language in English is, in Japanese, "inability to request." (*irai suru koto ga dekinai*). Here the state is only required to provide counsel when the defendant is unable to procure their own counsel. Under the Cabinet Order to Provide for

Assets under Article 36-2 of the Code of Criminal Procedure and the Standard Amount under Paragraph 1 of Article 36-3,[467] the threshold for eligibility is set at assets of JPY 500,000 (approximately $5,000).

Until quite recently, state-funded lawyers were only available for defendants post-indictment. Those arrested have always been free to engage lawyers, and local bar associations have tried to develop systems for supporting indigent accused at the pre-charge stage of the process. Judicial System Reform saw the introduction of state-funded lawyers for arrestees charged with serious crimes in 2006, and the range of offenses eligible for such lawyers has been expanded.[468] Since 2016 all suspects who have been detained by judicial warrant (which is required in order to detain a person for more than 72 hours after arrest) are entitled to state-provided counsel. However, there is still no right to a state-funded lawyer during the first three days following arrest.

Also, the right to the assistance of counsel does not include having counsel present during interrogations. As already noted at Article 34, under CCP Article 39(3), police and prosecutors are entitled to schedule meetings between suspects and their lawyers based on the needs of their investigation.

Article 38: Protection Against Self-Incrimination and Forced Confessions

Mari Hirayama

Article 38.

(1) No person shall be compelled to testify against himself.

(2) Confession made under compulsion, torture or threat, or after prolonged arrest or detention shall not be admitted in evidence.

(3) No person shall be convicted or punished in cases where the only proof against him is his own confession.

Confessions in Japanese criminal procedure

"The Confession is the Queen of Evidence" is a maxim of criminal procedure that has long been applicable in most countries. It is particularly true in Japan, which lacks a general system of plea bargaining and police and prosecutors depend heavily on confessions to make their case. The ability to procure confessions is facilitated by CCP rules which allow a suspect to be held in custody after arrest for up to 23 days before a charging decision must be made. Under the CCP, such pre-trial detentions are considered a form of investigative tool and lawyers may be blocked from seeing detained clients until police and prosecutors are finished interrogating them.[469] Moreover, the 23-day clock may be re-set by making a new arrest for a different (but often related) offense, a practice known as *bekken taiho*. This means police and the prosecutors have ample time to interrogate suspects. Prolonged detentions are identified as a powerful tool for generating confessions, including false confessions which have generated numerous high profile wrongful (or at least questionable) convictions.[470]

This "Japanese way of Criminal Procedure"—frequently referred to in Japan as *hitojichi shihō* or "hostage-based justice" (the "hostage" being the suspect) has been criticized by a variety of international organizations. Notable among these is the UN Committee Against Torture (CAT), which monitors implementation of the Convention against Torture and Other Cruel, Inhuman or Degrading Treatment or Punishment (which Japan ratified in Convention in 1998).[471]

In response to CAT demands in 2013 that the Government of Japan identify concrete safeguards to prevent forced confessions, which are clearly prohibited by Article 15 of the Convention, the GOJ explained that confessions obtained by threatening are prohibited by both the constitution and the CCP. Yet this begs the question of how coerced confessions seem to play an important role in the criminal justice system, a fact that received significant international attention when Nissan CEO Carlos Ghosn was arrested and detained for alleged financial reporting violations.[472] The GOJ does not seem too concerned about this international criticism, and the Ministry of Justice has published counterarguments asserting that interrogations in Japan are properly conducted and confessions not coerced.[473]

Article 38 in theory and practice

The first paragraph of Article 38 establishes a privilege against self-incrimination that will seem familiar to those versed in the Fifth Amendment to the US constitution. The "no person shall," formulation makes it clear that the protection applies not only to suspects and defendants, but also to witnesses. The Japanese corollary to "testify against himself" might be more accurately translated "give testimony disadvantageous to himself." This is understood to refer to any statement which incriminates the speaker, in a way that may either result in his conviction or being sentenced more severely.[474]

However, the "disadvantageous" element in the Japanese text means that the protection has been found not to apply to certain types of statements, such as confirmation of a suspect's name.[475] The clear reference to "statements" in the Japanese means that taking fingerprints, bodily measurements, pictures and other activities which may tend to incriminate a suspect are excluded from the protection.

On similar grounds, the Supreme Court has also held that compelling breathalyzer tests from suspected drunk drivers did not violate Article 38(1), since it involved measuring alcohol levels in the breath rather than "statements." In other words, extracting evidence from a suspect's body does not constitute a "statement."[476] While the Supreme Court has not addressed the subject, there are lower court rulings stating that polygraph examinations are also unlikely to violate a suspect's privilege against self-incrimination or right to remain silent.[477]

One issue is whether the prohibition on compulsion in the first paragraph of Article 38 establishes a constitutional right to remain silent. Such a right has been enacted legislatively through the CCP, which requires that suspects be informed of the right before an interrogation begins.[478] However, the Supreme Court and many scholars alike have been reluctant to clearly establish the right to be informed of a right to remain silent as a constitutional requirement, and has rejected the idea that a confession can be excluded as evidence merely because the defendant was not informed of the right.[479]

As already noted, since pre-charge detention is a category of investigative tool, even if a suspect in a custody exercises his right to remain silent, interrogators can continue to interrogate him, and there is no right to have a lawyer present during interrogations (see discussion at Article 34). Under Article 198(1) of the CCP prosecutors or police may demand "a suspect to appear in their offices and interrogate said person when it is necessary for the investigation of a crime; provided however, that the suspect may, except in cases where said person is under arrest or under detention, refuse to appear or after said person has appeared, may withdraw at any time." This is understood as establishing a duty on the part of suspects in custody to "endure" interrogations. Many scholars, consider this a problematic interpretation, since such a duty could potentially make a right to remain silent meaningless. The Supreme Court has not ruled on the matter, but lower court decisions have referred to suspects having such a duty.[480]

Paragraph (2) of Article 38 would seem to specifically address the concerns of the CAT described above. Not only does it clearly prohibit confessions procured "under compulsion, torture or threat," but specifically addresses confessions made "after prolonged arrest or detention."[481] Moreover, the constitutional prohibition is further bolstered by the CCP, Article 319(1), which states that: "Confession under compulsion, torture, threats, after unduly prolonged detention or *when there is doubt about it being voluntary may not be admitted as evidence*" (emphasis added). In practice, this means that confessions may be excludable not only if they were procured in violation of the prohibitions in Article 38(2), but also if they are obtained through deception, promise of benefits, exhaustion or other factors.[482]

The exclusion of confessions about which there are doubts as to their voluntariness is thus clearly anticipated by Japan's system of criminal justice. The question is thus under what circumstances confessions are excluded and how frequently. For example, the Supreme Court has questioned the voluntariness of a confession procured based on a prosecutor's promise to suspend an indictment.[483] The Court has also rejected the voluntariness of confessions made based on false statements by police about a confession made by a suspect's wife and accomplice, finding it to be a form of psychological coercion.[484]

As for confessions procured after prolonged detentions, there are instances of very early Supreme Court cases rejecting as unconstitutional confessions coming after months of detention.[485] Yet very early in its history the Court also ruled that even if the confession was procured after prolonged detention, it was not invalidated if it was clear that there was no causal relationship between the detention and the confession.[486]

Accordingly, at some trials, the voluntariness of confessions may be a significant point of dispute. However, having confessed, the burden of proving coercion generally falls on the defendant. This may result in "he-said-she-said" conflicting testimony by defendants and investigators (police or prosecutors), with judges often being inclined to believe the latter. Moreover, Japanese criminal trials have traditionally been very heavily focused on documentary evidence, including written confessions. The longstanding practice has been for confessions procured from interrogations to be written by the investigator and acknowledged by the defendant, a practice which ensures the confession contains a recitation of facts that is favorable to the prosecution. It also makes it possible to procure multiple confessions.[487]

With the introduction in 2009 of the *saiban'in* system of citizen lay judges participating in serious criminal trials, it was impossible to expect average citizens to read thick dossiers to determine whether confessions were obtained voluntarily (also see discussion at Article 32). After much debate (and public scandals calling into question the integrity of prosecutorial investigations), 2019 amendments to the CCP made mandatory the recording of interrogations in cases to be tried before the lay judge system (which account for only 2 percent of all criminal trials) and certain other special cases. While this was meaningful in that it brought transparency into the interrogation rooms in serious cases and spared lay judges the task of reading confessions written by professional investigators, there are still some concerns that the process can be used to coerce defendants to help "stage" convincing confessions that may still not be voluntary.[488]

Corroborating evidence

Paragraph (3) of Article 38 prohibits convictions based on confessions alone. This has been legislatively enacted through CCP 319, which further clarifies that the prohibition applies even if the confession is freely made in open court.[489] Together they establish a rule known as the "Corroborating Evidence Requirement" In general, Japanese judges operate based on what is known as a "Principle of Free Evaluation of Evidence" (*jiyū shinshō shugi*), which allows them to give weight to evidence as they please.[490] This rule thus establishes an exception to that principle intended to prevent excessive focus on confessions and avoid wrongful convictions. In practice, however, it does not appear to be difficult to procure evidence that corroborates a confession.

What about confessions by a defendant at a trial? Article 38(3) does not address this. According to the Supreme Court, Article 38(3) does not cover confessions in open court at trial, therefore convicting a defendant when a confession at a trial is the only incriminating evidence does not violate Article 38(3).[491] Some people may claim this is because there is a high expectation of voluntariness in a confession at a trial, and even if a defendant proffers a false statement, their lawyer is there, ready to correct them. A similar view is that judges are in the best position to evaluate whether a defendant is telling the truth or not, as the Court is hearing directly from the defendant. This is, however, an underestimation of the pressure the defendant may experience at a trial and assumes a high degree of faith in judges. A defendant may give a confession under pressure even at the trial.

CCP Article 319(2) states that evidence corroborating a confession is required regardless of whether the confession was made in open court. Thus, in practice a confession at a trial also needs corroborating evidence anyway under CCP. A significant difference is that a violation of CCP presents less scope for appeals to the Supreme Court than a constitutional violation (CCP 405 (1)). How to deal with a confession at a trial has much to do with a discussion whether Japan should introduce an arraignment system as used in the United States.

Note that the requirement for additional evidence corroborating a confession by a defendant does not extend to a confession by an accomplice who is not a co-defendant.[492] Nor does it apply to witness testimony.

Finally, the Court has found a violation of Article 38 (and Article 31) to occur when a court uses evidence of a defendant's uncorroborated confession about an offense other than the one for which he is being tried as grounds for imposing a particularly strict punishment for the latter.[493]

Applicability to administrative proceedings

Article 38 is clearly concerned with criminal proceedings. However, as with the search and seizure provisions of Article 35, there is some question about whether the constitutional protection extends to administrative proceedings. Although numerous regulatory regimes involve requirements that license holders or other persons enjoying government privileges provide information or reports, including those of a character which could be incriminating, the Supreme Court has generally been reluctant to extend Article 38 to such contexts.[494]

Article 39: Prohibition on Double Jeopardy and Ex Post Facto Laws

Mari Hirayama

> **Article 39.**
> No person shall be held criminally liable for an act which was lawful at the time it was committed, or of which he has been acquitted, nor shall he be placed in double jeopardy.

The Japanese version of Article 39 is actually comprised of two sentences, so it may help to imagine a full stop after "acquitted" in the English. The first half of the first sentence prohibits retroactive punishments and, by extension *ex post facto* laws.

The complex and seemingly duplicative nature of the remainder of Article 39 is a result of the drafting history. Article XXXVII(2) of the GHQ Draft stated "No person shall be twice placed in jeopardy for the same offense," while what became the Article 39 prohibition on retroactive punishments was contained in Article XXXIX. The Japanese government added the "or of which he had been acquitted" language to Article 39 and deleted the reference to double jeopardy on the assumption it was now redundant. GHQ, however, requested the double jeopardy language be reinstated, so it was added as at the end of Article 39.[495]

Retroactive punishment and ex post facto *laws*

The prohibition of *ex post facto* laws and retroactive punishment is based on the fundamental legal principle of *nulla poena sine lege* (Latin for "no punishment without law") which is reflected in many constitutions and enshrined in Article 8 of the French Declaration of the Rights of Man of 1789. This principle was at least partially reflected in Article 23 of the Meiji Constitution, which required punishments to be according to law, but did not clearly prohibit their retroactive application. By contrast, the Article 39 prohibition is reflected in (for example) Article 6 of the Japanese Penal Code, which stipulates that when a punishment is changed by law after the commission of a crime, the lesser punishment shall be applied.

The prohibition of retroactive punishment clearly applies to substantive criminal law, but what about procedural law? Here the Supreme Court has been more accommodating, ruling very early in its history that an amendment to a procedural law, which "merely restricts some of the grounds for appeal to the Supreme Court" does not contravene the wording of Article

39, "even if it is somewhat more disadvantageous to the accused than the procedural law at the time of the act was committed."[496]

A more recent example comes from the victims' rights movement, which has been growing since the late 1990s and whose lobbying has led to amendments to the CCP to extend or abolish the statute of limitations for some offenses. A 2010 amendment completely abolished the statute of limitations for murder (which had previously been 15 years), extended the statute of limitations for other serious crimes and applied these changes retroactively. In response to a challenge brought by a defendant prosecuted for a murder-robbery committed more than 15 years prior to the prosecution (which would have been barred by the old statute of limitations), the Supreme Court ruled that such retroactive changes to statutes of limitations does not violate the Article 39 ban on ex *post-facto* laws, or the due process guarantee of Article 31, so long as the amendments took place prior to the expiry of the statutory period previously applicable to the acts in question.[497] There is some criticism of this ruling, since this is a retroactive application that clearly has a significant effect on the accused, with some scholars saying that the Article 39 prohibition on ex *post-facto* criminal laws should apply not only to substantive laws but also to procedural law provisions having a substantive impact.[498]

Another question arises as to whether Article 39 applies to changes in precedent; i.e., can a defendant be found guilty based on a change in Supreme Court interpretive precedent rendered after the act in question. In a case involving its interpretation of the prohibition on collective action by local public servants contained in the Local Public Service Act, the Supreme Court held this not to violate Article 39.[499] Limiting the prohibition on *ex post facto* laws to legislative acts is consistent with the understanding that Japanese Supreme Court precedents are not "law" as the term is used in Article 39 (or elsewhere in the constitution).

Non bis in idem *and double jeopardy*

As with other civil law jurisdictions Japan follows the principle of *non bis in idem* ("not twice the same thing"—*ichiji fusairi* in Japanese) in criminal procedure. This includes applying it only after all appeals have been exhausted. In the Japanese system, on initial appeal an appellate court can review fact finding and evaluate additional evidence. This means prosecutors can and do make appeals from judgments they find objectionable, including acquittals. This is different from the US system where the Fifth Amendment and the guarantee of a jury trial cause double jeopardy to attach much earlier and prohibit prosecutorial appeals of trial outcomes.

There are several theories as to what the seemingly duplicative prohibitions of double jeopardy mean. One holds that they are collectively the source of the civil law version of the *non bis in idem* principle. Another theory is that the latter half of the first sentence (third clause, in the English) provides for *non bis in idem*, which prohibits trying the same offense twice, while the second sentence (final clause) prohibits the government from trying to punish the same act twice (i.e., by prosecuting it as a different offense). Yet another theory holds that these the two clauses together establish a US-style prohibition on double jeopardy, though this would make the first clause unnecessary. Insofar as prosecutors can and do make appeals that are adjudicated by the courts (CCP Article 351(1) clearly states "The public prosecutor or the accused may appeal"), this last view is entirely theoretical.

The Supreme Court, for its part has upheld prosecutorial appeals, even when brought not against acquittals, but against sentences considered too lenient. In a case involving a defendant convicted of violating the Public Offices Election Act and fined by the trial court, but sentenced to imprisonment by the high court upon appeal by prosecutors, the Supreme Court rejected arguments that Article 39 works in the same way as the double jeopardy prohibition of the Fifth Amendment to the US constitution (and that Article 351 of the CCP was unconstitutional). In doing so it essentially endorsed the civil law view of *non bis in idem*, holding that the entire process of a trial including all appeals constituted a single continuing "jeopardy," and it was the repetition of this process that was prohibited by Article 39. Interpreted this way, an appeal by prosecutors against an acquittal or lenient sentencing by a lower court, does not expose a defendant to double jeopardy and thus does not violate Article 39.[500]

Double jeopardy and administrative sanctions

Article 39 refers to *criminal* sanctions, so it is unclear whether it prevents punishment under penal provisions to be imposed together with non-penal administrative penalties (such as administrative fines). In a tax evasion case, the Supreme Court upheld the imposition of criminal penalties together with supplemental taxes on the grounds that they were of a different character; the criminal penalty being a sanction against antisocial behavior, while the additional taxes were an administrative measure intended to prevent evasion of tax obligations. On that basis the Court found the imposition of dual sanctions not to violate the "double punishment" prohibition of Article 39.[501]

Article 40: The Right to Seek Redress For Wrongful Arrest or Detention

Mari Hirayama

> **Article 40.**
> Any person, in case he is acquitted after he has been arrested or detained, may sue the State for redress as provided by law.

Law enforcement agencies make mistakes. Sometimes the wrong person can be arrested for a crime, detained, prosecuted and, in the worst-case scenario, convicted.[502] Needless to say, it is not just enough to release those erroneously ensnared in the criminal justice system; they need a concrete remedy in the form of compensation. The Meiji Constitution was silent on such compensation, but it was available under the (old) Criminal Compensation Act of 1931, which was modeled after a German law.

Article 40 of the present constitution guarantees the right of a person who has been arrested or detained and subsequently acquitted to seek compensation from the state. The English version of Article 40 is somewhat misleading. First the Japanese only refers to "demanding" (*motomeru*) compensation, not bringing a legal action in court as is implied by the English "sue." Second, as discussed at the Editorial Note on page 143, the English terms "arrest" and "detain" are an additional source of potential confusion.

Third, the Japanese is unambiguous that the right to demand compensation applies only after being "acquitted by a trial." The natural interpretation is that the right to seek compensation is conditioned on a final verdict of acquittal. As noted at Article 39, in Japan prosecutors can appeal an acquittal and thus further appeals may need to be exhausted before it is "final."

A more expansive interpretation would be that "acquittal" refers to any situation where a person is deprived of their freedom by the State but the matter is never brought to trial, because of a mistake or suspicions that prove groundless. Under that interpretation the term "acquittal" would have a substantive, rather than procedural meaning.

Article 40 is implemented legislatively through the (new) Criminal Compensation Act (CCA) of 1950. It takes a middle ground in providing for compensation after acquittals, but also allowing those whose indictments are dismissed (with or without prejudice) to claim redress under the Act if it can be established that they would likely have been acquitted at trial.[503] This is a slightly broader standard than "acquittal at trial" under Article 40, but much narrower than "substantive acquittal."[504]

In 1956 the Supreme Court confirmed that those who are arrested or detained but are not prosecuted are not entitled to compensation under Article 40 of the constitution. However, it also acknowledged a possible exception in the case of *bekken taiho* (see discussions at Articles 33 and 28), where a suspect is arrested for one offense and, once under detention, investigated and subsequently prosecuted for a different offense; if acquitted of the latter offense he could be entitled to compensation for the arrest and detention attributable to the first offense.

Article 4(1) of the CCA establishes a range of compensation from JPY 1,000–12,500 per day of arrest or detention to be decided by the Court which issued the acquittal, taking into consideration the type and the duration of the detention, as well as loss of property and profits, mental anguish and physical injury suffered as a result.[505] Claims must be filed within 3 years of the acquittal being finalized.[506]

Compensation under the CCA is separate from compensation which can be obtained for tort claims against the state under the State Redress Act (see discussion at Article 17). Compensation under the latter is possible for wrongful detentions if the defendant can prove that the law enforcement officials were acting intentionally or negligently. However, the CCA makes it impossible to "double dip" by providing for reductions in compensation under the CCA to the extent compensation is received for the same reason under other laws such as the State Redress Act.[507]

In addition to the CCA, the MOJ has established "Regulations for Compensation of Suspects," which provides for compensation in situations where a suspect has been detained but then released because it is clear they are not guilty.[508]

The Code of Civil Procedure also provides that the acquitted can seek compensation of legal fees and other amounts not covered by the CCA.[509]

Finally, a separate law—the Act on Compensation for Juvenile Cases provides for a system analogous to the CCA for compensation in the juvenile justice system, which is operated through the family court system.[510] Under this law, if a family court declines to commence a hearing or finds it unnecessary to subject a juvenile to rehabilitation by reason of there having been no offense or delinquent behavior, the juvenile can seek compensation from the state for any period of detention.

Notes

[1] For a detailed discussion of this see Ōkubo, T., The Concept of Rights in Modern Japan, in Jenco, L.K., et al., (Eds.) (2020), 394.

[2] Whereas the very idea of putting any rights into the Meiji Constitution was a source of contention in the debate in the Privy Council leading up to its creation, in contrast there were a number of social movements in favor of robustly enshrining rights operating at the same time. On the former see Ukai, N. (1956). On the latter, see Hamano, S.B. (1999), 422–23.

[3] See for example Wagatsuma, S. (1951).

[4] For a discussion of this, see Hamano, S.B. (1999), 426–30.

[5] Supreme Court, Grand Bench Judgment of October 4, 1978. As noted at Article 14, the Court had already made a general statement about foreign nationals enjoying equal protection in a 1964 case.

[6] Supreme Court, 3rd Petty Bench Judgment of December 15, 1995. Fingerprinting was (and still is) required for non-citizens obtaining residency in Japan. Refusal to be fingerprinted also resulted in the *Kathleen Morikawa Case*, which held that non-Japanese residents do not have a right of "sojourn"—to leave Japan temporarily and return—as discussed at Article 22.

[7] Supreme Court, Grand Bench Judgment of November 26, 1969.

[8] Matsui, S. (2011), 141.

[9] Ibid., 135–40.

[10] See for example Law, D.S. (2009), 1546–48 for a review of some of these.

[11] Most famously in the *Lady Chatterley's Lover case*, discussed at Article 21.

[12] Matsui, S. (2011), 141.

[13] Supreme Court, 2nd Petty Bench Judgment of May 30, 2011.

[14] 5,000 Yen was awarded in one case involving the violation of voting rights in the *Overseas Voting Rights Case*.

[15] Matsui, S. (2011), 145. Notably it does not require the Diet to act immediately.

[16] *Nationality Act Case*.

[17] Supreme Court, Grand Bench Judgment of April 5, 1961.

[18] Supreme Court, 3rd Petty Bench judgment of March 10, 2015; Nationality Act, Article 12, Family Register Act, Article 104.

[19] Supreme Court, Grand Bench Judgment of July 11, 1951.

[20] Supreme Court, 1st Petty Bench Judgment of March 13, 1997.

[21] GHQ Draft, Article XI.

[22] *E.g.*, the *Niigata Prefecture Public Safety Ordinance* Case discussed at Article 21. *See also* Supreme Court, 3rd Petty Bench Judgment of February 1, 1955; Supreme Court, 3rd Petty Bench Judgment of May 10, 1955. For a detailed discussion of the development of the public welfare standard in these cases see Beer, L.W., The Public Welfare Standard and Freedom of Expression in Japan, in Henderson, D.F. (Ed.) (1968), 205–38.

[23] *See e.g.*, Basic Act on Education, Article 2, Medical Care Act, Articles 1–2, Public Assistance Act, Article 3, Shōgaisha kihonhō [Basic Act for Persons with Disabilities], Article 3.

[24] Ashibe, N. (2019), 120–21. The judicial normative nature of this Article was approved by the Supreme Court in the *Kyoto Prefectural Federation of Student Unions Case* discussed later.

[25] Ashibe, N. (2019), 121; Satō, K. (1995), 448.

[26] Hashimoto, K. (1988), 168, 216; Uchino, M. (1991), 316.

[27] Tonami, K. (1996), 18.

[28] In recent years, however, the understanding that individual human rights are derived as concrete rights from the abstract right of Article 13 is also prevalent. Takahashi, K. (2020), 148–49.

[29] As to indigeneity, in 1997 the Sapporo District Court recognized that respecting people "as individuals" may mean respecting the implications that come from their being an indigenous minority group. This does not change the prevailing understanding that it is only individuals, not groups, who enjoy human rights under the constitution of Japan, but nevertheless importantly implicates group membership status as warranting constitutional respect in appropriate circumstances. Sapporo District Court decision of March 27, 1997, translation Levin, M.A. (1999); Levin, M.A. (2001), 484–88; Tsunemoto, T. (1998).

[30] Ashibe, N. (2019), 122–23. Academic theories show the possibility of various new rights even if they are not explicitly stated in the constitution. In recent public discourse about the possibility of constitutional amendment, it is often argued that the constitution was established more than 70 years ago and does not

include rights such as the right to privacy or environmental rights and that, therefore, amendment is necessary to guarantee these new rights. Given the fact that judicial precedents have shown a very restrained understanding of the scope of the right to the pursuit of happiness, there is a certain logic to amendments that identify "new human rights." However, even if such amendments were made, they would likely be drafted in a very simple way, such as "Environmental rights shall be guaranteed." It would thus still be necessary to interpret what is guaranteed by the "environmental rights," leading back to theories similar to those currently being made about Article 13 and other provisions. In the end, it is important to consider the meaning of guaranteeing "new human rights" through the Article 13, regardless of whether or not there is explicit text.

31 *Griswold v. Connecticut*; 381 U.S. 479 (1965).

32 Supreme Court, Grand Bench judgment of December 24, 1969 (translation by author).

33 Supreme Court, 3rd Petty Bench judgment of April 14, 1981 (translation by author).

34 Maki, M., *Dai goshō—hōkatsuteki kihonken* [Comprehensive fundamental rights], in Yasunishi, F., et al. (2018), 96.

35 Gyōsei Kikan no Hoyū suru Kojin Jōhō ni Kansuru Hōritsu [Law for the Protection of Personal Information Held by Administrative Organs], Law No. 58/2003; Kojin Jōhō no Hogo ni Kansuru Hōritsu [Personal Information Protection Act], Law no. 57 of 2003. In 2022, as part of the legal framework to implement measures for the formation of a digital society, the former act, together with another law relating to data privacy were merged into the latter, creating a new Personal Information Protection Act.

36 Supreme Court, 1st Petty Bench judgment of March, 6, 2008.

37 Supreme Court, 2nd Petty Bench judgment of September 12, 2003.

38 Note the Supreme Court rejected the request for an injunction without referring to personal rights and upheld only the claim for damages. Supreme Court judgment of December 16, 1981.

39 Ashibe, N. (2019), 128.

40 Tonami, K. (1996).

41 The Supreme Court avoided the constitutional question in a case challenging a high school's rules regarding *inter alia*, hair styles, on the grounds that it was a private school so there was no state action. Supreme Court, 1st Petty Bench judgment of July 1996. In 2021 the Osaka District Court upheld the rules of a prefectural high school that required students with naturally brown hair to die it black. *See, e.g.*, May, T. (2021, February 19). Japanese student forced to dye her hair black wins, and loses, in court. *The New York Times*. Retrieved June 16, 2022, from https://www.nytimes.com/2021/02/19/world/asia/japan-hair-school.html.

42 Supreme Court, 3rd Petty Bench judgment of February 29, 2000.

43 Act on Special Cases in Handling Gender Status for Persons with Gender Identity Disorder, Article 3(1).

44 Supreme Court, 2nd Petty Bench decision of January 23, 2019.

45 *Kazoku* [peers] is the term used to refer to the European-style hereditary aristocracy whose members bore titles such as "baron" or "marquis," and who were created by an 1884 imperial edict (the *Kazokurei*). *Kizoku* (peerage, in the English) is a term with a much older provenance used to describe imperial courtiers. Under the Meiji system, however, it referred to those who sat in the House of Peers, which included not only the *kazoku*, but also imperial princes, imperial appointees, high tax payers and academics. Not all *kizoku* had a heritable status. Thus, in the English "peers" can be considered a reference to the aristocracy, while "peerage" to those sitting in the House of Peers (including the aristocrats).

46 The cost became prohibitive and the pension was eliminated in 1941.

47 Recipients of the Order of Culture for contribution to literature and the arts typically do enjoy a lifetime stipend from the government. The constitutional issue is avoided (?) by having them separately designated by the Minister of Education (not the emperor) as a "Person of Cultural Merit" entitled to a pension under the Person of Cultural Merit Pension Act (Bunka Kōrōsha Nenkin Hō, Law no. 125 of 1951). *See also*, "So-Called Egalitarian Japan is still Honor-Bound", in Jones, C.P.A. (2019) 317.

48 In Japanese the term used in Articles 14(1) and 24(2) to where the English uses "equality" is *byōdō*, while that used in Article 24(1) is *dōtō*. The latter term could be said to have a more rigid nuance (e.g., objective equality as opposed to subjective), but "equal" is probably the best translation of both.

49 Supreme Court, Grand Bench judgment of May 27, 1964 (18 *Minshū* 676) (translation by author).

50 Ibid.

51 Note a different term is used to denote religious faith in both the English and Japanese versions of Article 20.

[52] E.g., Supreme Court, 3rd Petty Bench judgment of March 24, 1981. Although not a constitutional case, the Court referenced Article 14(1) as grounds for finding rules of employment that discriminated based on gender void under Article 90 of the Civil Code ("A juristic act with any purpose which is against public policy is void.") A 2006 ruling the Court used a similar rationale to strike down customary rules of a village that denied commonage rights (see Civil Code, arts. 263 and 294) to village women who married outside the village, got divorced and returned to the village without reassuming their maiden name. The Kyoto District Court found worker compensation rules that compensated women more highly than men for facial disfigurement was found unconstitutional; it was not appealed by the government, which changed the rules. Kyoto District Court judgment of May 27, 2010, 2093 *Hanji* 72. The prohibition on discrimination in employment has been legislatively implemented (with questionable efficacy, some might say) primarily through the Equal Opportunity in Employment Act. (Koyō no Bunya ni Okeru Danjo no Kintō na Kikai Oyobi Shogū no Kakuhotō ni Kansuru Hōritsu), Law no. 113 of 1972.

[53] See 1964 Supreme Court case cited supra at note [49].

[54] During the drafting process, the Japanese side unsuccessfully sought to eliminate the provisions of what became Article 14 specifically banning the aristocracy on the grounds that the prohibition of discrimination based on *monchi* would suffice for that purpose. Moore, R., & Robinson, D. (2004), 130. Article XIII of the GHQ Draft also contained a sentence declaring "All natural persons are equal before the law." This was ultimately changed to the current "all the [Japanese] people," but not before it was successfully used as an argument for removing the provision granting equal protection to aliens, on the grounds it was redundant since they were "natural persons."

[55] Because the *burakumin* were often associated with specific geographic locations which have in some ways been perpetuated through affirmative action programs directly targeting such communities, place of origin/domicile (within Japan) has sometimes been used as a basis for informal discrimination that persists to this day. In September 2021 the Tokyo District Court issued an injunction and award of damages against a publisher that published a list of "*burakumin* place names" on the Internet. "Tokyo court orders firm to partially delete online discriminated place names list." *The Mainichi* (n.d.). Retrieved June 16, 2022, from https://mainichi.jp/english/articles/20210928/p2a/00m/0na/014000c. One of the interesting manifestations of this is that "where are they from?" may be a problematic question in some contexts. Similarly, Japanese paperwork rarely involves forms where one is required to fill in a place of birth. Both lines of inquiry are associated with discrimination based on family origin or social status. The problems of *burakumin* identity in modern Japan are illustrated in Tōson Shimazaki's famous 1906 novel "The Broken Commandment" (*Hakai*).

[56] GHQ Draft, Articles XIII and XVI. The term used in Article XVI to express "alien" was *gaikokujin* (literally "person from other countries"), which is still the term almost universally used to refer to non-Japanese persons. See Moore, R., & Robinson, D. (2004), 130–31.

[57] It is common to cite a 1964 Grand Bench judgment containing a statement by the Supreme Court to the effect that Article 14 of the constitution also applies to non-Japanese people. Supreme Court, Grand Bench judgment of November 18, 1964. However, reading the case reveals that the statement is being made in the context of an appeal challenging convictions for failure to pay import duties on items imported indirectly by the defendants by purchasing them from members of the US forces in Japan, who through the Status of Forces Agreement with Japan were able to import such items free of Japanese customs duties. The equal protection argument thus essentially involved a challenge to the special *privileges* enjoyed by US service personnel and their families, and was easily rejected by the Supreme Court. Note also, the Japanese term *gaikokujin* is commonly translated as "foreigner," and both are sometimes controversial, possibly due to the connotations of "otherness" they convey. The term is nonetheless a legal term rendered in the Japanese government's English translation as "foreign national" and defined as "a person who does not have Japanese nationality." Shutsunyūkoku Kanri Oyobi Nanmin Nintei Hō [Immigration Control and Refugee Recognition Act], Cabinet Order No. 319 of October 4, 1951, article 2(ii). Note that although this law had its origins in one of the so-called "Potsdam Orders" issued during the Occupation to implement the Potsdam Declaration, it was converted to a law through the Law on Orders Relating to the Ministry of Foreign Affairs issued in connection with the acceptance of the Potsdam Declaration. (Potsudamu Sengen no Judaku ni Tomonai Hassuru Meirei ni Kansuru Ken ni Motoduku Gaimushō Kankei Shomeirei no Sochi ni Kansuru Hōritsu), Law no. 126 of 1952.

[58] Supreme Court, 1st Petty Bench judgment of March 2, 1989 (pension eligibility); Supreme Court, 2nd Petty Bench judgment of July 18, 2014 (public assistance), Supreme Court, 2nd Petty Bench judgment of

November 29, 2004; Supreme Court, April 28, 1992 (eligibility for military pension benefits). A Taishō-period law enabling the government to restrict foreign acquisition and ownership of land remains in force, but has never been implemented through the necessary Cabinet orders during the post war period. Gaikokujin Tochihō [Foreigner Land Act], Law no. 41 of 1925. A more recent act limits the acquisition by non-Japanese persons of lands near military bases or other strategic locations. Jūyō Shisetsu Shūhen Oyobi Kokkyō Ritōtō ni Okeru Tochitō no Riyōjōkyō no Chōsa Oyobi Riyō no Kiseitō ni Kansuru Hōritsu [Law on the Use, Investigation of Usage and Limitation on Use of Land, etc. Near Critical Facilities and on Border Areas and Insular Areas], Law no. 84 of 2021. Note that with respect to benefits programs an added consideration may be that even if the constitution's reference to rights enjoyed by *kokumin* (Japanese) is generally considered as extending to non-Japanese, that alone does not prevent the Diet from crafting legislation that only applies to *kokumin*, either explicitly or implicitly through the use of the same term in statutes. For example, the national pension scheme is established pursuant to a statute that could literally be translated as the "Japanese People's Pension Act" (*Kokumin Nenkinhō*). The Supreme Court also discriminates on the basis of nationality by refusing to engage otherwise qualified non-Japanese lawyers and other professionals as court mediators, despite its own rules not specifying citizenship as a requirement. Minji Chōtei Iin Oyobi Kaji Chōteiin Kisoku [Civil and Family Court Mediator Rules], Supreme Court Rule No. 5 of 1973. *See, e.g., Asahi Shinbun*. (2022, April 19). *Chōteiin, Gaikokuseki Mitomenu Saikōsai* [Supreme Court does not recognize foreigners as court mediators]. Retrieved June 16, 2022, from https://www.asahi.com/articles/DA3S15271542.html.

59 Japanese citizens can get married, adopt or dissolve these relationships non-contentiously by simply filing paperwork with the family registry; physically being in Japan is not even required. Family Register Act, Article 40. If no Japanese citizens are involved, the same changes of status would require different procedures, essentially "work-arounds." This is not only because non-Japanese are excluded from the family register system, but because Japan's choice of law statute applies "home country" law to the family status of non-Japanese residents. *See,* Hō no Tekiyō ni Kansuru Tsūsokuhō [Act on General Rules for Applications of Laws], Law no. 78 of 2006.

60 Article 200 mandated punishments ranging from imprisonment without defined term (effectively life imprisonment) or death for such murders. Article 199 gives a range of five years' imprisonment to death for other murders.

61 As the defendant was impoverished, her lawyer—who subsequently represented Ron McLean in the *McLean Case*—reportedly accepted a rucksack full of potatoes in lieu of fees. Kanda, N. (2016, March 16). *"Chichikoroshi no Musume" wo Sukutta Nihon Hatsu no Hōrei Iken Hanketsu* [The "Patricidal Daughter" saved by japan's first ruling of statutory unconstitutionality]. *Nikkei Business.* Retrieved June 16, 2022, from https://business.nikkei.com/atcl/report/15/120100058/120200001/?P=2.

62 Supreme Court, Grand Bench judgments of October 11 and 25, 1950.

63 Except for one dissenting judge, the majority agreed the provision was unconstitutional but a number of judges rendered separate opinions articulating different rationales.

64 The defendant was sentenced to a short prison sentence but with a suspension. It may be simply that in a case where virtually any observer would have considered the defendant to have already suffered enough, the Court simply found the constitution a useful tool for overcoming a statutory impediment that unduly restricted judicial discretion in sentencing and prevented the Court from achieving the "correct" result.

65 Supreme Court, 1st Petty Bench judgment of September 26, 1974.

66 After the Court found Article 200 unconstitutional prosecutors simply did not bring charges under it.

67 One Supreme Court judge recused himself because he had been previously head of the Civil Affairs Bureau of the Ministry of Justice, which had oversight over the Civil Code, including proposed amendments.

68 Supreme Court, Grand Bench decision of July 5, 1995; Supreme Court, 1st Petty Bench decision of January 27, 2000, 2nd Petty Bench decision of March 28, 3rd Petty Bench judgment of March 31, 2003, 1st Petty Bench decision of October 14, 2003, and 2nd Petty Bench decision of September 30, 2009.

69 The formulation in the 1995 inheritance judgment was: "Differentiation in the legal treatment on the grounds of the difference in economic, social, and other various factual relations concerning individuals is not against this provision [i.e., Article 14(1)], insofar as the differentiation is reasonable."

70 Upon closer scrutiny, the "family has changed" part of the Court's rationale seems strained. The decedent in the 2013 case died in 2001—just six years after the Court upheld the Article 900 proviso in 1995. The 1995 case in turn arose from a 1988 death.

[71] Japan's ratification of both conventions preceded the 1995 decision; but apparently not soon enough to influence its outcome; the UNCRC prohibition on discrimination based on legitimacy was noted by the dissent. Note that in referencing Japan's ratification of the two treaties, the 2013 Court did not go so far as to suggest they might have force as law. See discussion at Article 98 regarding the treatment of international law in Japanese courts.

[72] Specifically, Court 1996 bill prepared by the Ministry of Justice through its Legislative Council which included a number of changes to the family provisions of the Civil Code, including elimination of the Article 900 proviso. The bill was never enacted, however, so rather than "legislative history" it is more likely "legislation that should have been." Interestingly, the Court in the *Lineal Ascendant Murder Case* also referenced a past legislative proposal to remove the provisions in question, even though it never became law.

[73] Supreme Court, Grand Bench judgment of October 15, 1958; Supreme Court, Grand Bench judgment of October 23, 1985. Thirteen is the age of consent under the Penal Code and criminal punishments for "consensual" sexual contact with minors above that age are imposed primarily through prefectural ordinances.

[74] See discussion at note [55].

[75] Tokyo High Court judgment of September 16, 1997, 986 *Hanrei Taimuzu* 206.

[76] For example, Article 3 of the Labor Standards Act prohibits discrimination in terms of employment based on nationality, creed or social status. The title of the 2013 "Promotion of the Elimination of Discrimination against Persons with Disabilities Act" speaks for itself as does that of the 2014 "Promotion of the Elimination of Buraku Discrimination. Act" Shōgai wo Riyū to Suru Sabetsu no Kaishō no Suishin ni Kansuru Hōritsu [Promotion of the Elimination of Discrimination against Persons with Disabilities Act], Law no. 65 of 2013; Buraku Sabetsu no Kaishō no Suishin ni Kansuru Hō [Promotion of the Elimination of Buraku Discrimination Act], Law no. 109 of 2014.

[77] Meiji Constitution, Article 10.

[78] Supreme Court, Grand Bench Judgment of February 9, 1955.

[79] Supreme Court, 2nd Petty Bench Judgment of February 26, 1993.

[80] Supreme Court, 3rd Petty Bench Judgment of February 28, 1995.

[81] Supreme Court, Grand Bench Judgment of September 14, 2005.

[82] Supreme Court, 1st Petty Bench Judgment of July 13, 2006.

[83] Supreme Court, Grand Bench Judgment of March 23, 2011.

[84] Supreme Court, Grand Bench Judgment of November 20, 2013; Supreme Court, Grand Bench Judgment of November 25, 2015; Supreme Court, Grand Bench Judgment of December 19, 2018.

[85] Supreme Court, Grand Bench Judgment of November 10, 1999 (53 *Minshū* 1577).

[86] Supreme Court, Grand Bench Judgment of April 25, 1973.

[87] Supreme Court, 2nd Petty Bench Judgment of December 7, 2012.

[88] Supreme Court, Grand Bench judgment of January 26, 2003.

[89] Rules excluding non-Japanese from public service jobs exist in other spheres including, for example, the seemingly innocuous role of court-appointed conciliators and family mediators.

[90] POEA, Article 46.

[91] Supreme Court, 3rd Petty Bench judgment of June 1, 1948; Supreme Court, 1st Petty Bench judgment of November 9, 1950, Supreme Court, 2nd Petty Bench judgment of March 28, 1997.

[92] Act No. 13 of 1947.

[93] Tokyo District Court judgment of January 15, 2014. (1420 *Hanta* 268).

[94] Article 1(2) of the State Redress Act allows the state to seek compensation from its own officials where its liability stems from their gross negligence.

[95] Yūsei hō [Postal Act], Law no. 165 of 1947 (Articles 68 and 73).

[96] Act No. 45 of April 24, 1907, Article 12(2).

[97] Supreme Court, Grand Bench judgment of April 2, 1969.

[98] Supreme Court, Grand bench judgment of November 16, 2011.

[99] Matsui, S. (2011), 187.

[100] Supreme Court, Grand Bench judgment of February 12, 1958.

[101] Supreme Court, Grand Bench judgment of February 15, 1961.

[102] Supreme Court, 3rd Petty Bench judgment of July 4, 1989.

[103] Supreme Court, Grand Bench judgment of July 4, 1956.

[104] Supreme Court, 2nd Petty Bench judgment of July 15, 1988.

[105] Supreme Court, Grand Bench judgment of December 12, 1973.
[106] Supreme Court, 3rd Petty Bench judgment of March 19, 1996.
[107] Supreme Court, Grand Bench judgment of June 22, 1983.
[108] Supreme Court, 2nd Petty Bench judgment of September 10, 1993.
[109] Supreme Court, 1st Petty Bench judgment of July 14, 2005.
[110] Supreme Court, 3rd Petty Bench judgment of June 14, 2011; Supreme Court, 3rd Petty Bench judgment of June 21, 2011.
[111] Supreme Court, 1st Petty Bench judgment of June 6, 2011.
[112] So is the language. The Japanese term for "religion" in the first sentence of Paragraph (1) is *shinkyō* (religious belief and practice) while the term used in the rest of Article 20 is *shūkyō*, which refers to religion itself. This is a significant distinction. For example, the First Amendment to the United States constitution uses the same term, "religion," in both the Establishment Clause and the Free Exercise Clause. Volumes have been written about what the term means in each context. Because Article 20 uses *shinkyō* in the free exercise sentence and *shūkyō* in the context of what would be called "establishment" in the US it is clearer that the religious freedom/free exercise referred to in Article 20 includes the freedom to believe in and practice religion.
[113] *See, e.g.*, Hardacre, H. (1989); Ravitch, F.S. (2013).
[114] Ibid. (both sources).
[115] Supreme Court, Petty Bench judgment of December 22, 1994.
[116] Supreme Court, Grand Bench judgment of June 1, 1988.
[117] Other members of the deceased's family were reportedly in favor of enshrinement, and he had been given a Buddhist funeral.
[118] The offerings cost relatively small sums of money and consisted of twigs from a specific type of tree, the sakiki tree, wrapped with folded white papers. This sort of offering to a Shinto Shrine is called *tamagushi.*
[119] The Endorsement Test was a popular test in Establishment cases in the US at that time and the Japanese Supreme Court borrowed the concept, but adapted it to the Japanese context.
[120] The Court also noted that government officials may give *saisen* (a gift of money given when people visit temples or shrines). This practice is still used today. A recent example being Prime Minister Yoshihide Suga's gift to the Yasakuni Shrine in April 2021.
[121] Supreme Court, 3rd Petty Bench judgment of February 16, 1993.
[122] Meiji Constitution, Article 29: "Japanese subjects shall, within the limits of law, enjoy the liberty of speech, writing, publication, public meetings and associations."
[123] The most notorious was the Chian Ijihō [Peace Preservation Act], of 1925, which banned publication of any attacks on the essence of the body politics, the imperial capitalist system heralded by the emperor. It was an attempt to control the thought of the public, especially skeptics and critics, and force them to convert to actively support the imperial government system under the emperor.
[124] Supreme Court. Grand Bench judgment of June 11, 1986.
[125] Supreme Court, Grand Bench judgment of December 6, 2017 (holding that Article 64 of the Broadcasting Act which mandates every household with a television set enter into a mandatory contract with the NHK, Japan's public broadcaster, and pay the required contract fees, does not violate Article 21).
[126] Supreme Court, 3rd Petty Bench decision of January 31, 2017 (holding that Google is entitled to the protection of freedom of expression since it provides search results based on its own algorithm and is performing a vital function in facilitating the flow of information in the cyberspace).
[127] In the *Yodogō Hijacking News Redaction Case* the Supreme Court held that pretrial detainees have a right to receive information and can be prevented from getting access to newspaper articles only when there is a plausible likelihood to cause intolerable problem for maintaining order.
[128] Supreme Court, Grand Bench decision of November 26, 1969 (The *Hakata Station TV Film Production Case*, holding that the right to gather information should be respected in light of the spirit of Article 21).
[129] Supreme Court, 3rd Petty Bench decision of February 16 (holding that the right of access to criminal records is not guaranteed by Article 21).
[130] Supreme Court, 1st Petty Bench judgment of September 8, 1983 (holding that the corporation's disciplinary action against its employee for distributing documents criticizing it outside of the office and outside of the working hours as reasonable and not violating public order). This is an inevitable consequence of the *Mitsubishi Resin Case* discussed at Article 19, in which the Court held that the constitution is not directly applicable to private corporations.

[131] *See* Matsui, S. Judicial Review of Restrictions on Constitutional Rights in Japan: Highly Ad Hoc, Contextualized, and Deferential. In Yap, P.J. (Ed.) (2020), 140.
[132] Supreme Court, Grand Bench judgment of March 13, 1957.
[133] Penal Code, Article 175.
[134] In some cases, the Court has found restrictions as being merely incidental and sustained the resulting infringement on freedom of expression without any serious inquiry. For instance, the Public Office Election Act prohibits door-to-door canvassing, thereby severely limiting the ability of candidates for political office to interact directly with voters. When challenged on constitutional grounds in the *Door-to-Door Canvassing Case*, the Court found the ban on door-to-door canvassing during the election campaign period to be a merely incidental impairment of the freedom of expression and sustained the total ban on it. Supreme Court, Grand Bench judgment of April 23, 1969.
[135] Supreme Court, Grand Bench judgment of November 6, 1974.
[136] See also Supreme Court, Grand Bench judgment of November 6, 1974.
[137] Mitchell, R.H. (1983).
[138] Supreme Court, Grand Bench judgment of December 12, 1984 (38 *Minshū* 1308). *See also* Supreme Court, Grand Bench judgment of December 12, 1984. Kanzeihō [Custom Act], Law no. 60 of 1954.
[139] Supreme Court, 3rd Petty Bench judgment of March 16, 1993.
[140] Supreme Court, Grand Bench judgment of June 11, 1986.
[141] Supreme Court, 3rd Petty Bench judgment of September 24, 2002.
[142] NPSA, Article 100.
[143] NPSA, Article 109(1)(xii). Supreme Court, 1st Petty Bench decision of May 31, 1978. When Okinawa was returned to Japan in 1972, there was an official agreement between the US and Japan pursuant to which the US was obligated to cover various expenses relating to the return, but there was speculation that Japan had secretly agreed to pay them instead. The document in question was diplomatic cable revealing the existence of such a confidential agreement.
[144] SDF Act, Articles 59 & 111; Nichibei Sōgo Bōei Enjo Kyōteitō nI Tomonau Himitsu Hogohō [Secret Protection Act based on Japan-United States Mutual Security Assistance Agreement], of 1954.
[145] Penal Code, Articles 77, 106, 107, 108 and 117.
[146] Bakuhatsubutsu Torishimari Bassoku [Explosives Control Declaration], of 1884.
[147] Penal Code, Article 61.
[148] Hakai Katsudō Bōshihō [Subversive Activities Prevention Act], Law no. 240 of 1952, Articles 38, 39 and 40.
[149] Supreme Court, Grand Bench judgment of May 18, 1949.
[150] See also Supreme Court, 1st Petty Bench judgment of January 19, 1950.
[151] Supreme Court, 2nd Petty Bench judgment of September 28, 1990.
[152] Subversive Activities Prevention Act, arts. 4(2).
[153] POEA, Articles 129, 138 and 142.
[154] Supreme Court, Grand Bench judgment of April 6, 1955; Supreme Court, Grand Bench judgment of April 23, 1969.
[155] *See* Matsui, S. Election Campaign Regulation and the Supreme Court of Japan. In Yap, P.J. (Ed.) (2017), 115.
[156] Civil Code, Article 709.
[157] Penal Code, Article 230-2.
[158] Supreme Court, 1st Petty Bench judgment of May 7, 1959.
[159] Supreme Court, Grand Bench judgment of June 25, 1969.
[160] Supreme Court, 1st Petty Bench, judgment of June 23, 1966.
[161] *New York Times v. Sullivan*, 376 U.S. 254 (1964).
[162] Supreme Court, 1st Petty Bench decision of March 15, 2010.
[163] Supreme Court, 3rd Petty Bench judgment of February 8, 1994.
[164] Shiji Seiteki Gazō Kiroku no Teikyōtō ni Yoru Higai no Bōshi ni Kansuru Hōritsu [Act on Prevention of Harms from Provision of Private Sexual Images], Law no. 26 of 2014. See Matsui, S. (2015).
[165] Penal Code, Article 231.
[166] Supreme Court, Grand Bench judgment of October 15, 1969.
[167] Supreme Court, 2nd Petty Bench judgment of November 28, 1980.

[168] Supreme Court, 3rd Petty Bench judgment of February 19, 2008.
[169] Supreme Court, 3rd Petty Bench decision of July 16, 2001.
[170] Supreme Court, 1st Petty Bench judgment of July 16, 2020. Although obscenity is strictly regulated in law, explicit sexual images are ever-present in everyday life, easily visible in newspapers or weekly magazines and can be accessible while on public transportation or in regular bookstores. Many feminists have criticized the over-sexualization of women in Japan and have especially condemned the availability of pornography depicting rape and sexual assault against women, often times portraying the women as eventually enjoying the assault. It appears that the Japanese attitude towards sex and pornography is more tolerant and greatly differs from western attitudes. *See*, Allison, A. (2000). See also McLelland, M., Sex, Censorship, and Media Regulation in Japan: A Historical Overview. In McLelland, M., & Mackie, V. (Eds.) (2014), 402.
[171] Jidō Baishun, Jidō Poruno ni Kakawaru Kōitō no Kisei Oyobi Shobatsu Narabini Jidō no Hogotō ni Kansuru Hōritsu [Child Prostitution and Child Pornography and Protection of Children Act], Law no. 52 of 1999.
[172] Child Prostitution and Child Pornography and Protection of Children Act, Article 9.
[173] Supreme Court, 1st Petty Bench decision of January 27, 2020. However, in this case, defendant used pictures of real children to create computerized graphic images of child pornography. The Supreme Court ultimately held that the images thus created constituted child pornography.
[174] Honpōgai Shusshinsha ni Taisuru Futō na Sabetsuteki Gendō no Kaishō ni Muketa Torikumi ni Kansuru Hōritsu [Act Concerning Facilitation of Countermeasures to Eliminate Discriminatory Practices against Persons Born in Other Countries], Law no. 68 of 2016.
[175] The Supreme Court upheld the Osaka City anti-hate speech ordinance which authorized the city to take administrative countermeasures against hate speech. Supreme Court, 3rd Petty Bench judgment of February 15, 2022.
[176] Okugai Kōkokubutsu Hō [Outdoor Advertisement Regulation Act], Law no. 189 of 1949.
[177] Supreme Court, Grand Bench judgment of December 18, 1968; Supreme Court, 1st Petty Bench judgment of May 29, 1975.
[178] Supreme Court, 3rd Petty Bench judgment of March 3.
[179] Minor Offenses Act, Article 1(33).
[180] Supreme Court, Grand Bench judgment of June 17, 1970.
[181] *See, e.g.,* Ōsaka-fu Kakuseiki ni Yoru Bōsōon no Kisei Nikansuru Jōrei [Osaka Ordinance on Regulation of Loud Noise by the Use of Loud-speakers], of 1993.
[182] Supreme Court, Grand Bench judgment of December 23, 1953, 7 *Minshū* 1561,
[183] Supreme Court, Grand Bench judgment of November 24, 1954.
[184] Supreme Court, Grand Bench judgment of July 20, 1960.
[185] Supreme Court, Grande Bench judgment, July 20, 1960; Supreme Court, 3rd Petty Bench judgment of June 18, 1974; Supreme Court, 3rd Petty Bench judgment of September 30, 1975.
[186] Supreme Court, 3rd Petty Bench judgment of November 16, 1982.
[187] Local Autonomy Act, Article 240.
[188] Supreme Court, 3rd Petty Bench judgment of March 7, 1995.
[189] Supreme Court, 2nd Petty Bench judgment of March 15, 1996.
[190] Kangokuhō [Prison Act], of 1908, Article 31. This statute has been replaced by the Keiji Shūyō Shisetsu Oyobi Hishūyōshatō no Shogū ni Kansuru Hōritsu [Act on Criminal Detention Facilities and Treatment of Their Inmates], of 2006, which contains corresponding provisions at Articles 206–209.
[191] This holding is quite contrasting with another decision of the Supreme Court, which held that the refusal to grant a permit for inmate to send a private letter to a newspaper illegal since there was no such plausible harms. Supreme Court, 1st Petty Bench judgment of March 23, 2006.
[192] See also Supreme Court of Japan, 1st Petty Bench judgment of April 13, 1995.
[193] Photography and recording are still prohibited.
[194] Supreme Court, 2nd Petty Bench decision of January 30, 1989; Supreme Court, 2nd Petty Bench decision of July 9, 1990.
[195] Supreme Court, 3rd Petty Bench decision of October 3, 2006.
[196] Supreme Court, 3rd Petty Bench decision of February 16, 1990; Supreme Court, 2nd Petty Bench decision of October 27 (holding that the right of access to criminal record after the conclusion of the case is not directly protected by Article 21).

[197] Gyōsei kikan no hoyū suru jōhō no kōkai ni kansuru hōritsu [Access to Information Held by Administrative Organizations Act], Law no. 42 of 1999.
[198] Hōsōhō [Broadcasting Act], Law no. 132 of 1950, Article 3.
[199] Broadcasting Act, Article 4.
[200] Note that the Japanese term is *kessha*, which refers to organization.
[201] Sometimes freedom of association is invoked in support of the right to create highly intimate and personal relationships, such as family. In Japan, however, most family-related issues are discussed in the context of the right of personal autonomy under Article 13 and the right to family relationships consistent with essential equality of sexes and individual dignity under Article 24.
[202] In order to create a religious corporation for the purpose of spreading religious beliefs, conducting religious ceremonies or educating and training believers, it is necessary to follow the requirements of the Religious Corporations Act, which includes being certified by the prefectural or national government, depending on the geographic scope of activities. Religious corporations enjoy various privileges including tax exemptions, but are subject to decertification and judicial dissolution if they engage in conduct harmful to the public welfare or inconsistent with the law. Shūkyō Hōjinhō [Religious Corporations Act], Law no. 126, Articles 5, 80, 81.
[203] Seitō Kōfukin no Kōfu o Ukeru Seitōtō ni Taisuru Hōjinkaku no Fuyo ni Kansuru Hōritsu [Act on the Grant of Corporate Status to Political Parties (etc.) Receiving Political Party Grants], Law no. 106 of 1994. Seiji Shikin Kiseihō [Political Spending Regulation Act], Law no. 194 of 1948.
[204] The Supreme Court has rejected challenges to electoral rules favoring candidates affiliated with political parties, though without reference to Article 21. Supreme Court, 3rd Petty Bench judgment of December 18, 2001 (without referring to Article 21).
[205] Subversive Activities Prevention Act, Articles 5 and 7.
[206] Ibid., Article 8.
[207] Supreme Court, 1st Petty Bench judgment of January 30, 1996.
[208] After the religious corporation was dissolved, a filing was made against the Ōmu organization under the Subversive Activities Prevention Act, but ultimately dismissed by the National Public Safety Commission.
[209] Penal Code, Articles 133 and 134.
[210] Yūbinhō [Postal Act], Law no. 165 of 1947, Articles 7, and 8 ; Denki tsūshin jigyōhō [Telecommunication Service Act], Law no. 86 of 1984, Articles 3 and 4.
[211] Fusei akusesu kōi no kinshitō ni kansuru hōritsu [Illegal Access Prohibition Act], Law no. 128 of 1999, Articles 3–7.
[212] Code of Criminal Procedure, Article 222-2; Hanzai Sōsa no Tame no Tsushin Bōju ni Kansuru Hōritsu [Wiretapping Act], Law no. 137 of 1999.
[213] Tokutei Denki Tsūshin Ekimu Teikyōsha no Songai Baishō Sekinin no Seigen Oyobi Hasshinsha Jōhō no Kaiji ni Kansuru Hōritsu [Act on Liability Limitation of Designated Telecommunication Service Provers and Disclosure of Sender Information], Law no. 137 of 2001.
[214] Itō, H. (1978), 49.
[215] *Lochner v. New York*, 198 U.S. 45 (1905)
[216] Kumamoto District Court judgment of May 11, 2001, 1748 *Hanji* 30. The Koizumi administration declined to appeal and subsequently settled with the plaintiffs.
[217] Supreme Court (1st Petty Bench), 26 June 2003, 1831 Hanji 94.
[218] Supreme Court, 3rd Petty Bench judgment of January 22, 1985.
[219] Supreme Court, Grand Bench judgment of December 25, 1957; Supreme Court, 1st Petty Bench judgment of November 16, 1992.
[220] Ryoken Hō [Passport Act], Law no. 267 of 1951, Article 13(1)(v) [now (viii)].
[221] Supreme Court, Grand Bench judgment of September 10, 1958.
[222] Passport Act, Articles 5(2) and 19(1)(iv).
[223] Tokyo High Court judgment of September 6, 2017. Supreme Court, 1st Petty Bench judgment of March 15, 2018.
[224] Nationality Act, Article 13(1).
[225] Nationality Act, Articles 11. 14 and 15. There do not appear to be any instances of the government ever exercising this power.
[226] Translation from Japan courts website: https://www.courts.go.jp/app/hanrei_en/detail?id=42.

[227] Supreme Court, Grand Bench judgment of November 22, 1972.
[228] Examples of "public welfare" economic regulations upheld by the Supreme Court based on the *Public Market Act Case* include: (1) a system for stabilizing the price of raw silk through use of an import monopoly (which devastated the Nishijin Necktie industry in Kyoto (Supreme Court, 3rd Petty Bench judgment of February 6, 1990); (2) a system for licensing tobacconists that favored the disabled and war widows (Supreme Court, 2nd Petty Bench judgment of June 25, 1993); (3) prohibitions on the import of specific refined petroleum products resulting in it only being possible to import unrefined petroleum (Supreme Court. 1st Petty Bench judgment of March 28, 1996); (4) compulsory insurance for farmers (Supreme Court, 3rd Petty Bench judgment of April 26, 2005); and (5) limits on medical institutions eligible for participation in medical insurance scheme to only those hospitals with the number of beds conforming to the government's regional medical plans (Supreme Court. 1st Petty Bench judgment of September 8, 2005).
[229] Supreme Court, Grand Bench judgment of April 30, 1975.
[230] Translation from Japan courts website: https://www.courts.go.jp/app/hanrei_en/detail?id=1911.
[231] Ashibe, N. (2019) 235–36.
[232] *Pharmaceutical Affairs Act Case.*
[233] Supreme Court, Grand Bench judgment of January 26, 1955.
[234] Supreme Court, 2nd Petty Bench judgment of January 20, 1989.
[235] Supreme Court, 3rd Petty Bench judgment of March 7, 1989.
[236] *Shuzeihō* [Liquor Tax Act], law no. 6 of 1953.
[237] Supreme Court, 3rd Petty Bench judgment of February 8, 2000.
[238] Supreme Court, 1st Petty Bench judgment of March 18, 2021.
[239] This was not the first time the Supreme Court addressed the regulation of on-line pharmacies. In a 2013 ruling the Court struck down certain restrictions imposed by Ministry of Health, Labour and Welfare regulations issued under the Pharmaceutical Affairs Act. However, although it did mention possible implications for the right to choose one's occupations, its ruling was based on the ministry exceeding the scope of the rule-making authority delegated to it by the Act.
[240] Article 5(3). Kunst und Wissenschaft, Forschung und Lehre sind frei. Die Freiheit der Lehre entbindet nicht von der Treue zur Verfassung.
[241] Article XXII of the GHQ Draft guaranteed "academic freedom and choice of occupation" together.
[242] Constitution Investigation Association, "Outline of Constitution Draft," December 26, 1945. This draft was translated into English and circulated within GHQ. Its states as follows in Japanese: "No law may be promulgated which interferes with the freedom of speech, education, art, or religion of the people."
[243] Available at National Diet Library website: https://www.ndl.go.jp/constitution/e/shiryo/03/046shoshi.html.
[244] Takayanagi, K., et al. (Eds.). (1972). (Vol. 1), 204.
[245] Ibid., (Vol. 2.)
[246] Ibid., (Vol. 1), 204.
[247] *See*, Marshall, B.K. (1992).
[248] Under the Meiji Constitution, the sovereign was the emperor. However, the political science scholar Sakuzō Yoshino still aimed to advance democracy under the Meiji system. Yoshino introduced the term "democracy" to Japan and is the father of the Japanese term originally used to express it (*mimpon shugi*, which is different from the term which prevailed—*minshushugi*). Yoshino sought to reconcile the democratic flourishing of the Taishō Period (1912–1926) which was characterized by increased power accruing to political parties with the inviolable sovereign emperor of the Meiji Constitution,
[249] After the war, reflecting on the prewar government pressure on academic freedom, Article 23 of the constitution provided for academic freedom. Immediately after the war, the Maintenance of the Public Order Act was repealed and GHQ was moderate toward communists. However, when the Cold War structure began, there was a movement, led by the Civil Affairs Bureau of GHQ, to expel those associated with communists from public office. This is called the *gyakkō* or "reverse course."
[250] Somewhat ironically, during the Occupation Minobe was appointed to the Privy Council and was the sole member of that body to vote against the adoption of the new constitution.
[251] Ashibe, N. (2019), 173.
[252] School Education Act, Article 83(1) (translation by author).

[253] The Minobe and Takigawa cases involved professors at imperial universities, which in the postwar period became part of a network of national (public) universities across the country. However, these were converted into "national university corporations" in 2003. Article 23 nonetheless continues to apply to such corporations, as well as to private universities.
[254] Science Council of Japan. (2012). Nippon Gakujutsu Kaigi. Retrieved June 16, 2022, from https://www.scj.go.jp/ja/member/iinkai/gunjianzen/index.html.
[255] Hito ni Kansuru Kurōn Gijutsutō ni Kansuru Hōritsu [Human Cloning Techniques Regulation Act], Law no. 146 of 2000.
[256] Gordon, B.S. (2014). Gordon had grown up in Japan and was one of the few people on the US drafting team who understood Japanese. "The Only Woman in the Room" is the title of her 1998 memoir.
[257] For example, until its amendment during the Occupation, the penal code criminalized adultery but only when committed by married women.
[258] Into the 21st century children born in wedlock were recorded in the family register using terms that denoted birth order (e.g., "eldest son," "second daughter"), while those born outside of marriage were not, making illegitimacy readily apparent from registry extracts. This form of discriminatory record-keeping was eliminated through a 2004 amendment to the Family Register Act.
[259] In a trio of decisions issued in 2014, the Supreme Court rejected the use of DNA evidence by mothers and their children to rebut the Article 772 presumption of paternity. Supreme Court, 1st Petty Bench judgments (3) of July 17, 2014. At the time of writing (2022) the MOJ had published the outline of amendments to the Civil Code that would both eliminate the remarriage prohibition period for women and the presumption of paternity of a former husband.
[260] At the time of writing the decision does not appear to have been published, probably because the Court merely rejected an appeal without addressing the merits. Reporting can be found at, for example, *Chakushutsu Hinin "Otto Nomi" Gōken ga Kakutei, Saikōsai ga Jōkoku Shirizokeru* [Constitutionality of "Husband Only" legitimacy denial affirmed, Supreme Court rejects appeal]. *Nihon Keizai Shinbun,* (2020, February 7). Retrieved June 16, 2022, from https://www.nikkei.com/article/DGXMZO55395290X00C20A2CR8000/ For a summary of other recent paternity cases see Jones, C.P.A. (2015).
[261] In addition, in the past the family register was essentially a public document, so it was easy for any person to examine another's family background. It could thus be said to have functioned as a pre-Internet system of "social credit" until increased concern for privacy resulted in access to third party registry details being severely limited.
[262] Marriages (and most divorces) are accomplished through registration in the family register (Civil Code Article 739), but this is only possible if at least one of the persons involved is Japanese and has a family registry. If two non-Japanese persons seek to get married (or divorced) in Japan, it requires separate procedures determined in part by "home country law" relating to personal status. Act on General Rules for Application of Laws, Articles 24 and 27.
[263] A common reason for non-registration of births is fear of domestic violence. Women who have fled an abusive husband may be reluctant to file a birth registry (and seek a divorce) for fear that he may be able to find her through the linkage between the family register system and separate system of resident registration.
[264] The facts of the 1995 case overruled by the 2013 case illustrate the persistence of some more traditional Japanese family practices, one of which is the adoption as a son of a daughter's husband by families that have no sons of their own. The 1995 case involved a claim by a child born out of wedlock to the estate of a mother who had gone through several "trial" unions as part of an effort to find a husband who would also be acceptable as an adopted son. Delaying a marriage registration until pregnancy or birth has also been a common practice which obviated the need to go through a divorce if a wife proved to be barren.
[265] Supreme Court, Grand Bench judgment of December 16, 2015, 69 *Minshū* 2586.
[266] Two of the three female justices on the Court at the time joined in a concurring opinion to this effect. The other dissented, expressing the view that the appellants should be awarded damages due to legislative inaction resulting in the alleged constitutional violations. See also, Tsuji, Y. (2017).
[267] Supreme Court, Grand Bench decision of June 23, 2021.
[268] *See, e.g.*, NHK News. (2021, April 21). *Kaigaikon fūfu kon'in seiritsu mitomerumo bessei no koseki kisai mitomezu, Tōkyō Chisai* [Tokyo District Court: Recognizes validity of couple's marriage abroad but not registration of different surnames in family registry]. Retrieved June 16, 2022, from https://www.nhk.or.jp/politics/articles/statement/58802.html

[269] Marriage involves the creation of a new family register and when both spouses are Japanese, the question is which one's surname will be used for the registration. When a Japanese person marries a foreign spouse (s)he may establish a new registration either under the spouse's surname, or retain his/her surname. The difference is there is no requirement that the foreign spouse have the same surname, since (s)he does not have a family register, other than appearing as a notation ("husband/wife") in the Japanese spouse's.

[270] At the time of writing, the MOJ had announced an outline of proposed amendments to the Civil Code that would eliminate the Article 733 prohibition entirely.

[271] Supreme Court, 3rd Petty Bench decision of December 10, 2013. The case only arose because the family registry officials knew from the father's register details that he had previously been a woman and was thus incapable of fathering the child. However, infertility simply put him in the same position as any other couple using donor sperm to conceive, so the real problem was arguably the registry administrators exceeding their authority, though the Court did not address this facet of the case. Thus, the case can also be seen as another confirmation of the Civil Code restriction of the power to deny paternity to husbands only, even if family registry administrators were in possession of information relevant to the question.

[272] Some municipalities and prefectures have used their authority over their system of registering residents to issue documents granting official recognition to same-sex couples. See, e.g., McKirdy, E. (2015, April 1). Shibuya, Tokyo Recognizes Same-Sex Partnerships. CNN. Retrieved June 17, 2022, from https://edition.cnn.com/2015/04/01/asia/japan-shibuya-same-sex-relationships-recognized/index.html. This does not create a "legal" marriage, and has only the limited impact of entitling such couples to enjoy the limited range of benefits and privileges which the local government is by law able to accord married couples, and whatever benefits businesses wish to accord to them.

[273] Sei Doitsu Sei Shōgai no Seibetsu no Toriatsukai no Tokurei ni Kansuru Hōritsu [Act on Special Cases in Handling Gender Status for Persons with Gender Identity Disorder], Law no. 111 of 2003, Article 3.

[274] Shigemura, H. (2015).

[275] As with same-sex partnerships, local governments have also used their limited scope of authority over the residence registry to grant a modicum of "official" status to defacto marriages through the registration process.

[276] Supreme Court, Grand Bench Judgment of September 2, 1987. The couple in question had been separated for 35 years; the husband was the spouse "at fault" for having an affair with a woman with whom he subsequently made a new family. Despite this change of precedent, Japan is still unusual compared to many western countries in that, on the one hand it is exceptionally easy to get a *consensual* divorce by merely filing paperwork with the family registry (Civil Code, Article 764), but on the other, it can still be arduous and time consuming to procure a judicial divorce over the objections of the other spouse. The Civil Code (Article 770) only recognizes limited grounds for judicial divorce, one of which is essentially "if the Court thinks a divorce should be granted."

[277] Equal Opportunity in Employment Act, Article 9(1).

[278] The Supreme Court commonly frames the mandate in such terms. For example see the following language from the *Remarriage Restriction Case*: "*...article 24, paragraph (2) of the constitution leaves it primarily to the Diet's reasonable legislative discretion to establish specific systems for those matters concerning marriage and the family...*" For further analysis, see Tsuji, Y., (2018).

[279] Jidō Fukushi Hō [Child Welfare Act], Law No. 164 of 1947; Rōjin Fukushi Hō [Elderly Welfare Act], Law No. 133 of 1958; Shintai Shōgaisha Fukushi Hō [Disabled Welfare Act], Law No. 283 of 1949.

[280] National Health Insurance Act; Koyō Hoken Hō [Employment Insurance Act], Law No. 116 of 1974; Kaigo Hoken Hō [Long-Term Care Insurance Act], Law No. 123 of 1997.

[281] Chiiki Hoken Hō [Community Health Act], Law No. 101 of 1947; Shokuhin Eisei Hō [Food Sanitation Act], Law No. 233 of 1947; Kankyō Kihon Hō [Basic Environment Act], Law No. 91 of 1993; Taiki Osen Bōshi Hō [Air Pollution Control Act], Law No. 97 of 1968.

[282] 283 Hōgaku Kyōkai., (1953). 488.

[283] *E.g.*, Ashibe, N. (2019), 279.

[284] *E.g.*, Ōsuga, A. (1984), 71.

[285] *E.g.*, Munesue, Y. *Seizonken no gutaiteki kenrisei* [Concrete rights theory of the welfare right]. In Hasebe, Y. (Ed.) (1995).

[286] Supreme Court, Grand Bench judgment of September 29, 1948.

[287] Supreme Court, Grand Bench judgment of May 24, 1967. Translation in Itō, H., & Beer, L.W. (Eds.). (1978), 130.
[288] Translation in Itō, H., & Beer, L.W. (Eds.). (1978), 134.
[289] Supreme Court, Grand Bench judgment of July 7, 1982.
[290] Jidō Teate Fuyō Hō [Child Rearing Allowance Act], Law No. 238 of 1961. The case pertained to what at the time it was filed was Article 4(3)(iii) of the law, which was excised in a 1973 amendment, but did not affect her pre-amendment eligibility.
[291] English translation from Japan courts website at: https://www.courts.go.jp/app/hanrei_en/detail?id=68.
[292] Ashibe, N. (2019), 280.
[293] Osaka High Court judgment of November 10, 1975 (26 *Gyōshū* 1268). Translation by authors.
[294] Nakamura, M. *Dai nijūgojō—kokumin no seizonken, kuni no shakai hoshōteki gimu* [Article 25: People's welfare right, the government obligations regarding social security]. In Higuchi, Y., et al. (1997), 159.
[295] Supreme Court, 3rd Petty Bench judgment of February 28, 2012.
[296] Ōsaka Bengoshikai Kankyō Kenkyūkai (1973).
[297] Osaka High Court, 27 November 1975, 797 *Hanrei Jihō* 36; Supreme Court, Grand Bench judgment of December 16, 1981.
[298] Environmental rights are often included in proposals for constitutional revision. For more on this, see discussion at Article 13.
[299] Ashibe, N. (2019), 281–82.
[300] Ibid.
[301] Ibid.
[302] Sakamoto, M. (1993), 236; Matsui, S., (2007), 592.
[303] Hōgaku Kyōkai (Ed.). (1953), 449.
[304] Horio, T. (1971), 155–58.
[305] Supreme Court, Grand Bench judgment of May 21, 1976. In this case, the defendants who opposed the National Junior High School Achievement Test, (which was introduced in 1960 at the direction of the Ministry of Education) were prosecuted for breaking into a junior high school and assaulting the principal in order to prevent its implementation. The background of the case was influenced by the social situation at the time, when the State was promoting policies (e.g., the implementation of evaluation of teachers, the strict implementation of textbook authorizing) to strengthen its control over education.
[306] Prior to World War II, the textbook authorization system prevailed for junior high schools, while elementary schools were required to use national textbooks for all subjects from 1903. After the war, under the School Education Act, a system of official certification of textbooks for use in elementary and junior high schools was established and continues to be in operation today.
[307] This theory was adopted in the initial judgment of the second *Ienaga Textbook Case*. Tokyo District Court judgment of July 17, 1970, 604 *Hanrei Jihō* 29.
[308] This was adopted by the initial court in the first *Ienaga Textbook Case*. Tokyo District Court judgment of July 16, 1974, 751 *Hanrei Jihō* 47. Note: The first textbook case was filed before the second, but the second was decided earlier due to the differing nature of the claim.
[309] Supreme Court, 3rd Petty Bench judgment of March 16, 1993. In the third *Ienaga Textbook Case*, Supreme Court held that government interference in the content of textbooks was illegal if it had gone beyond what was "necessary and reasonable". Supreme Court, 3rd Petty Bench judgment of August 29, 1997.
[310] Article 83 (1) of the current Act, Article 52 at the time the case was decided (the wording was the same in the prior version of the provision)).
[311] Article 4 of the Basic Act on Education mandates equality of educational opportunity.
[312] See also the Shiritsu Gakkōhō [Private School Act], Law no. 270 of 1949.
[313] As discussed in the Introduction to Chapter III, the prevailing theory is that the "people" in Article 26 (and elsewhere) means Japanese citizens only. According to the government, parents of non-Japanese people are not legally obligated to send their children to school. Based on the International Covenant on Economic, Social and Cultural Rights and the Convention on the Rights of the Child, however, the Japanese government has also taken the position that it is desirable to allow foreign children to attend public schools if they want to do so. In practice, therefore, they are allowed to attend public compulsory education schools. In such cases, no tuition is charged, and textbooks are distributed free of charge. The Supreme Court has not ruled on this issue.

[314] One example of the problem is whether parents who object to certain classes or ceremonies should be allowed to refuse to send their children to school as part of their educational freedom. For example, the Tokyo District Court has ruled that even if Parents' day on Sunday conflicted with church meetings, it would be permissible as a compelling restriction based on reasonable grounds. Tokyo District Court of March 20, 1986, 37 *Gyōshū* 347.
[315] Supreme Court, Grand Bench judgment of February 26, 1964. Note the Japanese term for "free" used in Article 26 is *mushō*, which means "without compensation" and is etymologically unrelated to words such as "freedom" or "liberty."
[316] Gimukyōiku Shōgakkō no Kyōkayōtosho no Mushō Sochi ni Kansuru Hōritsu [Law on Measures for Free Textbooks For Schools Providing Compulsory Education], Law no. 82 of 1963.
[317] Kōtō Gakkōtō Shūgaku Shienkin ni Kansuru Hōritsu [Act on the Payment of Schooling Subsidies for High School, etc.], Law no. 18 of 2010.
[318] Private employers are not required to have a mandatory retirement age, but 60 has been common in both private and public employment. In recent years, however, employers are required to provide employment up to the age of 65.
[319] Interestingly, Article XXV of the GHQ Draft only saw fit to guarantee the right to work for *men*. This was rendered gender neutral in the Japanese translation and stayed that way.
[320] Rōdō Keiyakuhō [Labor Contract Act], Law no. 128 of 2007.
[321] Kōreishatō no Koyō no Anteitō ni Kansuru Hōritsu [Law for the Stabilization of Employment of Elderly Persons], Law no. 68 of 1971. To be clear, the law only requires *opportunities* to be made available, and the requirement is satisfied even if the post retirement age employment is a non-managerial position at greatly reduced benefits. At the time of writing amendments had been passed that would extend this obligation to the age of 70.
[322] Kaisha Bunkatsu ni Tomonau Rōdō Keiyaku Shōkei ni Kansuru Hōritsu [Law on the Succession to Labor Contracts upon Company Splits], Law no. 103 of 2000.
[323] Shōgaisha no Koyō no Sokushintō nI Kansuru Hōritsu [Act for the Promotion (etc.) of Employment of Persons with Disabilities], Law No. 123 of 1960.
[324] Saiteichinginhō [Minimum Wage Act], Law no. 37 of 1959; Rōdō Anzen Eiseihō [Industrial Health and Safety Act], Law No. 57 of 1973; Rōdōsha Saigai Hoshō Hokenhō [Worker Accident Compensation Insurance Act], Law no. 50 of 1947; Shitsugyohokenhō [Unemployment Insurance Act],Law no. 116 of 1974; Shokugyō Anteihō [Employment Security Act], Law no. 41 of 1947; Equal Opportunity in Employment Act (1972); Tanjikan Rōdōsha Oyobi Yūki Koyō Rōdōsha no Koyō Kanri no Kaizentō ni Kansuru Hōritsu [Law for the Improvement of Personnel Management and Conversion of Employment Status for Part-Time Workers and Fixed-Term Workers], Law No. 76 of 1993; Rōdōsha Hakenjigyō no Tekisei na Un'ei no Kakuho Oyobi Hakenrōdōsha no Shūgyō Jōken no Seibitō ni Kansuru Hōritsu [Act for Securing the Proper Operation of Worker Dispatching Undertakings and Improved Working Conditions for Dispatched Workers], Law no. 88 of 1985 (The "Worker Dispatch Act"). Unlike the small number of statutes such as the National Pension Act and the Public Assistance Act containing statements of a legislative intent to implement the minimum standard of living guarantee contained in Article 25 of the constitution (and thus cited in support of the "program provision" theory of constitutional interpretation), almost none of the myriad of employment-related statutes reference the constitution or Article 27. Of the employment laws named above, the only one mentioning the constitution is the Equal Opportunity in Employment Act, Article 1 of which references the constitutional guarantee of equal protection under the law.
[325] Supreme Court, 2nd Petty Bench judgment of April 25, 1975. As mentioned at Article 12, Article 1 of Japan's Civil Code prohibits the abuse of private rights.
[326] Supreme Court, 2nd Petty Bench judgment of January 31, 1977.
[327] Supreme Court, 1st Petty Bench judgment of July 22, 1974; Supreme Court, 2nd Petty Bench judgment of July 14, 1986. *See also*, Scheer, K.M. Labor Law—Abuse of Employer's Right to Transfer Employees. In Bälz, M., et al. (Eds.) (2012).
[328] Article 19 contains provisions imposing restrictions on the non-renewal of fixed term contracts. See also, Upham, F.K. (2011).
[329] As discussed at Article 36, Japan's penal code provides for a variety of punishments including imprisonment with labor and imprisonment without labor. In 1958 the Supreme Court rejected a challenge to a

sentence of imprisonment without labor on the grounds it deprived the convict of their constitutional right to work under Article 27(1). Supreme Court, Grand Bench judgment of September 10, 1958.

[330] Chian Keisatsuhō [Security Police Act], Law no. 36 of 1900 (repealed in 1945). As documented by Gordon (1991), there was nonetheless a vibrant and politically active labor movement in prewar Japan at least until the passage of the Peace Preservation Law in 1925.

[331] NPSA, Article 98; LPSA, Article 37.

[332] On this point it is worth noting that even though the Japanese Communist Party (JCP) is a well-established mainstream political party that routinely wins enough votes to be a reasonably significant minority presence in both chambers of the Diet, it is still considered by the police and the MOJ's Public Security Intelligence Agency to be an organization worthy of continued investigation for possible subversive or destructive activities. *See, e.g.* Kōan Chōsa Chō [Public Security Intelligence Agency]. (n.d.). *Kyōsantō ga Habōhō ni Motozuku Chōsa Taishō Dantai de aru to suru Tōchō Kenkai* [This agency's view that the Communist Party is a target of investigation under the Subversive Activities Prevention Act]. Retrieved June 17, 2022, from http://www.moj.go.jp/psia/habouhou-kenkai.html. The annual Police White Paper always contains a section on the JCP in a chapter that also discusses extreme right and left wing groups, the Ōmu Doomsday Cult and other problematic phenomena. In fact, an entire book could likely be written on the theme of "The Cold War in the Japanese Supreme Court," which would involve taking many of the famous Supreme Court cases—which are usually described in highly sanitized, politically neutral terms—and adding key facts which reveal many to involve instances of police or other government actors targeting communists, socialists or union organizers.

[333] The Japanese version can arguably be read as establishing collective bargaining as one form of acting collectively while acknowledging "other" forms of collective acts are also possible.

[334] Rōdō Kumiai Hō [Labor Union Act], Law no. 174 of 1949, Article 7. The Supreme Court has also specifically confirmed that the provisions of Article 7 of the Labor Union Act are intended to implement Article 28 of the constitution. Supreme Court, 3rd Petty Bench judgment of April 9, 1968.

[335] Supreme Court, 1st Petty Bench judgment of December 14, 1989. Specifically the Court rejected union shop provisions in collective bargaining agreements that required termination of employment of workers who left the union but joined or formed other unions.

[336] Supreme Court, Grand Bench judgment of December 4, 1968; Supreme Court, 2nd Petty Bench judgment of February 2, 2007.

[337] Supreme Court, 3rd Petty Bench judgment of November 28, 1975.

[338] Osaka High Court Judgment of June 26, 2015, 2278 *Hanrei Jihō* 32.

[339] Labor Union Act, Article 7(ii).

[340] Labor Union Act, Article 7(iv), Article 19, *et seq.*

[341] Labor Union Act, Article 8.

[342] Supreme Court, Grand Bench judgment of April 2, 1969; Supreme Court, Grand Bench judgment of November 15, 1950; Supreme Court, Grand Bench judgment of April 25, 1973.

[343] Rōdōkankei Chōseihō [Labor Relations Adjustment Act], Law no. 25 of 1946. For example, under Articles 8 and 37, "public interest workers" (those in the post, transportation, utility, medical or public health spheres) are required to give prior notice of strikes in the public gazette. The Law Relating to the Regulation of the Means of Conducting Strikes in Electrical Coal Mining Businesses imposes what appears to be an almost outright prohibition on strikes, though without establishing any penalties for violation. Denki Jigyō Oyobi Sekitan Kōgyō ni Okeru Sōgi Kōi no Kisei ni Kansuru Hōritsu, Law no. 71 of 1953. The Mariner Act prohibits strikes by maritime workers on Japanese-flagged ships in foreign ports. Funaudohō [Mariner Act], Law no. 100 of 1947, Article 30.

[344] NPSA, Article 98; Local Public Service Act, Article 37.

[345] NPSA, Articles 108-2, 108-3; LPSA, Articles 52, 53.

[346] NPSA, Article 108-2, LPSA, Article 52.

[347] NPSA, Article 110(1), LPSA, Article 61(4).

[348] Supreme Court, Grand Bench judgment of April 8, 1953.

[349] Supreme Court, Grand Bench judgment of October 26, 1966.

[350] Supreme Court, Grand Bench judgment of April 2, 1969 (23 *Keishū* 305); Supreme Court, Grand Bench judgment of April 2, 1969 (23 *Keishū* 685).

[351] Supreme Court, Grand Bench judgment of April 25, 1973.

[352] The most recent instance can be found in: International Labour Organization. (2018, June 9). *Reports of the Committee on Freedom of Association: 386th report*. 333rd Session of the ILO Governing Body: Reports of the Committee on Freedom of Association: 386th Report. Retrieved June 17, 2022, from https://www.ilo.org/gb/GBSessions/GB333/WCMS_631904/lang—en/index.htm
[353] Labor Union Act, Article 1(2).
[354] In 2020 a labor organization filed a suit against the state under the State Redress Act on the basis of law enforcement activities against union members that resulted in dozens of arrests. *See, e.g.*, Rengō News Agency. (2020, August 24). *Kansai Namakon no Kokubai Soshō Hajimaru / Tōkyō Chisai / Genkokura Kumiai Dan'atsu no Futōsei Uttae* [Kansai Namakon's state redress lawsuit begins / Tokyo District Court / Plaintiffs allege improper union suppression]. Retrieved June 17, 2022, from https://www.rengo-news-agency.com/2020/08/24/関西生コンの国賠訴訟始まる-東京地裁-原告ら組合弾圧の不当性訴え/.
[355] Civil Code, Article 206 *et. seq.*
[356] Supreme Court, Grand Bench judgment of April 22, 1987.
[357] Shinrinhō [Forest Act], Law no. 249 of 1951.
[358] The conception of institutional guarantee is derived from German constitutional theory on "institutionelle Garantie" or "Institutsgarantie" advocated by scholars such as Carl Schmitt.
[359] Note that the Japanese constitution's prohibition on post-facto laws applies only to those imposing criminal punishments (see Article 39).
[360] Supreme Court, Grand Bench judgment of July 12, 1978.
[361] This was accomplished through a now-defunct law pre-dating the constitution which required landlords to sell land to tenant farmers at a price based on the price of rice. Jisakunō Sōsetsu Tokubetsu Sotchihō [Special Law for the Fostering of Owner-farmers], Law no. 21 of 1946.
[362] The buy-back was enabled through the Agricultural Land Act prior to its amendment in 1971. Nōchihō [Agricultural Land Act], Law no. 229 of 1952.
[363] Kokuyū Nōchitō no Uribarai ni Kansuru Tokubetsu Sochihō [Special Act Relating to the Sale of State-owned Agricultural Land, etc.], Law no. 50 of 1971.
[364] Ashibe, N. (2019) 235
[365] Supreme Court, Grand Bench judgment of February 13, 2002.
[366] Kinyū Shōhin Torihiki Hō [Financial Instruments and Exchange Act], Law no. 25 of 1948, Article 164. This provision was modeled after Section 16(b) of the US Securities Exchange Act of 1934.
[367] English translation from Japan courts website at: https://www.courts.go.jp/app/hanrei_en/detail?id=68.
[368] Examples include: Supreme Court, 2nd Petty Bench judgment of November 27, 2006 (upholding provisions of the Consumer Contract Act), and Supreme Court, 1st Petty Bench judgment of April 23, 2009 (involving a statutory provision enabling a supermajority of owners of condominium buildings to affect the property rights of objecting owners; unlike the *Forest Act Case*, the case involved property which *was* impossible to subdivide further).
[369] Supreme Court, Grand Bench judgment of June 26, 1963.
[370] The Court was also rendering its decision based on provisions of the Local Autonomy Act which were subsequently deleted.
[371] Supreme Court, Grand Bench Judgment of December 23, 1953; Supreme Court, 2nd Petty Bench judgment of January 22, 1954.
[372] The Expropriation of Land Act also specifically includes housing developments of at least 50 dwellings as a public purpose that may justify expropriation. Tochi Shūyōhō [Expropriation of Land Act] Law no. 219 of 1951, Article 3(xxx).
[373] Supreme Court, Grand Bench judgment of November 27, 1968.
[374] Under the holding of the *River Area Restriction Case*, the fact that the regulations under which shops and restaurants were subject to pandemic restrictions did not contain provisions providing for compensation should not prevent them from being able to seek compensation for the restrictions on their property rights.
[375] Supreme Court, Grand Bench Judgment of December 23, 1953, 7 *Minshū* 1523; Supreme Court, 2nd Petty Bench judgment of January 22, 1954.
[376] Supreme Court, 1st Petty Bench judgment of October 18, 1973.
[377] Expropriation of Land Act, Articles 68 *et. seq.*
[378] Supreme Court, 3rd Petty Bench judgment of June 11, 2002.

[379] Under the Expropriation of Land Act (Articles 51 *et sec.*), compensation decisions are made by prefectural Compensation Committees.
[380] Tokyo District Court judgment of May 18, 1984, 527 *Hanta* 165; Osaka District Court judgment of September 30, 1987, 1255 *Hanji* 45.
[381] Tokyo High Court judgment of December 18, 1992, 1644 *Hanji* 42. Only one victim and his parents appealed. Supreme Court, 2nd Petty Bench judgment of June 1998 granted his appeal and vacated the judgment denying his claim.
[382] Supreme Court (Grand Bench), 10 October 1960 (Imperial Order to Return the Properties of the Allied Powers), 14 *Minshū* 2441; Supreme Court (Grand Bench), 27 November 1968, 22 *Minshū* 2808 (Treaty Of Peace With Japan, Article 14, paragraph (a), clause 2, item (I)[each of the Allied Powers shall have the right to seize, retain, liquidate or otherwise dispose of all property, rights and interests of (a) Japan and Japanese nationals, (b) persons acting for or on behalf of Japan or Japanese nationals, and (c) entities owned or controlled by Japan or Japanese nationals, which on the first coming into force of the present Treaty were subject to its jurisdiction.].)
[383] Tsuji, Y., (2018). The Meiji Constitution contained two duties: the duty to serve in the military (Article 20) and to pay taxes (Article 21).
[384] Sendai High Court. July 23, 1983. (The legal principle of taxation stipulated in Article 84 of the constitution should be applied to local taxes to the effect that the requirements for taxation, procedural rules, etc. should be determined by ordinance, and in this sense, the tax ordinance principle is a requirement under the constitution.) As noted at Article 84, the ability of municipal and prefectural governments to set taxes is provided for by statute in any case.
[385] Supreme Court, Grand Bench judgment of March 27, 1985.
[386] Okudaira, Y. (1993).
[387] Editors of statutory compilations and annotations add explanatory titles to constitutional provisions. For Article 31 it is common to see titles such as "*Tekisei tetsuzuki no hoshō*" (Guarantee of due process), which describe the provision in terms of due process. Even this Japanese term (which does not appear in the Constitution), refers to "procedural" process. Interestingly, the commonly used Japanese translation of the US constitution translates "due process" into Japanese more broadly as "*hō no tekisei na katei*," presumably to reflect notions of substantive due process. Constitutional scholars often use the phrase *Dyū purosesu*, possibly to avoid confusion between the two.
[388] Satō, K. (1995), 399.
[389] Penal Code, Article 49. Confiscation is a supplementary punishment sometimes imposed in addition to primary punishments such as imprisonment. This case is also interesting in that the Court allowed the primary offenders to maintain an appeal based on the confiscation of party belonging to third parties (who never participated in the trial). The Court's holding resulted in the Diet immediately passing a special law providing for a mechanism of giving notice and an opportunity to participate in cases where third party property is subject to confiscation. Keiji Jiken ni Okeru Daisansha Shoyūbutsu no Bosshū no Tetuzuki ni Kansuru Ōkyū Sochi Hō [Emergency Law Relating to Procedures for the Confiscation of Third Party Property in Criminal Cases], Law no. 138 of 1963.
[390] Supreme Court, Grand Bench judgment of April 28, 1965. See Penal Code, Article 197-5.
[391] Supreme Court, Grand Bench judgment of March 12, 1948.
[392] The process of expropriating land for the construction of Narita International Airport was badly executed and resulted in a prolonged campaign of radicalized activities by present and former landowners as well as student activists and anarchist groups. The law in question in this case involved the construction of "battle forts" on land owned by sympathetic farmers near the airport for use to interfere with airport activities. These were the structures subject to the administrative orders. *See, e.g.,* Apter, D.E., & Sawa, N. (1984).
[393] Supreme Court, Grand Bench judgment of July 1, 1992.
[394] Shingata Infuruenzatō Taisaku Tokubetsu Sochihō [Law for Special Measures in Response to New Types of Influenza etc.], Law no. 31 of 2012.
[395] Note that the Japanese term for "court" (*saibansho*) literally means place of trials (*saiban*), while judges are *saibankan* (trial officials). By contrast, these terms have no etymological connection to the Japanese word for "courtroom" (*hōtei*).
[396] The clause has its genesis as a part of Article XXXII of the GHQ Draft, which went on to become Article 31.

[397] Supreme Court, Grand Bench decision of July 6, 1960. This case involved a wartime law requiring mandatory court conciliation of disputes of monetary claims, with the conciliation result having the same effect as a confirmed judgment but without the opportunity for a trial.
[398] Supreme Court, Grand Bench decision of June 30, 1965.
[399] Supreme Court, Grand Bench judgment of December 23, 1953 (upholding an Article 32 challenge to a lower court's refusal to entertain a suit involving the rejection of a request to use a public space on a specific date on the grounds the date was already passed and the matter thus moot); Supreme Court, Grand Bench judgment of December 7, 1960 (upholding the rejection of a suit by a member of a municipal assembly challenging their expulsion from the body on the grounds that their term of office had already expired).
[400] Supreme Court, Grand Bench decision of September 18, 1950.
[401] This includes family court proceedings as described above, but also summary proceedings in minor criminal cases, certain tax court dispositions, and criminal proceedings in which defendants admit their guilt and waive certain rights of appeal in exchange for lighter punishments. Supreme Court, Grand Bench decision of July 29, 1948; Supreme Court, Grand Bench decision of December 3, 1969 and Supreme Court, 3rd Petty Bench judgment of July 14, 2009.
[402] Baishinhō [Jury Act], Law no. 50 of 1923; Baishinhō no Teishi ni Kansuru Hōritsu [Jury Act Suspension Act], Law no. 88 of 1943. Article 3(3) of the Court Act of 1947 specifically anticipates the possibility of the resumption of the jury system through separate legislation. See also Dobrovolskaia, A. (2008).
[403] Supreme Court, Grand Bench judgment of November 16, 2011.
[404] Supreme Court, 3rd Petty Bench decision of March 10, 1977.
[405] Tokyo High Court judgment of September 22, 2021. (D1-Law Case Number: 28293459) (reporter citation pending]. The government did not appeal this judgment.
[406] Article 213 of the CCP allows anyone to make an arrest for a crime in progress.
[407] Supreme Court, 3rd Petty Bench decision of January 29, 1996.
[408] Supreme Court, Grand Bench judgment of December 14, 1955.
[409] Supreme Court, Grand Bench judgment of April 6, 1955; Supreme Court, 2nd Petty Bench decision of August 9, 1977. The Court has also declined to reject the use of confessions obtained in such circumstances. Supreme Court, 3rd Petty Bench judgment of July 12 1983.
[410] Supreme Court, 3rd Petty Bench decision of April 30, 1974.
[411] The present immigration law anticipates detentions pursuant to a "detention order," a term that is both different from "warrant" but also uses a specific term for detention (*shūyō*) that applies only in the immigration context. Shutsunyūkoku Kanri Oyobi Nammin Ninteihō [Immigration Control and Refugee Recognition Act], and Cabinet Order No. 319 of October 4, 1951, Article 37.
[412] The Japanese term is "*Seitō na*" which might be better translated "proper," "valid" or "legitimate."
[413] CCP, Articles 203–205.
[414] Similar grounds are used for denying bail to defendants after a prosecution has been initiated. CCP Article 89.
[415] Japanese criminal procedure does not use an American style "arraignment" where a suspect makes an initial appearance before a judge.
[416] The "any person" wording in the English version of Article 34 is misleading. The Japanese version essentially says "upon demand" without specifying "by whom." Thus, despite the "any person" of the English, the ability to demand is generally considered limited to the suspect/defendant, his counsel, and other interested parties.
[417] Keijisoshō Kisoku [Rules of Criminal Procedure], Supreme Court Rule no. 32 of 1948, Article 85-3.
[418] In the high-profile case of former Nissan Chairman Carlos Ghosn, a demand was used and simply ended in a vague statement of the grounds for his detention that was highly criticized by his defense counsel. That said, his subsequent dramatic escape to Lebanon from house arrest in Japan doubtless validated that he was, in fact, a flight risk!
[419] Jinshin Hogohō [Habeas Corpus Act], Law no. 199 of 1948.
[420] Jinshin Hogo Kisoku [Habeas Corpus Rules], Supreme Court Rule no. 22 of 1948. *See also,* Satō, K. (2020), 375–76. Jones, C.P.A., (2017). In 1954 the Supreme Court rejected a petition for *habeas corpus* relief filed on behalf of Japanese convicted of war crimes by the Tokyo War Crimes Tribunal on the grounds that their imprisonment was the result of proceedings outside the scope of the constitution. Supreme Court, Grand Bench decision of April 26, 1954, 8 *Minshū* 848.

[421] Supreme Court, Grand Bench judgment of November 11, 1949.
[422] That lawyers can meet their counsel outside the presence of jailers or other officials may seem obvious, but it is actually an exception from the otherwise strict controls imposed on visits between those in detention and outsiders, including family members which, in the case of non-Japanese persons may require the use of translators to ensure facility administrators can understand what is being said. The Supreme Court has held that the right to meet counsel privately is required by Article 34. Supreme Court, Grand Bench judgment of March 24, 2001.
[423] Under CCP Article 39(2) discussions with and the sharing of documents with counsel may be subject to restrictions to the extent necessary "prevent the flight of the accused or the suspect, the concealment or destruction of evidence, or the sending or receiving of articles which may hinder safe custody." Under CCP Article 39(3), during the pre-charge detention stage, prosecutors or police may "designate the date, place and time" of a suspect's meeting with counsel or the exchange of documents to the extent necessary for their investigation. In other words, investigators may literally decline to allow counsel to meet a detained client because they haven't finished interrogating him for the day.
[424] The Japanese term for "seizure" used in the constitution (*ōshū*) is different from that used in the CCP, which is "*sashiosae*."
[425] Ashibe, N. (3rd edition) (2002), 227 (translation by author).
[426] Satō, K. (2020), 359. (translation by author).
[427] That said, according to judicial statistics, virtually all requests for search, seizure and other similar warrants are granted (not counting those that are withdrawn by the requesting authority), and there are no formal means of challenging the issuance of warrants or underlying probable cause.
[428] Supreme Court, Grand Bench decision of July 29, 1958. (translation by author).
[429] Supreme Court, Grand Bench judgment of April 27, 1955.
[430] Supreme Court, Grand Bench judgment of June 7, 1961.
[431] Ibid.
[432] Supreme Court, Grand Bench judgment of March 15, 2017.
[433] Supreme Court, 1st Petty Bench judgment of September 7, 1978.
[434] Supreme Court, Grand Bench judgment of November 22, 1972; Supreme Court, Grand Bench judgment of July 1, 1992.
[435] Supreme Court, 3rd Petty Bench judgment of June 20, 1978. Keisatsu Shokumu Shikkōhō [Police Duties Execution Act], Law no. 136 of 1948. Under Article 2(1) of this law, "[a] police official may stop and question any person who is suspected on reasonable grounds of having committed or being about to commit a crime or who is deemed to possess information on a crime which has already been committed or is about to be committed, judging reasonably on the basis of unusual behavior and/or other surrounding circumstances." Note that conceptually, Japanese police are deemed to have two roles: judicial and administrative. In the former capacity they conduct investigations, make arrests, and engage in other activities that may lead to a criminal trial. In the latter they perform various ministerial duties such as report on traffic accidents, issue various documents and so forth.
[436] Penal Code, Articles 11–17. Persons who are unable to pay penal fines may perform labor in a penal institution instead (Article 18).
[437] Penal Code, Article 19.
[438] Supreme Court, Grand Bench judgment of June 30, 1948 (translation by author).
[439] Supreme Court, Grand Bench judgment of March 12, 1947 (translation by author).
[440] Supreme Court, Grand Bench judgment of April 6, 1955.
[441] Lay Judge Act, Article 2(1).
[442] Osaka District Court judgment of October 31th 2011 (1397 *Hanta* 104).
[443] Note that as discussed at Article 15, the Japanese term is *kōmuin*, which is rendered "public official" in other provisions.
[444] Satō, K. (2020), 376.
[445] Penal Code, Article 195.
[446] CCP, Article 262. This is one of the few ways to circumvent the great discretion prosecutors have to *not* prosecute cases. Since prosecutors have the power to both arrest and interrogate suspects, the potential for them to abuse their powers and abuse suspects is the same as for police.

[447] United Nations High Commissioner for Refugees. (n.d.). Concluding observations on the second periodic report of Japan, adopted by the Committee at its Fiftieth Session (6–31 May 2013). Refworld. Retrieved June 17, 2022, from https://www.refworld.org/publisher,CAT,,JPN,51dfe6614,0.html
[448] Ibid.
[449] Code of Criminal Procedure, Article 247.
[450] Confusingly, defendants in *civil* cases are called *hikoku* and the media frequently refers to *criminal* defendants using this term also.
[451] 2018 amendments to the CCP established a new limited form of plea bargaining for use in cases involving specific categories of offense, and whereby the accused can receive leniency in exchange for cooperating with investigators in a way that helps them arrest and prosecute *other* criminals. CCP Article 350-2. The arrest and prosecution of Carlos Ghosn, the former CEO of Nissan Motors was one of the first cases resulting from cooperation under this procedure.
[452] No special significance should be attached to the use of "tribunal" instead of "court" in the English version of Article. 37. The term *saibansho* (court) is used throughout the constitution in the Japanese version, including Article 37.
[453] Supreme Court, Grand Bench judgment of May 26, 1948. Translation by author.
[454] For example, Article 20 of the Code of Criminal Procedure disqualifies judges from hearing cases in which they have any involvement or connections, and Articles 21–25 establishes the procedure by which the defense or the prosecution can seek to have a judge removed for potential bias. Article 13 of the Supreme Court's Criminal Procedure Regulations states that judges may recuse themselves if they feel they cannot be impartial. Similar provisions intended to ensure the impartiality of lay judges are also provided in the Lay Judge Act.
[455] Supreme Court, Grand Bench judgment of December 22, 1948. Among other things, the court acknowledged that:

> *Suppose for the sake of argument that the trial in this case was not speedy and violated the constitutional provision. What would be the result? If the delay was due to the judge presiding over the trial, then that judge should naturally be held responsible through judicial administration and otherwise. But if the argument is that because the trial was illegal because it was not speedy and that therefore the judgment of the court of second instance should be vacated, then the only remedy is to remand. But that would simply further delay the progress of the trial, and paradoxically cause the constitutional guarantee to be betrayed. For that reason, even if there was a violation of Article 37(1), it is clear that it would not affect the judgment, so we must understand it as not being grounds for an appeal to this court.* (Translation by Colin P.A. Jones)

[456] Supreme Court, Grand Bench judgment of December 20, 1972. The *Takada Case* was an incident of factionalism within the ethnic Korean community that escalated to violence and the burning of a police box. It involved charges being brought against 31 defendants but some of them were involved in other "public security" incidents as well, making the resulting proceedings complicated.
[457] Supreme Court, 1st Petty Bench judgment of August 6, 1975.
[458] Saiban no Jinsokuka nI Kansuru Hōritsu [Act on the Expediting of Trials], Law no. 107 of 2003, Article 2.
[459] In the absence of a jury or jury-like system, Japanese trials are conducted through a series of hearings that may be weeks apart. The need to have concentrated proceedings in at least some trials in order to minimize the time lay judges were inconvenienced was one of the significant procedural changes wrought by the *saiban'in system.*
[460] Supreme Court, 3rd Petty Bench judgment of November 29, 1955.
[461] Code of Criminal Procedure, Articles 157-2, 157-3 and 157-4.
[462] Supreme Court, 1st Petty bench judgment of April 14, 2005. In addition, in the case of physical shielding between witness and defendant, the Court held that since defense counsel could still see the witness, "the defense counsel will not be prevented from observing the witness's attitude while giving a statement." This is possible because in Japanese courts defense lawyers do not sit next to the defendant.
[463] Supreme Court, Grand Bench judgment of July 29, 1948.
[464] Ibid.
[465] The Japanese term for "counsel" used in Article 37(3) and the CCP is *bengonin* which is different from the term used to describe licensed attorneys (*bengoshi*). Under the CCP, *bengonin* is generally used synonymously

for *bengoshi*, but under CCP Article 31(1) there is an exception which makes it possible for a non-lawyer to act as "counsel" in family or summary court criminal cases with the permission of the Court.

[466] There is an interesting difference in thinking about criminal procedure in Japan and the United States regarding the relationship between the state and the individual. In the US, the adversarial relationship between the state and suspects is considered to begin at the time of arrest, and this is reflected in the interpretation of the right to counsel attaching at the time of arrest—"at all times." On the other hand, in Japanese Criminal Procedure, the adversarial relationship with the state is only really serious after a prosecution is brought and a defendant faces trial. That is one of the reasons why the constitution only guarantees the right for a lawyer at state expense for those who are indicted.

[467] Articles 1 and 2. E-Gov. (n.d.). *Cabinet Order to Provide for Assets under Article 36-2 of the Code of Criminal Procedure and the Standard Amount under Paragraph (1) of Article 36-3*. Hōrei Kensaku. Retrieved July 22, 2022, from https://elaws.e-gov.go.jp/document?lawid=418CO0000000287_20150801_000000000000000.

[468] Under the Comprehensive Legal Support Act (2004), the Japan Legal Support Center (also known as *Hō-terasu*) has been established in each judicial district, and lawyers register with the center within the jurisdiction of the bar association where they are registered. The Center pays for counsel in criminal cases based on a set fee schedule.

[469] Under Japanese criminal law, prosecutors and assistant prosecutors are included within the scope of officials who may conduct arrests and interrogations.

[470] There does not appear to be any rules of reason or proportionality which prevent prolonged detention from being used in the case of relatively minor offenses. Thus, suspects who refuse to confess may be detained for a prolonged period of time when they would likely only pay a fine or receive a suspended sentence if they simply confessed. The pre-charge detention regime thus provides police and prosecutors a powerful tool for punishing criminal suspects before they are convicted or even put on trial.

[471] United Nations. (n.d.). Convention Against Torture and Other Cruel, Inhuman or Degrading Treatment or Punishment. OHCHR. Retrieved June 27, 2022, from https://www.ohchr.org/en/instruments-mechanisms/instruments/convention-against-torture-and-other-cruel-inhuman-or-degrading. Ministry of Foreign Affairs of Japan. (n.d.). Gōmon tō Kinshi Jōyaku [Convention Against Torture]. Retrieved June 27, 2022, from https://www.mofa.go.jp/mofaj/gaiko/gomon/index.html#:~:text=関西生コンの国賠訴訟始まる-東京地裁-原告ら組合弾圧の不当性訴え/

[472] *See, e.g.*, Ripley, W. (2019, January 21). Carlos Ghosn case puts Japan's system of "hostage justice" under scrutiny. Retrieved June 17, 2022, from https://edition.cnn.com/2019/01/20/business/carlos-ghosn-japan-justice-system/index.html

[473] Ministry of Justice. (n.d.). *Wagakuni no keiji shihō ni tsuite, kokunaigai kara no samazama na goshiteki ya goshitsumon ni okotaeshimasu.* [Answering foreign and domestic objections and questions regarding our criminal justice system.]. Retrieved June 17, 2022, from https://www.moj.go.jp/hisho/kouhou/20200120QandA.html#Q6.

[474] Supreme Court, Grand Bench judgment of February 20, 1957.

[475] Ibid.

[476] Supreme Court, 1st Petty Bench judgment of January 30, 1997.

[477] Tokyo High Court judgment of June 30, 1966 (19 *Kōkei* 447).

[478] CCP, Articles 198(2), 291(3) and 311(1).

[479] Supreme Court, Grand Bench judgment of July 14, 1948; Supreme Court, 3rd Petty Bench judgment of November 21, 1950.

[480] Tokyo District Court judgment of December 9, 1974 (6 *Keisaigeppō* 1270). The Supreme Court has not directly addressed this "duty of suspects to endure interrogation" but in response to arguments that no such duties exist has held that "the interpretation that the suspect in custody has a duty to be present for interrogation and to stay for interrogation does not necessarily mean that the suspect is deprived of the right against self-incrimination." Supreme Court, Grand Bench judgment of March 24, 1999. Therefore, the Supreme Court can be seen to have at least tacitly acknowledged a duty on the part of suspects to endure interrogation.

[481] Note, as discussed at Article 36, Japanese law lacks a statutory definition of "torture."

[482] The exclusion of problematic confessions is extended to documents contains admissions of potentially disadvantageous facts through CCP Article 322.

[483] Supreme Court, 2nd Petty Bench judgment of July 11, 1966. Note that under Article 248 of the CCP prosecutors have broad discretion to suspend prosecutions.

[484] Supreme Court, Grand Bench judgment of November 25, 1970. The prosecution then used the husband's confession to procure one from the wife. Despite the court's ruling in this case, this practice of deceptively procuring "cross-confessions" (known as "*kirichigae jinmon*") continues.
[485] Supreme Court, Grand Bench judgment of July 19, 1948. *See also*, Supreme Court, Grand Bench judgment of November 2, 1949.
[486] Supreme Court, Grand Bench judgment of June 23, 1948.
[487] In the so-called "Hakamada Case," Iwao Hakamada was convicted of a 1966 multiple homicide after prolonged interrogation that included beatings and denial of food and access to a toilet. Investigators procured 45 written confessions from Hakamada (who is now in the Guinness Book of World Records for spending the more time on death row than anyone in history). Of these the trial court rejected 44 on the grounds they were coerced, but he was convicted on the basis of the remaining one. *See, e.g.*, Brennan, D. (2018, June 11). A death row prisoner freed after 45 years might be going back to jail. *Newsweek*. Retrieved June 17, 2022, from https://www.newsweek.com/death-row-prisoner-freed-after-45-years-might-be-going-back-jail-970348. He was granted a new trial just before this book was published. Curry, J. (2023, March 23), Japanese man granted retrial after 45 years on death row, *The Guardian*. retrieved April 6, 2023 from https://www.theguardian.com/world/2023/mar/13/japanese-man-iwao-hakamada-granted-retrial-45-years-on-death-row.
[488] Miyazawa, S. & Hirayama, M. (2017).
[489] There is some debate about whether Article 38(3) goes so far as to prohibit convictions based solely on a confession made in open court, including an early Supreme Court suggesting this was not the case. Supreme Court, Grand Bench judgment of July 29, 1948. Since the CCP establishes a clear statutory prohibition on such convictions it is arguably an academic debate.
[490] CCP, Article 318.
[491] Supreme Court, Grand Bench judgment of July 29, 1948. In an early case the Supreme Court also found the use of a written statement by the defendant prepared by a police officer based on his comments as evidence to "corroborate" a confession to violate Article 38. Supreme Court, Grand Bench judgment of July 12, 1950 4 *Keishū* 1298.
[492] Supreme Court, Grand Bench judgment of May 18, 1949.
[493] Supreme Court, Grand Bench judgment of July 5, 1965.
[494] *See, e.g.*, Supreme Court 2nd Petty Bench judgment of July 16, 1954.
[495] Aoi, M. *Dai sanjūkyūjō—sokyū shobatsu no kinshi, ichiji fusairi* [Article 39—forbidding retroactive punishment and double jeopardy]. In Serizawa, H., et al. (Eds.) (2011), 287. Aoi cited Takayanagi, K., et al. (Eds.) (1972), 189, 191–92.
[496] Supreme Court, Grand Bench judgment of April 26, 1950 (Translation by author).
[497] Supreme Court, 1st Petty Bench judgment of December 3, 2015.
[498] Satō, K. (2020), 387.
[499] Supreme Court, 2nd Petty Bench judgment of November 18, 1996.
[500] Supreme Court, Grand Bench judgment of September 27, 1950.
[501] Supreme Court, Grand Bench judgment of April 30, 1958.
[502] The "he" in "he is acquitted" of Article 40 is not reflective of the Japanese, which is expressed in gender neutral terms.
[503] CCA, Article 25. Note that such dismissals are extremely rare.
[504] While outside the scope of Article 40, Article 4(3) of the CCA also provides for compensation of up to JPY30 million for wrongful executions in death penalty cases, and remedies for wrongfully imposed fines and confiscations (Articles 5 and 6). So far there have been no instances of a person being executed and subsequently exonerated
[505] CCA, Article 4(2). By way of example, one of the most infamous wrongful conviction cases in Japan is the *Ashikaga Case* (1990) in which the defendant served 17½ years of a sentence of imprisonment with labor for an indefinite term, after being wrongfully convicted of raping and murdering a little child. He was ultimately granted a new trial and acquitted in 2010, and awarded approximately JPY 80,000,000 in compensation the following year.
[506] CCA, Article 7.
[507] CCA, Article 5(2). A well-known example of tort redress is the *Himi Case*, which involved a wrongful conviction for rape. The exoneree sued Toyama Prefecture and the state for illegal and coercive investigation conducted by the Toyama Prefectural Police Officers and the Prosecutors of the District Prosecution Office

and was awarded almost JPY 20 million in damages. However, the Court only found Toyama Prefecture liable, not the prosecutors or police who conducted the interrogation. Toyama District Court judgment of March 9, 2015 (unreported).
[508] Kensatsuchō [Public Prosecutors Office]. (n.d.). *Highisha Hoshō Kitei* [Regulations on Compensation of Suspects] (Ministry of Justice Directive). Retrieved June 17, 2022, from https://www.kensatsu.go.jp/content/000127550.pdf. Note that this may seem like a generous expansion by the MOJ (which is run by prosecutors) of the right to compensation. However, since it is framed as a directive, it does not create any right on the part of suspects to demand compensation, but rather authorizes prosecutors to grant compensation when considered appropriate.
[509] CCP, ch. 16.
[510] Shōnen no Hogojiken ni Kakawaru Hoshō ni Kansuru Hōritsu [Act on Compensation for Juvenile Cases], Law no. 84 of 1992.

Chapter IV
The Diet
Articles 41–64

Introduction

Koji Higashikawa

Chapter IV of the constitution deals with the Diet, the legislature of Japan. Although the constitution establishes a three-way separation of powers, the Diet appears superior—the "highest organ of state power" and the "sole law-making organ of the State" (Article 41). This reflects the constitution's relocation of sovereignty to the Japanese people and their elected representatives. As will be seen in the following articles, the Diet performs several important functions in addition to legislation.

The Imperial Diet under the Meiji Constitution

"Deliberative assemblies shall be widely established and all matters decided by open discussion" was one of the mandates of the Meiji emperor in his Charter Oath of 1868. With the dissemination of knowledge of how western countries were governed, demands for a national, representative assembly became an important factor in post-Restoration politics. These were ultimately met with the promulgation of the Meiji Constitution, which established the Imperial Diet, the predecessor of the current Diet. There is limited continuity between the two Diets. The Imperial Diet had two houses: the elected House of Representatives (*Shūgiin*; the same name as under the current constitution) and the appointed House of Peers (*Kizokuin*). Under the Meiji Constitution the Imperial Diet performs certain functions of government in tandem with the ministers of state and the judicature, but without a well-developed separation of powers.

In contrast, the present Diet is different from the Imperial Diet in many ways, most of which can be explained by the status of the emperor. Under the Meiji Constitution, the emperor was the holder of absolute sovereign power (*sōransha*) (Article 4), and enacted laws "with the consent of" the Imperial Diet (Article 5). Due to his status as *sōransha*, the emperor had a veto over bills that were passed by both chambers of the Imperial Diet, which could be exercised by the emperor not giving assent (*saika*) (Article 6). Furthermore, under the Meiji Constitution the emperor could rule by decree in certain circumstances without the support of the Imperial Diet (Articles 8 and 9). The emperor monopolized the power to command the army and navy without interference from the legislature (Articles 11 and 12), except through the budget process. The emperor also had the power to declare or conclude wars, and to conclude treaties that became self-executing without the approval of the Imperial Diet (Article 13). All these powers are now denied to the emperor under the current constitution because he is no longer the sovereign of the State.

In terms of representativeness, the Imperial Diet was more like a chamber established through the grace of the emperor himself. The members of the House of Peers were mostly appointed, and representative of the upper class of the people of the time, including princes of the imperial family, the hereditary nobility, distinguished academicians and so forth.[1] The House of Peers was expected to side with the emperor and his government rather than the people, providing constraint upon the possible excess of democracy in the political arena. As was the case in many other countries at the time, even membership in the House of Representatives and those entitled to vote for them were limited to those who paid a substantial amount of tax, which at the time of the first House of Representatives elections in 1890 amounted to only 1.13 percent of the population. Universal male suffrage was not enacted until 1925, and female suffrage was never achieved under the Meiji Constitution except for the brief period during the postwar Occupation before the current constitution came into force.

Under the Meiji Constitution, what is now called "the executive branch," in the form of the Cabinet, the Privy Council and the military were established based on the unquestionable authority of the emperor without any dependencies on the legislature (other than through its limited control of the budgetary process). The Cabinets were thus substantially immunized from political pressure from the Imperial Diet, and some were dubbed "cabinets of aloofness" (*chōzen naikaku*). Although a more democratic government based on party politics appeared for a limited time during the Taishō period, the government under the Meiji Constitution turned into a government of fascists that was eventually ruled by the military.

The Diet under the Constitution of Japan

GHQ had a set of goals in the drafting of the new constitution, one of which was to strengthen the power of the legislature and thereby democratize the political process in Japan. The Imperial Diet debated and approved the current constitution, effectively voting itself out of existence. The postwar constitution establishes the Diet as a sort of hybrid system consisting of Westminster parliamentary government and American-style separation of powers. As in the British system, the prime minister is elected from the members of the Diet, meaning the party that wins a general election for the House of Representatives also appoints the prime minister, absent unusual circumstances.

The Diet is vested with the legislative power in Chapter IV, and the Cabinet and the Judiciary are vested with the executive power in Chapter V, and the judicial power in Chapter VI, respectively. This fact shows that the Japan embraces the American style of separation of powers, though the degree of which is not so rigid as the one in the United States government. The government powers in Japan are essentially equally divided into the three branches, with each serving as a check-and-balance against the other two. The ideal of separation of powers, in parallel with the rule of law, is important for the protection of fundamental human rights.

Among other things, Article IV sets forth the basic constitutional parameters of the legislative process. This process is further detailed in the Diet Act. However, it is important to appreciate that except for brief interregnums, the same political party—the Liberal Democratic Party (LDP)—has controlled both houses of the Diet for most of the period from 1955 to the present. This means that to a certain degree the LDP has often been able to conduct a significant part of the "real" legislative process, consisting of coordinating within the party and relevant industry and bureaucracy stakeholders, before submitting a bill to the Diet; when it does so, it is generally confident of being able to muster the necessary votes to pass it.

At the same time, it has been rare for the LDP to have more than two-thirds of the seats in the House of Representatives, which is required to override the rejection by the House of Councillors. There have also been periods when the LDP lost control of the House of Councillors, while retaining control of the House of Representatives. Thus, productive communications between the two houses, regardless of who controls them have occasionally been necessary, as anticipated by the constitution. Thus, the criticism by some that the Diet is a "deliberative body that does not really deliberate" may be too harsh. That said, non-LDP Diet members can generally only play a limited role, often forced to focus on dilatory procedural tactics and asking difficult questions, with limited expectation of actually legislating.

Article 41: The Diet Defined

Koji Higashikawa

Article 41.
The Diet shall be the highest organ of state power, and shall be the sole law-making organ of the State.

Chapter IV starts with two clear statements about the Diet contained in Article 41: (1) it is the highest organ of state power, and (2) it is the sole law-making organ of the State. In spite of the simplicity, what these words imply about the government system and in real world politics is not obvious, and academics have developed several different theories on their meanings. What follows are the most typical questions and the prevailing answers to them.

"The highest organ of state power"

These words lead to two different questions: what is "state power" (*kokken*),[2] and why is the Diet described as being its pinnacle? Under the constitution, the sovereign right (*shuken* or "sovereignty") resides with the people, as is clearly stated in the Preamble and Article 1 and the sovereignty of the people is an ideal underpinning the entire constitution, but how *shuken* relates to *kokken* is not clear from the text of the constitution.

It is possible to adumbrate a possible definition of *kokken* that renders it synonymous with the sovereign power of the state and its government system as a whole. Under this definition, the ultimate authority and legitimacy are drawn from the people, not from the emperor, as was the case under the Meiji Constitution. The Diet is the highest organ of the state power in that it sits in the highest position in the government that has sovereign power of the state. Why the highest? Because under Article 43, the members of the Diet are elected by the Japanese people in whom sovereign power is vested. This prevailing theory focuses on a somewhat symbolized view of the Diet rather than one based on the legally cognizable authorities granted to it. Under this theory, the "highest organ of state power" language of Article 41 is considered a *"seijiteki-bishō,"* a "political encomium." This means that the language does not necessarily need to be interpreted as establishing the Diet as higher than the other branches of government in a formal hierarchy.

"The sole law-making organ of the state"

The "sole law-making" part establishes two important constitutional rules. The first rule is that only the Diet may enact the laws, and the constitution locates the legislative powers exclusively in the Diet. The second rule is that the legislative process shall be finalized by the Diet itself, and no other organs of the state are to interfere in it.

These two rules lead to several theoretical questions. First, does the "sole law-making" language require that all laws be enacted by the Diet? The simple answer is "yes," but this requires an inquiry into what is meant by "law-making" and "law." An answer is implied by Article 73(vi) which allows the Cabinet to enact cabinet orders (*seirei*), "in order to execute the provisions of this constitution and of the law," subject to the caveat that no such order may include penal provision without explicit authorization by law—law passed by the Diet. This is understood as meaning that a law passed by the Diet is required in order to either limit the rights of the people, impose duties on them or establish penalties or other detriments as well as provide benefits. This is called "the principle of the Diet as the source of substantial laws" (*kokkai chūshin rippō no gensoku*).[3] As long as the principle is well observed, it would be fair to assume that the constitution admits the delegation of legislative power to other organs of the state.

In practice, legislative delegation of subsidiary rule-making authority to ministries and other government institutions is common, just as in other countries.[4] In some cases, the Supreme Court has also been extremely permissive of the delegation of rule-making authority, such as the 1974 *Sarufutsu Case* in which it upheld the National Public Service Act delegation to the National Personnel Authority of broad powers to make rules defining political activities by public servants punishable by criminal penalties.[5] In that case four judges dissented, in part over objections to the delegation to an agency of the authority to define the elements of a crime in a sphere which involves substantial restraints on rights protected by the constitution. Since that case was decided, the Court has sometimes sustained objections to administrative rules deemed to exceed the authority delegated by the Diet.[6]

Furthermore, there are still ongoing debates with respect to laws, rules, and ordinances by local entities as to whether they are within the meaning of making of "law" (see discussion at Article 94). Similarly, the precedence of laws passed by the Diet and the rules passed by individual Diet chambers under Article 58(2) and by the Supreme Court, under Article 77 is the subject of some debate, though it is largely academic, since there appear to have been few instances of conflict.[7]

The second issue arising under Article 41 is the degree to which other organs of government can be involved in the legislative process. As discussed at Article 7, the emperor now plays only a symbolic role in the legislative process through the promulgation of laws. Similarly, before a law is sent to the emperor for promulgation it must be signed by the prime minister and other responsible ministers pursuant to Article 74. However, the signature is also considered a symbolic requirement that has nothing to do with the validity of the law. Once a bill has been passed by the Diet it takes effect as law. This is called "the principle of the Diet as the exclusive law-making authority" (*kokkai tandoku rippō no gensoku*). As discussed at Article 59, in reality the Cabinet plays a dominant role in the drafting and vetting of a great deal of the legislation passed by the Diet. The Cabinet also has been the primary sponsor of bills that ultimately become law. This might be constitutionally problematic because it appears that the executive branch of the government is penetrating into the domain of the legislative branch. The constitution, however, does not prohibit the Cabinet from submitting legislative proposals (see Article 72), and as long as a bill is considered by both houses and otherwise follows the process mandated by the constitution its origins are unimportant.

Article 42: The Bicameral System

Koji Higashikawa

Article 42.
The Diet shall consist of two Houses, namely the House of Representatives and the House of Councillors.

Article 42 provides that there shall be two houses in the Diet, both autonomous and independent from each other, as recognized in Articles 55 and 56. And both houses are the representatives of the same constituency: the Japanese electorate. The historical background of the introduction of the bicameral system in Japan reveals why the second house in the Diet is unique and different from the second houses in other countries.

The birth of the House of Councillors

As noted in the Introduction to Chapter IV, the Imperial Diet was bicameral, but one chamber, the House of Peers, with limited exceptions, was not elected. In the process of drafting the current constitution there were two competing arguments with regards to the composition of the new Diet. The GHQ Draft simply envisioned that the undemocratic House of Peers would be eliminated, leaving a unicameral legislature comprised solely of the House of Representatives (GHQ Draft, Article XLI). The American drafters thought retaining the unelected House of Peers would hinder the process of full democratization of the Diet. On the other side, Japanese government negotiators insisted on maintaining a bicameral system in the interests of avoiding overly drastic changes in the structure of the Diet and preserving the diversity of opinions that would be heard through two chambers and their different constituencies. After a series of negotiations, the Japanese side prevailed in retaining a bicameral Diet, subject to GHQ's condition that members of the second chamber be elected, the Americans prioritizing fostering democratic institutions over enforcing a particular design. As a result, under the new constitution the House of Peers was replaced by the House of Councillors.

The House of Councillors: a "third way" of bicameralism?

This historical background has resulted in Japan's Diet having an unusual form of bicameralism in two respects; constituencies and function. This can be seen through comparisons to the UK Parliament and the US Congress.

The UK's House of Lords is comprised of a mixture of hereditary peers, life peers appointed by the government and the bishops of the Church of England, and thus can be seen as representing a particular class and community of constituents. In contrast, the House of Councillors is comprised of members directly elected by the Japanese people, giving it strong legitimacy equal to that of the House of Representatives.

The House of Councillors also differs from the US Senate where seats are allocated equally to states regardless of population, presenting a different form of representation from that of the House of Representatives. While the Senate has legislative powers that are essentially co-equal to those of the House of Representatives it performs a number of other constitutional functions such as consenting to presidential appointments to federal judgeships and agencies, as well as the ratification of treaties.[8] By contrast, the House of Councillors is in some ways inferior to the House of Representatives (which can pass budgets, designate the prime minister and even pass legislation over the objections of the other chamber; see Articles 59, 60, 61, and 67), but apart from these anti-deadlock provisions, the two chambers exercise essentially the same powers. Moreover, since it is not subject to dissolution the House of Councillors functions as a caretaker legislature when the House of Representatives has been dissolved pending an election (see Article 54).

Thus, compared to its US and UK counterparts, Japan's Diet can be seen as offering a "third way" of bicameralism, one which both exists within a unitary political system rather than a federal system and in which the second chamber represents a constituency that is much more similar to that of the first (i.e., the electorate, based on population). Under this "third way," however, it can be a challenge to justify the existence of the second legislative chamber. This has been particularly so, since the LDP (or a coalition led by the LDP) have controlled both houses of the Diet for most of the postwar period. It has thus been very rare for the two houses to be at odds or deadlocked, and the House of Councillors has sometimes been criticized as merely parroting the House of Representatives.

Such criticism aside, the constitution results in two distinctions between the two chambers in terms of representation. The first one is the differing terms of office of their members (Articles 45 and 46). The second is that the House of Representatives is subject to dissolution while the House of Councillors is not (Articles 7, 45, 54 and 69). In addition, the Diet has legislatively established different systems for the elections for each house, which further give them a different character. In particular, the electoral districts and manner of allocating votes ensures that even smaller minority parties are reliably able to obtain seats in the House of Councillors at least.

Moreover, the constitution arguably gives the Diet the power to legislatively differentiate the constituencies represented by its two chambers by the manner in which it structures elections and draws up electoral districts. Despite the resulting malapportionment of voting power, the Supreme Court has been sympathetic to efforts to make the House of Councillors somewhat representative of individual prefectures.[9]

As already noted, the constitution renders the House of Representatives the superior chamber in some key respects. Nonetheless, the House of Councillors has tools to resist the House of Representatives (see discussion at Article 59), and the brief instances where the two chambers have been controlled by different parties have been characterized by gridlock.[10] It thus seems fair to say that the House of Councillors can act as a constraint on the tyrannical majoritarian rule that could arise from a unicameral system, even though the both chambers represent essentially the same constituency and have similar functions and authorities.

Article 43: Composition of the Diet

Koji Higashikawa

Article 43.

(1) Both Houses shall consist of elected members, representative of all the people.
(2) The number of the members of each House shall be fixed by law.

"Representative of all the people"

Article 43 provides for the characteristics of the members of both houses. In the Japanese version it is clear that it is the elected members, not the houses that are "representative of all the people." There has been a fair amount of academic discussions on what this phrase means. The prevailing consensus is that "representative" does not mean the type of relationship such as between an attorney and client, where the attorney acts on client instructions, can be discharged for failing to do so, and the acts of the attorney are imputed to the client. This "agency" type of representation does not apply in the constitutional context.

Article 43 does require that Diet members be elected by the people. Once elected, however, Diet members are not constrained by any preference or mandate expressed by those who voted for them. The "of all the people" part of Article 43 can thus be understood as *rejecting* a theory of mandate-based representation, and instead requiring that Diet members represent the people in Japan as a whole, not just a particular constituency or region. Under this view Diet members are free to pursue their political beliefs in performing their duties. Most scholars thus understand the language of Article 43 as making Diet members *politically* representative, subject to being held to account by voters at the next election. Diet members thus retain their political freedom, but the Diet as a whole should function in a way that mirrors the wishes of the people in Japan as a whole—including reflecting the changes of demography or other social conditions. This is referred to as "*sociological* representativeness," distinguishable from "political representativeness."

These views remain academic, as there is no significant jurisprudence on the "representative of all the people" language. The benefit of the sociological representativeness theory is in the emphasis it brings to the electoral system by which diverse interests should be suitably reflected in electoral results. How they conduct an election affects who is going to win, which party is favored, and the extent to which the people's voices are heard are all important.

Political parties and the constitution

The constitution speaks nothing of political parties except implicitly through the Article 21 guarantee of freedom of association. Political parties, however, play a crucial role in Japanese politics, by functioning as a medium for integrating various opinions and interest into cohesive policies.[11] The current electoral systems for both Diet chambers as defined in detail by the Public Offices Election Act (POEA) is premised on party politics. Among other things, the POEA imposes various stringent restrictions on campaigning activities by individual candidates for office (see discussion at Article 21), but gives political parties broader leeway in various respects.[12]

Some Diet members are elected through a proportional representation system as described in Article 47. Their candidacy is based on the membership of the party to which the candidate belongs. So what if an elected member leaves, or is expelled from, the party after the election? It is arguable that the member is not an elected member in Article 43(1) anymore because he or she lacks the prerequisite to be "elected." Once elected in an election, however, the member is supposed to be a representative of all people, along with being a member of a political party. Academics do not reach an agreement on this conundrum, while in practice a member who lost party membership has been allowed to maintain the seat as an independent. But Article 99-2 of the POEA prohibits an elected member from transferring to another political party after the election.

Article 44: Qualifications of Members and Voters

Koji Higashikawa

> **Article 44.**
> The qualifications of members of both Houses and their electors shall be fixed by law. However, there shall be no discrimination because of race, creed, sex, social status, family origin, education, property or income.

The Meiji Constitution established no parameters relating to eligibility to vote or the composition of the Imperial Diet. This meant the unelected House of Peers was literally beyond the reach of the average person, many of whom may have not been qualified for any involvement in the House of Representatives in the Imperial Diet either, because eligibility for the franchise could be set by law to exclude people based on gender or wealth.

Articles 44 and 47 of the present constitution also delegate to legislation regarding the fine details of eligibility to vote and run for seats in the Diet. However, Article 44 does provide a clear assumption that there will be electors, and further prohibits the Diet from using its legislative powers to discriminate in granting the franchise. Thus, although the way elections are conducted can be changed by laws in response to possible shifts in the political environment in the future, Article 44 sets a threshold that, in tandem with Article 15, the Diet may not exceed. Though the expansion of the franchise started even before World War II, the introduction of universal adult suffrage has developed in parallel with this constitutional commitment.

Qualifications and discrimination

The POEA provides for the qualifications of the members of both houses and the electors. The minimum age for being a member of the House of Representatives is 25, while the age for the House of Councillors is 30.[13] Every citizen aged 18 or over has the right to vote.[14]

The proviso to Article 44 essentially restates the key anti-discrimination provisions of Article 14(1) as also being equal protection requirements with regard to political participation. It also adds additional categories of prohibited discrimination: education, property and income, all of which were used to restrict the franchise under the Meiji Constitution.

Because Japan has a comprehensive system of resident registration, voters in Japan do not have to separately register to vote as is the case in the US or the UK, though this linkage of registration to voting also led to the disenfranchisement of overseas voters addressed in the *Overseas Voting Rights Case* discussed at Article 15.

Several issues arise under the anti-discrimination provisions of Article 44. First, under the POEA, a candidate for public office has to post a significant bond (three or six million yen in the case of Diet seats, depending on the type of seat). This is forfeited if a candidate does not get more than a designated proportion of votes.[15] According to one court ruling, this is intended to discourage the use of electoral campaigns as publicity stunts.[16] While such bonds impose a significant financial burden on running for political office, the Supreme Court has upheld the requirements, though without articulating a rationale.[17]

A second issue is the provisions of the POEA which disenfranchise those convicted of serious crimes and violations of electoral laws.[18] The suspension of political rights is regarded as a reasonable restraint upon those convicted, and the Supreme Court has found such sanctions reasonable.[19] However some activists and scholars contend the systematic suspension of voting rights to be constitutionally problematic, and that certain types of offenders should be allowed to vote, depending on the crime for which they are convicted.

Also, as discussed at the Introduction to Chapter III, the "people" in the constitution refers to the Japanese people. In the context of political rights this means that only Japanese citizens are allowed to participate in the election as candidates and voters. Limiting the franchise to citizens is the norm in many other countries. However, in the Japanese context there is a unique issue: the rights of the ethnic Korean community, whose members were born and raised in Japan but, because of the linkage of Japanese citizenship to parenthood (see discussion at Article 10), are only deemed "special permanent residents." Such persons are born and grow up in Japan and pay taxes but are not eligible to vote (unless they naturalize as Japanese).[20]

In the past, persons subject to adult guardianship orders (*seinen hi kōken nin*) were not eligible to vote. However, this restriction was removed through legislative amendments shortly after a lower court found the restriction unconstitutional in 2013.[21]

Vote dilution by malapportionment

As also discussed at Article 15, vote dilution, the devaluation of one vote caused by the unequal allocation of voters per legislative seat, is an inherent problem in electoral districting, short of designating the entire country a single district (as was the case for some seats in the House of Councillors). Although it is probably an impossible task to achieve true equality in the number of voters across all electoral districts, governments in most democratic countries generally have to do their best effort to ensure elections are fair in terms of the number of voters represented by a voting district. A well-known example of the effort is the one-person, one-vote principle in the United States, which was developed in a Supreme Court case and its progeny.[22] This principle of one-person, one-vote seems well appreciated in Japan from the manner it is described in constitutional treatises. Individual Japanese Supreme Court judges also recognize the principle. However, when acting collectively through the Supreme Court, they have routinely allowed to persist in both Diet chambers severe disparities in voter representation between seats in different districts. In short, the one-person, one-vote principle is recognized in Japan, but not enforced, despite the equal-protection guarantee of Article 14 and the non-discrimination mandate of both that article and Article 44.

Why is this so? Both the Supreme Court of Japan and the Liberal Democratic Party, which has been able to perpetuate its control of the Diet in part through such malapportionment, have given a variety of reasons justifying at least some degree of malapportionment. These can be summarized as two basic forms of justification which the Court has used in other contexts but have played a particularly important role in the manner it has addressed this issue: the doctrine of legislative discretion (*rippō sairyō*) and the legal doctrine of ruling on special circumstances (*jijō hanketsu no hōri*).

Legislative discretion *(rippō sairyō)*

As explained at Article 47, the constitution establishes no clear mandates regarding electoral districts or how elections should be conducted; rather it clearly defers such matters to legislation. Thus, it is at the discretion of the Diet to establish electoral districts and voting systems, meaning that *not* changing them also falls within the Diet's discretion, even in the face of demographic change.

To the Diet, however, this doctrine proved a good excuse to ignore the growing disparity between the voting power of rural and urban voters caused mostly by the migration of rural populations to cities during the postwar economic boom. The result of this was that rural, agricultural and politically conservative rural voters enjoyed greater representatives, and were also leading supporters of the LDP which controlled it. The LDP has of course been consistently reluctant to ease the disparity to their political detriment.

As for the judiciary, the grant of legislative discretion being clear from the text of Article 47, it has been very difficult for the Supreme Court of Japan to draw a line between permissible and impermissible levels of disparity. Accordingly, the Supreme Court has held that the judicial branch should defer to the discretion by the Diet, unless the disparity is so obvious as to be unconstitutional.[23] In effect, the Diet has misused the legislative discretion granted to it by the constitution for the benefit of the LDP, and the Supreme Court of Japan has been bewildered by that exercise of discretion.

The legal doctrine of ruling in special circumstances *(jijō hanketsu no hōri)*

Despite being permissive of disparities between the voting power of electoral districts, the Supreme Court of Japan has on occasion found instances in which the disparity is too egregious to be ignored. Even so, the Supreme Court has been baffled in consideration of the mess that would be triggered by the invalidation of the electoral map. Actually, the Court has never struck down an electoral map, while in two instances the Court has found severe disparities to be unconstitutional, but declined to do anything about it (see discussion at Article 15).

The Court has also sometimes declared the level of inequality between electoral districts to be in a "state of unconstitutionality" (*iken jōtai*), a form of signalling to the Diet that it is a constitutional problem the legislature should solve. This has been justified by the doctrine of ruling by special circumstances, under which the Court may maintain the legality of an act in spite of its formal ruling on the act to be unconstitutional. In the malapportionment cases, for example, the laws that have passed the Diet whose members were elected in the election that was declared unconstitutional by the Supreme Court of Japan, should have been null and void. In that case, there would be no validly constituted Diet to legislate a new electoral map, if the members lost the seats due to the ruling. In some American states, retired judges in the jurisdiction could be appointed to draw a new electoral map when the state legislature is not able to do so. However, the Diet is the sole law-making organ in Japan, and no one can replace it in performing its roles under Articles 41 and 47. To avoid this impasse, the only option available to the Supreme Court of Japan is to keep warning the Diet to do the right thing. These warnings have not always been taken seriously by the members of the Diet.

From 2011 to 2015, the Supreme Court of Japan held in three separate cases in terms of three different elections that the disparities were in a "state of unconstitutionality" but not void.[24] Because of the cumulative effects of three consecutive rulings in such a short period, the Diet took another step to ease the disparity for the map of the elections for the House of Representatives. Under the new allocation method (based on the Adams Method, originally proposed by John Quincy Adams for the US Congress), the disparity was lowered to 1:1.956, the lowest since 1949. The Supreme Court of Japan held in 2018 that this degree of disparity was permissible, emphasizing that the partial introduction of the Adams Method adequately proved the Diet's effort to minimize the disparity and maintain it at less than 1:2.0 in the future.[25]

With respect to the elections for the House of Councillors, the Supreme Court of Japan had been more forgiving of disparities in representation, which have ranged from 1:3 to 1:5.85 in recent decades. According to the Court, the members of the House of Councillors were somewhat regarded as representatives based on prefectures in practice, even though the members should be representatives of all the people in theory. Since the start of the 21st century, the Court has tweaked this prefectural representative character and been willing to examine the disparity carefully. Applying a more lenient standard to the election for the House of Councillors, however, the Court has held the disparity around 1:3 constitutional under the current apportion scheme.[26]

Article 45: Term of Members of the House of Representatives

Koji Higashikawa

Article 45.
The term of office of members of the House of Representatives shall be four years. However, the term shall be terminated before the full term is up in case the House of Representatives is dissolved.

The Meiji Constitution did not define the terms of office of members of the Imperial Diet, meaning they were subject to laws or edicts that could be changed. Articles 45 and 46, which establish defined tenures for members of the House of Representatives and the House of Councillors, respectively are thus understood as a sort of safeguard for the members of both houses, and a constitutional mandate that the government shall hear the voice of the electorate at predetermined intervals.

That said, the constitutional safeguard for the members of the House of Representatives has been largely theoretical, since they almost never serve their full four-year term. In fact, except for the election of 1976, as of writing, all the general elections for the House of Representatives under the present constitution have been called because of dissolution rather than the expiry of the four-year term. The dissolution of the House of Representatives, however, is incorporated into the mechanism of "checks and balances" which underpins the separation of powers in the constitution. It has not been used to usurp the seats of member of opposing parties.[27]

Their term of office being two years shorter than that of members of the House of Councillors, and subject to the constant threat of dissolution, members of the House of Representatives are expected to be more sensitive to voter sentiments and advocate on their behalf in order to be reelected. This stronger connection to the people through weaker job security is, somewhat paradoxically, another basis for House of Representatives being considered the superior of the two houses.

The term of all members of the House of Representatives starts and ends at the same time, regardless of the reason for the election (i.e., expiration of term or the dissolution). When a vacancy arises in a seat in the House of Representatives due to death, resignation or other circumstances, a special election is held to choose a replacement, who only sits for the remainder of the term, not a new four-year period.

Article 46: Term of Members of the House of Councillors

Koji Higashikawa

Article 46.
The term of office of members of the House of Councillors shall be six years, and election for half the members shall take place every three years.

The term of office of members of the House of Councillors is six years. That chamber is not subject to dissolution for any reason. This greater job security is not intended to give a higher status compared to members of the House of Representatives. It is understood that the constitution gives the longer term and freedom from political pressure to the members of the House of Councillors, a design which gives that chamber more continuity and stability than the more important but more unpredictable House of Representatives.[28]

Continuity and stability are also reflected in the electoral system used for the House of Councillors. With half of the members subject to election every three years, the potential number of newcomers to the chamber can never exceed half of its total membership. Of course, many incumbents are re-elected.[29] Even a significant change in political balance of power reflected by a single House of Councillors election would be mitigated by the half of the membership not up for election until the next cycle. This gradual adjustment of the House of Councillors to electoral sentiment and the political environment is part of the constitutional design. Because of this unique mixture of the characteristics of entrenchment from political influence and commitment to people's sovereignty, the House of Councillors is sometimes called "the House of Reason," in contrast to "the House of Majoritarianism"—the House of Representatives.

Article 47: The Election of Diet Members

Koji Higashikawa

> **Article 47.**
> Electoral districts, method of voting and other matters pertaining to the method of election of members of both Houses shall be fixed by law.

Legislative discretion (rippō sairyō)—*again*

Despite containing a number of provisions ensuring state power is exercised directly or indirectly through elected representatives, the constitution is silent on how elections should be conducted, leaving the fine detail to legislative discretion. Article 47 is simply a statement of this discretion; that all electoral system "shall be fixed by law."[30] Why not provide rules for such things directly in the constitution? Because the constitutionalizing of electoral rules would make it difficult for the Diet to deal with demographic change and the transformation of the political environment, which could render any constitutionally-mandated electoral system obsolete or dysfunctional, and less responsive to the people's voice.

The electoral system adopted for Diet elections created pursuant to Article 47 is expressed primarily in the POEA. The following is a brief summary of its key features as of the time of writing (2021–2022).

Electoral Districts

The House of Representatives

At the time of writing, the POEA sets the number of the members of the House of Representatives at 465. Of these, 289 are elected from single-member districts based on a "first-past-the-post" system. Electoral districts are generally based on municipal boundaries, meaning US-style gerrymandering rarely happens. The remaining 176 seats are elected through a D'Hondt-style proportional representation system in which votes are cast for political parties within 11 larger regional electoral districts and allocated to candidates in the order designated by their parties. Voters in House of Representatives elections thus have two votes: one for the single-member district in which they reside, and the other in the proportional representation system, which is a vote for a political party rather than a candidate. Under this system a candidate who loses in their electoral district may still win a seat through the proportional representation vote.

This combination of two different systems is a product of political compromise. Until the POEA was amended in 1994, members in the House of Representatives were elected from electoral districts represented by two-to-five seats. This meant the same large political party might have multiple candidates in one district and the candidates therein had to compete with each other for votes. This often led to aggressive intra-party factional rivalry among the candidates that carried over into post-electoral politics and was seen as a factor in various corruption scandals which fostered the change to single-member districts. However, multi-seat districts also had the benefit of ensuring minority parties could gain some seats. The post-1994 system was thus intended to reduce intra-party electoral contests while ensuring continued representation in the Diet for smaller parties.

The House of Councillors

The number of seats in the House of Councillors is 248[31] of which 148 are elected from electoral districts defined primarily by prefectural boundaries, with each allocated two or a higher even number of seats.[32] The prefectural-based electoral districts represent an effort to differentiate the constituency of the House of Councillors from that of the House of Representatives.

The remaining 100 seats in the chamber are chosen based on a proportional representation system with the entire nation as a single electoral district. As with House of Representatives elections voters cast two votes: one for the representative from their district, and the other for the proportional representation pool. Under this system voters can cast their vote either for a political party, or a specific candidate, if any, who is named in the list prepared by a political party.

Method of voting

Voting methodology is a highly complex subject involving a variety of issues and technical choices: choice of transferable and non-transferable votes, write-in ballots vs. checkbox ballots, manual voting vs. mechanical/computerized and so forth. Some choices relate to the convenience of electoral authority (automated vote tabulation, for example), while others relate to voter needs and ensuring the realization of the electorate's constitutional rights to vote (also see discussion at Article 15). On this point, the POEA provides for early voting and absentee voting.[33] The POEA provides also for some special voting methods including voting at home or by mail; proxy voting for the handicapped, elderly, or infirmed; and braille voting for visually-impaired voters.[34] Until 1998 Japanese citizens living abroad were not able to vote in Diet elections. A constitutional challenge was brought by a group of overseas residents, alleging, *inter alia*, that the legislative non-feasance (see discussion at Chapter III) in the Diet's failure to legislatively provide for voting abroad violated their right to vote. After the filing of this case, the government amended the POEA to allow citizens abroad to vote in the proportional systems for both the House of Representatives and the House of Councillors, but not for their electoral districts. The appellants contended this amendment was insufficient and left them subject to unconstitutional unequal treatment. In its

2005 judgment in the *Overseas Voting Rights Case*, the Supreme Court issued one of its rare conclusions that statutory provisions were unconstitutional. In doing so it held that the state had no compelling interest in not allowing overseas nationals to vote, recognized a claim to tort damages for legislative nonfeasance, and ordered electoral authorities to ensure overseas citizens were accorded full voting rights in the next election.

As discussed at Article 44, in the context of the *Malapportionment Cases* "legislative discretion" has frequently served as a convenient excuse for the courts to do nothing to remedy the Diet's failure to address outdated aspects of the electoral system. In the *Overseas Voting Rights Case*, the Supreme Court, however, sided with voters and resulted in the introduction of full overseas voting for Diet elections.[35] At the time it was decided, it was only the 7th case in which the Supreme Court of Japan held a statutory provision unconstitutional on its face.

Other rules and regulations

"Other rules and regulations" encompass a variety of rules and regulations related to election process. The subject of those rules and regulations varies from housekeeping matters to controversial rules that have something to do with constitutional norms. Notable differences from other democratic countries are regulations on campaigns. For instance, the POEA prohibits door-to-door visiting to solicit support in a campaign and regulates the place and amount of posters or other materials that a candidate may display or distribute, which would be allowed in the United States or the United Kingdom. Academics regard that these rules and regulations are inconsistent with the freedom of electoral campaign, a subcategory of freedom of expression (see Article 21).

Article 48: Prohibition of Concurrent Membership in Diet Houses

Koji Higashikawa

> **Article 48.**
> No person shall be permitted to be a member of both Houses simultaneously.

Article 48 prohibits any person from being a member of both houses of the Diet concurrently and is a corollary of the implied mandate of bicameralism contained in Article 42. The House of Representatives and the House of Councillors are autonomous and independent from each other. Although Article 44 gives the Diet broad discretion to regulate the membership of each chamber, Article 48 establishes an absolute bar on concurrent tenures by the same person in both houses.

Article 48 (and other articles of the constitution) are silent as to whether the same person can occupy a Diet seat and a role elsewhere in government, e.g., as a judge or government official. From the standpoint of separation of powers, such "double hatting" is problematic and legislatively prohibited. For example, Article 52 of the Court Act provides that a judge may not concurrently be a member of the Diet, and Article 39 of the Diet Act prohibits members from concurrently being a public official for any national, prefectural or municipal government body, with limited exceptions applied to national government officials when approved by a joint resolution of both houses. Of course, an exception to this is that Diet members may serve in the Cabinet. As discussed at Articles 67 and 68, the prime minister and a majority of the ministers of state must be chosen from the members of the Diet.

Article 49: Salary of Diet Members

Koji Higashikawa

> **Article 49.**
> Members of both Houses shall receive appropriate annual payment from the national treasury in accordance with law.

It may seem odd to readers in 21st century that a constitutional provision is needed for seemingly obvious prospect: that Diet members should be compensated for the role. It is more easily understood in the historical context of the election system under the Meiji Constitution, where qualifications for membership in both houses were at first exclusively limited to men of property. Many may have thought of the role as an honorable duty rather than a job or profession, and likely did not *need* to be paid for their service, given the limited scope of the franchise until 1925.[36] The Meiji Constitution was thus silent on compensation for legislators. The Legislature Act did provide for elected Diet members, using instead the term "*saihi*"—annual payment—rather than "*kyūyo*"—salary.

The term "*saihi*" is still used in the Japanese version of Article 49 (and in Article 35 of the Diet Act). However, the nature of the "annual payment" is generally understood to be a salary (*kyūyo*), and is paid monthly just as for other public servants. As discussed at Article 44, the constitution now prohibits financial qualifications for Diet membership. Article 49 builds on this by ensuring that Diet members receive compensation from the government sufficient to both meet their personal living expenses and facilitate their activities as legislators. This constitutionally mandated financial security for Diet members also helps them maintain their independence, in theory at least. In reality, most Diet members (or those aspiring to such roles) can never have enough money and thus tend to become dependent on financial support from political parties and interest groups, subject to the restrictions set by the POEA and the Political Funds Control Act.[37] Nevertheless, by providing a certain level of financial independence to legislators, Article 49 has made obsolete the notion of them as agents, politically bound to the desire of a narrow constituency.

Whether described as a salary, annual payment, monetary support for the activity as a legislator, or reimbursement for expenses incurred during the term of service, the payments to Diet members should be an amount appropriate to the office of the "highest organ of the state power." Perhaps for that reason, but also as a reflection of the balance of power between bureaucrats and legislators at the time the constitution was drafted, the Diet Act mandates that all Diet members should be paid at least as much as the highest paid member of the public service.[38]

Article 50: Freedom from Arrest

Koji Higashikawa

> **Article 50.**
> Except in cases provided by law, members of both Houses shall be exempt from apprehension while the Diet is in session, and any members apprehended before the opening of the session shall be freed during the term of the session upon demand of the House.

Article 50 establishes one of the constitutional privileges accorded to members of both houses. Comparable protections were set forth in Article 53 of the Meiji Constitution.

History books are full of examples from around world of kings or other government officials seeking to forcibly silence the voice of the people and their representatives. The ideals of free speech and protection from arbitrary arrest have become widely expected protections enjoyed by all persons, but these parts of the constitution serve as a reminder that they originate in part from parliamentary privileges as a response to tyrannical government.

This privilege against apprehension applies "while the Diet is in session," which means when the body is not adjourned. One exception to this rule is during emergency sessions of the House of Councillors under Article 54(2), which are considered to be excluded from the scope of the Diet being "in Session" as derived from the interpretation of Article 52. However, the view of scholars is that members attending such sessions should also enjoy the privilege since they would be deliberating urgent issues of national importance on behalf of the Diet as a whole. That understanding is now affirmed in Article 100 of the Diet Act. Since emergency session of the House of Councillors have only been held twice very early in the history of the constitution (1952 and 1953) the scope of the privilege has not been tested extensively.

Taiho: *Arrest or apprehension?*

As discussed at the Editorial Note in Chapter III at page 143, the use of the terms "apprehend" and "arrest" in the English version of the constitution is confusing because it diverges from the Japanese. In the Japanese versions of Article 50 (and Article 33) the term used for "apprehend" is "*taiho*," which is more commonly translated "arrest" and is the same term used in the Code of Criminal Procedure. The English "apprehend," however may better reflect the academic understanding of the provision, which is that it applies not just to criminal arrest, but also deprivations of physical freedom by a judicial or administrative order. Under this view the purpose of the privilege is to ensure Diet members enjoy freedom from efforts of other parts of the government to suppress them through detention.

Article 50 does not mean Diet members are completely immune from arrest or criminal prosecution while the Diet is in session. It clearly anticipates that the Diet itself can legislate exceptions to the privilege. The Diet Act currently provides for two exceptions. The first is when the arrest is for a crime in progress committed outside the chamber in which the arrestee is a member.[39] Even when the crime takes place inside the chamber, the arrest may not be made, unless the president of the house decrees to do so under the authority set in the rules of the respective house.

The second is when the house in which the member sits consents to the arrest.[40] As discussed at Article 33, normally an arrest warrant would be necessary, and normally a judge would be able to issue one based on probable cause. However, the Diet Act requires the judge to first send a written request to the Cabinet, which must in turn seek the consent to the arrest from the applicable chamber, which refers it to its steering committee for review and consent. The meeting of this committee would normally be held in secret.[41] So far in the constitution's history there have been about around twenty incidents of prosecutors requesting permission to arrest sitting Diet members, most of which resulted in consent being granted.

Article 51: Immunity for Members' Speech and Votes

Koji Higashikawa

> **Article 51.**
> Members of both Houses shall not be held liable outside the House for speeches, debates or votes cast inside the House.

Article 51 provides another safeguard from attempts to silence or intimidate Diet members. Unrestrained and frank exchange of opinions among the members of the houses are fundamental to democratic governments. Diet members are also vested with constitutional powers to ask questions and demand information from the Cabinet and its ministers (see Article 63). These communications may involve robust, aggressive or even offensive criticism directed at the government or other factions of the Diet. As seen in the Bill of Rights of 1689 in England, freedom of speech for the members of the legislature is an old and common privilege found in the constitutions of democratic countries, including Japan.[42] Article 52 of the Meiji Constitution contained a similar though much more qualified privilege.[43]

The privilege applies to members of both houses. One question that arises is whether the privilege applies to Diet members speaking in a chamber in their capacity as a minister of state (see Article 63), or also to ministry officials doing so on his or her behalf. The common understanding among academics is that it does not in either case.[44]

Article 51 specifically refers to "speeches, debates or votes cast inside the House" as being subject to the privilege, but this is thought to be an indicative rather than exclusive list, and should be interpreted to include any behavior of a member that expresses his or her opinion on a given matter. The privilege is also not considered to be limited to speech or acts physically taking place within the premises of the Diet, but extends to the member's activities, wherever they are conducted. In short, the privilege is not for the benefit of the Diet or its individual houses as institutions, but for individual members in their capacity as representatives of the people.[45]

"Shall not be liable outside the House" means that the members are immune from criminal prosecution or civil claims brought by anyone. This includes immunity for defamatory statements made in the Diet, and members who make such statements are protected according to Article 51. However, the privilege only protects the member making the defamatory statement from liability; it is not clear whether it bars defamation claims against the state brought under the State Redress Act based on the statement (see discussion at Article 17).[46]

Obviously, Article 51 does not prevent Diet members from being held responsible for their words and deeds through the electoral process or by their political party, or from being criticized by citizens or other politicians. Article 51 thus does not provide immunity from the political consequences of making ill-advised or offensive remarks. However, since Article 58(2) clearly grants each house of the Diet the power to punish its members for disorderly conduct, the Article 51 immunity does not apply to such disciplinary actions from within their chamber.

Article 52: Ordinary Sessions

Koji Higashikawa

Article 52.
An ordinary session of the Diet shall be convoked once per year.

The Diet is not in session throughout the year. The starting from its convocation to when it closes is called a "session" (*kai*). The constitution provides for three different types of Diet sessions: ordinary sessions (provided for in Article 52), extraordinary sessions (Article 53), and special sessions. Special sessions are not named as such in the constitution but that is the term used in Article 1(3) of the Diet Act to describe the session convoked after a House of Representatives election for the primary purpose of choosing a new prime minister. Article 54 also provides for "emergency sessions" of the House of Councillors, but these are not considered "Diet sessions" and are referred to using a slightly different Japanese term.

Diet sessions are numbered, starting from the first session under the present constitution, but the number does not distinguish between types of sessions. For example, when this was written in March of 2023 the 211th Diet session was in process and it was an ordinary session. Both houses open and close at the same time so numbers do not distinguish between the two.[47]

Two principles relating to the system of Diet sessions

The adoption of the session system has resulted in the emergence of two basic principles, neither of which is based on or even implied from any constitutional provisions. The first one is the so-called "principle of non-continuity of Diet sessions" (*kaiki fukeizoku no gensoku*), and it is formally articulated in Article 68 of the Diet Act. This principle holds that each Diet session is independent, meaning a bill or agenda that is not resolved in one session cannot be continued into the next one.[48] If debate over a controversial bill becomes intense and prolonged, members of the chamber debating it may fail to reach a conclusion before the current session expires. If that happens, the process has to be started anew at the next session: what has already been discussed and agreed may not be used as the baseline for the deliberation in the next session.

There is some justification behind the principle. To the majority party, the principle generates inefficiency in the conduct of a house's business. After all, absent an intervening election, the members of a house at a new session are the same as those at the previous one, yet they still need to rebuild a prior consensus. If continuity across sessions bridging an election were allowed, however, it would mean agreements made by older members could be used to bind or limit newly-elected members with respect to a bill continued from the session. Conversely, for members of minority parties, the principle can be an effective tool to defeat bills they do not like. If they can delay the legislative process and hold out until the session term expires, the bill fails and has to be started over in the next session. When the majority party wishes to avoid such a result or the bill is time sensitive, the minority members can use its leverage to negotiate compromises.[49]

The second one is the so-called "principle of no turning back" (*ichiji fusaigi no gensoku*), meaning no matter can be debated more than once in the same session. It is like a legislative version of *res judicata*, the rule which prohibits a party from re-litigating the same issue after it has been conclusively adjudicated. This principle was clearly provided for in Article 39 of the Meiji Constitution but the current constitution has no corollary provision, nor are there such provisions in the Diet Act or the rules of either Diet house. One leading constitutional scholar has posited that the principle was not written down to avoid potential conflicts with the second vote at the House of Representatives provided in Article 59(2).[50]

Timing and duration of ordinary sessions

Under the Diet Act, an ordinary session must be convoked in January and has a term of 150 days, which can be extended once if agreed by both houses.[51] An ordinary session also terminates if one of the chambers is up for election. Ordinary sessions are usually the longest type of Diet agenda, and are when the Diet conducts most of its routine business. The most important agenda item for ordinary sessions is passing the national budget for new fiscal year, which starts in April of the same year. Because of this, ordinary sessions are often nicknamed *yosan kokkai* ("budget sessions").

Article 53: Extraordinary Sessions

Koji Higashikawa

> **Article 53.**
> The Cabinet may determine to convoke extraordinary sessions of the Diet. When a quarter or more of the total members of either House makes the demand, the Cabinet must determine on such convocation.

Extraordinary sessions are another type of Diet session anticipated by the constitution. They can be understood from two different perspectives: the convenience of the Cabinet, and the Diet control over the Cabinet and executive power.

Since ordinary sessions last only 5 months (unless extended), the Cabinet would be unable to operate a government requiring legislative action if the Diet is closed for the latter half of the year. Article 53 solves this problem by vesting in the Cabinet the power to convoke the Diet for additional sessions.[52]

Article 53 also enables the Diet to meet for deliberation when enough of its members think it is necessary. The threshold of only "a quarter or more of the total members of either House" is understood to protect members of minority parties who demand the convocation over the opposition of a majority in either house (or both).

However, even when an extraordinary session is demanded by the requisite number of Diet members, the final determination as to whether to convoke it is in the hands of the Cabinet. Diet members may include a date in their demand, but it is not binding and Article 53 does not set a deadline for the Cabinet to convoke an extraordinary session after receipt of such a demand. Moreover, it is generally thought the Cabinet can satisfy the requirement by convoking an ordinary session (which it must do every year anyways) or a special session (if there is a House of Representatives election); if the Cabinet considers it reasonable to delay (some might say "ignore") the convocation demand until one of these other types of session is convoked.[53]

In reality, the Cabinet's discretion to schedule even extraordinary sessions demanded by Diet members has sometimes been misused to avoid responding to criticism or pressure from opposition parties.[54] It is very difficult to draw a clear line between a reasonable delay and intended laziness, and there have been multiple examples (including in recent history) of Cabinets ignoring demands made under Article 53. There is also nothing to stop the Cabinet from acceding to the demand and then immediately dissolving the House of Representatives.[55]

Article 54: Dissolution of the House of Representatives

Koji Higashikawa

Article 54.

(1) When the House of Representatives is dissolved, there must be a general election of members of the House of Representatives within forty (40) days from the date of dissolution, and the Diet must be convoked within thirty (30) days from the date of the election.

(2) When the House of Representatives is dissolved, the House of Councillors is closed at the same time. However, the Cabinet may in time of national emergency convoke the House of Councillors in emergency session.

(3) Measures taken at such session as mentioned in the proviso of the preceding paragraph shall be provisional and shall become null and void unless agreed to by the House of Representatives within a period of ten (10) days after the opening of the next session of the Diet.

Article 54 provides that a general election for the House of Representatives must be held within 40 days from the day of its dissolution and the Diet must be convoked within 30 days of that election. It is thus a constitutional requirement that the Diet be convened within 70 days of a House of Representatives election being called.[56]

Although the term does not appear in the constitution, the Diet session following a House of Representatives election is called a "special session."[57] Special sessions can be very short because the only business they conduct may be choosing a prime minister and Diet officials. That said, however, special sessions can be combined with ordinary sessions, depending on the timing of the election.[58] Note that in connection with the Article 70 requirement that the Cabinet resign en masse upon convocation of the Diet after a House of Representatives election, the constitution denies the Cabinet the ability to immediately dissolve the House of Representative again (because, for example, it does not like those who just won the election).[59] In accordance with the principle of concurrent activity, implicit due to the bicameralism, which is provided in Article 42, Article 54(2) mandates closure of the House of Councillors after dissolution of the House of Representatives. However, it also provides for the convocation of an emergency session of the House of Councillors by the Cabinet if necessary to deal with urgent matters that cannot wait for the House of Representatives to be reconstituted. Although not a constitutional limitation, under the Diet Act, the Cabinet specifies the matters to be deliberated at an emergency sessions and members of the House of Councillors may not propose any bill or matter for resolution.[60]

Under paragraph (3) of Article 54, any matter passed at an emergency session must be renewed shortly after a full Diet can convene or it will expire. Emergency sessions by the House of Councillors, and the decisions thereof, are thus like the special spare tires provided with many passenger cars; intended to tide the driver over until (s)he can get to a safe place and replace it with a proper one. By comparison, the Meiji Constitution (Article 8) enabled the emperor to legislate by ordinances when the legislature was not sitting, "in consequence of urgent necessity to preserve the public safety or to prevent calamity," subject to the possibility of subsequent nullification by Diet when it next convened. Article 54(2) can thus be seen as an effort to preserve a more limited continuation of emergency powers that preserves bicameralism.[61] However, so far in the Diet's history only two emergency sessions have been held, and neither involved national emergency where people's lives were at stake.[62]

Article 55: Disputes over Qualifications of Members

Koji Higashikawa

> **Article 55.**
> Each House shall judge disputes related to qualifications of its members. However, in order to deny a seat to any member, it is necessary to pass a resolution by a majority of two-thirds or more of the members present.

Pursuant to Article 47, elections for Diet members are to be held according to laws passed by the Diet. This means that dispute related to electoral outcomes are legal disputes subject to judicial resolution. Under Article 44, the qualification of Diet members is also left to definition by law. However, Article 55 carves out disputes related to qualification of Diet members as beyond the scope of the judicial power and allows each house to determine the resolution of such disputes internally. This is an autonomous power of each Diet house and their resolutions are not amenable to judicial review. Article 55 thus establishes a rare and narrow exception to the scope of the judicial power (see discussion at Chapter VI).

Perhaps because it is so narrowly tailored, Article 55 has been dormant since its birth; there have been no incidents of disputes being resolved by either Diet chamber. Even if it were not dormant, Article 55 imposes a stringent hurdle to actually denying a seat to a member in case of disputes over qualifications. The super-majority requirement of Article 54 is the same as for expelling a member under in Article 58. This is to prevent a dominant party or coalition from using majority rule to arbitrarily challenge the qualifications of members of minority parties.

Article 56: Quorum and Votes Needed

Koji Higashikawa

Article 56.

(1) Business cannot be transacted in either House unless one-third or more of total membership is present.

(2) All matters shall be decided, in each House, by a majority of those present, except as elsewhere provided in the Constitution, and in case of a tie, the presiding officer shall decide the issue.

Article 56 sets out the quorum requirements for both houses to commence business, as well as the voting threshold for deciding matters and a mechanism for breaking deadlocks through the vote of the presiding officer (which is the same term in Japanese translated as "president" in Article 58(1)). The requirements of the article speak only to the thresholds to open the Diet sessions and the rule for the determination in the houses and nothing more. Instead, the Diet Act and rules of each chamber provide for more detailed procedural requirements that generate some academic debate. For example, "one-third or more of total membership" is the constitutional quorum requirement. The number of seats in each chamber is set by the Diet Act, but do those numbers mean "total membership"? If a vacancy occurs, should it be taken into account for purposes of tallying the "total membership" for quorum requirements? What if a member abstains from voting or casts a blank or invalid vote, should they be counted? Academics have various views on some of these questions, but the general answer is likely that each house can set detailed rules pursuant to their autonomous power to do so under Article 58(2). In a 1962 decision the Supreme Court declined to intervene in a dispute over the validity of a vote in the Diet based on uncertainty about whether the quorum requirement had been satisfied.[63]

The "quorum" required under the article here is the one for either house, which means the one needed to open the plenary session (*honkaigi*) at which all members are present; the requirement does not apply to committees or other bodies within the chambers. With respect to the quorum for committees, the number of members of which is much smaller than that of the plenary session, the Diet Act provides for the heightened thresholds in order to prevent a small group of members from deciding all matters before the committee.[64]

One area of uncertainty arising under Article 56 is constitutional amendments. Neither Article 56 nor Article 96 designates a specific quorum for the Diet to commence deliberations on a constitutional amendment. Article 96 requires two-thirds of both houses to approve an amendment, but there are debates about whether this means the quorum for debate is also two-thirds, or whether the Article 56 quorum is enough. Since no constitutional amendments have been formally debated, the issue has yet to arise.

Article 57: Public Access to Deliberations

Koji Higashikawa

Article 57.

(1) Deliberation in each House shall be public. However, a secret meeting may be held where a majority of two-thirds or more of those members present passes a resolution therefor.

(2) Each House shall keep a record of proceedings. This record shall be published and given general circulation, excepting such parts of proceedings of secret session as may be deemed to require secrecy.

(3) Upon demand of one-fifth or more of the members present, votes of the members on any matter shall be recorded in the minutes.

A democratic government needs transparency in its business. As a branch of the government established by "trust of the people" who have "sovereign power," the Diet is required by Article 57 to deliberate in public and to keep records of the proceedings (including how individual members vote, if required under paragraph (3)) and make them available to the people. These requirements are considered relevant to the rights to information and freedom of the press under Article 21. Access to such information helps the people evaluate the performance of Diet members and helps them decide how to vote in a next election.

Unfortunately, the principle of open meetings (*kaigi kōkai no gensoku*) in the Diet has not been fully realized for two reasons. First, paragraph (1) is understood to apply only to plenary sessions. Plenary sessions are often formalities with little or no debate, since by the time a matter is brought to the session it has already been deliberated at the meeting of the relevant committee(s), and the outcome of the vote is already known. Second, the constitutional mandate of openness does not extend to meetings of the committees of both houses where much of the Diet's day-to-day business is conducted. While spectators are able to watch the plenary meetings, Article 52 of the Diet Act prohibits committees from allowing spectators other than journalists and those permitted by the chair of the committee, even though committee meetings are where most of the substantive legislative process is conducted. Even joint committee meetings under Article 59(3) of the constitution are closed to observers by the Diet Act.[65]

This is not to say the first two paragraphs of Article 57 are meaningless. First, the threshold for secret meetings is quite high compared to the Meiji Constitution, under which it was possible on a majority vote or when demanded by the government. No secret plenary sessions have been held since the birth of the current constitution. Some committee meetings have been held in secret, which is possible under the Diet Act through a simple majority vote of the committee members.[66]

Secondly, information technologies have made the open-to-the-public process so easy, and now it is possible to watch the plenary sessions of both houses and some meetings of primary committees via live streaming through a mobile device.[67] In terms of paragraph (2), all the records of proceedings are well kept in organized format, and now available on-line.[68] These rapid developments of information technologies seems to have changed the perception that the government process could be kept secret for some cause which is favorable to the government. Limited seating capacity or other reasons are no longer justifiable in keeping the people away from the Diet building.

Article 58: Autonomous Powers of Diet Houses

Koji Higashikawa

Article 58.

(1) Each House shall select its own president and other officials.

(2) Each House shall establish its rules pertaining to meetings, proceedings and internal discipline, and may punish members for disorderly conduct. However, in order to expel a member, a majority of two-thirds or more of those members present must pass a resolution thereon.

Under the Meiji Constitution (Article 51), each chamber of the Imperial Diet had the ability to make its own rules, but it was limited to matters anticipated by the constitution and the Legislature Act and other internal housekeeping matters. Similarly, the rules governing selection of the heads of the two houses and punishment of members for misconduct were also by legislation. This meant each house was subject to potential external political interference. Article 58 wards off the threat of such encroachment by granting each house constitutional autonomy over each chamber in recognition of the separation of powers.

Who is included in "other officials"

First, an issue of terminology must be addressed. The word "officials" appears in a number of places in the English version of the constitution (e.g., Articles 7, 15, etc.). However, the Japanese term (*yakuin*) used in Article 58 is different from that used elsewhere, and would be more commonly translated "officers" (i.e., of a corporate body).[69]

Beyond the presiding officer (president) of each chamber, the coverage of Article 58 is not clear from its text. Who are the "other officials"? The Diet Act defines the deputy presiding officer, temporary presiding officer, chairs of standing committees, and the secretary general as the "officials" (officers) of each house.[70]

As shown above and elsewhere in this Chapter, the Diet Act (or other legislation) often fills in gaps and gray areas left by the broad strokes of the constitution. In doing so it seems to leave the autonomy the constitution notionally grants to each individual house and has limited the power to make miscellaneous rules in spheres not covered by the Diet Act. Yet there is a basic question as to whether a rule of one house could prevail with a conflicting provision of the Diet Act (or other legislation passed by the Diet). On one hand, Diet legislation is considered to be inferior to the rules that each house establishes for their own governance because of their constitutional provenance, at least as long as they are rules related to "meetings, proceedings and internal discipline." On the other hand, rules (*kisoku*) are generally considered to be subordinate to laws (*hōritsu*) in the hierarchy of laws and regulations in Japan. Moreover, laws usually require the consent of both houses, while the house rules are made within one house for that house only. Both positions are equally strong. In practice, however, it would be fair to say that though the constitutional mandate in terms of separation of powers should not be misevaluated, the autonomous power has been used to make supplemental rules in most cases.

Punishment of Diet members

Each house may punish its members for disorderly conduct, including being absent from the sessions without just cause, disclosing information discussed in a closed meeting, and inappropriate remarks which diminish the integrity of the house.[71] A member can be punished regardless of where the problematic behavior or statements take place, if the conduct or remarks were made in the course of performing the activities of a Diet member. Both houses have standing disciplinary committees. The types of punishments which may be imposed are admonition in open session, requiring an apology in open session, suspension of attendance for a specific period, and expulsion.[72] As per paragraph (2), expulsion requires a two-thirds majority vote of the applicable house. Expulsion results in the member losing their status as a Diet member, but does not hinder the expelled member from seeking to be elected to the Diet again.[73] These punishments are thought to be outside the scope of judicial review because they are reflected in the constitutional design.[74]

Article 59: Legislative Process and Superiority of the House of Representatives

Koji Higashikawa

Article 59.

(1) A bill becomes a law on passage by both Houses, except as otherwise provided by the Constitution.

(2) A bill which is passed by the House of Representatives, and upon which the House of Councillors makes a decision different from that of the House of Representatives, becomes a law when passed a second time by the House of Representatives by a majority of two-thirds or more of the members present.

(3) The provision of the preceding paragraph does not preclude the House of Representatives from calling for the meeting of a joint committee of both Houses, provided for by law.

(4) Failure by the House of Councillors to take final action within sixty (60) days after receipt of a bill passed by the House of Representatives, time in recess excepted, may be determined by the House of Representatives to constitute a rejection of the said bill by the House of Councillors.

Article 59 is comprised of four paragraphs but addresses just two basic issues: the legislative process and how to resolve deadlocks between the two houses.

The legislative process

A bill becomes a law when both houses agree to the bill with a majority vote of the members present, as per Article 56. There are three exceptions to this general rule, only one of which is mentioned in Article 59. The first is a "measure" passed by the House of Councillors in an emergency session under Article 54. The second is a special law which affects only one municipality or prefecture and thus also requires a local referendum, as discussed at Article 95. Finally, there is the exception provided for in paragraph (2) of Article 59, which enables a two-thirds majority of the House of Representatives to pass a law in face of objections from the House of Councillors.

Cabinet-initiated legislation

Despite the Article 41 designation of the Diet as the "sole law-making" organ of the state, the majority of bills submitted to the Diet and successfully passed into law are drafted and submitted by the Cabinet.[75] However, it is not clearly stated anywhere in the constitution that the Cabinet has such a power of submission (the Japanese version of it, at least—the Japanese term for "bill" (*hōritsuan*) used in Article 59 is different from that used in Articles 63 and 72). In the past there were academic debates on the constitutionality of this practice. In reality, it is appropriate for the Cabinet to propose legislation because it sits atop the Cabinet Legislation Bureau (CLB, which is considered to consist of "the best and the brightest" government legal experts) as well as other ministries and agencies constituting a significant pool of expertise in legislation. And the fact that legislation originates from the Cabinet does not change the constitutional rule that Diet approval is still required for it to become law. Nor has the practice resulted in the usurping of Diet members' power to propose bills in their houses.[76] It would be safe to say that both politicians and academics agree that the long-standing practice of cabinet-initiated legislation is now constitutionally permissible.

The process of preparing a bill for submission by the Cabinet is very rigorous: it is drafted by the ministry or ministries having jurisdiction over the subject matter, and then reviewed by the Cabinet Legislation Bureau for consistency of formatting, usage and conformity with existing laws and the constitution. Once it has gone through all agency approvals, it must be approved unanimously by the Cabinet (see Article 66). The bill is then submitted to one of the two chambers (usually the House of Representatives). Note that under Article 60 a different process is followed for draft budgets.

Legislation by Diet members

Each Diet chamber has its own process for initiating and evaluating legislation. Although each chamber has its own internal legislation bureau to support them, most Diet members do not have (or have access to) the same legal expertise and drafting experience as executive branch agencies. Thus, the Diet process for drafting bills is not as rigorous, which may be one reason for the high failure rate of Diet-initiated bills. Diet rules and practices also limit the ability of individual members to initiate legislative proposals, including minimum thresholds of support from other members of their chamber (which can be substantial), and support of the member's party.[77] The Diet Act provides that absent special urgency, all legislative proposals are first discussed at the relevant house committee(s) in either house.[78] The committee deliberates the bill preliminarily and refers it to the plenary session upon the decision of the committee.[79]

The superiority of the House of Representatives

In several places the constitution anticipates the possibility of deadlocks between the two Diet chambers and provides mechanisms for getting out of them. Collectively they render the House of Representatives the superior of the two chambers. The legislative override contained in Article 59 is one of these mechanisms.

A bill first approved by the House of Councillors but rejected by the House of Representatives fails. On the other hand, if the House of Councillors does not approve a bill passed by the House of Representatives, the House of Representatives has three possible options, depending on the circumstances.[80] The first option is to use its legislative override to vote the bill into law notwithstanding the House of Councillors' objections, but this is only possible if the requisite super-majority threshold can be met. The second is to hold a meeting of a joint committee of both houses pursuant to paragraph (3) and attempt to negotiate a resolution. Finally, if the House of Councillors does not formally reject the bill within the period specified in paragraph (4), the House of Representatives may pursue the two preceding options based on deemed rejection. If the joint committee option is not pursued or fails to achieve a compromise and the super-majority vote is not feasible, the House of Representatives' bill fails. The option of a joint committee would seem the preferred choice for resolving deadlocks, and is also the method mandated for deadlocks in choosing a prime minister, passing a budget or approving treaties (see Articles 67, 60 and 61). Given the importance and urgency of some legislative matters, an effort should be made to reach agreement. If a joint committee is not able to find a way out of the impasse, the stronger superiority of the House of Representatives applies. The house does not have to have the second vote of two-thirds or more majority to override the decision of the House of Councillors. The latest decision by the House of Representatives, even with simple majority vote, becomes the final decision of the Diet.

In reality, the two-thirds supermajority vote by the House of Representative has not been extensively used nor has the joint committee process. This is in part because the ruling Liberal Democratic Party has controlled both chambers for most of the period since 1955 making recourse to these deadlock-breaking measures unnecessary. At the same time, it has also been rare for the LDP or LDP-led coalition to control a two-thirds majority in the House of Representatives.

Article 60: Deliberation on Budgets

Koji Higashikawa

Article 60.

(1) The budget must first be submitted to the House of Representatives.

(2) Upon consideration of the budget, when the House of Councillors makes a decision different from that of the House of Representatives, and when no agreement can be reached even through a joint committee of both Houses, provided for by law, or in the case of failure by the House of Councillors to take final action within thirty (30) days, the period of recess excluded, after the receipt of the budget passed by the House of Representatives, the decision of the House of Representatives shall be the decision of the Diet.

The government spends money. The way the government spends money and how much it spends has direct influences on the economy and the people's welfare. Therefore, the control of national finances by the representatives of the people is an integral aspect of a government established by the people.[81]

Article 60 establishes the process by which budgets are approved. The budget is drafted and submitted to the Diet by the Cabinet (see Article 73). It is deliberated by both houses but Article 60 accords superiority to the House of Representatives on this matter. This superiority includes two elements: The House of Representatives is the first chamber to receive and decide on the budget, and can override the objections from the House of Councillors in the event of disagreement. This mechanism prevents deadlock and government shutdowns resulting from a lack of funding.

The Meiji Constitution (Article 65) also required budgets to be first submitted to the House of Representatives, the rationale being that since they were so relevant to the lives of all the people, budget bills should be deliberated first by the more representative chamber.

This rationale arguably does not apply under the current constitution where both chambers consist of elected representatives of the people. The rationale under the current constitution is understood to come from the fact that the House of Representations has a stronger connection with the Cabinet (which prepares the draft budget pursuant to Articles 73(5) and 86) and the existence of which is effectively defined by the House of Representatives electoral cycle.[82]

Unlike in the event of disagreements between the two houses on bills under Article 59, a joint committee of both houses is mandatory when they cannot agree on a proposed budget. On the other hand, a two-thirds majority vote is not required for the House of Representatives to override the House of Councillors. The constitution simply regards the decision of the House of Representatives as the decision of the Diet. The mandatory joint session of both houses is, therefore, thought to be granted to the House of Councillors in compensation for the lower threshold for House of Representatives overrides.

See discussion at Article 86 regarding the legal character of the budget.

Article 61: Ratification of Treaties

Koji Higashikawa

> **Article 61.**
> The second paragraph of the preceding article applies also to the Diet approval required for the conclusion of treaties.

Article 61 provides the mechanism by which the Diet ratifies treaties negotiated and signed by the Cabinet. Under the Meiji Constitution, foreign policy and the execution of treaties, including the declaration and the conclusion of war, were parts of the emperor's prerogatives and conducted without direct oversight (other than financial) from the Imperial Diet. Under the current constitution, the power over foreign policy is vested in the Cabinet (see Article 73). However, the Cabinet cannot conclude a treaty without the approval of the Diet. The Diet is thus not necessarily wholly subordinate to the Cabinet in managing foreign affairs. The Diet approval requirement under Article 61 is perhaps best understood as a variation of a check and balance mechanism between the Diet and the Cabinet.

The process for ratification of treaties is basically the same as the enactment of laws: the treaty can be submitted to either house first for deliberation and approval and both should approve the ratification by a majority vote. The main difference is that treaties follow Article 60 rather than Article 59 when deadlocks need to be resolved. This means the House of Representatives does not need to wait 60 days to deem inaction a rejection, or have to muster a two-thirds majority to override rejection by the House of Councillors. The process leading to the conclusion of a treaty is significantly different from the enactment of domestic laws, involving time consuming, often secret negotiations stages between diplomats and other government officials. It is thus logical to minimize the ability of the Diet to frustrate these negotiations intentionally or through a deadlock, while at the same time ensuring the people's representatives have a veto over treaties.

The constitution is unclear on whether the Diet has the power to propose amendments to treaties submitted for ratification. There are two principal academic theories which offer different answers to this question. The first holds that insofar as Article 61 provides for a mandatory joint session in the event of disagreement between the two chambers, it is reasonable to extrapolate a constitutional interpretation that allows both houses to impose conditions on ratification during the mandatory joint session. The second is that for the Diet to be able to make changes to the text of the treaties would be an encroachment upon the Cabinet's powers to conclude a treaty. Moreover, such amendments cannot be effective to the party country unless the treaty party agrees to them. The academic debate is not settled yet, but has had no impact in practice, since there have been no instances of the Diet attempting such amendments.

Article 62: Investigations by the Diet

Koji Higashikawa

> **Article 62.**
> Each House may conduct investigations in relation to government, and may demand the presence and testimony of witnesses, and the production of records.

As the highest organ of the state, the houses are charged with deliberating and deciding important matters. Such decisions should be based on proper information. While it may be difficult to define what information is "proper," Diet members need to have some confidence that they are acting on credible information in the course of reaching any determinations. While they may routinely rely on information provided by government agencies, it may not always be credible. The Diet chambers thus need independent powers to conduct investigations.[83]

The Meiji Constitution was silent as to investigation powers of the Imperial Diet. The old House Act (Articles 72–75) provided for some limited powers, but they were not sufficient to enable the legislature to thoroughly investigate the conduct of government affairs. The Imperial Diet had no power to call officials from ministries or lower levels of government to answer questions, nor the ability to compel witnesses to testify. The government was able to deny the Imperial Diet access to information, even when requested to provide it.[84]

Article 62 grants independent powers of investigation to each house and ways it can be used. The methods of investigation specified are similar to those commonly used in a courtroom trial process: compelling a witness to appear and give testimony, and the production of documents. The details are set forth in the Law on the Oaths and Testimony (etc.) of Witnesses before Diet Chambers, which establishes criminal penalties for non-compliance but also recognizes testimonial privileges (such as against self-incrimination or arising within certain relationships) and provides for the protection of materials designated as classified materials by the government.[85] The Diet Act also gives each chamber the authority to demand government agencies provide information, and the rules of individual chambers allow legislative committees to summon "reference witnesses" (*sankōnin*), though these are not backed by criminal sanctions.[86]

Although technically not included within the scope of the Diet's constitutional investigation powers, the Diet Act vests individual Diet members with the power to submit questions to the Cabinet; this may be particularly significant for small minority parties that have limited direct input on legislation, but are able to use such questions to hold the government to account.[87] Answers to questions are typically prepared by officials in the relevant ministry and approved by the Cabinet before being given. In some cases they may present the "government view" of issues of constitutional interpretation that have not been resolved by the Court.

The nature of investigation power

There are two main theories about the nature of the investigation power. The scope of the power varies depending on which theory is applied. One theory is that the investigation power is an independent power inherent to the Diet as the highest organ of state power, a power separate from the legislative, budgeting and other powers accorded to the Diet and its chambers in the constitution. Under this view, the houses can investigate whatever they wish, including (for example) investigating crimes. However, this "independent power theory" was heavily criticized as early as 1949 when the House of Councillors conducted an investigation of a controversial judicial decision, resulting in a formal protest against this encroachment on the judicial power from the Supreme Court.[88]

The other view is that the investigation power is ancillary to the other powers of the Diet and thus limited in scope to the extent necessary to exercise such powers. This "ancillary power theory" has been articulated in at least one lower court ruling and is widely accepted by academics.[89]

The question still remains, however, as to what constitutes "ancillary" to the power granted to the Diet houses. Arguably, in addition to the power to enact laws and pass budgets, in order to perform these functions properly it needs broad oversight over the activities of the administrative branch.[90] In reality the houses seem able to conduct virtually any kinds of investigation relating to issues of national governance, though they may not (should not) conduct investigations of political scandals for the purpose of intervening in police investigations or influencing prosecutorial decisions regarding indictments. The houses may, nonetheless, conduct investigations in parallel with such investigation for the purpose of finding and disclosing information about a scandal in furtherance of the people's right to know about such things. Thus, whether an investigation on a given issue is permissible as an exercise of an "ancillary" investigation power, depends on the purpose of the investigation.

Whichever theory is taken, the political reality is that the investigation power seems to be reduced to a political tool rather than a means of gathering information necessary to legislate. Moreover, the ability to use the investigation power to investigate political scandals has been limited because of the parliamentary cabinet system; the same party that controls the Cabinet also controls one or both houses of the Diet, meaning one is unlikely to investigate the other rigorously. While minority parties may push for investigations, they are likely to be overwhelmed by the majority in each chamber.

The politicization and majority dominance over investigations have been mitigated by a "preliminary investigation system" that was introduced in the House of Representatives in 1998. Under it, upon the demand of 40 or more members, the president of the House of Representatives is required to establish a committee to conduct a preliminary investigation on a specific subject upon the demand of 40 members or more, and to direct the committee to publish a report on the results.[91]

Article 63: Accountability of Ministers in the Diet

Koji Higashikawa

Article 63.
The Prime Minister and other Ministers of State may, at any time, appear in either House for the purpose of speaking on bills, regardless of whether they are members of the House or not. They must appear when their presence is required in order to give answers or explanations.

Article 63 establishes the right and duty of cabinet members to speak in either house. On its face, the provision appears to facilitate the process of deliberation within the Diet chambers. However, the purpose of the provision must be framed in the context of Japan's parliamentary cabinet system.

The Meiji Constitution (Articles 54) gave ministers of state the right but not the obligation to attend and speak in the Imperial Diet. The Cabinet had no constitutionally defined status or relationship to the Diet, and its ministers were individually responsible to the emperor. Imposing an obligation on ministers of state to answer questions from the Diet, Article 63 is another aspect of the present constitution's general rejection of the Meiji Constitution's balance of powers, as is its replacement with a system where the Diet and the Cabinet have a more balanced relationship, one in which the Diet can compel cabinet members to disclose information needed by the Diet.[92]

For the first fifty years of the present constitution's history, ministers of state were able to delegate the task of answering questions to ministry bureaucrats, as was the practice under the Meiji Constitution. In 1999, however, the Diet Act was amended to greatly limit such delegations in the interests of forcing cabinet members to take greater responsibility.[93]

According to Articles 48 and 68, it is theoretically possible that either house asks a minister to appear in the house where the minister does not hold a seat. "[R]egardless of whether they are members of the House or not" fills these loopholes and ensure the member whom either house asks to appear to be present in the house.

Article 64: Impeachment of Judges

Koji Higashikawa

Article 64.
(1) The Diet shall set up an impeachment court from among the members of both Houses for the purpose of trying those judges against whom removal proceedings have been instituted.
(2) Matters relating to impeachment shall be provided by law.

As discussed in Chapter VI, the constitution embraces judicial independence and affords strong protections to individual judges against retribution from the political branches of government. Judges can be removed by the judiciary if they are physically or mentally incompetent (Article 78), or by the voters in the case of Supreme Court judges (Article 79). Otherwise, the only way a judge can be removed is through *public* impeachment under Article 78. This requirement protects judges from political pressure or unfounded accusations of wrongdoing and other considerations that could otherwise affect how they decide trials. Article 64 thus establishes the means by which another branch of government (the Diet) can remove a judge.

From the people's point of view, the impeachment of judges can be thought of as a form of constitutional right; Article 15 recognizes "the inalienable right" of the people to dismiss public officials, which includes judges.

A court or any organization within the judicial branch would not be appropriate to judicial impeachment due to possible concern of influence from colleagues. Executive agencies or organs are expressly prohibited from being involved in disciplinary action against judges under Article 78, so the only remaining venue for the judicial impeachment process is the Diet, the members of which are representatives of the people.

The constitution was drafted with caution about the partisan influence within the Diet. Consequently, Article 64 grants to the Diet only the power to set up the judicial impeachment court and legislatively establish how it will operate. That means the Court is independent from the Diet, though the members of the Court are chosen from Diet members in both houses (seven from each for a total of 14).

The details of the impeachment are set forth in the Judge Impeachment Act. The independence of the Court from the Diet is provided in Articles 4 and 19 of the Act. Among other things this means the Court can continue a trial in process even when the Diet is not in session.

Notes

1 The House of Peers did have some seats that were elected for a fixed term of years from the ranks of high-tax payers. *Kizokuinrei* [House of Peers Edict], edict no. 11 of 1889, Article 1. Shortly before the end of World War II seats in the chamber were also established for suitable representatives of Japan's colonies in Korea and Taiwan.

2 Note the term *kokken* is also used in Article 9, where it is rendered in English as "the sovereign right of the nation."

3 Every principle has its own exception, and some exceptions are constitutionally designed, such as the rules for the Supreme Court of Japan (Article 77), or the rules for the houses of the Diet (paragraph (2) of Article 58).

4 Given that much of the legislation passed into law is drafted primarily by the bureaucrats who will be responsible for administering it after passage, it is unsurprising that they often delegate detailed rule-making to themselves, pursuant to ministerial or agency regulations that do not need to go through the rigors of the legislative process.

5 Supreme Court Grand Bench judgment of November 6, 1974.

6 *See, e.g.*, Supreme Court 3rd Petty Bench judgment of July 9, 1991 (invalidation of administrative rules regarding visitation between suspects in pre-trail detention and minors as exceeding scope of the Prison Act), Supreme Court 1st Petty Bench judgment of January 31, 2002 (invalidating implementing regulations under the Child Rearing Allowance Act, which provides for subsidies to single mother households, that rendered children in certain de facto marriages ineligible).

[7] That said, some consider the Supreme Court's use of its rule-making powers to have substantially reduced the scope of relief under Japan's Habeas Corpus Act of 1948. *See* Jones, C.P.A. From Great Writ to Tuning Fork; How Habeas Corpus was Tamed in Japan (2017). Perhaps not coincidentally, *habeas corpus* relief is rarely a subject of Japanese constitutional discourse.

[8] Note that appointments to numerous important Japanese government institutions, such as the Bank of Japan and the Fair Trade Commission must be approved by both chambers of the Diet. However this is not a constitutional requirement, but rather a function of the relevant legislation (e.g., the Bank of Japan Act, the Anti-Monopoly Act and so forth).

[9] Supreme Court Grand Bench judgment of April 27, 1983. More recently, the Supreme Court might not be so supportive of this concept, having held that the Diet should prioritize minimizing the disparity of voting power over endorsing the representation of each prefecture. Supreme Court, Grand Bench judgment of October 17, 2012.

[10] In addition to the challenges differing control of the two houses imposes on the legislative process, various statutes require both houses to consent to appointments to leadership posts in various government institutions, such as the Bank of Japan and the ability to agree on them can thus become an additional source of political gridlock.

[11] The Supreme Court discusses the importance of political parties at length in the *Yawata Steel* case, discussed in the Introduction to Chapter III.

[12] POEA, ch. 13, ch. 14-3.

[13] POEA, Article 10.

[14] The minimum age for voters used to be 20 (the age of majority), but was lowered to 18 in 2016. The age of majority was also lowered to 18 in 2022.

[15] POEA, Articles 92–94.

[16] Kobe District Court judgment of August 7, 1996, 1600 *Hanrei Jihō* 82.

[17] There are reportedly two unreported "*mikudari hanketsu*" ("three line" *pro forma* judgments rejecting appeals without any detailed explanation) from 1999 which uphold the requirement. Doubtless in part because the Court has not rendered a considered judgment on the subject, constitutional litigation challenging the requirement continues. Supreme Court, Grand Bench judgment of November 11, 1999.

[18] POEA, Article 11.

[19] Supreme Court, Grand Bench judgment of February 9, 1955.

[20] As noted at Article 15, the Supreme Court has indicated it would be constitutionally permissible for the Diet to allow non-citizens to participate in local elections.

[21] Tokyo District Court judgment of March 14, 2013 (2234 *Hanrei Jihō* 29).

[22] Reynolds v. Sims, 377 U.S. 533 (1963).

[23] *See generally* Supreme Court Grand Bench judgment of April 14, 1976.

[24] Supreme Court Grand Bench judgment of March 23, 2011, 65 *Minshū* 755 (holding the ratio of 1:2.304 as the state of unconstitutionality), Supreme Court Grand Bench judgment of November 20, 2013, 67 *Minshū* 1503 (holding 1:2.425 as the state of unconstitutionality), Supreme Court Grand Bench judgment of November 25, 2015, 69 *Minshū* 2035 (holding 1:2.129 as the state of unconstitutionality).

[25] Supreme Court Grand Bench judgment of December 19, 2018, 72 *Minshū* 1240.

[26] *See, e.g.*, Supreme Court Grand Bench judgment of November 18, 2020 (finding a 1:3.002 disparity in House of Councillors representation as constitutional).

[27] One notable case on this regard is the dissolution in August 2005, by Prime Minister Koizumi, whose top political agenda at that time was the privatization of Japan's Post Office (and massive postal banking system). Having encountered considerable opposition from Diet members from within his own party, such that he experienced a rare rejection in the House of Councillors, Koizumi dissolved the House of Representatives. This was supposedly to seek the public's views on postal privatization, but in reality Koizumi used it as an opportunity to put up candidates supportive of his agenda in districts of LDP members who had been opposed. His effort was successful and resulted in the House of Councillors supporting the bills when resubmitted. Some commentators consider this a constitutionally questionable use of the dissolution power because Koizumi dissolved the House of Representatives who supported his agenda, and the dissolution had no legal but, instead, a political impact on members of the House of Councillors who rejected the privatization.

[28] Higuchi, et al. (1988), 890.

[29] With the general election taking place every three years, the half of the members of the House of Councillors serving in the first term had to be subject to the first general election. This was the only exception for the shortened term. *See* Article 102.
[30] The Japanese term used to express "fixed" is *sadameru*, a legal term which would more commonly be translated "determined" or "provided for."
[31] POEA, Article 4.
[32] Each district has an even number of seats so that half are always up for election every three years (see Article 46).
[33] POEA, Articles 48-2, 49.
[34] POEA, Articles 47, 48. *See also* the discussion of the *Postal Voting Case* at Article 15.
[35] At the time of writing overseas voters still did not participate in retention elections for judges on the Supreme Court. See discussion at Article 79.
[36] Once universal male suffrage was introduced for the House or Representatives there was criticism that limited compensation for its members was a form of suppression of small or proletarian political parties.
[37] *Seiji Shikin Kisei Hō* [Political Funds Control Act], Law No. 194 of 1948.
[38] Diet Act, Article 35.
[39] Diet Act, Article 33.
[40] Diet Act, Article 34.
[41] *See* Kinoshita, S., & Tadano, M. (Eds.) (2019), 502.
[42] Japan's Supreme Court has nonetheless declined to recognize a similar privilege for members of prefectural and municipal assemblies. Supreme Court, Grand Bench judgment of May 24, 1967.
[43] Specifically, it clearly did not apply to speeches or publications outside the Diet. ("When, however, a Member himself has given publicity to his opinions by public speech, by documents in print or in writing, or by any other similar means, he shall, in the matter, be amenable to the general law").
[44] Tokyo High Court judgment of December 26, 1959 (213 *Hanrei Jihō* 46).
[45] Lower court cases involving incidents of violence within the Diet premises suggested the scope of the privilege could be interpreted very broadly, but declined to do so in the cases at bar. Tokyo District Court judgment of January 22, 1962 (297 *Hanrei Jihō* 7); Tokyo District Court judgment of January 21, 1966 (8 *Kakei* 44): Tokyo High Court judgment of December 17, 1969 (22 *Kōkei* 924), and Tokyo High Court judgment of December 17, 1969 (22 *Kōkei* 924).
[46] In the *Hospital Director Suicide Case*, which involved a tort claim against the state by the spouse of a person allegedly driven to suicide by a purportedly defamatory statement by a Diet member, the Supreme Court rejected the claim based on the circumstances and noted that:

> *in order to find the State's liability for damages for such act by a Diet member, there must be special circumstances where it is obvious that the Diet member has exercised the authority vested in him/her contrary to the purport thereof, including cases where the Diet member has alleged the facts for an illegal or inappropriate purpose irrespective of his/her duties, or has knowingly alleged false facts.*

[47] The type of session is indicated after the ordinal numbers. For instance, the 203rd Extraordinary Session means the 203rd Diet session and the type of the session is an extraordinary session, not that the extraordinary session that has been held 203 times. *See* The House of Representatives, Japan. (n.d.). *Kokkai Kaiki Ichiran* [Table of Sessions of the Diet]. Shugiin.go.jp. Retrieved June 27, 2022, from https://www.shugiin.go.jp/internet/itdb_annai.nsf/html/statics/shiryo/kaiki.htm
[48] The principle is not absolute. Articles 47(2) and 68 of the Diet Act allow for exceptions if a chamber determines that a specific matter needs ongoing consideration while the Diet is closed, in which case the matter can be carried over to the next session.
[49] *See* Diet Act, Article 47, para. 2, Article 68.
[50] Itō, M. (1995), 449–50.
[51] Diet Act, Articles 2, 10, and 12.
[52] Extraordinary sessions must also be convoked within 30 days of either chamber due to expiry of the applicable term of office, unless an ordinary or special session is convoked. *See* Diet Act, Article 2-3.
[53] Doi, M., in Kawagishi, N., et al. (2020), Vol. 3, 661.

[54] For example, in 2015 the Abe administration declined to convoke an extraordinary session using the justification that the prime minister was busy dealing with diplomatic issues—in spite of the constitutionally valid demand by opposition (the real reason may have been to avoid criticism over political scandals).
[55] Prime Minister Abe did just this in 2017 when opposition demanded an extraordinary session in order to grill him and other government officials about a political scandal. After three months' delay, the extraordinary session was convened, but Abe then immediately dissolved the House of Representatives, effectively depriving the opposition of the opportunity to criticize his administration in the Diet.
[56] There is an academic debate whether or not the election after 41 days from the day of dissolution is constitutionally permissible. Article 133 of the Diet Act provides for the special rule for calculating the period of the date. It includes the starting day in the calculation, which would otherwise be excluded. However, there was one election that was held after 41 days of dissolution under the interpretation that the day of dissolution was to be excluded. As to this one-day late election, which was triggered by Prime Minister Tarō Asō in the summer of 2009, no constitutional challenge was made. *See* Doi, M., in Kawagishi, N., et al. (2020), Vol. 3, 674–75. The bottom line is that the constitution does not prescribe how to calculate the period for constitutional matters.
[57] Article 1 of the Diet Act uses the term, defining it by reference to Article 54. Confusingly, a Diet session convoked due to the expiry of the term of a house's members (rather than dissolution) is a referred to as an "extraordinary session" in the Diet Act (Article 2-3).
[58] Diet Act, Article 2-2.
[59] Higuchi, et al. (1988), 935.
[60] *See* Diet Act, Articles 99, 101.
[61] Some statutes specifically anticipate the convocation of emergency sessions. *See, e.g.,* Act on the Peace and Independence of Japan and Maintenance of the Nation and the People's Security in Armed Attack Situations etc., Article 9, para. 4; Basic Act on Disaster Management, Article 109-2.
[62] One was necessary in connection with the appointment of members of the board of election in charge of a retention referendum for Supreme Court judges under Article 79. The second was needed in order to pass a provisional budget and extend the effect of laws set to expire before the new Diet session started.
[63] Supreme Court Grand Bench judgment of March 7, 1962.
[64] Diet Act, Article 49. *See* Itō, M. (1995), 456, and Hashimoto, K. (1980), 514.
[65] Diet Act, Article 97.
[66] Diet Act, Article 52(2).
[67] House of Representatives, Japan. (n.d.). House of Representatives Internet TV. Retrieved June 27, 2022, from https://www.shugiintv.go.jp/; House of Councillors, Japan. (n.d.). House of Councillors Internet Deliberation Relay. Retrieved June 27, 2022, from https://www.webtv.sangiin.go.jp/webtv/index.php.
[68] National Diet, Japan. (n.d.). *Kokkai Kaigiroku Kensaku Shisutemu* [National Diet Minutes Search System]. Retrieved June 27, 2022, from https://kokkai.ndl.go.jp/#/.
[69] Note also that while the English version of the constitution uses "President" to express the Japanese term *gichō*, in the English translation of the Diet Act the term used is "Presiding Officer."
[70] Diet Act, Article 16. Despite the clarity of the provision, it is arguable whether the Secretaries General, who are in charge of the administration of their respective houses, are not an "official" in the constitutional meaning because they are elected from those who are not Diet members. (See Diet Act, Article 27). The question has not been contested in court so far, but the uncertainty still remains.
[71] *See* Diet Act, Article 124, the Rules of the House of Representatives, Article 238, the Rules of the House of Councillors, Article 235-36.
[72] Diet Act, Article 122.
[73] The English term "expulsion" suggests the punishment is physical exclusion from the Diet chamber. The Japanese term (*jomei*) would actually be better rendered something like "to have your name stricken from the rolls" and is thus clearer that it involves an actual loss of membership status.
[74] With respect to sanctions against members of prefectural and municipal assemblies, the Supreme Court recently reversed an earlier precedent to find them amenable to judicial review. Supreme Court, Grand Bench judgment of November 25, 2020.
[75] In any given year cabinet-submitted bills typically account for approximately 80 percent of the bills passed into law. In this respect the legislative process shows remarkable continuity with the Imperial Diet under the Meiji Constitution, where a similar ratio prevailed. *See* Ōmori, M., & Kamata, K. (Eds.) (2011). In fact

there is a seemingly oxymoronic term—*giin rippō* ("legislation by legislators")—used to describe legislation originating from within the Diet.

[76] The constitution does not provide the submission power of the members of the Diet, either, taking it for granted. Note, however, that the submission by a single member is not allowed. Article 56 of the Diet Act requires certain numbers of members to agree on the submission. This is thought to be preventing a bill as "pork" (*omiyage-hōan*) to make up the member's fake political achievement.

[77] Article 56 of the Diet Act requires the support of 20 members for a bill in the House of Representatives and 10 in the House of Councillors, unless the bill requires fiscal appropriations, in which case the threshold is 50 members and 20. In addition, House of Representatives practice is that a proposed bill also requires the approval of the proponent member's political faction (*kaiha*), meaning it will not be accepted if the members are dissident in the faction. A court challenge to this requirement was rejected on the grounds that it was a matter relating to the autonomy of the Diet chamber. Tokyo High Court judgment of June 18, 1997 (1618 *Hanrei Jihō* 71).

[78] A committee in the houses and the research committee in the House of Councillors can propose a bill (Diet Act, Articles 50-2, 54-4).

[79] An urgent bill or matter may proceed to the plenary session directly when the house decides it to be necessary upon the request of the sponsor(s). *See* Diet Act, Article 56(2).

[80] The House of Councillors can agree to the House of Representatives's bill with some amendments; this situation should be distinguished from when there is an outright rejection of the bill by the House of Councillors. In that case, the amended bill may be passed into law by the House of Representative with a simple majority vote when they agree with the amendment pursuant Article 59(1).

[81] The matter related to the national budget is provided in Article 60, while the powers of the Diet over finance are provided in Chapter 8. It is probably because the constitution recognizes the superiority of the House of Representatives on this matter, which are recognized as well in terms of legislative power (Article 59) and treaty approval (Article 61) in the same Chapter.

[82] Shishido, J., in Kawagishi, N., et al. (2020), Vol. 3, 805.

[83] Note that the English version of Article 62 refers to investigations in relation to *government*. The Japanese is *kokusei* which might be more appropriately translated "the governance of the nation."

[84] Higuchi, et al. (1988), 984–85.

[85] Giin ni Okeru Shōnin no Sensei Oyobi Shōgentō ni Kansuru Hōritsu, Law No. 225 of 1947. Note that the house powers of investigation are understood not to extend to the full panoply of police powers such as forcibly entering homes, confiscation or arrest. *See, e.g.*, Sapporo High Court judgment of August 23, 1955, 8 *Kōkei* 845.

[86] Diet Act, Article 104; the Rules of the House of Councillors, Articles 42-3 and 186; the Rules of the House of Representatives, Articles 45-3 and 85-2.

[87] Diet Act, ch. VIII.

[88] The so-called *Urawa Incident* involved a woman driven to despair by debt and marital issues attempted to commit suicide with her three children. The children died but she survived and was prosecuted for murder but given a very lenient sentence. The House of Councillors used its investigation power to call the woman, her husband and the prosecutor to testify about the case.

[89] Tokyo District Court judgment of July 24, 1980, (12 *Keigetsu* 538).

[90] This view has also been articulated in a lower court opinion. Sapporo High Court judgment of August 12, 1961, 14 *Kōkei* 459.

[91] *See* The Rules of the House of Representatives, Articles 56-3 and 56-2 (in case of being initiated by the president).

[92] Note that rather than "question" the GHQ Draft (Article LVI) used the term "interpellations," which implied accountability of a Minister for the question and a more inquisitive process by Diet members. Note also that when they do appear in a chamber, cabinet members are not limited to speaking about legislation before the chamber. *See* Ōishi, M. (2008), 163.

[93] Diet Act, Article 69(2).

Chapter V
The Cabinet
Articles 65–75

Introduction

Colin P.A. Jones

Overview

Chapter V defines the Cabinet. Read together with Chapter IV (the Diet) and Chapter VI (the Judiciary), it is easy to discern a US-style tripartite "separation of powers" structure in the constitution but even easier to be misled as to the degree of separation. This is further facilitated by the confusing use of the term "executive power" in the English version of Article 65, as discussed at that article.

Insofar as the political party that controls the Diet also controls the Cabinet, the "separation of powers" between the two is less meaningful than in a presidential system of government. In 2016 Prime Minister Shinzō Abe was widely ridiculed for describing himself as the "head of the legislative branch."[1] But as the leader of the party controlling a majority in both Diet chambers, he might have just been describing political reality, particularly given the dominant role played by the Cabinet in making many of the legislative proposals that become law, as discussed at Articles 59 and 73.[2]

That the constitution contains an entire chapter devoted to the Cabinet is itself a form of refutation of the Meiji constitutional system. Article IV of the Meiji Constitution was comprised of only two articles, one describing the role of ministers of state (Article 55) and the other the Privy Council (Article 56).[3] The word "cabinet" does not appear anywhere in the document.

The first cabinet (*naikaku*) with a prime minister was established in 1885, several years before the Meiji Constitution was even promulgated. However, the historical experience of those who created that constitution was that a person or institution formally defined as exercising some of the emperor's powers would ultimately usurp more of them, as had happened with the shoguns. Not only were the structures and operations of cabinets under the Meiji system not "constitutional"—in that they were not defined by the constitution, they were not even "legal," in the sense that they were governed by imperial mandates rather than legislation passed by the Imperial Diet. Lack of constitutional foundations can be seen as a reason why cabinets under the Meiji Constitution were weak, but this might also be seen as a design choice.

Under Article 55 of the Meiji Constitution ministers of state advised and were responsible to the emperor, not the prime minister or the Cabinet as a body. Cabinets failed frequently, and were unable to control the disastrous military adventurism which led Japan into war. Many of the provisions of Chapter V of the current constitution can be seen as efforts to remedy perceived deficiencies in the way cabinets were constituted and functioned under the previous one.

The structure of the administrative branch

The Cabinet sits atop the ministries, agencies, commissions and other organizations comprising the nation's central government, excluding those parts coming under the jurisdiction of the Diet, the judiciary, or the Board of Audit. A brief description of these apparatuses will be helpful in understanding the discussion that follows.

Beyond what is set forth in Chapter V, the finer details of the Cabinet and its procedures are set forth in the Cabinet Act of 1947. That the Cabinet is governed by a law passed by the Diet is itself a significant difference from the Meiji system.

The Cabinet Act also makes clear that the term "cabinet" refers to more than just its members—the ministers of state—but to the institutions that support them. The most important of these is the Cabinet Secretariat, itself a ministry of sorts that manages the cabinet affairs. The Cabinet Secretariat is a nexus of centralized strategic planning and administration, as well as inter-agency coordination. Its head, the Chief Cabinet Secretary is a minister of state and one of the most powerful people in the government after the prime minister.

The Cabinet Act also sets the size of the Cabinet (narrowly defined). The default setting under the Act has long been that cabinets should consist of the prime minister and no more than 14 other ministers of state. However, the law contains a proviso to the effect that in special circumstances this can be expanded by an additional three members. More obscure, supposedly temporary provisional exceptions expand the number of ministers of state to a maximum of 20.

At the time of writing the Cabinet of Prime Minister Fumio Kishida consisted of him and 20 other ministers of state. In addition, there were a large number of vice ministers and parliamentary secretaries, all political roles typically filled by Diet members. Cabinet posts are commonly used as political rewards for the prime minister's political allies, with rotations being common. For example, over two dozen people held the position of Minister of Justice during the 2000–2020 period.

Discussing cabinet ministers in English can be confusing because the Japanese term for "minister of state" (*kokumudaijin*) has no etymological relationship to the term for "ministry" (*shō*). Thus, there are a number of positions that by law are filled by a "minister of state" who sits in the Cabinet but not atop a ministry. Examples include the Chief Cabinet Secretary and the Chairman of the National Public Safety Commission. In addition, there are a large number of "minister without portfolio"-type positions that, pursuant to their organizational statutes, are also required to be filled by a minister of state. All told there are several dozen minister of state positions. The problem of the numerical limit on ministers of state in the Cabinet is resolved through double- and triple-hatting. For example, in the Cabinet of Prime Minister Yoshihide Suga, Finance Minister Tarō Aso also held three other ministerial posts as well as being deputy prime minister.

Ministries are a basic components of the national government. At the time of writing there were eleven ministries: Finance (MOF), Foreign Affairs (MOFA), Defense (MOD), Justice (MOJ), Internal Affairs and Communications (MIC), Environment (ME), Agriculture, Forestry and Fisheries (MAFF), Land, Infrastructure Transport and Tourism (MLIT), Education, Culture, Sports, Science and Technology (MEXT), Health, Labour and Welfare (MHLW) and Economy, Trade and Industry (METI).

In addition to the ministries, which each have portfolios over areas of governance that are generally apparent from their titles, there is the Cabinet Office. This is in many ways similar to a ministry, but encompassing a diverse range of bureaus, committees and agencies, all sitting under the prime minister, but with a number of additional ministers of state for specific issues. Significant agencies sitting under the Cabinet Office include the Financial Services Agency, which regulates the finance industry, and the Imperial Household Agency, which manages the affairs of the imperial family.

Most government institutions follow the organizational mandates of the National Administrative Organization Act.[4] In addition, the details of specific institutions are provided in either a special statute (e.g., the Ministry of Finance Establishment Act of 1948) or within a broader regulatory statute, such as the Police Act, which provides the organizational details of both the National Public Safety Commission and the National Police Agency.[5]

The Cabinet Legislation Bureau

One institution attached to the Cabinet that merits special attention is the Cabinet Legislation Bureau. It performs a number of important functions relevant to the government, which are set forth in its establishing legislation. First, it reviews all legislative proposals submitted by the Cabinet to the Diet, for consistency and format. Second, it provides legal advice to the Cabinet and its ministries; while not clearly stated, this naturally includes interpretations of laws including the constitution. Third, it helps the Cabinet and its members respond to questions from Diet members, including as to questions of statutory or constitutional interpretation.[6] To the extent these roles involve constitutional interpretations, absent Supreme Court rulings on the subject the CLB view may by default be the most definitive "official" interpretation of a particular question of constitutional law. That this may be politicized was demonstrated in 2013 when Prime Minister Abe broke established norms by appointing a favored person as head of the CLB and thereby engineering a change in its interpretation of Article 9 that was formalized in the cabinet resolution discussed in the following section.

Cabinet decision-making

The Cabinet typically meets twice a week with additional meetings as necessary. Formal minutes (which have only been made public since 2014) reveal these meeting to be short but often involving a large number of decisions. Obviously, these meetings are simply formalizing a consensus that in some cases may have been arrived at through long contentious meetings held outside the public view.

Decisions are reflected in cabinet resolutions (*kakugi kettei*), and cover the vast range of roles performed by the Cabinet and the agencies below it. *Kakugi kettei* may include approving legislative proposals, cabinet orders, honors, official responses to interpellations from the Diet, numerous appointments, and the numerous acts in matters of state requiring the emperor's seal and signature and thus also the advice and approval of the Cabinet (see Article 6). Cabinet resolutions passed at a meeting are signed by all ministers of state, and the use of signed circular resolutions without meetings is also common.

Although the substantive answer may be prepared by the CLB, the formal response to questions asked by Diet members to the Cabinet (or individual cabinet members) are formalized in a cabinet resolution. Insofar as the Cabinet is already announcing statutory and constitutional interpretations through this process, it is not a great leap for cabinet resolutions to be used to *change* the government's interpretation. As discussed at Article 9, Prime Minister Shinzō Abe's cabinet did this in 2014 in connection with formalizing the change of interpretation of whether the constitution permitted Japan to engage in collective self-defense activities. Similarly controversial was a 2020 cabinet resolution used to reinterpret statutes relating to the retirement age of prosecutors specifically and public servants generally in order to retain a politically favored senior prosecutor who had reached statutory retirement age.[7]

Article 65: The Administrative (Executive) Power

Colin P.A. Jones

> **Article 65.**
> Executive power shall be vested in the Cabinet.

Article 65 presents an example of where the English version can mislead in a subtle but important way. In the Japanese the Cabinet is vested with the *gyōseiken*, which would more accurately be translated "the administrative power," and is consistent with other terminology used in Chapter V, such as "administrative branches" in Article 72. Accordingly, the remainder of this chapter discussion will also use the term "administrative power" despite the English text's use of "executive power."

The distinction is not merely semantic. The starting point for Japanese constitutionalism is the Meiji Constitution, under which all sovereign powers were vested in the emperor. The emperor was not merely executing the laws passed by the Imperial Diet; he exercised numerous prerogatives that were not subject to legislative control, including the organization and control of the military. Thus, the answer to the question of "what is the administrative power under Article 65?" should logically be rooted in the sovereignty of the emperor and the powers derived from it, at the time sovereignty was realigned with the Japanese people.

One view, which might be called the "remainder theory" is that it consists of what is left after the deduction of the legislative and judicial powers. If one assumes all powers of government were originally vested in the emperor (the premise of the Meiji Constitution), then transferred to the Japanese people and further distributed to the three branches of government through the present Constitution, then the Cabinet would get the leftovers. This theory would see the Cabinet vested with various inherent, implied and other residual powers. However, it potentially conflicts with the Article 41 designation of the Diet as the highest organ of state power.

Some scholars are of the view that the administrative power is, in fact, the executive power—as in the power to execute the law. This theory holds that the administration of government all takes place within a framework of law, including the constitution and various other statutes which establish and govern administrative institutions. Thus, on a certain level whatever the Cabinet and the institutions under it are doing is essentially "executing the law." This view is criticized for ignoring the political character of the Cabinet, and failing to distinguish between the bureaucracy and the Cabinet which is supposed to control it. This view is also hard to reconcile with Article 73(i), where faithful execution of the law is merely one of many roles accorded the Cabinet.

A third view is that the administrative power is the power to govern (*shissei*). Under it the administrative institutions under the Cabinet can be thought of as executing the law, but the Cabinet itself provides political leadership that determines the direction of the country, with some proponents drawing attention to the "manage affairs of state" language of Article 73(i) in support. This theory reconciles the different character of administrative institutions and their professional bureaucracies on the one hand and the political Cabinet on the other. Resolution of the potential conflict with the "highest organ" designation of the Diet is sought through a theory of power sharing between the legislative and administrative branches.

There is no Supreme Court jurisprudence to help resolve these interesting theoretical puzzles.

Independent administrative commissions

Another question arising under Article 65 involves a category of administrative bodies collectively known as administrative commissions. These were an Occupation-era innovation based on US models of independent regulatory commissions. Examples of such bodies which have survived until the present day include the Fair Trade Commission (the competition regulator), the National Personnel Authority (which administers the national civil service) and the more recently-created Personal Information Protection Commission (the data privacy authority).[8] While their organization depends on the specific body, typically their leadership is appointed by the prime minister, subject to the consent of both chambers of the Diet. These leaders serve fixed terms and are protected from arbitrary dismissal to various degrees by their incorporating statutes. For example, commissioners of the National Personnel Authority can only be removed by impeachment by the Supreme Court.[9]

Bureaucracies are generally expected to be politically neutral, and the organization of some bodies in this fashion is intended to provide an additional level of isolation from partisan politics, particularly changes in cabinets. However, while establishing administrative institutions that are structurally isolated from the Cabinet is a perfectly rational goal, it is constitutionally suspect given the "vested in the Cabinet" language of Article 65.

Arguments in favor of the constitutionality of such bodies are that Article 65 lacks any sort of language of exclusivity as found in Article 41 as to the legislative power and Article 76 as to the judicial, and there is thus more flexibility in allocating the executive powers, including through sharing some of it with the Diet. Moreover, to the extent the Diet is the highest organ of state power, it should be within its powers to create such bodies to administer the law. The question is largely academic in any case, since administrative commissions have existed for decades and there has been no jurisprudence to suggest they should not.

Article 66: The Prime Minister and Ministers of State

Colin P.A. Jones

Article 66.

(1) The Cabinet shall consist of the Prime Minister, who shall be its head, and other Ministers of State, as provided for by law.

(2) The Prime Minister and other Ministers of State must be civilians.

(3) The Cabinet, in the exercise of executive power, shall be collectively responsible to the Diet.

In its historical context, Article 66 can be seen as remedying multiple perceived defects of cabinets under the Meiji system. These were: (1) the prime minister was merely a "first among equals" with no special powers over other cabinet members, (2) the ministers of the army and navy were generals and admirals on active service and thus subject to the influence of their institutions, (3) it was possible for military officers to become prime minister and fill other ministerial roles contemporaneously, the most famous example being Hideki Tōjō, and (4) each minister was only accountable individually to the emperor, who was accountable to no one.

The first paragraph of Article 66 clearly renders the prime minister the head of the Cabinet. Etymologically, the Japanese term *shuchō* ("head") denotes a leader at the top of a hierarchy—more than just first among equals.

The "as provided by law" in paragraph (1) formally subordinates the Cabinet to the Diet, which has the power to determine its composition. As noted in the Introduction to this Chapter the laws relevant to the composition of the Cabinet include the Cabinet Act as well as the statutes constituting the various ministries and other administrative bodies.

Civilian requirement

The requirement that the prime minister and other ministers of state must be civilians was added to the constitution late in the process at the insistence of the Far Eastern Commission. A new Japanese term for civilian ("*bunmin*") had to be created anew to satisfy the FEC's demands.[10]

Since Article 9 suggests that Japan cannot have a military, and that therefore anyone joining a cabinet could only ever be a "civilian," there is some debate about what paragraph (2) means. One theory that was more relevant earlier in the postwar period was that the language excluded from cabinet service those who had *previously* served in the imperial military. However, since conscription during and prior to the war meant most males above a certain age would have been excluded by this interpretation, more refined versions of the theory held that it excluded only those who had formerly been career soldiers or naval personnel, or that it was career military personnel who were ideologically militaristic. This last version was the initial official government interpretation of the language, and actually prevented a former admiral of the Imperial Navy from joining the Cabinet in 1954.

Today the interpretation of the language is concerned primarily with the eligibility of former SDF personnel to serve as ministers of state. Several former SDF personnel have now served as ministers of state without incident. In a 2001 response to a Diet interpellation regarding one such instance, the government reaffirmed its interpretation regarding former members of the imperial military (which would have been only of historical interest) but distinguished the SDF as a different type of military. Under the government's interpretation, the language only prevents SDF personnel on active duty from serving in cabinets and all former SDF persons satisfy the "civilian" requirement.[11]

Collective responsibility to the Diet

Paragraph (3) enhances the democratic accountability of the Cabinet, and prevents the type of situation that arose under the Meiji Constitution whereby a single minister could diverge from the rest of the Cabinet by asserting his own separate responsibility to the emperor. The practice is for all cabinet resolutions to be unanimous, but that is not an inevitable requirement of the collective responsibility mandate. It would not be clearly unconstitutional to have cabinet decisions made by a simple majority of the cabinet members, and for all of them to still be collectively responsible to the Diet. On the other hand, members are free to resign if they disagree with a decision, and the prime minister also has the power to remove dissenters (Article 68(2)), as has happened occasionally.

It is largely undisputed that "responsibility" in paragraph (3) refers to *political* responsibility rather than any sort of actionable legal liability. While the constitution, Diet practice and the political process in general provide a number of avenues by which the Diet can pursue the responsibility of the Cabinet, this does not extend to criminal or civil liability.

An interpretive issue under paragraph (3) of Article 66 arises from the reference to the Diet: does it mean that the Cabinet is responsible only to the Diet as a collective of both chambers, or to each of the chambers separately? It can and occasionally does happen that the two Diet chambers are controlled by different political parties or coalitions, so this is not an entirely theoretical question. However, since only the House of Representatives has the power to force a cabinet to resign by a vote of non-confidence under Article 69, it could be argued that ultimately the Cabinet is only responsible to that chamber. However, such an interpretation requires ignoring the clear language of the constitutional text.

The collective responsibility of the Cabinet provided for in paragraph (3) is not considered a bar against the Diet (either an individual house or acting collectively) from pursuing the responsibility of individual cabinet members. A diet chamber may do so by passing a "resolution questioning the responsibility" (*monseki ketsugi*) of individual cabinet ministers who say or do stupid things. Such resolutions are of political significance only and have no legal effect.

Article 67: Designation of Prime Minister; Priority of House of Representatives

Colin P.A. Jones

> **Article 67.**
> (1) The Prime Minister shall be designated from among the members of the Diet by a resolution of the Diet. This designation shall precede all other business.
> (2) If the House of Representatives and the House of Councillors disagree and if no agreement can be reached even through a joint committee of both Houses, provided for by law, or the House of Councillors fails to make designation within ten (10) days, exclusive of the period of recess, after the House of Representatives has made designation, the decision of the House of Representatives shall be the decision of the Diet.

Article 67 sets forth the basic mechanism for choosing the prime minister. It mandates that doing so takes precedence over all other activities of a newly-constituted Diet (i.e., immediately after a House of Representatives election).

Under the Meiji Constitution the prime minister was often not a Diet member, and the GHQ draft did not require this either. The requirement that the prime minister be chosen from the Diet membership was one of the changes added by the Far Eastern Commission late in the process.

The provisions in paragraph (2) prevent a deadlock in the event the two Diet chambers are controlled by different parties. The ability of the House of Representatives to appoint a prime minister over the objections of the House of Councillors is one of several constitutional provisions which establishes the former as the superior chamber. Note however, that while Article 67 gives the House of Representatives the final say over the selection of the prime minister, it does not actually require that he be a member of that chamber. Some scholars have argued that it is an implicit requirement of Article 67, though so far it has been an entirely academic question, since prime ministers under the current constitution have always been chosen from the House of Representatives.

Article 68: Appointment of Ministers of State by Prime Minister

Colin P.A. Jones

> **Article 68.**
> (1) The Prime Minister shall appoint the Ministers of State. However, a majority of their number must be chosen from among the members of the Diet.
> (2) The Prime Minister may remove the Ministers of State as he chooses.

Article 68 ensures the Cabinet is democratically accountable by requiring a majority of its members to be Diet members. This requirement was also added late in the drafting process at the insistence of the Far Eastern Commission. By contrast, the GHQ Draft would have required all ministers of state to be approved by the Diet, similar to the US system of Senate confirmation of presidential appointments.[12]

Although the constitution still allows for the possibility of a cabinet with a significant number of members drawn from outside the Diet, in practice such appointments are rare. Typically, all ministerial posts are filled by Diet members, usually from the House of Representatives.

Under the Meiji Constitution the prime minister lacked the ability to remove a minister of state, meaning that the only solution for irresoluble disagreement between members of a cabinet was its dissolution. Paragraph (2) of Article 68 is in essence a remedy to this deficiency since it empowers the prime minister to remove intransigent colleagues, subject to the formal requirement of attestation of the removal by the emperor under Article 7.

Since Paragraph (2) seems to leave removals to the discretion of the prime minister alone, there is academic debate over whether removals are subject to the "advice and approval" of the Cabinet which otherwise applies to acts in matters of state under Article 7. The prevailing view appears to be that the advice and approval requirement does apply, meaning that a cabinet decision is required to remove a minister, though the minister being removed would naturally not participate.

Article 69: No-Confidence Votes and Dissolution of the House of Representatives

Colin P.A. Jones

Article 69.
If the House of Representatives passes a non-confidence resolution, or rejects a confidence resolution, the Cabinet shall resign en masse, unless the House of Representatives is dissolved within ten (10) days.

Article 69 is one of the constitution's more problematic provisions, since it only clearly anticipates premature dissolutions of the House of Representatives resulting from a vote of no-confidence against the Cabinet by that chamber. In reality, dissolutions have occurred numerous times over the seven decades of the constitution's history, but only four instances were triggered by no-confidence votes.[13] The constitutional basis for other dissolutions is a matter of debate, but government practice references Article 7 as the basis in the relevant procedural documentation (see discussion at Article 7).[14]

The constitution is also silent as to who is substantively responsible for dissolution. Under Article 7 it is one of the roles of the emperor, but, given his symbolic role, it cannot be one that he has any discretion in performing. The accepted view is that the power of dissolution being vested in the Cabinet is the only logical interpretation. Some have argued that the House of Representatives could vote to dissolve itself, which would presumably be accomplished through a simple majority vote, even though it would result in all of its members losing their seats contrary to the supermajority voting requirements applicable to the expulsion of members under Article 58. The proposition has never been tested.

In the real world, decades of parliamentary practice have rendered it beyond debate that a general power to dissolve the House of Representatives exists, and is exercised by the prime minister as a political tool. That said, questions remain about whether there are any constraints on the use of the power. Timing the dissolution of the House of Representatives so that the election coincides with a triennial House of Councillors election has been criticized, but was upheld by a lower court.[15]

No-confidence/confidence resolutions must be clearly framed as such. The rejection by the Diet of a budget or bill cannot be deemed a no-confidence vote. As noted at Article 66, individual Diet houses may sometimes pass resolutions of no-confidence against individual ministers of state.

Article 70: Cabinet to Resign After Elections or Vacancy in Post of Prime Minister

Colin P.A. Jones

Article 70.
When there is a vacancy in the post of Prime Minister, or upon the first convocation of the Diet after a general election of members of the House of Representatives, the Cabinet shall resign en masse.

Article 70 makes it clear that a cabinet cannot exist without a prime minister and must resign if that is the case. Vacancies may arise through death, of course, but also due to the prime minister losing his or her status as a Diet member. It is unclear what happens if a vacancy arises due to the prime minister's resignation, though there is no logical reason why Article 70 should not apply in that situation also.

A vacancy does not arise for purposes of Article 70 merely because the prime minister is temporarily incapacitated or otherwise unavailable (due to travel abroad or other reasons). In such cases another member of the Cabinet exercises the powers pursuant to a predetermined delegation of authority to other cabinet ministers pursuant to Article 9 of the Cabinet Act. It is now common for the first cabinet minister in the line of succession to also be given the title "deputy prime minister," though this position has no constitutional or even statutory basis.

Prime ministers have died in office twice: Ōhira in 1980 and Obuchi in 2000. Ōhira died after the House of Representatives had been dissolved (during a rare "double election" timed to coincide with the House of Councillor election), resulting in temporary confusion about when the Cabinet should resign (it did the day after his death). Obuchi was suddenly incapacitated by a stroke that caused him to fall into a coma from which he never recovered; he passed away the following month.[16]

Article 71: Continuity of Cabinet until New Prime Minister Appointed

Colin P.A. Jones

Article 71.
In the cases mentioned in the two preceding articles, the Cabinet shall continue its functions until the time when a new Prime Minister is appointed.

Article 71 provides that if the Cabinet resigns for any of the reasons specified in Articles 69 or 70, it nonetheless continues to function in a caretaker capacity until a new prime minister has been appointed by the Diet. The constitution being silent on the subject, there are different theories as to the extent to which the caretaker cabinet can exercise the various powers granted under the constitution. Most scholars agree that a caretaker cabinet should not be able to take significant actions such as dissolving the House of Representatives, proposing major legislation or signing treaties. In 1947 and 1948 delays in forming a cabinet resulted in the prime ministers (Tetsu Katayama in 1947 and Shigeru Yoshida in 1948) performing the Cabinet functions alone for a period of time. To avoid this unusual result, the practice now is to appoint the prime minister and other cabinet ministers at essentially the same time.

Article 72: Duties of the Prime Minister

Colin P.A. Jones

Article 72.
The Prime Minister, representing the Cabinet, submits bills, reports on general national affairs and foreign relations to the Diet and exercises control and supervision over various administrative branches.

Proposing Legislation

The English version of Article 72 disguises the existence of a basic constitutional question: does the Cabinet actually have the ability to propose legislation to the Diet? While the English term "bill" used here is the same as in Article 59 ("A *bill* becomes a law on passage by both Houses…"), in Japanese different terms are used in the two places. In Article 59 it is "*hōritsuan,*" a very specific term literally meaning "proposed law." In Article 72 (and Article 63) the term used is *gian* which might be better translated "matter proposed for deliberation."

Thus, while the English version clearly appears to vest in the Cabinet a role in initiating legislation, the Japanese version is less clear. Compared to *hōritsuan*, *gian* is arguably a much broader term which could naturally be assumed to include legislative proposals. On the other hand, it would also not be unreasonable to expect a constitution to clearly set forth something as fundamental as a cabinet role in legislation if one was intended. After all, the Cabinet's role in submitting proposed treaties and budgets to the Diet is clearly provided for in Articles 73 and 86, respectively, despite the fact that they would also fall within the rubric of *gian*. Moreover, absent clear language simply assuming a cabinet role in the legislative process would seem inconsistent with the Article 41 designation of the Diet as the *sole* law-making organ of the state. By contrast, Article 38 of the Meiji Constitution clearly anticipated government-proposed legislation.

Nonetheless, interpretive issues relating to the "*gian*" remain, and could be potentially significant. For example, it is unclear whether it can be interpreted as allowing the Cabinet to propose constitutional amendments, particularly given the wording of Article 96 which requires amendments to initiate from the Diet.

Reporting on foreign affairs and supervising administrative branches

The English version of Article 72 also potentially misleads because it seems clear that the prime minister represents the Cabinet in all three of the functions enumerated (submitting proposals, reporting on foreign affairs and administering administrative branches). However, the Japanese version can be plausibly read so that the "representative" language applies only to submitting *gian*. Under the reading the Cabinet submits its proposals through representation by the prime minister, but the prime minister performs the other two roles independently of the Cabinet.

The generally accepted interpretation is that "representing the Cabinet" applies to all of the roles enumerated in Article 72. This interpretation has significant implications for the amount of leadership which may be exercised individually by the prime minister when it comes to the "exercise and control and supervision over various administrative branches" part of the article. In other words, can the prime minister override a minister to demand that his or her ministry take a particular course of action? Or does the "representative" language require all supervisory activities to be taken through a cabinet resolution? The interpretive question is effectively resolved through the Cabinet Act which requires the administration and supervision function to be performed in accordance with policies agreed by a unanimous Cabinet decision (*kakugi*).[17]

The question of the scope of the prime minister's ability to exercise influence over individual ministries was addressed by the Supreme Court in a 1995 judgment relating to the *Lockheed Scandal*, which involved bribery of various Japanese officials—including Prime Minister Kakuei Tanaka—to ensure the purchase of aircraft from the US aerospace company Lockheed. One of the questions addressed by the Court was whether it was within the scope of the powers and duties of the prime minister to "work on" the transport minister to secure the purchase of aircraft from a particular supplier. This question needed to be answered because Japan's penal code defined bribery in terms of influencing a government official in connection with their official duties.

The Court essentially tried to have it both ways by ruling:

> [A] *decision of a cabinet meeting is necessary for the prime minister to exercise control and supervision over various administrative branches. However, it is appropriate to construe that considering the position and the power and duties of the prime minister mentioned above, even in the absence of a decision of a cabinet meeting, the prime minister is at least entitled to give guidance and advice to various administrative agencies to deal with their tasks in accordance with given*

policies, as long as the guidance and advice of the prime minister do not infringe upon the explicit intentions of the cabinet. Therefore, it cannot be denied that the … prime minister's working on the transport minister to do as mentioned above is, generally speaking, within the power and duties of the prime minister as an instruction of the prime minister.[18]

The degree to which formal cabinet decisions are a prerequisite to the prime minister's exercise of his power to control and supervise administrative branches remains the subject of debate.

Article 73: Functions of the Cabinet

Colin P.A. Jones

Article 73.
The Cabinet, in addition to other general administrative functions, shall perform the following functions:
(i) Administer the law faithfully; conduct affairs of state.
(ii) Manage foreign affairs.
(iii) Conclude treaties. However, it shall obtain prior or, depending on circumstances, subsequent approval of the Diet.
(iv) Administer the civil service, in accordance with standards established by law.
(v) Prepare the budget, and present it to the Diet.
(vi) Enact cabinet orders in order to execute the provisions of this Constitution and of the law. However, it cannot include penal provisions in such cabinet orders unless authorized by such law.
(vii) Decide on general amnesty, special amnesty, commutation of punishment, reprieve, and restoration of rights.

Article 73 sets forth *some* of the Cabinet's constitutional responsibilities, but also refers to a largely undefined category of "other general administrative functions." Other articles of the constitution allocate additional roles to the Cabinet yet they are quite specific and thus hard to reconcile with "general administrative functions." There is thus some debate about what the expression means, which ties into the broader debate about what constitutes the "administrative (executive) power," as discussed at Article 65.

It helps to read Article 73 in comparison with the Meiji Constitution. All of the functions enumerated in Article 73 have clear corollaries in powers of the emperor under Chapter I of the Meiji charter, with the exception of the power to prepare budgets, which nonetheless implicitly resided in the emperor under its Chapter VI. In a historical context, therefore, Article 73 of the present constitution could be understood as being the result of decisions about where to relocate substantive powers of government away from the emperor. However, it would be a mistake to approach interpretation solely from this perspective.

Administer the law; conduct affairs of state

Clause (i) adds to the linguistic confusion described at Article 65. The Japanese term used to express "administer" is *shikkō*, which is typically translated "execute." Accordingly, in the Japanese version "executing the laws" is a subset of the administrative powers of the Cabinet, rather than administering the laws being part of the executive powers.

Other linguistic issues are worth noting: (i) "affairs of state" in clause (i) of Article 73 is expressed using the same Japanese term (*kokumu*) as in Article 72, where the English is "national affairs," and (ii) "conduct" does not adequately convey the nuance of the Japanese *sōri*, which might more accurately be translated over "preside over all important aspects of." It is also a component of the Japanese term used in the constitution to refer to the prime minister—*sōri daijin*.

Under some interpretations, the "conduct affairs of state" language refers to the administrative (executive) function, and may even include a component of broad political leadership. Others, however, consider the language as referring to affairs relating to the legislative and judicial functions (e.g., the signing of laws under Article 74), and ensuring that the other branches of government are able to perform their respective roles properly.

By requiring the Cabinet to faithfully execute the law, the constitution forestalls it from declining to execute laws that it disagrees with or considers unconstitutional. The Cabinet would not be required to execute laws that have been judicially determined to be unconstitutional, though there is some debate over to the extent to which the Cabinet would be bound to accept such a ruling beyond the scope of the case which resulted in that judgment.

Manage foreign affairs

Under Article 13 of the Meiji Constitution the declarations of war, cessation of hostilities and execution of treaties were imperial prerogatives, effectively vesting in the emperor (and his advisors) largely unrestricted powers to conduct Japan's foreign policy. Although Article 7 of the current constitution involves the emperor in some aspects of foreign policy (attesting the ratification of treaties and receiving ambassadors), these roles are all conducted with the advice and approval of the Cabinet, and Article 73 clearly vests substantive foreign policy powers in the Cabinet. One theory holds that the Cabinet is the country's "head of state" under international law, though in diplomatic practice this role falls to the emperor.

Conclude treaties

Treaties are discussed at Articles 61 and 98. With respect to Article 73, it should be noted that there is a tension between clauses (ii) and (iii) as to what sort of agreements with foreign countries or their governments constitute "treaties" and must be ratified by the Diet (and thus made public), and which do not and fall into the province of the Cabinet's authority to manage foreign affairs (and if necessary, can be concluded in secret). It is generally accepted that the title of the instrument is not dispositive, and also that requiring all agreements entered into with foreign nations would be unworkable. The government interpretation is that three categories of international agreements need to be submitted to the Diet for ratification:

(i) those which would have a legal effect in Japan and thus implicate the legislative powers of the Diet under Article 41; (ii) those involving financial obligations and implicating the requirement Article 65; and (iii) agreements establishing a basic relationship between Japan and another country. [19]

Administer the civil service

The English version of this clause is misleading because the Japanese term "*kanri*" would typically not be translated "civil service." In fact, it is the same term as is used in in clause (v) of Article 7, where it is rendered in English as "official." But it is also different from the term used in Article 15, which refers to "public officials" in English, and *kōmuin* in Japanese. *Kōmuin* is the standard term used to refer to government workers, including in the National Public Servant Act. By contrast, *kanri* is a somewhat archaic term rooted in the Meiji system and even older Chinese imperial terminology, but which is rarely used in statutes passed since the constitution took effect.[20]

The practical scope of *kanri* is problematic. It cannot just be a synonym for *kōmuin*, since "public officials" as used in Article 15 includes Diet members and other elected officials who could not be "administered" by the Cabinet. In addition, currently the categories of "officials" whose appointments are attested by the emperor under Article 7 include Supreme Court judges (other than the chief judge) and some high court judges. [21] But the basic principle of separation of powers would seem to make it difficult to include them in the universe of civil servants administered by the Cabinet under Article 73. A similar interpretive problem arises with judicial employees and Diet employees, even though these are generally governed by the NPSA as categories of "special" public servants. *Kanri* does not include prefectural and municipal public servants, who are referred to by a different, even more obscure term in Article 93.

Still more confusion arises in the English version due to the use of the term "administer" which in Japanese is another comparatively obscure term (*shōri*) which has nothing to do linguistically with the Japanese terms for "administration" or "execute." "Oversee" or "be responsible for" might be a closer rendering.

There is also a debate over whether *shōri* includes the power to hire and remove civil servants, which of course depends on how the term *kanri* is interpreted. An interpretation that allowed the Cabinet to remove judicial or legislative branch employees would seem problematic. In practice, much of the responsibility for the day-to-day administration of the national public service has been delegated to the National Personnel Authority—the bureaucracy which runs the bureaucracy. Under the current constitution, appointments and dismissals of most public servants is subject to the conditions set forth in the NPSA. The extremely broad legislative delegation to the National Personnel Authority of rule-making authority (including the power to establish criminal penalties for some violations) was challenged and upheld in the *Sarufutsu Case.*

Prepare the budget

This is discussed in more detail in Chapter VII, particularly Article 86.

Enact cabinet orders

The Meiji Constitution accorded the emperor broad powers to make rules—both in the form of decrees that had the force of law during national emergencies, and in the form of edicts and prescripts regarding matters that were outside the scope of Diet legislation. Although some prewar imperial edicts were converted into Cabinet orders as part of the transition to the current constitutional system and remain in force today, these are exceptional cases.

It would be a mistake to interpret clause (vi) as simply moving the emperor's authority to rule by decree to the Cabinet. In point of fact the current constitution does not vest in the Cabinet emergency powers such as those enjoyed by the emperor under Article 8 of the Meiji Constitution. The so-far unsuccessful efforts of the ruling Liberal Democratic Party to develop public support for constitutional amendment have focused heavily on the supposed need for such emergency powers, citing examples such as the March 11, 2011 earthquake/nuclear disaster and, more recently, the Covid-19 pandemic, which saw Japanese leaders at all levels of government struggle with a lack of powers to impose or enforce lockdowns and other restrictions.

While clause (vi) may appear to clearly vest rule-making powers in the Cabinet, the language must be read in conjunction with the Article 41 designation of the Diet as the *sole* law-making organ of the state. Accordingly, the ability to issue cabinet orders is limited to the extent necessary to execute laws passed by the Diet, or when there has been a legislative delegation to the Cabinet (or government agency under it) of authority to do so by the Diet. In that sense the proviso regarding the use of cabinet orders to impose criminal penalties is simply an additional limitation on the Cabinet within a framework that already imposes a prerequisite of Diet legislative action for cabinet rule-making.

The extent to which the Diet can use legislation to delegate rule-making authority (including the ability to establish criminal penalties for violations) to the Cabinet or government institutions under it has been the subject of both academic debate and constitutional litigation. In the *Sarufutsu Case*, the Supreme Court upheld the legislative delegation to the National Personnel Authority of broad powers to establish rules punishing public servants for engaging in political activities.[22]

In a number of instances, however, the Supreme Court has found the exercise of delegated powers by administrative branch authorities to have exceeded the scope of delegation. For example, in a 2013 ruling, it invalidated Ministry of Health, Labour and Welfare rules prohibiting the sale of non-prescription medicines over the Internet, on the grounds that the Pharmacy and Medical Device Act under which these rules were passed did not include any requirement that such medicines be sold in physical stores.[23]

Clause (vi) refers to both laws *and* the constitution. There is thus a remaining question as to whether the Cabinet could issue orders to implement provisions of the constitution without Diet authorization. There is in fact a single instance of this happening. In 1955 the Cabinet used a cabinet order to resuscitate in modified form the Ordinance on Medals of Honor, a prewar imperial edict governing the award of official honors.[24] The system of imperial honors had been abolished during the Allied Occupation. Its restoration was not a popular enough subject at the time to gain the support of the Diet, yet a system of honors is clearly anticipated by Article 7 of the constitution. Hence it was reinstated through a cabinet order. Constitutional scholars grumble about this, but it is the only such instance.

Note that the "execute" in clause (vi) is "*jisshi*" in Japanese. This is different from terms rendered "execute" or "executive" elsewhere in the constitution, and might be better translated "implement."

Decide on amnesties

Under Article 16 of the Meiji Constitution the power to grant amnesties and other merciful dispensations to criminals was a prerogative of the emperor.[25] Now this power is clearly vested in the Cabinet and exercised in accordance with the Amnesty Act. The Amnesty Act provides for five categories of dispensations ranging from general amnesties to restoration of rights lost due to conviction. Whatever category of dispensation is granted by the Cabinet under Clause (vii) must be attested by the emperor (Article 7(vi)).[26]

Article 74: Signature of Laws and Orders

Colin P.A. Jones

> **Article 74.**
> All laws and cabinet orders shall be signed by the competent Minister of State and countersigned by the Prime Minister.

Under the Meiji Constitution, all laws and edicts had to be countersigned by a minister of state.[27] Under the current constitution, the emperor's role is limited to promulgating laws and regulations, with signatures required from the responsible minister of state and a co-signature of the prime minister. Note that in the Japanese version it is quite clear that both signatures are "required" (*hitsuyō to suru*). However, the signature is considered necessary as an indicator of responsibility, rather than as part of the legislative process; laws passed by the Diet would have force even without ministerial signatures.

Article 74 is silent on the subject of whether ministerial signatures are also required for treaties or proposed constitutional amendments. The government does not appear to have developed a firm position, though ministers and the prime minister do sign at least some treaties and conventions.

Article 75: Ministers of State Immune from Prosecution

Colin P.A. Jones

> **Article 75.**
> The Ministers of State, during their tenure of office, shall not be subject to legal action without the consent of the Prime Minister. However, the right to take that action is not impaired hereby.

Article 75 is intended to both preserve the unity of the Cabinet and protect it from politically-motivated prosecutions. While the use of the English term "legal action" suggests ministers of state are immune from civil actions during their tenure, the Japanese term used (*sotsui*) refers only to criminal actions. There is some uncertainty as to whether it refers only to prosecutions or also includes arrest and detention as well. A 1959 Tokyo High Court case held that the 1948 arrest and detention of a member of the Ashida Cabinet did not violate Article 75, but this ruling is open to criticism and the Supreme Court has not made any definitive rulings on the subject. [28]

There is debate about whether the prime minister must have a valid reason for refusing to consent to legal action, or whether he is free to exercise the power for any reason. Under the latter view he is subject only to the political consequences of refusing to consent. [29]

A potentially critical ambiguity in Article 75 is that it leaves unclear whether "Minister of State" includes the prime minister. On the one hand it is ridiculous to expect the prime minister to consent to his own prosecution, since interpreting the constitution in this way would effectively give the prime minister total immunity. On the other, it would be odd for the prime minister to be more susceptible to criminal prosecutions than other cabinet members.[30]

Notes

1 *See, e.g.*, Watanabe, T. (2016, June 9). *Abe Shushō no "Rippōfu no Chō" hatsugen ga Kokkai gijiroku kara kesareru* [Prime Minister Abe's "Head of the Legislative Branch" statement stricken from Diet record]. Retrieved June 30, 2022, from https://news.yahoo.co.jp/byline/watanabeteruhito/20160609-00058635. He made a similar statement again in 2018. Asahi Shimbun. (2018, November 2). "'*Watashi wa rippōfu no chō' mata iimachigae, chokugo ni shazai.* [Prime Minister Abe 'I am the head of the legislative branch' gaffe again, apologizes immediately]." Retrieved June 29, 2022, from https://www.asahi.com/articles/ASLC23T54LC2UTFK00S.html.

2 Those who have just finished diligently reading the discussion of Chapter IV would likely struggle to answer the question "who is the head of the legislative branch in Japan?" because constitutionally there is no such position, just the presidents of the individual Diet chambers.

3 Ministers of state are also mentioned in Article 54 of the Meiji Constitution, which states that they may "take seats and speak in either House [of the Imperial Diet]."

4 Kokka Gyōsei Soshiki Hō [National Administrative Organization Act], Law no. 120 of 1948.

5 Zaimushō Setchi Hō [Ministry of Finance Establishment Act], Law no. 95 of 199; Keisatsuhō [Police Act], Law no. 162 of 1954.

6 Naikaku Hōseikyoku Setchihō [Cabinet Legislation Bureau Establishment Act], Law no. 252 of 1952, Article 3.

7 *The Mainichi*. (2020, May 13). *No records kept on meetings about extending Japan Prosecutors' Retirement.* Retrieved June 29, 2022, from https://mainichi.jp/english/articles/20200513/p2a/00m/0na/004000c.

8 The National Personnel Authority which oversees the entirety of the national public service, should not be confused with the Cabinet Personnel Bureau, which exercises centralized control over top level management positions in the administrative branch.

9 NPSA, Articles 9, 194

10 Under the Meiji system, the emperor had two types of officials—military officials (*bukan*) and civil officials (*bunkan*)—but not a term to distinguish the military from the non-military outside the scope of officialdom. The "*bu*" in "*bukan*" is also a component of various military terms, as well as the "force" (*buryoku*) in paragraph (1) of Article 9. The more generic term for military personnel is "*gunjin*" which includes the element *gun* (army). *Gun* is a component of the "forces" in "land, sea and air forces" proscribed by paragraph (2) of Article 9. The inability to use traditional terminology—even in opposition to a term like "civilian"—is thus a penumbra of the constraints imposed by Article 9.

11 The House of Representatives, Japan. (2001, May 22). *Cabinet response to House of Representatives question 151 No. 66*. Shugiin.go.jp. Retrieved June 29, 2022, from https://www.shugiin.go.jp/internet/itdb_shitsumon.nsf/html/shitsumon/b151066.htm.

[12] GHQ Draft, Article LXI.
[13] The four instances occurred in 1949 and 1953 (causing the downfall of the second and fourth Yoshida cabinets), 1980 (the Ōhira Cabinet) and 1992 (the Miyazawa Cabinet). All four involved a non-confidence resolution; there have been no instances of a dissolution occurring due to the Diet's refusal to pass a confidence resolution.
[14] Matsui, S. (2011), 101.
[15] Nagoya High Court judgment of March 25, 1987 (unreported).
[16] Until a new prime minister (Yoshirō Mori) was appointed on April 5, the functions of prime minister were exercised by Chief Cabinet Secretary Mikio Aoki, whom Obuchi supposedly named as his proxy immediately before losing consciousness, a scenario regarded with incredulity by many at the time.
[17] Cabinet Act, Article 6.
[18] Supreme Court, Grand Bench Decision of February 22, 1995. English translation available at: Courts in Japan. (n.d.). *Details of 1987 (a) 1351: Judgments of the Supreme Court.* Retrieved June 29, 2022, from https://www.courts.go.jp/app/hanrei_en/detail?id=194. Note that Tanaka had already passed away by the time the Court rendered this judgment, which was rendered in connection with the trials of Japanese company executives implicated in the bribery scandal.
[19] Statement of Foreign Minister Ōhira to House of Coucillors Foreign Affairs Committee, February 20, 1974.
[20] The NPSA only uses the term in its "purpose" clause to reference Article 63(i), and in references to the titles of imperial edicts relating to the public service that predate the new constitutional system.
[21] In addition, Article 46 of the Courts Act renders persons "incompetent to be appointed ordinary government officials [*kanri*] according to other laws" ineligible to be judges, suggesting judges may be a "special" category of *kanri* (as was the case under the Meiji system).
[22] Supreme Court, Grand Bench judgment of November 6, 1974. The Court revisited the question in a 2012 judgment in which it upheld the punishment of a low level national public servant for the crime of distributing communist party literature in his free time. Supreme Court, 2nd Petty Bench judgment of December 7, 2012.
[23] Supreme Court, 2nd Petty Bench judgment of January 11, 2013.
[24] Hōshō Jōrei [Ordinance on Medals of Honor], Grand Council of State order No. 63 of 1881, available at: *Meiji Jūyonen Dajōkan Fukoku Dai Rokujūnigō (Hōshō Jōrei).* E-Gov. (n.d.). Retrieved June 29, 2022, from https://elaws.e-gov.go.jp/document?lawid=114DF0000000063.
[25] The Meiji Constitution does not mention reprieves, however.
[26] Amnesties remain closely tied to the imperial system in that widespread amnesties and commutations have been a feature of major transitions in the imperial family, such as dynastic changes or the marriage of the crown prince.
[27] Meiji Constitution, Article 55(2).
[28] Tokyo High Court, 26 December 1959, *Hanrei jihō* 213, 46. The interpretation of Article 75 could potentially result in different cabinet members being treated differently depending upon whether they are Diet members as well (and thus protected by the immunities granted by Articles 50 and 51). Arguably the best construction of Article 75 would be one which results in Cabinet Members all being treated the same.
[29] Note also that the proviso in the second sentence of Article 75 is thought to result in any applicable statute of limitations being tolled during the relevant period. Whether the tolling applies throughout a Minister's tenure, or only commences from the time the prime minister refuses to consent to prosecution is a subject of debate.
[30] Around the time that it seemed possible that Ichirō Ozawa, once head of the Democratic Party of Japan, might become prime minister, despite being doggedly pursued by prosecutors for allegedly misreporting political donations, it seemed possible that the interpretation might assume serious importance. In an August 2010 *Yomiuri Shinbun* article, a source within the prosecutorial agency was reported as expressing the view that consent would not be required to prosecute the prime minister if it had been authorized by the Prosecutorial Review Commission (an institution composed of randomly-selected citizens and empowered to overturn prosecutorial decisions not to prosecute). This article is referenced in: Okuyama, T. (2010, August 30). *Sōridaijin no sotsui wa dekiruka? Ozawa-shi no daihyōsen shutsuba de kenpō giron* [Can the Prime Minister be prosecuted? Constitutional debate from Mr. Ozawa's candidacy for party leadership]. Asahi Judiciary. Retrieved June 29, 2022, from https://webronza.asahi.com/judiciary/articles/2710083000001.html Ozawa was prosecuted as the result of a decision by the Prosecutorial Review Commission but acquitted at trial in 2012. He never became prime minister.

Chapter VI
The Judiciary
Articles 76–82

Introduction

Giorgio Fabio Colombo and *Mark Levin*

Historical overview

Though civil and criminal adjudicatory processes had operated in Japan for centuries, the roots of the present-day court system in Japan can be traced back to 1872, when an ordinance from the newly-established Ministry of Justice created a national court structure in the country. Other early Meiji innovations, such as the establishment in 1875 of a Great Court of Cassation (*Daishin'in*) based on the French Cassation, contributed to the shaping of the court system.[1] With the passage in 1896 of the Court Organization Law,[2] heavily influenced by German models, the Japanese judicial system gained its modern features at the same time as the other features of government under the Meiji constitutional system took shape.[3]

In the Meiji Constitution, Chapter V was devoted to "The Judicature," while in the current constitution, Chapter VI deals with "The Judiciary." The Japanese term (*shihō*) used is the same in both texts, meaning the difference is primarily one of changing the English to match a more contemporary (and possibly American) reading. Under the Meiji system the Ministry of Justice was named the *shihōshō*, as it administered the justice system, including the courts.[4] The overlap of the judiciary and the executive was thus a feature of the Meiji system.

As discussed later in this chapter, the highly bureaucratic organization of the Japanese judiciary born under the Meiji reforms may still be observed in contemporary Japan, and continued close ties and cooperation between the judiciary and the Ministry of Justice is a key element in understanding how the Japanese judicial system operates today.

Consistent with the idea of a state centered around the emperor which was the foundation of the Meiji Constitution, and the attendant rejection of any fundamental separation of powers, the Judiciary was not a fully autonomous governmental organ. This is clear from Article 57, which reads "The Judicature shall be exercised by the Courts of Law according to law in the name of the Emperor." Moreover, perhaps more importantly for practical purposes, judges were subject to the administrative authority of the Ministry of Justice. Remedying this was a matter of primary concern for both Allied and Japanese reformers involved with drafting the current constitution, as evidenced in several provisions of the document.[5]

Under the Meiji system, the consistency of jurisprudence in Japanese courts was supervised from above by the Great Court of Cassation. In that capacity the Court served as a "judge of judgments," and was the court of final instance entrusted with checking the correctness of reasoning and application of the law by the lower courts. The Meiji Constitution (Article 61) also allowed for administrative courts, specifically devoted to disputes between the subjects and the state administration, subject to different regulations and involving different personnel than the regular courts.

Both these features were removed under the present constitution due to the American influence on reshaping judicial organization during the Occupation; the Great Court of Cassation was replaced by the Supreme Court loosely modeled on the US corollary and part of an entirely separate judiciary, and the system of administrative courts system abolished. The Court Organization Act was replaced with the Court Act of 1947.

Hanrei: *Japanese courts and* stare decisis

Similar to the European continental models from which the system was primarily derived, Japanese law rejects the principle of *stare decisis*; precedents (*hanrei*)—including those of the Supreme Court—are not formally a source of law.[6] As noted at Article 41 the Diet is "the sole law-making organ of the State." That said, however, just as in other Civil law countries, the importance of case decisions—particularly those coming from the highest judicial body in the land—cannot be underestimated. In some instances, importance may be accorded by statute. For example, under the principal procedural codes, the failure of a lower court judgment to follow a precedent from the Supreme Court—or other higher courts—may constitute grounds for appeals.[7] Even the Supreme Court itself has to follow its own decisions insofar as Petty Benches are not allowed to change prior decisions issued by the Court sitting in its Grand Bench composition (see Article 79 below). Moreover, Supreme Court judgments in particular are an important subject of study for law students.

On one hand, while not fully binding *de jure*, judgments of higher courts are most often *de facto* faithfully observed by lower courts.[8] On the other hand, the ability of lower courts to disregard prior decisions allows for judicial innovation to happen also at the lower levels in the administration of justice. Thus, even lower court decisions are often studied and referenced as useful examples of interpretation of specific provisions of law or applications in novel cases, particularly when the Supreme Court has not addressed the matter. Both these opposing and symmetrical phenomena confer a significant role to the judiciary in the evolution of the law of Japan.

What's not in the constitution

There have been few judicial decisions interpreting provisions of Chapter VI. Nor are the role of precedent or other distinctive features of the judiciary and its function readily apparent from the text of the constitution. These must be discerned from statutes such as the Court Act, the procedural codes and the practice of judicial administration.

As we shall see, the constitution only provides for some basic principles regarding the organization and role of the judiciary. The only court explicitly mentioned in the constitutional text is the Supreme Court, and the only judge its chief judge. The detailed organization of the judiciary is left to the law, and to the internal regulatory power of the judiciary itself: in this latter regard, the Supreme Court is vested with significant tasks and prerogatives (see Article 77).

The Japanese judicial organization is the fascinating product of a system squarely rooted in the continental legal tradition, and largely influenced by German and other continental European models, which had been transformed by the injections of elements coming from the American experience. More recently, the system has been substantially revisited following the deliberations and recommendations of the Justice System Reform Council at the turn of the millennium.[9]

The result is indeed very interesting for the scholar of comparative law, but may be to some extent puzzling, especially for students and practitioners from common law jurisdictions. Unlike in the common law system where most judges are appointed from the ranks of experienced lawyers and may serve their entire judicial tenure in the same court, nearly all Japanese judges are career professionals who spend most of their working life in the judiciary in various places and roles: they are effectively a specialized form of bureaucrats (as is the case in some continental legal systems also). The procedural system, especially in civil matters, features hybridized American influences, but is still modeled primarily after the inquisitorial tradition of continental Europe.

Philosophical role of judges

In 1999, the Cabinet established the Justice System Reform Council, a body whose purpose was "defining the role of judicature in Japan in the 21st century." The Council, chaired by a famous and highly respected professor of constitutional law, proposed many initiatives to detach Japan from its traditional continental model (such as the reform of legal education, the strengthening of ADR, etc.).

However, notwithstanding these recent reforms, the Japanese judiciary is still firmly set in the civil law tradition. Judges—the ones who have passed the national bar exam, at least—are perceived as a bureaucratic elite:[10] they mostly start their careers soon after completing their studies, most spend their entire professional life in the judiciary, and they are not supposed to actively engage in legal debate, but rather to apply the law. To use a French expression liked by comparative lawyers, the judge is *la bouche de la loi* ("the mouth of the law"): they are supposed to *interpret* and *apply* the law, but not to *create* it. This representation, however, fails to fully convey the complexity of the role of the judiciary in Japan: in spite of a very conservative image, and somehow in contrast with the black letter rule of the monopoly of legislative power on the Diet, Japanese judges—not only at the Supreme Court level—do indeed create, if not laws, norms, and their role is fundamental in the developing of the legal system.[11]

Yet, the judiciary has been criticized, especially in recent years, for its detachment from the general public: judgments are still written in a fairly obscure, esoteric jargon; judges are said to be "detached from the society" and as such unaware of the problems common people encounter in their daily lives. Irrespective of the validity of these criticisms, it must be remembered that these features are not the fruit of mistakes on the Japanese legislator, but rather intended elements of a system designed by jurists for jurists: Japanese judges do not write judgment for the lay people, but for their fellow judges and for lawyers. A certain degree of insulation is not undesirable when judges have just to apply the law: it is indeed the legislator who has to feel the pulse of societal needs and amend regulations if appropriate.

As a part of the millennial reforms, the idea of bringing justice closer to the general public moved to counter the traditional idea of the judge-bureaucrat in Japan: there is a push for judgments to use a more accessible language; enhancing the diversity of background in prospective judges was a key element of the law school reform; the introduction of the lay-judge system (*saiban'in seido*) had the primary purpose of enabling ordinary citizens to see and understand the inner working of the legal system.

Article 76: The Judicial Power

Giorgio Fabio Colombo and *Mark Levin*

Article 76.

(1) The whole judicial power is vested in a Supreme Court and in such inferior courts as are established by law.

(2) No extraordinary tribunal shall be established, nor shall any organ or agency of the Executive be given final judicial power.

(3) All judges shall be independent in the exercise of their conscience and shall be bound only by this Constitution and the laws.

The judicial power

In order to understand the boundaries of the judicial power granted by the constitution to the Supreme Court and to the inferior courts established by law, one needs indeed to look at the statutory framework regulating the court system. In this regard, the Court Act plays a fundamental role. Article 3(1) of the Act states "Courts shall, except as specifically provided for in the Constitution of Japan, decide all legal disputes, and have such other powers as are specifically provided for by law." For most practical purposes this has come to define the scope of the judicial power.

The limits of the judicial power

While the constitution does not clearly define the scope of the judicial power, there are cases and theories which point to some of its limits, some of which have been imposed in case decisions by the judiciary itself. First there are the matters which the constitution clearly locates elsewhere, such as the resolution of disputes involving the qualifications of Diet members and impeachment trials (see Articles 55 and 64).

The "all legal disputes" language of Article 3 of the Court Act is understood as confirming a "case or controversy" requirement in the exercise of the judicial power. It is not possible to bring an action for the purposes of ascertaining constitutionality on its own: a party must have an actual, justiciable case involving infringement of a right. This principle has been affirmed in the *National Police Reserve* case in which the Supreme Court avoided ruling on the constitutionality of the precursor to Japan's Self-Defense Forces by ruling it had no power to rule on abstract issues of constitutionality.[12]

Next, based on general principles of international law recognized by the Supreme Court (and its predecessor) foreign diplomats are generally not subject to the jurisdiction of Japanese courts.[13] Within the context of the Japan-US defense treaty, Japan has ceded to the US primary judicial jurisdiction over US personnel and property in Japan. In the *Sunagawa Case* the Supreme Court declined to involve itself in disputes over the constitutionality of US forces in Japan. [14] Perhaps not coincidentally, the Court has never ruled on the constitutionality of Japan's own Self-Defense Forces (see discussion at Article 9).

In the *Tomabechi Case*, the Court avoided becoming involved in questions about the authority to dissolve the House of Representatives (see also discussions at Articles 7 and 69). The Court has also refused to involve itself in the internal disputes of Diet chambers, and while it has not been litigated, academic theory holds that courts would similarly be unable to intervene in cabinet proceedings. Where the Diet or the Cabinet is given discretion to make decisions by the constitution or a law, courts will generally not second guess decisions made within the scope of that discretion. The Supreme Court has been particularly deferential to legislative discretion in numerous contexts.

Finally, the Court has sometimes in the past refused to get involved in disputes involving the internal affairs of certain types of communities or organizations to the extent they do not affect outsiders in society at large. Called the "partial society theory" (*bubunshakairon*), the Court has applied this logic to disputes involving such diverse groupings as municipal assemblies, religious corporations and political parties, though not always consistently and not without criticism at the lack of any constitutional founding for this form of timidity.[15]

Courts established by the law

The first paragraph of Article 76 prevents the establishment of courts of special jurisdiction or free-standing administrative law courts outside the system headed by the Supreme Court. However, paragraph (2) anticipates the possibility of a preliminary adjudication by "administrative organs" (but these are not "courts").

With this it is clear that the judiciary is a separate and self-standing branch of government, as such not under the control of the executive. However, as discussed *infra*, there are many points of contact and friction between the judiciary and the executive branch. The issue of political independence of the Japanese judges has been one of the most debated points in the legal scholarship on Japan.[16] Judicial autonomy is also a topic of interest to lawyers and other practitioners.

Article 76 is clear in its purpose of consolidating the entire judicial power under the Supreme Court and inside a system of tribunals created legislatively. Its drafters chose to abolish the separate administrative court system which existed under the Meiji Constitution. No longer would the government enjoy the privilege of having disputes with it resolved in a forum it controlled. Article 76 explicitly forbids the creation of "extraordinary tribunals," such as courts martial (which would be potentially problematic under Article 9 also), and deprives the executive of any final adjudicative authority.

The structure of the judicial system

The details of the organization and regulation of the court system are provided for in the Court Act, which establishes the following four-tier hierarchy: First at the top there is the Supreme Court (*Saikō saibansho*), which is discussed in more detail at Article 79. Below it are the eight high courts (*kōtō saibansho*), some of which have branches, including a special branch for intellectual property disputes: the Intellectual Property High Court (*Chiteki-zaisan kōtō saibansho*), attached to the Tokyo High Court. Under the high courts, there are fifty district courts (*chihō saibansho*), one in each of Japan's 47 prefectures (except for Hokkaidō prefecture, which has four due to its size). These also have 203 branches to ensure coverage of the entire territory of Japan. Also immediately below the high courts there are the family courts (*katei saibansho*) which are distributed geographically in the same fashion as district courts. At the bottom, under the district courts are a total of 438 summary courts (*kan'i saibansho*).

While high courts also have "original" jurisdiction in certain specific types of cases (e.g., electoral disputes), they mainly serve as appellate fora for decisions by lower courts, and the court of final appeal for cases originating from summary courts.

One feature which often surprises the American-trained lawyer is that on the first level of appeal, the appellate court (which is usually the high court, or a district court in the case of appeals from a summary court) can re-evaluate the evidence, entertain new evidence, and modify the findings of fact.

The initial jurisdiction for most types of civil, criminal, and administrative cases rests with the district courts. Minor civil claims and petty crimes which constitute the majority of the judiciary's criminal caseload are first heard by the summary courts, and domestic disputes (including inheritance) and juvenile criminal cases initiate in the family courts.

Independence and freedom of conscience

The last paragraph of Article 76 relates to one of the most intensely debated issues on the subject of the Japanese judiciary: the independence of the judiciary. Opinions on the subject vary greatly: some scholars argue that the Japanese judges enjoy a decent level of independence, even if it is not perfect.[17] Some see issues but do not construe them as problems, but rather as a *feature*.[18] Still others underline the failings in a system which allows for a certain degree of political interference in the judiciary.[19] In any case, the debate here is not yet settled.[20]

In considering the debate it is important to distinguish between the independence of the judiciary from other branches of government (the Cabinet or the Diet), and the independence of individual judges *within* the judiciary (i.e., the judicial hierarchy and the bureaucracy that administers it); some accounts conflate the two. Pragmatically speaking, the latter investigation is probably more significant, since the judicial bureaucracy has various ways of deftly steering the behavior of judges. Given the language of Article 76, there are arguably constitutional dimensions to there being influences other than law and conscience affecting the outcome of trials.

When it comes to straightforward political interference the judiciary has long fought for its autonomy from other parts of the government: this has been established as early as 1891, when the President of the Great Court of Cassation rejected the pressure of the government to render a judgment based on an unreasonable interpretation of the law in order to impose a suitably harsh punishment in a diplomatically sensitive case.[21] Shortly after the new constitution was established, the new Supreme Court also stood up to the legislative branch in the *Urawa Incident*, discussed at Article 62.[22]

However, the matter is significantly more complicated when the pressure on a judge is exerted from inside the judiciary, even for political reasons, through instrumental mechanisms of administrative control.[23] This happened, for example, in the *Naganuma Nike Case*,[24] which involved a dispute over the constitutionality of an SDF missile base being constructed in Hokkaidō (see discussion at Article 9).

The initial trial was heard at the Sapporo District Court and the chief judge of that court, Kenta Hiraga, wrote a letter to the judge presiding over the case, Shigeo Fukushima, captioned as "friendly advice from a senior colleague" not to issue a judgment declaring the proposed base unconstitutional.[25] Fukushima ignored him, holding for the plaintiffs, and then going public with the memo. Hiraga received a formal warning from the Supreme Court for his ostensible interference, but his career otherwise continued on an upwards trajectory. [26] Fukushima, whose ruling of unconstitutionality was overturned on appeal, was sternly admonished for having been open with the matter and then posted to various provincial cities for a period of twelve years before he ultimately resigned from the courts.[27] The so-called "Hiraga Letter" remains a piece of Japanese constitutional history, and the incident illustrates the tension between the ideal expressed in Article 76(3)—that judges are bound only by the law and their conscience—and the reality of being a judge within a large bureaucracy. Known instances of outright interference such as this have been rare. However, the institutional design of the Japanese judiciary empowered through the constitutional language of Article 77 discussed below, and the laws and regulations effectuating Article 77's provisions grant judges in administrative roles the ability to capably transmit their views on the correct way to address both organizational *and substantive* matters in both open and covert manners.

The career path of judges and the ability of judicial administrators to influence it is thus another area where institutional or political positions and pressures may come into play. Given the ample discretion the Supreme Court's *jimusōkyoku* (General Secretariat) enjoys in dealing with appointments, confirmation, and transfers, some scholars have argued that employment tools may be used to reward compliant judges and punish rebellious ones.[28] This will be discussed at Article 80.

Finally, notwithstanding the language of paragraph (3) of Article 76, the constitution is understood to permit the use of juries or other systems of lay participation in helping decide the outcome of trials. This is discussed in more detail at Article 32.

Article 77: The Supreme Court's Regulatory Power

Giorgio Fabio Colombo

Article 77.

(1) The Supreme Court is vested with the rule-making power under which it determines the rules of procedure and of practice, and of matters relating to attorneys, the internal discipline of the courts and the administration of judicial affairs.

(2) Public procurators shall be subject to the rule-making power of the Supreme Court.

(3) The Supreme Court may delegate the power to make rules for inferior courts to such courts.

Article 77 provides the Supreme Court of Japan with a number of significant powers relating to the functioning of the whole judicial system. Its regulatory prerogatives extend to the courts as legal institutions, but also judges and public prosecutors and even to attorneys.[29]

No provisions comparable to Article 77 existed in the Meiji text and administration of the courts was left to the Ministry of Justice. The rationale behind the provision's inclusion in the present constitution was to enhance the autonomy of the judiciary and of the judicial process in general and to enable the courts to administer themselves. While the Court has not actually exercised its rule-making powers to regulate lawyers and prosecutors (other than within the scope of the trial process), that it could do so (maybe) establishes that *they* cannot regulate the Court or judges. As noted in the Introduction to Chapter VI, under the Meiji system judges were subject to administration by prosecutors.

A side effect of this broad rule-making authority is that the courts can regulate matters central to the administration of justice and as such potentially capable of infringing on people's rights. In this regard, the scope of the regulatory power of the Supreme Court had been debated in the past, as several commentators had argued that such power could not extend to invade the sphere of the legislator (under the principle known as "statutory priority" or "statutory reserve") by creating rules on key matters such as procedural guarantees in criminal trial. The idea is that the internal matters pertaining to the administration of judicial affairs and the discipline of the courts are reserved to the regulatory powers of the Supreme Court.[30] This seems to be the prevailing (and correct) opinion, though it is not clear which specific issues could be otherwise considered outside the scope of the Supreme Court's purview.[31]

Despite this grant, the principal source of procedural rules comes in the form of laws such as the Code of Civil Procedure and the Code of Criminal Procedure. As to the judicial system, the Court Act also establishes some of the basic rules regarding the functioning of the courts. Nevertheless, the Supreme Court plays a pivotal role in structuring and managing the operations of courts around the country.[32] In this sense it is important to understand that in addition to being a court (or rather several courts, comprised of three Petty Benches of five judges each and the Grand Bench when they sit *en banc*), the Supreme Court is also a bureaucracy devoted to administering the court system nationwide (and administering the Legal Training and Research Institute where lawyers, judges and prosecutors are trained).

As a bureaucracy the Supreme Court is much larger than the 15 judges who sit on the benches, consisting of the administrators who oversee the bureaucracy (primarily judges) as well as thousands of other court employees. The nerve center of the bureaucracy is the *Saikō saibansho jimusōkyoku* (General Secretariat of the Supreme Court). Within the General Secretariat there are three sections and seven bureaus, which together handle the administrative side of the judiciary (e.g., financing, relations with the public, etc.) The General Secretariat is responsible for drafting regulations that are then approved by the Supreme Court Judicial Assembly.

The "contempt" power in Japanese courtrooms

Japanese judges lack the broad contempt powers of their common law counterparts. A specific statute—the Act on Preserving Order in Courtrooms—empowers judges to impose penal fines or terms of imprisonment on persons disrupting the order of the courtroom.[33] Since these sanctions are imposed summarily in the course of unrelated proceedings, some of the procedural protections of Chapter III are implicated. In a 1958 decision, however, the Grand Bench rejected challenges based on Articles 32, 33, 34 and 37 of the constitution, finding the punishments under the Act to be of a special character, existing outside the realm of both criminal and administrative sanctions.[34]

Article 78: Removal of Judges and Disciplinary Measures

Giorgio Fabio Colombo

> **Article 78.**
> Judges shall not be removed except by public impeachment unless judicially declared mentally or physically incompetent to perform official duties. No disciplinary action against judges shall be administered by any executive organ or agency.

Overview

As is common in most countries, judges in Japan enjoy a high degree of job security. Those who become judges by passing the national bar exam normally enter the ranks of the judiciary just after completing their training and either leave mid-career voluntarily to become lawyers or notaries, or retire at the statutory retirement age, which for most judges is 65.[35]

The Court Act expands on the protections accorded to judges under the constitution. Under Article 48 of the Act, judges may not be removed, transferred, reassigned, suspended or subjected to reductions in compensation against their will. In reality a judicial career—a successful one at least—involves regular reassignments to different geographic locations, courts and posts, one of the features of administration by the Supreme Court's General Secretariat that subjects judges to subtle control.

There are four instances in which a judge may be forced to leave the bench before retirement age: First, in the case of Supreme Court judges only, when they are removed through the electoral process described at Article 79 (which has never happened); Second, in the case of lower court judges only, if they are not reappointed after the expiry of their ten-year term of appointment (see Article 80); Third, when they are judicially declared to be mentally or physically incompetent (see discussion below). The fourth is impeachment by the Judge Impeachment Court established in the Diet under Article 64. Article 78 thus shields individual judges from intervention from the executive branch,[36] and restricts the scope of intervention from the legislative branch and even the judicial branch itself.

Impeachment

The impeachment procedure is regulated by the Judge Impeachment Act. Under that law it may be activated "externally," by a member of the general public filing a petition to impeach a judge with the Judge Impeachment Court (see Article 64). Impeachments may also be generated "internally" from within the judiciary, since the law also requires the chief judges of high, district and family courts to notify the Supreme Court if they become aware of any impeachable behavior by judges below them, and for the Supreme Court to petition the impeachment court if it is aware of grounds for doing so.[37] Grounds for impeachment are vaguely defined: "significant breach of professional obligations or gross neglect in the performance of duties" or "misconduct significantly unbecoming a judge, whether or not in the scope of official duties."[38]

An impeachment petition is first evaluated by the Judge Impeachment Committee, which is composed of ten members of the House of Representatives and ten of the House of Councillors. The Committee investigates the matter in non-public proceedings, and if it finds the claim to be grounded, it moves to impeach the judge. If two-thirds or more of the members vote in favor of prosecution, the case is then transferred to a Judge Impeachment Court, composed by seven members of the House of Representatives and seven of the House of Councillors, and it is tried publicly. The procedure is closed by a decision on whether or not to remove the impeached judge: if a majority of more than two-thirds of the members of the Court decide to remove, the judge is immediately expelled from the judiciary. Removal through impeachment renders a judge who has passed the bar exam ineligible to register as an attorney.[39] They are, however, allowed to file a request to recover their qualification (Article 38), either after five years or when new evidence is found.[40] Judgments of the Court are published.

While many petitions to impeach judges are filed, the number resulting in prosecutions are few, and those resulting in removal even fewer (seven instances as of the time of writing).[41] Cases resulting in removal have involved judges accepting gifts in the forms of golf clubs and tailor-made suits from a party, solicitation of underage prostitutes, and stalking female court employees.[42]

Incapacity and disciplinary measures

Article 78 clearly states judges can be removed if they are incapacitated. It also implicitly anticipates disciplinary action (short of "removal") against judges is possible, just not by executive organs and agencies. This prerogative is reserved to the judiciary itself, pursuant to the Judges Status Act, which establishes the procedures for disciplinary actions against judges as well as for finding them mentally or physically incapable of performing their duties.[43]

The disciplinary procedure is not an alternative to the impeachment described above, but may be a precursor.[44]

Judges who commit inappropriate acts may be subject to disciplinary trials. These trials are conducted behind closed doors at the high court having jurisdiction over the judge in which the Court sits if a lower court, or the Supreme Court if a judge of a high court. The judge does not lose their status, and the punishment in itself it is very mild—an admonishment[45] or an administrative fine of 10,000 yen or less, But the matter is actually quite serious and may attract significant media attention. As discussed at Article 80, judges in Japan are elite public servants of considerably prestigious social standing; as such, they are considered bound to higher standards of conduct than ordinary citizens.[46]

Article 79: The Supreme Court

Giorgio Fabio Colombo

Article 79.

(1) The Supreme Court shall consist of a Chief Judge and such number of judges as may be determined by law; all such judges excepting the Chief Judge shall be appointed by the Cabinet.

(2) The appointment of the judges of the Supreme Court shall be reviewed by the people at the first general election of members of the House of Representatives following their appointment, and shall be reviewed again at the first general election of members of the House of Representatives after a lapse of ten (10) years, and in the same manner thereafter.

(3) In cases mentioned in the foregoing paragraph, when the majority of the voters favors the dismissal of a judge, he shall be dismissed.

(4) Matters pertaining to review shall be prescribed by law.

(5) The judges of the Supreme Court shall be retired upon the attainment of the age as fixed by law.

(6) All such judges shall receive, at regular stated intervals, adequate compensation which shall not be decreased during their terms of office.

Composition of the Supreme Court

The Supreme Court is composed of 14 judges and the chief judge. While the judges are appointed by the Cabinet, the chief judge is formally appointed directly by the emperor, subject to the advice and approval of the Cabinet (see discussion at Article 6). In practice the chief judge may play a significant role in advising the Cabinet as to which candidates to appoint to the other judgeships.

According to the Court Act, to be eligible to be a judge on the Supreme Court, a candidates must be over the age of forty and at least ten of the judges must have the requisite years of experience as a judge, lawyer, prosecutor and/or law professor.[47] As of July 2021, only three justices on the Court were women and in the whole history of the Supreme Court, only seven women judges have served, accounting for just 4 percent of all Japanese Supreme Court judges. Hisako Takahashi was the first woman to be appointed, in 1994.

Justices on Japan's Supreme Court who were appointed from within the judiciary have often spent only a portion of their careers as judges in adjudicating cases, but instead spent a significant portion of their careers in administrative and management roles in the courts or on secondment to other parts of the government. [48]

Moreover, not all Supreme Court judges have previously been judges. Appointments are made not only from the ranks of the three branches of the legal profession that pass the national bar exam (*hōsō*—some judges and public prosecutors, and attorneys), but also academia and the upper bureaucracy. In fact, there has developed an unwritten system of allocating seats among these constituencies that has been kept roughly in place since a conservative ideological shift was achieved in 1973. Former judges dominate (typically accounting for about six seats, including the chief judge), former prosecutors (two, currently three), lawyers (four, who are frequently former presidents of one of the larger bar associations), legal scholars (one) and bureaucrats (two, one of whom is often a former diplomat to ensure the Court is equipped with expertise on public international law).[49] As Professor Lawrence Repeta has noted, "lifetime government employees hold a commanding ten-to-five majority on the Grand Bench, along with majorities on each of the three Petty Benches."[50]

Whatever route is taken, an appointment as a Supreme Court judge represents the apex of any legal career. However, Supreme Court judges are subject to mandatory retirement at the age of 70, and since in practice all appointments are of people in their mid-sixties (the statutory retirement age for judges, prosecutors and other public servants generally ranging from 60–65), the judges have fairly short tenures of about five years. [51]

The Supreme Court consists of three in Petty Benches (*shōhōtei*—literally "small courtroom"), each composed of five judges and the Grand Bench (*daihōtei*—"large courtroom") where all fifteen members sit *en banc*. Whether a case is heard by a Petty Bench or the Grand Bench is set forth in the Court Act (Article 10) and supplemented by Supreme Court Regulations: a Petty Bench may not consider cases that (1) require a determination of the constitutionality of a law, order, rule or disposition (unless the question has already been dealt with by the Grand Bench and the Petty Bench intends to follow the precedent); (2) when a law, order, rule or order is to be decided as unconstitutional, or (3) would be decided contrary to a previous judgment of the Supreme Court.[52]

A description of the Court would not be complete without mentioning the *chōsakan* (research judges). These are a team of approximately forty well-regarded and experienced mid- and more senior-career judges who assist the Supreme Court judges with legal research and drafting.[53] Being appointed to a *chōsakan* post is often the hallmark of a successful judicial career.

While the principle of *stare decisis* is not applied, precedents from the Supreme Court carry a very strong authoritative value. Another role of some *chōsakan* is to sit with judges from each Petty Bench, in what is called "Committee of Judicial Precedents" to decide how and where to publish the judgments rendered by the Court. [54]

Supreme Court judges: Dismissal by public vote; retirement; remuneration

Article 79 establishes a system of retention elections for Supreme Court judges, appointments of each of which are "reviewed by the people" on the occasion of the first House of Representatives election following their appointment. The same applies every ten years thereafter.

If the majority of voters decide to remove a judge, they are dismissed. In theory this system allows for popular democratic control of the Supreme Court. However, in practice it has serious limits. First, since practice for decades has been that those appointed to the Supreme Court judges are already in their mid-sixties, they undergo only a single review before reaching retirement age. Second, since the general public knows nothing about individual judges (starting with their names) the number of voters who express their desire to remove a specific judge from the Supreme Court is limited and blank votes are considered as being in favor of retention.[55] As a result, no Supreme Court judge has ever been dismissed by popular vote. In the *Overseas Voters Right to Review Supreme Court Judges Case* the Supreme Court held the failure to enable citizens living abroad to vote in these retention elections to violate the constitution.

Hence, the normal way for a judge to leave the Supreme Court is to reach the mandatory retirement age of 70. Voluntary retirement or death of course may also terminate a Supreme Court judge's career before the end of their tenure.

As explicitly stipulated by the constitution, Supreme Court judges need to be remunerated, and their remuneration cannot be decreased during their tenure. This reduces the ability of other branches of government to pressure the Court financially. Legislation further provides that the chief judge and the prime minister receive the same annual salary and other justices on the Supreme Court receive the same annual salary as cabinet members, thereby reconfirming the equality of the two branches of government: this is made clear by the comparison between the Judges Remuneration Act and the Special Employees Remuneration Act.

Functioning of the Supreme Court

One of the striking features of the Supreme Court is the number of judgments it issues every year: in fiscal year 2020 (April 2020–March 2021), the Court issued 4,262 decisions in civil matters, and 1,882 in criminal cases. While the overwhelming majority of the judgements are simple and plain rejections of appeals, they account for a significant part of the workload of just 15 judges. That they are able to manage this burden is on the one hand remarkable, but on the other indicates a structural framework in which the *chōsakan* research judges play an important role, including in shaping the direction of the Court's jurisprudence.

The docket numbers above also represent an improvement over past practice in civil cases. Prior to the adoption in 1996 of the present Code of Civil Procedure, appeals from high court judgments could be had as a matter of right based on alleged error in constitutional interpretation or application of law.[56] The present Code allows the Court more flexibility in declining appeals, giving it more control over its docket. Similar rules apply in the criminal sphere.

In looking at Supreme Court docket numbers it is important to bear in mind that not only is it charged with final interpretation of the constitution (see discussion at Article 81), but it is also charged with giving final interpretive guidance on other Japanese laws—the Civil Code being a prime example—as well. Supreme Court precedents are thus an important subject of study in most basic areas of law, and cases without any constitutional dimension are part of its docket.

One other feature of the Japanese Supreme Court that will seem normal to Americans but differentiates it from the majority of other civil law jurisdictions and even lower courts in Japan is that pursuant to Article 11 of the Court Act Supreme Court judges are each required to express their opinion. In many cases they merely sign the "opinion of the Court." However, in some judgments it is possible to read concurring or even dissenting opinions. Those concurring and dissenting opinions may be important and, in some instances, reflect what ultimately becomes the majority view in a future case.[57]

Article 80: Inferior Courts

Giorgio Fabio Colombo

Article 80.

(1) The judges of the inferior courts shall be appointed by the Cabinet from a list of persons nominated by the Supreme Court. All such judges shall hold office for a term of ten (10) years with privilege of reappointment, provided that they shall be retired upon the attainment of the age as fixed by law.

(2) The judges of the inferior courts shall receive, at regular stated intervals, adequate compensation which shall not be decreased during their terms of office.

The legal profession and the judiciary in Japan

Before describing the appointment of judges of the lower courts pursuant to Article 80, it is necessary to give a short explanation about the legal professions in Japan. First there are a variety of licensed legal professions and specialized roles within government that in countries like the United States might all be counted as lawyers. Of these, only a limited universe are "trial-related" legal professionals who pass the national bar exam and become judges, lawyers or prosecutors (referred to collectively as *hōsō*).

In the Meiji period Japan followed the French model, with different professional paths for judges and prosecutors and attorneys. Then, in the 1920s, in line with the reforms inspired by the German approach, it adopted a system by which candidates wishing to become lawyers, judges, or public prosecutors, all took the same unified test (the national bar exam): it was only after passing the exam that their professional paths diverged. After completing their post-exam training, judges and prosecutors need to be appointed, while lawyers need to register with a bar association.

An important change happened in 1949 as part of the Occupation-era reforms, when lawyers were freed from the supervision of the Ministry of Justice and put under the regulation of self-governing bar associations. The new Court Act (Articles 41–44) was revised in order to allow prosecutors and lawyers to be appointed as judges. While appointments from the former category are not rare, those from the latter are very uncommon. It was only in 1988 that the Supreme Court started inviting lawyers to apply for the bench, but the number of successful applications is still very low.[58]

The year 2004 saw the introduction of a system of a professional graduate law schools loosely modelled on those in the United States. Prior to this, there were few formal qualifications for taking the national bar exam, so many took it but few passed. Since the number of passers was functionally limited to about 500 per year for several decades and then rose gradually thereafter, the pass ratc routinely hovered between one and three percent. The new system trades a higher bar exam pass rate (or rather, more passing slots) for a requirement that applicants for the national bar exam to either be law school graduates or pass a highly competitive "preliminary examination."

Candidates who successfully pass the bar exam are eligible to enter the *Shihō-kenshū-jo*, the Supreme Court's Legal Training and Research Institute (LTRI) for a one-year course of training, graduation from which is the fastest and most certain route to becoming a *hōsō*.[59] While at the LTRI trainees may apply or be "scouted" by teaching staff to become judges or prosecutors. Compared to the LTRI class size every year (approximately 1500 in recent years) the number of positions for new judges and prosecutors is small (less than a few dozen of each), meaning the government employers can be picky, and the vast majority of graduates become lawyers either by choice or by default. Commentators have argued that this serves as an informal process to filter potentially subversive candidates out of the government legal professions.[60] As mentioned in the discussion at Article 76. summary court judges, who are "judges" for constitutional purposes, have not all passed the bar exam, follow a different appointment track and have different pay scales.[61]

Appointment—reappointment—career track

For those entering the judiciary from the LTRI, they are appointed as assistant judges (*hanji-ho*). By law, such judges are not allowed to preside over cases alone, sitting as junior members on panels of three judges (and on which they cannot preside).[62] A statute provides that after five years' service the Supreme Court may designate assistant judges to exercise the same powers as full-fledged judges.[63] The English version of Article 80 suggests reappointment is a "privilege" for a lower court judge, but the Japanese only says that reappointment is possible.

There are various theories as to the degree to which a judge is somehow entitled to be reappointed (should (s)he so wish), and thus the degree to which judicial administrators can get rid of judges they don't like by the simple expedient of not seeking their reappointment from the Cabinet. The prevailing view (followed by the Supreme Court) is that reappointments are discretionary, and in the past allegedly politically-motivated non-reappointments have received attention.[64] However, the Court's ability to use its discretion may have been limited by the introduction in 2003 Lower Court Judge Nominating Committees comprised of judges, prosecutors, lawyers and academics. These committees vet appointments (and reappointments) and make recommendations to the Supreme Court, which must notify the applicable committee if it does not follow them.[65]

In subsequent terms after reappointment a judge is a full-fledged judge (*hanji*).[66] The vast majority of members of the judiciary enjoy a fairly stable career: their professional success is determined by a number of factors, though there has been debate over the level of transparency underlying the annual evaluation judges receive. Judges are normally transferred every three years, and some courts and posts are more prestigious than others: the Tokyo District and High Court are most prestigious and influential, and administrative postings to the Supreme Court are a good sign. By contrast, a series of postings to regional cities or family courts may be a bad sign, or even a form of punishment.[67]

Judges may also be seconded to other parts of the government, even for extensive portions of their "judicial" careers. At any given time over one hundred judges are on secondment to other branches of government, through an arrangement which sees them temporarily appointed prosecutors. In this capacity they may act as defense counsel for the government in constitutional or administrative litigation, spend time at a Japanese embassy abroad, or assist in the drafting or review of legislation by executive or legislative branch institutions.

The appointment of judges of inferior courts is an example of constitutionally framed cooperation between the executive branch and the Supreme Court across constitutional separation of powers.[68] As already mentioned at Article 77, the most significant body for the management of the judiciary is the General Secretariat of the Supreme Court. Based on feedback from the Lower Court Judicial Appointment Advisory Committees, The General Secretariat prepares a list which is submitted to the Supreme Court for approval, and then sent to the Cabinet. As is clear from the language of Article 80, the Cabinet has no voice in the choice of the names to be put on the list or appoint judges who are not on the list. There is an interpretive debate as to whether the Cabinet's power of appointment is substantive such that it could refuse to appoint individual judges despite their inclusion on the Supreme Court's list. Since this has apparently never happened it is a strictly academic debate.[69] Hence, the reality is that for most purposes the career judges working as judicial bureaucrats in the Supreme Court's General Secretariat, under the leadership of its Secretary General and through the operations of its Personnel Affairs Bureau, substantially decides who should serve as a judge.[70]

Judicial Compensation

As with Supreme Court judges under article 79, all lower court judges also enjoy constitutional protections around their compensation. However, this does not extend to being immune from general pay reductions that affect the entire public service based on recommendations of the National Personnel Authority, since these do not target specific judges or the judiciary (and were agreed to by the judicial conference of the Supreme Court when such a pay decrease was implemented at the turn of the millennium).

The constitutional protection of compensation does not extend to salary increases, however. While the judiciary has a tenure-based compensation system, individual personnel evaluations result in some judges advancing through the pay scale more quickly than others.[71]

Article 81: Judicial Review

Giorgio Fabio Colombo

> **Article 81.**
> The Supreme Court is the court of last resort with power to determine the constitutionality of any law, order, regulation or official act.

Overview

Article 81 is a very significant provision of the constitution in that it establishes the judiciary—the Supreme Court, at least—as the final arbiter of what the constitution means with respect to government conduct, a very significant power. This is a significant departure from the Meiji system, under which the Grand Court of Cassation rejected the idea that it could find a statute unconstitutional, though the possibility was subsequently debated by academics nonetheless.[72]

That the Americans prepared a draft constitution containing a clear allocation of the power of constitutional review to a new Japanese Supreme Court is unsurprising. That they may have had some reservations on the subject based on what at the time would have been the recent history of the US Supreme Court obstructing the legislative agenda of the elected branches of government is reflected in Article LXIII, which would have allowed a 2/3 majority of the Diet to overturn a Supreme Court ruling of constitutionality unless it related to Chapter III.

The American officials in the drafting process were generally unfamiliar with the legal systems of civil law countries which have dealt with constitutional review differently than the United States. As a result, a significant feature of the Japanese system is the absence of a separate constitutional court entrusted specifically with the role of reviewing the constitutionality of laws and administrative acts, though such tribunals are common in many civil law systems. In fact, Japan is one of a very few civil law-rooted jurisdictions which continues to not have a separate constitutional court, but instead deals with constitutional challenges within the framework of the mainstream judiciary applying US-style "case or controversy" requirements. This aspect as well may be ascribed to the American influence on the Japanese constitution.[73] The adoption of the constitution thus saw Japan abandon the previous model based on the French *Cassation* (which basically served as "judge of judgments" but had no power of constitutional judicial review) and created a Supreme Court with the final word on the constitutionality of laws and regulations.

Article 81 is silent on whether lower courts also have the power of constitutional review. However, that does not mean the Supreme Court has a monopoly on that role: that lower courts are fully entitled to rule on constitutionality has never been seriously in doubt and was a basic assumption in the procedural codes and Supreme Court rules drafted around the same time as the constitution. In a 1950 judgment the Supreme Court acknowledged that confirming whether laws and regulations comply with the constitution is within the purview of the lower courts.[74]

Guidance for the exercise of the judicial review provided for in Article 81 can also be found in the Supremacy Clause contained in Article 98(1), which contains a similar but not identical list of items that are void if they violate provisions of the constitution.

Judicial review in action

The formulation of judicial review in Article 81 is very broad, as it allows the Court to review the constitutionality not only of legislation and regulations, but also of executive acts and orders. Absent from this listing is treaties, and there are various theories on whether courts could find a treaty unconstitutional. In practice the only time the issue has come up is in the *Sunagawa Case* (see Article 9), in which the Supreme Court declined to opine on the constitutionality of the US-Japan defense treaty.

"Law" (*hōritsu*) refers to legislative acts passed by the Diet (see Article 59), but is also understood to include ordinances (*jōrei*) passed by prefectural and municipal assemblies. "orders" (*meirei*) and "rules" (*kisoku*) have distinct meanings but together cover the vast body of regulations created by administrative agencies and orders of such agencies, as well as rules of the Diet chambers and the Supreme Court.[75] "Official act" in Japanese is *shobun*, which is more commonly translated "disposition;" it refers to the vast range of government acts (rejection of permit applications, expenditures of public funds, grants regulatory privileges and so forth), and which affect the rights or duties of the people within the framework of a statutory regime.[76]

There are a number of hurdles to bringing constitutional challenges. These include first the interpretation of a number of the rights guaranteed by the constitution as legislative mandates or otherwise not amenable to direct judicial relief (see discussion at Chapter III introduction). The courts have also been restrictive in recognizing standing to challenge government actions. Finally, courts have adopted approaches that may be familiar to American constitutional scholars, such as a form of "mootness" to avoid ruling on constitutional challenges if it is unnecessary to do so to decide a case.

When the Supreme Court does find a constitutional violation has occurred, it can typically be categorized in one of two ways: (1) *hōrei iken* (unconstitutional law or regulation)—a finding that a statutory or regulatory provision violates the constitution (discussed in more detail below; and (2) *tekiyō iken* (application contrary to the constitution)—the law or regulatory provision is upheld, but its application to the plaintiff/appellant in the case at bar is found unconstitutional.[77]

Considering the broad US-style power of constitutional review the Supreme Court enjoys, one might expect it to be frequently used to find problematic laws and regulations unconstitutional. It is actually quite the opposite, as the Court has consistently shown a great degree of restraint over the decades. In the span of more than 70 years, the Supreme Court has ruled statutory provision unconstitutional in only eleven instances. Moreover, as the list below demonstrates, some of the cases of statutory unconstitutionality seem to involve the application of constitutional review to fine tune statutory minutiae rather than dramatic vindications of civil rights. All decisions were issued by the Supreme Court sitting in its Grand Bench composition.

Unconstitutionality rulings

Hōrei iken cases

The Lineal Ascendant Murder Case (1973)

The Court found that the Penal Code provision of Article 200, which provided for a much harsher penalty for the homicide of a relative compared to that of another person violated the equality clause under Article 14 of the constitution. (See discussion at Article 14).

The Pharmaceutical Affairs Act Case (1975)

In this case it was decided that the restriction to open a pharmacy in a place too close to another one violated the freedom to choose one own's occupation provided for by Article 22 of the constitution. (See discussion at Article 22).

House of Representatives Malapportionment Case I (1976) and House of Representatives Malapportionment Case II (1985)

In both these cases the Court found that a significant disproportionality in the number of voters between electoral districts compared to the number of representatives they elected violated the equal protection guarantee of Article 14 and the provision about electors of Article 44.

Both these cases are significant also because they involve the application of what is commonly referred to as "*jijō hanketsu*," i.e., ruling taking into account the circumstance of the case. A provision is found to be unconstitutional, but the Court does not go beyond a mere acknowledgment of this fact, as further action (in these cases, the invalidation of the concerned election and the consequent disqualification of the Diet and its operations) would be too disruptive "taking into account the circumstances." (See discussion at Articles 15 and 44).

The Forest Act Case (1987)

The Court found that some restriction to the partition of joint interest in forest land violated the right to property protected by Article 29 of the constitution. (See discussion at Article 29).

The Postal Act Case (2002)

In this case it was decided that the blanket waiver of tort liability of postal employees violates the right to obtain compensation from the State provided for by Article 17 of the constitution. (See discussion at Article 17).

The Overseas Voting Rights Case (2005)

Provisions of the Public Office Election Act restricting the right of Japanese living abroad to vote for the Diet election violate both the right to universal suffrage (Article 15) and Article 43 and 44 about the elections. (See discussion at Article 15).

The Nationality Act Case (2008)

A provision of the Nationality Act which differentiated the treatment of children of Japanese fathers and non-Japanese mothers based on whether the father acknowledged the child before or after birth was found in violation of the equality clause of Article 14. (See discussion at Article 10).

The Out-of-Wedlock Inheritance Rights Discrimination Case (2013)
Article 900 of the Civil Code, which provided that children born out of wedlock were entitled only to half of the statutory share of those born in wedlock violates Article 14 of the constitution. (See discussion at Article 14).

The Women-only Remarriage Prohibition Period Case (2015)
The Court found that Article 733 of the Civil Code, which prohibited women (only) to remarry for a period of 180 days after the dissolution of a previous marriage was unconstitutional as the period was too long. The Court shortened the period to 100 days. (See discussion at Article 24).

Overseas Voters Right to Review Supreme Court Judges Case (2022)
The Court found that Japanese citizens abroad had a right to vote in the retention elections mandated for Supreme Court judges under Article 79 (see also discussion at Article 15).

Being so few in number, these cases have taken on a special significance in being the focus of attention in the pedagogy of any student of the law in Japan. The list of cases is commonly known in law study and an important focus of attention in studies for professional law school admission and the bar exam.

Tekiyō iken cases

In addition to the *hōrei iken* cases mentioned above, the Supreme Court has also issued "unconstitutionality-of-application" *tekiyō iken* rulings in thirteen cases. Some of these are quite technical and/or no longer relevant, but the three most recent (including the *Ehime Tamagushi Case* and the *Sunagawa Sorachibuto Shrine Case*) involved the use of public funds or property for religious purposes and are discussed at Articles 20 and 89.[78]

The uses of judicial review

A simple majority (eight judges) of the Grand Bench is required to render a ruling of unconstitutionality.[79] When this happens, a notice is published in the Official Gazette, and a copy of the Court's ruling is sent to the Cabinet and, if it involves finding a statutory provision unconstitutional, the Diet.[80] The legislature is expected to amend the statute, which sometimes happens, but in the *Lineal Ascendant Murder Case,* the unconstitutional provision remained in the Penal Code for twenty years before being removed.

The Court's limited use of its power to strike down legislative and administrative acts is the subject of much debate, particularly among American observers. However, there are arguably several additional ways in which the judiciary uses its power of judicial constitutional review.

The first is in the Supreme Court's use of judgments *upholding* laws and administrative acts to articulate interpretive doctrines and parameters that may be relevant (and cited) in future cases. Japanese students of constitutional law are required to study far more Supreme Court precedents than those mentioned above and this is one reason; constitutional law textbooks are full of ringing statements of constitutional principles from Supreme Court judgments rendered in cases where the constitutional challenge was ultimately unsuccessful.

Lower courts have also occasionally issued rulings declaring something to be unconstitutional while finding in favor of the government on other grounds, typically that the plaintiff has not suffered any actual damages. The "unconstitutional" portion of the ruling may be mere *dicta* that has no legal force and such judgments have the benefit (to the judge issuing such rulings, at least) of being impossible for the government to appeal (because they won).

Finally, courts increasingly seem to be taking the middle ground; declaring that a particular state of affairs is not unconstitutional now, but might be in the future, or are in an unconstitutional state, but not so unconstitutional as to be void. Combined with the increased use of tort claims against the state based on legislative non-feasance (see Introduction to Chapter III), this gives courts an ability to, on the one hand, express support for constitutional challenges, while at the same time finding that the plaintiffs have not suffered actionable damages, or that the Diet should be given more time to act. In this context, constitutional litigation that seems hopeless (because of the very low success rate for such challenges) can perhaps be better understood as a form of lobbying activity. Insofar as the Court has found a number of constitutional guarantees to be essentially mandates to the legislature rather than the source of concrete legal rights that can be vitiated directly through litigation (see Chapter III), this is also consistent.

Why is the Supreme Court so "conservative"?

There are several likely reasons behind the reluctance of the Supreme Court to use its power of constitutional review to invalidate legislative and administrative acts. The most important is probably deference towards the Diet as the "sole law-making organ of the State" (see Article 41) and to the Cabinet as well. This attitude sometime is taken to its extremes in what is known as the "political question doctrine" (*tōchi kōi ron*).[81] This doctrine was first developed in the famous (or notorious) *Sunagawa Case*, discussed at Article 9. Many commentators have openly criticized the judgment, as they consider the employment of the "political question doctrine" a clever sleight of hand to dodge touchy decisions in highly sensitive matters.[82]

Another reason may lay in the simpler fact that the Cabinet Legislation Bureau (see Introduction to Chapter V), does a thorough job of vetting draft legislation originating from the Cabinet before it is submitted to the Diet for deliberation. This vetting would of course include ensuring the proposed laws are at least consistent with the CLB's interpretation of the constitution.[83] From a substantive point of view, this ensures that a preliminary control over the constitutionality of laws is already carried out (albeit by another branch of government). In point of fact, most of the statutory provisions found by the Supreme Court were in laws that originated in the Diet, which lacks the same level of institutional quality control as is provided by the CLB.[84]

A third reason may be due to the potentially disruptive impact of unconstitutionality rulings. A basic issue faced by the courts in electoral malapportionment cases—even in instances where the Court has found discrepancies so significant as to be outright unconstitutional—is that for the Court to declare the relevant Diet election void would potentially invalidate everything done by the government based on that election, starting from the selection of a prime minister. Similarly, in the *Out-of-Wedlock Inheritance Rights Discrimination Case*, although the Court found the discriminatory rules of inheritance in the Civil Code unconstitutional, it was careful to make it clear that its ruling only applied to estates that had not been settled yet.

A fourth reason may be that the administrative control of judges and the process by which they and the majority of other Supreme Court judges achieve that status—i.e., long years of government service—makes them both conservative and sympathetic to the government point of view. Some scholars have also identified a correlation between successful judicial careers and support of majoritarian (LDP) policies.[85]

Finally, the judiciary's power of judicial review also needs to be considered in conjunction with the supremacy clause in Article 98.

Article 82: Open Courts

Mari Hirayama

Article 82.

(1) Trials shall be conducted and judgment declared publicly.

(2) Where a court unanimously determines publicity to be dangerous to public order or morals, a trial may be conducted privately, but trials of political offenses, offenses involving the press or cases wherein the rights of people as guaranteed in Chapter III of this Constitution are in question shall always be conducted publicly.

Public trials

Article 82 is quite similar to Article 59 of the Meiji Constitution. One significant difference, however, is that the Meiji charter gave judges much greater discretion to conduct trials behind closed doors.

The "publicly" requirement of Article 82(1) means trial must be held in such a way that anyone can observe them. The Supreme Court has confirmed the importance of this "openness principle," holding that: "[b]y making trials open to the public, we seek to ensure that trials are conducted fairly as a system, and by doing so, we can ensure public confidence in trials."[86] In practice this means the general public is free to observe trials, as are members of the press. However, the Supreme Court's rules of criminal procedure prohibit live broadcasts of trials, and even the taking of photographs or recordings is tightly restricted.[87]

The constitutionality of restrictions on photography in courts was upheld by the Supreme Court in 1958 in the *Hokkai Times Case*, in connection with an appeal by a newspaper cameraperson challenging a fine imposed by a judge for taking pictures without permission.[88] As discussed at Article 21, in the *Courtroom Note-Taking Case*, while denying that courtroom spectators have a right to take notes during proceedings, the Supreme Court ruled that the act of note-taking by courtroom spectators should be respected by the courts and only restricted in exceptional cases. On the day of the ruling the Court also issued instructions to courts throughout the country to repeal rules requiring approval for courtroom note-taking. As a result, observers in courtrooms are generally free to take notes.

Proceedings that are not "trials" do not need to be public

As noted in the Introduction to this book and discussed at Article 32, "trial" (*saiban*) has a specific meaning in Japan's procedural codes and refers only to proceedings with oral arguments, evaluation of testimony and other evidence, which result in a "judgment" (*hanketsu*) by the Court based on the motions of the parties. There are several broad categories of proceedings which are *not* considered trials and thus do not need to be conducted publicly.

First, the adjudication of juvenile criminal cases is considered to prioritize the development and rehabilitation of juveniles. In order to protect their privacy such proceedings are not open to the public.[89] This has been found by a lower court not to violate Article 82, but there is no Supreme Court ruling on the subject.[90] In response to complaints from victims' rights groups, the law was amended in 2008 to enable victims of serious crimes committed by juveniles to watch the proceedings.[91]

Second, with respect to criminal proceedings, the Supreme Court has ruled that although "proceedings to determine the existence and scope of the right to punishment" require a trial and judgment conducted in an open court, petitions for a retrial are outside the scope of such proceedings and do not need to be adjudicated publicly, held in open court.[92]

Third, with respect to civil trials, the Supreme Court has ruled that "trials of purely litigation cases where finally facts are confirmed and the existence of the rights and obligations claimed by the parties are determined, regardless of the intentions of the parties," must be conducted publicly and the judgment must be declared in open court.[93] A corollary of this is that there is a large category of civil proceedings deemed "non-contentious" and thus not conducted publicly. Some are defined in the Non-Contentious Case Procedures Act,[94] but they also include the vast majority of family and inheritance disputes which are heard in family courts which are not open to the public.[95]

Fourth, the Supreme Court has held that Article 82 does not extend to proceedings for the disciplining of judges under the Judicial Status Act.[96]

Fifth, pretrial proceedings do not need to be open to the public.[97] In any case, the Japanese version of paragraph (1) does not require the entire trial to be public, only the "adversarial" or "confrontational" (*taishin*) portion.

Sixth, pursuant to 2004 amendments to the Patent Act and the Unfair Competition Prevention Act, testimony relating to trade secrets may be closed to the public.

Finally, in the context of challenges to the refusal of administrative departments to disclose information in response to Japan's Information Disclosure Act, there has been some discussion of whether it would be possible for courts to conduct an *in camera* review of the information in question to evaluate the legitimacy of the government's grounds for refusal without disclosing it to the petitioner as well. The Supreme Court, however, has refused to create such a procedure absent clear statutory authorization.[98] However, in doing so the Court seems to have suggested that *in camera* review provided for by statute would not violate Article 82.

Trial records

The right of the public to observe trials does not extend to access to trial records. The Final Criminal Case Records Act tightly restricts access to records in criminal trials, which are maintained by the relevant public prosecutors' office after the trial is finished.[99] The Supreme Court has rejected challenges to denials of access to records under this Act.[100]

Exceptions

Although the "open court" principle is widely accepted in many countries, trials conducted publicly may also result in human rights violations in the form of invasions of privacy and unwanted publicity on the part of persons such as crime victims. The International Covenant on Civil and Political Rights, for example, states that a trial may be closed to the press and the public for a variety of reasons, including when it is necessary in the interests of the private life of the parties concerned or in special circumstances where its disclosure would be prejudicial to the interests of justice (Article 14 (1)). The openness principle exists in relation to other competing interests.

Paragraph (2) of Article 82 establishes a limited range of instances when a court may create an exception to the principle of open trials. Article 82(2) provides the limited grounds on which a judge or panel of judges acting unanimously may close a trial to the public.[101] However, even in this case, the judgment must always be conducted in an open court.

The term "dangerous to public order or morals" in paragraph (2) is understood to mean when there is a risk of harm to public safety or a risk of a significantly bad effect on people's minds.[102] Under Article 22 of the Personal Status Litigation Act of 2003 a family court litigation can be closed upon the unanimous consent of the Court if necessary in order to ensure a proper trial in cases involving serious secrets of one's private life.

Examples of crimes which must always be tried publicly include insurrection, instigation of foreign aggression and offenses related to foreign relations (Penal Code Articles 77, 81 and 92 *et seq.*) As to what sort of offenses might be included in "offenses involving the press," there are various theories. One suggests it includes any crime where publication is an element of the offense, such as electoral offenses involving improper use of media.[103] Another leading theory holds that it more broadly refers to any crime committed through publication, such as sedition or the distribution of obscene content.[104] Such offenses must be tried in open court to ensure freedom of publication is not unreasonably infringed, since it is one of the most important means of expression. Today, however, the means of public expression are no longer limited to publication in print but also include movies, television, and social networking sites. There is thus a strong argument that offenses involving other forms of expression beyond "publication" should be subject to the absolute public trial requirement.[105]

Finally, cases wherein the rights of people as guaranteed in Chapter III are in question, is understood to apply to all cases involving potential violations of the rights guaranteed by the constitution, whether substantive or procedural, and whether civil, criminal or administrative trials. [106]

Notes

[1] Itō, H. (1970). Itō, H. (2010), 19. The very first usage of the word currently used for court of law, *saibansho* (literally "place of trials") is recorded in 1872, when it was used for a division of the Ministry of Justice in charge of dispute resolution for the city of Tokyo (the Tōkyō *Saibansho*), Röhl, W. (Ed.) (2005), 717.

[2] Saibansho Kōseihō [Court Organization Act], Law No. 6 of 1890.

[3] Röhl, W. (Ed.) (2005), 655.

[4] Possibly because under the present constitution *shihō* was formally denoted a separate branch of government, while the Ministry of Justice retained its English name, in Japanese it was changed to *Hōmushō*, which would be more accurately rendered as "Ministry of Legal Affairs." Note that *Shihōshō* the previous name is also used as the Japanese translation of the US Department of Justice.

[5] Hellegers, D.M., (2001), 645–56.

[6] Merryman, J.H. (2007), 47.

[7] *See, e.g.*, Code of Civil Procedure, Article 318, Code of Criminal Procedure, Article 405.

[8] Colombo, G.F. (2015).

[9] Justice System Reform Council. (2001). Recommendations of the Justice System Reform Council: For a Justice System to Support Japan in the 21st Century (D. Foote, trans.) available at http://www.kantei.go.jp/foreign/judiciary/2001/0612report.html; Prime Minister of Japan and his Cabinet. Retrieved June 30, 2022, from https://japan.kantei.go.jp/policy/sihou/singikai/990612_e.html; Levin, M.A., & Mackie, A. (2013).

[10] Takahashi, H. (2009), 50; Law, D.S. (2009), 1556.

[11] Itō, H. (1990); Kozuka, S. (2009); Upham, F.K. (2011).

[12] See also, Matsui, S. (2010).

[13] Supreme Court, 2nd Petty Bench judgment of July 21, 2005; Grand Court of Cassation Decision of December 28, 1928, 56 Minshū 729.

[14] The *Tomabechi Case* discussed at Articles 3 and 7 was a similar example of the Court avoiding a resolution on the grounds the matter was fundamentally a political question.

[15] Tsujimura, M., & Yamamoto, H. (Eds.). (2018), 317; Shibutani, H. (2017), 599.

[16] Law, D.S. (2009).Ramseyer, J.M., & Rasmusen, E.B. (2010). Fujita, T. (2011).

[17] Haley, J.O. (1995); Haley, J.O., in Foote, D.H. (Ed.) (2008), 99–135.

[18] Ramseyer, J.M., & Rasmusen, E.B. (2010).

[19] Law, D.S. (2009).

[20] Upham, F.K. (2005); Matsui, S. (2011), 129.

[21] The case is known as the "Ōtsu incident." Röhl, W. (2005), 784; Jones, C. P. A. (2019, January 2). How the Last Czar Shaped Japan's Courts. *The Japan Times*. Retrieved June 30, 2022, from https://www.japantimes.co.jp/community/2019/01/02/issues/last-czar-shaped-japans-courts/.

[22] See also, Tsuji, Y. (2020), 79–80; Fujita, T. (2011); and Matsui, S. (2011), 127.

[23] Miyazawa, S. (1991); Levin, M.A. (2011); Levin, M.A., in Ageishi, K., Ōtsuka, H., Musashi, K., & Hirayama, M. (Eds.). (2017), 735–55.

[24] Tsuji, Y. (2011), 72–73.

[25] The case was one of the most significant cases of constitutional law regarding war and peace in Japan in the late 1960s, at least comparable to the US Guantánamo Bay litigation in the 2000s if not even more significant for Japan in its time. The advice shared why Hiraga thought the government's position in the case should be upheld and how the rationale could be circumspectly crafted. Levin, M.A. (2011), footnote 83, 283.

[26] To be clear, administrative / organizational management is entirely understandable in the setting here. It is the instrumental and politically ideological use of such authority to accomplish substantive legal results imposing on judges' independence to decide according to their own consciences, that has drawn the criticism of Levin and the various other authors cited above.

[27] Matsui, S. (2011), 128.

[28] Ramseyer, J.M., & Rasmusen, E.B. (2006): Law, D.S. (2009), 1549.

[29] The Japanese term kensatsukan is rendered "procurator" in the English version of the Constitution. While that term may be familiar to Europeans, it is more commonly translated into English as "prosecutor," since prosecuting criminal offenses is the primary role of such officials.

[30] Tsuji, Y. (2011), 0; Levin, M.A., in Ageishi, K., Ōtsuka, H., Musashi, K., & Hirayama, M. (Eds.). (2017), 735–55.

31 For the impact of judicial rule-making on the implementation of Japan's *Habeas Corpus Act*, see: Jones, C.P.A. (2017b).
32 Abe, M. (1995), 307; Levin, M.A. (2011), 275.
33 Hōtei no Chitsujo Iji ni Kansuru Hōritsu [Act on the Preservation of Order in Courtrooms], Law no. 286 of 1952.
34 Supreme Court, Grand Bench judgment of October 15, 1958, 12 *Keishū* 3291.
35 Court Act, Article 50. Retirement age for summary court judges and Supreme Court judges is set at 70. Under the Court Act (Articles 42 and 44), lawyers and prosecutors with suitable experience may also be appointed as judges. A few such appointments are made from the bar every year, but they are the exception rather than the rule. As part of an "prosecutor-judge exchange program" (*hanken kōryū*) program, prosecutors may also spend some time in the judiciary, though they stopped acting as judges in criminal cases in 2012 due to criticism of the practice. Also, as explained under Article 76, summary court judges follow a different career path.
36 The Japanese term used to express "executive organ or agency" is *gyōseikikan*, which simply means "administrative institution," and needs to be read in conjunction with the meaning of the "executive" (administrative) power as discussed at Article 65.
37 Judge Impeachment Act, Article 15.
38 Judge Impeachment Act, Article 2.
39 Attorney Act, Article 7. *See also* Yanase, N. (2014), 7–8.
40 Judge Impeachment Act, Article 38.
41 Matsui, S. (2011), 126. Ii, T. (2013).
42 Tsuji, Y. (2011), 77–80.
43 Saibankan Bungenhō [Judges Status Act] Law No. 27 of 1947.
44 If impeachment proceedings are pending, a disciplinary proceeding regarding the same matter must be temporarily suspended until the outcome of the impeachment is reached. Judges Status ct, Article 10.
45 Judges are also subject to less severe administrative warnings from their judicial superiors outside the scope of these proceedings, under Article 21 of the Regulations for inferior courts.
46 Haley, J.O. The Japanese Judiciary: Maintaining Integrity, Autonomy, and the Public Trust. In Foote, D.H. (Ed.) (2008). A bit more critical is Law, D.S. (2011), 1436–1437. Among all disciplinary proceedings held to date, two have attracted particular attention. The first was the case of assistant Judge Kazushi Teranishi. In 1998 he was disciplined with a warning for publishing an opinion about a proposed legislation about wiretapping and for participating in an event as a member of the audience after being denied permission from his court to attend as a speaker, in violation of the Court Act's prohibition on political activities by judges (Article 52). Judge Teranishi appealed to the Supreme Court on claiming the prohibition violated his freedom of expression but the Court confirmed the result as constitutional on the grounds that the political neutrality of judges is deemed essential to preserve the public trust in the judiciary. (Supreme Court Grand Bench decision of December 1, 1998.) The second high-profile case is that of Judge Kiichi Okaguchi, a high court judge who was particularly active on Twitter. Known by the general public as the "underwear judge," he had posted a picture of himself wearing white briefs only. Judge Okaguchi attracted both informal criticism and formal warnings for his inappropriate use of social media. At the time of writing impeachment proceedings against him were pending.
47 Court Act, Article 41.
48 Nishikawa, S. (2010).
49 Okudaira, Y. Forty Years of the Constitution and its Influences: Japanese, American, and European. In Luney, P.R. & Takahashi, K. (Eds.) (1993), 24; Repeta, L. (2011).
50 Repeta, L. (2011), 1743.
51 Nishikawa, S. (2010).
52 By defining the scope of cases which Petty Benches may not hear, the Court Act effectively establishes a universe of cases which *must* be heard by the Grand Bench. The Supreme Court's rules also make it possible for the presiding judge of a Petty Bench to refer a case to the Grand Bench for resolution in certain circumstances. Saikōsaibansho Saiban Jimushori Kisoku [Rules on Administration of Supreme Court Trials], Supreme Court Rule No. 6 of 1947, Article 9.
53 The closest US counterpart would be judicial law clerks, but law clerks in the US are not judges. The *chōsakan* are themselves career judges, but to be clear, not themselves Supreme Court judges. Law, D.S. (2009), part III C; Kamiya, M. (2011).
54 Chōsakan often publish articles about the rationale behind cases they assist the Supreme Court in resolving.

[55] In recent years, as a part of the movement to bring justice closer to the people encouraged by the Justice System Reform Council in 2001, the website of the Supreme Court showcases detailed profiles of each judges: they are not limited to their professional background, but include information to make them more personable in the eyes of the general public such as their motto, hobbies, and favourite books.
[56] Ōta, S. (2001), 571.
[57] For example, as discussed at Article 14, the *Out-of-Wedlock Inheritance Case* discussed was a reversal in 2013 of a 1995 Grand Bench decision in which there was a significant dissent.
[58] Oda, H. (2009), 74.
[59] Until 1998 the LTRI training lasted 24 months, but in connection with the introduction of the law school system it was shortened to 12. It is also possible to qualify as a lawyer without going to the LRTI.
[60] Law, D.S. (2009), 1552.
[61] Japanese law formally recognizes six categories of judge: The Chief Judge of the Supreme Court, Supreme Court Judge, High Court Chief Judge, judge, assistant judge and summary court judge.
[62] Court Act, Article 27.
[63] Hanjiho no Shokken No Tokureitō ni Kansuru Hōritsu [Law Relating to Special Exceptions (etc.) for the Duties of Assistant Judge], Law no. 146 of 1948.
[64] The most well-known case is that of Judge Yasuaki Miyamoto, who was a member of a liberal, left wing organization known as the Young Lawyers' Guild (political activity is formally forbidden for judges, but affiliating with such organizations is not). However, starting in 1969 in what came to be called the "Blue Purge," the Supreme Court actively sought to restrain young leftist judges or drive them out of the judiciary. Against this backdrop Miyamoto name was not recommended for reappointment. The decision not to confirm Miyamoto has been criticized by generation of scholars, as the instrumental use of reappointments is seen as yet another tool again by which the Supreme Court may steer the behavior of judges who, under Article 76, should instead be bound only by the law and their conscience. That said, it is not clear how frequently this tool is actually used: Judge Terashima, whose case is discussed at Article 78, was reappointed twice after his formal warning and remained a judge until retiring in 2020.
[65] Kakyūsaibansho Saibankan Shimei Shimon Iinkai Kisoku [Lower Court Judge Nomination Advisory Committee Rules], Supreme Court Rule no. 6 of 2003, Article 4.
[66] Although all are referred to using the generic term *saibankan* (judges), Japanese law distinguishes between six types of judges: assistant judges (*hanjiho*), full judges (*hanji*), High Court chief judges (*Kōtōsaibansho chōkan*), Supreme Court judges (*saikōsaibansho hanji*), Chief Judge of the Supreme Court (*saikōsaibansho chōkan*) and summary court judges (*kan'i saibansho saibankan*).
[67] Tsuji, Y. (2020), 104–5.
[68] Foote, D.H. (2011).
[69] Okudaira, Y, supra note 48, 16; Matsui, S. (2011), 125. In 2003, in order to limit this wide discretionary power in appointment (and re-appointment), an advisory board composed of both members of the *hōsō* and academics was established.
[70] Foote, D.H. (2011).
[71] Ramseyer, J. M., Do School Cliques Dominate Japanese Bureaucracies? Evidence from Supreme Court Appointments (February 1, 2011). Harvard Law and Economics Discussion Paper No. 687, Available at SSRN: https://ssrn.com/abstract=1767276 or http://dx.doi.org/10.2139/ssrn.1767276.
[72] Grand Court of Cassation judgment of July 11, 1913, 19 *Keiroku* 790; Kinoshita, S., & Tadano, M. (Eds.) (2019), 660.
[73] Records show debate among Allied officials as to whether the Supreme Court should have absolutely final review over all executive branch or legislative decisions, but no mention of devising another court for such matters apart from the ordinary judiciary. Hellegers, D.M., (2001), 645–56.
[74] Supreme Court, 1 February 1950, 4 Keishū 73.
[75] The Japanese term for order (*meirei*) has a special meaning in the parlance of administrative law and applies not just to orders issued by administrative bodies, but to the rules and regulations they pass as well, including (for example) Cabinet Orders.
[76] Supreme Court, 1st Petty Bench judgment of February 24, 1955; Supreme Court, 1st Petty Bench judgment of October 20, 1964. In Japanese administrative law "dispositions" have a more specific meaning within the context of, *inter alia*, that Administrative Case Litigation Act, under which it is possible to challenge or revoke a disposition. Gyōseijiken Soshōhō [Administrative Case Litigation Act], Law no. 139 of 1962, Article

8. This renders *shobunsei* (dispositivity) a basic precondition to many forms of administrative challenges and a subject of rigorous academic debate.

[77] Some commentators also refer to *shobun iken* (unconstitutional disposition) and *unyō iken* (unconstitutional operation), which are additional different variants of unconstitutional acts under statutes or regulations that are themselves found constitutional. Kinoshita, S., & Tadano, M. (Eds.), (2019), 671.

[78] There are also *tekiyō iken* relating to confessions and corroborating evidence (see Article 38] as well as the *Confiscation of Third Party Property Case* discussed at Article 31, and the *Takada Case*, discussed at Article 37. There are also two cases in this category addressing the continued applicability of Occupation-era regulations after the coming into force of the Treaty of San Francisco. Supreme Court, Grand Bench judgment of July 22, 1953; Supreme Court, Grand Bench judgment of April 27, 1955.

[79] Saikō Saibansho Saiban Jimu Shori Kisoku [Administrative Rules for Supreme Court Trials], Supreme Court Rules no. 6 of 1947, Articles 12 and 14.

[80] Tsuji, Y. (2017), 174

[81] Chen, P.L., & Wada, J.T. (2017).

[82] Ibid., 364.

[83] It is not unusual for a former Director General of the CLB to be appointed to the Supreme Court.

[84] Satō, J. (2008).

[85] Ramseyer, J.M., & Rasmusen, E.B. (2001).

[86] Supreme Court, Grand Bench judgment of March 8, 1989.

[87] Article 215 of Supreme Court's Rules of Criminal Procedure state that "Photographing, recording, or broadcasting in the courtroom shall not be permitted without the permission of the court." Similar rules apply to civil trials (Rules of Civil Procedure, Article 77). While this suggests that individual judges are free to allow such behavior, as is illustrated by the discussion elsewhere in this chapter (including the discussion of the *Courtroom Note-Taking Case* at Article 21), the reality is that virtually all judges would be expected to follow rules set and disseminated by the judicial bureaucracy on subjects such as this.

[88] Supreme Court, Grand Bench decision of February 17, 1958. Note the constitutional challenge in this case was based on Article 21 rather than 82.

[89] Shōnenhō [Juvenile Act], Law no. 168 of 1948, Article 22(2).

[90] Takamatsu High Court decision of August 5, 1954, 7 *Kōkei* 1255.

[91] Juvenile Act, Article 22-4.

[92] Supreme Court, Grand Bench decision of July 5, 1967,

[93] Supreme Court, Grand Bench decision of July 6, 1960. Translation by author.

[94] Hishōjiken Tetsuzukihō [Non-Contentious Case Procedures Act], Law no. 51 of 2011. The Supreme Court upheld the non-applicability of Article 82 to proceedings under an earlier version of the same law. Supreme Court, Grand Bench decision of December 27, 1966.

[95] The Domestic Relations Case Procedure Act imposes mandatory court-sponsored conciliation on a broad range of divorce and related proceedings, all of which are non-public (Articles 33 and 257). The Supreme Court upheld the non-applicability of Article 82 to marital proceedings under the precursor to this law. Supreme Court, Grand Bench decision of June 30, 1965. The Personal Status Litigation Act provides for special rules for cases involving potential changes in personal status (e.g, divorce) and which are not resolved through proceedings under the Domestic Case Procedure Act. Despite clearly being litigation, courts have broad discretion to close these proceedings, which appears to be a routine practice. Jinji Soshōhō [Personal Status Litigation Act], Law no. 109 of 2003, Article 22

[96] Supreme Court, Grand Bench decision of December 1, 1998.

[97] Supreme Court, Grand Bench decision of November 8, 1948.

[98] Supreme Court, 1st Petty Bench decision of January 15, 2009.

[99] Keiji Kakutei Soshō Kirokuhō [Confirmed Criminal Case Record Act], Law no. 64 of 1987.

[100] See, e.g., Supreme Court, 3rd Petty Bench decision of February 16, 1990.

[101] Under Article 70 of the Courts Act, the Court must give the reason for closing the trial before ordering observers to leave.

[102] *See, e.g.*, Ashibe, N., & Miyazawa, S. (1978), 700.

[103] Ibid.

[104] Hōgaku Kyōkai (Ed.) (1954), 1254.

[105] Sugihara, Y. (1989), 394.

[106] Ibid.

Chapter VII
Finance
Articles 83–91

Introduction

Yūichirō Tsuji

The nine articles comprising Chapter VII collectively vest the national government with financial power. Through these provisions the government exercises its power to raise, manage, and use money.

Article 83 establishes the basic principle underlying the chapter, which is referred to as "fiscal constitutionalism." The financial powers of government influence people's lives and are manifested in the powers to impose and collect taxes, borrow money, and spend and manage the use and distribution of funds.

Chapter VII seeks to prevent the exercise of this power from unduly burdening the people. "No taxation except by law" is another general principle established by the Chapter, which requires government finances to be under the control of the democratically-elected Diet (see Articles 30 and 43). Moreover, unlike under the Meiji Constitution, there are no exceptions to this latter principle.

The finance provisions of the Meiji Constitution had 11 provisions (Chapter VI: Articles 62 to 72) and also espoused the basic principle that there would be no taxation without law (Article 62(1)).[1] The Imperial Diet needed to pass a statute to impose a new tax or modify an existing one, and its consent was also needed in order to incur national debt or other liabilities chargeable to the National Treasury (Article 62(3)). Imperial Diet approval was also required for the annual budget (Article 64(1)).

However, the Meiji Constitution contained several exceptions to the principle of taxes requiring a legal basis. First, Article 62(2) excluded "all administrative fees or other revenue having the nature of compensation" from the scope of taxes or rates that needed to have a statutory basis. Second, Article 66 provided that expenses of the imperial house (which became a huge financial conglomerate in its own right) did not require the approval of the Imperial Diet. Third, if the Imperial Diet could not be convoked, Article 70(1) permitted emergency financial measures to be taken by imperial ordinance in cases of urgent need for the maintenance of public safety. Fourth, Article 71 permitted the government to use the prior year's budget if the Imperial Diet failed to pass a new one. Finally, under Article 76 of the Supplementary Rules contained in Chapter VII of the Meiji Constitution the approval of the Imperial Diet was not required for expenditures appertaining to the power of the emperor, expenditures that had arisen through the effect of law, or spending attaining to the legal obligations of the government and which predated the constitution.

The Meiji Constitution was thus designed to limit the ability of the Imperial Diet to use "the power of the purse" to keep the emperor's government in check. For example, if the Imperial Diet failed to pay for all of the warships the navy wanted, the emperor could use his considerable financial resources to pay for at least some of them instead. Chapter VII is thus in many ways a refutation of the Meiji Constitution's fiscal system, though as we shall see some elements of the old system—such as the Board of Audit—were also retained.

Article 83: Administration of Finances Decided by Diet

Yūichirō Tsuji

Article 83.
The power to administer national finances shall be exercised as the Diet shall determine.

The power to administer national finances overlaps with the budgetary power of the Diet (see Article 60). Under the principle of fiscal constitutionalism, the Diet controls the budget. The budget is not considered a "law" (*hōritsu*) because it deals with accounts, does not bind the people directly, has a limited duration (one year) and is passed through a different procedure (see Articles 59 and 60). However, fiscal constitutionalism does not require that Diet consent to all exercises of all financial powers, as discussed later in this chapter.

The Bank of Japan

Significant financial powers are exercised by the Bank of Japan. The Bank of Japan (BOJ) is Japan's only central bank and is a special corporation whose status is defined by the Bank of Japan Act.[2] It is not a government agency or joint stock company. As the nation's central bank, its purpose is to issue banknotes and regulate the national currency and finance. It also facilitates the settlement of funds between banks and other financial institutions and maintains order in credit markets.

The BOJ conducts three basic types of financial activities. First, it engages in operations related to treasury funds (government funds) deposited with it by the national government, including receipts and disbursements, accounting, management of government deposits and receipt, disbursement and custody of government securities. Second, it conducts activities related to the issuance, settlement, and distribution of payments of principal and interest on government bonds. Finally, it engages in transactions with the government, such as the purchase and sale of government bonds.

The Policy Board is the BOJ's top decision-making body. It decides on policies related to currency and monetary control and sets the basic policy for the conduct of the Bank's other operations. Comprised of various categories of Bank officers appointed in various ways depending on the category, by law the Bank's leadership is intended to be isolated from political pressure. Bank officers serve for fixed terms and may not be removed except in extraordinary circumstances.[3]

There is a question of whether this independence granted to the Bank of Japan violates Article 65 of the constitution, which vests administrative powers in the Cabinet, not a central bank designed specifically to be independent of cabinet control.[4] The CLB has issued an interpretation that the BOJ is constitutional because the Diet retains ultimate control through its ability to veto key personnel appointments, as well as through the exercise of its budgetary, legislative and other powers.[5] In other words, it is constitutional for the same reason that independent administrative committees are (see discussion at Article 65).[6] Under this view, the constitutionality of the BOJ is dependent on the ability of the Cabinet and the Diet to exercise final control over its personnel and budget. By extension this means that it would be constitutionally permissible for either the Minister of Finance or the Cabinet as a whole to assume direct oversight of BOJ operations if given such authority by the Diet, to which the Cabinet would then be responsible. Whether this would be an acceptable arrangement for a nation's central bank is questionable, and the practice of appointing former top MOF officials to leadership positions at the BOJ has raised questions about its independence.[7]

Fiscal investment and loan programs vs. fiscal constitutionalism

Fiscal Investment and Loan Programs (FILP) is a collective reference to government-led financing activities by which funds raised from sources such as government bond issuances and government-linked savings institutions (including the postal savings network) are used to fund special public corporations, help local governments build social capital and to provide loans on advantageous terms to small and medium-sized enterprises.

FILPs typically offer long-term, low-interest funding to facilitate large, long-term risky projects that are difficult for the private sector to finance unassisted. FILPs were frequently used to regulate the economy and to function as grants to boost certain projects in furtherance of government policies. FILPs are a category of *tokubetsu kaikei* or "special accounts" since they are separate from the national budget and controlled primarily by the MOF and the Cabinet, not the Diet. By the mid-1990s the FILP program had become so large that it was called "the second budget." This changed with the passage of a 2001 law requiring FILP plans to be reported to the Diet.[8] This is now done, but the plans do not require Diet approval. This is problematic from the standpoint of fiscal constitutionalism.

Local government and finance

The Diet—comprising the elected representatives of the people—is the institution which sets the tax burdens of the people. Tax revenues are spent on social security, repayment of government bonds, public works, education, science and technology, defense and local tax subsidies.

Article 92 of the constitution gives prefectural and municipal governments the power to regulate their own organization and operations. Article 223 of the Local Autonomy Act provide that local governments have the power to levy and collect local taxes. The Local Tax

Act establishes that local taxes must be based on ordinances adopted by the applicable local government.[9]

Municipal and prefectural governments collect taxes from residents and local businesses and use the revenue to provide public services closely related to daily life, such as education, police, fire, sanitation and public assistance. However, economic conditions may differ greatly between regions and thus, the revenues of individual prefectures and municipalities. The national government grants subsidies to local governments to reduce disparities and ensure a minimum level of service in public programs, most of which are established by national law but left to local governments to administer.

Article 84: Taxes to Have a Legal Basis

Yūichirō Tsuji

> **Article 84.**
> No new taxes shall be imposed or existing ones modified except by law or under such conditions as law may prescribe.

Article 84 establishes the basic principle that all taxes require a foundation in law. it. As with the Meiji Constitution (Article 63), Article 84 permits "perennial" taxation, which is to say that even though budgets must be passed by the Diet every year, the laws by which tax revenues expended in accordance with the budgets do not themselves need to be renewed annually. Additional legislative action is only needed to impose new taxes, or change the conditions of taxation. That said, perennial taxation is not a constitutional requirement either; the Diet may establish a one-year (or other limited duration) tax by statute. Extending such a tax would, of course, require a further Diet resolution.

Definition of "tax" and the Public Finance Act

"Tax" as used in Article 84 is understood to be any means by which a national, prefectural or municipal government imposes compulsory monetary contribution obligations on people for purposes of funding governmental spending. As per the Article 84 mandate, taxes are imposed through statutes. Article 3 of the Public Finance Act, the principal law governing the administration of national finances, provides that in addition to taxes, "all levies and monopoly prices or business rates in businesses that legally or practically belong to the State's monopoly, which are collected by the State under the State's authority" must also have a statutory basis. This effectively expands the requirement that there be a legislative basis for taxes, to include all other levies and even amounts paid in respect of legislatively sanctioned monopolies, such as water and sewer services.

That said, there is an interpretive controversy over the relationship between Articles 83 and 84 of the constitution on one hand and the Public Finance Act on the other. One interpretation holds that the expansive scope of Article 3 of the Public Finance Act is required by principle of fiscal constitutionalism articulated in Article 83 of the constitution, but thus by extension not required by the "no taxation without law" principle of Article 84. Under this interpretation Article 84 only applies, as its wording suggests, to taxes, i.e., amounts forcibly and unilaterally collected from the people by the government and used for governmental spending.

A competing interpretation is that Article 3 of the Act is required by Article 84, and that Article 84 requires Diet action to impose any amount collected by the government and used for any governmental purposes. Under this interpretation, the scope of Article 84 legislation requirement is not limited to traditional "taxes" but extends to other amounts collected by the government as well.[10]

A third interpretation is that Article 3 of the Act reflects a legislative policy mandated by the constitution. In other words, Article 84 requires the Diet to provide statutory clarity as to how taxes are assessed, calculated and collected; tax rules must be so clear that they can be understood *a priori* by taxpayers.

In practice, the fine details of tax policy are provided for in the applicable cabinet order anticipated in the delegating provisions in the relevant tax statute. Such delegations should be clear and address every possible case. In practice, a great deal of tax law is implemented through interpretive directives (*tsūtatsu*) from the National Tax Agency (which sits under the MOF) to local tax offices.[11] The NTA can use such directives, which are merely communications from superior tax regulators to inferior tax administrators, to change interpretations and effectively impose new or modified taxes, fiscal constitutionalism notwithstanding.

This is clearly problematic from the perspective of Article 84; however, the use of interpretive directives as a form of tax regulation was upheld by the Supreme Court many decades ago in the *Pachinko Case*. Pachinko is a Japanese form of entertainment that involves using a pachinko machine to shoot balls onto a peg board to win points and prizes that can be exchanged for cash, making it a two-step form of gambling. Under the Excise Tax Act of 1940, pachinko machines were not originally subject to taxation as "entertainment devices."[12] In 1951 the Tokyo Tax Bureau issued an interpretive directive declaring them to be entertainment devices and henceforth subject to taxation. This directive was merely a notification circulated among tax administrators, and as such did not technically directly impact the rights or duties of citizens. Of course, it had an indirect effect on those who were required to start paying excise taxes on pachinko machines. The Supreme Court rejected challenges asserting that this was the imposition of a new tax without a statutory basis on the grounds that the change in interpretation was consistent with a correct interpretation of the Excise Tax Act.[13]

Some constitutional scholars have criticized this ruling, pointing out that the directive indirectly impacts the rights and duties of the citizenry and imperils the rule of law.

Local taxes

The definition of tax in Article 84 also covers prefectural and municipal taxes. These may be imposed by the relevant governments by passing ordinances (See Chapter VIII), though most sources of local tax revenues also have a statutory foundation such as the Local Tax Act, and ordinances of the local government. In a 1962 case, the Supreme Court upheld the imposition of taxes based only on an ordinance passed by the local assembly, on the grounds that such assemblies had democratic legitimacy through their elected representatives.[14]

Accordingly, for purposes of satisfying the Article 84 requirement, a local ordinance is equivalent to a statute.

The Asahikawa Health Insurance Ordinance Case

Japan has a national health insurance scheme but it is administered by municipalities. Under the National Health Insurance Act, municipalities are required to collect funds from insured households, but have discretion to do so in the form of either "health insurance taxes" or "health insurance premiums."[15] When imposed as taxes, they clearly fall within the definition of Article 84. What about when they are imposed as premiums? Even as premiums, they are payment obligations constituting a public duty imposed through municipal ordinances within a statutory framework; payment is essentially mandatory.[16] Thus, Article 84 should arguably also apply to health insurance premiums, given their tax-like character, its purpose in funding state-subsidized health care, and the need for prior notice as to applicability and amount due. The Supreme Court held as much in the *Asahikawa Health Insurance Ordinance Case*, finding that Article 84 applies to national health insurance premiums, even though they are not "taxes." It also upheld the Asahikawa City ordinance which delegated to the mayor authority to set premium rates and give public notice of the same, finding that it was consistent with both the National Health Insurance Act (Article 81) and Article 84 of the constitution.[17]

Article 85: Diet Authorization Required For Expenditures and Debts

Yūichiro Tsuji

Article 85.
No money shall be expended, nor shall the State obligate itself, except as authorized by the Diet.

Article 85 reinforces the Article 83 principle of fiscal constitutionalism by applying it to government expenditures. The term expend/expenditure (*shishutsu*) is defined in Article 2(1) of the Public Finance Act as "the payment of cash to satisfy the various needs of the state" (translation by author).[18] The requirement of Diet authorization is also consistent with Article 60 requirements regarding the budget.

The government may cause the state to assume debts in order to meet its financial needs. The full procedure to assume debts is not provided for in the constitution. Essentially there are two principal methods, both set forth in the Public Finance Act: one is statutory,[19] the other budgetary.[20] Under the Public Finance Act, state expenditures to fund public works, investment or loan programs can be financed through the issuance of government bonds or other borrowings, up to the amount authorized by the Diet through statutes.[21] Statutory resolution is required for public loans for financial purposes; they will be reimbursed from the following year. This is the statutory method of assuming debts.

Budgetary methods of incurring debt include the issuance of short-term securities by the Ministry of Finance and short-term loans from the BOJ, which must be repaid from state revenues the same fiscal year.[22] However, the principal budgetary method of assuming obligations is through a budget approved by Diet resolution pursuant to Article 60.[23]

Article 86: Budget

Yūichiro Tsuji

Article 86.
The Cabinet shall prepare and submit to the Diet for its consideration and decision a budget for each fiscal year.

Overview

Article 86 sets forth the requirements for budgetary approval and establishes the general principle for the budget, or rather budgets, as discussed below. Budgets cover general income and expenditures for the applicable fiscal year as well as ongoing expenditures. They also include the rules used to estimate national revenues and expenditures for the applicable fiscal year.[24]

Single year budgeting and its exceptions; types of budget

Article 86 is understood as requiring a single national general account to be prepared each fiscal year. This is called the single year budget principle. This does not mean there must be a single budget, since the Diet may pass supplementary budgets in a single fiscal year.[25] Rather, it is a limit on the ability of the Diet to budget beyond the coming fiscal year or to use multi-year budgets to limit the discretion of future Diets. Although the language of Article 86 is unequivocal, the Public Finance Act establishes what are essentially several exceptions to this limitation.

With the scope of government activities becoming broader and more complex, the management of the funding of large projects carried out over multiple years has become increasingly difficult to reconcile with the principle of single-year budgeting. In response, the Public Finance Act (Article 13) permits the establishment of "special accounts" that are separate from the general account and which may be used for specific projects or for the use of funds from specific sources. These special accounts must be authorized by law, but are managed independently of the general account by national, prefectural or municipal governments and may help give a clearer picture of how specific funds or projects are being managed fiscally.

Article 68 of the Meiji Constitution allowed the government to ask the Imperial Diet to consent to a "continuing expenditure fund" to be used to meet special requirements over a predetermined number of years. However, successive governments abused this power to weaken the control of the legislature. This history may explain why Article 86 does not mention continuing (ongoing) expenditures. Article 12 of the Public Finance Act is consistent with Article 86 in requiring the expenditure of funds to be completed within the fiscal year for which they are budgeted.

However, Article 14-2(1) of the Act establishes exceptions which allow the Diet to approve expenditures over several years for construction, manufacturing or other multi-year projects. Another minor exception to the annual budgeting requirement of Article 86 is Article 41 of the Public Finance Act which allows a surplus from one year to be incorporated into revenue in the following year.[26]

The Public Finance Act does not allow for a general deficit covering government bonds. Article 4(1) notes that expenditure should comprise spending other than governmental bonds and debt. If necessary, the Diet can pass a special statute for bonds to finance deficits, in exception to Article 4(1). It is controversial for the ruling party to issue deficit financing bonds frequently, and there is no provision for fiscal soundness in the Constitution of Japan.

In March 2011, the Great East Japan Earthquake occurred. Under special legislation a reconstruction bond was issued to cover reconstruction costs. Issuance was limited from 2011 to 2015, and the government had to pay within 25 years. The appropriate use and transparency of reconstruction bonds have been the subject of some debate.

Law or not? The nature of the budget

There is an interpretive dispute about the nature of the budget under Article 86. Unlike other countries such as the United States where the budget is passed as a form of legislation, the Japanese constitution seems to establish the budget as a separate animal, which is passed through a different process from most laws.[27] That still leaves open the question of the character of the budget: is it a form of law? It is not an entirely theoretical question either, since the expenditure of funds anticipated by a budget must be conducted according to a law (Article 85), but it is possible for discrepancies to develop between the two. It is also relevant to the question of whether the Diet can amend a budget proposed by the Cabinet.

One interpretative view is that that the budget is the same as a statute. This is consistent with the principle of fiscal constitutionalism. And although the budget does not directly affect the rights and duties of the people (one common conceptualization of what comes under the rubric of "law"), it is consistent with the Article 73(iv) requirement that the civil service be administered "in accordance with standards established by law." Under this view the different procedural provenance of the budget is a matter of technicalities, and there is no danger of mismatch arising between the statute and the budget arising, since if both are laws, then the latter in time will naturally prevail.

Under a different interpretation, the budget is not a law. Rather it is an administrative measure, a financial plan expressing the will of the Cabinet to the Diet. Once approved by the latter it is binding as between the two branches, but has no impact on the people in the way laws do. This was the prevailing view of the nature of the budget under the Meiji Constitution.

A third interpretation endorses the legal nature of the budget as something which binds government action, but acknowledges that it has a different form and character from statutory law. According the budget legal status is consistent with fiscal constitutionalism. Although the budget only controls governmental action within the applicable fiscal year, whereas a statute binds the people until it expires or is repealed, this distinction does not mean the budget lacks the character of a legal norm.

With respect to the Meiji Constitution, Professor Toshiyoshi Miyazawa has explained that the budget was one form of national law, but one that was different from other acts passed by the Imperial Diet.[28] This notion remained in the current constitution. In other words, the budget is not just an estimate of revenue and expenditure, but a form of legal norm in the sense that it gives the executive branch the authority to spend in the manner set forth in the budget.

Revising the budget

Although the principle of fiscal constitutionalism reflected in Chapter VII makes it clear that Diet approval is required for budgeting and expenditures, it is silent as to whether the Diet can amend a budget after it has been submitted by the Cabinet, as it can with a statute. The legal character of the budget is thus relevant to whether it can be amended. Under the "administrative measure" of the budget, the Diet does not have the ability to propose a budget, so it would not logically have the ability to amend it either.

In practice, the Diet can and does amend budgets. In the course of "considering" budgets, the Diet may propose two types of amendments: increases or decreases. There are no constraints on the Diet reducing the budget. This contrasts with Article 67 of the Meiji Constitution, which prohibited reducing expenditures if they were based "upon the powers appertaining to the emperor" or "such expenditures as may have arisen by the effect of law, or that appertain to the legal obligations of the Government." Under current law, the Diet may also increase the budget, subject to certain conditions.[29]

However, there is controversy over the extent to which the Diet may amend the budget. If one accepts the view that the budget is a special form of law, then the Diet may revise the budget without any limitation, just as it can any other law, and this is consistent with the principle of fiscal constitutionalism is enshrined in Chapter VII. A more nuanced interpretation is that since the Diet has final responsibility for management of the nation's finances, it may revise the budget but subject to limits. In other words, the Diet may carry out amendments to "fine tune" the budget, but cannot revise it so much that it becomes a totally different budget and infringes the exclusive power of the Cabinet to initiate budgets. This is similar to the government view, which is that the Diet is thought to have the power to amend the budget to the extent it does not damage the power of the Cabinet to propose the budget.[30]

Since the proposed budget must be submitted to the House of Representatives first (Article 60), that chamber also has the ability to pass a special resolution asking the Cabinet to "restructure" it. This can effectively force the Cabinet to amend it (on the expectation that otherwise the Diet will reject the proposed budget).[31]

Mismatches between budgets and statutes

Since the constitution establishes different procedures for passing statutes and budgets, there is a possibility of a mismatch between the two. That is unless the budget is viewed as being the same as a statute, in which case there is no mismatch, since the latter in time supplants the former. Under other competing interpretations, there are three possible mismatch scenarios. The first is the situation where a statute requiring a budgetary allocation has been passed, but the budget has not. In that case, its duty under Article 73(i) to administer the law faithfully would seem to require the Cabinet to propose a supplementary or provisionary budget or develop other solutions.

The second scenario is when there is no statute required to implement budgetary provisions. In such a case the Cabinet would need to submit a necessary legislative proposal to the Diet, though the Diet is free not to pass it.

The third scenario is where the Diet passes a statute requiring budgetary expenditures but subsequently reduces the budget so as to make its implementation impossible. In this case the Diet needs to resolve the incongruity by revising or repealing the statute.

Article 87: Unforeseen Expenses

Yūichirō Tsuji

Article 87.

(1) In order to provide for unforeseen deficiencies in the budget, a reserve fund may be authorized by the Diet to be expended upon the responsibility of the Cabinet.

(2) The Cabinet must get subsequent approval of the Diet for all payments from the reserve fund.

Under the Meiji Constitution (Article 67) the establishment of a reserve fund to cover "unavoidable" shortfalls was mandatory. Under Article 87 it is optional, as a means of handling "unforeseen" deficiencies.

Article 87 is silent on the details, which are filled out in the Public Finance Act, Article 24 of which provides that the Cabinet may include a reserve fund in the revenue and expenditure budget (which thus requires Diet approval). The Cabinet is responsible for managing and using the reserve fund to cover deficits and other unexpected or new expenses.

As described in the preceding section on Article 86, a supplemental budget may be used to address unforeseen expenses in the middle of the fiscal year. However, because it takes time for the Cabinet to compose a supplementary budget and for the Diet to deliberate on it, the Cabinet may set aside a certain amount of unrestricted funds in the budget at the beginning of the fiscal year as a reserve fund which provides flexibility in responding to disasters and other emergencies. The inclusion of reserve funds in the expenditure and revenue budget is left to the discretion of the Cabinet.[32] Reserve funds are managed by the Ministry of Finance, and utilized in accordance with requests from other ministries.[33]

Reserve funds mean that there are funds budgeted for unknown uses, which is problematic from the standpoint of Article 85. The second paragraph of Article 87 addresses this by requiring subsequent parliamentary approval of expenditures from the reserve fund.[34] However, since the money is already spent, the impact of the Diet refusing to ratify such expenditures is political; the prime minister and his cabinet can be held politically responsible at the next election. There have been several instances when the Diet has declined to ratify emergency expenditures, including in 2006 and 2007 when reserve funds were used for politically controversial purposes such as counter-terrorism activities and humanitarian and reconstruction assistance in Iraq.

Article 88: Finances of the Imperial Household

Yūichirō Tsuji

Article 88.
All property of the Imperial Household shall belong to the State. All expenses of the Imperial Household shall be appropriated by the Diet in the budget.

Together with Article 8, Article 88 served the purpose of eliminating and preventing the resurgence of the imperial household as a concentration of wealth and political power, as it had been under the Meiji system. This was accomplished primarily by transferring the property of the imperial household as well as its income and expenditures to control by the Diet. Nonetheless, the emperor and other members of the imperial house need to maintain a suitable degree of prestige in their public and private lives.

The expenses of the imperial household include a portion of the living expenses of imperial families and the business of the imperial court. These are approved by the Diet. The Imperial Household Finance Act establishes three categories of expenses of the imperial household and its members. First there are *naitei-hi* (or "inner court expenses"), which are the living expenses of imperial family members and include an allowance to each member defined as having imperial family status as per the Imperial House Law. These are not treated as public funds under the control of the Imperial Household Agency, the government agency which administers the imperial family. There are also *kōzoku-hi*, which are allowances given to members of the imperial house in order to maintain their prestige, including one-time lump sums paid upon reaching adulthood and establishing their own homes, and when separating from the imperial family due to marriage or other reasons under the Imperial House Law. These are also outside the jurisdiction of the Imperial Household Agency.

All remaining expenses are *kyūtei-hi* (or "court expenses") and are managed by the Imperial Household Agency and used in furtherance of the performance of official duties by members of the imperial families. Examples include the costs of entertaining foreign monarchs and heads of state, as well as security and administrative costs.[35] Diet control does not extend to private property acquired by members of the imperial family, or their private expenditures.

Note that Article 88 requires the approval of the Diet in the form of the budget, meaning it can be approved by the House of Representatives alone (Article 60). By contrast, the Diet approval required under Article 8 for giving property to the imperial household is not budgetary.

An interesting gray area under Article 88 is the status of religious structures within the imperial palace and imperial graves. The former are considered to be private property of the imperial family, while the land and buildings comprising the latter are considered public property appertaining to the imperial household.

Article 89: Use of Public Funds For Religious Purposes Prohibited

Frank S. Ravitch

Article 89.
No public money or other property shall be expended or appropriated for the use, benefit or maintenance of any religious institution or association, or for any charitable, educational or benevolent enterprises not under the control of public authority.

Under the Meiji Constitution the government funded, and gave property to, Shintō shrines that suited the government's needs and also funded a variety of programs supporting State Shintō.[36] Moreover, the government used its power through the Shrine Act to defund and close many traditional and local Shintō Shrines in favor of shrines that reinforced State Shintō.[37] Buddhism, the dominant religion at the start of the Meiji period, was also repressed.

This was not lost on GHQ when it was drafting and negotiating the new constitution. Nor was it lost on those who were harmed by the prior system's support for State Shintō and the retribution meted out against those who spoke out against it. Thus, in addition to Article 20, which protects religious freedom and supports the separation of politics and religion, the constitution includes Article 89, which is aimed specifically at government financial support for religion (including use of property). Article 89 was designed to erect an additional barrier against government support for religion, as had happened during the Meiji era.

Much of the analysis under Article 20(1) and Article 20(3) also applies to Article 89. Thus, both the *Tsu City Groundbreaking Ceremony Case* and the *Ehime Tamagushi Case*, discussed at Article 20 also referenced Article 89. As a general matter the analysis is the same under both Articles.

The 21st century has seen additional cases in which both Article 20 and Article 89 were applied. But in some of these cases the underlying issues were more focused on the question of whether the government can give free use of property to a religious group. Significantly, one of the most important recent cases included a more direct discussion of Article 89 and what it requires.

In the *Sunagawa Sorachibuto Shrine Case*, the city of Sunagawa gave a neighborhood religious association called the *ujiko* the use of city owned property for use as a Shintō Shrine without requesting any compensation from the association.[38] This was challenged by a resident of the city as violating the constitution.

On appeal, the Supreme Court applied the endorsement analysis from the *Ehime Tamagushi Case* (see Article 20) and asked how the situation would be viewed from the public's perspective. It held that the city's actions violated both Article 20 and Article 89 and explained that the analysis under these Articles overlap. The fact that the shrine was originally taken over by the city at the request of a local citizen who had donated the land (for tax reasons) did not change this analysis. The Court acknowledged the religious nature of Shintō shrines and the problems raised by perceived government favoritism toward the shrine. In holding that the use of a government meeting building to house a religious shrine, especially without any compensation, would be viewed from the public's perspective as favoring Shintoism, the Court provided a more in-depth discussion of Article 89 itself than prior cases had done:

Article 89 of the constitution can be construed to prohibit the state's or local public entity's connection with religion in cases where its connection with religion in terms of appropriating public property for use, etc. is found to be beyond the limit that is deemed to be reasonable, in light of the social and cultural conditions of our country, in relation to the fundamental purpose of the system of securing [the] *guarantee of freedom of religion.*

The act of the state or a local public entity to offer national or public land for the use as a site of a religious facility without compensation should be, in general, deemed to constitute offering of a benefit to the religious organization, etc. which has established said religious facility, and it raises a conflict with Article 89 of the constitution.[39]

The Court also explained that context is very important when considering whether offering public land for use of a religious facility without compensation violates Article 89. In this regard the Court explained:

[I]*t is appropriate to construe that judgment should be made comprehensively in light of socially accepted ideas, while taking into consideration various factors, including the nature of the religious facility in question, the circumstances where the land in question has been offered for the use as the site of the relevant facility without compensation, the manner of offering without compensation, and the public's evaluation of such practice.*[40]

The Court held that the situation in the case violated these principles. It noted, however, that it would be inappropriate to require the mayor to remove the shrine immediately because it would make it very hard for the *ujiko* group (*ujiko* refers to those who live within a shrine's parish area who maintain the shrine) to carry out its religious activities, which would harm the religious freedom of members of the group. Remanding the case to see whether any "rational and realistic alternative means" other than total removal of the shrine was possible, the Court noted several possible alternatives, including a grant, transfer for compensation, or lease at fair market value. The Court itself seemed to favor a remedy that involved compensation or a lease at fair market value, but since it also mentioned a grant, it is not clear what would be required. A Petty Bench of the Court ultimately approved a lease at fair market value.[41]

In another judgment rendered the same day, but involving a different shrine in Sunagawa City, the Court upheld a transfer by the municipal government to a neighborhood association of a Shintō shrine and the small parcel of land on which it sat.[42] The transfer of the land and shrine had been challenged by municipal residents as a violation of Article 20(3) and Article 89. Interestingly, the Court noted that given the religious nature of a Shintō Shrine, the city might be viewed by the public to be favoring a religion. The Court explained, however, that the land had originally belonged to the predecessor of the same neighborhood association, which had donated it to the city to build housing for public school teachers, but the housing was no longer there. As a result, the land transfer to the association was viewed by the Court as a return of land given to the city for a specific purpose that was no longer being served. Under these facts the Court considered the transfer an acceptable way to avoid problems under Article 20 and Article 89 that would have existed had the city continued to own land used by the shrine free of charge. Thus, despite the seeming similarities, the facts of the case were decisively different from the facts in the *Sunagawa Sorachibuto Shrine Case*.

In 2021, the Court addressed similar issues in the context of a religion other than Shintō for the first time, in a case from Okinawa involving a Confucian temple.[43] The government of the city of Naha allowed the temple to build a new facility in a public park without paying any rent or fees. The Court held that this violated both Article 20 and Article 89, following the reasoning from the *Sunagawa Sorachibuto Shrine Case* to hold that allowing the temple to build on and occupy the land in a public park without paying rent unconstitutionally promoted religion. While some might argue that Confucianism is a philosophy, not a religion, the Court held that the performance of rites at the temple had enough of a religious function to be covered under Article 20 and Article 89, but did so without specifically holding that Confucianism is a religion.[44] The Court also distinguished the temple from historical religious sites that are able to be on public land without fees because of their historical nature and longstanding presence at their locations (the temple was built in the park in 2013).

These cases help illustrate the fact that the context and history of any land transfer, financial support, or other benefit given to a religious entity will be important to the analysis under Article 89 (and Article 20). The Court will consider the issue from the perspective of whether the public would view the government as favoring religion, and the Court has not been afraid to find that a violation has occurred.

Article 90: Review by Board of Audit

Yūichirō Tsuji

Article 90.

(1) Final accounts of the expenditures and revenues of the State shall be audited annually by a Board of Audit and submitted by the Cabinet to the Diet, together with the statement of audit, during the fiscal year immediately following the period covered.

(2) The organization and competency of the Board of Audit shall be determined by law.

The final account (*kessan*) is a reconciliation of actual revenues and expenditures against the budget for a fiscal year. Constitutionally, however, while the budgets have a legal status, the final accounts do not—they are a reporting exercise and have no impact on the legal effect of the applicable budget. Such reporting is nonetheless consistent with fiscal constitutionalism, and serve the useful purpose of reviewing the budget to determine if it was appropriate.

The Board of Audit is one of the few government agencies specifically mentioned by the constitution. First established under the Ministry of Finance in 1880, under the Meiji constitutional system it reported directly to the emperor and was outside the control of the government.[45] Under the present constitution the three Inspectors comprising the Board are appointed by the Cabinet with the consent of both houses of the Diet and attestation by the emperor.[46] They are otherwise independent, serving fixed terms and only subject to removal in extraordinary circumstances.[47]

The Board of Audit reviews the validity and legality of the final accounts of the revenue and expenditure, and makes an inspection report. The final account is audited and submitted to each House of the Diet for their respective review. The Diet chambers may not revise the report, and even if they reject the final account as reported by the Board, it does not change the expenditure and revenue, which have already been completed by the time the audit is finished.

Note that the English version of Article 90 lacks a crucial "all" at the beginning ("*All* final accounts…") which would make it more accurately reflect the Japanese. This is important because in the Japanese version it is clear that the audit requirement extends to all government institutions and activities. This helps explain why there is some dispute over whether the Board of Audit is exempt from Japan's national secrecy law, the Protection of Specially Designated Secrets Act. The law does not currently contain any special exceptions to the secrecy of sensitive government activities that would permit the Board to conduct its audit of the financial aspects of those activities.[48]

Article 91: Cabinet to Report on National Finances Annually

Yūichirō Tsuji

> **Article 91.**
> At regular intervals and at least annually the Cabinet shall report to the Diet and the people on the state of national finances.

Article 91 adds to the ability of the Diet to get information from the Cabinet (see Articles 62, 63 and 72), by imposing upon it a specific duty to report on the state of national finances. In practice this constitutional obligation is satisfied first through a speech by the Minister of Finance that is delivered at the opening of the new ordinary Diet session every January.[49]

Article 91 is further implemented through provisions of the Public Finance Act requiring the Cabinet to publish details of the budget once it has been approved, and to report to the Diet and the people on the status of budget implementation and other financial matters.[50]

Article 91 is not interpreted as giving the people the power to demand access to the financial reports of the Cabinet. It is up to the Diet to hold the Cabinet politically responsible for failing to report the necessary information to the people.

Notes

1 Note that although the chapter title is "Finance" in the English version of both constitutions, in the Japanese they are different. In the Meiji Constitution the title is "*kaikei*" which is typically translated "accounts" or "accounting." In the present constitution it is "*zaisei*" a more sophisticated term meaning "finance," "financial affairs" or "fiscal policy."

2 Nihon Ginkō Hō [Bank of Japan Act], Law no. 67 of 1942.

3 Bank of Japan Act, Articles 14, 16, 21, 23, 24 and 25.

[4] If the Bank's operation constitutes an exercise of executive power, the question arises as to what control the Cabinet should retain over the Bank to ensure compatibility with Article 65 of the constitution. The government's position on this issue is that, as in the case of the Administrative Board, if control is retained at least through personnel and budgetary matters, the Bank is under the control of the Cabinet and is not unconstitutional in relation to Article 65.

[5] Statement by Masahiro Sakata, then 3rd Head of the Cabinet Legislation Bureau, at the Financial Systems Research Council, Bank of Japan Act Revision Subcommittee (6th session) (January 14, 1997); and at the House of Councillors Committee on Finance (May 7, 1997). Under Article 23 of the BOJ Act, the members of the bank's Policy Board are appointed by the Cabinet with the consent of both chambers of the Diet.

[6] The Fukui District Court confirmed the constitutionality of the Board of Independent Administrative Commission on September 6, 1952; Bank of Japan Trial Law Volume 3, No. 9, 1823

[7] Satō, K. (2020), 589–91. When the Bank of Japan Act was revised in 1997, the question arose as to how to explain the independence of the Bank of Japan under the theory of the "remainder theory" of the administrative power (see discussion at Article 65). Sato criticizes the remainder theory used by the government to justify the status of the BOJ, arguing instead that although central banking is a task that the national government is responsible for, it is not an administrative function that belongs to the Cabinet. Accordingly, it is an area permitting broad legislative discretion. He also points out that even if the central bank is independent of the Cabinet, it does not violate Article 65 of the constitution, so long as the bank is ultimately subject to control by the Diet. Satō argues that the BOJ's powers could be determined through legislation and that the BOJ could also be constituted as a private corporation. If the government has the authority to appoint personnel to the BOJ, it is constitutional to grant the BOJ that is independent of the Cabinet. Pointing to clashes between the BOJ and the MOF over revisions to the Bank of Japan Act impacting the Bank's independence, Yamawaki argues that to maintain the independence of financial policy, the central bank must be independent because it could otherwise be distorted at the will of the Ministry of Finance. The report of the Central Bank Study Group did not clarify whether the Ministry of Finance should approve the Bank's budget to carry out its mandate. Yamawaki, T. (1998), 85–86, 91, 95–96.

[8] Tokubetsu Kaikei ni Kansuru Hōritsu [Special Account Act], Law no. 23 of 2007.

[9] Chihōzeihō [Local Tax Act], Law no. 226 of 1950, Article 3.

[10] Kobayashi, N. (1968), 185.

[11] Local taxes are administered by the MIC rather than the National Tax Agency.

[12] The Excise Tax Act was repealed with the passage of the Consumption Tax Act in 1989 under the administration of Prime Minister Noboru Takeshita.

[13] Supreme Court, 2nd Petty Bench judgment of March 28, 1948.

[14] Supreme Court, Grand Bench judgment of February 21, 1962.

[15] National Health Insurance Act, Article 76. The distinction between tax or premium does not greatly impact implementation of the national scheme, but does tie back to different statutes and involves some fine differences, such as in terms of statutes of limitation and priority against other creditors.

[16] National Health Insurance Act, Article 81.

[17] Supreme Court, Grand Bench judgment of March 1, 2006. The case involved various other constitutional challenges based on allegedly discriminatory impact on impoverished citizens through premium rates and mechanisms for reducing them, all of which were rejected.

[18] Note though substantively the same, the structure of the Japanese version of Article 85 is different. A more direct translation might be "The expenditure of state funds and the assumption of debts by the state is required to be based on a resolution of the Diet."

[19] Public Finance Act, Article 15(1).

[20] Public Finance Act, Article 15(2).

[21] Public Finance Act, Article 4(1). When such borrowings are used to finance public works, the scope of the public works must also be approved by the Diet each fiscal year (Article 4(3)).

[22] Public Finance Act, Article 7.

[23] Public Finance Act, Article 15.

[24] Japan's fiscal year starts on April 1 and runs to March 31 of the following calendar year. Public Finance Act, Article 11.

[25] The Public Finance Act provides that the "budget" should be comprised of a main budget and supplementary and provisional budgets. The main budget covers the general and special accounts. The supplementary

budget covers additional and revised budgets which may be necessary to cover shortfalls. The Cabinet may also submit a provisional budget before formal approval of the main budget. Once the budget is approved by the Diet, the provisional budget loses its effect, and any measures based on the provisional budget are assumed to be spent by the main budget. In practice, the provisional budget is limited to minimum expenditure to cover necessary legal spending and salaries for public officials and is necessitated by the mismatch between the fiscal year and the legislative calendar.) In the Meiji Constitution, the government could the implement the previous year's budget if the Imperial Diet could not approve the new budget.

[26] Public Finance Act, Articles 41 & 42.

[27] Unlike legislative proposals, the budget must originate from the Cabinet (Article 73), can be passed by a simple majority of the House of Representatives in the face of opposition from the House of Councillors (Articles 59 and 60), and is not a category of government act that must be promulgated by the emperor (Article 7). Note that Article 59(1) clearly anticipates exceptions to the law-making process it mandates, based on other provisions of the constitution.

[28] Miyazawa, T. (1942), 255–56. *See also*, Satō, I. (1984), 1124; Miyazawa, T. (1942), 256 (arguing the budget is a form of law). Sasaki, S. (1930), 637 (arguing budget is an administrative matter not a legal form).

[29] Under of the Diet Act, at least 50 members in the House of Representatives, or 20 members in the House of Councillors must support a legislative bill that would have the effect of increasing the budget, or to take up a motion to amend the budget (Article 57 and 57-2). Under Article 57-3, each chamber (or its relevant committee) "must afford the Cabinet an opportunity to give its opinion" on amendments to legislative bills that would increase the budget.

[30] Cabinet Legislation Bureau Director Hideo Sanada 23, February in 1977 in response to the House of Representatives Budget Committee. Asano, I., and Sugihara, Y. (Eds.) (2003). 485.

[31] This is a rare occurrence, however, and has only happened twice in the history of the current constitution.

[32] Public Finance Act, Articles 24, 29.

[33] Public Finance Act, Articles 24, 35.

[34] For example, in 2020, the Cabinet decided to make expenditures from the reserve funds of a supplementary budget to address the spread of Covid-19 by helping municipalities secure isolation accommodation for people with mild cases and to pay for vaccines for developing countries in Africa and elsewhere. Reserve funds were also used to pay for repairs of damage caused by heavy rains. The Diet approved these expenditures.

[35] Kōshitsu Keizaihō [Imperial Household Finance Act], Law no. 4 of 1947.

[36] These programs included educational curricula reinforcing fealty to the emperor and State Shintō, events and holidays that reinforced State Shintō, and gifts from the imperial household for home shrines. The government also supported a series of charitable, educational, and benevolent associations that fostered nationalism and State Shintō. *See, e.g.* Hardacre, H. (1989); Ravitch, F.S. (2013).

[37] Within Shintō there is a huge pantheon of divine beings worshipped at various shrines throughout the country. They can be categorized in various ways, but one is to distinguish between: (1) Shrines to deities related to nature, family ancestors and local ancestors, and (2) Shrines to deities having a connection to the imperial family, including those mentioned in the *Kojiki* or the *Nihonshoki*, two of Japan's oldest surviving historical accounts, including the divine ancestors of the imperial family. State Shintō was implemented in part by supporting and emphasizing the latter and diminishing or suppressing the former even though the former was more central to the lived religion of many Japanese.

[38] The shrine consisted of a *torii* (the gate to a Shintō Shrine), a *jishingū* (stone monument to the deity that is seen as protecting the local area), a *hokora* (small Shintō Shrine), and a sign noting that the shrine was in the building. A religious association called the *Ujiko* managed the property and performed festivals and rituals but paid no compensation to the city for the use of the property.

[39] English translation from Japan courts website at: https://www.courts.go.jp/app/hanrei_en/detail?id=1048.

[40] Ibid.

[41] Supreme Court, 1st Petty Bench judgment of February 16, 2012.

[42] Supreme Court, Grand Bench judgment of January 20, 2010 (64 *Minshū* 128).

[43] Supreme Court, Grand Bench Judgment of February 24, 2021.

[44] One judge dissented, expressing the view that the activities at the temple were a form of custom rather than religious practice.

[45] Article 72 of the Meiji Constitution established the Board of Audit as performing a similar audit function.

[46] Kaikei Kensain Hō [Board of Audit Act], Law no. 73 of 1947, Articles 1, 2, 4 and 5.
[47] Board of Audit Act, Article 5.
[48] Jones, C.P.A. (2019). Japan's Board of Audit: Unlikely Guardians of the Constitution?, in Jones, C.P.A. (2019).
[49] At this time the prime minister also delivers an administrative policy speech, the Minister of Foreign Affairs delivers a speech about foreign affairs, and the diplomatic speech, the Minister of Finance delivers a fiscal speech, and the Minister of State for Economic and Fiscal Policy delivers a speech about the state of the economy. The speeches also present an opportunity to Diet members to ask questions to the ministers about policy. Notwithstanding one of them satisfying a postwar constitutional requirement, these speeches have a longstanding tradition dating back to the first convocation of the Imperial Diet in 1890.
[50] Public Finance Act, Article 46. The government also publishes numerous other official monthly reports relevant to the state of government finance, balance of payments and the state of economy.

Chapter VIII
Local Self Government
Articles 92–95

Introduction

Tōru Enoki

Introduction

The tiers of governance below the national government are carried out through what are described as "local public entities" in the constitution. Chapter VIII addresses the subject of self-government without further defining the term. The term "local" is also likely to confuse, since the Japanese term is *chihō*, which is more commonly translated "region" or "the countryside." The term "local government" as used in the constitution and elsewhere thus includes what might be more accurately called "regional" governments which are known as prefectures and encompass multiple municipalities.

Local self-government in Japan: Past, present and future

Before the establishment of the modern state after the Meiji Restoration, the shogunate functioned as a central government with individual domains (*han*) headed by lords owing allegiance and obedience to the shogun, who was also the largest domain lord. With the restoration the *han* were abolished by converting them into prefectures which, after some consolidation, remain to this day.

The Meiji Constitution did not contain any provisions on local self-government. However, the government under it established a system of cities, towns, villages, counties and prefectures between 1888 and 1890. Under these systems, the applicable administrative units were granted a certain degree of local self-governance. However, the national government retained strong control over the regions; for example, prefectural governors were appointed from among national administrative officials. The lower tiers of government were thus part of a system of top-down control by the national government.

By contrast, the present constitution devotes an entire chapter to the subject of "Self-Government," reflecting in part the American drafters' views of the importance of democracy in local government. A chapter guaranteeing local autonomy was thus part of the political democratization that formed a keynote in the new constitution. Chapter VIII guarantees a form of government in which public affairs closely related to the residents' daily lives are handled by residents of that area, through elected representative bodies.[1] The Constitution of Japan has four articles on local self-government, namely Articles 92 to 95. Article 92 sets forth the basic principles of local self-government. Article 93 provides for the establishment of local assemblies as organs of proceedings and the direct election of heads and members, among others. Article 94 defines the powers of the local government. Lastly, Article 95 provides some protection of local autonomy from national legislation targeting specific prefectures or municipalities.

The details of local government are provided for in the Local Autonomy Act (LAA). It establishes two tiers of local public bodies below the national government: prefectures and municipalities (cities, towns and villages). Thus, Japan has three tiers of government: national, prefectural, and municipal. "Local public entities" refers to prefectures and municipalities. The details of their organization, powers and responsibilities are set forth in the LAA. Japan has 47 prefectures (including Tokyo) which are the intermediary tier and encompass multiple municipalities.[2] Municipalities are the smallest unit of Japan's basic local government and are further subdivided by into cities, towns, and villages depending on population, with Tokyo having "special wards" discussed in more detail at Article 92. As of the time of writing there were approximately 1700 municipalities in Japan.

Municipal governments deal with truly local matters, while prefectural governments deal with matters that may affect multiple municipalities (such as river management, major roads and the police). Municipal governments are also charged with implementing various national government programs. Most major cities in Japan (those with a population of 500,000 or more) are "designated cities," a category designated by the Cabinet under the LAA. Designated cities are delegated numerous authorities otherwise exercised by prefectural governments. Thus, Japanese people are likely to interact with government mostly at the municipal level.

Under the constitution both prefectures and municipalities were reconstituted with elected executives and assemblies. However, elements of the prewar system of top-down control remained, with local governments devoting much of their time and energy to implementing national government policies and programs. This was accomplished through the legislative or regulatory delegation by ministries and other national institutions of policy implementation to local government heads. This subjected elected prefectural and municipal governments to control by unelected central government bureaucrats in connection with matters closely related to the daily lives of residents of municipalities and prefectures.

In this context, one of the most important developments in local government in Japan was the passage in 1999 of the Promotion of Decentralization Reform Act.[3] This substantially amended the LAA to clarify the division of responsibilities between the national and local governments, encapsulated in the following statement:

> *the national government shall play an important role in the implementation of policies and projects that must be carried out on a nationwide scale or from a national perspective, and other roles that should be played by the national government, and shall share the roles appropriately with local governments, based on the principle of leaving as much as possible of the administration close to the residents to local governments.*[4]

Before the 1999 amendments, the national government was constantly intervening in the affairs of local governments. Now, the involvement of the national government in the affairs of local governments has been subject to greater definition and transparency (see discussion at Article 94).

That said, however, there are still certain statutory functions of the national government the performance of which are delegated to local governments by statute or cabinet order. For example, the family registration system in which births, deaths, marriages, divorces and so forth are recorded (see discussion at Article 24) is under the jurisdiction of the Ministry of Justice. However, day-to-day operations are handled by municipalities, subject to oversight and guidance from the MOJ through its network of Legal Affairs Bureaus to ensure registrations are performed properly and uniformly nationwide.[5]

In addition, while prefectural governors are no longer appointed by the central government as under the Meiji Constitution, at any given time there are a large number of national government officials seconded to prefectural and municipal governments, including as vice-governors and vice-mayors.[6] Thus, although decentralization reform has been implemented legislatively, national government involvement in municipal and prefectural governance remains significant. Recent years have also seen an effort to reduce duplication of government functions through a program of merging municipalities, the number of which has dropped by approximately half since the beginning of the Heisei era in 1989. Legislators and regulators have also long been evaluating the possibility of converting to a more federal system, which would see the 47 prefectures combine into a dozen or so "states" or "provinces" with a much higher degree of autonomy than prefectures have now.

Article 92: The Principle of Local Autonomy

Tōru Enoki

Article 92.
Regulations concerning organization and operations of local public entities shall be fixed by law in accordance with the principle of local autonomy.

The meaning of "the principle of local autonomy"

Article 92 stipulates the general principles of local autonomy.[7] This is understood as consisting of two elements: the autonomy of local public entities (see the Chapter introduction for the meaning of this term) and of the people who live in them. The autonomy of residents is a democratic element in which their will forms the basis for local self-government. On the other hand, the autonomy of local public entities is a liberal and decentralized element in which local governance is entrusted to an organization independent of the national government. Local self-governance is thus carried out pursuant to the will and responsibility of that organization itself.

There are three principal theories used to conceptualize the constitutional guarantee of local autonomy: (1) the inherent rights theory; (2) the recognition theory; and, (3) the institutional guarantee theory.

The inherent rights theory holds that local governments have inherent rights, just as individuals have inherent and inalienable rights against the state. In the past, the dominant view of academic circles was to deny this theory. However, in recent years, it has been re-evaluated as a basis for emphasizing the independent rule-making and financial roles of local governments. However, the nature and extent of local autonomy under the inherent rights theory is not always clear.

The recognition theory holds that local autonomy exists to the extent recognized by the state. This theory does not attach any great significance to "the principle of local autonomy" under Article 92.[8] Almost no one supports this theory because it renders the constitution's guarantee of local autonomy meaningless.

Under the institutional guarantee theory, the constitution does not guarantee fundamental rights of local governments (as under the inherent rights theory), but rather accords them institutional protections under public law. According to this theory, the "principle of local autonomy" in Article 92 refers to the essential elements and core of the system of local government, which cannot be infringed even by national laws. It is not clear, however, what the "essential elements" or the core are.

It is said that the inherent rights theory and institutional guarantee theory do not result in a significant difference in understanding the "the principle of local autonomy" because they are both unclear. They do affect how the structure of the state is understood: is it a federation of autonomous organizations or a centralized state?[9] This is a question that remains unresolved by judicial or other governmental interpretation.

The meaning of "local public entities"

The constitution uses the term "local public entities" without definition. The LAA establishes two basic types: ordinary local public entities and special local public entities. The former are prefectures and municipalities and the latter are "special local entities," the most significant of which are the 23 municipalities (called "special wards") comprising metropolitan Tokyo. The lack of definition in the constitution raises two questions: (1) whether the constitution requires (by guaranteeing) the two-tier system of ordinary local entities (i.e., prefectures and municipalities); and, (2) whether "local public entities" in the constitution include special local public entities, in particular Tokyo's special wards.

As to the first question, the generally-accepted view is that while the constitution guarantees a two-tier system, so long as it does not contravene the "principle of local autonomy" articulated in Article 92, the form of the higher level of ordinary local entity is left to legislative policy; it does not need to be a "prefecture." This is an important consideration in the context of ongoing deliberations regarding the possible abolition of prefectures and replacement with a more federal system of "state"-like regional governments discussed in the Chapter Introduction.

As for the second question, some explanation of special wards is required. Currently these only exist in Tokyo,[10] and for the most part function as municipalities (some refer to themselves as "cities" in English) but with a different allocation of roles and responsibilities between prefecture and municipality than in other prefectures and municipalities.[11]

For constitutional purposes, the most significant difference between special wards and cities, towns and villages is that from 1949 until 1975, the chief executives of Tokyo's special wards were not elected.[12] When this was challenged in court as a violation of Article 93, the Supreme Court declared that special wards were not "local public entities" as defined in the constitution, which the Court declared referred to "local public entities that have a social basis in that its residents live together economically and culturally and have a sense of community" and having "a considerable degree of autonomous legislative power, autonomous administrative power, autonomous financial power, and other basic elements of local autonomy."[13]

Thus, although the executives of Tokyo's special wards are currently elected, it is not—or perhaps was not—a constitutional requirement, and at least as far as Tokyo is concerned the standard "two-tiered" system of elected local governments is not necessarily guaranteed by the constitution.[14] After decades of using elections to choose special ward executives and assemblies, and with the passage of 2012 making possible the establishment of special wards in other large municipalities,[15] the better interpretation would be that special wards in Tokyo and elsewhere should be understood as "local public entities" under the constitution.[16]

Article 93: Organization of Local Public Entities

Tōru Enoki

Article 93.

(1) The local public entities shall establish assemblies as their deliberative organs, in accordance with law.

(2) The chief executive officers of all local public entities, the members of their assemblies, and such other local officials as may be determined by law shall be elected by direct popular vote within their several communities.

The LAA provides for two other types of special local public entities in addition to Tokyo's special wards: (1) associations of local public bodies and (2) financial wards. The former are administrative associations or cross-regional federations through which multiple municipalities cooperate in the performance of certain functions such as firefighting, water, sewage and garbage disposal. Functions delegated to such associations are no longer performed by the municipalities involved.[17] The latter are organizations established to administer specific assets, such as forests, cemeteries, reservoirs, hot springs, residential land and fields, or public facilities, such as irrigation canals and community centers, owned by some areas (residents) of a municipality. Some financial wards are the result of municipal mergers and offered a means of preserving community control over specific assets that would otherwise fall under the complete control over the merged entity. It is clear that these two types of "special local public bodies" are not "local public entities" for purposes of Article 93, and thus do not need to have elected assemblies or executives.

At the same time, however, there is also no dispute that such entities do not fall under the category of "local public entities" under Article 94. There are different views on whether these organizations are "local public entities" under Article 92 of the constitution, but the prevailing one is that the "local public entities" under Article 92 are the same as those under Articles 93 and 94: all should be understood to have the same meaning. Moreover, "associations of local public bodies" and "financial wards" do not fall under the "local public entities" as used in Article 92. We thus think that they do not fall under the category of "local public entities" under the constitution.[18]

Dual representation system in local politics

The constitution provides for a "dual representation" system in local politics consisting of the assemblies and chief executives of each ordinary local public entity (see discussion at Article 92). Paragraph (1) of Article 93 requires that all (ordinary) local public entities (i.e., prefectural and municipal governments) have assemblies, and paragraph (2) requires that these assemblies be directly elected. Note that although the term used for assembly (*gikai*) is a generic term commonly used to refer to legislative bodies, in the context of the constitution it refers to assemblies that enact ordinances (see Article 94).

Under paragraph (2) of Article 93, all ordinary local public entities also have chief executive officers (governors in prefectures and mayors in municipalities) who are also directly elected by local residents. This means that, unlike the national government, which has a parliamentary cabinet system in which the executive and at least one house of the legislature are controlled by the same party, the local government system mandated by the constitution makes it possible to have a local assemblies and executives in opposition due to differences in their political affiliations.

The LAA establishes basic parameters followed by all local public entities. Assembly members and chief executives each serve four-year terms, but are subject to recall by the electorate, who may also demand the dissolution of their local assemblies.[19] Textually, Article 93(2) also anticipates the possibility of the election of "such other local officials as may be determined by law." In the past there were instances of local school board officials being elected but this is no longer the case. The "such other" language is not interpreted as requiring that other local officials be elected, and under current practice electoral roles are uniformly limited to the executives and assembly members.[20]

Assemblies as deliberative organs

The reference to "deliberative organs" means that assemblies are the organs that decide the will of individual local public entities. However, unlike the Diet, which is "the highest organ of state power" (see Article 41), is granted broad autonomy and its members vested with special immunities (see Articles 50 and 51), the Supreme Court has declined to find local assemblies and their members as enjoying similar privileges.[21]

Direct democratic system

Article 93(2) guarantees community residents the right to directly elect the heads of local governments and members of local assemblies.[22] It likewise provides for referendums on special laws (Article 95). The constitution thus envisages the residents' active involvement in local governance. This system of direct democracy is further implemented through the LAA, which makes it possible for residents to demand their local assembly be dissolved, for the dismissal of assemblies or executives to be dismissed, for the enactment, amendment or abolition of local ordinances, and for audits of their local government.[23]

There are also examples of local public entities holding referenda on issues such as the construction and hosting of nuclear power plants or US military bases, the pros and cons of mergers with other municipalities, and the reorganization of local municipal bodies. However, the results of such referendums are not considered to be legally binding, although it goes without saying the assembly and the chief executive should respect the results. There was a case regarding this matter, in which the residents of a municipality claimed damages for a mayor's decision to accept the relocation of the US military's offshore heliport base in Okinawa, in the face of the majority of residents indicating their opposition in a referendum. The Naha District Court ruled that the mayor was not legally obligated to follow the referendum's result and if the result of the referendum was legally binding, it might lead to a result that is inconsistent with the indirect democracy system, which is a fundamental principle of current national law.[24]

A more recent (2019) referendum in Okinawa Prefecture similarly revealed the majority of prefectural residents opposing the reclamation of land in order to relocate a US Marine Corps air base to Henoko in Nago City. However, the results of such referenda not being considered legally binding, the national government continues to push ahead with the construction of the new base at Henoko.

Article 94: Functions of Local Public Entities

Tōru Enoki

Article 94.
Local public entities shall have the right to manage their property, affairs and administration and to enact their own regulations within law.

Functions and affairs of local public entities

Under the constitution the national government has the legislative, executive and judicial powers of the state. Within this framework, Article 94 stipulates the scope of autonomy that local public entities (municipal and prefectural governments) have in managing their own property and affairs. An example of this is municipal and prefectural ordinances (*jōrei*), the "regulations" referenced in Article 94.[25] A local ordinance is an independent "law" enacted by local governments based on its autonomy, therefore, the ordinance only applies within the jurisdictional boundaries of the local public entity that enacted it.[26] Local public entities have the authority to make independent decisions regarding their internal organization, legislation, administration, and finance. However, local public entities do not have their own constitutions, nor do they have any judicial powers.

Subsequent to its amendment in 1999 (see discussion in Chapter Introduction), the LAA categorizes the "autonomy functions" that municipal and prefectural governments may perform as being either (1) functions that would otherwise be performed by the national government but which are delegated to lower tiers of governments by statute and thus need to be handled with particular care and consistency, and (2) other functions.[27] Involvement of higher levels of government in the affairs of lower tiers of government (i.e., the national in prefectural and municipal, the prefectural in municipal) is limited to those cases provided for by law.[28]

The 1999 amendments to the LAA also established The Central and Local Government Dispute Management Council, an independent organization whose purpose is to resolve disputes arising between the national government and local governments, or between local governments.[29] If the head of a local government is dissatisfied with the involvement of the national government, he or she may file a request for review with the council. If council resolution is unsuccessful, further recourse is possible through the courts.[30] Litigation is possible in some instances where the council resolution is not accepted. Moreover, if the national government has demanded that a local government take corrective action against an illegal act, but the said corrective action is not taken, the national government may sue the local government in an action for the declaration of illegality of inaction.[31]

Local government ordinances: Meaning and basis

The meaning of the phrase "their own regulations" in Article 94 is the subject of multiple interpretations but the prevailing view of constitutional scholars is that it includes not just ordinances enacted by resolution of the local assembly, but also rules and regulations issued by chief executives and administrative committees. These are essentially the three categories of local rules anticipated by the LAA.[32]

As also discussed at Article 31, concerning the basis for the right of local governments to enact regulations, in the *Osaka Anti-Prostitution City Ordinance Case* the Supreme Court ruled that:

> *Regulations enacted by local public entities are nothing other than self-governing legislation that is directly authorized by Article 94 of the Constitution to be enacted within the scope of the law, based on the principle of local autonomy guaranteed by the Constitution as an indispensable component of democratic political organization* (Article 92).[33]

Limitations on the power to enact local regulations

There are two limitations on the ability of local governments to enact regulations. The first is that matters covered by local governments in their regulations must be within the scope of local autonomy functions. The second is that regulations are limited by the scope of national law.

Regulations within the scope of local autonomy functions

So long as they are relevant to the exercise of local autonomy, local governments have broad authority to make rules. Regulations passed within the scope of local autonomy functions can even impose restrictions on residents' basic human rights (subject to constitutional constraints, of course).

Matters outside the scope of local autonomy functions include matters defined by law as the national government affairs, those where the law requires uniformity throughout the country, those related to the formation of private law relationships such as marriages or divorce, the definition of criminal offenses and their punishment, and those relevant to the interests of the entire country as opposed to a particular region.

Even within the scope of local autonomy, the ability of local governments to regulate is subject to constitutional constraints with respect to property rights, criminal penalties and taxation.

Property rights

As discussed at Article 29, restrictions on property rights must be based on law and there is thus a question about whether property rights can be restricted through local ordinances. In the *Nara Prefectural Reservoir Ordinance Case*, a farmer who continued farming atop a communal levee after passage of a local ordinance prohibiting doing so challenged his conviction.[34] On appeal the Supreme Court ruled that:

> *the act of using the reservoir levees to cause the destruction or collapse of the reservoir is outside the scope of the lawful exercise of property rights protected by the Constitution and the Civil Code, and prohibiting and punishing such an act with the ordinance does not violate or deviate from the Constitution and laws.*

It is unclear, however, whether the Court was saying that the act of using land above reservoir levees (which could cause them to collapse and damage the reservoir) (1) is not a property right guaranteed by the constitution, or (2) is a constitutionally-protected property right, but one which can be limited by regulation. Academic theories hold that even constitutionally-protected property rights can be restricted through local ordinances, which are democratically-established norms enacted by local assemblies.[35] In practice it is not uncommon for local ordinances to regulate property rights (see discussion at Article 29).

Penalties

As discussed at Article 31, the constitution prohibits the imposition of penalties "except according to procedure established by law." Article 73(vi) also prohibits the use of cabinet orders to impose punishments without authorization by law. Thus, it is not clear from the text of the constitution whether local governments can use local regulations to impose criminal penalties. Article 14(3) of the LAA authorizes municipal and prefectural government to pass ordinances containing penal provisions with punishments no greater than two years imprisonment with labor or a fine of 1 million yen. Most academic theories also hold that Article 94 empowers the use of local ordinances to impose penalties without such delegation.

Taxation

The constitution requires that all taxes have a foundation in law (see Article 84). However, this is not an impediment to local governments imposing taxes through ordinances. The

Supreme Court has ruled that local governments are "constitutionally programmed to be the subject of taxing power."[36] Article 3(1) of the Local Tax Act states that "[l]ocal governments shall make decisions on the tax items, taxable entities, tax bases, tax rates, and other matters concerning the levy and collection of local taxes in accordance with the local ordinances."[37] This conforms to Article 84 of the constitution. However, the Supreme Court has also held that when laws (such as the LAA and Local Tax Act) establish rules for "tax items, taxable entities, tax bases, tax rates, and other matters" local governments must follow them, which is also consistent with Article 84.[38]

Regulation within the scope of law

The second limit on regulation by local governments is that they must be "within the scope of the law."[39] The LAA also makes it clear that local governments may enact ordinances regarding local affairs (see discussion above) so long as they do not conflict with national laws and regulations.[40]

One question is whether local governments can enact ordinances that set stricter standards than those provided in national laws and regulations. Another is whether they can enact regulation in areas where there is no national law. In point of fact, local governments have been issuing such ordinances since the 1950s to regulate pollution more aggressively than the national government. Similarly, municipal and prefectural ordinances granting public access to government information existed over a decade before the Diet passed the Disclosure of Information Held by Administrative Agencies Act.

The Supreme Court addressed the relationship between local ordinances and national laws in the *Tokushima City Public Safety Ordinance Case*.[41] In it the Court explained that an analysis of the purpose, object, content and effect of ordinances and laws had to be compared in order to understand whether they were in conflict. For example, it would be possible for an ordinance to conflict with even the absence of national law governing the matter if the absence was because of a legislative intent by the Diet to leave the matter unregulated. By contrast, overlapping laws and ordinances can co-exist if the ordinance serves a different purpose from the law and does not interfere with the purpose of the law, or if the ordinance has a consistent purpose with the law.

Some statutes specifically permit local ordinances to set stricter local standards than those provided for in the law. Examples include the Air Pollution Control Act and the Noise Regulation Act.[42]

Article 95: Special Laws

Tōru Enoki

Article 95.
A special law, applicable only to one local public entity, cannot be enacted by the Diet without the consent of the majority of the voters of the local public entity concerned, obtained in accordance with law.

Since the Diet is the "sole law-making organ of the State" (Article 41), it can normally legislate without the participation of other institutions. However, Article 95 establishes an exception in the case of law affecting only one municipality or prefecture; such "special laws" must also be approved by the voters of the applicable local public entity. This requirement prevents the Diet from imposing burdensome legislation on specific communities.

The framing of "special laws" as "applicable only to one local public entity" does not mean laws that only affect a single entity, but rather laws targeting specific local public entities. Thus, the referendum requirement can apply to laws impacting several local public entities.

A number of special laws were passed early in post war history. One is the Hiroshima Peace Memorial City Construction Act of 1949. No special laws requiring Article 95 referenda have been passed since 1952.

Notes

1 Supreme Court, Grand Bench judgment of March 27, 1963, *Keishū* 17, 121.

2 Tokyo is commonly described as Japan's "capital city," which is partially incorrect since it is a prefecture, not a city, and none of the municipalities comprising Tokyo prefecture is named "Tokyo." By contrast, both Kyoto and Osaka are prefectures which encompass cities also named Kyoto and Osaka as well as other municipalities..

3 Chihō Bunkatsu no Suishin wo Hakaru Tame no Kankei Hōritsu no Seibitō ni Kansuru Hōritsu [Promotion of Decentralization Reform Act], Law no. 87 of 1999.

4 LAA, Articles 1-2(ii). Translation by author.

5 *See*, The Ministry of Justice, Japan. (n.d.). *Family registration*. Retrieved July 4, 2022, from https://www.moj.go.jp/EN/MINJI/koseki.html

6 Every year, the Cabinet Secretariat releases a "Report on the status of personnel exchanges between the national government and local governments." For the material released on March 10, 2021, please refer to Cabinet Secretariat. (2021, March 10). *Kuni to chihō kōkyō dantai to no aida no jinji kōryū no jisshi jōkyō* [Report on the status of personnel exchanges between the national government and local governments]. Cabinet Secretariat Homepage. Retrieved July 4, 2022, from https://www.cas.go.jp/jp/gaiyou/jimu/jinjikyoku/.

7 Note that "local self-government" as used in the title of Chapter VIII and "local autonomy" as used in Article 92 are expressed in Japanese using the same term (*chihō jichi*).

8 Note the Japanese term used to express "principle" is *honshi*, which could also be translated "main purpose" or "principle objective."

9 Nakamura, M. *Dai jūhachi shō: Chihōjichi* [Chapter 18: Local self-government]. In Nonaka, T., et al. (2012), 363–65.

10 Since the passage of the Law Relating to the Establishment of Special Wards in Large Metropolitan Areas, it has been theoretically possible to establish special wards elsewhere. Daitoshi Chiiki ni Okeru Tokubetsuku no Secchi ni Kansuru Hōritsu, Law no. 80 of 2012.

11 For example, outside of Tokyo's special wards, municipalities are responsible for administering the water supply, sewerage, and firefighting, but in Tokyo they are managed by the metropolitan government rather than the special wards themselves.

12 Under the LAA during this period, special ward heads were selected by the special ward assemblies with the consent of the Tokyo prefectural governor.

13 Supreme Court, Grand Bench judgment of March 27, 1963 (17 *Keishū* 121).

14 Takahashi, K. (2020), 415; Shishido, J. *Dai jūyon shō: Chihōjichi* [Chapter 14: Local self-government]. In Watanabe, Y., et al. (2020), 423–24.

15 Daitoshi Chiiki ni Okeru Tokubetsuku no Secchi ni Kansuru Hōritsu [Establishment of Special Wards in Large Metropolitan Areas Act], Law no. 80 of 2012.

16 See note 14.

17 Articles 286–291-13 of LAA.

[18] Nonaka, T., et al. (2012), 370–71.

[19] LAA, Articles 76, 80, 81, 93 & 140.

[20] The "as may be determined by law" means that prefectural and municipal governments are not able to establish elective positions through local ordinances.

[21] Supreme Court, Grand Bench judgment of May 24, 1967 (21 *Keishū* 505). "[T]here is no basis for understanding that the same principles of parliamentary autonomy are recognized for local assemblies as for the Diet. There is likewise no basis that the constitution guarantees the so-called immunity for local assembly members' statements." This case involved criminal charges brought against members of the Saga Prefectural Assembly for activities directed at obstructing its process. Their defense involved arguments to the effect that their status as assembly members gave them constitutionally-guaranteed immunities.

[22] Article 94 of the LAA stipulates that "A town or village may, by its ordinance, establish a general meeting of the electorate, in lieu of an assembly." In June 2017, the mayor of Okawa Village in Kochi Prefecture announced that he would consider abolishing the village assembly and instead establish a village general meeting. However, the investigation was suspended. Since the electorate organizes the general meeting in the municipality, it is understood the assembly is "their deliberative organ" under Article 93 of the constitution. The constitutionality of the general meeting was questioned to the government by a member of the House of Representatives. The House of Representatives, Japan. (2018, February 7). *Shitsumon honbun jōhō* [Text of question]. Shugiin.go.jp. Retrieved July 4, 2022, from https://www.shugiin.go.jp/internet/itdb_shitsumon.nsf/html/shitsumon/a196057.htm

[23] LAA, Articles 76–88, 242.

[24] Naha District Court judgment of May 9, May 2000, 1746 *Hanrei Jihō* 122.

[25] The English term "regulation" is used in Articles 16 and 81 (where the Japanese is *kisoku*, which is more commonly translated "rule"), and in Article 92 (where the Japanese is *ni kansuru jikō*, which would be more commonly translated "matters relating to").

[26] Some national government agencies have model ordinances and encourage prefectures to adopt them, resulting in many prefectures having very similar local rules. For example, regulations on outdoor advertisement are governed by Okugai Kōkokubutsu Hō (Outdoor Advertisement Act. Law No. 189/1949), which applies nationwide. And actual regulations on outdoor advertisement are carried out by local governments on their own by establishing ordinances and regulations. The Ministry of Land, Infrastructure, Transport and Tourism (MLIT) has published a model ordinance "as technical advice on the operation of Outdoor Advertisement Act for reference by local governments with the aim of supporting the accurate operation of the system based on that Act." These regulations have been implicated in litigation over freedom of expression (see discussion at Article 21). See Ministry of Land, Infrastructure, Transport and Tourism. (2018, September 27). Okugai Kōkokubutsu Jōrei Gaidorain [Outdoor Advertisement Regulations Guidelines]. Retrieved July 4, 2022, from https://www.mlit.go.jp/toshi/townscape/toshi_townscape_tk_000024.html

[27] Article 2(8), 2(9).

[28] Ibid.

[29] LAA, Articles 250-7, et. seq.

[30] Article 251-5.

[31] Article 251-7. For more information on the 1999 amendment to the LAA to handle disputes arising between the national government and local governments or between local governments, please refer to the following references. See Nonaka, T., et al. (2012), 378–79; Shibutani, H. (2017), 757–58; Takahashi, K. (2020), 418–22; Watanabe, Y., et al. (2020), at 437–40.

[32] Articles 14(1), 15(1) 96(1)(i) and 138-4(2). See Nonaka, T., et al. (2012), 380–81; Shibutani, H. (2017), 759.

[33] Translation by author.

[34] Naraken Tameike no Hozen ni Kansuru Jōrei, [Nara Prefecural Ordinance concerning the Preservation of Reservoirs], Ordinance of Nara Prefecture No. 38/1954.

[35] Hōgaku Kyōkai (ed.) (1953), 568; Ashibe, N. (2019), 382.

[36] Supreme Court, 1st Petty Bench judgment of March 21, 2013.

[37] Chihōzeihō [Local Tax Act], Law no. 226 of 1950.

[38] Supreme Court, 1st Petty Bench judgment of March 21, 2013.

[39] The Japanese version of "within law" in Article 94 is *hōritsu no han'inai,* which could be more rendered in English more artfully as "within the limits of the law."

[40] Local Government Act, Article 14(1).

[41] Supreme Court, Grand Bench judgment of September 10, 1975. Shūdan Kōshin Oyobi Shūdan Shiikōdō ni Kansuru Jōrei [Ordinance Relating to Group Marching and Demonstration Activities], Ordinance of Tokushima City No.3/1952.

[42] Taiki Osen Bōshi Hō [Air Pollution Control Act], Law no. 97 of 1968, Article 4(1); *Sōon Kisei Hō* [Noise Regulation Act], Law no 98 of 1968 (Article 4(2)).

Chapter IX
Amendments
Article 96

Tetsuji Matsumoto

Article 96.

(1) Amendments to this Constitution shall be initiated by the Diet, through a concurring vote of two-thirds or more of all the members of each House and shall thereupon be submitted to the people for ratification, which shall require the affirmative vote of a majority of all votes cast thereon, at a special referendum or at such election as the Diet shall specify.

(2) Amendments when so ratified shall immediately be promulgated by the Emperor in the name of the people, as an integral part of this Constitution.

Historical background

The Constitution of Japan has never been amended since its birth, as an amendment in toto of the Meiji Constitution, which itself had never been amended until then. Article 73 of the Meiji Constitution required proposed amendments to be submitted by Imperial Order, but proposed amendments could not be debated by either House unless a quorum comprising at least two-thirds of its membership was present, and a two-thirds supermajority requirement was required to approve it. The two-thirds threshold for amendment under Article 96 appear to have been inherited from the Meiji Constitution.

The GHQ drafting team initially considered imposing heavy restrictions on the people's right of amendment—their initial internal draft would have prohibited any until 1955 and only allowed them thereafter if proposed by a 2/3 vote of the Diet and subsequently ratified by not less than a 3/4 vote of the Diet.[1] A subsequent internal draft required a 3/4 vote of both Diet chambers and a popular referendum. The provision that was ultimately proposed in the GHQ Draft (Article LXXXIX) became Article 96, subject to a few minor changes relating to bicameralism and permitting "a special referendum" for ratification.

Although at the time of writing the present constitution has never been amended, various proposals have been in the Diet and elsewhere, but none have come even close to going anywhere. Well-known examples include:

- A comprehensive set of amendments proposed by the LDP in 2012

- Amendments proposed by the *Sankei* and *Yomiuri* newspapers in 2013 and 2014, respectively
- A 2012 proposal by Prime Minister Abe to first "just" amend Article 96 to make the amendment process easier
- A 2017 proposal by Abe to amend Article 9 to add language acknowledging the existence of the SDF
- More limited amendment proposals by the LDP focused on (1) acknowledging the SDF, (2) adding language providing emergency powers to the government (3) expanding educational rights and (4) House of Councillors electoral districting.

Initiation by the Diet

Under Article 96 only the Diet can initiate the amendment process but amendments successfully passing through that process must be submitted to the people for ratification. It is not clear whether the "all the members" of each House requirement means: (1) the statutory number of members of the applicable chamber, or (2) the actual number of members, which accounts for deaths, resignations and other vacancies (also see discussion at Article 56). It is up to each chamber to decide, though in practice they have never had to.

The constitution is silent as to the form and manner of amendment initiatives. Article 68-III of the Diet Act requires that a separate amendment proposal (a "Preliminary Draft Amendment") be made for each "relevant matter." Article 68-II requires a Preliminary Draft Amendment to secure the support of at least one hundred members of the House of Representatives, or fifty in the House of Councilors to be formally submitted to the chamber for consideration and debate.

Finally, Article 102-VI of the Diet Act establishes a Commission on the Constitution in each house of the Diet, and amendment proposals can also be initiated by these commissions (Article 102-VII(1)). Significantly, there is no provision in any relevant statutes which gives the Cabinet the power to propose a Preliminary Draft Amendment to the Constitution of Japan.

Ratification by the people

The procedure for holding the popular referendum to approve amendments initiated by the Diet is set forth in the Constitutional Amendment Procedures Act.[2] Under the Act (Article 3), Japanese nationals aged 18 and above are eligible to vote in the referendum approving a proposed constitutional amendment. A "majority" of this population could mean a majority of: (1) all eligible voters; (2) all votes cast; or, (3) all valid votes cast. The Act adopts (3) as the standard for approving an amendment. Some scholars argue there should also be a minimum turnout requirement for a ratification vote to be effective.

If an amendment is initiated by the Diet pursuant to Article 96, a Board of Public Information on the National Referendum must be established within the Diet for the purpose of a "undertaking affairs concerning public information" about the proposed amendment (Diet Act, Article 102-XI).[3] The Constitutional Amendment Procedures Act establishes a wide range of restrictions on the freedom of expression of public servants, teachers and university professors, as well as broadcast activities in connection with a constitutional referendum.[4] Some scholars consider this combination of government-led narrative about the nature of the amendment and restrictions on the ability to freely express contrary views to be unconstitutional.

Promulgation by the emperor

Both Article 96(2) and Article 7 require amendments to be promulgated by the emperor. The "in the name of the people" formulation is thought to show the amendments as being based upon the will of the Japanese people, in whom sovereign power resides.

The "as an integral part of this Constitution" language may seem to have no substantive meaning. However, one view holds it helps support the view that the amendment process cannot be used to completely rewrite the constitution—in the same manner as its own birth from the Meiji Constitution—since wholesale amendments could not reasonably be called an integral part of the current constitution.

Limits on constitutional amendments

As the preceding discussion suggests, whether there are limits on the substance and scope of constitutional amendment has been the subject of fierce academic and political controversies. For illustrative purposes, here are examples of some of the arguments made regarding possible limits.

First, the sovereignty of the people enshrined in the present constitution might make it impossible to use the amendment process to return sovereignty to the emperor. This is a reasonable argument: the power of amendment should not be able to change who ultimately has the power to make the constitution. This logic, however, potentially calls into question the validity of the Constitution of Japan itself, which accomplished a transfer of sovereignty through the amendment process of the Meiji Constitution.[5]

A second argument is based on "amendment" meaning that the fundamental identity of the constitution should remain unchanged. Under this view it would be impossible as a matter of law to make amendments that have the effect of abandoning the fundamental premises of the constitution, such as the protection of natural and inherent rights of the people. A related but different theory is that some fundamental rules (in German, constitutional theorists such as H. Kelsen used the word *Grundnorm* in hypothetical meaning supporting the law's effect but some Japanese scholars used it in substantive meaning) such as popular sovereignty, protection of human rights, or even pacifism limit not only the power of amendments, but the constitution-making power itself.

A third theory is textual, and based on the wording of specific language in the constitution which might be interpreted as limits on amendments to specific provisions. For example, Article 11 describes the fundamental human rights conferred on the people by the constitution as "eternal and inviolate rights." This could be read as a prohibition on amendments that take away those rights. Article 97's reference to constitutional rights "to be held for all time inviolate" could also be read as a limit on amendments. Similarly, Article 9's renunciation of war "forever" could also be viewed as prohibiting amendment of that provision. A related theory is that amendments to such provisions which prohibit amendment are not possible.

Finally, it could be argued that amendments to the amendment procedure mandated by Article 96 (and, for that matter, Article 7) are prohibited. If constitutional provisions regulating amendments procedure are to be understood as self-imposed restrictions by the Japanese people, who are vested with the constitution-making power, it may be reasonable to infer that it is impossible for the people to amend these provisions through the amendment process. This last theory of inherent limits on amendments may be the least theoretical of those discussed above, since Prime Minister Shinzō Abe tried unsuccessfully to popularize the idea of first "just" amending Article 96 to make it easier to amend other parts of the constitution.

On this point, it should be remembered that Article 96 imposes two basic procedural requirements on constitutional amendments: an initiative approved by 2/3 majorities of both houses of the Diet, and the ratification by the people through a simple majority vote. The latter requirement seems likely to be beyond the reach of amendment through the amendment process. The former may be too, at least politically: Prime Minister Abe's proposal was harshly criticized and subsequently abandoned.

There may nonetheless be substantial differences between the two procedural requirements of Article 96, at least in terms of their amenability to amendment. One leading scholar carefully limits the scope of this prohibition to the substantive part of procedural provisions; in other words, it would be possible to amend Article 96 in a way that changed the threshold of approval required in the Diet, but not in a way that eliminated the popular referendum from the process.[6]

Other commentators have suggested that the requirement that amendments be initiated through a super-majority Diet vote renders the sovereign people of a democratic society as "prisoners" of a mechanism for deciding what the constitution should be that was devised by GHQ decades ago. In this respect, it should be noted that while a single political party (the Liberal Democratic Party) has controlled both houses of the Diet for most of the postwar period, it has nonetheless been impossible for them (or any other party or coalition) to achieve the 2/3 majority in both houses necessary to amend the constitution. On the other hand, the electoral laws can be amended with a simple majority of both Houses (or a supermajority of the House of Representatives), and such amendments could be used to introduce all-single constituency systems to constitute the entire composition of both houses (see Chapter IV) and facilitate the formation of the requisite supermajorities.

For any of the hypothetical limits on amendments posited above to be effective, they would need to be raised in judicial challenges to amendments actually proposed or made. Yet this again raises questions about the validity of the constitution itself, given its provenance as an amendment of the Meiji Constitution, if similar limits are thought to apply to that process.

If one assumes validity rooted in the support and sovereignty of the people which emerged during the period between the acceptance of the Potsdam Declaration in August of 1945 and the birth of the constitution in 1946, it could be argued that constitutional amendments beyond the limits described above could also be valid based on other, different circumstances. In such a case, at the very least such amendments would have been supported by the vote of a majority of the people through the referendum required under Article 96(1), a process that was absent from the birth of the current constitution.

Notes

[1] Takayanagi, K., et al. (Eds.) (1972), Vol. 1, 134.

[2] Nihon Kokukenpō no Kaisei Tetuzuki ni Kansuru Hōritsu [Constitutional Amendment Procedure Act], Law no. 51 of 2007. The fact that no such law existed for the first six decades of the constitution's existence is evidence of the longstanding political resistance to constitutional amendment.

[3] Some of the Committee's roles are defined in more detail in the Constitutional Amendment Procedure Act, Article 11 *et. seq.*

[4] Constitutional Amendment Procedure Act, Articles 100-2, 102, 103, 105-108.

[5] See discussion at Article 1 regarding the "August Revolution" theory.

[6] Satō, K. (2020), 52.

Chapter X
Supreme Law
Articles 97–99

Introduction

Andrea Ortolani

Overview

The three articles comprising Chapter X establish the constitution as the supreme law of the nation, though not without raising some questions about the status of international law. These three articles seem of paramount importance, as they articulate fundamental constitutional principles found in legal systems of most, if not all, modern liberal democracies.

Some commentators, however, have expressed reservations about or even openly criticized these articles for a variety of reasons. For example, one would expect fundamental provisions affecting the interpretation of the entire document to appear at the beginning, ideally in the preamble or first chapter. This would be a legitimate expectation especially in the case of texts with an important symbolic value and a profound political impact such as constitutions. In the Japanese constitution, however, this chapter appears at the end, sandwiched between the provisions on amendment and the now meaningless supplementary provisions of Chapter XI. While in principle the binding force of provisions of law does not depend on their position within the text, the location of Chapter X nonetheless appears a bit unusual and possibly diminishes its perceived importance. A common explanation is that the drafters felt that these provisions had to be included, but they did not find a better position in the document, so they placed them where they are for lack of better alternatives.[1]

Similarly, in the final report of the Commission on the Constitution, several commissioners expressed the view that Chapter X did nothing more than repeat matters already dealt with in other articles, or state obvious things such as that the constitution should be upheld and respected, and that it is superior to other laws and regulations. In fact, the majority view was that all three articles of Chapter X were either unnecessary or wrongly placed, and they should be eliminated in the event of amendment.[2]

Right to resistance and state of emergency

Japanese constitutional law scholars usually analyze the relation between the provisions of Chapter X and the doctrine of the right to resistance (*teikōken*), and the issues related to the validity of the constitution during a state of emergency.

Several modern constitutions include provisions declaring that people have inviolable rights. Interpreting these provisions according to the Lockean notion of social contract would imply that the governed have a natural right to resist the government when it breaches the social contract reflected in the constitution, i.e., when their fundamental and unalienable rights are grossly violated but the legal system does not provide any remedies. The provisions on inviolable rights however are often vague, seldom interpreted on the basis of the Lockean doctrine, and their enforcement is subject to political pressures and institutional obstacles. It would even be of dubious practical utility for any legal system to include a provision explicitly empowering people to disobey the law and resist the government, even in limited and particular conditions. This would also contradict the premise of the right to resistance, namely that the legal system does not provide any procedure to rectify egregious violations of fundamental rights. Revolts and revolutions are by definition events occurring outside and against the existing legal order. Moreover, the paradoxical nature of a doctrine according to which, in order to uphold the constitutional structure of a state and the fundamental freedoms of the people, it is legitimate to infringe those very freedoms and subvert that very structure, is clear.

The current Japanese constitution does not have an explicit provision on the right of resistance, but the provisions of Chapter X, in particular Articles 97 and 99, have been interpreted as offering at least an implicit hint of this theory. The issue is debated by scholars.[3] The Sapporo District Court also mentioned the right of resistance in a judgment of 1962 about the right to demonstrate without first obtaining a permit.[4] It held that the conditions for its exercise are that: (1) the resistance is not motivated just by a simple violation of a constitutional provision, but by a serious violation of the basic democratic order, putting at risk the survival of the constitution itself; (2) the violation is objectively illegal; and, (3) the legal system does not grant any means to preserve the legal order, so that the right of resistance is a last resort measure to restore the constitutional order.[5] On the other hand, the provisions of Article 12, and in particular the plea to "refrain from any abuse of these freedoms and rights," can be seen as a denial of the existence of extra-legal or extra-constitutional means to guarantee those freedoms and rights.

Another issue relevant to Chapter X is the doctrine of the state of emergency (*kokka kinkyūken*): situations where the existence of the state is in peril due to war, insurrections, natural disasters or other exceptional events, and the government seeks to justify taking action to preserve the order, even disregarding some of the fundamental rights and principles (such as separation of powers) guaranteed by the constitution. The Meiji Constitution had three provisions related to the doctrine of the state of emergency: Article 8 on the power of the emperor to issue imperial ordinances in the place of law in consequence of an urgent necessity to maintain public safety or to avert public calamities "when the Imperial Diet is not sitting"; Article 14 on the declaration of the state of siege; and, Article 31 on the powers appertaining to the emperor in times of war or in cases of a national emergency.

The current constitution has no provisions related to the state of emergency. Neither the emperor nor the Cabinet is able to issue emergency ordinances. Depending on the situation the Cabinet can convoke extraordinary sessions of the Diet or emergency sessions of the House of Councillors (see Articles 53 and 54), but the law-making power remains with the legislative branch in all cases.

Scholars are divided on the issue whether the absence of provisions addressing the state of emergency implies the rejection of the doctrine. Some scholars hold that the absence means that the government shall never have the powers to set aside the constitutional provisions, even in situations of emergency. Others have argued that even in absence of an express provision, a norm granting the government extraordinary powers in case of emergency is implied by the fact that the survival of the state and the preservation of the constitution are supreme goals that can justify deviations from the rule of law, as long as they are limited to the smallest extent and do not last for an extended period of time.[6]

Textual references to the state of emergency can be found in a number of statutes, including the Police Act and the SDF Act.[7] It is possible that these references were made in anticipation of other legislation introducing explicit provisions on the state of emergency. In general, they seem to maintain implicitly that in certain circumstances the state has the power to act beyond constitutional limits.

This tendency can be seen as well in several statutes on emergency situations enacted since 2003, collectively going under the name of "*yūji rippō*," for example in the Act Concerning the Measures for Protection of the People in Armed Attack Situations, etc., of 2004.[8] Moreover, especially in the aftermath of the earthquake, tsunami and nuclear disaster of March 11, 2011, and during the Covid-19 pandemic, conservative politicians have used the absence of emergency powers as an argument in support of constitutional amendment. At the time of writing there were no new specific proposals.

Article 97: Durability of Fundamental Human Rights

Andrea Ortolani

> **Article 97.**
> The fundamental human rights by this Constitution guaranteed to the people of Japan are fruits of the age-old struggle of man to be free; they have survived the many exacting tests for durability and are conferred upon this and future generations in trust, to be held for all time inviolate.

In the GHQ Draft this provision was placed in the chapter on the rights and duties of the people, as Article X, but the Japanese government wanted to have Chapter III contain only provisions on the protection of fundamental human rights. GHQ agreed but requested it be included somewhere in the constitution. Hence, in the final version it was placed in the current position near the end, its text unchanged from the GHQ draft.

This history may explain why the article bears little if any direct connection to the title of Chapter X, "Supreme Law." One could argue it articulates a reason why the fundamental human rights enshrined in the constitution shall be the supreme law of the land: because these rights are eternal and inviolable. On the other hand, it does not offer explicitly a concrete procedure in order to ensure that the provisions of the constitution, being supreme, shall prevail over conflicting laws, regulations or government practices. This provision repeats in part ideas expressed in Articles 11 and 12. The wording used in Articles 11 and 97 however is slightly different: in Article 11 the "eternal and inviolate rights" shall be "conferred (*ataerare-ru*) upon the people," while in Article 97 the "fundamental human rights" are "guaranteed" (*hoshō*) and "conferred ... in trust" (*shintaku sareta mono de aru*).

The word translated here as "trust" is "*shintaku*" in Japanese, which is the standard term used for the legal arrangement typical of Anglo-American law in which a person (settlor) gives some assets to a party (trustee) who must keep and use it in the interest of a third party (beneficiary). There are different views on the implications of this lexical choice. Some commentators have suggested that God or a deity can be seen as the settlor, the current and future Japanese citizens as trustees and all mankind as beneficiary.[9] The prevailing view however is that the use of the word trust does not necessarily imply a direct and technical reference to the relative legal doctrine, but is intended just as a general reminder that the enjoyment of fundamental rights is a matter to be treated with the uttermost respect. [10]

There is little question that the fundamental human rights (*kihonteki jinken*) of Article 97 are the same as those in Article 11, as the same expression is used in both articles. Some scholars also expressed the idea that the rights mentioned in the article are not only the fundamental rights explicitly mentioned by the constitution, but all fundamental human rights, according to natural law theories.[11] These rights are, according to Article 97, "fruits of the age-old struggle of man to be free." This expression might sound familiar to legal scholars, even if a bit magniloquent, as it evokes the foundational texts of western constitutionalism, such as the United States Declaration of Independence or the French Declaration of the Rights of Man and of the Citizen of 1789. Kenzō Takayanagi, a Japanese scholar of Anglo-American law, defined Article 97 as "a collection of aphorisms suitable for ethics papers."[12] In fact, the words of Article 97 bear little connection with the actual circumstances from which it originated. The western documents mentioned above were the direct result of internal political struggles or of revolutionary and violent uprisings, in which the victorious forces got what they wanted. On the contrary, Japanese citizens regained basic human rights and fundamental freedoms thanks to a defeat and the subsequent occupation by foreign forces. If anything, it was the struggle not of the Japanese people, but of Allied forces, which put an end to the militaristic regime and brought this constitution and these fundamental human rights to Japan.

Despite these critiques, the article exerts its importance in the overall interpretation of the general spirit of the constitution, reinforcing the values expressed by Article 11. When cited in judgments, Article 97 often appears together with Article 11.[13]

Article 98: Supremacy Clause

Andrea Ortolani

Article 98.

(1) This Constitution shall be the supreme law of the nation and no law, ordinance, imperial rescript or other act of government, or part thereof, contrary to the provisions hereof, shall have legal force or validity.

(2) The treaties concluded by Japan and established laws of nations shall be faithfully observed.

Article 98 is the only article in Chapter X bearing a direct connection with the title of the chapter. The first paragraph declares the supremacy of the constitution but does not go into details as to how the supremacy of the constitution shall be assured. In part this task is left to Article 81 and in part to the Court Act (see discussion at Chapter VI).

Article 76 of the Meiji Constitution did contain a provision in part corresponding to Article 98. By stipulating that "existing [provisions] shall, so far as they do not conflict with the present Constitution, continue in force," Article 76 implied that provisions in conflict with the constitution shall not continue in force. The constitution was thus declared superior to other laws. There were no provisions on international law and on the position of treaties in the domestic constitutional order.

In Article XC of the GHQ draft, the corresponding provision read "This Constitution and the laws and treaties made in pursuance hereof shall be the supreme law of the nation, and no public law or ordinance and no imperial rescript or other governmental act, or part thereof, contrary to the provisions hereof shall have legal force or validity," clearly echoing the first part of Article VI(2) of the United States constitution.[14] This version would have put the laws and treaties "made in pursuance" of the constitution at the same level of the constitution in the hierarchy of the sources of law.

Such a conceptualization of the sources of law would have been uncommon in the panorama of modern constitutional law theory. The hierarchy usually sees constitutional provisions as sources of highest rank, then on a lower rank the provisions of statutes and other acts approved or sanctioned by representative assemblies, which must be in conformity with the constitution, and then administrative provisions and other acts of the government, which must be in conformity with the constitutional norms and with statutory law. The GHQ intention was twofold: on the one hand, to stress the principle of the rule of law and the need for all governmental action to be in conformity with the provisions of the constitution, on the other, the reference to international law was intended to ensure that Japan kept its international commitments.

This provision was however changed in the parliamentary discussions on the constitution, and the part on "the laws and treaties made in pursuance hereof" was expunged. The reference to international treaties became the second paragraph of Article 98. This might have had many goals. On one hand, not equating international law with the constitution obfuscates in part the significance of international law. On the other hand, the decision to make an explicit reference to international law might have had, in part, the goal to express Japan's atonement for past violations and its commitment to international law for the future, and in part to provide international law with a formal foothold in the constitution, ensuring it had binding force in the national legal system. International treaties are not mentioned in Article 81 on the Supreme Court's power of judicial review, nor in paragraph (1) of Article 98, and this raises the issue whether international treaties can be subject to judicial review by the Supreme Court.[15]

The notion of "contrary to" (*ni han suru*) the provisions of the constitution mentioned in this article is substantially equivalent to the notion of "constitutionality" under Article 81 (*kenpō ni tekigō suru ka shinai ka*). The acts that must be in conformity with the constitution are those already mentioned in Article 81, i.e., statutes *(hōritsu)* passed by the Diet, orders, rules and other dispositions (see discussion at Article 81). Article 98 also mentions *shōchoku*, that is imperial rescripts and other acts of the emperor predating the constitution but retained in effect under it. It also uses the catch-all expression "or other act of government" (*sono hoka no kōi*). This seems broader in scope than "other official acts" (*shobun*) as used in Article 81. It is also commonly interpreted as referring to ordinances or regulations (e.g., *jōrei*) of local governments. It can also apply to non-legislative acts of the Houses of the Diet, and to judgments of courts.[16] Finally, by explicitly stating "or part of" (*mata wa ichibu wa*) the provision makes it clear that partial unconstitutionality does not invalidate the entirety of a law or regulation.[17]

Given the language of Article 98, some scholars questioned the validity under the current constitution of the statutes and regulations approved before its enactment, suggesting that the notion of supremacy of the constitution implies the invalidation of legislation predating it.[18] There is, after all, no constitutional language specifically preserving the validity of laws and regulations pre-dating the constitution. Moreover, the institutions of the Meiji Constitution and the legislative procedures which followed differ from those mandated by the present constitution, hence all the previous legislation could be seen as technically unconstitutional. In comparative perspective however, the automatic abrogation of old laws is not what routinely happens with the enactment of new constitutions.[19] Nor did this occur in Japan; specific laws were abrogated during the Occupation, but this was by plan and on a case-by-case basis, rather than an automatic function of the new constitution. Moreover, transitional laws and ordinances passed at the time specifically gave the force of law to all cabinet orders passed by the Japanese government through December 31, 1947.[20] In the same fashion, an Occupation-era cabinet ordinance gave force to all imperial rescripts that remained in force at the time by converting them into cabinet orders.[21] The Grand Bench of the Supreme Court confirmed as early as 1948 and 1949 that laws (*hōritsu*) duly passed under the Meiji Constitution continued being valid and effective as long as their content was not in conflict with the new constitutional provisions.[22] In a judgment of 1950 in which the constitutionality of the Food Control Act of 1942 was at stake, the Court affirmed that the effectiveness of an act does not depend on whether it was passed before or after the enactment of the constitution.[23]

International law and the constitution

The Meiji Constitution mentioned treaties in Article 13: "The Emperor declares war, makes peace and concludes treaties." Treaties were introduced in the domestic legal system upon promulgation by the emperor, and although no provision explicitly dealt with their validity, the general interpretation was that they had domestic legal force by the emperor's prerogative power.[24]

In the current constitution, the second paragraph of Article 98 addresses the interaction between the constitution and international law—both treaties (which is interpreted as referring to all international agreements) and "established laws of nations," which refers to rules of customary international law. While Articles 7, 61, and 73 address the process by which the Japanese government enters into treaties, Article 98 addresses what international law means, though arguably raises more questions than answers.

Whether Japanese courts can directly use provisions of international law in their decisions, without a specific, domestic, legal instrument that introduces them formally in the Japanese legal system is still open to question. Article 98 seems to give the provisions of international law the foothold required to have binding force in the domestic legal system. In addition, since Article 73 provides that international treaties must be approved by the Diet, and Article 7 that treaties are promulgated by the emperor, treaties are clearly a source of law recognized by the constitution.

While the majority of scholars seem to accept the principle of indirect application of international law, the precedents of inferior courts are not clear-cut. In theory, self-executing treaties should be valid and have force of law in the domestic legal system without the need of further legislation, but this has not always been the case. In practice, Japanese courts have sometimes rejected, sometimes endorsed the direct application of provisions of international treaties in domestic cases. For example, the Supreme Court has rejected the direct domestic application of Article 9 of the International Covenant on Economic, Social and Cultural Rights on "the right of everyone to social security."[25] On the other hand, in a judgment of 2009 it considered whether domestic tax provisions were compatible with the Japan-Singapore Double Tax Avoidance Agreement, hinting at the fact that these provisions of international law can have a direct effect on domestic law.[26]

The Courts have also referenced international law as grounds for the decision when it is relevant and useful in the interpretation, especially when the international norms declared principles, standards or other norms that could be used in the interpretation of the domestic norm. Sometimes however it seems that international treaties were cited just as a reference in order to confirm outcomes that would have been reached even without the influence of the international provision.[27]

This issue is intertwined with the issue of which source has a position of primacy: treaties or the constitution. One theory holds that treaties are superior, since in order for paragraph (2) of Article 98 to mean anything, treaties have to be at least equal to if not a higher order of law than the constitution. As a consequence, under this theory any domestic law contrary to international law should be invalid, and the fact that paragraph (1) of Article 98 does not mention international law as "the supreme law of the nation" is understood as a logical consequence of the mandate in paragraph (2) regarding the faithful observance of international law. Repetition of the latter's superiority would be superfluous.[28]

By contrast, the theory of the primacy of the constitution is based on the fact that the validity of international treaties in the domestic legal system derives from the action of organs established and governed by the constitution. Logically, international law cannot be placed in a higher position than the organs that have control over its validity, even more so it cannot be placed above the document that establishes those organs. Moreover, the constitution prescribes the complex procedure of Article 96 for its revision, while recognition of treaties can be enacted via a much easier procedure: a decision of the Cabinet and a simple approval of the Diet. Recognizing the supremacy of international law over the constitution, in this view, would be illogical as it would, at least in theory, give the government and its parliamentary majority a way to circumvent the complex constitutional revision procedure via the adoption of international treaties.[29]

The leading case on the issue of which source of law is in a position of primacy is the *Sunagawa Case*. This is discussed in more detail at Article 9 but can be briefly summarized here as the Supreme Court declaring the government's decision to become a party to a defense treaty a highly political question directly related to national defense and the safety of the country, and therefore not subject to judicial review, absent clear constitutional violations.

Article 99: Obligation to Respect and Uphold the Constitution

Andrea Ortolani

Article 99.
The Emperor or the Regent as well as Ministers of State, members of the Diet, judges, and all other public officials have the obligation to respect and uphold this Constitution.

Article 99 is a direct and logical corollary of the constitution being the supreme law of the land. Many modern constitutions have similar provisions either in the preamble or in supplementary provisions.

By contrast, the Meiji Constitution provided that "Our Ministers of State, on Our behalf, shall be held responsible for the carrying out of the present Constitution, and Our present and future subjects shall forever assume the duty of allegiance to the present Constitution." Under the Meiji Constitution, only the ministers of state had the responsibility of "carrying out" (*shikō* in the original) its mandates. Moreover, the Meiji Constitution did not just grant rights to the subjects (*shinmin*) of the emperor, but also burdened present and future subjects with a duty of allegiance to the constitution, that is to the state. Given that the state was identified with the emperor who bestowed the Meiji Constitution on the nation, the duty of allegiance to the constitution was virtually the same as the duty of allegiance to the emperor. The difference with current Article 99 is clear. Other parts of the present constitution establish that sovereignty resides in the people, and Article 99 reflects this by imposing on the emperor and other government officials a duty to respect it.[30] Therefore, even if the emperor retains his position as a "symbol of the State and of the unity of the people" (Article 1), logically and ideologically there is no room to assert a duty of allegiance to the emperor either directly or through the constitution.

In the current text, other political actors, such as ministers and members of the Diet, and all civil servants and public employees, including civil servants of local public entities and incorporated administrative agencies, bear the same duty to respect and uphold the constitution.[31] The text of Article 99 makes use of two different words, "respect" (*sonchō*) and "uphold" (*yōgo*). However, most scholars do not attach a deep meaning to this lexical choice and treat these words as quasi-synonymous, as both words refer in general to the duty of not contravening the constitution.

The duty (or duties) articulated in Article 99 might sound quite abstract and of limited effectiveness, as the constitution does not establish any clear sanctions for violations. In this respect it may seem more like an ethical duty, related to a vague notion of political responsibility, rather than a legal duty originating from a binding provision of law. However, it may be simply a matter of the details of implementation being left to legislation, just as is the case with many other provisions of the constitution. Article 97 of the National Public Service Act, for example, provides that upon their commencement of office, "[o]fficials must take an oath of service, as provided for by Cabinet Order." The relevant cabinet order provides for an oath in which officials swear to comply with the constitution. Moreover, the National Public Service Act provides that, except as provided for by rules of the National Personnel Authority, "a person who, on or after the date of the enforcement of the Constitution of Japan, formed or belonged to a political party or other organization which advocated the overthrow by force of the Constitution of Japan or the government established thereunder" may not be eligible to assume a government position, and violations are punishable by disciplinary action including dismissal.[32] Sanctions against judges are discussed at Article 78.

Can persons in the categories listed in Article 99 push for revisions of constitutional provisions? Would this infringe Article 99 and the duty to "respect and uphold" the constitution? The general consensus is that ministers of state and other politicians do not violate Article 99 if they advocate for constitutional revision through non-violent means, according to the procedure of Article 96. In this regard, politicians can use their freedom of speech quite widely and have expressed deep criticism of the constitution they are supposed to uphold and under which they serve. For example, just days before becoming prime minister for the second time, Shinzō Abe called Japan's constitution "pathetic" (*mittomonai*), but this did not prevent him from assuming office and eventually becoming Japan's longest serving prime minister. In general, however, it must be said that it would be illogical for the Constitution to foresee at Article 96 a procedure for its revision, and then prohibit the very persons who have the power to use this provision from discussing constitutional revision and making use of such procedure.

Moreover, prime ministers and other members of the Diet can be removed through electoral processes. The situation is different for unelected civil servants. Words or actions in favor of constitutional revision might contravene their duty of non-partisan loyalty to the constitution, impairing the public trust in the impartiality of their office. Judges do not have power to submit proposals of constitutional revision. Members of the judiciary involved in political activities or other forms of campaigning for constitutional revision would commit a violation of their duties.

Notes

1 Ejima, A. *Dai Jūshō: Saikō Hōki* [Chapter 10: Supreme Law]. In Tsujimura, M. & Yamamoto, H. (Eds.) (2018), 447.

2 Maki, J.M. (1980), 354.

3 Ejima, A., supra note 1, 448.

4 Sapporo District Court, Judgment of 18 January 1962, Collection of lower court criminal cases, 4 n. 1–2, 69.

[5] Kurata, M. *Dai Jūshō: Saikō Hōki* [Chapter 10: Supreme Law]. In Kinoshita, S. & Tadano, M. (Eds.) (2019), 774; Ejima, A., supra note 1, 448.
[6] Kurata, M. supra note 5, 775.
[7] Police Act, Article 71; SDF Act, Article 78.
[8] Buryoku Kōgeki Jitaitō ni Okeru Kokumin no Hogo no Tame no Sochi ni Kansuru Hōritsu [Act Relating to Measures Taken to Protect the People in the Event of Situations such as Armed Attacks, etc.], Act 112 of 2004.
[9] Ejima, A., supra note 1, 450; Kurata, M. supra note 5, 777.
[10] Ejima, A., supra note 1, 450.
[11] Kurata, M. supra note 5, 776.
[12] *Kenpō Chōsakai Hōkokusho* [Report of the Constitutional Research Group], in *Hōritsu jihō zōkan*, p. 374, quoted in Yamashita, T. *Dai Jūshō: Saikō Hōki* [Chapter 10: Supreme Law]. In Urata, K. & Ōsuga, A. (Eds.) (1994), 240.
[13] Ibid.
[14] "This Constitution, and the Laws of the United States which shall be made in Pursuance thereof; and all Treaties made, or which shall be made, under the Authority of the United States, shall be the supreme Law of the Land…"
[15] Ejima, A., supra note 1, 451. Note also that the statute under which Japan's Ministry of Foreign Affairs is constituted specifically lists interpreting treaties and foreign affairs as one of the ministry's roles. Gaimushō Secchi Hō [Ministry of Foreign Affairs Establishment Act], Law no. 94 of 1999, Article 4(1) (v).
[16] Kurata, M. supra note 5, 779.
[17] The Japanese uses the expression "*zenbu mata wa ichibu*" which could be more clearly translated "in its entirety or in part."
[18] Hasegawa and Yamashita, cited in Ejima, A., supra note 1, 453.
[19] Ejima, A., supra note 1, 454.
[20] Nihonkoku Kenpō Shikō no Sai Gen ni Kōryoku o Yūsuru Meirei no Kitei no Kōryokutō ni Kansuru Hōritsu [Law on the Effectiveness, etc. of the Provisions of Orders Currently in Force upon the Implementation of the Constitution of Japan], Law no. 72 of 1947. Among other things this act (which took effect the same day as the Constitution) abolished a number of laws and regulations relating to the peerage.
[21] Nihonkoku Kenpō Shikō no Sai Gen ni Kōryoku o Yūsuru Chokurei no Kitei no Kōryokutō ni Kansuru Seirei [Cabinet Order on the Effectiveness, etc. of the Provisions of the Imperial Ordinances Currently in Force upon the Implementation of the Constitution of Japan], Cabinet Order no. 14 of 1947.
[22] Supreme Court, Grand Bench judgment of June 23, 1948; Supreme Court, Grand Bench judgment of April 6, 1949.
[23] Supreme Court, Grand Bench judgment of February 1, 1950. Despite its wartime provenance, the Food Control Act remained in force until 1995 (subject to various amendments, of course).
[24] Satō, I. Treaties and the Constitution. In Henderson, D.F. (Ed.) (1968), 169.
[25] Ejima, A., supra note 1, 456; Supreme Court, 1st Petty Bench judgment of March 2 1989 [*Shōmu geppō* 35-9, 1754].
[26] Ejima, A., supra note 1, 456; Supreme Court, 1st Petty Bench judgment of October 29 2009 [*Minshū* 63-8, 1881].
[27] Ejima, A., supra note 1, 456. For example, in the *Kyoto North Korean School Case*, demonstrators held rallies outside a school for children of North Korean descent, yelling slurs with the help of loudspeakers and damaging school property. They were criminally prosecuted and convicted. The school sued the demonstrators in tort, claiming that their actions were illegal under the International Convention on the Elimination of All Forms of Racial Discrimination (ICERD) of which Japan is a party. The Tokyo District Court granted ¥12 million, which is an unusually high amount for such cases, explaining that the acts of racial discrimination required an increased amount of damages. The Osaka High Court upheld the outcome of the decision and the amount of damages, but on different grounds, denying that the acts of the defendants were illegal under the ICERD. The Supreme Court affirmed the decision of the High Court (Kyoto District Court, April 21, 2011; Osaka High Court, October 28, 2011; Supreme Court, 3rd Petty bench, decision of December 9 2014; Kotani, J. (2018), 612). In the *Otaru Onsen Case*, the Sapporo District Court denied the direct application of international law, but admitted that international law can be used as a reference standard for the interpretation of

domestic law (Sapporo District Court, November 11 2002, confirmed by Sapporo High Court, September 16, 2004). Webster, T. (2010), 263.

[28] Some may wonder why international law is not included in the "law" in paragraph (1). This is confusion caused by the English version. In Japanese international law (*kokusaihō*) is a form of law, but the "law" referenced in paragraph (1) is *hōritsu, i.e.,* a statute passed by the Diet pursuant to the process set forth in the constitution (see Article 59). Also note that the Japanese corresponding to "faithfully observed" is "*seijitsu ni junshu suru koto o hitsuyō to suru,*" which might be more accurately translated "faithful compliance is required."

[29] Regardless of the two competing theories, the Potsdam Declaration of 1945 (which resulted in the end of World War II for Japan), and the Treaty of San Francisco of 1951 (the formal peace treaty by which Japan regained full sovereignty over its territory) are generally recognized by most scholars as having a position uniquely superior to the constitution: Kurata, M. supra note 5, 782.

[30] Interestingly, the draft for the amendment of the Constitution of Japan, presented by the LDP in April 2012, rewrites this article, adding in a newly established first paragraph the provision "All people shall respect this constitution," and deleting "the Emperor or the Regent" in the second paragraph from the list of persons who have the duty to respect and uphold the constitution.

[31] "Official" as used in Article 99 is *kōmuin* or "public servant," the same term as is used in Articles 15, 16, 17 and 36. The "all other public officials" language coming at the end of a sentence starting with "The Emperor" and the corresponding Japanese formulation both raise the interesting, but unlikely to be definitively answered question of whether that means the emperor is also a "public official."

[32] NPSA, Articles 38 & 83. Local public servants are similarly bound by analogous provisions in the Local Public Service Act (Articles 16, 32 and 29).

Chapter XI
Supplementary Provisions
Articles 100–103

Introduction

Colin P.A. Jones

The provisions of Chapter XI were transitional in nature and have no substantive effect today. They are thus mainly of historical interest.

Article 100: Effectiveness and Transitional Measures

Colin P.A. Jones

Article 100.

(1) This Constitution shall be enforced as from the day when the period of six months will have elapsed counting from the day of its promulgation.

(2) The enactment of laws necessary for the enforcement of this Constitution, the election of members of the House of Councillors and the procedure for the convocation of the Diet and other preparatory procedures necessary for the enforcement of this Constitution may be executed before the day prescribed in the preceding paragraph.

The constitution was promulgated in the fall of 1946 on November 3, the birthday of the Meiji emperor (now celebrated as "Culture Day"). It took effect six months later on May 3, 1947, the anniversary of which is also a national holiday.

Since the House of Councillors did not exist under the Meiji Constitution, it was considered necessary to specifically anticipate and ratify the passage of laws by the soon-to-disappear Imperial Diet relating to necessary elections and other preparatory measures.

Article 101: Transitional Measure Pending Formation of House of Councillors

Colin P.A. Jones

> **Article 101.**
> If the House of Councillors is not constituted before the effective date of this Constitution, the House of Representatives shall function as the Diet until such time as the House of Councillors shall be constituted.

Article 101 anticipated the possibility of the constitution taking effect before the House of Councillors was constituted. This problem did not arise so the provision proved unnecessary.

Article 102: Transitional Measure for House of Councillors Term of Office

Colin P.A. Jones

> **Article 102.**
> The term of office for half the members of the House of Councillors serving in the first term under this Constitution shall be three years. Members falling under this category shall be determined in accordance with law.

Under Article 46 members of the House of Councillors are elected for six-year terms, staggered so that 50 percent of the membership is up for election every three years. Article 102 provided the mechanism by which this staggering was commenced: by designating half of those elected in the first elections to the chamber to serve a term of only three years.

Article 103: Preservation of Official Positions in Transition

Colin P.A. Jones

> **Article 103.**
> The Ministers of State, members of the House of Representatives and judges in office on the effective date of this Constitution, and all other public officials who occupy positions corresponding to such positions as are recognized by this Constitution shall not forfeit their positions automatically on account of the enforcement of this Constitution unless otherwise specified by law. When, however, successors are elected or appointed under the provisions of this Constitution, they shall forfeit their positions as a matter of course.

Although the Allied Occupation of Japan involved a significant purge of politicians and officials considered responsible for the rise of militarism, this was not accomplished through the transition to the new constitution. Article 103 specifically preserved the status of elected representatives, ministers of state, judges and other officials through the transition. A noteworthy omission is any reference to the emperor. Since his role is clearly provided for elsewhere in the constitution references may have been unnecessary, though retaining the emperor as a constitutional institution did not necessarily require retention of a specific emperor (i.e., Hirohito; see discussion at Chapter I: Introduction).

Appendices

Appendix 1
Constitution of the Empire of Japan

(Japanese)

大日本帝国憲法

告文

皇朕レ謹ミ畏ミ
皇祖
皇宗ノ神霊ニ誥ケ白サク皇朕レ天壌無窮ノ宏謨ニ循ヒ惟神ノ宝祚ヲ承継シ旧図ヲ保持シテ敢テ失墜スルコト無シ顧ミルニ世局ノ進運ニ膺リ人文ノ発達ニ随ヒ宜ク
皇祖
皇宗ノ遺訓ヲ明徴ニシ典憲ヲ成立シ条章ヲ昭示シ内ハ以テ子孫ノ率由スル所ト為シ外ハ以テ臣民翼賛ノ道ヲ広メ永遠ニ遵行セシメ益々国家ノ丕基ヲ鞏固ニシ八洲民生ノ慶福ヲ増進スヘシ茲ニ皇室典範及憲法ヲ制定ス惟フニ此レ皆
皇祖
皇宗ノ後裔ニ貽シタマヘル統治ノ洪範ヲ紹述スルニ外ナラス而シテ朕カ躬ニ逮テ時ト倶ニ挙行スルコトヲ得ルハ洵ニ
皇祖
皇宗及我カ
皇考ノ威霊ニ倚藉スルニ由ラサルハ無シ皇朕レ仰テ
皇祖
皇宗及
皇考ノ神祐ヲ祷リ併セテ朕カ現在及将来ニ臣民ニ率先シ此ノ憲章ヲ履行シテ愆ラサラムコトヲ誓フ庶幾クハ
神霊此レヲ鑒ミタマヘ

憲法発布勅語

朕国家ノ隆昌ト臣民ノ慶福トヲ以テ中心ノ欣栄トシ朕カ祖宗ニ承クルノ大権ニ依リ現在及将来ノ臣民ニ対シ此ノ不磨ノ大典ヲ宣布ス
惟フニ我カ祖我カ宗ハ我カ臣民祖先ノ協力輔翼ニ倚リ我カ帝国ヲ肇造シ以テ無窮ニ垂レタリ此レ我カ神聖ナル祖宗ノ威徳ト並ニ臣民ノ忠実勇武ニシテ国ヲ愛シ公ニ殉ヒ以テ此ノ光輝アル国史ノ成跡ヲ貽

シタルナリ朕我カ臣民ハ即チ祖宗ノ忠良ナル臣民ノ子孫ナルヲ回想シ其ノ朕カ意ヲ奉体シ朕カ事ヲ奨順シ相与ニ和衷協同シ益々我カ帝国ノ光栄ヲ中外ニ宣揚シ祖宗ノ遺業ヲ永久ニ鞏固ナラシムルノ希望ヲ同クシ此ノ負担ヲ分ツニ堪フルコトヲ疑ハサルナリ

大日本帝国憲法

朕祖宗ノ遺烈ヲ承ケ万世一系ノ帝位ヲ践ミ朕カ親愛スル所ノ臣民ハ即チ朕カ祖宗ノ恵撫慈養シタマヒシ所ノ臣民ナルヲ念ヒ其ノ康福ヲ増進シ其ノ懿徳良能ヲ発達セシメムコトヲ願ヒ又其ノ翼賛ニ依リ与ニ倶ニ国家ノ進運ヲ扶持セムコトヲ望ミ乃チ明治十四年十月十二日ノ詔命ヲ履践シ茲ニ大憲ヲ制定シ朕カ率由スル所ヲ示シ朕カ後嗣及臣民及臣民ノ子孫タル者ヲシテ永遠ニ循行スル所ヲ知ラシム

国家統治ノ大権ハ朕カ之ヲ祖宗ニ承ケテ之ヲ子孫ニ伝フル所ナリ朕及朕カ子孫ハ将来此ノ憲法ノ条章ニ循ヒ之ヲ行フコトヲ愆ラサルヘシ

朕ハ我カ臣民ノ権利及財産ノ安全ヲ貴重シ及之ヲ保護シ此ノ憲法及法律ノ範囲内ニ於テ其ノ享有ヲ完全ナラシムヘキコトヲ宣言ス

帝国議会ハ明治二十三年ヲ以テ之ヲ召集シ議会開会ノ時ヲ以テ此ノ憲法ヲシテ有効ナラシムルノ期トスヘシ

将来若此ノ憲法ノ或ル条章ヲ改定スルノ必要ナル時宜ヲ見ルニ至ラハ朕及朕カ継統ノ子孫ハ発議ノ権ヲ執リ之ヲ議会ニ付シ議会ハ此ノ憲法ニ定メタル要件ニ依リ之ヲ議決スルノ外朕カ子孫及臣民ハ敢テ之カ紛更ヲ試ミルコトヲ得サルヘシ

朕カ在廷ノ大臣ハ朕カ為ニ此ノ憲法ヲ施行スルノ責ニ任スヘク朕カ現在及将来ノ臣民ハ此ノ憲法ニ対シ永遠ニ従順ノ義務ヲ負フヘシ

御名御璽

明治二十二年二月十一日

内閣総理大臣　伯爵　黒田清隆

枢密院議長　伯爵　伊藤博文

外務大臣　伯爵　大隈重信

海軍大臣　伯爵　西郷従道

農商務大臣　伯爵　井上　馨

司法大臣　伯爵　山田顕義

大蔵大臣兼内務大臣　伯爵　松方正義

陸軍大臣　伯爵　大山　巌

文部大臣　子爵　森　有礼

逓信大臣　子爵　榎本武揚

大日本帝国憲法

第1章　天皇

第1条　大日本帝国ハ万世一系ノ天皇之ヲ統治ス

第2条　皇位ハ皇室典範ノ定ムル所ニ依リ皇男子孫之ヲ継承ス

第3条　天皇ハ神聖ニシテ侵スヘカラス

第4条　天皇ハ国ノ元首ニシテ統治権ヲ総攬シ此ノ憲法ノ条規ニ依リ之ヲ行フ

第5条　天皇ハ帝国議会ノ協賛ヲ以テ立法権ヲ行フ

第6条　天皇ハ法律ヲ裁可シ其ノ公布及執行ヲ命ス

第7条　天皇ハ帝国議会ヲ召集シ其ノ開会閉会停会及衆議院ノ解散ヲ命ス

第8条　天皇ハ公共ノ安全ヲ保持シ又ハ其ノ災厄ヲ避クル為緊急ノ必要ニ由リ帝国議会閉会ノ場合ニ於テ法律ニ代ルヘキ勅令ヲ発ス
2　此ノ勅令ハ次ノ会期ニ於テ帝国議会ニ提出スヘシ若議会ニ於テ承諾セサルトキハ政府ハ将来ニ向テ其ノ効力ヲ失フコトヲ公布スヘシ

第9条　天皇ハ法律ヲ執行スル為ニ又ハ公共ノ安寧秩序ヲ保持シ及臣民ノ幸福ヲ増進スル為ニ必要ナル命令ヲ発シ又ハ発セシム但シ命令ヲ以テ法律ヲ変更スルコトヲ得ス

第10条　天皇ハ行政各部ノ官制及文武官ノ俸給ヲ定メ及文武官ヲ任免ス但シ此ノ憲法又ハ他ノ法律ニ特例ヲ掲ケタルモノハ各々其ノ条項ニ依ル

第11条　天皇ハ陸海軍ヲ統帥ス

第12条　天皇ハ陸海軍ノ編制及常備兵額ヲ定ム

第13条　天皇ハ戦ヲ宣シ和ヲ講シ及諸般ノ条約ヲ締結ス

第14条　天皇ハ戒厳ヲ宣告ス
2　戒厳ノ要件及効力ハ法律ヲ以テ之ヲ定ム

第15条　天皇ハ爵位勲章及其ノ他ノ栄典ヲ授与ス

第16条　天皇ハ大赦特赦減刑及復権ヲ命ス

第17条　摂政ヲ置クハ皇室典範ノ定ムル所ニ依ル
2　摂政ハ天皇ノ名ニ於テ大権ヲ行フ

第2章　臣民権利義務

第18条　日本臣民タル要件ハ法律ノ定ムル所ニ依ル

第19条　日本臣民ハ法律命令ノ定ムル所ノ資格ニ応シ均ク文武官ニ任セラレ及其ノ他ノ公務ニ就クコトヲ得

第20条　日本臣民ハ法律ノ定ムル所ニ従ヒ兵役ノ義務ヲ有ス

第21条　日本臣民ハ法律ノ定ムル所ニ従ヒ納税ノ義務ヲ有ス

第22条　日本臣民ハ法律ノ範囲内ニ於テ居住及移転ノ自由ヲ有ス

第23条　日本臣民ハ法律ニ依ルニ非スシテ逮捕監禁審問処罰ヲ受クルコトナシ

第24条　日本臣民ハ法律ニ定メタル裁判官ノ裁判ヲ受クルノ権ヲ奪ハルヽコトナシ

第25条　日本臣民ハ法律ニ定メタル場合ヲ除ク外其ノ許諾ナクシテ住所ニ侵入セラレ及捜索セラルヽコトナシ

第26条　日本臣民ハ法律ニ定メタル場合ヲ除ク外信書ノ秘密ヲ侵サルヽコトナシ

第27条　日本臣民ハ其ノ所有権ヲ侵サルヽコトナシ
2　公益ノ為必要ナル処分ハ法律ノ定ムル所ニ依ル

第28条　日本臣民ハ安寧秩序ヲ妨ケス及臣民タルノ義務ニ背カサル限ニ於テ信教ノ自由ヲ有ス

第29条　日本臣民ハ法律ノ範囲内ニ於テ言論著作印行集会及結社ノ自由ヲ有ス

第30条　日本臣民ハ相当ノ敬礼ヲ守リ別ニ定ムル所ノ規程ニ従ヒ請願ヲ為スコトヲ得

第31条　本章ニ掲ケタル条規ハ戦時又ハ国家事変ノ場合ニ於テ天皇大権ノ施行ヲ妨クルコトナシ

第32条　本章ニ掲ケタル条規ハ陸海軍ノ法令又ハ紀律ニ牴触セサルモノニ限リ軍人ニ準行ス

第3章　帝国議会

第33条　帝国議会ハ貴族院衆議院ノ両院ヲ以テ成立ス

第34条　貴族院ハ貴族院令ノ定ムル所ニ依リ皇族華族及勅任セラレタル議員ヲ以テ組織ス

第35条　衆議院ハ選挙法ノ定ムル所ニ依リ公選セラレタル議員ヲ以テ組織ス

第36条　何人モ同時ニ両議院ノ議員タルコトヲ得ス

第37条　凡テ法律ハ帝国議会ノ協賛ヲ経ルヲ要ス

第38条　両議院ハ政府ノ提出スル法律案ヲ議決シ及各々法律案ヲ提出スルコトヲ得

第39条　両議院ノ一ニ於テ否決シタル法律案ハ同会期中ニ於テ再ヒ提出スルコトヲ得ス

第40条　両議院ハ法律又ハ其ノ他ノ事件ニ付キ各々其ノ意見ヲ政府ニ建議スルコトヲ得但シ其ノ採納ヲ得サルモノハ同会期中ニ於テ再ヒ建議スルコトヲ得ス

第41条　帝国議会ハ毎年之ヲ召集ス

第42条　帝国議会ハ三箇月ヲ以テ会期トス必要アル場合ニ於テハ勅命ヲ以テ之ヲ延長スルコトアルヘシ

第43条　臨時緊急ノ必要アル場合ニ於テ常会ノ外臨時会ヲ召集スヘシ
2　臨時会ノ会期ヲ定ムルハ勅命ニ依ル

第44条　帝国議会ノ開会閉会会期ノ延長及停会ハ両院同時ニ之ヲ行フヘシ
2　衆議院解散ヲ命セラレタルトキハ貴族院ハ同時ニ停会セラルヘシ

第45条　衆議院解散ヲ命セラレタルトキハ勅令ヲ以テ新ニ議員ヲ選挙セシメ解散ノ日ヨリ五箇月以内ニ之ヲ召集スヘシ

第46条　両議院ハ各々其ノ総議員三分ノ一以上出席スルニ非サレハ議事ヲ開キ議決ヲ為ス事ヲ得ス

第47条　両議院ノ議事ハ過半数ヲ以テ決ス可否同数ナルトキハ議長ノ決スル所ニ依ル

第48条　両議院ノ会議ハ公開ス但シ政府ノ要求又ハ其ノ院ノ決議ニ依リ秘密会ト為スコトヲ得

第49条　両議院ハ各々天皇ニ上奏スルコトヲ得

第50条　両議院ハ臣民ヨリ呈出スル請願書ヲ受クルコトヲ得

第51条　両議院ハ此ノ憲法及議院法ニ掲クルモノヽ外内部ノ整理ニ必要ナル諸規則ヲ定ムルコトヲ得

第52条　両議院ノ議員ハ議院ニ於テ発言シタル意見及表決ニ付院外ニ於テ責ヲ負フコトナシ但シ議員自ラ其ノ言論ヲ演説刊行筆記又ハ其ノ他ノ方法ヲ以テ公布シタルトキハ一般ノ法律ニ依リ処分セラルヘシ

第53条　両議院ノ議員ハ現行犯罪又ハ内乱外患ニ関ル罪ヲ除ク外会期中其ノ院ノ許諾ナクシテ逮捕セラルヽコトナシ

第54条　国務大臣及政府委員ハ何時タリトモ各議院ニ出席シ及発言スルコトヲ得

第4章　国務大臣及枢密顧問

第55条　国務各大臣ハ天皇ヲ輔弼シ其ノ責ニ任ス
2　凡テ法律勅令其ノ他国務ニ関ル詔勅ハ国務大臣ノ副署ヲ要ス

第56条　枢密顧問ハ枢密院官制ノ定ムル所ニ依リ天皇ノ諮詢ニ応ヘ重要ノ国務ヲ審議ス

第5章　司法

第57条　司法権ハ天皇ノ名ニ於テ法律ニ依リ裁判所之ヲ行フ
2　裁判所ノ構成ハ法律ヲ以テ之ヲ定ム

第58条　裁判官ハ法律ニ定メタル資格ヲ具フル者ヲ以テ之ニ任ス
2　裁判官ハ刑法ノ宣告又ハ懲戒ノ処分ニ由ルノ外其ノ職ヲ免セラルヽコトナシ
3　懲戒ノ条規ハ法律ヲ以テ之ヲ定ム

第59条　裁判ノ対審判決ハ之ヲ公開ス但シ安寧秩序又ハ風俗ヲ害スルノ虞アルトキハ法律ニ依リ又ハ裁判所ノ決議ヲ以テ対審ノ公開ヲ停ムルコトヲ得

第60条　特別裁判所ノ管轄ニ属スヘキモノハ別ニ法律ヲ以テ之ヲ定ム

第61条　行政官庁ノ違法処分ニ由リ権利ヲ傷害セラレタリトスルノ訴訟ニシテ別ニ法律ヲ以テ定メタル行政裁判所ノ裁判ニ属スヘキモノハ司法裁判所ニ於テ受理スルノ限ニ在ラス

第6章　会計

第62条　新ニ租税ヲ課シ及税率ヲ変更スルハ法律ヲ以テ之ヲ定ムヘシ
2　但シ報償ニ属スル行政上ノ手数料及其ノ他ノ収納金ハ前項ノ限ニ在ラス
3　国債ヲ起シ及予算ニ定メタルモノヲ除ク外国庫ノ負担トナルヘキ契約ヲ為スハ帝国議会ノ協賛ヲ経ヘシ

第63条　現行ノ租税ハ更ニ法律ヲ以テ之ヲ改メサル限ハ旧ニ依リ之ヲ徴収ス

第64条　国家ノ歳出歳入ハ毎年予算ヲ以テ帝国議会ノ協賛ヲ経ヘシ
2　予算ノ款項ニ超過シ又ハ予算ノ外ニ生シタル支出アルトキハ後日帝国議会ノ承諾ヲ求ムルヲ要ス

第65条　予算ハ前ニ衆議院ニ提出スヘシ

第66条　皇室経費ハ現在ノ定額ニ依リ毎年国庫ヨリ之ヲ支出シ将来増額ヲ要スル場合ヲ除ク外帝国議会ノ協賛ヲ要セス

第67条　憲法上ノ大権ニ基ツケル既定ノ歳出及法律ノ結果ニ由リ又ハ法律上政府ノ義務ニ属スル歳出ハ政府ノ同意ナクシテ帝国議会之ヲ廃除シ又ハ削減スルコトヲ得ス

第68条　特別ノ須要ニ因リ政府ハ予メ年限ヲ定メ継続費トシテ帝国議会ノ協賛ヲ求ムルコトヲ得

第69条　避クヘカラサル予算ノ不足ヲ補フ為ニ又ハ予算ノ外ニ生シタル必要ノ費用ニ充ツル為ニ予備費ヲ設クヘシ

第70条　公共ノ安全ヲ保持スル為緊急ノ需用アル場合ニ於テ内外ノ情形ニ因リ政府ハ帝国議会ヲ召集スルコト能ハサルトキハ勅令ニ依リ財政上必要ノ処分ヲ為スコトヲ得

2　前項ノ場合ニ於テハ次ノ会期ニ於テ帝国議会ニ提出シ其ノ承諾ヲ求ムルヲ要ス

第71条　帝国議会ニ於テ予算ヲ議定セス又ハ予算成立ニ至ラサルトキハ政府ハ前年度ノ予算ヲ施行スヘシ

第72条　国家ノ歳出歳入ノ決算ハ会計検査院之ヲ検査確定シ政府ハ其ノ検査報告ト倶ニ之ヲ帝国議会ニ提出スヘシ

2　会計検査院ノ組織及職権ハ法律ヲ以テ之ヲ定ム

第7章　補則

第73条　将来此ノ憲法ノ条項ヲ改正スルノ必要アルトキハ勅命ヲ以テ議案ヲ帝国議会ノ議ニ付スヘシ

2　此ノ場合ニ於テ両議院ハ各々其ノ総員三分ノ二以上出席スルニ非サレハ議事ヲ開クコトヲ得ス出席議員三分ノ二以上ノ多数ヲ得ルニ非サレハ改正ノ議決ヲ為スコトヲ得ス

第74条　皇室典範ノ改正ハ帝国議会ノ議ヲ経ルヲ要セス

2　皇室典範ヲ以テ此ノ憲法ノ条規ヲ変更スルコトヲ得ス

第75条　憲法及皇室典範ハ摂政ヲ置クノ間之ヲ変更スルコトヲ得ス

第76条　法律規則命令又ハ何等ノ名称ヲ用ヰタルニ拘ラス此ノ憲法ニ矛盾セサル現行ノ法令ハ総テ遵由ノ効力ヲ有ス

2　歳出上政府ノ義務ニ係ル現在ノ契約又ハ命令ハ総テ第六十七条ノ例ニ依ル

Appendix 2
Constitution of the Empire of Japan

(English Translation)

Imperial Oath at the Sanctuary of the Imperial Palace

We, the Successor to the prosperous Throne of Our Predecessors, do humbly and solemnly swear to the Imperial Founder of Our House and to Our other Imperial Ancestors that, in pursuance of a great policy co-extensive with the Heavens and with the Earth, We shall maintain and secure from decline the ancient form of government.

In consideration of the progressive tendency of the course of human affairs and in parallel with the advance of civilization, We deem it expedient, in order to give clearness and distinctness to the instructions bequeathed by the Imperial Founder of Our House and by Our other Imperial Ancestors, to establish fundamental laws formulated into express provisions of law, so that, on the one hand, Our Imperial posterity may possess an express guide for the course they are to follow, and that, on the other, Our subjects shall thereby be enabled to enjoy a wider range of action in giving Us their support, and that the observance of Our laws shall continue to the remotest ages of time. We will thereby to give greater firmness to the stability of Our country and to promote the welfare of all the people within the boundaries of Our dominions; and We now establish the Imperial House Law and the Constitution. These Laws come to only an exposition of grand precepts for the conduct of the government, bequeathed by the Imperial Founder of Our House and by Our other Imperial Ancestors. That we have been so fortunate in Our reign, in keeping with the tendency of the times, as to accomplish this work, We owe to the glorious Spirits of the Imperial Founder of Our House and of Our other Imperial Ancestors.

We now reverently make Our prayer to Them and to Our Illustrious Father, and implore the help of Their Sacred Spirits, and make to Them solemn oath never at this time nor in the future to fail to be an example to our subjects in the observance of the Laws hereby established.

May the Heavenly Spirits witness this Our solemn Oath.

Imperial Speech on the Promulgation of the Constitution

Whereas We make it the joy and glory of Our heart to behold the prosperity of Our country, and the welfare of Our subjects, We do hereby, in virtue of the supreme power We inherit from Our Imperial Ancestors, promulgate the present immutable fundamental law, for the sake of Our present subjects and their descendants.

The Imperial Founder of Our House and Our other Imperial Ancestors, by the help and support of the forefathers of Our subjects, laid the foundation of Our Empire upon a basis, which is to last forever. That this brilliant achievement embellishes the annals of Our country, is due to the glorious virtues of Our Sacred Imperial Ancestors, and to the loyalty and bravery of Our subjects, their love of their country and their public spirit. Considering that Our subjects are the descendants of the loyal and good subjects of Our Imperial Ancestors, We doubt not but that Our subjects will be guided by Our views, and will sympathize with all Our endeavours, and that, harmoniously cooperating together, they will share with Us Our hope of making manifest the glory of Our country, both at home and abroad, and of securing forever the stability of the work bequeathed to Us by Our Imperial Ancestors.

The Constitution of the Empire of Japan

Having, by virtue of the glories of Our Ancestors, ascended the throne of a lineal succession unbroken for ages eternal; desiring to promote the welfare of, and to give development to the moral and intellectual faculties of Our beloved subjects, the very same that have been favoured with the benevolent care and affectionate vigilance of Our Ancestors; and hoping to maintain the prosperity of the State, in concert with Our people and with their support, We hereby promulgate, in pursuance of Our Imperial Rescript of the 12th day of the 10th month of the 14th year of Meiji, a fundamental law of the State, to exhibit the principles, by which We are guided in Our conduct, and to point out to what Our descendants and Our subjects and their descendants are forever to conform.

The right of sovereignty of the State, We have inherited from Our Ancestors, and We shall bequeath them to Our descendants. Neither We nor they shall in future fail to wield them, in accordance with the provisions of the Constitution hereby granted.

We now declare to respect and protect the security of the rights and of the property of Our people, and to secure to them the complete enjoyment of the same, within the extent of the provisions of the present Constitution and of the law.

The Imperial Diet shall first be convoked for the 23rd year of Meiji, and the time of its opening shall be the date, when the present Constitution comes into force.

When in the future it may become necessary to amend any of the provisions of the present Constitution, We or Our successors shall assume the initiative right, and submit a project for the same to the Imperial Diet. The Imperial Diet shall pass its vote upon it, according to the conditions imposed by the present Constitution, and in no otherwise shall Our descendants or Our subjects be permitted to attempt any alteration thereof.

Our Ministers of State, on Our behalf, shall be held responsible for the carrying out of the present Constitution, and Our present and future subjects shall forever assume the duty of allegiance to the present Constitution.

[His Imperial Majesty's Sign-Manual.]

[Privy Seal.]
The 11th day of the 2nd month of the 22nd year of Meiji.
(Countersigned)

Count Kuroda Kiyotaka,
Minister President of State.
Count Ito Hirobumi,
President of the Privy Council.
Count Okuma Shigenobu,
Minister of State for Foreign Affairs.
Count Saigo Tsukumichi,
Minister of State for the Navy.
Count Inouye Kaoru,
Minister of State for Agriculture and Commerce.
Count Yamada Akiyoshi,
Minister of State for Justice.
Count Matsugata Masayoshi,
Minister of State for Finance, and Minister of State for Home Affairs.
Count Oyama Iwao,
Minister of State for War.
Viscount Mori Arinori,
Minister of State for Education.
Viscount Enomoto Takeaki,
Minister of State for Communications.

The Constitution of the Empire of Japan

Chapter I. The Emperor

Article 1. The Empire of Japan shall be reigned over and governed by a line of Emperors unbroken for ages eternal.

Article 2. The Imperial Throne shall be succeeded to by Imperial male descendants, according to the provisions of the Imperial House Law.

Article 3. The Emperor is sacred and inviolable.

Article 4. The Emperor is the head of the Empire, combining in Himself the rights of sovereignty, and exercises them, according to the provisions of the present Constitution.

Article 5. The Emperor exercises the legislative power with the consent of the Imperial Diet.

Article 6. The Emperor gives sanction to laws, and orders them to be promulgated and executed.

Article 7. The Emperor convokes the Imperial Diet, opens, closes and prorogues it, and dissolves the House of Representatives.

Article 8. The Emperor, in consequence of an urgent necessity to maintain public safety or to avert public calamities, issues, when the Imperial Diet is not sitting, Imperial Ordinances in the place of law.
(2) Such Imperial Ordinances are to be laid before the Imperial Diet at its next session, and when the Diet does not approve the said Ordinances, the Government shall declare them to be invalid for the future.

Article 9. The Emperor issues or causes to be issued, the Ordinances necessary for the carrying out of the laws, or for the maintenance of the public peace and order, and for the promotion of the welfare of the subjects. But no Ordinance shall in any way alter any of the existing laws.

Article 10. The Emperor determines the organization of the different branches of the administration, and salaries of all civil and military officers, and appoints and dismisses the same. Exceptions especially provided for in the present Constitution or in other laws, shall be in accordance with the respective provisions (bearing thereon).

Article 11. The Emperor has the supreme command of the Army and Navy.

Article 12. The Emperor determines the organization and peace standing of the Army and Navy.

Article 13. The Emperor declares war, makes peace, and concludes treaties.

Article 14. The Emperor proclaims the law of siege.
(2) The conditions and effects of the law of siege shall be determined by law.

Article 15. The Emperor confers titles of nobility, rank, orders and other marks of honor.

Article 16. The Emperor orders amnesty, pardon, commutation of punishments and rehabilitation.

Article 17. A Regency shall be instituted in conformity with the provisions of the Imperial House Law.
(2) The Regent shall exercise the powers appertaining to the Emperor in His name.

Chapter II. Rights and Duties of Subjects

Article 18. The conditions necessary for being a Japanese subject shall be determined by law.

Article 19. Japanese subjects may, according to qualifications determined in laws or ordinances, be appointed to civil or military offices equally, and many fill any other public offices.

Article 20. Japanese subjects are amenable to service in the Army or Navy, according to the provisions of law.

Article 21. Japanese subjects are amenable to the duty of paying taxes, according to the provisions of law.

Article 22. Japanese subjects shall have the liberty of abode and of changing the same within the limits of the law.

Article 23. No Japanese subject shall be arrested, detained, tried or punished, unless according to law.

Article 24. No Japanese subject shall be deprived of his right of being tried by the judges determined by law.

Article 25. Except in the cases provided for in the law, the house of no Japanese subject shall be entered or searched without his consent.

Article 26. Except in the cases mentioned in the law, the secrecy of the letters of every Japanese subject shall remain inviolate.

Article 27. The right of property of every Japanese subject shall remain inviolate.
(2) Measures necessary to be taken for the public benefit shall be any provided for by law.

Article 28. Japanese subjects shall, within limits not prejudicial to peace and order, and not antagonistic to their duties as subjects, enjoy freedom of religious belief.

Article 29. Japanese subjects shall, within the limits of law, enjoy the liberty of speech, writing, publication, public meetings and associations.

Article 30. Japanese subjects may present petitions, by observing the proper forms of respect, and by complying with the rules specially provided for the same.

Article 31. The provisions contained in the present Chapter shall not affect the exercise of the powers appertaining to the Emperor, in times of war or in cases of a national emergency.

Article 32. Each and every one of the provisions contained in the preceding Articles of the present Chapter, that are not in conflict with the laws or the rules and discipline of the Army and Navy, shall apply to the officers and men of the Army and of the Navy.

Chapter III. The Imperial Diet

Article 33. The Imperial Diet shall consist of two Houses, a House of Peers and a House of Representatives.

Article 34. The House of Peers shall, in accordance with the Ordinance concerning the House of Peers, be composed of the members of the Imperial Family, of the orders of nobility, and of those persons, who have been nominated thereto by the Emperor.

Article 35. The House of Representatives shall be composed of Members elected by the people, according to the provisions of the Law of Election.

Article 36. No one can at one and the same time be a Member of both Houses.

Article 37. Every law requires the consent of the Imperial Diet.

Article 38. Both Houses shall vote upon projects of law submitted to it by the Government, and may respectively initiate projects of law.

Article 39. A Bill, which has been rejected by either the one or the other of the two Houses, shall not be again brought in during the same session.

Article 40. Both Houses can make representations to the Government, as to laws or upon any other subject. When, however, such representations are not accepted, they cannot be made a second time during the same session.

Article 41. The Imperial Diet shall be convoked every year.

Article 42. A session of the Imperial Diet shall last during three months. In case of necessity, the duration of a session may be prolonged by the Imperial Order.

Article 43. When urgent necessity arises, an extraordinary session may be convoked, in addition to the ordinary one.
(2) The duration of an extraordinary session shall be determined by Imperial Order.

Article 44. The opening, closing, prolongation of session and prorogation of the Imperial Diet, shall be effected simultaneously for both Houses.
(2) In case the House of Representatives has been ordered to dissolve, the House of Peers shall at the same time be prorogued.

Article 45. When the House of Representatives has been ordered to dissolve, Members shall be caused by Imperial Order to be newly elected, and the new House shall be convoked within five months from the day of dissolution.

Article 46. No debate can be opened and no vote can be taken in either House of the Imperial Diet, unless not less than one third of the whole number of the Members thereof is present.

Article 47. Votes shall be taken in both Houses by absolute majority. In the case of a tie vote, the President shall have the casting vote.

Article 48. The deliberations of both Houses shall be held in public. The deliberations may, however, upon demand of the Government or by resolution of the House, be held in secret sitting.

Article 49. Both Houses of the Imperial Diet may respectively present addresses to the Emperor.

Article 50. Both Houses may receive petitions presented by subjects.

Article 51. Both Houses may enact, besides what is provided for in the present Constitution and in the Law of the Houses, rules necessary for the management of their internal affairs.

Article 52. No Member of either House shall be held responsible outside the respective Houses, for any opinion uttered or for any vote given in the House. When, however, a Member himself has given publicity to his opinions by public speech, by documents in print or in writing, or by any other similar means, he shall, in the matter, be amenable to the general law.

Article 53. The Members of both Houses shall, during the session, be free from arrest, unless with the consent of the House, except in cases of flagrant delicts, or of offences connected with a state of internal commotion or with a foreign trouble.

Article 54. The Ministers of State and the Delegates of the Government may, at any time, take seats and speak in either House.

Chapter IV. The Ministers of State and the Privy Council

Article 55. The respective Ministers of State shall give their advice to the Emperor, and be responsible for it.
(2) All Laws, Imperial Ordinances, and Imperial Rescripts of whatever kind, that relate to the affairs of the State, require the countersignature of a Minister of State.

Article 56. The Privy Councillors shall, in accordance with the provisions for the organization of the Privy Council, deliberate upon important matters of State, when they have been consulted by the Emperor.

Chapter V. The Judicature

Article 57. The Judicature shall be exercised by the Courts of Law according to law, in the name of the Emperor.
(2) The organization of the Courts of Law shall be determined by law.

Article 58. The judges shall be appointed from among those, who possess proper qualifications according to law.
(2) No judge shall be deprived of his position, unless by way of criminal sentence or disciplinary punishment.
(3) Rules for disciplinary punishment shall be determined by law.

Article 59. Trials and judgments of a Court shall be conducted publicly. When, however, there exists any fear that, such publicity may be prejudicial to peace and order, or to the maintenance of public morality, the public trial may be suspended by provisions of law or by the decision of the Court of Law.

Article 60. All matters, that fall within the competency of a special Court, shall be specially provided for by law.

Article 61. No suit at law, which relates to rights alleged to have been infringed by the illegal measures of the executive authorities, and which shall come within the competency of the Court of Administrative Litigation specially established by law, shall be taken cognizance of by a Court of Law.

Chapter VI. Finance

Article 62. The imposition of a new tax or the modification of the rates (of an existing one) shall be determined by law.
(2) However, all such administrative fees or other revenue having the nature of compensation shall not fall within the category of the above clause.
(3) The raising of national loans and the contracting of other liabilities to the charge of the National Treasury, except those that are provided in the Budget, shall require the consent of the Imperial Diet.

Article 63. The taxes levied at present shall, in so far as are not remodelled by new law, be collected according to the old system.

Article 64. The expenditure and revenue of the State require the consent of the Imperial Diet by means of an annual Budget.
(2) Any and all expenditures overpassing the appropriations set forth in the Titles and Paragraphs of the Budget, or that are not provided for in the Budget, shall subsequently require the approbation of the Imperial Diet.

Article 65. The Budget shall be first laid before the House of Representatives.

Article 66. The expenditures of the Imperial House shall be defrayed every year out of the National Treasury, according to the present fixed amount for the same, and shall not require the consent thereto of the Imperial Diet, except in case an increase thereof is found necessary.

Article 67. Those already fixed expenditures based by the Constitution upon the powers appertaining to the Emperor, and such expenditures as may have arisen by the effect of law, or that appertain to the legal obligations of the Government, shall be neither rejected nor reduced by the Imperial Diet, without the concurrence of the Government.

Article 68. In order to meet special requirements, the Government may ask the consent of the Imperial Diet to a certain amount as a Continuing Expenditure Fund, for a previously fixed number of years.

Article 69. In order to supply deficiencies, which are unavoidable, in the Budget, and to meet requirements unprovided for in the same, a Reserve Fund shall be provided in the Budget.

Article 70. When the Imperial Diet cannot be convoked, owing to the external or internal condition of the country, in case of urgent need for the maintenance of public safety, the Government may take all necessary financial measures, by means of an Imperial Ordinance.
(2) In the case mentioned in the preceding clause, the matter shall be submitted to the Imperial Diet at its next session, and its approbation shall be obtained thereto.

Article 71. When the Imperial Diet has not voted on the Budget, or when the Budget has not been brought into actual existence, the Government shall carry out the Budget of the preceding year.

Article 72. The final account of the expenditures and revenues of the State shall be verified and confirmed by the Board of Audit, and it shall be submitted by the Government to the Imperial Diet, together with the report of verification of the said Board.
(2) The organization and competency of the Board of Audit shall be determined by law separately.

Chapter VII. Supplementary Rules

Article 73. When it has become necessary in future to amend the provisions of the present Constitution, a project to that effect shall be submitted to the Imperial Diet by Imperial Order.
(2) In the above case, neither House can open the debate, unless not less than two thirds of the whole number of Members are present, and no amendment can be passed, unless a majority of not less than two thirds of the Members present is obtained.

Article 74. No modification of the Imperial House Law shall be required to be submitted to the deliberation of the Imperial Diet.
(2) No provision of the present Constitution can be modified by the Imperial House Law.

Article 75. No modification can be introduced into the Constitution, or into the Imperial House Law, during the time of a Regency.

Article 76. Existing legal enactments, such as laws, regulations, Ordinances, or by whatever names they may be called, shall, so far as they do not conflict with the present Constitution, continue in force.
(2) All existing contracts or orders, that entail obligations upon the Government, and that are connected with expenditure, shall come within the scope of Article 67.

Appendix 3
The Potsdam Declaration

Proclamation Defining Terms for Japanese Surrender
Issued, at Potsdam, July 26, 1945

1. We—the President of the United States, the President of the National Government of the Republic of China, and the Prime Minister of Great Britain, representing the hundreds of millions of our countrymen, have conferred and agree that Japan shall be given an opportunity to end this war.
2. The prodigious land, sea and air forces of the United States, the British Empire and of China, many times reinforced by their armies and air fleets from the west, are poised to strike the final blows upon Japan. This military power is sustained and inspired by the determination of all the Allied Nations to prosecute the war against Japan until she ceases to resist.
3. The result of the futile and senseless German resistance to the might of the aroused free peoples of the world stands forth in awful clarity as an example to the people of Japan. The might that now converges on Japan is immeasurably greater than that which, when applied to the resisting Nazis, necessarily laid waste to the lands, the industry and the method of life of the whole German people. The full application of our military power, backed by our resolve, will mean the inevitable and complete destruction of the Japanese armed forces and just as inevitably the utter devastation of the Japanese homeland.
4. The time has come for Japan to decide whether she will continue to be controlled by those self-willed militaristic advisers whose unintelligent calculations have brought the Empire of Japan to the threshold of annihilation, or whether she will follow the path of reason.
5. Following are our terms. We will not deviate from them. There are no alternatives. We shall brook no delay.
6. There must be eliminated for all time the authority and influence of those who have deceived and misled the people of Japan into embarking on world conquest, for we insist that a new order of peace, security and justice will be impossible until irresponsible militarism is driven from the world.
7. Until such a new order is established and until there is convincing proof that Japan's war-making power is destroyed, points in Japanese territory to be designated by the Allies shall be occupied to secure the achievement of the basic objectives we are here setting forth.

8. The terms of the Cairo Declaration shall be carried out and Japanese sovereignty shall be limited to the islands of Honshu, Hokkaido, Kyushu, Shikoku and such minor islands as we determine.
9. The Japanese military forces, after being completely disarmed, shall be permitted to return to their homes with the opportunity to lead peaceful and productive lives.
10. We do not intend that the Japanese shall be enslaved as a race or destroyed as a nation, but stern justice shall be meted out to all war criminals, including those who have visited cruelties upon our prisoners. The Japanese Government shall remove all obstacles to the revival and strengthening of democratic tendencies among the Japanese people. Freedom of speech, of religion, and of thought, as well as respect for the fundamental human rights shall be established.
11. Japan shall be permitted to maintain such industries as will sustain her economy and permit the exaction of just reparations in kind, but not those which would enable her to re-arm for war. To this end, access to, as distinguished from control of, raw materials shall be permitted. Eventual Japanese participation in world trade relations shall be permitted.
12. The occupying forces of the Allies shall be withdrawn from Japan as soon as these objectives have been accomplished and there has been established in accordance with the freely expressed will of the Japanese people a peacefully inclined and responsible government.
13. We call upon the government of Japan to proclaim now the unconditional surrender of all Japanese armed forces, and to provide proper and adequate assurances of their good faith in such action. The alternative for Japan is prompt and utter destruction.

Appendix 4
Instrument of Surrender

We, acting by command of and in behalf of the Emperor of Japan, the Japanese Government and the Japanese Imperial General Headquarters, hereby accept the provisions set forth in the declaration issued by the heads of the Governments of the United States, China, and Great Britain on 26 July 1945 at Potsdam, and subsequently adhered to by the Union of Soviet Socialist Republics, which four powers are hereafter referred to as the Allied Powers.

We hereby proclaim the unconditional surrender to the Allied Powers of the Japanese Imperial General Headquarters and of all Japanese armed forces and all armed forces under the Japanese control wherever situated.

We hereby command all Japanese forces wherever situated and the Japanese people to cease hostilities forthwith, to preserve and save from damage all ships, aircraft, and military and civil property and to comply with all requirements which may be imposed by the Supreme Commander for the Allied Powers or by agencies of the Japanese Government at his direction.

We hereby command the Japanese Imperial Headquarters to issue at once orders to the Commanders of all Japanese forces and all forces under Japanese control wherever situated to surrender unconditionally themselves and all forces under their control.

We hereby command all civil, military and naval officials to obey and enforce all proclamations, and orders and directives deemed by the Supreme Commander for the Allied Powers to be proper to effectuate this surrender and issued by him or under his authority and we direct all such officials to remain at their posts and to continue to perform their non-combatant duties unless specifically relieved by him or under his authority.

We hereby undertake for the Emperor, the Japanese Government and their successors to carry out the provisions of the Potsdam Declaration in good faith, and to issue whatever orders and take whatever actions may be required by the Supreme Commander for the Allied Powers or by any other designated representative of the Allied Powers for the purpose of giving effect to that Declaration.

We hereby command the Japanese Imperial Government and the Japanese Imperial General Headquarters at once to liberate all allied prisoners of war and civilian internees now under Japanese control and to provide for their protection, care, maintenance and immediate transportation to places as directed.

The authority of the Emperor and the Japanese Government to rule the state shall be subject to the Supreme Commander for the Allied Powers who will take such steps as he deems proper to effectuate these terms of surrender.

Signed at TOKYO BAY, JAPAN at 0903 I on the SECOND day of SEPTEMBER, 1945.

[Signature blocks of the Japanese representatives omitted]

Accepted at TOKYO BAY, JAPAN at 0908 I on the SECOND day of SEPTEMBER, 1945, for the United States, Republic of China, United Kingdom and the Union of Soviet Socialist Republics, and in the interests of the other United Nations at war with Japan.

[Signature blocks of MacArthur as SCAP and representatives of the United States, Republic of China, United Kingdom, USSR, Australia, Canada, France, the Netherlands and New Zealand omitted]

Appendix 5
The "MacArthur Notes"

(February 3, 1946)[1]

(Three basic points stated by Supreme Commander Allied Powers to be "musts" in constitutional revision.)

I

Emperor is at the head of the state.

His succession is dynastic.

His duties and powers will be exercised in accordance with the Constitution and responsive to the basic will of the people as provided therein.

II

War as a sovereign right of the nation is abolished. Japan renounces it as an instrumentality for settling its disputes and even for preserving its own security. It relies upon the higher ideals which are now stirring the world for its defense and its protection.

No Japanese Army, Navy, or Air Force will ever be authorized and no rights of belligerency will ever be conferred upon any Japanese force.

III

The feudal system of Japan will cease.

No rights of peerage except those of the Imperial family will extend beyond the lives of those now existent.

---

1 The version available on the National Diet Library website is undated.

No patent of nobility will from this time forth embody within itself any National or Civic power of government.

Pattern budget after British system.

Appendix 6
The "GHQ Draft"

(February 13, 1946)

CONSTITUTION OF JAPAN

We, the Japanese People, acting through our duly elected representatives in the National Diet, determined that we shall secure for ourselves and our posterity the fruits of peaceful cooperation with all nations and the blessings of liberty throughout this land, and resolved that never again shall we be visited with the horrors of war through the action of government, do proclaim the sovereignty of the people's will and do ordain and establish this Constitution, founded upon the universal principle that government is a sacred trust the authority for which is derived from the people, the powers of which are exercised by the representatives of the people, and the benefits of which are enjoyed by the people; and we reject and revoke all constitutions, ordinances, laws and rescripts in conflict herewith.
Desiring peace for all time and fully conscious of the high ideals controlling human relationship now stirring mankind, we have determined to rely for our security and survival upon the justice and good faith of the peace-loving peoples of the world. We desire to occupy an honored place in an international society designed and dedicated to the preservation of peace, and the banishment of tyranny and slavery, oppression and intolerance, for all time from the earth. We recognize and acknowledge that all peoples have the right to live in peace, free from fear and want.
We hold that no people is responsible to itself alone, but that laws of political morality are universal; and that obedience to such laws is incumbent upon all peoples who would sustain their own sovereignty and justify their sovereign relationship with other peoples.
To these high principles and purposes we, the Japanese People, pledge our national honor, determined will and full resources.

CHAPTER I The Emperor

Article I. The Emperor shall be the symbol of the State and of the Unity of the People, deriving his position from the sovereign will of the People, and from no other source.

Article II. Succession to the Imperial Throne shall be dynastic and in accordance with such Imperial House Law as the Diet may enact.

Article III. The advice and consent of the Cabinet shall be required for all acts of the Emperor in matters of state, and the Cabinet shall be responsible therefor.
The Emperor shall perform only such state functions as are provided for in this Constitution. He shall have no governmental powers, nor shall he assume nor be granted such powers. The Emperor may delegate his functions in such manner as may be provided by law.

Article IV. When a regency is instituted in conformity with the provisions of such Imperial House Law as the Diet may enact, the duties of the Emperor shall be performed by the Regent in the name of the Emperor; and the limitations on the functions of the Emperor contained herein shall apply with equal force to the Regent.

Article V. The Emperor appoints as Prime Minister the person designated by the Diet.

Article VI. Acting only on the advice and with the consent of the Cabinet, the Emperor, on behalf of the people, shall perform the following state functions:
Affix his official seal to and proclaim all laws enacted by the Diet, all Cabinet orders, all amendments to this Constitution, and all treaties and international conventions;
Convoke sessions of the Diet;
Dissolve the Diet;
Proclaim general elections;
Attest the appointment or commission and resignation or dismissal of Ministers of State, ambassadors and those other state officials whose appointment or commission and resignation or dismissal may by law be attested in this manner;
Attest grants of amnesty, pardons, commutation of punishment, reprieves and rehabilitation;
Award honors;
Receive ambassadors and ministers of foreign States; and
Perform appropriate ceremonial functions.

Article VII. No grants of money or other property shall be made to the Imperial Throne, and no expenditures shall be made by the Imperial Throne, unless authorized by the Diet.

CHAPTER II Renunciation of War

Article VIII. War as a sovereign right of nation is abolished. The threat or use of force is forever renounced as a means for settling disputes with any other nation. No army, navy, air force, or other war potential will ever be authorized and no rights of belligerency will ever be conferred upon the State.

CHAPTER III Rights and Duties of the People

Article IX. The people of Japan are entitled to the enjoyment without interference of all fundamental human rights.

Article X. The fundamental human rights by this Constitution guaranteed to the people of Japan result from the age-old struggle of man to be free. They have survived the exacting test for durability in the crucible of time and experience, and are conferred upon this and future generations in sacred trust, to be held for all time inviolate.

Article XI. The freedoms, rights and opportunities enunciated by this Constitution are maintained by the eternal vigilance of the people and involve an obligation on the part of the people to prevent their abuse and to employ them always for the common good.

Article XII. The feudal system of Japan shall cease. All Japanese by virtue of their humanity shall be respected as individuals. Their right to life, liberty and the pursuit of happiness within the limits of the general welfare shall be the supreme consideration of all law and of all governmental action.

Article XIII. All natural persons are equal before the law. No discrimination shall be authorized or tolerated in political, economic or social relations on account of race, creed, sex, social status, caste or national origin.
No patent of nobility shall from this time forth embody within itself any national or civic power of government.
No rights of peerage except those of the Imperial dynasty shall extend beyond the lives of those now in being. No special privilege shall accompany any award of honor, decoration or other distinction; nor shall any such award be valid beyond the lifetime of the individual who now holds or hereafter may receive it.

Article XIV. The people are the ultimate arbiters of their government and of the Imperial Throne. They have the inalienable right to choose their public officials and to dismiss them. All public officials are servants of the whole community and not of any special groups.
In all elections, secrecy of the ballot shall be kept inviolate, nor shall any voter be answerable, publicly or privately, for the choice he has made.

Article XV. Every person has the right of peaceful petition for the redress of grievances for the removal of public officials and for the enactment, repeal or amendment of laws, ordinances or regulations; nor shall any person be in any way discriminated against for sponsoring such a petition.

Article XVI. Aliens shall be entitled to the equal protection of law.

Article XVII. No person shall be held in enslavement, serfdom or bondage of any kind. Involuntary servitude, except as a punishment for crime, is prohibited.

Article XVIII. Freedom of thought and conscience shall be held inviolable.

Article XIX. Freedom of religion is guaranteed to all. No religious organization shall receive special privileges from the State, nor exercise political authority.
No person shall be compelled to take part in any religious acts, celebrations, rites or practices.
The State and its organs shall refrain from religious education or any other religious activity.

Article XX. Freedom of assembly, speech and press and all other forms of expression are guaranteed. No censorship shall be maintained, nor shall the secrecy of any means of communication be violated.

Article XXI. Freedom of association, movement and choice of abode are guaranteed to every person to the extent they do not conflict with the general welfare. All persons shall be free to emigrate and to change their nationality.

Article XXII. Academic freedom and choice of occupation are guaranteed.

Article XXIII. The family is the basis of human society and its traditions for good or evil permeate the nation. Marriage shall rest upon the indisputable legal and social equality of both sexes, founded upon mutual consent instead of parental coercion, and maintained through cooperation instead of male domination. Laws contrary to these principles shall be abolished, and replaced by others viewing choice of spouse, property rights, inheritance, choice of domicile, divorce and other matters pertaining to marriage and the family from the standpoint of individual dignity and the essential equality of the sexes.

Article XXIV. In all spheres of life, laws shall be designed for the promotion and extension of social welfare, and of freedom, justice and democracy.
Free, universal and compulsory education shall be established.
The exploitation of children shall be prohibited.
The public health shall be promoted.
Social security shall be provided.
Standards for working conditions, wages and hours shall be fixed.

Article XXV. All men have the right to work.

Article XXVI. The right of workers to organize and to bargain and act collectively is guaranteed.

Article XXVII. The right to own property is inviolable, but property rights shall be defined by law, in conformity with the public welfare.

Article XXVIII. The ultimate fee to the land and to all natural resources reposes in the State as the collective representative of the people. Land and other natural resources are subject to the right of the State to take them, upon just compensation therefor, for the purpose of securing and promoting the conservation, development, utilization and control thereof.

Article XXIX. Ownership of property imposes obligations. Its use shall be in the public good. Private property may be taken by the State for public use upon just compensation therefor.

Article XXX. No person shall be apprehended except upon warrant issued by a competent officer of a court of law specifying the offense upon which the person is charged, unless he is apprehended while committing a crime.

Article XXXI. No person shall be arrested or detained without being at once informed of the charges against him nor without the immediate privilege of counsel; he shall not be held incommunicado; he shall not be detained without adequate cause; and upon demand of any person such cause must be immediately shown in open court in his presence and the presence of his counsel.

Article XXXII. No person shall be deprived of life or liberty, nor shall any criminal penalty be imposed, except according to procedures established by the Diet, nor shall any person be denied the right of appeal to the courts.

Article XXXIII. The right of the people to be secure in their persons, homes, papers and effects against entries, searches and seizures shall not be impaired except upon judicial warrant issued only for probable cause, and particularly describing the place to be searched and the person or things to be seized.
Each search or seizure shall be made upon separate warrant issued for the purpose by a competent officer of a court of law.

Article XXXIV. The infliction of torture by any public officer is absolutely forbidden.

Article XXXV. Excessive bail shall not be required, nor cruel or unusual punishments inflicted.

Article XXXVI. In all criminal cases the accused shall enjoy the right to a speedy and public trial by an impartial tribunal.
He shall be permitted full opportunity to cross-examine all witnesses, and he shall have the right of compulsory process for obtaining witnesses on his behalf at public expense.
At all times the accused shall have the assistance of competent counsel who shall, if the accused be unable to secure the same by his own efforts, be assigned to his use by the government.

Article XXXVII. No person shall be declared guilty of a crime except by a court of competent jurisdiction.
No person shall be twice placed in jeopardy for the same offense.

Article XXXVIII. No person shall be compelled to testify against himself.
No confession shall be admitted in evidence if made under compulsion, torture or threat, or after prolonged arrest or detention.
No person shall be convicted or punished in cases where the only proof against him is his own confession.

Article XXXIX. No person shall be held criminally liable for an act lawful at the time it was committed.

CHAPTER IV The Diet

Article XL. The Diet shall be the highest organ of state power and shall be the sole law-making authority of the State.

Article XLI. The Diet shall consist of one House of elected representatives with a membership of not less than 300 nor more than 500.

Article XLII. The qualifications of electors and of candidates for election to the Diet shall be determined by law, and in determining such qualifications there shall be no discrimination because of sex, race, creed, color or social status.

Article XLIII. Members of the Diet shall receive adequate compensation from the national treasury as determined by law.

Article XLIV. Members of the Diet shall in all cases, except those specified by law, be free from arrest while attending the sessions of the Diet or while travelling to and from such sessions; and for any speech, debate, or vote in the Diet, they shall not be held legally liable elsewhere.

Article XLV. The term of the members shall be four years, but it may be terminated at an earlier date by dissolution of the Diet as provided herein.

Article XLVI. The method of election, apportionment, and voting shall be determined by law.

Article XLVII. The Diet shall convene at least once in every year.

Article XLVIII. The Cabinet may call special sessions and shall do so on petition of not less than twenty per cent of the members of the Diet.

Article XLVIX. The Diet shall be the sole judge of the elections and the qualifications of its members. The denial of a seat to anyone who is certified to have been elected and whose right to the seat has been questioned shall require the vote of a majority of the members present.

Article L. A quorum to transact business shall consist of not less than one-third of all the members. Except as otherwise provided herein all actions of the Diet shall be by majority vote of those present. In case of a tie the presiding officer shall cast the deciding vote.

Article LI. The Diet shall choose its presiding officer and other officials. It may determine the rules of its proceedings, punish members for disorderly behavior and expel them. On a motion for expulsion of a member a vote of not less than two-thirds of the members present shall be required to effect such expulsion.

Article LII. No law shall be passed except by bill.

Article LIII. The deliberations of the Diet shall be public, and no secret sessions shall be held. The Diet shall maintain and publish a record of its proceedings and this record shall be made available to the public. The individual votes of members on any question shall be recorded in the journal upon the demand of twenty per cent of those present.

Article LIV. The Diet shall have the power to conduct investigations, to compel the attendance and testimony of witnesses and the production of records, and to punish for refusal to comply.

Article LV. The Diet by a majority vote of those present shall designate the Prime Minister. The designation of a Prime Minister shall take precedence over all other business of the Diet. The Diet shall establish the several Ministries of State.

Article LVI. The Prime Minister and the Ministers of State whether or not they hold seats in the Diet may at any time appear before that body for the purpose of presenting and arguing bills, and shall appear when required to answer interpellations.

Article LVII. Within ten days after the passage of a resolution of non-confidence or the failure to pass a resolution of confidence by a majority of the total membership of the Diet, the Cabinet shall resign or order the Diet to dissolve. When the Diet has been ordered dissolved a special election of a new Diet shall be held not less than thirty days nor more than forty days after the date of dissolution. The newly elected Diet shall be convoked within thirty days after the date of election.

Article LVIII. The Diet shall constitute from among its members a court of impeachment to try members of the judiciary against whom removal proceedings have been instituted.

Article LIX. The Diet shall enact all laws necessary and proper to carry into execution the provisions of this Constitution.

CHAPTER V The Cabinet

Article LX. The executive power is vested in a Cabinet.

Article LXI. The Cabinet consists of a Prime Minister, who is its head, and such other Ministers of State as may be authorized by the Diet.
In the exercise of the executive power, the Cabinet is collectively responsible to the Diet.

Article LXII. The Prime Minister shall with the advice and consent of the Diet appoint Ministers of State.
The Prime Minister may remove individual Ministers at will.

Article LXIII. Whenever a vacancy occurs in the office of Prime Minister or upon the convening of a new Diet, the Cabinet shall collectively resign and a new Prime Minister shall be designated. Pending such designation, the Cabinet shall continue to perform its duties.

Article LXIV. The Prime Minister introduces bills on behalf of the Cabinet, reports to the Diet on general affairs of State and the status of foreign relations, and exercises control and supervision over the several executive departments and agencies.

Article LXV. In addition to other executive responsibilities, the Cabinet shall:
Faithfully execute the laws and administer the affairs of State;
Conduct foreign relation;
Conclude such treaties, international conventions and agreements with the consent of the Diet by prior authorization or subsequent ratification as it deems in the public interest;
Administer the civil service according to standards established by the Diet;
Prepare and submit to the Diet an annual budget;
Issue orders and regulations to carry out the provisions of this Constitution and the law, but no such order or regulation shall contain a penal provision; and
Grant amnesty, pardon, commutation of punishment, reprieve and rehabilitation.

Article LXVI. The competent Minister of State shall sign and the Prime Minister shall countersign all acts of the Diet and executive orders.

Article LXVII. Cabinet Ministers shall not be subject to judicial process during their tenure of office without the consent of the Prime Minister, but no right of action shall be impaired by reason hereof.

CHAPTER VI Judiciary

Article LXVIII. A strong and independent judiciary being the bulwark of the people's rights, the whole judicial power is vested in a Supreme Court and in such inferior courts as the Diet shall from time to time establish.
No extraordinary tribunal shall be established, nor shall any organ or agency of the Executive be given final judicial power.
All judges shall be independent in the exercise of their conscience and shall be bound only by this Constitution and the laws enacted pursuant thereto.

Article LXIX. The Supreme Court is vested with the rule-making power under which it determines the rules of practice and of procedure, the admission of attorneys, the internal discipline of the courts, the administration of judicial affairs, and such other matters as may properly affect the free exercise of the judicial power.
Public procurators shall be officers of the court and subject to its rule-making power.
The Supreme Court may delegate the power to make rules for inferior courts to such courts.

Article LXX. Removals of judges shall be accomplished by public impeachment only and no disciplinary action shall be administered them by any executive organ or agency.

Article LXXI. The Supreme Court shall consist of a chief justice and such number of associate justices as may be determined by the Diet. All such justices shall be appointed by the Cabinet and shall hold office during good behavior but not after the attainment of the age of

70 years, provided however that all such appointments shall be reviewed at the first general election held following the appointment and thereafter at every general election held immediately following the expiration of ten calendar years from the next prior confirmation. Upon a majority vote of the electorate not to retain the incumbent the office shall become vacant. All such justices shall receive, at regular, stated intervals, adequate compensation which shall not be decreased during their terms of office.

Article LXXII. The judges of the inferior courts shall be appointed by the Cabinet from a list which for each vacancy shall contain the names of at least two persons nominated by the Supreme Court. All such justices shall hold office for a term of ten years with privilege of reappointment and shall receive, at regular, stated intervals, adequate compensation which shall not be decreased during their terms of office. No judge shall hold office after attaining the age of 70 years.

Article LXXIII. The Supreme Court is the court of last resort. Where the determination of the constitutionality of any law, order, regulation or official act is in question, the judgment of the Supreme Court in all cases arising under or involving Chapter III of this Constitution is final; in all other cases where determination of the constitutionality of any law, ordinance, regulation or official act is in question, the judgment of the Court is subject to review by the Diet. A judgment of the Supreme Court which is subject to review may be set aside only by the concurring vote of two-thirds of the whole number of representatives of the Diet. The Diet shall establish rules of procedure for reviewing decisions of the Supreme Court.

Article LXXIV. In all cases affecting ambassadors, ministers and consuls of foreign states, the Supreme Court has exclusive original jurisdiction.

Article LXXV. Trials shall be conducted and judgment declared publicly. Where, however, a court unanimously determines publicity to be dangerous to public order or morals, a trial may be conducted privately, but trials of political offenses, offenses of the press, and cases wherein the rights of citizens as reserved in Chapter III of this Constitution are in question, shall be conducted publicly without exception.

CHAPTER VII Finance

Article LXXVI. The power to levy taxes, borrow money, appropriate funds, issue and regulate the value of coins and currency shall be exercised through the Diet.

Article LXXVII. No new taxes shall be imposed or existing ones modified except by action of the Diet or under such conditions as the Diet may prescribe.
All taxes in effect at the time this Constitution is promulgated shall continue to be collected under existing regulations until changed or modified by the Diet.

Article LXXVIII. No contract shall be entered into in the absence of an appropriation therefor, nor shall the credit of the State be pledged except as authorized by the Diet.

Article LXXIX. The Cabinet shall prepare and submit to the Diet an annual budget setting forth the complete government fiscal program for the next ensuing fiscal year, including all proposed expenditures, anticipated revenues and borrowings.

Article LXXX. The Diet may disapprove, reduce, increase or reject any item in the budget or add new items.
The Diet shall appropriate no money for any fiscal year in excess of the anticipated income for that period, including the proceeds of any borrowings.

Article LXXXI. In order to provide for unforeseen deficiencies in the budget a reserve fund may be authorized to be expended under the direct supervision of the Cabinet.
The Cabinet shall be held accountable to the Diet for all payments from the reserve fund.

Article LXXXII. All property of the Imperial Household, other than the hereditary estates, shall belong to the nation. The income from all Imperial properties shall be paid into the national treasury, and allowances and expenses of the Imperial Household , as defined by law, shall be appropriated by the Diet in the annual budget.

Article LXXXIII. No public money or property shall be appropriated for the use, benefit or support of any system of religion, or religious institution or association, or for any charitable, educational or benevolent purposes not under the control of the State.

Article LXXXIV. A final audit of all expenditures and revenues of the Sate shall be made annually by a board of audit and submitted by the Cabinet to the Diet during the fiscal year immediately following the period covered.
The organization and competency of the board of audit shall be determined by the Diet.

Article LXXXV. At regular intervals and at least annually the Cabinet shall report to the Diet and the people on the state of public finances.

CHAPTER VIII Local Government

Article LXXXVI. The governors of prefectures, the mayors of cities and towns and the chief executive officers of all other subordinate bodies politic and corporate having taxing power, the members of prefectural and local legislative assemblies, and such other prefectural and local officials as the Diet may determine, shall be elected by direct popular vote within their several communities.

Article LXXXVII. The inhabitants of metropolitan areas, cities and towns shall be secure in their right to manage their property, affairs and government and to frame their own charters within such laws as the Diet may enact.

Article LXXXVIII. The Diet shall pass no local or special act applicable to a metropolitan area, city or town where a general act can be made applicable, unless it be made subject to the acceptance of a majority of the electorate of such community.

CHAPTER IX Amendments

Article LXXXIX. Amendments to this Constitution shall be initiated by the Diet, through a concurring vote of two-thirds of all its members, and shall thereupon be submitted to the people for ratification, which shall require the affirmative vote of a majority of all votes cast thereon at such election as the Diet shall specify.

Amendments when so ratified shall immediately be proclaimed by the Emperor, in the name of the People, as an integral part of this Constitution.

CHAPTER X Supreme Law

Article XC. This Constitution and the laws and treaties made in pursuance hereof shall be the supreme law of the nation, and no public law or ordinance and no imperial rescript or other governmental act, or part thereof, contrary to the provisions hereof shall have legal force or validity.

Article XCI. The Emperor, upon succeeding to the Throne, and the Regent, Ministers of State, Members of the Diet, Members of the Judiciary and all other public officers upon assuming office, shall be bound to uphold and protect this Constitution.

All public officials duly holding office when this Constitution takes effect shall likewise be so bound and shall remain in office until their successors are elected or appointed.

CHAPTER XI Ratification

Article XCII. This Constitution shall be established when ratified by the Diet by roll-call vote of two-thirds of the members present.

Upon ratification by the Diet, the Emperor shall immediately proclaim, in the name of the People, that this Constitution has been established as the supreme law of the nation.

Milo E. Rowell
Lt. Col AUS

Appendix 7
The Constitution of Japan
(Japanese)

日本国憲法

日本国民は、正当に選挙された国会における代表者を通じて行動し、われらとわれらの子孫のために、諸国民との協和による成果と、わが国全土にわたつて自由のもたらす恵沢を確保し、政府の行為によつて再び戦争の惨禍が起ることのないやうにすることを決意し、ここに主権が国民に存することを宣言し、この憲法を確定する。そもそも国政は、国民の厳粛な信託によるものであつて、その権威は国民に由来し、その権力は国民の代表者がこれを行使し、その福利は国民がこれを享受する。これは人類普遍の原理であり、この憲法は、かかる原理に基くものである。われらは、これに反する一切の憲法、法令及び詔勅を排除する。

日本国民は、恒久の平和を念願し、人間相互の関係を支配する崇高な理想を深く自覚するのであつて、平和を愛する諸国民の公正と信義に信頼して、われらの安全と生存を保持しようと決意した。われらは、平和を維持し、専制と隷従、圧迫と偏狭を地上から永遠に除去しようと努めてゐる国際社会において、名誉ある地位を占めたいと思ふ。われらは、全世界の国民が、ひとしく恐怖と欠乏から免かれ、平和のうちに生存する権利を有することを確認する。

われらは、いづれの国家も、自国のことのみに専念して他国を無視してはならないのであつて、政治道徳の法則は、普遍的なものであり、この法則に従ふことは、自国の主権を維持し、他国と対等関係に立たうとする各国の責務であると信ずる。

日本国民は、国家の名誉にかけ、全力をあげてこの崇高な理想と目的を達成することを誓ふ。

第一章　天皇

第一条　天皇は、日本国の象徴であり日本国民統合の象徴であつて、この地位は、主権の存する日本国民の総意に基く。

第二条　皇位は、世襲のものであつて、国会の議決した皇室典範の定めるところにより、これを継承する。

第三条　天皇の国事に関するすべての行為には、内閣の助言と承認を必要とし、内閣が、その責任を負ふ。

第四条　天皇は、この憲法の定める国事に関する行為のみを行ひ、国政に関する権能を有しない。

②　天皇は、法律の定めるところにより、その国事に関する行為を委任することができる。

第五条　皇室典範の定めるところにより摂政を置くときは、摂政は、天皇の名でその国事に関する行為を行ふ。この場合には、前条第一項の規定を準用する。

第六条　天皇は、国会の指名に基いて、内閣総理大臣を任命する。

②　天皇は、内閣の指名に基いて、最高裁判所の長たる裁判官を任命する。

第七条　天皇は、内閣の助言と承認により、国民のために、左の国事に関する行為を行ふ。

一　憲法改正、法律、政令及び条約を公布すること。

二　国会を召集すること。

三　衆議院を解散すること。

四　国会議員の総選挙の施行を公示すること。

五　国務大臣及び法律の定めるその他の官吏の任免並びに全権委任状及び大使及び公使の信任状を認証すること。

六　大赦、特赦、減刑、刑の執行の免除及び復権を認証すること。

七　栄典を授与すること。

八　批准書及び法律の定めるその他の外交文書を認証すること。

九　外国の大使及び公使を接受すること。

十　儀式を行ふこと。

第八条　皇室に財産を譲り渡し、又は皇室が、財産を譲り受け、若しくは賜与することは、国会の議決に基かなければならない。

第二章　戦争の放棄

第九条　日本国民は、正義と秩序を基調とする国際平和を誠実に希求し、国権の発動たる戦争と、武力による威嚇又は武力の行使は、国際紛争を解決する手段としては、永久にこれを放棄する。

②　前項の目的を達するため、陸海空軍その他の戦力は、これを保持しない。国の交戦権は、これを認めない。

第三章　国民の権利及び義務

第十条　日本国民たる要件は、法律でこれを定める。

第十一条　国民は、すべての基本的人権の享有を妨げられない。この憲法が国民に保障する基本的人権は、侵すことのできない永久の権利として、現在及び将来の国民に与へられる。

第十二条　この憲法が国民に保障する自由及び権利は、国民の不断の努力によつて、これを保持しなければならない。又、国民は、これを濫用してはならないのであつて、常に公共の福祉のためにこれを利用する責任を負ふ。

第十三条　すべて国民は、個人として尊重される。生命、自由及び幸福追求に対する国民の権利については、公共の福祉に反しない限り、立法その他の国政の上で、最大の尊重を必要とする。

第十四条　すべて国民は、法の下に平等であつて、人種、信条、性別、社会的身分又は門地により、政治的、経済的又は社会的関係において、差別されない。

②　華族その他の貴族の制度は、これを認めない。

③　栄誉、勲章その他の栄典の授与は、いかなる特権も伴はない。栄典の授与は、現にこれを有し、又は将来これを受ける者の一代に限り、その効力を有する。

第十五条　公務員を選定し、及びこれを罷免することは、国民固有の権利である。

②　すべて公務員は、全体の奉仕者であつて、一部の奉仕者ではない。

③　公務員の選挙については、成年者による普通選挙を保障する。

④　すべて選挙における投票の秘密は、これを侵してはならない。選挙人は、その選択に関し公的にも私的にも責任を問はれない。

第十六条　何人も、損害の救済、公務員の罷免、法律、命令又は規則の制定、廃止又は改正その他の事項に関し、平穏に請願する権利を有し、何人も、かかる請願をしたためにいかなる差別待遇も受けない。

第十七条　何人も、公務員の不法行為により、損害を受けたときは、法律の定めるところにより、国又は公共団体に、その賠償を求めることができる。

第十八条　何人も、いかなる奴隷的拘束も受けない。又、犯罪に因る処罰の場合を除いては、その意に反する苦役に服させられない。

第十九条　思想及び良心の自由は、これを侵してはならない。

第二十条　信教の自由は、何人に対してもこれを保障する。いかなる宗教団体も、国から特権を受け、又は政治上の権力を行使してはならない。

②　何人も、宗教上の行為、祝典、儀式又は行事に参加することを強制されない。

③　国及びその機関は、宗教教育その他いかなる宗教的活動もしてはならない。

第二十一条　集会、結社及び言論、出版その他一切の表現の自由は、これを保障する。

②　検閲は、これをしてはならない。通信の秘密は、これを侵してはならない。

第二十二条　何人も、公共の福祉に反しない限り、居住、移転及び職業選択の自由を有する。

②　何人も、外国に移住し、又は国籍を離脱する自由を侵されない。

第二十三条　学問の自由は、これを保障する。

第二十四条　婚姻は、両性の合意のみに基いて成立し、夫婦が同等の権利を有することを基本として、相互の協力により、維持されなければならない。

②　配偶者の選択、財産権、相続、住居の選定、離婚並びに婚姻及び家族に関するその他の事項に関しては、法律は、個人の尊厳と両性の本質的平等に立脚して、制定されなければならない。

第二十五条　すべて国民は、健康で文化的な最低限度の生活を営む権利を有する。

②　国は、すべての生活部面について、社会福祉、社会保障及び公衆衛生の向上及び増進に努めなければならない。

第二十六条　すべて国民は、法律の定めるところにより、その能力に応じて、ひとしく教育を受ける権利を有する。

②　すべて国民は、法律の定めるところにより、その保護する子女に普通教育を受けさせる義務を負ふ。義務教育は、これを無償とする。

第二十七条　すべて国民は、勤労の権利を有し、義務を負ふ。

②　賃金、就業時間、休息その他の勤労条件に関する基準は、法律でこれを定める。

③　児童は、これを酷使してはならない。

第二十八条　勤労者の団結する権利及び団体交渉その他の団体行動をする権利は、これを保障する。

第二十九条　財産権は、これを侵してはならない。

②　財産権の内容は、公共の福祉に適合するやうに、法律でこれを定める。

③　私有財産は、正当な補償の下に、これを公共のために用ひることができる。

第三十条　国民は、法律の定めるところにより、納税の義務を負ふ。

第三十一条　何人も、法律の定める手続によらなければ、その生命若しくは自由を奪はれ、又はその他の刑罰を科せられない。

第三十二条　何人も、裁判所において裁判を受ける権利を奪はれない。

第三十三条　何人も、現行犯として逮捕される場合を除いては、権限を有する司法官憲が発し、且つ理由となつてゐる犯罪を明示する令状によらなければ、逮捕されない。

第三十四条　何人も、理由を直ちに告げられ、且つ、直ちに弁護人に依頼する権利を与へられなければ、抑留又は拘禁されない。又、何人も、正当な理由がなければ、拘禁されず、要求があれば、その理由は、直ちに本人及びその弁護人の出席する公開の法廷で示されなければならない。

第三十五条　何人も、その住居、書類及び所持品について、侵入、捜索及び押収を受けることのない権利は、第三十三条の場合を除いては、正当な理由に基いて発せられ、且つ捜索する場所及び押収する物を明示する令状がなければ、侵されない。

②　捜索又は押収は、権限を有する司法官憲が発する各別の令状により、これを行ふ。

第三十六条　公務員による拷問及び残虐な刑罰は、絶対にこれを禁ずる。

第三十七条　すべて刑事事件においては、被告人は、公平な裁判所の迅速な公開裁判を受ける権利を有する。

②　刑事被告人は、すべての証人に対して審問する機会を充分に与へられ、又、公費で自己のために強制的手続により証人を求める権利を有する。

③　刑事被告人は、いかなる場合にも、資格を有する弁護人を依頼することができる。被告人が自らこれを依頼することができないときは、国でこれを附する。

第三十八条　何人も、自己に不利益な供述を強要されない。

②　強制、拷問若しくは脅迫による自白又は不当に長く抑留若しくは拘禁された後の自白は、これを証拠とすることができない。

③　何人も、自己に不利益な唯一の証拠が本人の自白である場合には、有罪とされ、又は刑罰を科せられない。

第三十九条　何人も、実行の時に適法であつた行為又は既に無罪とされた行為については、刑事上の責任を問はれない。又、同一の犯罪について、重ねて刑事上の責任を問はれない。

第四十条　何人も、抑留又は拘禁された後、無罪の裁判を受けたときは、法律の定めるところにより、国にその補償を求めることができる。

第四章　国会

第四十一条　国会は、国権の最高機関であつて、国の唯一の立法機関である。

第四十二条　国会は、衆議院及び参議院の両議院でこれを構成する。

第四十三条　両議院は、全国民を代表する選挙された議員でこれを組織する。

②　両議院の議員の定数は、法律でこれを定める。

第四十四条　両議院の議員及びその選挙人の資格は、法律でこれを定める。但し、人種、信条、性別、社会的身分、門地、教育、財産又は収入によつて差別してはならない。

第四十五条　衆議院議員の任期は、四年とする。但し、衆議院解散の場合には、その期間満了前に終了する。

第四十六条　参議院議員の任期は、六年とし、三年ごとに議員の半数を改選する。

第四十七条　選挙区、投票の方法その他両議院の議員の選挙に関する事項は、法律でこれを定める。

第四十八条　何人も、同時に両議院の議員たることはできない。

第四十九条　両議院の議員は、法律の定めるところにより、国庫から相当額の歳費を受ける。

第五十条　両議院の議員は、法律の定める場合を除いては、国会の会期中逮捕されず、会期前に逮捕された議員は、その議院の要求があれば、会期中これを釈放しなければならない。

第五十一条　両議院の議員は、議院で行つた演説、討論又は表決について、院外で責任を問はれない。

第五十二条　国会の常会は、毎年一回これを召集する。

第五十三条　内閣は、国会の臨時会の召集を決定することができる。いづれかの議院の総議員の四分の一以上の要求があれば、内閣は、その召集を決定しなければならない。

第五十四条　衆議院が解散されたときは、解散の日から四十日以内に、衆議院議員の総選挙を行ひ、その選挙の日から三十日以内に、国会を召集しなければならない。

②　衆議院が解散されたときは、参議院は、同時に閉会となる。但し、内閣は、国に緊急の必要があるときは、参議院の緊急集会を求めることができる。

③　前項但書の緊急集会において採られた措置は、臨時のものであつて、次の国会開会の後十日以内に、衆議院の同意がない場合には、その効力を失ふ。

第五十五条　両議院は、各々その議員の資格に関する争訟を裁判する。但し、議員の議席を失はせるには、出席議員の三分の二以上の多数による議決を必要とする。

第五十六条　両議院は、各々その総議員の三分の一以上の出席がなければ、議事を開き議決することができない。

②　両議院の議事は、この憲法に特別の定のある場合を除いては、出席議員の過半数でこれを決し、可否同数のときは、議長の決するところによる。

第五十七条　両議院の会議は、公開とする。但し、出席議員の三分の二以上の多数で議決したときは、秘密会を開くことができる。

②　両議院は、各々その会議の記録を保存し、秘密会の記録の中で特に秘密を要すると認められるもの以外は、これを公表し、且つ一般に頒布しなければならない。

③　出席議員の五分の一以上の要求があれば、各議員の表決は、これを会議録に記載しなければならない。

第五十八条　両議院は、各々その議長その他の役員を選任する。

②　両議院は、各々その会議その他の手続及び内部の規律に関する規則を定め、又、院内の秩序をみだした議員を懲罰することができる。但し、議員を除名するには、出席議員の三分の二以上の多数による議決を必要とする。

第五十九条　法律案は、この憲法に特別の定のある場合を除いては、両議院で可決したとき法律となる。

②　衆議院で可決し、参議院でこれと異なつた議決をした法律案は、衆議院で出席議員の三分の二以上の多数で再び可決したときは、法律となる。

③　前項の規定は、法律の定めるところにより、衆議院が、両議院の協議会を開くことを求めることを妨げない。

④　参議院が、衆議院の可決した法律案を受け取つた後、国会休会中の期間を除いて六十日以内に、議決しないときは、衆議院は、参議院がその法律案を否決したものとみなすことができる。

第六十条　予算は、さきに衆議院に提出しなければならない。

②　予算について、参議院で衆議院と異なつた議決をした場合に、法律の定めるところにより、両議院の協議会を開いても意見が一致しないとき、又は参議院が、衆議院の可決した予算を受け取つた後、国会休会中の期間を除いて三十日以内に、議決しないときは、衆議院の議決を国会の議決とする。

第六十一条　条約の締結に必要な国会の承認については、前条第二項の規定を準用する。

第六十二条　両議院は、各々国政に関する調査を行ひ、これに関して、証人の出頭及び証言並びに記録の提出を要求することができる。

第六十三条　内閣総理大臣その他の国務大臣は、両議院の一に議席を有すると有しないとにかかはらず、何時でも議案について発言するため議院に出席することができる。又、答弁又は説明のため出席を求められたときは、出席しなければならない。

第六十四条　国会は、罷免の訴追を受けた裁判官を裁判するため、両議院の議員で組織する弾劾裁判所を設ける。

②　弾劾に関する事項は、法律でこれを定める。

第五章　内閣

第六十五条　行政権は、内閣に属する。

第六十六条　内閣は、法律の定めるところにより、その首長たる内閣総理大臣及びその他の国務大臣でこれを組織する。

②　内閣総理大臣その他の国務大臣は、文民でなければならない。

③　内閣は、行政権の行使について、国会に対し連帯して責任を負ふ。

第六十七条　内閣総理大臣は、国会議員の中から国会の議決で、これを指名する。この指名は、他のすべての案件に先だつて、これを行ふ。

②　衆議院と参議院とが異なつた指名の議決をした場合に、法律の定めるところにより、両議院の協議会を開いても意見が一致しないとき、又は衆議院が指名の議決をした後、国会休会中の期間を除いて十日以内に、参議院が、指名の議決をしないときは、衆議院の議決を国会の議決とする。

第六十八条　内閣総理大臣は、国務大臣を任命する。但し、その過半数は、国会議員の中から選ばれなければならない。

②　内閣総理大臣は、任意に国務大臣を罷免することができる。

第六十九条　内閣は、衆議院で不信任の決議案を可決し、又は信任の決議案を否決したときは、十日以内に衆議院が解散されない限り、総辞職をしなければならない。

第七十条　内閣総理大臣が欠けたとき、又は衆議院議員総選挙の後に初めて国会の召集があつたときは、内閣は、総辞職をしなければならない。

第七十一条　前二条の場合には、内閣は、あらたに内閣総理大臣が任命されるまで引き続きその職務を行ふ。

第七十二条　内閣総理大臣は、内閣を代表して議案を国会に提出し、一般国務及び外交関係について国会に報告し、並びに行政各部を指揮監督する。

第七十三条　内閣は、他の一般行政事務の外、左の事務を行ふ。

一　法律を誠実に執行し、国務を総理すること。

二　外交関係を処理すること。

三　条約を締結すること。但し、事前に、時宜によつては事後に、国会の承認を経ることを必要とする。

四　法律の定める基準に従ひ、官吏に関する事務を掌理すること。

五　予算を作成して国会に提出すること。

六　この憲法及び法律の規定を実施するために、政令を制定すること。但し、政令には、特にその法律の委任がある場合を除いては、罰則を設けることができない。

七　大赦、特赦、減刑、刑の執行の免除及び復権を決定すること。

第七十四条　法律及び政令には、すべて主任の国務大臣が署名し、内閣総理大臣が連署することを必要とする。

第七十五条　国務大臣は、その在任中、内閣総理大臣の同意がなければ、訴追されない。但し、これがため、訴追の権利は、害されない。

第六章　司法

第七十六条　すべて司法権は、最高裁判所及び法律の定めるところにより設置する下級裁判所に属する。

②　特別裁判所は、これを設置することができない。行政機関は、終審として裁判を行ふことができない。

③　すべて裁判官は、その良心に従ひ独立してその職権を行ひ、この憲法及び法律にのみ拘束される。

第七十七条　最高裁判所は、訴訟に関する手続、弁護士、裁判所の内部規律及び司法事務処理に関する事項について、規則を定める権限を有する。

②　検察官は、最高裁判所の定める規則に従はなければならない。

③　最高裁判所は、下級裁判所に関する規則を定める権限を、下級裁判所に委任することができる。

第七十八条　裁判官は、裁判により、心身の故障のために職務を執ることができないと決定された場合を除いては、公の弾劾によらなければ罷免されない。裁判官の懲戒処分は、行政機関がこれを行ふことはできない。

第七十九条　最高裁判所は、その長たる裁判官及び法律の定める員数のその他の裁判官でこれを構成し、その長たる裁判官以外の裁判官は、内閣でこれを任命する。

②　最高裁判所の裁判官の任命は、その任命後初めて行はれる衆議院議員総選挙の際国民の審査に付し、その後十年を経過した後初めて行はれる衆議院議員総選挙の際更に審査に付し、その後も同様とする。

③　前項の場合において、投票者の多数が裁判官の罷免を可とするときは、その裁判官は、罷免される。

④　審査に関する事項は、法律でこれを定める。

⑤　最高裁判所の裁判官は、法律の定める年齢に達した時に退官する。

⑥　最高裁判所の裁判官は、すべて定期に相当額の報酬を受ける。この報酬は、在任中、これを減額することができない。

第八十条　下級裁判所の裁判官は、最高裁判所の指名した者の名簿によつて、内閣でこれを任命する。その裁判官は、任期を十年とし、再任されることができる。但し、法律の定める年齢に達した時には退官する。

②　下級裁判所の裁判官は、すべて定期に相当額の報酬を受ける。この報酬は、在任中、これを減額することができない。

第八十一条　最高裁判所は、一切の法律、命令、規則又は処分が憲法に適合するかしないかを決定する権限を有する終審裁判所である。

第八十二条　裁判の対審及び判決は、公開法廷でこれを行ふ。

②　裁判所が、裁判官の全員一致で、公の秩序又は善良の風俗を害する虞があると決した場合には、対審は、公開しないでこれを行ふことができる。但し、政治犯罪、出版に関する犯罪又はこの憲法第三章で保障する国民の権利が問題となつてゐる事件の対審は、常にこれを公開しなければならない。

第七章　財政

第八十三条　国の財政を処理する権限は、国会の議決に基いて、これを行使しなければならない。

第八十四条　あらたに租税を課し、又は現行の租税を変更するには、法律又は法律の定める条件によることを必要とする。

第八十五条　国費を支出し、又は国が債務を負担するには、国会の議決に基くことを必要とする。

第八十六条　内閣は、毎会計年度の予算を作成し、国会に提出して、その審議を受け議決を経なければならない。

第八十七条　予見し難い予算の不足に充てるため、国会の議決に基いて予備費を設け、内閣の責任でこれを支出することができる。

②　すべて予備費の支出については、内閣は、事後に国会の承諾を得なければならない。

第八十八条　すべて皇室財産は、国に属する。すべて皇室の費用は、予算に計上して国会の議決を経なければならない。

第八十九条　公金その他の公の財産は、宗教上の組織若しくは団体の使用、便益若しくは維持のため、又は公の支配に属しない慈善、教育若しくは博愛の事業に対し、これを支出し、又はその利用に供してはならない。

第九十条　国の収入支出の決算は、すべて毎年会計検査院がこれを検査し、内閣は、次の年度に、その検査報告とともに、これを国会に提出しなければならない。

②　会計検査院の組織及び権限は、法律でこれを定める。

第九十一条　内閣は、国会及び国民に対し、定期に、少くとも毎年一回、国の財政状況について報告しなければならない。

第八章　地方自治

第九十二条　地方公共団体の組織及び運営に関する事項は、地方自治の本旨に基いて、法律でこれを定める。

第九十三条　地方公共団体には、法律の定めるところにより、その議事機関として議会を設置する。

②　地方公共団体の長、その議会の議員及び法律の定めるその他の吏員は、その地方公共団体の住民が、直接これを選挙する。

第九十四条　地方公共団体は、その財産を管理し、事務を処理し、及び行政を執行する権能を有し、法律の範囲内で条例を制定することができる。

第九十五条　一の地方公共団体のみに適用される特別法は、法律の定めるところにより、その地方公共団体の住民の投票においてその過半数の同意を得なければ、国会は、これを制定することができない。

第九章　改正

第九十六条　この憲法の改正は、各議院の総議員の三分の二以上の賛成で、国会が、これを発議し、国民に提案してその承認を経なければならない。この承認には、特別の国民投票又は国会の定める選挙の際行はれる投票において、その過半数の賛成を必要とする。

② 憲法改正について前項の承認を経たときは、天皇は、国民の名で、この憲法と一体を成すものとして、直ちにこれを公布する。

第十章　最高法規

第九十七条　この憲法が日本国民に保障する基本的人権は、人類の多年にわたる自由獲得の努力の成果であつて、これらの権利は、過去幾多の試錬に堪へ、現在及び将来の国民に対し、侵すことのできない永久の権利として信託されたものである。

第九十八条　この憲法は、国の最高法規であつて、その条規に反する法律、命令、詔勅及び国務に関するその他の行為の全部又は一部は、その効力を有しない。

② 日本国が締結した条約及び確立された国際法規は、これを誠実に遵守することを必要とする。

第九十九条　天皇又は摂政及び国務大臣、国会議員、裁判官その他の公務員は、この憲法を尊重し擁護する義務を負ふ。

第十一章　補則

第百条　この憲法は、公布の日から起算して六箇月を経過した日から、これを施行する。

② この憲法を施行するために必要な法律の制定、参議院議員の選挙及び国会召集の手続並びにこの憲法を施行するために必要な準備手続は、前項の期日よりも前に、これを行ふことができる。

第百一条　この憲法施行の際、参議院がまだ成立してゐないときは、その成立するまでの間、衆議院は、国会としての権限を行ふ。

第百二条　この憲法による第一期の参議院議員のうち、その半数の者の任期は、これを三年とする。その議員は、法律の定めるところにより、これを定める。

第百三条　この憲法施行の際現に在職する国務大臣、衆議院議員及び裁判官並びにその他の公務員で、その地位に相応する地位がこの憲法で認められてゐる者は、法律で特別の定をした場合を除いては、この憲法施行のため、当然にはその地位を失ふことはない。但し、この憲法によつて、後任者が選挙又は任命されたときは、当然その地位を失ふ。

Appendix 8
The Treaty of San Francisco

Treaty of Peace with Japan

WHEREAS the Allied Powers and Japan are resolved that henceforth their relations shall be those of nations which, as sovereign equals, cooperate in friendly association to promote their common welfare and to maintain international peace and security, and are therefore desirous of concluding a Treaty of Peace which will settle questions still outstanding as a result of the existence of a state of war between them;

WHEREAS Japan for its part declares its intention to apply for membership in the United Nations and in all circumstances to conform to the principles of the Charter of the United Nations; to strive to realize the objectives of the Universal Declaration of Human Rights; to seek to create within Japan conditions of stability and well-being as defined in Articles 55 and 56 of the Charter of the United Nations and already initiated by post-surrender Japanese legislation; and in public and private trade and commerce to conform to internationally accepted fair practices;

WHEREAS the Allied Powers welcome the intentions of Japan set out in the foregoing paragraph;

THE ALLIED POWERS AND JAPAN have therefore determined to conclude the present Treaty of Peace, and have accordingly appointed the undersigned Plenipotentiaries, who, after presentation of their full powers, found in good and due form, have agreed on the following provisions:

Chapter 1: Peace

Article 1

(a) The state of war between Japan and each of the Allied Powers is terminated as from the date on which the present Treaty comes into force between Japan and the Allied Power concerned as provided for in Article 23.

(b) The Allied Powers recognize the full sovereignty of the Japanese people over Japan and its territorial waters.

Chapter II: Territory

Article 2

(a) Japan recognizing the independence of Korea, renounces all right, title and claim to Korea, including the islands of Quelpart, Port Hamilton and Dagelet.

(b) Japan renounces all right, title and claim to Formosa and the Pescadores.

(c) Japan renounces all right, title and claim to the Kurile Islands, and to that portion of Sakhalin and the islands adjacent to it over which Japan acquired sovereignty as a consequence of the Treaty of Portsmouth of 5 September 1905.

(d) Japan renounces all right, title and claim in connection with the League of Nations Mandate System, and accepts the action of the United Nations Security Council of 2 April 1947, extending the trusteeship system to the Pacific Islands formerly under mandate to Japan.

(e) Japan renounces all claim to any right or title to or interest in connection with any part of the Antarctic area, whether deriving from the activities of Japanese nationals or otherwise.

(f) Japan renounces all right, title and claim to the Spratly Islands and to the Paracel Islands.

Article 3

Japan will concur in any proposal of the United States to the United Nations to place under its trusteeship system, with the United States as the sole administering authority, Nansei Shoto south of 29deg. north latitude (including the Ryukyu Islands and the Daito Islands), Nanpo Shoto south of Sofu Gan (including the Bonin Islands, Rosario Island and the Volcano Islands) and Parece Vela and Marcus Island. Pending the making of such a proposal and affirmative action thereon, the United States will have the right to exercise all and any powers of administration, legislation and jurisdiction over the territory and inhabitants of these islands, including their territorial waters.

Article 4

(a) Subject to the provisions of paragraph (b) of this Article, the disposition of property of Japan and of its nationals in the areas referred to in Article 2, and their claims, including debts, against the authorities presently administering such areas and the residents (including juridical persons) thereof, and the disposition in Japan of property of such authorities and residents, and of claims, including debts, of such authorities and residents against Japan and its nationals, shall be the subject of special arrangements between Japan and such authorities. The property of any of the Allied Powers or its nationals in the areas referred to in Article 2 shall, insofar as this has not already been done, be returned by the administering authority in the condition in which it now exists. (The term nationals whenever used in the present Treaty includes juridical persons.)

(b) Japan recognizes the validity of dispositions of property of Japan and Japanese nationals made by or pursuant to directives of the United States Military Government in any of the areas referred to in Articles 2 and 3.

(c) Japanese owned submarine cables connection Japan with territory removed from Japanese control pursuant to the present Treaty shall be equally divided, Japan retaining the Japanese terminal and adjoining half of the cable, and the detached territory the remainder of the cable and connecting terminal facilities.

Chapter III: Security

Article 5

(a) Japan accepts the obligations set forth in Article 2 of the Charter of the United Nations, and in particular the obligations

> (i) to settle its international disputes by peaceful means in such a manner that international peace and security, and justice, are not endangered;
>
> (ii) to refrain in its international relations from the threat or use of force against the territorial integrity or political independence of any State or in any other manner inconsistent with the Purposes of the United Nations;
>
> (iii) to give the United Nations every assistance in any action it takes in accordance with the Charter and to refrain from giving assistance to any State against which the United Nations may take preventive or enforcement action.

(b) The Allied Powers confirm that they will be guided by the principles of Article 2 of the Charter of the United Nations in their relations with Japan.

(c) The Allied Powers for their part recognize that Japan as a sovereign nation possesses the inherent right of individual or collective self-defense referred to in Article 51 of the Charter of the United Nations and that Japan may voluntarily enter into collective security arrangements.

Article 6

(a) All occupation forces of the Allied Powers shall be withdrawn from Japan as soon as possible after the coming into force of the present Treaty, and in any case not later than 90 days thereafter. Nothing in this provision shall, however, prevent the stationing or retention of foreign armed forces in Japanese territory under or in consequence of any bilateral or multilateral agreements which have been or may be made between one or more of the Allied Powers, on the one hand, and Japan on the other.

(b) The provisions of Article 9 of the Potsdam Proclamation of 26 July 1945, dealing with the return of Japanese military forces to their homes, to the extent not already completed, will be carried out.

(c) All Japanese property for which compensation has not already been paid, which was supplied for the use of the occupation forces and which remains in the possession of those forces at the time of the coming into force of the present Treaty, shall be returned to the Japanese Government within the same 90 days unless other arrangements are made by mutual agreement.

Chapter IV: Political and Economic Clauses

Article 7

(a) Each of the Allied Powers, within one year after the present Treaty has come into force between it and Japan, will notify Japan which of its prewar bilateral treaties or conventions with Japan it wishes to continue in force or revive, and any treaties or conventions so notified shall continue in force or by revived subject only to such amendments as may be necessary to ensure conformity with the present Treaty. The treaties and conventions so notified shall be considered as having been continued in force or revived three months after the date of notification and shall be registered with the Secretariat of the United Nations. All such treaties and conventions as to which Japan is not so notified shall be regarded as abrogated.

(b) Any notification made under paragraph (a) of this Article may except from the operation or revival of a treaty or convention any territory for the international relations of which the notifying Power is responsible, until three months after the date on which notice is given to Japan that such exception shall cease to apply.

Article 8

(a) Japan will recognize the full force of all treaties now or hereafter concluded by the Allied Powers for terminating the state of war initiated on 1 September 1939, as well as any other arrangements by the Allied Powers for or in connection with the restoration of peace. Japan also accepts the arrangements made for terminating the former League of Nations and Permanent Court of International Justice.

(b) Japan renounces all such rights and interests as it may derive from being a signatory power of the Conventions of St. Germain-en-Laye of 10 September 1919, and the Straits Agreement of Montreux of 20 July 1936, and from Article 16 of the Treaty of Peace with Turkey signed at Lausanne on 24 July 1923.

(c) Japan renounces all rights, title and interests acquired under, and is discharged from all obligations resulting from, the Agreement between Germany and the Creditor Powers of 20 January 1930 and its Annexes, including the Trust Agreement, dated 17 May 1930, the

Convention of 20 January 1930, respecting the Bank for International Settlements; and the Statutes of the Bank for International Settlements. Japan will notify to the Ministry of Foreign Affairs in Paris within six months of the first coming into force of the present Treaty its renunciation of the rights, title and interests referred to in this paragraph.

Article 9

Japan will enter promptly into negotiations with the Allied Powers so desiring for the conclusion of bilateral and multilateral agreements providing for the regulation or limitation of fishing and the conservation and development of fisheries on the high seas.

Article 10

Japan renounces all special rights and interests in China, including all benefits and privileges resulting from the provisions of the final Protocol signed at Peking on 7 September 1901, and all annexes, notes and documents supplementary thereto, and agrees to the abrogation in respect to Japan of the said protocol, annexes, notes and documents.

Article 11

Japan accepts the judgments of the International Military Tribunal for the Far East and of other Allied War Crimes Courts both within and outside Japan, and will carry out the sentences imposed thereby upon Japanese nationals imprisoned in Japan. The power to grant clemency, to reduce sentences and to parole with respect to such prisoners may not be exercised except on the decision of the Government or Governments which imposed the sentence in each instance, and on recommendation of Japan. In the case of persons sentenced by the International Military Tribunal for the Far East, such power may not be exercised except on the decision of a majority of the Governments represented on the Tribunal, and on the recommendation of Japan.

Article 12

(a) Japan declares its readiness promptly to enter into negotiations for the conclusion with each of the Allied Powers of treaties or agreements to place their trading, maritime and other commercial relations on a stable and friendly basis.

(b) Pending the conclusion of the relevant treaty or agreement, Japan will, during a period of four years from the first coming into force of the present Treaty

(1) accord to each of the Allied Powers, its nationals, products and vessels

(i) most-favoured-nation treatment with respect to customs duties, charges, restrictions and other regulations on or in connection with the importation and exportation of goods;

(ii) national treatment with respect to shipping, navigation and imported goods, and with respect to natural and juridical persons and their interests–such treatment to include all matters pertaining to the levying and collection of taxes, access to the courts, the making and performance of contracts, rights to property (tangible and intangible), participating in juridical entities constituted under Japanese law, and generally the conduct of all kinds of business and professional activities;

(2) ensure that external purchases and sales of Japanese state trading enterprises shall be based solely on commercial considerations.

(c) In respect to any matter, however, Japan shall be obliged to accord to an Allied Power national treatment, or most-favored-nation treatment, only to the extent that the Allied Power concerned accords Japan national treatment or most-favored-nation treatment, as the case may be, in respect of the same matter. The reciprocity envisaged in the foregoing sentence shall be determined, in the case of products, vessels and juridical entities of, and persons domiciled in, any non-metropolitan territory of an Allied Power, and in the case of juridical entities of, and persons domiciled in, any state or province of an Allied Power having a federal government, by reference to the treatment accorded to Japan in such territory, state or province.

(d) In the application of this Article, a discriminatory measure shall not be considered to derogate from the grant of national or most-favored-nation treatment, as the case may be, if such measure is based on an exception customarily provided for in the commercial treaties of the party applying it, or on the need to safeguard that party's external financial position or balance of payments (except in respect to shiping and navigation), or on the need to maintain its essential security interests, and provided such measure is proportionate to the circumstances and not applied in an arbitrary or unreasonable manner.

(e) Japan's obligations under this Article shall not be affected by the exercise of any Allied rights under Article 14 of the present Treaty; nor shall the provisions of this Article be understood as limiting the undertakings assumed by Japan by virtue of Article 15 of the Treaty.

Article 13

(a) Japan will enter into negotiations with any of the Allied Powers, promptly upon the request of such Power or Powers, for the conclusion of bilateral or multilateral agreements relating to international civil air transport.

(b) Pending the conclusion of such agreement or agreements, Japan will, during a period of four years from the first coming into force of the present Treaty, extend to such Power treatment not less favorable with respect to air-traffic rights and privileges than those exercised by any such Powers at the date of such coming into force, and will accord complete equality of opportunity in respect to the operation and development of air services.

(c) Pending its becoming a party to the Convention on International Civil Aviation in accordance with Article 93 thereof, Japan will give effect to the provisions of that Convention applicable to the international navigation of aircraft, and will give effect to the standards, practices and procedures adopted as annexes to the Convention in accordance with the terms of the Convention.

Chapter V: Claims and Property

Article 14

(a) It is recognized that Japan should pay reparations to the Allied Powers for the damage and suffering caused by it during the war. Nevertheless it is also recognized that the resources of Japan are not presently sufficient, if it is to maintain a viable economy, to make complete reparation for all such damage and suffering and at the same time meet its other obligations. Therefore,

1. Japan will promptly enter into negotiations with Allied Powers so desiring, whose present territories were occupied by Japanese forces and damaged by Japan, with a view to assisting to compensate those countries for the cost of repairing the damage done, by making available the services of the Japanese people in production, salvaging and other work for the Allied Powers in question. Such arrangements shall avoid the imposition of additional liabilities on other Allied Powers, and, where the manufacturing of raw materials is called for, they shall be supplied by the Allied Powers in question, so as not to throw any foreign exchange burden upon Japan.

2. (I) Subject to the provisions of subparagraph (II) below, each of the Allied Powers shall have the right to seize, retain, liquidate or otherwise dispose of all property, rights and interests of

(a) Japan and Japanese nationals,

(b) persons acting for or on behalf of Japan or Japanese nationals, and

(c) entities owned or controlled by Japan or Japanese nationals,

which on the first coming into force of the present Treaty were subject to its jurisdiction. The property, rights and interests specified in this subparagraph shall include those now blocked, vested or in the possession or under the control of enemy property authorities of Allied Powers, which belong to, or were held or managed on behalf of, any of the persons or entities mentioned in (a), (b) or (c) above at the time such assets came under the controls of such authorities.

(II) The following shall be excepted from the right specified in subparagraph (I) above:

(i) property of Japanese natural persons who during the war resided with the permission of the Government concerned in the territory of one of the Allied Powers, other than territory occupied by Japan, except property subjected to restrictions during the war and not released from such restrictions as of the date of the first coming into force of the present Treaty;

(ii) all real property, furniture and fixtures owned by the Government of Japan and used for diplomatic or consular purposes, and all personal furniture and furnishings and other private property not of an investment nature which was normally necessary for the carrying out of diplomatic and consular functions, owned by Japanese diplomatic and consular personnel;

(iii) property belonging to religious bodies or private charitable institutions and used exclusively for religious or charitable purposes;

(iv) property, rights and interests which have come within its jurisdiction in consequence of the resumption of trade and financial relations subsequent to 2 September 1945, between the country concerned and Japan, except such as have resulted from transactions contrary to the laws of the Allied Power concerned;

(v) obligations of Japan or Japanese nationals, any right, title or interest in tangible property located in Japan, interests in enterprises organized under the laws of Japan, or any paper evidence thereof; provided that this exception shall only apply to obligations of Japan and its nationals expressed in Japanese currency.

(III) Property referred to in exceptions (i) through (v) above shall be returned subject to reasonable expenses for its preservation and administration. If any such property has been liquidated the proceeds shall be returned instead.

(IV) The right to seize, retain, liquidate or otherwise dispose of property as provided in subparagraph (I) above shall be exercised in accordance with the laws of the Allied Power concerned, and the owner shall have only such rights as may be given him by those laws.

(V) The Allied Powers agree to deal with Japanese trademarks and literary and artistic property rights on a basis as favorable to Japan as circumstances ruling in each country will permit.

(b) Except as otherwise provided in the present Treaty, the Allied Powers waive all reparations claims of the Allied Powers, other claims of the Allied Powers and their nationals arising out of any actions taken by Japan and its nationals in the course of the prosecution of the war, and claims of the Allied Powers for direct military costs of occupation.

Article 15

(a) Upon application made within nine months of the coming into force of the present Treaty between Japan and the Allied Power concerned, Japan will, within six months of the date of such application, return the property, tangible and intangible, and all rights or interests of any kind in Japan of each Allied Power and its nationals which was within Japan at any time between 7 December 1941 and 2 September 1945, unless the owner has freely disposed thereof without duress or fraud. Such property shall be returned free of all encumbrances and charges to which it may have become subject because of the war, and without any charges for its return. Property whose return is not applied for by or on behalf of the owner or by his Government within the prescribed period may be disposed of by the Japanese Government as it may determine. In cases where such property was within Japan on 7 December 1941, and cannot be returned or has suffered injury or damage as a result of the war, compensation will be made on terms not less favorable than the terms provided in the draft Allied Powers Property Compensation Law approved by the Japanese Cabinet on 13 July 1951.

(b) With respect to industrial property rights impaired during the war, Japan will continue to accord to the Allied Powers and their nationals benefits no less than those heretofore accorded by Cabinet Orders No. 309 effective 1 September 1949, No. 12 effective 28 January 1950, and No. 9 effective 1 February 1950, all as now amended, provided such nationals have applied for such benefits within the time limits prescribed therein.

(c) (i) Japan acknowledges that the literary and artistic property rights which existed in Japan on 6 December 1941, in respect to the published and unpublished works of the Allied Powers and their nationals have continued in force since that date, and recognizes those rights which have arisen, or but for the war would have arisen, in Japan since that date, by the operation of any conventions and agreements to which Japan was a party on that date, irrespective of whether or not such conventions or agreements were abrogated or suspended upon or since the outbreak of war by the domestic law of Japan or of the Allied Power concerned.

(ii) Without the need for application by the proprietor of the right and without the payment of any fee or compliance with any other formality, the period from 7 December 1941 until the coming into force of the present Treaty between Japan and the Allied Power concerned shall be excluded from the running of the normal term of such rights; and such period, with an additional period of six months, shall be excluded from the time within which a literary work must be translated into Japanese in order to obtain translating rights in Japan.

Article 16

As an expression of its desire to indemnify those members of the armed forces of the Allied Powers who suffered undue hardships while prisoners of war of Japan, Japan will transfer its assets and those of its nationals in countries which were neutral during the war, or which were at war with any of the Allied Powers, or, at its option, the equivalent of such assets, to the International Committee of the Red Cross which shall liquidate such assets and distribute the resultant fund to appropriate national agencies, for the benefit of former prisoners of war and their families on such basis as it may determine to be equitable. The categories of assets described in Article 14(a)2(II)(ii) through (v) of the present Treaty shall be excepted from transfer, as well as assets of Japanese natural persons not residents of Japan on the first coming into force of the Treaty. It is equally understood that the transfer provision of this Article has no application to the 19,770 shares in the Bank for International Settlements presently owned by Japanese financial institutions.

Article 17

(a) Upon the request of any of the Allied Powers, the Japanese Government shall review and revise in conformity with international law any decision or order of the Japanese Prize Courts in cases involving ownership rights of nationals of that Allied Power and shall supply copies of all documents comprising the records of these cases, including the decisions taken and orders issued. In any case in which such review or revision shows that restoration is due, the provisions of Article 15 shall apply to the property concerned.

(b) The Japanese Government shall take the necessary measures to enable nationals of any of the Allied Powers at any time within one year from the coming into force of the present Treaty between Japan and the Allied Power concerned to submit to the appropriate Japanese authorities for review any judgment given by a Japanese court between 7 December 1941 and such coming into force, in any proceedings in which any such national was unable to make adequate presentation of his case either as plaintiff or defendant. The Japanese Government shall provide that, where the national has suffered injury by reason of any such judgment, he shall be restored in the position in which he was before the judgment was given or shall be afforded such relief as may be just and equitable in the circumstances.

Article 18

(a) It is recognized that the intervention of the state of war has not affected the obligation to pay pecuniary debts arising out of obligations and contracts (including those in respect of bonds) which existed and rights which were acquired before the existence of a state of war, and which are due by the Government or nationals of Japan to the Government or nationals of one of the Allied Powers, or are due by the Government or nationals of one of the Allied Powers to the Government or nationals of Japan. The intervention of a state of war shall equally not be regarded as affecting the obligation to consider on their merits claims for loss or damage to property or for personal injury or death which arose before the existence of a state of war, and which may be presented or re-presented by the Government of one of the Allied Powers to the Government of Japan, or by the Government of Japan to any of the Governments of the Allied Powers. The provisions of this paragraph are without prejudice to the rights conferred by Article 14.

(b) Japan affirms its liability for the prewar external debt of the Japanese State and for debts of corporate bodies subsequently declared to be liabilities of the Japanese State, and expresses its intention to enter into negotiations at an early date with its creditors with respect to the resumption of payments on those debts; to encourage negotiations in respect to other prewar claims and obligations; and to facilitate the transfer of sums accordingly.

Article 19

(a) Japan waives all claims of Japan and its nationals against the Allied Powers and their nationals arising out of the war or out of actions taken because of the existence of a state of war, and waives all claims arising from the presence, operations or actions of forces or authorities of any of the Allied Powers in Japanese territory prior to the coming into force of the present Treaty.

(b) The foregoing waiver includes any claims arising out of actions taken by any of the Allied Powers with respect to Japanese ships between 1 September 1939 and the coming into force of the present Treaty, as well as any claims and debts arising in respect to Japanese prisoners of war and civilian internees in the hands of the Allied Powers, but does not include Japanese claims specificially recognized in the laws of any Allied Power enacted since 2 September 1945.

(c) Subject to reciprocal renunciation, the Japanese Government also renounces all claims (including debts) against Germany and German nationals on behalf of the Japanese Government and Japanese nationals, including intergovernmental claims and claims for loss or damage sustained during the war, but excepting (a) claims in respect of contracts entered into and rights acquired before 1 September 1939, and (b) claims arising out of trade and financial relations between Japan and Germany after 2 September 1945. Such renunciation shall not prejudice actions taken in accordance with Articles 16 and 20 of the present Treaty.

(d) Japan recognizes the validity of all acts and omissions done during the period of occupation under or in consequence of directives of the occupation authorities or authorized by Japanese law at that time, and will take no action subjecting Allied nationals to civil or criminal liability arising out of such acts or omissions.

Article 20

Japan will take all necessary measures to ensure such disposition of German assets in Japan as has been or may be determined by those powers entitled under the Protocol of the proceedings of the Berlin Conference of 1945 to dispose of those assets, and pending the final disposition of such assets will be responsible for the conservation and administration thereof.

Article 21

Notwithstanding the provisions of Article 25 of the present Treaty, China shall be entitled to the benefits of Articles 10 and 14(a)2; and Korea to the benefits of Articles 2, 4, 9 and 12 of the present Treaty.

Chapter VI: Settlement of Disputes

Article 22

If in the opinion of any Party to the present Treaty there has arisen a dispute concerning the interpretation or execution of the Treaty, which is not settled by reference to a special claims tribunal or by other agreed means, the dispute shall, at the request of any party thereto, be referred for decision to the International Court of Justice. Japan and those Allied Powers which are not already parties to the Statute of the International Court of Justice will deposit with the Registrar of the Court, at the time of their respective ratifications of the present Treaty, and in conformity with the resolution of the United Nations Security Council, dated 15 October 1946, a general declaration accepting the jurisdiction, without special agreement, of the Court generally in respect to all disputes of the character referred to in this Article.

Chapter VII: Final Clauses

Article 23

(a) The present Treaty shall be ratified by the States which sign it, including Japan, and will come into force for all the States which have then ratified it, when instruments of ratification have been deposited by Japan and by a majority, including the United States of America as the principal occupying Power, of the following States, namely Australia, Canada, Ceylon, France, Indonesia, the Kingdom of the Netherlands, New Zealand, Pakistan, the Republic of the Philippines, the United Kingdom of Great Britain and Northern Ireland, and the United States of America. The present Treaty shall come into force of each State which subsequently ratifies it, on the date of the deposit of its instrument of ratification.

(b) If the Treaty has not come into force within nine months after the date of the deposit of Japan's ratification, any State which has ratified it may bring the Treaty into force between itself and Japan by a notification to that effect given to the Governments of Japan and the United States of America not later than three years after the date of deposit of Japan's ratification.

Article 24

All instruments of ratification shall be deposited with the Government of the United States of America which will notify all the signatory States of each such deposit, of the date of the coming into force of the Treaty under paragraph (a) of Article 23, and of any notifications made under paragraph (b) of Article 23.

Article 25

For the purposes of the present Treaty the Allied Powers shall be the States at war with Japan, or any State which previously formed a part of the territory of a State named in Article 23, provided that in each case the State concerned has signed and ratified the Treaty. Subject to the provisions of Article 21, the present Treaty shall not confer any rights, titles or benefits on any State which is not an Allied Power as herein defined; nor shall any right, title or interest of Japan be deemed to be diminished or prejudiced by any provision of the Treaty in favour of a State which is not an Allied Power as so defined.

Article 26

Japan will be prepared to conclude with any State which signed or adhered to the United Nations Declaration of 1 January 1942, and which is at war with Japan, or with any State which previously formed a part of the territory of a State named in Article 23, which is not a signatory of the present Treaty, a bilateral Treaty of Peace on the same or substantially the same terms as are provided for in the present Treaty, but this obligation on the part of Japan will expire three years after the first coming into force of the present Treaty. Should Japan make a peace settlement or war claims settlement with any State granting that State greater advantages than those provided by the present Treaty, those same advantages shall be extended to the parties to the present Treaty.

Article 27

The present Treaty shall be deposited in the archives of the Government of the United States of America which shall furnish each signatory State with a certified copy thereof.

IN FAITH WHEREOF the undersigned Plenipotentiaries have signed the present Treaty.

DONE at the city of San Francisco this eighth day of September 1951, in the English, French, and Spanish languages, all being equally authentic, and in the Japanese language.

[signatory details omitted, but treaty was signed by the following countries: Argentina, Australia, Belgium, Bolivia, Brazil, Cambodia, Canada, Ceylon, Chile, Colombia, Costa Rica, Cuba, the Dominican Republic, Ecuador, Egypt, El Salvador, Ethiopia, France, Greece, Guatemala, Haiti, Honduras, Indonesia, Iran, Iraq, Laos, Lebanon, Liberia, the Grand Duchy of Luxembourg, Mexico, the Netherlands, New Zealand, Nicaragua, Norway, Pakistan, Panama, Peru, the Republic of the Philippines, Saudi Arabia, Syria, Turkey, the Union of South Africa, the United Kingdom of Great Britain and Northern Ireland, the United States of America, Uruguay, Venezuela, Viet-Nam and Japan]

Bibliography

Japanese-language sources

Ageishi, K., Ōtsuka, H., Musashi, K. & Hirayama, M. (Eds.). (2017). *Gendai Nihon no hōkatei—Miyazawa Setsuo sensei koki kinen (jōkan)* [The legal process in contemporary Japan: A festschrift in honor of Professor Setsuo Miyazawa's 70th birthday (Vol.1)]. Tokyo: Shinzansha.

Arai, M., Sokabe, M., Sasaki, K. & Yokodaidō, S. (2021). *Kenpō I sōron/tōchi* [The Constitution of Japan Vol. 1: General theory and system of government]. (2nd ed.). Tokyo: Nippon Hyōronsha.

———. (2016) *Kenpō II jinken* [The Constitution of Japan Vol. 2: Constitutional rights]. Tokyo: Nippon Hyōronsha.

Asano, I., and Sugihara, Y. (Eds.). (2003). *Kenpō tōbenshū (1947–1999)* [A collection of answers on the Constitution (1947–1999)]. Tokyo: Shinzansha.

Ashibe, N. (2019). *Kenpō* [The Constitution]. (Takahashi, K., Ed.). (7th ed.). Tokyo: Iwanami Shoten.*

———. (2002). *Kenpō* [The Constitution]. (Takahashi, K., Ed.). (3rd ed.). Tokyo: Iwanami Shoten.

Ashibe, N. & Miyazawa, S. (1978). *Zentei Nihonkoku kenpō* [Fully revised Constitution of Japan]. Tokyo: Nippon Hyōronsha.

Ashibe, N., Nonaka, T., Ebashi, T., Takami, K., Tomatsu, H., Takahashi, K. & Urabe, N. (Eds.). (2000). *Chūshaku kenpō (1) Sōsetsu · Jōyu · Daimei · Zenbun dai ichijō—dai kyūjō* [The annotated constitution (1) Overview; imperial edict; title; Preamble; Articles one through nine]. Tokyo: Yūhikaku.

Endō, M. (2013). *Koseki to kokuseki no kingendaishi* [The modern history of the family register and citizenship]. Tokyo: Akashi Shoten.

Hasebe, Y. (Ed.). (1995). *Rīdinguzu gendai no kenpō* [Readings in modern constitutional law]. Tokyo: Nippon Hyōronsha.

Hasebe, Y., Ishikawa, K. & Shishido, J. (Eds.). (2019). *Kenpō hanrei hyakusen I* [Leading cases in constitutional law (Vol. 1)]. (7th ed.). Tokyo: Yūhikaku.*

———. (2019). *Kenpō hanrei hyakusen II* [Leading cases in constitutional law (Vol. 2)]. (7th ed.). Tokyo: Yūhikaku.*

Hashimoto, K. (1988). *Nihonkoku kenpō (kaitei ban)* [The Constitution of Japan (revised ed.)]. Tokyo: Yūhikaku.*

———. (1980). *Nihonkoku kenpō* [The Constitution of Japan]. Tokyo: Yūhikaku.

Hatake, M. (2006). *Kenpō kyūjō—kenkyū to giron no saizensen* [Article 9 of the constitution—the front line of research and debate]. Tokyo: Seirinshoin.

Higuchi, Y. (2021). *Kenpō* [The constitution]. (4th ed.). Tokyo: Keisōshobō.*

Higuchi, Y., Satō, K., Nakamura, M. & Urabe, N. (2004) *Chūkai hōritsugaku zenshū—Kenpō IV—Dainanajūrokujō-daihyakusanjō* [The complete work of the commentary on jurisprudence: The constitution IV—Articles 76–103]. Tokyo: Seirinshoin.*

———. (1998) *Chūkai hōritsugaku zenshū—Kenpō III—Daiyonjūichijō-dainanajūgojō* [The complete work of the commentary on jurisprudence: The constitution III—Articles 41–75]. Tokyo: Seirinshoin.*

———. (1997) *Chūkai hōritsugaku zenshū—Kenpō II—Dainijūichijō-daiyonjūjō* [The complete work of the commentary on jurisprudence: The Cconstitution II—Articles 21–40]. Tokyo: Seirinshoin.*

———. (1994). *Chūkai hōritsugaku zenshū—Kenpō I—Enbun, dai ichijō-dainijūjō* [The complete work of the commentary on jurisprudence: The constitution I—Preamble, Articles 1–20]. Tokyo: Seirinshoin.*

Hōgaku Kyōkai (Ed.). (1954). *Chūkai Nihonkoku kenpō gekan* [The annotated Constitution of Japan (Vol. 2)]. Tokyo: Yūhikaku.

———. (1953). *Chūkai Nihonkoku kenpō jōkan* [The annotated Constitution of Japan (Vol. 1)]. Tokyo: Yūhikaku.

Horio, T. (1971). *Gendai kyōiku no shisō to kōzō* [The theory and structure of modern education]. Tokyo: Iwanami Shoten.

Hōsei Shitsumu Kenkyūkai. (2018). *Shintei wākubukku hōsei shitsumu* [Revised workbook (of) legislative drafting]. (2nd ed.). Tokyo: Gyōsei.

Hotta, S. (2020). *Higisha torishirabe to jihaku* [Suspect investigation and confession]. Tokyo: Kōbundō.

Ishimura, O., Urata, I. & Serizawa, H. (Eds.). (2012). *Jidai o kizanda kenpō hanrei* [Era-defining constitutional precedents]. Tokyo: Shōgakusha.

Itō, M. (1995). *Kenpō* [The Constitution]. (3rd ed.). Tokyo: Kōbundō.

Kawaguchi, A. (2017). *Futatsu no kenpō to Nihonjin* [Two constitutions and the Japanese people]. Tokyo: Yoshikawa Kobunkan

Kawagishi, N., Komamura, K., Sakaguchi, S., Shishido, J. & Doi, M. (2020). *Chūshaku Nihonkoku kenpō (3): Kokumin no kenri oyobi gimu (2—Kokkai* [Japanese constitutional law annotated, Vol. 3: The rights and obligations of the people (2)—National Diet]. (Y. Hasebe, Ed.). Tokyo: Yūhikaku.

———. (2020). *Chūshaku Nihonkoku kenpō (2): Jūjō–ijūyonjō* [Japanese constitutional law annotated, Vol. 2: Articles 10 to 24]. (Y. Hasebe, Ed.). Tokyo: Yūhikaku.

Kempōteki Keiji Tetsuzuki Kenkyūkai, (Ed.), (1997). *Kempōteki keiji tetsuzuki* [Constitutional criminal procedure]. Tokyo: Nippon Hyōronsha.

Kimura, S. (2022). *Kimura Sōta no kenpō no shinte 3* [Sōta Kimura's new approach to the constitution 3]. Naha: Okinawa Times.

———. (2019). *Kimura Sōta no kenpō no shinte 2* [Sōta Kimura's new approach to the constitution 2]. Naha: Okinawa Times.

———. (2017). *Kimura Sōta no kenpō no shinte* [Sōta Kimura's new approach to the constitution]. Naha: Okinawa Times.

Kinoshita, S. & Itō, T. (2017). *Kihon kenpō 1—Kihonteki jinken* [Basic constitution I: Basic human rights]. Tokyo: Nippon Hyōronsha.

Kinoshita, S. & Tadano, M. (Eds.). (2019). *Shin kommentāru kenpō* [A new commentary on the constitution]. (2nd ed.). Tokyo: Nippon Hyōronsha.

Kobayashi, N. (1968). *Kenpō kōgi (ge)* [Lectures on the constitution (Vol. 2.)]. Tokyo: Tōkyō Daigaku Shuppankai.

Matsui, S. (2022). *Nihonkoku kenpō* [The Constitution of Japan]. (4th ed.). Tokyo: Yūhikaku.*

Miyazawa, T. (1942). *Kenpō ryakusetsu* [An outline of the constitution]. Tokyo: Iwanami Shoten.

Nishikawa, S. (2013). *Kore de wakatta! Naikaku hōseikyoku—Hō no bannin ka kenryoku no jijo ka* [Now I get it! The Cabinet Legislation Bureau—Guardians of the law, or maidservants of power?]. Tokyo: Gogatsu Shobō.

———. (2010). *Saibankan kambu jinji no kenkyū: "Keirekiteki shigen" o tegakari to shite* [Research on personnel management of the judiciary: Using "Career Path Resources" as a guide]. Tokyo: Gogatsu Shobō.

———. (2005). *Nihon shihō no gyakusetu—Saikōsai jimu sōkyoku no "Saiban shinai saibankan" tachi* [The paradox of Japanese justice—The Supreme Court Secretariat's "Judges who don't judge"]. Tokyo: Gogatsu Shobō.

———. (2003). *Kono kuni no seiji o kaeru keikaku kensain no senzairyoku* [The Board of Audit's hidden power to change this nation's politics]. Tokyo: Gogatsu Shobō.

———. (2002). *Rippō no chūsū—Shirarezaru kanchō—Shin naikaku hōseikyoku* [The
center of legislation: The Unknown government office—The new Cabinet Legislation Bureau]. Tokyo: Gogatsu Shobō.

Nonaka, T., Nakamura, M., Takahashi, K. & Takami, K. (2012). *Kenpō I* [The Constitution II]. (5th ed.). Tokyo: Yūhikaku.

———. (2012). *Kenpō II* [The Constitution II]. (5th ed.). Tokyo: Yūhikaku.

Nosaka, Y. (2011). *Kenpō kihon hanrei wo yominaosu* [Rereading basic constitutional precedents]. Tokyo: Yūhikaku.

Ōishi, M. (2008). *Kenpō chitsujo e no tembō* [A prospect on the constitutional order]. Tokyo: Yūhikaku.

Ōishi, M. & Ōsawa, H. (Eds.). (2016). *Hanrei kenpō* [Constitutional law: Selected cases]. (3rd ed.) Tokyo: Yūhikaku.

Okudaira, Y. (1993). Tetsuzukiteki dyū purosesu hoshō motsu imi [The Meaning of Procedural Due Process Guarantees]. *Hōritsu Jihō, 65*(6), 44.

Ōmori, M. & Kamata, K. (Eds.). (2011). *Rippōgakukōgi* [Lecture on legislation]. (Supp.). Tokyo: Shōji Hōmu.

Ōsuga, A. (1984). *Seizonkenron* [Theory on the welfare right]. Tokyo: Nippon Hyōronsha.

Ōyama, R. (2011). *Nihon no kokkai—Shingi suru rippōfu e* [Japan's National Diet—Towards a deliberative legislature]. Tokyo: Iwanami Shinsho.

Repeta, L., Miyake, H., Yamagishi, K., Suzuki, I., Akiyama, M. & Kitamura, Y. (1991). *Memo ga torenai—Saikōsai ni idonda otokotachi* [No note-taking allowed—The men who challenged the Supreme Court]. (J. Hamada, Trans.). Tokyo: Yūhikaku.

Sakamoto, M. (2007). *Kenpō riron* [Constitutional theory]. Tokyo: Seibundō.

Sakata, M. (Ed.). (2013). *Seifu no kenpō kaishaku* [The government's interpretation of the constitution]. Tokyo: Yūhikaku.

Sasaki, S. (1930). *Nihon kenpō yōron* [Summary of the Constitution of Japan]. Tokyo: Kanasashi Hōryūdō.

Satō, I. (1984). *Kenpō (ge)* [The Constitution (Vol. 2)]. Tokyo: Yūhikaku.

Satō, K. (2020). *Nihonkoku kenpōron* [Japanese constitutional jurisprudence]. (2nd ed.). Tokyo: Seibundō.

———. (1995). *Gendai hōritsugaku kōza—Kenpō* [Lectures on modern jurisprudence—The Constitution of Japan]. (3rd ed.). Tokyo: Seirinshoin.

Serizawa, H., Ichikawa, M. & Sakaguchi, S. (Eds.). (2011). *Shin kihonhō kommentāru kempō—Heisei nijūninen made no hō kaisei ni taiō* [A new commentary on the basic law: The constitution—Reflecting changes in law up to the year Heisei 22]. Tokyo: Nippon Hyōronsha.*

Shibutani, H. (2017). *Kenpō* [The Constitution]. (3rd ed.). Tokyo: Yūhikaku.*

Shigemura, H. (2015). *Kazoku no arikata o meguru hō to saiban no kōsaku* [The Mixture of Law and Trial over the Family Strie (sic)—What the Family Ought to Be]. *Kinki Daigaku Tandai Ronshū, 48*(1), 23–42.

Shikama, R. (2021). *Kokubō to kokusaihō* [National defense and international law]. Tokyo: Good Books K.K.

Shimoyama, K., Tomooka, F. & Chikushi, K. (2017). *Gyōseihō* [Administrative law]. Tokyo: Nippon Hyōronsha.

Shinoda, H. (2019). *Kenpōgaku no yamai* [The sickness of constitutional scholarship]. Tokyo: Shinchōsha.

Sonobe, I. (2016). *Kōshitsuhō gairon—Kōshitsu seido no hōri to un'yō* [An outline of the law of the Imperial House—The Imperial House system in principle and practice]. (Reprint). Tokyo: Daiichi Hōki.

Sugihara, Y. (1989). *Kenpō II* [The Constitution II]. Tokyo: Yūhikaku.

———. (1987). *Kenpō I* [The Constitution I]. Tokyo: Yūhikaku.

Takahashi, K. (2020). *Rikken shugi to nihonkoku kenpō* [Constitutionalism and the Constitution of Japan]. (5th ed.). Tokyo: Yūhikaku.*

Takano, T. (2021). *Hitojichi shihō* [Hostage justice]. Tokyo: Kadokawa Shinsho.

Takayanagi, K., Ōtomo, I. & Tanaka, H. (Eds.). (1972). *Nihon koku kenpō seitei no katei II* [The process of enactment of the Constitution of Japan Vol. 2]. Tokyo: Yūhikaku.

———. (1972). *Nihon koku kenpō seitei no katei I* [The process of enactment of the Constitution of Japan Vol. 1]. Tokyo: Yūhikaku.

Tamura, S. (Ed.). (2018). *Shin bōei hōsei* [The defense legislation]. Tokyo: Naigai Shuppan, K.K.

Tanaka, S. (2012). *Kokkai shitsumon seido no kenkyū—Shitsumon shuisho 1890–2007* [Research into the Diet interpellation system—Memoranda of questions, 1890–2007]. Tokyo: Nihon Shuppan Network.

Tomatsu, H. (2008). *Kenpō soshō* [Constitutional litigation], (2nd ed.). Tokyo: Yūhikaku.

Tomatsu, H. & Isao, I. (2013). *Hanrei kenpō 1* [Constitutional case law 1]. Tokyo: Daiichi Hōki.

Tomita, K. (2011). *Buki yushutsu sangensoku* [The three principles of weapons exports]. *Jōhō to Chōsa*. Issue Brief Number 726. Tokyo: National Diet Library.

———. (1996). *Kōfuku tsuikyūken no kōzō* [The structure of the right to pursuit of happiness]. *Kōhō Kenkyū* [Public Law Review] 58.

Tsujimura, M. (2021). *Kenpō* [The constitution], (7th ed.). Tokyo: Nihon Hyoronsha.*

Tsujimura, M. & Yamamoto, H. (Eds.). (2018). *Gaisetsu kenpō kommentāru* [An outline of constitutional commentary]. Tokyo: Shinzansha.

Tsunemoto, T. (1998). *Hōkoku: Senjūminzoku to saiban: Nibutani Dāmu no hanketsu no kōsatsu* [Report: Indigenous peoples and courts: An examination of the Nibutani Dam decision]. *Journal of the Japanese Association of Human Rights Law* 9, 51.

Uchino, M. (1991). *Kenpō kaishaku no ronri taikei* [The logic and system of constitutional interpretation]. Tokyo: Nippon Hyōronsha.

Urata, I. (Ed.). (2017). *Seifu no kenpō kyūjō kaishaku—Naikaku hōseikyoku shiryō to kaisetsu* [The government's interpretation of the constitution's article nine—Materials from the Cabinet Legislation Bureau and their analysis]. (2nd ed.) Tokyo: Shinzansha.

Urata, K. & Ōsuga, A. (Eds.). (1994) *Nihonkoku kenpō (3): Naikaku; shihō; zaisei; chihō jichi; kaisei; saikō hōki; hosoku (shin hanrei kommentāru)* [The Constitution of Japan (3): The Cabinet; justice; finance; local self-government; supreme law; supplementary rules (new precedent commentary)]. Tokyo: Sanseidō.

Wada, M. (2010). *Ie seido no haishi* [The abolition of the *Ie* system]. Tokyo: Shinzansha.

Watanabe, Y., Shishido, J., Matsumoto, K. & Kudō, T. (2020). *Kenpō II: Sōron/tōchi* [The Constitution of Japan Vol. 2: General theory and system of government]. Tokyo: Nippon Hyōronsha.

Yamawaki, T. (1998). *Nippon ginkō no shinjitsu* [The truth about the Bank of Japan]. Tokyo: Daiyamondosha [DIAMOND, Inc.].

Yasuaki, C. (2012). *Naikaku anzen hoshō kikō no rekishiteki hensen kara Mita Nihonban NSC no kadai* [Issues in the Japan version NSC as seen from the historical transition of cabinet security institutions]. *Bōei Kenkyūjo Nyūsu 170*. Tokyo: Bōei Kenkyūjo [National Institute for Defense Studies].

Yasunishi, F., Maki, M. & Shishido, J. (2018). *Kempōgaku tokuhon* [Constitutional law reader]. (3rd ed.) Tokyo: Yūhikaku.

English and other language sources

Abe, M. (1995). The Internal Control of a Bureaucratic Judiciary: The Case of Japan. *International Journal of the Sociology of Law* 23(4), 303–20.

Allison, A. (2000). *Permitted and Prohibited Desires: Mothers, Comics, and Censorship in Japan.* Berkeley: University of California Press.

Apter, D.E. & Sawa, N. (1984). *Against the State: Politics and Social Protest in Japan.* Cambridge, MA: Harvard University Press.

Baldwin, F. & Allison, A. (Eds.). (2015). *Japan: The Precarious Future.* New York: NYU Press.

Bälz, M., Dernauer, M., Heath, C. & Petersen-Padberg, A. (Eds.). (2012). *Business Law in Japan—Cases and Comments.* Alphen aan den Rijn: Kluwer Law International.

Banno, J. (1992). *The Establishment of the Japanese Constitutional System* (J.A.A. Stockwin, trans.). Abingdon-on-Thames: Routledge. (Original work published 1971).

Barnes, D.A. (2017). *Architects of Occupation: American Experts and the Planning for Postwar Japan.* Ithaca, NY: Cornell University Press.

Beer, L.W. (1984). *Freedom of Expression in Japan: A Study in Comparative Law, Politics, and Society.* New York: Kodansha America, Inc.

———. (1983). Postwar Law on Civil Liberties in Japan. *Pacific Basin Law Journal* 2(1–2), 98–115.

Beer, L.W. & Maki, J.M. (2002). *From Imperial Myth to Democracy.* Boulder: University Press of Colorado.

Bix, H.P. (1982). Rethinking "Emperor-System Fascism": Ruptures and Continuities in Modern Japanese History. *Bulletin of Concerned Asian Scholars* 14(2), 2–19.

Chapman, D. & Krogness, K.J. (Eds.). (2014). *Japan's Household Registration System and Citizenship: Koseki, Identification and Documentation.* Abingdon-on-Thames: Routledge.

Chen, P.L. & Wada, J.T. (2017). Can the Japanese Supreme Court Overcome the Political Question Hurdle? *Washington International Law Journal Association* 26(2), 349–80.

Colombo, G.F. (2015). Nomophilacy and Beyond: Comparative Reflections on Judicial Precedents by Supreme Jurisdictions in Italy and Japan. *European Journal of Comparative Law and Governance* 2(4), 281–315.

Colombo, G.F. & Ortolani, A. (2019). "Il Giappone". In M. Mazza (Ed.), *I sistemi del lontano Oriente.* Milan: Wolters Kluwer Italia.

Dobrovolskaia, A. (2008). The Jury System in Pre-War Japan: An Annotated Translation of "The Jury Guidebook." *Asian-Pacific Law & Policy Journal* 9(2), 231–96.

Dower, J. (2000). *Embracing Defeat: Japan in the Wake of World War II*. New York City: W.W. Norton & Company.

Duus, P. (Ed.). (1989). *The Cambridge History of Japan, Vol. 6: The Twentieth Century*. Cambridge: Cambridge University Press.

Feldman, E.A. (2000). *The Ritual of Rights in Japan: Law, Society, and Health Policy*. Cambridge: Cambridge University Press.

Flaherty, D.E. (2013). *Public Law, Private Practice: Politics, Profit, and the Legal Profession in Nineteenth-Century Japan*. Cambridge, MA: Harvard University Asia Center.

Foote, D.H. (2011). The Supreme Court and the Push for Transparency in Lower Court Appointments in Japan. *Washington University Law Review* 88(6), 1745–63.

———. (1992). The Benevolent Paternalism of Japanese Criminal Justice. *California Law Review 80*(2), 317–90.

———. (1991). Confessions and the Right to Silence in Japan. *Georgia Journal of International and Comparative Law* 21(3), 415–88.

Foote, D.H. (Ed.). (2008). *Law in Japan: A Turning Point*. (Asian Law Series). Seattle: University of Washington Press.

Fujita, T. (2011). The Supreme Court of Japan: Commentary on the Recent Work of Scholars in the United States. *Washington University Law Review 88*(6), 1507–26.

Goodman, C.F. (2008). *The Rule of Law in Japan: A Comparative Analysis* (2nd ed.). Alphen aan den Rijn: Kluwer Law International.

Gordon, A. (1991). *Labor and Imperial Democracy in Prewar Japan*. Berkeley: University of California Press.

Gordon, B.S. (2014). *The Only Woman in the Room: A Memoir of Japan, Human Rights, and the Arts*. Chicago: University of Chicago Press.

Gresser, J., Fujikura, K. & Morishima, A. (1981). *Environmental Law in Japan*. Cambridge, MA: The MIT Press.

Haley, J.O. (1995). Judicial Independence in Japan Revisited. *Law in Japan* 25(1), 1–18.

———. (1994). *Authority without Power: Law and the Japanese Paradox*. Oxford: Oxford University Press.

Hamano, S.B. (1999). Incomplete Revolutions and Not So Alien Transplants: The Japanese Constitution and Human Rights. *University of Pennsylvania Journal of Constitutional Law* 1(3), 415–91.

Hardacre, H. (1989). *Shinto and the State, 1868–1988*. Princeton: Princeton University Press.

Hellegers, D.M. (2001). *We the Japanese People—World War II and the Origins of the Japanese Constitution* (Volumes 1 and 2). Redwood City: Stanford University Press.

Henderson, D.F. (Ed.). (1968). *The Constitution of Japan: Its First Twenty Years, 1947–67*. Seattle: University of Washington Press.

Herber, E. (2019). *Lay and Expert Contributions to Japanese Criminal Justice*. Abingdon-on-Thames: Routledge.

Higashikawa, K. (2021). Bold Solution from Easy Cases: The Development, Benefit, and Concern on Japanese Hate Speech Laws, *Michigan State International Law Review* 29, 261–303.

———. (2017). Japan's Hate Speech Laws: Translations of the Osaka City Ordinance and the National Act to Curb Hate Speech in Japan. *Asian-Pacific Law and Policy Journal* 19(1), 1–22.

———. (2016). Tying the Knot with a Surname? The Constitutionality of Japan's Law Requiring a Same Marital Name, *ConLawNOW* 7(1), 51–58.

Hozumi, N. (1912). *Ancestor Worship and Japanese Law* (2nd rev. ed.). Tokyo: Maruzen Kabushiki Kaisha.

Ii, T. (2013). Japan's Judicial System May Change, But Its Fundamental Nature Stays Virtually the Same? Recent Japanese Reforms on the Judicial Appointment and Evaluation. *Hastings International & Comparative Law Review* 36(1), 459–74.

Inoue, K. (1991). *MacArthur's Japanese Constitution*. Chicago: University of Chicago Press.

Itō, H. (2010). *The Supreme Court and Benign Elite Democracy in Japan*. Abingdon-on-Thames: Routledge.

———. (1990). Judicial Review and Judicial Activism in Japan. *Law and Contemporary Problems* 53(1), 169–79.

———. (1989). *The Japanese Supreme Court: Constitutional Policies*. Princeton: Markus Wiener Publishers.

———. (1970). How Judges Think in Japan. *The American Journal of Comparative Law* 18(4), 779.

Itō, H. & Beer, L.W. (Eds.). (1978). *The Constitutional Case Law of Japan: Selected Supreme Court Decisions, 1961–70*. Seattle: University of Washington Press.

Itō, Hirobumi. (1906). *Commentaries on the Constitution of the Empire of Japan*. (M. Itō, Trans.). Santa Barbara: Greenwood Press.

Jansen, M.B. (Ed.). (1989). *The Cambridge History of Japan, Vol. 5: The Nineteenth Century.* Cambridge: Cambridge University Press.
Jenco, L. K., Idris, M. & Thomas, M. C. (Eds.). (2020). *The Oxford Handbook of Comparative Political Theory.* Oxford: Oxford University Press.
Jitsuhara, T. (2017). Guarantee of the Right to Freedom of Speech in Japan—A Comparison with Doctrines in Germany. In Y. Nakanishi (Ed.), 169–91.
Johnson, D.T. (2001). *The Japanese Way of Justice.* Oxford: Oxford University Press.
Jones, C.P.A. (2019). *Obey, Not Know: Essays in Japanese Law and Society.* Kumamoto: Kurodahan Press.
———. (2017a). Japan's New Conspiracy Law Expands Police Power. *The Asia-Pacific Journal, Japan Focus* 15(16).
———. (2017b). From Great Writ to Tuning Fork; How Habeas Corpus was Tamed in Japan. *University of Pennsylvania Asian Law Review* 12(1), 407–61.
———. (2015). Nineteenth Century Rules over Twenty-First Century Reality—Legal Parentage under Japanese Law. *Family Law Quarterly* 49(1), 149–77.
———. (2014). Legitimacy-based Discrimination and the Development of the Judicial Power in Japan as Seen through Two Supreme Court Cases. *University of Pennsylvania East Asia Law Review* 9(2), 99–136.
———. (2013). Amakudari and Japanese Law. *Michigan State International Law Review* 40, 879–959.
———. (2005). Kaoru Inoue's *Shihō no Shaberisugi* (Blabbermouth Judiciary): Moral Relief, Legal Reasoning and Judicial Activism in Japan. *Emory International Law Review* 19(3), 1563.
Jones, C.P.A. & Ravitch, F.S. (2020). *The Japanese Legal System in a Nutshell.* St Paul: West Academic Publishing.
———. (2018). *The Japanese Legal System.* St Paul: West Academic Publishing.
Kamiya, M. (2011). Chōsakan: Research Judges Toiling at the Stone Fortress. *Washington University Law Review* 88(6), 1601–29.
Kasza, G.J. (1993). *The State and the Mass Media in Japan, 1918–1945.* Berkeley: University of California Press.
Kawai, K. (1960). *Japan's American Interlude.* Chicago: University of Chicago Press.
Keene, D. (2005). *Emperor of Japan: Meiji and His World, 1852–1912.* New York City: Columbia University Press.
Kingston, J. (2017). *Press Freedom in Contemporary Japan.* Abingdon-on-Thames: Routledge.
Kitagawa, J.M. (1966). *Religion in Japanese History.* New York: Columbia University Press.
Kitajima, N. (2012). The Protection of Reputation in Japan: A Systematic Analysis of Defamation Cases. *Law & Social Inquiry* 37(1), 89–118.
Koseki, S. (1997). *The Birth of Japan's Postwar Constitution* (R. Moore, trans.). New York City: Perseus. (Original work published 1989).
Kotani, J. (2018). Proceed with Caution: Hate Speech Regulation in Japan. *Hastings Constitutional Law Quarterly* 45(3), 603–22.
Kozuka, S. (2009). Judicial Activism of the Japanese Supreme Court in Consumer Law: Juridification of Society through Case Law. *Zeitschrift für Japanisches Recht/Journal of Japanese Law* 14(27), 81–90.
Law, D.S. (2011). Why Has Judicial Review Failed in Japan? *Washington University Law Review* 88(6), 1425–66.
———. (2009). The Anatomy of a Conservative Court: Judicial Review in Japan. *Texas Law Review* 87, 1545.
Levin, M.A. (2017). Speaking Truth to Power: Professor Setsuo Miyazawa's Impact on Overseas Understandings of the Japanese Judiciary. In Ageishi, K., Ōtsuka, H., Musashi, K. & Hirayama, M. (Eds.).
———. (2011). Civil Justice and the Constitution: Limits on Instrumental Judicial Administration in Japan. *Pacific Rim Law & Policy Journal* 20(2), 265–318.
———. (2001). Essential Commodities and Racial Justice: Using Constitutional Protection of Japan's Indigenous Ainu People to Inform Understandings of the United States and Japan. *New York University Journal of International Law and Politics* 33, 471–79.
Levin, M.A. (Trans.). (1999). Kayano et al. v. Hokkaido Expropriation Committee: 'The Nibutani Dam Decision'. *International Legal Materials,* 38, 394.
Levin, M.A. & Mackie, A. (2013). Truth or Consequences of the Justice System Reform Council: An English Language Bibliography from Japan's Millennial Legal Reforms. *Asian Pacific Law and Policy Journal* 14(3).
Luney, P.R. & Takahashi, K. (Eds.). (1993). *Japanese Constitutional Law.* Tokyo: University of Tokyo Press.
Maki, J.M. (1980). *Japan's Commission on the Constitution: The Final Report.* Seattle: University of Washington Press.

———. (1964). *Court and Constitution in Japan: Selected Supreme Court Decisions, 1948–60*. Seattle: University of Washington Press.
Marshall, B.K. (1992). *Academic Freedom and the Japanese Imperial University, 1868–1939*. Berkeley: University of California Press.
Martin, C. (2018). Striking the Right Balance: Hate Speech Laws in Japan, the United States, and Canada. *Hastings Constitutional Law Quarterly* 45(3), 455–532.
———. (2017). The Legitimacy of Informal Constitutional Amendment and the "Reinterpretation" of Japan's War Powers. *Fordham International Law Journal* 40(2), 427–522.
———. (2016). Change It to Save It: Why and How to Amend Article 9. *Ritsumeikan Journal of Peace Studies* 18.
———. (2010). Glimmers of Hope: The Evolution of Equality Rights Doctrine in Japanese Courts from a Comparative Perspective. *Duke Journal of Comparative & International Law* 20, 167–246.
———. (2008). Binding the Dogs of War: Japan and the Constitutionalizing of Jus Ad Bellum. *University of Pennsylvania Journal of International Law* 30(1), 267–358.
Matsui, S. (2021). Freedom of Expression in Japan: The Constitutional Framework of Protection. In Higaki, S. & Nasu, Y. (Eds.) *Hate Speech in Japan: The Possibility of a Non-Regulatory Approach*. Cambridge: Cambridge University Press.
———. (2018). *Law and Disaster: Earthquake, Tsunami and Nuclear Meltdown in Japan*. Abingdon: Routledge.
———. (2016). The Challenge to Multiculturalism: Hate Speech Ban in Japan. *UBC Law Review* 49(2), 427–84.
———. (2015). The Criminalization of Revenge Porn in Japan. *Washington International Law Journal* 24(2), 289–317.
———. (2011). *The Constitution of Japan: A Contextual Analysis*. London: Hart Publishing.
———. (2010). Why Is the Japanese Supreme Court So Conservative? *Washington University Law Review* 88(6), 1375–1423.
———. (2007). The Voting Rights of Japanese Citizens Living Abroad. *International Journal of Constitutional Law* 5(2), 332–42.
———. (1991). Freedom of Expression in Japan. *Osaka University Law Review* 38(13), 13–42.
McLelland, M. & Mackie, V. (Eds.). (2014). *Routledge Handbook of Sexuality Studies in East Asia*. Abingdon-on-Thames: Routledge.
Merryman, J.H. (2007). *The Civil Law Tradition: An Introduction to the Legal Systems of Europe and Latin America* (3rd ed.). Stanford: Stanford University Press.
Miller, F.O. (1965). *Minobe Tatsukichi, Interpreter of Constitutionalism in Japan*. Berkeley: University of California Press.
Mitchell, R.H. (1983). *Censorship in Imperial Japan*. Princeton: Princeton University Press. (1976). *Thought Control in Prewar Japan*. Ithaca, NY: Cornell University Press.
Miyazawa, S. (1992). *Policing in Japan: A Study on Making Crime*. Albany: SUNY Press.
———. (1991). Administrative Control of Japanese Judges. *Kobe University Law Review* 25, 45–61.
Miyazawa, S. & Hirayama, M. (2017). Introduction of Videotaping of Interrogations and the Lessons of the Imaichi Case: A Case of Conventional Criminal Justice Policy-Making in Japan. *Washington International Law Journal* 27(1), 149–76.
Miyazawa, S., and Feeley, M.M. (Eds.). (2002). *The Japanese Adversary System in Context: Controversies and Comparisons*. London: Palgrave Macmillan.
Moore, R. & Robinson, D. (2004). *Partners for Democracy: Crafting the New Japanese State under MacArthur*. Oxford: Oxford University Press.
Morioka, K. (2001). The Evolution of State Shinto. In K. Kasahara (Ed.), *A History of Japanese Religion* (P. McCarthy & G. Sekimori, trans.). Tokyo: Kosei Publishing Company.
Morris-Suzuki, T. (2012). Post-War Warriors: Japanese Combatants in the Korean War. *The Asia-Pacific Journal* 10(31), No. 1.
Muneo, N. (2014). The Overseas Dispatch of Japan's Self-Defense Forces and U.S. War Preparations. *The Asia-Pacific Journal* 12(31), No. 2. (Richard H. Minear, trans.).
Nakanishi, Y. (Ed.). (2017). *Contemporary Issues in Human Rights Law*. New York City: Springer.
Nasu, H. (2016). Japan's 2015 Security Legislation: Challenges to its Implementation under International Law. *International Law Studies* 92.
Oda, H. (2021). *Japanese Law* (4th ed.). Oxford: Oxford University Press.

———. (2009). *Japanese Law* (3rd ed.). Oxford: Oxford University Press.
Oppler, A.C. (2015). *Legal Reform in Occupied Japan: A Participant Looks Back*. Princeton: Princeton University Press.
Ōta, S. (2001). Reform of Civil Procedure in Japan. *The American Journal of Comparative Law* 49(4), 561–83.
Ramseyer, J.M. & Rasmusen, E.B. (2006). The Case for Managed Judges: Learning from Japan after the Political Upheaval of 1993. *University of Pennsylvania Law Review* 154(6), 1879–1930.
———. (2003). *Measuring Judicial Independence: The Political Economy of Judging in Japan*. Chicago: University of Chicago Press.
———. (2001). Why are Japanese Judges so Conservative in Politically Charged Cases? *American Political Science Review* 95(2), 331–44.
Ravitch, F.S. (2017). The Continued Relevance of Philosophical Hermeneutics in Legal Thought. In B.G. Slocum (ed.).
———. (2017). Secularism and Liberal Constitutionalism: Lessons from Japan. *Michigan State Law Review,* 149–61.
———. (2014). Visits by the Japanese Prime Ministers to the Yasukuni Shrine Analyzed Under Articles 20 and 89 of the Japanese Constitution. *Michigan State University International Law Review* (22)3, 713–29.
———. (2014). A Basic Introduction to Constitutional Free Exercise of Religion in the United States and Japan. *Doshisha Law Review* (64)85.
———. (2013). The Shinto Cases: Religion, Culture, or Both—The Japanese Supreme Court and Establishment of Religion Jurisprudence. *BYU Law Review* 2013(3), 505–20
———. (2011). The Unbearable Lightness of Free Exercise Under Smith: Exemptions, Dasein, and the More Nuanced Approach of the Japanese Supreme Court. *Texas Tech Law Review* 44, 259–79.
Repeta, L. (2015). "Personal Information," Media Control, and Government Power: Legislative Battles in Japan, 1999–2003. *Meiji Law Journal* 22, 9–35.
———. (2014). Raising the Wall of Secrecy in Japan—The State Secrecy Law of 2013. *Meiji Law Journal* 21, 13–34.
———. (2014). Police Surveillance of Muslims and Human Rights in Japan. *The Asia-Pacific Journal, Japan Focus* 12(39).
———. (2013). Japan's Democracy at Risk—The LDP's Ten Most Dangerous Proposals for Constitutional Change. *The Asia-Pacific Journal, Japan Focus* 11(28).
———. (2011). Reserved Seats on Japan's Supreme Court. *Washington University Law Review* 88(6), 1713–44.
———. (1989). Why We Sued the Judges. *Law in Japan* 22(49), 61–63.
Röhl, W. (Ed.). (2005). *History of Law in Japan since 1868*. Leiden: Brill Academic Publishers.
Rosen, D. (2014). Policing Political Speech: Japan's Mistrust of the Marketplace. *Michigan State International Law Review* 22(3), 799–814.
Ruoff, K. (2001). *The People's Emperor: Democracy and the Japanese Monarchy, 1945–1995*. Cambridge, MA: Harvard University Asia Center.
Samuels, R. J. (2004). Politics, Security Policy, and Japan's Cabinet Legislation Bureau: Who Elected These Guys, Anyway? *Japan Policy Research Institute Working Paper 99*.
Satō, J. (2008). Judicial Review in Japan: An Overview of the Case Law and an Examination of Trends in the Japanese Supreme Court's Constitutional Oversight. *Loyola of Los Angeles Law Review* 41(2), 603–28.
Slocum, B.G. (Ed.). (2017). *The Nature of Legal Interpretation: What Jurists can Learn about Legal Interpretation from Linguistics and Philosophy*. Chicago: University of Chicago Press.
Smith, E.M. (1993). Reporting the Truth and Setting the Record Straight: An Analysis of U.S. and Japanese Libel Laws. *Michigan Journal of International Law* 14(4), 871–904.
Steiner, K. (1965). *Local Government in Japan*. Redwood City: Stanford University Press.
Streenstrup, C. (1996). *A History of Law in Japan until 1868* (2nd ed.). Leiden: Brill Academic Publishers.
Takahashi, H. (2009). Career Judiciary, Judicial Reform, and Practicing Attorneys. *Zeitschrift für Japanisches Recht/Journal of Japanese Law* 14(27), 39–57.
Takahata, E. (2007). Religious Accommodation in Japan. *BYU Law Review* 2007(3), 729–50.
Takii, K. (2014). *Itō Hirobumi—Japan's First Prime Minister and Father of the Meiji Constitution*. Abingdon-on-Thames: Routledge.
———. (2007). *The Meiji Constitution: The Japanese Experience of the West and the Shaping of the Modern State* (D. Noble, Trans.). Tokyo: International House of Japan. (Original work published 2003).

Tanaka, J. (1959). Religion and the State under the Meiji and the Present Constitutions. In *Religion and the State in Japan*. Charlottesville: International Institute for the Study of Religions.
Tokikuni, Y. (1963). Obscenity and the Japanese Constitution. *Kentucky Law Journal* (51)4, 703–10.
Tsuji, Y. (2020). Independence of the Judiciary and Judges and Techniques of Interpretation in Japan. *Courts & Justice Law Journal* 2(1), 76–108.
———. (2018). Reflection of Public Interest in the Japanese Constitution: Constitutional Amendment. *Denver Journal of International Law and Policy* 46(2), 159–90.
———. (2018). Forced Sterilization and Abortion in Japan: Family and Constitution. *Bratislava Law Review* 2(2), 50–63.
———. (2017). Decisions that Declared Laws Unconstitutional and their Impact on Japanese Families. *ILSA Journal of International & Comparative Law* 24(1), 139–79.
———. (2011). Independence of the Judiciary and Judges in Japan. *Surugadai Hōgaku* 24(3), 63–82.
Ukai, N. (1956). The Individual and the Rule of Law under the New Japanese Constitution. *Northwestern University Law Review* 51(6), 733–44.
Upham, F.K. (2011). Stealth Activism: Norm Formation by Japanese Courts. *Washington University Law Review* 88(6), 1493–1505.
———. (2005). Political Lackeys or Faithful Public Servants? Two Views of the Japanese Judiciary. *Law & Social Inquiry* 30(2), 421–55.
———. (1987). *Law and Social Change in Japan*. Cambridge, MA: Harvard University Press.
Usaki, M. (1990). Restrictions on Political Campaigns in Japan. *Law and Contemporary Problems* 53(1), 133–56.
Van Wolferen, K. (1990). *The Enigma of Japanese Power*. New York: Vintage Books.
Von Mehren, A.T. (Ed.). (1964). *Law in Japan: The Legal Order in a Changing Society* (Modern Asia Edition). Cambridge, MA: Harvard University Press.
Wada, M. (2000). Abolition of the House (*ie*) Under the Occupation—Or the Two Faces of *Koseki*: A Janus. *Law in Japan* 26, 99–127.
Wagatsuma, S. (1951). Guarantee of Fundamental Rights under the Japanese Constitution. *Washington Law Review and State Bar Journal* 26(2), 145.
Ward, M.M. (2019). *Thought Crime: Ideology and State Power in Interwar Japan*. Durham, NC: Duke University Press.
Webster, T. (2010). International Human Rights Law in Japan: The View at Thirty. *Columbia Journal of Asian Law* 23(2), 241–68.
Wilson, J.W., Fukurai, H. & Maruta, T. (2015). *Japan and Civil Jury Trials: The Convergence of Forces*. Cheltenham: Edward Elgar Publishing.
Winkler, C.G. (2011). *The Quest for Japan's New Constitution: An Analysis of Visions and Constitutional Reform Proposals 1980–2009*. Abingdon-on-Thames: Routledge.
Yamagishi, K. (2008). Freedom of Religion, Religious Political Participation, and Separation of Religion and State: Legal Considerations from Japan. *BYU Law Review* 2008(3), 919–41.
Yanase, N. (2014). Overview of the Judge Impeachment System in Japan: Focusing on the Constitutional Design for the Impeachment Committee and Court. *Nihon University Comparative Law* 31, 1–17.
Yap, P.J. (Ed.). (2020). *Proportionality in Asia*. Cambridge: Cambridge University Press.
———. (2017). *Judicial Review of Elections in Asia*. Abingdon-on-Thames: Routledge.

Index

C

D

E

F

G

H

I

J

M

P

Q

R

S

T

U

V

W

Y

Index of Articles of the Constitution of Japan

For Product Safety Concerns and Information please contact our EU
representative GPSR@taylorandfrancis.com
Taylor & Francis Verlag GmbH, Kaufingerstraße 24, 80331 München, Germany

www.ingramcontent.com/pod-product-compliance
Ingram Content Group UK Ltd.
Pitfield, Milton Keynes, MK11 3LW, UK
UKHW050052200926
475702UK00019B/2789

* 9 7 8 1 0 4 1 1 8 7 2 0 2 *